STATISTICS
FOR
PSYCHOLOGY

Arthur Aron

State University of New York at Stony Brook

Elaine N. Aron

Pacifica Graduate Institute

Prentice Hall, Englewood Cliffs, New Jersey 07632

Library of Congress Cataloging-in-Publication Data

ARON, ARTHUR.
    Statistical methods in psychology / Arthur Aron, Elaine N. Aron.
        p.   cm.
    Includes bibliographical references and index.
    ISBN   0–13–845637–2
    1. Psychology—Statistical methods.   I. Aron, Elaine.   II. Title.
BF39.A69   1994
150'.72—dc20   92–45260
                                                      CIP

Executive editor: *Peter Janzow*
Production editor: *Joan Stone*
Interior design: *Maureen Eide*
Page layout: *Jayne Conte*
Copy editor: *B. F. Emmer*
Cover designer: *Jayne Conte*
Cover photo: *George Holton/The National Audubon Society Collection/Photo Researchers*
Photo editor: *Lorinda Morris-Nantz*
Photo researcher: *Melinda Reo*
Production coordinator: *Herb Klein*
Editorial assistant: *Marilyn Coco*

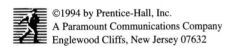©1994 by Prentice-Hall, Inc.
A Paramount Communications Company
Englewood Cliffs, New Jersey 07632

Acknowledgments appear on page xviii, which constitutes
a continuation of the copyright page.

Printed in the United States of America
10   9   8   7   6   5   4   3   2   1

ISBN 0-13-845637-2

Prentice-Hall International (UK) Limited, *London*
Prentice-Hall of Australia Pty. Limited, *Sydney*
Prentice-Hall Canada Inc., *Toronto*
Prentice-Hall Hispanoamericana, S.A., *Mexico*
Prentice-Hall of India Private Limited, *New Delhi*
Prentice-Hall of Japan, Inc., *Tokyo*
Simon & Schuster Asia Pte. Ltd., *Singapore*
Editora Prentice-Hall do Brasil, Ltda., *Rio de Janeiro*

Contents

1 Displaying the Order in a Group of Numbers   1

5 Some Key Ingredients for Inferential Statistics: The Normal Curve, Probability, and Population Versus Sample   133

6 Introduction to Hypothesis Testing   157

7 Hypothesis Tests With Means of Samples   181

8 Statistical Power and Effect Size   207

11 Introduction to the Analysis of Variance   311

12 The Structural Model in the Analysis of Variance   339

13 Factorial Analysis of Variance 367

14 Chi-Square Tests 415

17 Making Sense of Advanced Statistical Procedures in Research Articles 505

Appendix A
Overview of the Logic and Language of Psychology Research 533

Appendix B
Tables 545

Preface to the Instructor

The heart of this book was written over a summer in a small apartment near the Place Saint Ferdinand, having been outlined in nearby cafés and on walks in the Bois de Boulogne. It is based on our 25 years' experience teaching, doing research, and writing. We believe that this book is as different from the conventional lot of statistics books as Paris is from Calcutta, yet still comfortable and stimulating to the long-suffering community of statistics instructors.

The approach embodied in this text has been developed over two decades of successful teaching—successful not only in the sense that students have consistently rated the course (a statistics course, remember) as a highlight of their major but also in the sense that students come back to us years later saying, "I was light years ahead of my fellow graduate students because of your course," or "Even though I don't do research now, your course has really helped me read the journals in my field."

A Brief History of the Statistics Text Genre

In the 1950s and 1960s statistics texts were dry, daunting, and mathematical, quickly leaving most students behind. In the 1970s, there was a revolution—in swept the intuitive approach, with much less emphasis on derivations, proofs, and mathematical foundations. The approach worked. Students became less scared of the course and found the topic more accessible, if not quite clear.

The intuitive trend continued in the 1980s, adding in the 1990s some truly clear writing. A few texts have now also begun to encourage students to use the computer to do statistical analyses. However, discussions of intuitive understandings are becoming briefer and briefer. The standard is a kind of minimalism in which there is a cursory overview of the key idea and sometimes the associated "definitional" formula for each technique. Then come the procedures and examples for actually doing the computation, using another, "computational" formula.

Even with all this streamlining, or perhaps because of it, at the end of the course, most students cannot give a clear explanation of the logic behind the techniques they have learned. A few months later, they can rarely carry out the procedures either. Most important, the three main purposes of the introductory statistics course are not accomplished: Students are not able to make sense of the results of psychology research articles, they are poorly prepared for further courses in statistics (which courses must inevitably spend half the semester reteaching the introductory course), and the exposure to deep thinking that is supposed to justify the course's meeting general education requirements in the quantitative area has not occurred.

What We Have Done Differently

We continue to do what the best of the newer books are already doing well: emphasizing the intuitive, deemphasizing the mathematical, and explaining everything in clear, simple language. But what we have done differs from these other books in 11 key respects.

1. *The definitional formulas are brought back to center stage* because they provide a concise symbolic summary of the logic of each particular procedure. All our explanations, examples, and practice problems are based on these definitional formulas. (The numbers involved in practice problems are appropriately reduced to keep computations manageable).

Why this change? Because so far, statistic books have failed to adjust to technological reality. What is important is not that the students learn to calculate a *t* test with a large set of numbers—computers can do that for them. What is important is that students remain constantly aware of the underlying logic of the procedure. For example, consider the population variance—the average of the squared deviations from the mean. This concept is immediately clear from the definitional formula (once the student is used to the symbols): Variance $= \Sigma(X - M)^2/N$. Working problems using this formula constantly engrains the meaning in the student's mind. In contrast, the usual computational version of this formula serves only to obscure this meaning: Variance $= [\Sigma X^2 - (\Sigma X)^2/N]/N$. Working problems using this formula does nothing but teach the student the difference between ΣX^2 and $(\Sigma X)^2$!

Teaching computational formulas today is an anachronism. Researchers do their statistics on computers now. At the same time, the use of statistical software makes the understanding of the basic principles, as they are symbolically expressed in the definitional formula, more important than ever.

It is a mystery to us why statistics textbooks have not changed their methods with the advent of statistical software, but we are convinced that the change is overdue. Of course, because computational formulas are both historically interesting and occasionally needed—and because some instructors may feel naked without them—we still provide them, in a brief appendix to each chapter in which a computational formula would normally be introduced.

2. *Each procedure is taught both verbally and numerically—and usually visually as well—with the same examples being described in each of these ways.* Practice exercises, in turn, require the student to calculate results and make graphs or illustrations and also to write a short explanation in layperson's language of what the statis-

tic means. The chapter material, including at least two examples worked out in these different ways, completely prepares the student for the practice problems.

It is our repeated experience that these different ways of expressing an idea are very important for permanently establishing a concept in a student's mind. Many students of psychology are more facile with words than with numbers—in fact, some have a positive fear of all mathematics. Writing the lay-language explanation gives them an opportunity to do what they do best and, if they are having trouble, forces them to put the procedures in front of them in the verbal form they process best.

3. There is an *emphasis on statistical methods as a living, growing field of research.* We take the time to describe controversies and recent developments in simple terms. The goal is for students to see statistical methods as human efforts to make sense out of masses of data points; to see that statistics are not "given" by nature, not infallible, not perfect descriptions of the events they try to describe but rather constitute a language that is constantly improving through the careful thought of those who use it. We hope that this orientation will help them maintain a questioning, alert attitude while students and keep up with new developments in statistics as professionals.

4. The main goal of any introductory statistics course in psychology is to *prepare students to read research articles.* But in fact, the way a procedure such as a *t* test or an analysis of variance is described in a research article is often quite different from what the student expects on the basis of standard textbook discussions. Therefore, as this book teaches a statistical method, it also gives examples of how that method is reported in the journals. And the practice exercises also include excerpts from articles for the student to explain.

5. The book is unusually *up-to-date.* The fine points of statistical controversies are informed by the very latest studies. For example, the chapter on how to handle situations in which distributions are not normally distributed includes a clear discussion of computer-intensive methods (instead of being limited to the usual exclusive focus on nonparametric order statistics, which are not even used much these days). Similarly, the chapter on power and effect size—and continual references to power and effect size throughout the book—is consistent with the current emphasis on these topics in prominent recent articles in *American Psychologist, Psychological Bulletin,* and elsewhere.

6. *Chapter 16* is unique in that it *integrates the major techniques that have been taught,* explaining that the *t* test is a special case of the analysis of variance and that both the *t* test and the analysis of variance are special cases of correlation and regression. (In short, we introduce the general linear model.) In the past, when this point has been made at all, it has usually been only in advanced texts. But many students find it valuable for digesting and retaining what they have learned, as well as for sensing that they have penetrated deeply into the foundations of statistical methods.

7. The *final chapter looks at advanced procedures* without actually teaching them in detail. It explains in simple terms how to make sense out of these statistics when they are encountered in research articles. Most psychology research articles today use methods such as hierarchical and stepwise multiple regression, factor analysis, LISREL, analysis of covariance, and multivariate analysis of variance. Students completing the ordinary introductory statistics course are ill-equipped to comprehend most of the articles they must read to prepare a paper or study for a course. This chapter makes use of the basics that students have just learned to give a cursory understanding of these advanced procedures. It also serves as a reference guide that they can keep and use in the future when reading such articles.

8. The book is written to *appeal to the motivations that prompt a student to become a psychology major.* Our examples attempt to represent the diversity of psychology but emphasize topics or populations that students seem to find most interesting. The very first is from a real study in which 151 students in their first week of an introductory statistics class rate how much stress they feel they are under. Other examples emphasize clinical, organizational, and educational psychology while being sure to include sufficient interesting examples from experimental, social, developmental, and other fields to inspire students with the value of those fields.

In addition, we continually emphasize the usefulness of statistical methods and ideas as tools in the research process, never allowing students to feel that what they are learning is theory for the sake of theory. Appendix A provides an overview of research methods, giving the context in which statistics function. And as each technique is taught, its role in the research process is illustrated and underscored.

9. The accompanying *Student's Study Guide and Computer Workbook* focuses on mastering concepts and also includes instructions and examples for working problems using a computer. Most study guides focus on plugging numbers into formulas and memorizing rules (which is consistent with the emphasis of the textbooks they accompany). For each chapter, our *Student's Study Guide and Computer Workbook* provides learning objectives, a detailed chapter outline, the chapter's formulas (with all symbols defined), and summaries of steps of conducting each procedure covered in the chapter, plus a set of self tests, including multiple-choice, fill-in, and problem/essay questions. In addition, for each procedure covered in the chapter, the study guide furnishes a thorough outline for writing an essay explaining the procedure to a person who has never had a course in statistics. As a further study aid, it includes cutout flash cards of all the key terms.

Especially important, our *Student's Study Guide and Computer Workbook* provides the needed support for teaching students to conduct statistical analyses on the computer. There are special appendixes introducing the language and procedures of both SPSS/PC+ Studentware and MYSTAT (the student version of SYSTAT). Then, in each chapter corresponding to the text chapters, there is a section for each of these programs showing in detail how to carry out the chapter's procedures (including step-by-step instructions, examples, and illustrations of how each step of input and output appears on the computer screen), plus special activities for using the computer to deepen understanding. As far as we know, no other statistics textbook package provides this kind of flexibility or this much depth of explanation.

By the way, Prentice Hall is now selling and distributing all SPSS manuals, books, and student software. SPSS/PC+ Studentware, as well as SPSS for Windows Studentware, offers full-functioning student versions of the commercial SPSS software. The price for the software, including a student tutorial, is about that of a textbook. Further, these can be purchased at a discounted price with our *Statistics for Psychology,* as a unit. This seems to us like a very nice idea and a sensible plan for those of you who want to start your students analyzing data on the computer. We think such courses are valuable and exciting for students, getting them emersed sooner in the real joy of psychology research. Ask your Prentice Hall representative for more details if you would like to consider this option for your course.

10. We have written an *Instructor's Manual that really helps teach the course.* The *Manual* begins with a chapter summarizing what we have gleaned from our own teaching experience and from a review of the research literature on effectiveness in college teaching. The next chapter discusses alternative organizations of the course, including tables of possible schedules and a sample syllabus. Then each chapter, corresponding to the text chapters, provides full lecture outlines and *worked-out examples not found in the text* (in a form suitable for copying onto transparencies or for student handouts). These worked-out examples are particularly useful in that creating examples is one of the most difficult parts of preparing statistics lectures.

Also, in our teaching we have developed a teaching technique students really enjoy—we administer an anonymous questionnaire on the first day, on a topic of interest to them, and then analyze the class's responses throughout the quarter using the techniques of each chapter. The *Instructor's Manual* provides the questionnaire we have used for this purpose. (Or you can always develop one of your own—or even let them develop one with questions that would interest them.) If you do not wish to administer a questionnaire, for each text chapter the *Instructor's Manual* provides transparency masters based on results obtained with our classes, analyzed with whatever procedure is being studied in the text, following the steps described there. But if you use our questionnaire and provide us with a computer file of your class's data, we will analyze the results and quickly send back transparency masters based on your class's data. (We really do want to be helpful.)

11. Our *Test Bank and Answers to Set II Practice Problems makes preparing good exams easy.* We supply approximately 40 multiple-choice, 25 fill-in, and 10–12 problem/essay questions for each chapter. Considering that the emphasis of the course is so conceptual, the multiple-choice questions will be particularly useful for those of you who do not have the resources to grade essays. This supplement also includes answers to each textbook chapter's Set II practice problems, which are not given in the text. (The textbook provides answers to all Set I practice problems, including at least one example essay for each chapter.)

Keep in Touch

Our goal is to do whatever we can to help you make your course a success. If you have any questions or suggestions, please write or bitnet (**ARON@PSYCH1.PSY. SUNYSB.EDU** will do for both of us). Indeed, if you let us know you are teaching the course with this book, we will add you to our network of folks to be kept informed of any suggestions or comments we receive from others teaching the course (and our replies) and also send you periodic summaries of new developments in the statistical literature that relate to the material covered in the course. And if—heaven forbid—you should find an error somewhere, we promise that we will (a) fix it in the very next printing, (b) send out the details to everyone on the network, and (c) include your name with our thanks in the Introduction to the next edition.

Acknowledgments

First and foremost, we are grateful to our students through the years, who have shaped our approach to teaching by rewarding us with their appreciation for what we have done well, as well as their various means of extinguishing what we have done not so well. Indeed, during the past three years our students have patiently learned from photocopied drafts of this book (in lieu of the nicely printed textbooks enjoyed by those taking the course from other instructors), kindly scouring the pages in search of errors and confused wordings. (Offering them 3 test points per mistake found helped too.)

For getting us started on this project, we are grateful to our friend Bryan Strong, who encouraged us to undertake it in the first place, and to Brete Harrison, who guided the project through its initial development. We also appreciate the input and support from our friend John Touhey, who read several of the early draft chapters. The reviewers of the book at various stages have been extremely helpful in identifying weak points of logic and pedagogy, and their generosity of praise provided momentum when we occasionally became lost in the immensity of the project. We want to thank Michael L. Frank, Stockton State College; Martin A. Johnson, Missouri Western State College; Carol Pandey, L.A. Pierce College; Roger Bakeman, Georgia State University; Jeffrey S. Berman, Memphis State University; and Michael J. Scozzaro, SUNY College at Buffalo (who, of course, are not responsible for any weaknesses that remain). We are also grateful to Paul Sanders, who found many of the examples and did much of the research work on statistical controversies, and to Sami Corn, Josh Tager, Chuck Avery, and Scott Sokol, who put much effort into the typing and other details of preparing the manuscript. In addition, we are grateful to Elijah Aron, who painstakingly prepared the index. Finally, we want to express our appreciation to the people at Prentice Hall who made the book a reality, especially Peter Janzow, Senior Psychology Editor, who put so much energy and creativity into the project, and Joan Stone, Production Editor, who with great care and good nature oversaw the million details of making a pile of manuscript pages into this pleasant book.

Credits

CO-1, Spencer Grant/Photo Researchers; CO-2, Sohm/The Image Works; CO-3, Leonard Lee Rue III/Photo Researchers; CO-4, Robert Vincent, Jr./Photo Researchers; CO-5, Grant Heilman Photography; CO-6, Len Rue, Jr./Photo Researchers; CO-7, Grant Heilman Photography; CO-8, Thomas D. W. Friedmann/Photo Researchers; CO-9, Jen and Des Bartlett, Photo Researchers; CO-10, Animals Animals/Earth Scenes; CO-11, Tom Hollyman/Photo Researchers; CO-12, Calvin Larsen/Photo Researchers; CO-13, Okoniewski/The Image Works; CO-14, Barry L. Runk/Grant Heilman Photography; CO-15, H. Fouque/Photo Researchers; CO-16, Frank Siteman/Monkmeyer Press; CO-17, Carl Frank/Photo Researchers

Data on pages 100, 101, 272, 273, 301, 302, 331, 332, 401, 402, 437, and 483 based on tables in Cohen, J. (1988). *Statistical power analysis for the behavioral sciences* (2nd Ed.). Copyright © 1988 by Lawrence Erlbaum Associates, Inc. Reprinted by permission.

Introduction to the Student

The goal of this book is to have you *understand* statistical methods. Our emphasis is on meaning and concepts rather than on symbols and numbers.

This emphasis plays to your strength, as most psychology students are not lovers of calculus but are keenly attuned to ideas. And we want to underscore the following, based on our experience of over 20 years of teaching: We have never had a student who could pass other college-level psychology courses who could not also pass this course. (However, we will admit that passing this course often involves more work than passing others.)

In this introduction, we discuss why you are taking this course and how you can gain the most from it.

Why Learn Statistics?
(Besides It Being Required)

1. *Understanding statistical methods is crucial to being able to read the psychology research literature.* Nearly every course you will take as a psychology major emphasizes the results of research studies, and these are expressed in statistics. This is true not only of courses in fields like experimental, social, and developmental psychology. It is also true of courses in clinical and counseling psychology and in other applied areas such as organizational, health, and sports psychology. If you do not understand the basic logic of statistical methods—if you cannot make sense of the jargon, the tables, and the graphs that are at the heart of any research report—your reading of these articles will be very superficial. You will miss the subtleties, you will not be able to evaluate critically the conclusions drawn, and you will not be able to compare the outcomes of different studies.

2. *Understanding statistical methods is crucial to conducting psychological research.* Many psychology majors eventually decide to go on to graduate school. Graduate study in psychology—even in clinical and counseling psychology and other applied areas—almost always involves *conducting* research. Often learning to conduct research on your own is the entire focus of graduate study, and conducting research almost always involves using statistical methods. This course provides a solid foundation in these techniques. Further, by mastering the underlying logic and ways of thinking about statistics, you will be unusually well prepared for the advanced courses, which focus on the nitty-gritty of data analysis in the conduct of research.

Many psychology programs also offer opportunities for undergraduates to conduct research. Although the main focus of this course is understanding statistics, not using them, you will learn sufficient skills to carry out some kinds of data analyses (if you think through what these will be *before* you gather your data). Because it is the creativity of the hypotheses that counts—the statistics are only the means—there is no mathematical reason why you can't begin to make a real contribution to the body of psychological research right after you finish this course.

3. *Understanding statistical methods develops your analytic and critical thinking.* Psychology majors are often most interested in people and in improving things in the practical world. This does not mean that psychology majors avoid abstractions—indeed, the students we know are exhilarated most by the almost philosophical levels of abstraction where the secrets of human experience so often seem to hide. But even this kind of abstraction is often grasped only superficially at first, as slogans instead of useful knowledge. Of all the courses you are likely to take in psychology, this course will probably do the most to help you learn to think precisely, to evaluate information, and to apply logical analysis at a very high level.

How to Gain the Most From This Course

There are five things we can advise:

1. *Keep your attention on the concepts.* Treat this course less like a math course and more like a course in logic. When you read a section of a chapter, your attention should be on grasping the principles. When working the exercises, think about why you are doing each step. If you simply try to memorize how to come up with the right numbers, you will have learned very little of use in your future studies of psychology—nor you will do very well on the tests in this course.

2. *Be sure you know each concept before you go on to the next.* Statistics is cumulative; each new concept is built on the last one. Even within a chapter, if you have read a section and you don't understand it—*stop.* Reread it, rethink it, ask for help—do whatever you need to do to grasp it. (If you think that you have understood a section but are not sure, try working an appropriate problem from the end of the chapter.)

Having to read the material in this book over and over does not mean that you are stupid. Most students must read the material more than once. And each reading is much slower than reading an ordinary textbook. Statistics reading has to be pored over with clear, calm attention in order for it to sink in. Be sure to allow plenty of time for this kind of reading and rereading.

3. *Keep up.* Because the material is cumulative, if you fall behind in your reading or miss lectures, the lectures you then attend will be almost meaningless. And it will become harder and harder to catch up.

4. *Study especially intensely during the first half of the course.* Another implication of the cumulative nature of statistics is that it is most important to master the material at the start of the course. Everything else is built on it—yet the beginning of the semester is often when students study least seriously.

If you have mastered the first half of the course—not just learned the general idea, but really know it—the second half will be easier than the first. If you have not mastered the first half, the second half will be close to impossible.

5. *Help each other.* There is no better way to solidify and deepen your understanding of statistics than to try to explain it (with patience and respect) to someone who is having a harder time. And for those of you who are having a harder time, there is no better way to work the difficulties through than by learning from another student who has just learned it.

Thus we strongly suggest that you form study teams with one to three other students—preferably teams that include some members who expect this material to come easy to them and some who don't. Those who know the material well will really get the *most* if they form a group with some who fear that they won't get it at all—the latter will tax the former's supposed understanding enormously. For those who fear trouble ahead, you need to work with those who don't—the blind leading the blind is no way to learn. Also pick teammates who live near you so that it is easy for you to get together. And meet often—between each class, if possible.

In addition to learning from each other, succeeding together on a hard project can be a source of fun and a basis for real friendship. And when working together, remind each other often that how easily people learn statistics is not the major criterion for judging their worth as human beings. In other words, a group will help you avoid allowing any aspect of this course to become a basis for either arrogance or self-deprecation.

A Final Note

Believe it or not, we love teaching statistics. Time and again, we have had the wonderful experience of having beaming students come to us to say, "Professor Aron, I got a 90% on this exam. I can't believe it! Me, a 90 on a statistics exam!" Or the student who tells us, "This is actually *fun*. Don't tell anyone, but I'm actually enjoying . . . statistics, of all things!"[1]

Satisfactions like these have motivated us through the long process of writing this book. We truly want to make learning statistics come alive for you, or at least make it less of a burden than it has been for students in the past. To that end, we have put into this book everything we have learned about teaching statistics, including using earlier drafts with three different large classes and incorporating even the most minor suggestions of our students. Other statistics teachers and statistics experts have also pored over the manuscript and given us their input. So now it is ready for you. We fully expect you to do well in this course.

Arthur Aron
Elaine N. Aron

[1] It may seem hard to believe, but a teacher's feeling of success, including your professor's, is in seeing you learn, not in seeing you suffer. So if during the course you discover anything that your professor can do to make the class a more effective learning experience for you, don't be afraid to ask. (But ask, of course, with due consideration that your professor is also a human being with hurtable feelings. Also recognize that it is not always feasible to make changes in course structure halfway through a course.)

1

Displaying the Order in a Group of Numbers

WELCOME to this book on statistics. We imagine you to be like other psychology students we have known. You have chosen this major because you are fascinated by people—by the visible behaviors of the people around you, perhaps too by their inner life, including your own. Some of you are highly scientific sorts, others are more intuitive. Some of you are fond of math; others may be less so or even afraid of it. Whatever the category that you fall into, we welcome you all. And we want to assure you that if you give this book some special attention (a little more than most textbooks require), it along with your instructor will teach you statistics. Our confidence comes from the fact that the approach used in this book has successfully taught all sorts of students before you, including people who had taken statistics previously and done poorly. You will learn statistics and learn it well.

More important, we want to assure you that whatever your reason for studying psychology, this course is not a waste of time. You need statistics—to read the work of other psychologists; to do your own research, if you so choose; and to hone both your reasoning and your intuition. What is statistics really? It is a tool that has evolved from a basic thinking process that every psychologist—every human—employs: We observe a thing; we wonder what it means or what caused it; we have an insight or make an intuitive guess; we observe again, but now in detail, or we try making some little changes in the process to test our intuition. Then we face the eternal problem: What does our new observation mean in relation to our intuition? Was our hunch confirmed or not? What are the chances that what we have observed this second time will happen again and again, so that we can announce our insight to the world as something probably true?

In other words, statistics is a method of pursuing truth. If it is not your inclination to think that it can reveal "eternal truth," put it this way: It can at least tell you the likelihood that your hunch is true in this time and place, with these sorts of people. This pursuit of truth, or at least future likelihood, is the essence of psychology, of science, and of human evolution. Think of the first hypotheses: What will the mammoths do next spring? What will happen if I eat this root? It is easy to see how the accurate have survived. You are among them. Statistics is one good way to pursue accuracy and truth.

Psychologists use statistical methods to help them make sense of the numbers they collect when conducting research. The issue of how to design good research is a topic in itself, summarized in Appendix A. But in this book we shall confine ourselves to the statistical methods for making sense of the data collected through research.

The Two Branches of Statistical Methods

There are two main branches of statistical methods:

descriptive statistics

1. **Descriptive statistics,** which psychologists use to summarize and make understandable a group of numbers collected in a research study

inferential statistics

2. **Inferential statistics,** which psychologists use to draw conclusions that are based on the numbers actually collected in the research but go beyond them

In this chapter and the next three, we focus on descriptive statistics. Not only is the topic important in its own right, but understanding the techniques of descriptive statistics is also a necessary foundation for learning the techniques of inferential statistics, which is the focus of the remainder of the book.

Frequency Tables

In this chapter, we emphasize using tables and graphs to describe a group of numbers. As noted, the purpose of descriptive statistics is to make a group of numbers easy to comprehend. Obviously, tables and graphs help a great deal. Consider an example. Aron, Paris, and Aron (1993), as part of a larger study, administered a questionnaire to 151 students in an introductory statistics class during the first week of the course. One of the items on the questionnaire asked, "How stressed have you been in the last 2 1/2 weeks, on a scale of 0 to 10, with 0 being *not at all stressed* and 10 being *as stressed as possible*?" The 151 students' ratings were as follows:

4, 7, 7, 7, 8, 8, 7, 8, 9, 4, 7, 3, 6, 9, 10, 5, 7, 10, 6, 8, 7, 8, 7, 8, 7, 4, 5, 10, 10, 0, 9, 8, 3, 7, 9, 7, 9, 5, 8, 5, 0, 4, 6, 6, 7, 5, 3, 2, 8, 5, 10, 9, 10, 6, 4, 8, 8, 8, 4, 8, 7, 3, 8, 8, 8, 8, 7, 9, 7, 5, 6, 3 ,4, 8, 7, 5, 7, 3, 3, 6, 5, 7, 5, 7, 8, 8, 7, 10, 5, 4, 3, 7, 6, 3, 9, 7, 8, 5, 7, 9, 9, 3, 1, 8, 6, 6, 4, 8, 5, 10, 4, 8, 10, 5, 5, 4, 9, 4, 7, 7, 7, 6, 6, 4, 4, 4, 9, 7, 10, 4, 7, 5, 10, 7, 9, 2, 7, 5, 9, 10, 3, 7, 2, 5, 9, 8, 10, 10, 6, 8, 3

It takes quite a while just to read all the ratings in the list. And although scanning them gives some idea of the overall tendencies, it is hardly an accurate indication. One solution is to make a table showing how many students

BOX 1-1

Important Trivia for Poetic Statistics Students

The word *statistics* comes from the Italian word *statista,* a person dealing with affairs of state (from *stato*, "state"). It was originally called "state arithmetic," involving the tabulation of information about nations, especially for the purpose of taxation and planning the feasibility of wars.

Statistics derives from a wide variety of sources. The whole idea of collecting statistics came from governmental requirements but also from the need in ancient times to figure the odds of shipwrecks and piracy for the purpose of supplying marine insurance to encourage voyages of commerce and exploration to far-flung places. The modern study of mortality rates and life insurance descended from the 17th-century plague pits—counting bodies cut down in the bloom of youth. The theory of errors (covered in Chapter 4 in this book) began in astronomy, from stargazing; the theory of correlation (Chapter 3) in biology, from the observation of parent and child. Probability theory (Chapter 5) came to us from the tense environs of the gambling table. The theory of analysis of experiments (Chapters 9–13) began in breweries and out among waving fields of wheat, where correct guesses might determine not only the survival of a tasty beer but also of thousands of marginal farmers. Theories of measurement and factor analysis (Chapter 17) derived from personality psychology, where the depths of human character were first explored with numbers. And chi-square (Chapter 14) came to us from sociology, where it was often a question of class.

In the early days of statistics, in the 17th and 18th centuries, it was popular to use the new methods to prove the existence of God. For example, John Arbuthnot discovered that more male than female babies were born in London between 1629 and 1710. In what is considered the first use of a statistical test, he proved that the male birthrate was higher than could be expected by chance (assuming that 50:50 was chance in this case), concluding that there was a plan operating, since males face more danger to obtain food for their families, and such planning, he said, could only be done by God.

In 1767, John Michell also used probability theory to prove the existence of God when he argued that the odds were 500,000 to 1 against six stars being placed as close together as those in the constellation Pleiades—their placement had to have been a deliberate act of the Creator.

Statistics helped win the Revolutionary War for what became the United States. John Adams obtained critical aid from Holland by pointing out certain vital statistics, carefully gathered by the clergy in local parishes, demonstrating that the colonies had doubled their population every 18 years, adding 20,000 fighting men per annum. "Is this the case of our enemy, Great Britain?" Adams wrote. "Which then can maintain the war the longest?"

Similar statistics were observed by U.S. President Thomas Jefferson in 1786. He wrote that his people "become uneasy" when there are more of them than 10 per square mile and that given the population growth of the new country, within 40 years these restless souls would have filled up all of their country's "vacant land." Some 17 years later, Jefferson doubled the size of that "vacant land" through the Louisiana Purchase.

Statistics in the "state arithmetic" sense are legally endorsed by most governments today. For example, the first article of the U.S. Constitution requires a census.

Who said that statistics have no soul, no human side?

References: Peters (1987); Tankard (1984).

frequency table

used each of the 11 values the ratings can have, as we have done in Table 1-1. This is called a **frequency table** because it shows how frequently—how many times—each rating occurred. A frequency table can make the pattern of numbers clear at a glance. In this case, it is evident that most of these students rated their stress in the neighborhood of 7 or 8, with relatively few rating it very low.

Variables, Values, and Scores

value
variable

Another way of describing what a frequency table does is to say that it shows the frequency of each **value** of a particular **variable.** A value is simply a number, such as 4, -81, or 367.12, or it can be a category, such as male or female or the religion with which a person feels most affiliated.

A variable is a characteristic that can take on different values—in short, it can *vary*. In the example, the variable is level of stress, and it can have values of 0 through 10. Height is a variable, social class is a variable, score on a creativity test is a variable, type of therapy received by patients is a variable, speed on a reaction time test is a variable, number of people absent from work is a variable, and so forth.

score

On any variable, each individual studied has a particular number or **score** that represents that person's value on the variable. For example, Chris's score on the stress variable might have a value of 6; Pat's score might have a value of 8. We often use the word *score* for a particular person's value on a variable because much psychology research involves scores on some type of test.

Psychology research is about variables, values, and scores. We will be using this terminology throughout the book. Although the formal definitions are a bit abstract, in practice you will find that it is quite obvious what is meant when these words are used.

TABLE 1-1
Number of Individuals Using Each Value of the Stress Rating Scale

Stress Rating	Frequency
10	14
9	15
8	26
7	31
6	13
5	18
4	16
3	12
2	3
1	1
0	2

Note. Data from Aron, Paris, & Aron (1993).

How to Make a Frequency Table

Here are the three steps for making a frequency table:

1. Make a list down the page of each possible value, starting from the highest and ending with the lowest. In the stress rating results, the list goes from 10, the highest possible rating, down through 0, the lowest possible rating. (Even if one of the ratings between 10 and 0 had not been used—for example, if no one had given stress a 2 rating—you would still include that value of the stress variable in the listing and simply show it as having a frequency of 0.)

2. Go one by one through the group of scores you wish to describe, making a mark for each next to the corresponding value on your list. This is shown in Figure 1-1. It is a good idea to cross off each score as you tally it on the list.

3. Make a neat table showing how many times each value on your list occurs. Add up the number of marks beside each value. It is also wise to cross-check the accuracy of your work by adding up these totals to be sure that their sum equals the total number of scores.

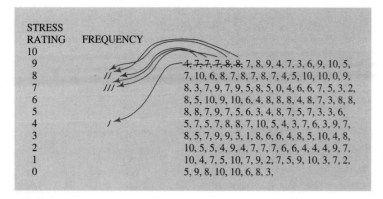

FIGURE 1-1
Creating a frequency table using the Aron et al. (1993) data set.

FIGURE 1-2
Creating a frequency table using the Moorehouse and Sanders (1992) data set.

A Second Example

As part of a larger study of children's attitudes toward learning and work, Martha Moorehouse and Paul Sanders (1992) had the teachers of 153 grade school students fill out a questionnaire that assessed the students' attitudes toward achievement. Typical items on the questionnaire were "Prefers new and challenging problems over easy problems" and "Is easily frustrated." The highest possible score on the test was 120, which represents a very positive attitude toward achievement. The lowest possible score was 24, which is the most negative possible attitude toward achievement. The scores for the 153 students were as follows:

> 77, 78, 98, 85, 59, 59, 59, 108, 86, 104, 111, 67, 77, 66, 70, 74, 65, 108, 92, 68, 95, 56, 87, 92, 73, 92, 106, 74, 97, 109, 69, 103, 113, 119, 45, 99, 111, 78, 95, 54, 68, 42, 65, 84, 80, 115, 44, 32, 107, 57, 118, 107, 30, 50, 63, 74, 76, 43, 25, 73, 115, 40, 45, 86, 113, 115, 111, 114, 94, 110, 96, 90, 112, 103, 108, 110, 82, 73, 101, 72, 61, 75, 67, 74, 55, 74, 69, 109, 87, 74, 112, 97, 91, 101, 105, 97, 107, 92, 100, 109, 114, 103, 107, 100, 117, 74, 120, 86, 105, 108, 115, 96, 97, 106, 110, 112, 95, 113, 71, 88, 94, 104, 95, 62, 104, 70, 64, 117, 116, 65, 82, 119, 115, 81, 107, 111, 118, 63, 53, 104, 112, 90, 74, 65, 79, 53, 115, 84, 93, 68, 70, 114, 91

Now let's follow the step-by-step procedure described earlier for making a frequency table.

1. Make a list down the left edge of a page of each possible value, starting from the highest and ending with the lowest. In this study, the values ranged from a possible high score of 120 to a possible low score of 24. Thus the first step would be to list these values down a page (perhaps using several columns so that you can have all the scores on a single page).

2. Go one by one through the group of scores you wish to describe, making a mark for each next to the corresponding value on your list. Figure 1-2 shows the result of this process.

3. Make a neat table showing how many times each value on your list occurred. Table 1-2 is the result.

120 - /	80 - /	40 - /
119 - //	79 - /	39 -
118 - //	78 - //	38 -
117 - //	77 - //	37 -
116 - /	76 - /	36 -
115 - ꟼꞪ /	75 - /	35 -
114 - ///	74 - ꟼꞪ ///	34 -
113 - ///	73 - ///	33 -
112 - ////	72 - /	32 - /
111 - ////	71 - /	31 -
110 - ///	70 - ///	30 - /
109 - ///	69 - //	29 -
108 - ////	68 - ///	28 -
107 - ꟼꞪ	67 - //	27 -
106 - //	66 - /	26 -
105 - //	65 - ////	25 - /
104 - ////	64 - /	24 -
103 - ///	63 - //	
102 -	62 - /	
101 - //	61 - /	
100 - //	60 -	
99 - /	59 - ///	
98 - /	58 -	
97 - ////	57 - /	
96 - //	56 - /	
95 - ////	55 - /	
94 - //	54 - /	
93 - /	53 - //	
92 - ////	52 -	
91 - //	51 -	
90 - //	50 -	
89 -	49 -	
88 - /	48 -	
87 - //	47 -	
86 - ///	46 -	
85 - /	45 - //	
84 - //	44 - /	
83 -	43 -	
82 - /	42 - /	
81 - /	41 -	

TABLE 1-2
Frequency Table for Attitudes Toward Achievement

Score	Frequency	Score	Frequency	Score	Frequency
120	1	88	1	56	1
119	2	87	2	55	1
118	2	86	3	54	1
117	2	85	1	53	2
116	1	84	2	52	0
115	6	83	0	51	0
114	3	82	2	50	1
113	3	81	1	49	0
112	4	80	1	48	0
111	4	79	1	47	0
110	3	78	2	46	0
109	3	77	2	45	2
108	4	76	1	44	1
107	5	75	1	43	1
106	2	74	8	42	1
105	2	73	3	41	0
104	4	72	1	40	1
103	3	71	1	39	0
102	0	70	3	38	0
101	2	69	2	37	0
100	2	68	3	36	0
99	1	67	2	35	0
98	1	66	1	34	0
97	4	65	4	33	0
96	2	64	1	32	1
95	4	63	2	31	0
94	2	62	1	30	1
93	1	61	1	29	0
92	4	60	0	28	0
91	2	59	3	27	0
90	2	58	0	26	0
89	0	57	1	25	1
				24	0

Note. Data from Moorehouse & Sanders (1992).

Grouped Frequency Tables

interval

grouped frequency table

Sometimes there are so many different possible values that the frequency table is too cumbersome to give a simple account of the information. The solution is to make groupings of values that include all cases within a certain **interval**. For example, in the Aron et al. (1993) study, instead of having a separate frequency figure for the students who rated their stress as 8 and another for those who rated it as 9, you could have a combined category of 8 and 9, which would include 41 individuals in this interval (the 26 ratings of 8 and the 15 of 9).

A frequency table that uses intervals is a **grouped frequency table.** Table 1-3 is a grouped frequency table for the stress ratings example. (However, in this case, since the full frequency table has only 11 different values, a grouped frequency table was not really necessary for clarity.)

TABLE 1-3
Grouped Frequency Table for Stress Ratings

Stress Rating Interval	Frequency
10–11	14
8–9	41
6–7	44
4–5	34
2–3	15
0–1	3

Note. Data from Aron, Paris, & Aron (1993).

Similarly, Table 1-4 is a grouped frequency table for the teachers' ratings of 153 students' attitudes toward achievement.

The grouped frequency table makes the information even more directly comprehensible than the ordinary frequency table does. Note, however, that the greater comprehensibility of a grouped frequency table is at the cost of losing some information—the details of the breakdown of frequencies within each interval.

How to Make a Grouped Frequency Table

Here are the four steps for making a grouped frequency table:

1. Subtract the lowest from the highest value to find the range. In the stress ratings, the range is 10 (10 – 0 = 10). In the attitudes toward achievement example, the range is 96 (120 – 24 = 96).

2. Divide the range by a reasonable interval size (use 2, 3, 5, 10, or a multiple of 10, if possible) until you achieve a result, after rounding up, that

TABLE 1-4
Grouped Frequency Table for Teachers' Ratings of 153 Grade School Students' Attitudes Toward Achievement

Interval	Frequency
120–129	1
110–119	30
100–109	27
90–99	23
80–89	13
70–79	23
60–69	17
50–59	10
40–49	6
30–39	2
20–29	1

Note. Data from Moorehouse & Sanders (1992).

represents a reasonable number of intervals (in general, no fewer than 5 and no more than 15). In the stress ratings example, dividing 10 by 2 gives 5, which is the lowest acceptable number of groupings.

Interval sizes of 2, 3, 5, 10, or a multiple of 10 are best because these are round, whole numbers. In the attitudes toward achievement example, dividing 96 by 2 gives 48, a rather large number of intervals. Dividing by 3 or 5 also gives too many intervals (32 or about 19). Dividing by 10 comes out to about 10 intervals, which is right in the middle of the desirable region for number of intervals. (Dividing by 20 would also be all right, but in this case we might not want to lose so much information as would result from summarizing our results into only five intervals.)

All intervals must be the same size. This is why the top interval in the stress ratings example is 10–11, even though no 11s can exist. Similarly, in the attitudes toward achievement example, the top interval is 120–129 and the bottom is 20–29, making all intervals come out to the same size. The only exception is when there are a few very extreme scores. In that case, the top or bottom interval may be an **open-ended interval**—for example, "50 and above" for ages of students in a college class or "70 and below" for IQ scores. Open-ended intervals should be avoided unless the extreme scores are very few and very extreme.

3. Make a list of the intervals, from highest to lowest, making the lower end of each interval equal to a multiple of the interval size. In the stress rating example, the first interval is 10–11, the next 8–9, and so forth. The numbers 10 and 8 are multiples of 2, the interval size. In contrast, 9–10 and 7–8 would not follow this convention. In the second example each interval starts with a multiple of 10.

Be sure that the intervals do not overlap. That is, you do not want intervals of 8–9 and 9–10 (where would a 9 go?).

4. Proceed as you would for an ordinary frequency table, going through the scores you wish to describe one at a time, making a mark by each interval, and proceeding through the usual steps to make a neat table. (If you have already made an ordinary frequency table, you can just add together the frequencies for the individual values that make up each interval.)

Additional Example of Making a Grouped Frequency Table

A grouped frequency table is especially helpful when the values include decimals, so that there are relatively few exact values with a frequency of more than 1. Consider the following fictional example, which is loosely based on the work of Inhoff, Lima, and Carroll (1984). These studies looked at the effects of context on the speed of reading ambiguous sentences, such as "The sun lay in spots on the field." We will look further at this research in a later chapter, but to begin with, let's consider the part of the research that required simply establishing that reading time is longer for ambiguous sentences. Reading time is measured in milliseconds (thousandths of a second) by an electronic device that determines whether the eyes are moving or pausing as it presents material to be read. The subjects, as usual, were college students. One hundred were presented with five ambiguous and five nonambiguous sentences.

open-ended interval

To illustrate the use of grouped frequency tables, consider the average time it took each subject to read the five ambiguous sentences:

27.2, 28.4, 26.3, 25.1, 25.4, 29.8, 26.1, 29.3, 28.7, 27.6, 25.8, 26.6, 28.6, 28.6, 25.8, 26.0, 26.3, 26.2, 27.3, 28.0, 27.9, 29.6, 25.8, 25.0, 28.2, 28.3, 29.0, 29.1, 28.7, 28.7, 27.4, 27.0, 25.2, 27.5, 29.9, 26.6, 25.8, 27.1, 25.1, 28.7, 28.7, 27.5, 28.5, 26.1, 25.4, 27.3, 29.6, 29.0, 27.5, 27.6, 29.3, 26.4, 28.5, 27.0, 25.6, 25.1, 28.3, 27.9, 27.6, 27.5, 28.6, 25.8, 28.7, 28.9, 28.9, 25.2, 25.9, 25.4, 25.4, 28.5, 28.3, 29.6, 29.3, 28.9, 29.2, 29.8, 25.9, 28.1, 27.8, 29.5, 29.6, 29.5, 25.6, 25.9, 28.7, 28.4, 28.4, 28.0, 26.5, 27.0, 26.1, 28.9, 28.3, 28.5, 25.2, 26.6, 27.4, 27.3, 28.8, 28.5

1. Subtract the lowest from the highest value to find the range. The highest (29.9) minus the lowest (25.0) is 4.9.

2. Divide the range by a reasonable interval size until you achieve a result, after rounding off, that represents a reasonable number of intervals (no fewer than 5, no more than 15). When dealing with a group of values in which the overall range is small, it is necessary to consider intervals that are decimals—but again trying to keep to common, regular units. In this example we might consider an interval size of 1, which would make 5 intervals. A better choice still would be to use .5, a quite common, regular kind of number, giving us 10 intervals.

Notice that there are relative advantages and disadvantages of different interval sizes you might select. To some extent the choice depends on the circumstances and is not a right-or-wrong, cut-and-dried situation.

3. Make a listing of the intervals, from highest to lowest, making the lower end of each interval equal to a multiple of the interval size. In this case, the intervals should run down the page from 29.5–29.9 and continue to 25.0–25.4. (Had the scores been reported to two decimal places, this could be reflected in the intervals, making them run from 29.50–29.99 down to 25.00–25.49.)

4. Proceed as you would for an ordinary frequency table, going through the scores you wish to describe one at a time, making a mark by each interval, and proceeding through the usual steps to make a neat table. Table 1-5 shows the result.

TABLE 1-5
Grouped Frequency Table for 100 Subjects' Average Time (in Milliseconds) to Read Ambiguous Sentences (Fictional Data)

Reading Time	Frequency
29.5–29.9	9
29.0–29.4	7
28.5–28.9	20
28.0–28.4	11
27.5–27.9	10
27.0–27.4	10
26.5–26.9	4
26.0–26.4	8
25.5–25.9	10
25.0–25.4	11

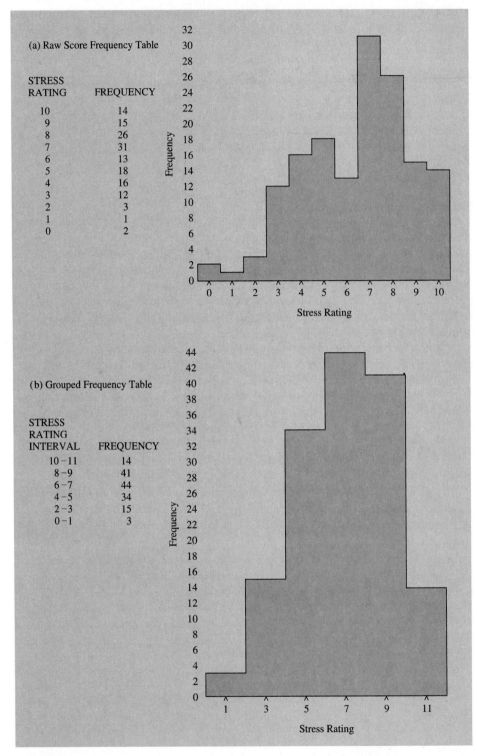

FIGURE 1-3
Histograms based on (a) a frequency table and (b) a grouped frequency table for the Aron et al. (1993) data.

Histograms

An effective way to convey numerical information concisely is with a graph. "A picture is worth a thousand words," it is said—and in some cases a thousand numbers. One widely used way of graphing the information in a frequency table is to make a bar chart in which the height of each bar corresponds to the frequency of each interval in the frequency table. You have probably seen many such graphs.

When these bars are put right next to each other, so that they look a bit like a city skyline, the graph is called a **histogram.** For example, Figure 1-3 shows two histograms based on the stress ratings example (one based on the ordinary frequency table and one based on the grouped frequency table).

histogram

How to Make a Histogram

Here are the four steps for making a histogram:

1. Make a frequency table (or a grouped frequency table).

2. Place the scale of intervals along the bottom of a page. The numbers should go from left to right, from lowest to highest. But in the case of a grouped frequency table, it is conventional to mark only the midpoint of each interval, placed in the center of each bar. (The midpoint is the number halfway between the start of the interval and the start of the next interval.)

3. Make a scale of frequencies along the left edge of the page. The scale should run from 0 at the bottom to the highest frequency in any interval.

4. Make a bar for each interval. The height of each bar corresponds to the frequency of the interval it represents.

Making a histogram is easiest if you use graph paper.

Additional Histogram Examples

Figure 1-4 shows a histogram based on the grouped frequency table for the students' attitudes toward achievement example, and Figure 1-5 shows the

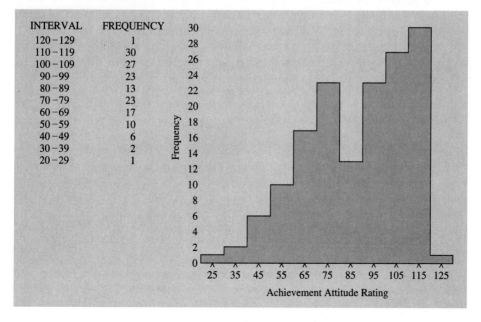

INTERVAL	FREQUENCY
120 – 129	1
110 – 119	30
100 – 109	27
90 – 99	23
80 – 89	13
70 – 79	23
60 – 69	17
50 – 59	10
40 – 49	6
30 – 39	2
20 – 29	1

FIGURE 1-4
Histogram for teachers' ratings of 153 students' attitudes toward achievement, based on grouped frequencies. (Data from Moorehouse & Sanders, 1992.)

11

FIGURE 1-5
Histogram for 100 subjects' average time to read ambiguous sentences, based on grouped frequencies (fictional data).

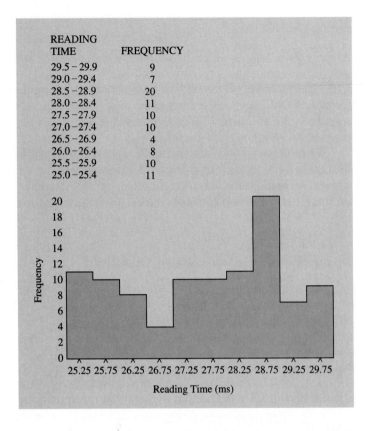

READING TIME	FREQUENCY
29.5 – 29.9	9
29.0 – 29.4	7
28.5 – 28.9	20
28.0 – 28.4	11
27.5 – 27.9	10
27.0 – 27.4	10
26.5 – 26.9	4
26.0 – 26.4	8
25.5 – 25.9	10
25.0 – 25.4	11

histogram based on the grouped frequency table for the ambiguous sentence reading time example.

Frequency Polygons

Yet another way to represent the information in a frequency table pictorially is to make a line graph in which the bottom of the graph shows the intervals (as in a histogram) and the line moves from point to point, with the height of each point showing the number of cases in that interval. This creates a kind of mountain peak skyline. This kind of graph is called a **frequency polygon.** Figure 1-6 shows the frequency polygons corresponding to the regular and grouped frequency tables in the stress ratings example.

frequency polygon

How to Make a Frequency Polygon

Here are the five steps for making a frequency polygon:

1. Make a frequency table (or a grouped frequency table).

2. Place the scale of intervals along the bottom, being sure to include one extra interval above and one extra interval below the intervals that actually have scores in them. The extra intervals are needed to be sure that the line starts and ends along the baseline of the graph, at zero frequency. This creates a closed or "polygon" figure. As with a histogram, mark the scale only at the midpoint of each interval.

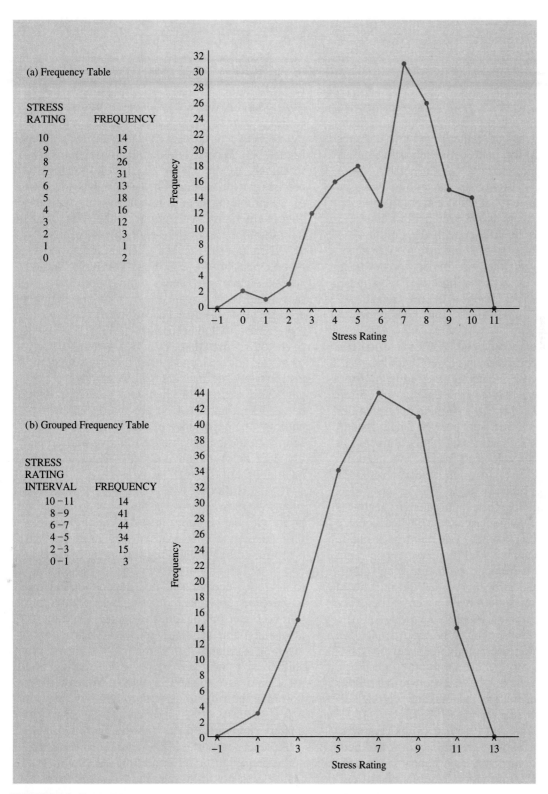

(a) Frequency Table

STRESS RATING	FREQUENCY
10	14
9	15
8	26
7	31
6	13
5	18
4	16
3	12
2	3
1	1
0	2

(b) Grouped Frequency Table

STRESS RATING INTERVAL	FREQUENCY
10 – 11	14
8 – 9	41
6 – 7	44
4 – 5	34
2 – 3	15
0 – 1	3

FIGURE 1-6
Frequency polygons based on (a) a frequency table and (b) a grouped frequency table for the Aron et al. (1993) data.

BOX 1-2

Math Anxiety, Statistics Anxiety, and You: A Message for Those of You Who Are Truly Worried About This Course

Many of you who are psychology majors are more eager to work with people than with numbers. You may, in fact, rather dread this statistics course, even to the point of having a full-blown case of "statistics anxiety" (Zeidner, 1991). So if you are going to tense up the minute you see numbers, we need to face that and resolve it now.

First, allow us to assure you that this course is a chance for a fresh start with the digits. Your past performance in (or avoidance of) geometry, trigonometry, calculus, or similar horrors need not influence in any way how well you grasp statistics. This is a largely different subject, one that is far more relevant to your goals of working with people.

Second, we recommend the work of Sheila Tobias, an expert on math anxiety who has written several books, including *Succeed with Math: Every Student's Guide to Conquering Math Anxiety* (1987). Tobias, a former math avoider herself, suggests that your goal be "math mental health," which she defines as "the willingness to learn the math you need when you need it" (p. 12). (Could it be that this course in statistics is one of those times?)

Tobias explains that math mental health is usually lost in elementary school, when you are called to the blackboard, your mind goes blank, and you are unable to produce the one right answer to an arithmetic problem. What confidence remained probably faded during timed tests, which you did not realize were difficult for everyone except the most proficient few.

Are you still reading this box? If so, we assume that you are among the statistics anxious. So let's close the door of the consulting room, so to speak, and have a heart-to-heart talk.

In studies of college students having difficulties with math (e.g., Dwinell & Higbee, 1991; Cooper & Robinson, 1989), test anxiety, math (and statistics) anxiety, general anxiety, and general low self-confidence each appeared to make an independent contribution to students' difficulties with math courses. That is, any of these, alone or together, could be at the root of your dread of this course.

Any kind of anxiety produces arousal, and one of the best understood relationships in psychology is between arousal and performance (see Figure 3-6). Whereas moderate arousal helps performance, too much or too little dramatically reduces performance. When arousal is the root of the problem, there is nothing wrong with the "hardware"—nothing wrong with your brain, your intelligence, or your studying of the material. When arousal exceeds a certain level, performance *must* go down. Things you have learned become harder to access; your mind starts to race, and this creates more anxiety, more arousal, and so on. The problem is how to reduce anxiety and arousal.

If you suspect that yours is a general anxiety or a lack of confidence, or if there is something else in your life causing you to worry, we suggest that it is time you tried your friendly college counseling center. If you are interested in psychology, the experience of receiving some counseling should be at least informative and probably very helpful (and it's free—which it won't be after you graduate!).

If your difficulty is test anxiety, whatever the subject, overprepare for a few tests so that you go in with the certainty that you cannot possibly fail, no matter how aroused you become. The best time to begin applying this tactic is the first test of this course—there will be no old material to review, success will not depend on having understood previous courses, and it will help you do better throughout the course. (You might also enlist the sympathy of your instructor or teaching assistant—bring in a list of what you've studied, state why you are being so exacting, and ask if you have missed anything.) Your preparation must be ridiculously thorough, but only for a few exams. After these successes, your test anxiety should decline.

Another important consideration is doing some preparing under conditions as similar to a real test as possible, making a special effort to duplicate the aspects that bother you most. If feeling rushed is the troubling part, once you think you are well prepared, set yourself a time limit for solving some homework problems. Make yourself write out answers fully and legibly—this may be part of what makes you feel slow during a test. If the presence of others bothers you, the sound of their scurrying pencils while yours is frozen in midair, do your practice test with others in your course. Even make it an explicit contest to see who can finish first.

If your anxiety dawns the moment you try to solve a problem with numbers in it, even when not taking a test, that is math anxiety, not test anxiety. Tobias suggests that the problem lies with the little thoughts we have while we work: "I don't understand this at all"; "I will never get it right"; "I am no good at this"; "I know I'm going to fail"—you know how it goes. All these self-recriminations raise your arousal to impossible levels, inevitably paralyzing your problem-solving processes.

A possible solution is a little Tobias (1987) trick you can try at home while solving statistics problems: Divide your sheet of paper in half, and work on the problem on the right-hand side; when you can't proceed any further, use the left side to note your thoughts and feelings. You won't be able to write down every elusive self-criticism, but in time you will at least recognize the patterns. You will be learning about yourself, and you will still be working on the problem—working on the psychological obstacles to solving it.

Thus maybe a note to yourself saying "I can't ever learn this" will be answered in time with the obvious self-counsel "Maybe it just takes time, like it said in the text." "I can never get this sort of problem" becomes "What is the pattern to these problems that I have so much trouble with?" "I didn't understand this in class either" becomes "Maybe there's someone that I could drop in on and get some help figuring this out."

Tobias claims that students who are good at math are not necessarily smarter than the rest of us, but they really know their strengths and weaknesses, their styles of thinking and feeling around a problem. They don't judge themselves harshly for mistakes; in particular they don't expect to understand things instantly. Allowing yourself to be a "slow learner" does not mean that you are less intelligent; it shows that you are growing in math mental health.

A final word about arousal. Some of us are more easily aroused by the same stimulation than others (Eysenck, 1981), and this is probably an inborn, temperamental difference (Thomas & Chess, 1977). We are in the process of doing research on this issue of highly sensitive people. Often such people are introverts, or the sort who avoid crowds and do not enjoy meeting strangers. They may be bothered inordinately by loud noise or other stimulation or by violence in the media, or they may just prefer a quiet life. They may be easily moved emotionally, crying at weddings, movies, and farewells. They seem "sensitive."

If this description fits you, it is very helpful to recognize it. For examples, if you think back to your childhood, you may recall being able when alone to hit a ball, speak French, or type as well as anyone, but all your skills vanished when under pressure, being observed, or feeling judged. Arousal was your problem, not innate ability.

Alas, there is considerable pressure due to being tested and judged in college, so you may have to accept that here, too, your performance in discussions or on tests will not always reflect what you actually know (which is, after all, what matters once you graduate). This simple act of self-acceptance—that you are no less smart but are more sensitive—may in itself help ease your arousal when trying to express your statistical knowledge.

In addition, you should do whatever you can to reduce arousal while studying or taking a test—quiet is probably better for you than a radio playing. And if you are not used to caffeine, do not drink it to stay up and study or on the morning of a test. Highly sensitive people are especially sensitive to caffeine, and unless you are very sleepy, it will usually hurt your performance more than help it.

All this talk about not being anxious can of course also make you anxious about being anxious. This can catch up with you at bedtime after you have decided that what you really need before the test is a good night's sleep. We heartily agree with that principle, but sleep is not always easy to come by. If you will stay in bed, however, with the lights off and your eyes closed for a full 8 hours, we think you'll find yourself surprisingly well rested for your test.

So good luck. We wish you all the best with this course.

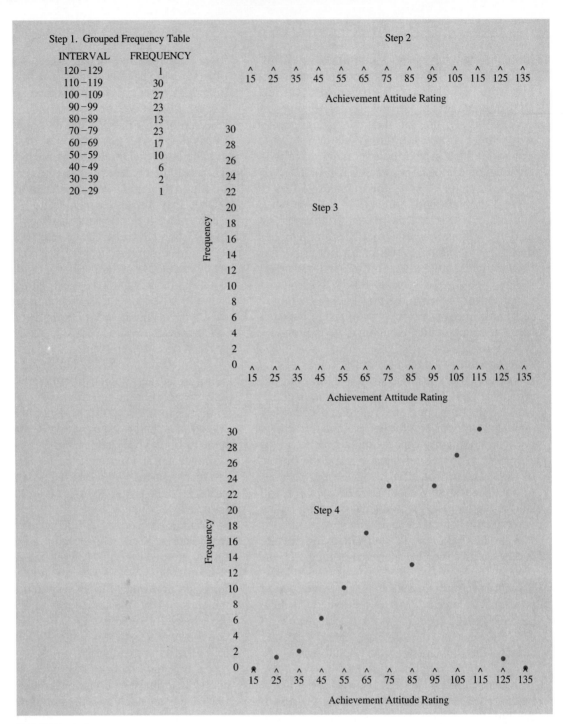

FIGURE 1-7

Five steps in constructing a frequency polygon based on the grouped frequency table for teachers' ratings of 153 students' attitudes toward achievement (based on data from Moorehouse & Sanders, 1992). Step 1: Make a frequency table. Step 2: Place the scale of intervals along the bottom. Step 3: Along the left of the page, make a scale of frequencies that runs from 0 at the bottom to the highest frequency in any interval. Step 4: Mark a point above the center of each interval corresponding to the frequency of that interval. Step 5: Connect the points with lines.

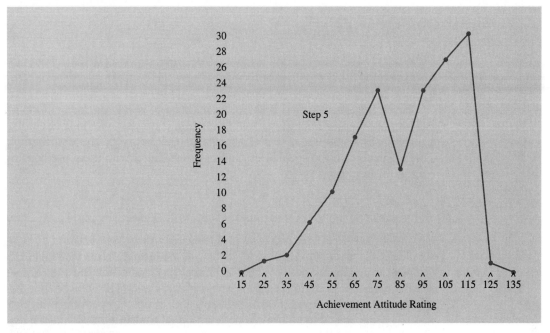

FIGURE 1-7 (*cont.*)

3. Along the left of the page, make a scale of frequencies that runs from 0 at the bottom to the highest frequency in any interval.

4. Mark a point above the center of each interval corresponding to the frequency of that interval.

5. Connect the points with lines.

Additional Frequency Polygon Example

Figure 1-7 shows the five steps in constructing a frequency polygon based on the grouped frequency table for the attitude toward achievement example.

Constructing a Frequency Polygon From a Histogram

If you have already made a histogram, you can make a frequency polygon merely by putting a point at the center of the top of each bar—plus endpoints at the centers of the intervals just below and just above the ones in the histogram—and connecting them. This is illustrated in Figure 1-8, using the example from the study of ambiguous sentence reading time.

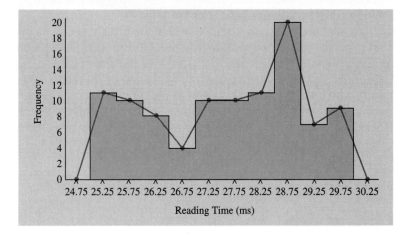

FIGURE 1-8
Constructing a frequency polygon from a histogram, using the histogram for 100 subjects' average time to read ambiguous sentences (fictional data).

17

Shapes of Frequency Distributions

frequency distribution

A frequency table, histogram, or frequency polygon describes a **frequency distribution.** Such representations show how the number of cases, or "frequencies," are spread out, or "distributed."

Psychologists also find it useful to describe in words the key aspects of the way numbers are distributed. In terms of a histogram or frequency polygon, the descriptions can be of aspects of the *shape* of the distribution. These aspects and the special terminology associated with them are considered in this section.

Unimodal and Bimodal Frequency Distributions

One important aspect of the shape of a frequency distribution has to do with whether it has only one main high "tower" in the histogram or one main high peak in the frequency polygon. For example, in the stress ratings, the single most common score is 7, giving a graph with only one high area. Such a distribution is called **unimodal.** A distribution with two major peaks is **bimodal.** Any distribution with two or more peaks is called **multimodal.**[1] Finally, a distribution in which all the values have about the same frequency is called **rectangular.** These frequency distributions are illustrated in Figure 1-9.

unimodal, bimodal
multimodal
rectangular

The information we collect in psychology research is usually approximately unimodal. Bimodal and other multimodal distributions turn up occasionally. For example, the distribution of number of employees whose names have come to the attention of higher level managers, distributed across different levels of quality of work, might be bimodal as it would include mainly employees whose quality of work was either of very poor or very high quality. The distribution of the number of children at each grade level attending an elementary school might be approximately rectangular (since there would be about the same number in first grade, second grade, and so on). These cases are illustrated in Figure 1-10.

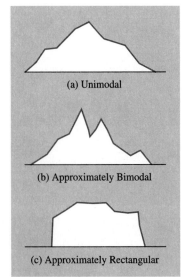

(a) Unimodal

(b) Approximately Bimodal

(c) Approximately Rectangular

FIGURE 1-9
Examples of (a) unimodal,
(b) approximately bimodal, and
(c) approximately rectangular
frequency polygons.

Symmetrical and Skewed Distributions

symmetrical, skewed

Another feature of the stress ratings example is that the distribution was lopsided, with more cases near the high end than near the low end. This is somewhat unusual. Most things we measure in psychology tend to have approximately equal numbers of cases on both sides of the middle. That is, most distributions are approximately **symmetrical** (if you folded them in half at the middle, the two halves would look the same).

Distributions such as the stress example, which are clearly not symmetrical, are said to be **skewed.** A skewed distribution has one side that is long and spread out, somewhat like a tail. The side with the *fewer* cases—the side that looks more like a tail—determines the direction of the skew. Thus a distribution in which there are too few cases to the right of the peak is said to be "skewed to the right." A distribution such as the stress example, which has too few cases at the low end, is skewed to the left. The other two exam-

[1]Strictly speaking, a distribution is bimodal or multimodal only if the peaks are exactly equal, but it is common practice to use these terms more informally to describe the general shape.

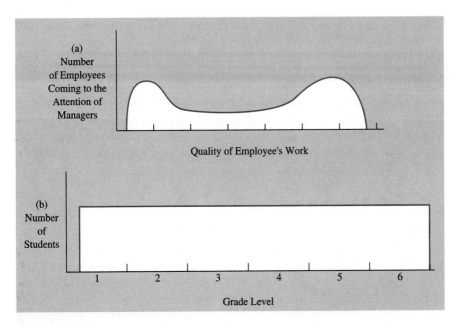

FIGURE 1-10
Fictional examples of distributions that are not unimodal. (a) A bimodal distribution representing the possible frequencies at different levels of quality of work of employees who come to the attention of higher level managers. (b) A rectangular distribution representing the possible frequencies of students at different grade levels in an elementary school.

ples we have examined in this chapter, the distributions of students' attitudes toward achievement and the time it takes to read ambiguous sentences, are both skewed slightly to the left as well. Figure 1-11 illustrates symmetrical and skewed distributions.

A distribution that is skewed to the right—the positive side of the middle—is also called *positively skewed*. A distribution skewed to the left—the negative side of the middle—is also called *negatively skewed*.

In practice, highly skewed distributions come up in psychology mainly when what is being measured has some upper or lower limit. For example, the distribution of the number of children in U.S. families is skewed to the

FIGURE 1-11
Examples of frequency polygons of distributions that are (a) approximately symmetrical, (b) skewed to the right (positively skewed), and (c) skewed to the left (negatively skewed).

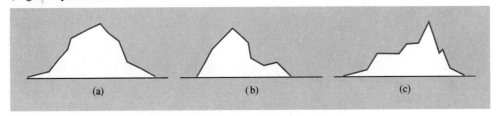

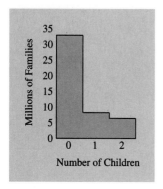

FIGURE 1-12
A distribution skewed to the right: number of children in U.S. families in 1988. (Data from U.S. Bureau of the Census, 1990.)

normal curve

kurtosis

right (see Figure 1-12) because it is not possible to have fewer than zero children! The situation in which many scores pile up at the low end because it is impossible to have a lower score is called a **floor effect.**

An example of a skewed distribution caused by an upper limit is illustrated in Figure 1-13, a distribution of adults' scores on a multiplication table test. This distribution is highly skewed to the left: Most of the scores pile up at the right, the high end (a perfect score). This is an example of a **ceiling effect.** The stress example also shows a mild ceiling effect: Many people had high levels of stress, the maximum rating was 10, and people often don't like to use ratings too near the maximum.

Normal and Kurtotic Distributions

Finally, a distribution can be described in terms of whether it is particularly flat or particularly peaked. The standard of comparison is a bell-shaped curve that is widely approximated in frequency distributions in psychological research and in nature generally. It is called the **normal curve,** and we will devote considerable attention to its characteristics in later chapters. For now, however, it is sufficient to note that the normal curve is a unimodal, symmetrical curve with the sort of bell shape shown in Figure 1-14a. All three of our main examples in this chapter approximate a normal curve in a very general way—although, as we noted, all are somewhat skewed to the left, and two of them have secondary high points. In our experience, most distributions that result from psychology research are actually closer to the normal curve than these three examples.

How peaked and pinched together or flat and spread out a distribution is in comparison to the normal curve is called its degree of **kurtosis.** (*Kurtosis* comes from the Greek word *kyrtos*, "curve.") Figure 1-14b illustrates a frequency distribution that is more spread out and flat than a normal curve. An extreme case would be a rectangular distribution. But a bimodal distribution can be an even more extreme case because it is even farther from being one-peaked like a normal curve. Figure 1-14c is an example of a frequency distribution that is much more single-peaked and pinched-together than a normal curve. An extreme case would be when all scores in a distribution have the same value.

FIGURE 1-13
A distribution skewed to the left: fictional distribution of adults' scores on a multiplication table test.

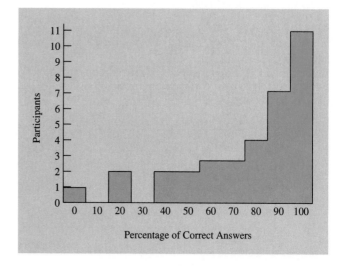

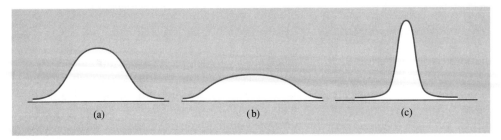

FIGURE 1-14
Examples of (a) normal, (b) kurtotic (too flat), and (c) kurtotic (too peaked) distributions.

Controversies and Limitations

The most serious controversy about the use of frequency tables, histograms, and frequency polygons is not among psychologists but among the general public. The use and misuse of these descriptive procedures by the media seem to have created skepticism about the trustworthiness of statistics in general and statistical tables and charts in particular. Everyone has heard that "statistics lie." In fact, people can and do lie with statistics. And although it is just as easy to lie with words, you may be less sure of your ability to recognize lies with numbers. In this section, we note two ways in which frequency tables and their graphic equivalents can be misused and tell how to recognize such misuses. (Much of this material is based on the excellent and entertaining discussion of these issues in Tufte, 1983.)

Failure to Use Equal Interval Sizes

A key requirement of a frequency table, as noted earlier, is that the interval sizes be equal. If they are not equal, the resulting table or graph can be very misleading. Tufte (1983) gives an example, shown in Figure 1-15, from the

FIGURE 1-15
Misleading illustration of a frequency distribution due to unequal interval sizes. (From *New York Times*, August 8, 1978, p. D-1. © 1978 by the New York Times Company. Reprinted by permission.)

BOX 1-3

Gender, Ethnicity, and Math Performance

From time to time, someone tries to argue that because some groups of people, on the average, excel at math, this means that these groups are inherently better at math (or statistics). The issue comes up about men versus women, about members of social classes, and about ethnic groups.

Regarding gender, in spite of an occasional claim to the contrary, there is no support for the idea that men are genetically better at math (Tobias, 1982). It is true that the very top performers in math have tended to be male. But even here the differences are slight, and the lowest performers are *not* more likely to be female, as would probably be the case if there were a genetic difference.

Tobias (1982) cites numerous studies providing nongenetic explanations for why women might not make it to the very top in math. For example, in a study of students identified by a math talent search, it was found that few parents arranged for their daughters to be coached before the talent exams. Sons were almost invariably coached. In another study of talented youths, parents of mathematically gifted girls were not even aware of their daughters' abilities, whereas parents of boys invariably were. And in general, girls tend to avoid math classes, according to Tobias, especially accelerated classes, because parents, peers, and even teachers often advise them against pursuing too much math. So even though women are earning more PhDs in math than ever before, it is not surprising that math is the field with the highest dropout rate for women.

As for women's performance in statistics, we checked the grades in our own introductory statistics classes and simply found no reliable difference for gender. Neither did Buck (1985), in an analysis of 13 semesters of elementary and advanced undergraduate statistics courses. To put it simply, women may have good reasons to expect difficulty with this course, but in a deeper sense there is no basis for that expectation.

Turning to the topic of ethnic differences, by the year 2000, fully 30% of U.S. youth will be African-American or Hispanic, yet in 1986 only 9 African-Americans and Hispanics received doctoral degrees in mathematics, and only a handful of the top 10,000 college freshmen in these populations indicated an interest in math as their major. There are plenty of obvious reasons for this situation that have nothing to do with genetics. Like women, people of color are frequently not encouraged to study higher math and often do not even have the opportunity by being tracked into vocational types of programs. Even more serious is the frequent inadequacy of the schools serving communities in which the majority are black or Hispanic. These schools typically have fewer advanced math courses, qualified math teachers, and resources for teaching math and science. The lack of PhDs from within these communities is likely to perpetuate the disadvantage. All of this makes it clear that the real problem is not genes but the attitudes that have fostered these inequalities in education. (There are some bright spots in this situation, however, such as the Algebra Project begun in Cambridge, MA, which is determined that all children of that city learn algebra at the middle school level so that they can enroll in college-

respectable (and usually accurate) *New York Times*. This chart gives the impression that commissions paid to travel agents dropped dramatically in 1978. However, a close reading of the graph shows that the third bar in each case is for only the first half of 1978, so that only half a year is being compared to each of the preceding full years. Assuming that the second half of 1978 was like the first half, the information in this graph actually suggests that 1978 would show an increase rather than a decrease. (For example, for Delta Airlines, the estimated full-year 1978 figure would be $72 million, much higher than 1977's $57 million.)

level courses in high school; see Moses, Kamii, Swap, & Howard, 1989). Clearly a massive change of attitude is needed on the part of everyone—educators, taxpayers, government, and all the rest of us—so that minds are not wasted as all too often they have been. In the meantime, what you can do for yourself is to battle as best as you can this idea that math is "naturally" harder for you. It is harder only because you were told it would be, because you were discouraged from taking higher math courses, because your math instruction was probably not as good as it could have been. Catching up may be difficult, but if you need to work harder, that says nothing at all about your potential to learn statistics.

To help you change your mind about your potential, we want you to understand that there is a widespread *mistaken* belief in our society that math is a rare and innate ability, a skill that you either have or lack, so why study a subject that you have no hope of mastering? This is a truly crippling idea and an erroneous one. There is no evidence for innate ability but much evidence for performance differences due to effort. (Effort is naturally increased if one is interested, and interest is increased if one has reason to expect success in understanding math.)

Still, for many of us, this wrong attitude persists. Tobias (1987) cites one study comparing students in Asia and the United States on an international mathematics test. The U.S. students were thoroughly outperformed, but more important was why: When the students were interviewed, it was found that Asian students saw math as an ability fairly equally distributed among people and thought that differences in performance were due to hard work. U.S. students persisted in the idea that mathematical ability is a rare, inborn talent.

Since in fact math almost never comes easily to anyone, thinking otherwise must work particularly against students who, because of gender or racial stereotypes or difficulty with English, are discouraged by lack of success early in their career with numbers.

Again, there is simply no evidence for any inherent difference, and the performance differences that do exist *need not predict anything at all about you.* You are an individual, with your own brain and determination. It may take much more work for you to do well in this class than it will for others. But it may be especially satisfying when you succeed in that hard work, when you have proved to yourself that you can master this subject matter and have modeled that achievement for others who will follow you.

Consider these words, from the former president of the Mathematics Association of America:

> The paradox of our times is that as mathematics becomes increasingly powerful, only the powerful seem to benefit from it. The ability to think mathematically—broadly interpreted—is absolutely crucial to advancement in virtually every career. Confidence in dealing with data, skepticism in analyzing arguments, persistence in penetrating complex problems, and literacy in communicating about technical matters are the enabling arts offered by the new mathematical sciences. (Steen, 1987, p. xviii)

Do not be left out because someone gave you the impression you could not or would not want to learn these "enabling arts."

Exaggeration of Proportions

Ordinarily, the height of a histogram or frequency polygon should begin at 0 or the lowest value of the scale and continue to the highest value of the scale, and the overall proportion of the graph should be about 1.5 times as wide as it is tall. This is illustrated in our stress ratings example. Note, however, what happens if we make the graph much taller or shorter (as shown in Figure 1-16). The impression is of either more or less difference between the intervals. The effect is like that of a fun house mirror—the true picture is distorted.

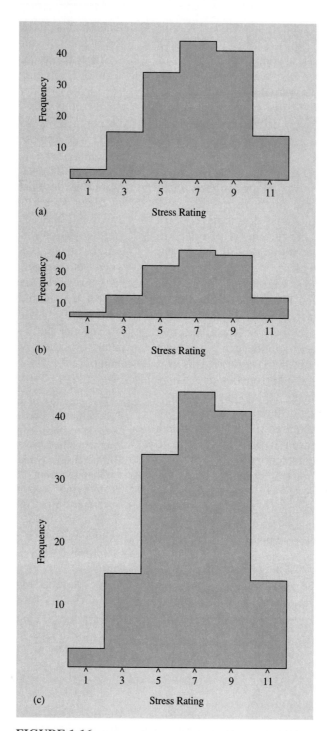

FIGURE 1-16
Histograms of students' stress ratings distorted from the desirable rule of width 1.5
times height. (Data from Aron et al., 1993.)

Of course, any particular shape is in a sense accurate. But the 1.5:1 scale has been adopted to give people a norm for comparison. Changing this proportion misleads the eye.

Frequency Tables, Histograms, and Frequency Polygons in Research Articles

Frequency tables, histograms, and frequency polygons are actually used by researchers mainly as an intermediary step in the process of more elaborate statistical analyses. On rare occasions, a frequency table of the kind we have been considering in this chapter will be presented in a study, particularly when it is set up to compare frequencies on two or more variables or for two or more groups.

As an example of a frequency table appearing in a article, Ann Beckingham and Bernard Lubin (1991) administered three forms of the Depression Adjective Check List (DACL) to each of 259 individuals between 60 and 74 years of age and to each of 136 individuals between 75 and 93 years old. (The DACL consists of 34 adjectives, each of which respondents either check or not check according to whether it applies to themselves.) Table 1-6 reproduces Beckingham and Lubin's frequency table, in which frequencies of numbers of words checked are shown separately for each age group, for each of three versions of the test. (Notice that in this example, the values are listed along the left edge from lowest to highest, which is not standard.)

Usually, however, when frequency tables appear in articles, it is in a situation in which the values of the variable are categories rather than numbers. For example, Tabachnick, Keith-Spiegel, and Pope (1991) mailed questionnaires to 500 men and 500 women who were members of the American Psychological Association and taught psychology at a university; 482 sent back the questionnaire with usable data. Table 1-7 reproduces one of their tables in which they show the frequencies for the various specialty areas.

Notice that this table showed both the number of cases in each category (the frequency) and also the percentages, which are very helpful in making sense of such a table. In fact, it is quite common for such tables to omit the raw numbers entirely and include only the percentages. For example, Table 1-8 is reprinted from an article by Fehr (1988), who asked 141 Canadian undergraduates to list as many features of the concept of "love" (or for some subjects, the concept "commitment") as came to mind during a 3-minute period. The table shows the percentage of subjects who listed various features.

Histograms and frequency polygons almost never appear in research articles (except in articles *about* statistics). However, the shape of the distribution of the scores collected in a study is sometimes commented on in the text of the article, particularly if the distribution seems to deviate from normal. For example, in the Beckingham and Lubin (1991) study of depression test scores among the elderly, the authors commented that the "distribution for all three lists is skewed to the left, most for list E and least for list F" (p. 409). (We consider additional examples of descriptions of the shape of distributions in Chapter 15, which focuses on statistical procedures when distributions are not normal.)

TABLE 1-6
Distribution of Raw Scores of the DACL Form E, F, G, by Age Group

	Age Group					
	60 to 74			75 to 93		
Score	E	F	G	E	F	G
1	32	10	26	6	4	8
2	14	12	22	6	2	8
3	26	12	14	10	4	2
4	14	12	10	5	7	9
5	23	16	22	12	4	7
6	21	23	19	10	8	6
7	16	21	16	14	17	12
8	21	18	19	14	5	7
9	19	32	24	9	13	17
10	20	24	19	6	18	10
11	16	29	17	10	17	15
12	9	20	14	8	12	8
13	7	9	10	14	7	12
14	7	7	6	0	9	7
15	6	7	7	3	4	2
16	4	3	3	2	0	0
17	1	2	3	3	0	0
18	1	0	3	1	2	0
19	1	0	3	0	0	0
20	0	0	1	0	0	2
21	1	2	0	1	0	2
22	0	0	0	1	0	0
23	0	0	1	0	2	0
24	0	0	0	0	0	2
25	0	0	0	0	1	0
26	0	0	0	0	0	0
27	0	0	0	1	0	0
Totals	259	259	259	136	136	136

Note. From Beckingham, A. C., & Lubin, B. (1991), tab. 5. Copyright, 1991, by Clinical Psychology Publishing Co. Reprinted by permission.

TABLE 1-7
Primary Specialty Areas of Psychologists Providing Usable Data

Specialty	n	%
Clinical	113	23.6
Experimental	85	17.7
Social	78	16.3
Developmental/Aging	67	14.0
Counseling	41	8.6
Industrial/Organization/Human Factors	27	5.6
Educational	16	3.3
Physiological and related	14	2.9
Personality	11	2.3
School	8	1.7
Other	19	4.0
No answer	3	0.6

Note. From Tabachnik, B. G., Keith-Spiegel, P., & Pope, K. S. (1991), tab. 3. Ethics of teaching: Beliefs and behaviors of psychologists as educators. *American Psychologist, 46,* 506–515. Copyright, 1991, by the American Psychological Association. Reprinted by permission of the author.

TABLE 1-8
Free Listing of Features of Love and Commitment

Feature	Percentage of Subjects	Feature	Percentage of Subjects
Love		*Love (continued)*	
Caring[a]	43.75	Gazing at the other	3.13
Happiness	29.17	Mutual	3.13
Want to be with other	28.13	Need each other	3.13
Friendship	22.92	Openness	3.13
Feel free to talk about anything	19.79	Patient	3.13
Warm feelings	16.67	Protectiveness	3.13
Accept other the way s/he is	15.63	Scary	3.13
Trust[a]	14.58	Sexual appeal	3.13
Commitment	13.54	Wonderful feelings	3.13
Sharing[a]	13.54	Admiration	2.08
Think about the other all the time[a]	13.54	Comfort	2.08
Sacrifice[a]	13.54	Want best for other	2.08
Understanding	12.50	Long-lasting[a]	2.08
Honesty[a]	11.46	*Commitment*	
Respect[a]	11.46		
Contentment[a]	10.42	Perseverance	34.83
Euphoria	10.42	Responsibility[a]	28.09
Put other first[a]	9.38	Living up to your word	23.60
Sexual passion	9.38	Devotion[a]	21.35
Supportiveness[a]	9.38	Faithfulness	19.10
Attachment[a]	8.33	Obligation	17.98
Closeness	8.33	Sacrifice[a]	15.73
Concern for the other's well-being[a]	8.33	Honesty[a]	14.61
Empathy	8.33	Love	14.61
Heart rate increases	8.33	Trust[a]	13.48
Helping[a]	8.33	Helping[a]	12.36
Feel good about self	7.29	Loyalty[a]	12.36
Forgiveness	7.29	A promise	12.36
Have a lot in common	7.29	Being there for the other in good and bad times	11.24
Miss other when apart	7.29	Mutual agreement	11.24
Feel relaxed with other	6.25	Caring[a]	10.11
Giving[a]	6.25	Give your best effort	10.11
Liking[a]	6.25	Put other first[a]	8.99
Security[a]	6.25	Respect[a]	8.99
Unconditional	6.25	Attachment[a]	7.87
Interest in the other	5.21	Attention focused on other	6.74
Intimacy	5.21	Concern for the other's well-being[a]	6.74
Laughing	5.21	Giving[a]	6.74
Loyalty[a]	5.21	Long-lasting[a]	6.74
Physical attraction	5.21	Reliable	6.74
Uncertainty	5.21	Sharing[a]	6.74
Affection[a]	4.17	Work toward common goals	5.62
Butterflies in stomach	4.17	Conscious decision	4.49
Compassion	4.17	Feel trapped	4.49
Dependency	4.17	Giving and taking	4.49
Do things for the other	4.17	Hard work	4.49
Excitement	4.17	Supportiveness[a]	4.49
Kind	4.17	Working out problems	4.49
Other is important	4.17	A high priority	3.37
Positve outlook	4.17	Liking[a]	3.37
Responsibilty[a]	4.17	Security[a]	3.37
See only the other's good qualities	4.17	Think about other all the time[a]	3.37
Touching	4.17	Affection[a]	2.25
Devotion[a]	3.13	Contentment[a]	2.25
Energy	3.13	Maturity	2.25

Note. Percentages based on 96 protocols for love, 89 protocols for commitment. From Fehr, B. (1988), tab. 1. Prototype analysis of the concepts of love and commitment. *Journal of Personality and Social Psychology, 55,* 557–579. Copyright, 1988, by the American Psychological Association. Reprinted by permission of the author.

[a]Feature shared by love and commitment.

Summary

Psychologists use the procedures of descriptive statistics to summarize and make understandable a group of numbers collected in a research study.

One approach to descriptive statistics is to organize the numbers into a frequency table in which each of the possible values is listed along the left from highest to lowest, accompanying each value by the number of cases that have that value.

However, when there are a large number of different values, a grouped frequency table will be more useful. It is like an ordinary frequency table except that the frequencies are given for intervals that include a range of values. An interval size should be selected so that (a) the total number of intervals is between 5 and 15; (b) the interval size is a common, simple number; and (c) each interval starts with a multiple of the interval size.

The distribution of frequencies can be illustrated graphically with a histogram, a kind of bar graph in which the height of each bar represents the frequency for a particular value or interval and there are no spaces between the bars. An alternative is a frequency polygon, in which a line connects dots, the height of each of which represents the frequency for a particular value or interval.

The general shape of the histogram or frequency polygon can be unimodal (having a single peak), bimodal, multimodal (including bimodal), or rectangular (having no peak); it can be symmetrical or skewed (having a long tail) to the right or the left; and compared to the bell-shaped normal curve, it can be kurtotic—too flat or too peaked.

Graphic displays of information presented to the general public are sometimes distorted in ways that mislead the eye, such as failing to use equal intervals and exaggerating proportions.

Frequency tables rarely appear in research articles. When they do, it is usually to compare distributions and often involves frequencies (and percentages) for various categories rather than for the different numerical values of a variable. Histograms and frequency polygons almost never appear in articles, though the shapes of distributions (normal, skewed, etc.) are occasionally described in words.

Key Terms

bimodal distribution	histogram	rectangular distribution
ceiling effect	inferential statistics	score
descriptive statistics	interval	skewed distribution
floor effect	kurtosis	symmetrical distribution
frequency distribution	multimodal distribution	unimodal distribution
frequency polygon	normal curve	value
frequency table	open-ended interval	variable
grouped frequency table		

Practice Problems

These problems involve computation (with the assistance of a calculator). Most real-life statistics problems are done on a computer. But even if you have a computer, do these by hand to ingrain the method in your mind.

For practice in using a computer to solve statistical problems, refer to the computer section of each chapter of the study guide that accompanies this text.

All data are fictional (unless an actual citation is given).

Answers to Set I are given at the back of the book.

SET I

1. These are the scores on a measure of sensitivity to smell administered to a group of chefs attending a national conference:

96, 83, 59, 64, 73, 74, 80, 68, 87, 67, 64, 92, 76, 71, 68, 50, 85, 75, 81, 70, 76, 91, 69, 83, 75

(a) Make a frequency table, (b) make a grouped frequency table, (c) make a histogram of the grouped frequencies, and (d) describe the general shape of the distribution.

2. The following scores are the number of minutes it took each of a group of 10-year-olds to complete a series of abstract puzzles:

24, 83, 36, 22, 81, 39, 60, 62, 38, 66, 38, 36, 45, 20, 20, 67, 41 87, 41, 82, 35, 82, 28, 80, 80, 68, 40, 27, 43, 80, 31, 89, 83, 24

Make (a) a grouped frequency table and (b) a histogram based on the grouped frequency table.

3. Suppose that 50 students were asked how many hours they had studied this weekend and they responded as follows:

11, 2, 0, 13, 5, 7, 1, 8, 12, 11, 7, 8, 9, 10, 7, 4, 6, 10, 4, 7, 8, 6, 7, 10, 7, 3, 11, 18, 2, 9, 7, 3, 8, 7, 3, 13, 9, 8, 7, 7, 10, 4, 15, 3, 5, 6, 9, 7, 10, 6

(a) Make a frequency table, (b) make a grouped frequency table, (c) make a frequency polygon based on the grouped frequency table, and (d) describe the shape of the distribution.

4. Describe the shapes of the three distributions illustrated.

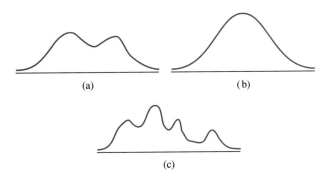

(a)

(b)

(c)

5. Draw an example of each of the following distributions: (a) symmetrical, (b) rectangular, and (c) skewed to the right.

6. Explain to a person who has never had a course in statistics what is meant by (a) a symmetric, unimodal distribution and (b) a negatively skewed unimodal distribution. (Be sure to explain in your first answer what is meant by a distribution as well.)

SET II

1. Following are the speeds of cars clocked by radar on a particular road in a 35-mph zone on a particular afternoon:

30, 36, 42, 36, 30, 52, 36, 34, 36, 33, 30, 32, 35, 32, 37, 34, 36, 31, 35, 20, 24, 46, 23, 31, 32, 45, 34, 37, 28, 40, 34, 38, 40, 52, 31, 33, 15, 27, 36, 40

(a) Make a frequency table, (b) make a grouped frequency table, (c) make a histogram of the grouped frequencies, (d) make a frequency polygon of the grouped frequencies, and (e) describe the general shape of the distribution.

2. Here are the number of holiday gifts purchased by 25 families randomly interviewed at a local mall at the end of the holiday season:

22, 18, 22, 26, 19, 14, 23, 27, 2, 18, 28, 28, 11, 16, 34, 28, 13, 21, 32, 17, 6, 29, 23, 22, 19

(a) Make a grouped frequency table, (b) make a frequency polygon of the grouped frequencies, and (c) describe the general shape of the distribution.

3. Indicate a book and page number of your choice (pick a page with at least 30 lines). Make a list of the number of words in each line; then use that list as your data set. (a) Make a frequency table, (b) make a grouped frequency table, (c) make a histogram of the grouped frequencies, (d) make a frequency polygon of the grouped frequencies, and (e) describe the general shape of the distribution.

4. Explain to a person who has never taken a course in statistics the meaning of (a) grouped frequency table and (b) histogram.

5. Give an example of something having these distribution shapes: (a) bimodal, (b) approximately rectangular, (c) positively skewed. Do not use an example given in this book or in class.

6. Find an example in a newspaper or magazine of a graph that misleads by failing to use equal interval sizes or exaggerating proportions.

2 The Mean, Variance, Standard Deviation, and Z Scores

As we noted in Chapter 1, the purpose of descriptive statistics is to make a group of scores understandable. And we looked at some ways of providing that understanding through tables and graphs—either a list of the distribution of scores over their possible range or a picture of that distribution. In this chapter, we consider the main statistical techniques for describing a distribution with numbers. These numbers are the mean, the variance, the standard deviation, and Z scores. The first indicates the average score, the second two describe the amount of variation in the scores, and the last describes a particular score in terms of its location in the distribution—specifically, by how much it varies from the average.

The Mean

Usually the best single number for describing a group of scores is the ordinary average, the sum of all the scores divided by the number of scores. In statistics, this is called the **mean.** The average or mean of a group of scores is sometimes said to show the **central tendency,** or the general typical or representative value of the group of scores.

mean

central tendency

Suppose that a psychotherapist noted how many sessions her last 10 clients had taken to complete brief therapy with her, and the numbers were as follows:

7, 8, 8, 7, 3, 1, 6, 9, 3, 8

The mean of these 10 scores is 6 (the sum of 60 sessions divided by 10 patients). That is, on the average, her last 10 clients had completed 6 sessions.

FIGURE 2-1
Mean of the distribution of the number of therapy sessions completed in a fictional example, illustrated through an analogy using blocks on a board balanced on a log.

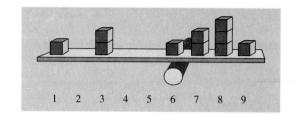

The information for the 10 clients is thus summarized by this single number.

Many students find it helpful to visualize the mean as a kind of balancing point for the distribution of scores. Try it by visualizing a board balanced over a log, like a rudimentary teeter-totter. On the board, imagine marks like a yardstick and piles of blocks distributed along the board, one for each score in the distribution. (This is a little like a histogram made of blocks.) The mean would be the point on the board where the weight of the blocks on each side would exactly balance. Figure 2-1 illustrates this for the case of our imaginary therapist's clients' sessions completed.

Some other examples are shown in Figure 2-2. Note that there need not even be a block right at the balance point—that is, the mean need not correspond to a value actually in the distribution. The mean is simply the average of the values, the balance point. The mean could even be a number that cannot possibly occur in the distribution, as in the case of a mean that is a deci-

FIGURE 2-2
Means of various fictional distributions illustrated using the analogy of blocks on a board balanced on a log.

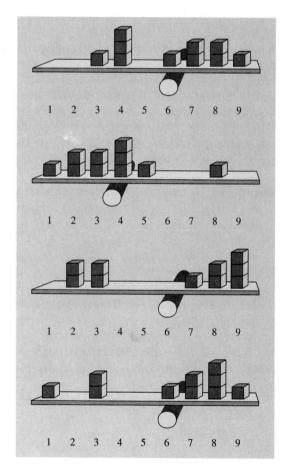

mal number when all the numbers in the distribution have to be whole numbers (2.3 children, for example). Also notice that the blocks can be very spread out or very close together and that they need not be spread out evenly. In any of these cases, it is still quite possible to mark a balance point. (Incidentally, this analogy to blocks balanced on a board on a log would in reality work precisely only if the board had no weight of its own.)

Formula for the Mean and Statistical Symbols

In the case of the mean, the computation is simple, and it is not really necessary to write it in symbols as a mathematical formula. However, some students find it easier to understand or remember a concept if it is expressed in the concise form of a formula. Because, the formula for the mean is so simple, it also provides a good opportunity for introducing the way formulas are written in statistics. When we get to more complicated procedures, formulas will simplify the task of expressing and comprehending what the procedure is and how it is calculated.

Thus the rule for computing the mean—add up all the scores and divide by the number of scores—can be expressed as the following formula:

$$M = \frac{\Sigma X}{N} \qquad (2\text{-}1)$$

M is a symbol for the mean. (Later you will learn another symbol for the mean, the Greek letter μ ("mu"), which is used in particular circumstances. A third symbol, $\overline{X}$, sometimes called "X-bar," is also widely used.)

Σ, the capital Greek letter "sigma," is the symbol for "sum of." It means "add up all the numbers" for whatever follows. It is the most common special arithmetic symbol used in statistics.

X refers to scores in the distribution of the variable X. We could have selected any letter, but if only one distribution is involved, it is customary to call it X. If, as will be necessary in some later chapters, you want to refer to two different distributions in the same formula, sometimes a second one, called Y, is used, and sometimes subscripts are used, as in X_1 and X_2. (In more formal, mathematical treatments of statistics, the symbols are a bit more complex still, in order to deal with complicated issues without being confusing. However, in books on statistics for psychologists, even fairly advanced texts, the symbols are kept simple, since the simpler form rarely creates ambiguities in the kinds of statistical formulas psychologists use.)

Thus ΣX means "the sum of X"—that is, these symbols direct you to add up all the scores in the distribution of the variable X. If X referred to number of therapy sessions in our example distribution, ΣX would equal 60, the sum of $7 + 8 + 8 + 7 + 3 + 1 + 6 + 9 + 3 + 8$.

N stands for *number* and is used in statistics to refer to the number of scores in a distribution. In our example, there are 10, so N equals 10.

Thus the formula says to divide the sum of all the scores in the distribution of the variable X by the total number of scores, N. In other words, divide 60 by 10. Put in terms of the formula:

$$M = \frac{\Sigma X}{N} = \frac{60}{10} = 6$$

FIGURE 2-3
Analogy of blocks on a board balanced on a fulcrum (using a histogram) illustrating the mean for 151 statistics students' ratings of their stress level. (Data from Aron et al., 1993.)

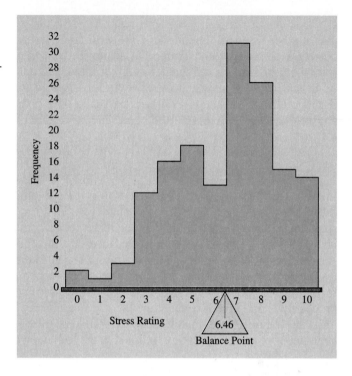

Additional Examples of Computing the Mean

Consider the examples from Chapter 1. The mean of the 151 statistics students' stress ratings (Aron et al., 1993) is computed by adding up all the ratings and dividing by the number of ratings.

$$M = \frac{\Sigma X}{N} = \frac{975}{151} = 6.46$$

This tells you that the average stress rating on the 10-point scale was 6.46, a figure clearly well above the middle of that scale. This can also be illustrated graphically, thinking of the histogram as a pile of blocks on a board and the mean of 6.46 as the point where a log underneath balances (see Figure 2-3). This single number is a considerable simplification of all the information in the set of stress scores.

Similarly, consider the teachers' ratings of grade school students' attitudes toward achievement (Moorehouse & Sanders, 1992). The original data, as we saw in Chapter 1, were as follows:

77, 78, 98, 85, 59, 59, 59, 108, 86, 104, 111, 67, 77, 66, 70, 74, 65, 108, 92, 68, 95, 56, 87, 92, 73, 92, 106, 74, 97, 109, 69, 103, 113, 119, 45, 99, 111, 78, 95, 54, 68, 42, 65, 84, 80, 115, 44, 32, 107, 57, 118, 107, 30, 50, 63, 74, 76, 43, 25, 73, 115, 40, 45, 86, 113, 115, 111, 114, 94, 110, 96, 90, 112, 103, 108, 110, 82, 73, 101, 72, 61, 75, 67, 74, 55, 74, 69, 109, 87, 74, 112, 97, 91, 101, 105, 97, 107, 92, 100, 109, 114, 103, 107, 100, 117, 74, 120, 86, 105, 108, 115, 96, 97, 106, 110, 112, 95, 113, 71, 88, 94, 104, 95, 62, 104, 70, 64, 117, 116, 65, 82, 119, 115, 81, 107, 111, 118, 63, 53, 104, 112, 90, 74, 65, 79, 53, 115, 84, 93, 68, 70, 114, 91

The frequency table, grouped frequency table, histogram, and frequency polygon that we constructed in Chapter 1 considerably simplified the pic-

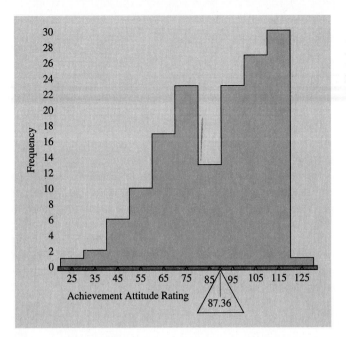

FIGURE 2-4
Analogy of blocks on a board balanced on a fulcrum (using a histogram) illustrating the mean for teachers' ratings of 153 grade school students' attitudes toward achievement. (Data from Moorehouse & Sanders, 1992.)

ture. But even with all that, a single-number summary could be useful too. Thus we can compute the mean in the usual way:

$$M = \frac{\Sigma X}{N} = \frac{13,366}{153} = 87.36$$

That is, if you add up all 153 scores, the "sum of X" comes to 13,366. Dividing this by the number of scores gives a mean attitudes score of 87.36. This is also illustrated in Figure 2-4.

Our other main example in Chapter 1 was about the time (in milliseconds) that it took for subjects to read ambiguous sentences. The mean is computed in the usual way:

$$M = \frac{\Sigma X}{N} = \frac{2,755}{100} = 27.55$$

Again, we have illustrated this graphically in Figure 2-5.

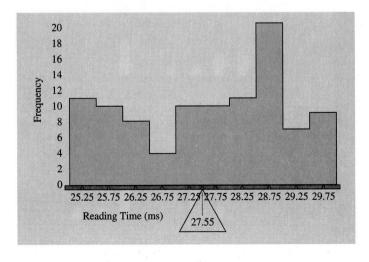

FIGURE 2-5
Analogy of blocks on a board balanced on a fulcrum (using a histogram) illustrating the mean for a fictional distribution of 100 subjects' time (in milliseconds) needed to read ambiguous sentences.

Alternative Measures of Central Tendency

mode

The mean is only one of several ways of describing central tendency, the typical or representative score. One alternative is the **mode,** the most common single number in a distribution. In our therapy sessions example, the mode is 8, since there are three cases of 8 sessions and no other number of sessions with as many cases. Another way to think of the mode is that it is the value with the largest frequency in a frequency table, the high point or peak of a distribution's frequency polygon or histogram (as shown in Figure 2-6).

In a perfectly symmetrical unimodal distribution (and a few other cases), the mode is the same as the mean. But when it is not the same, it generally corresponds less well than the mean to what we intuitively understand as central tendency as a good representative value. Also, it is possible to change some of the scores in a distribution (see Figure 2-7) without affecting the mode, whereas the mean is affected by any changes; hence the mean is more representative of all the numbers in the distribution. For these and other reasons, psychologists rarely use the mode.

FIGURE 2-6
Illustration of the mode as the high point in a distribution's histogram, using the fictional example of the number of therapy sessions completed by 10 patients.

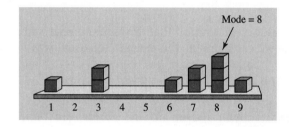

FIGURE 2-7
Illustration of the effect on the mean and on the mode of changing some scores, using the fictional example of the number of therapy sessions completed by 10 patients.

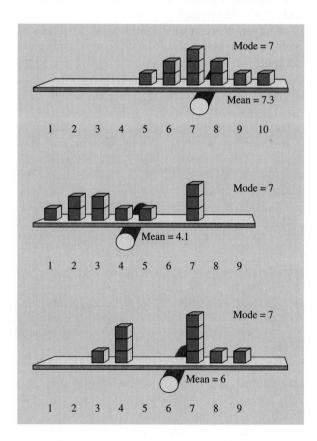

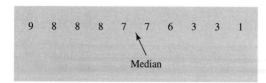

| 9 | 8 | 8 | 8 | 7 | 7 | 6 | 3 | 3 | 1 |

Median

FIGURE 2-8
Illustration of the median as the middle score when scores are lined up from highest to lowest, using the fictional example of the number of therapy sessions completed by 10 patients.

Another alternative to the mean is the **median.** If you line up all the scores from highest to lowest, the middle score is the median. As shown in Figure 2-8, if you line up the number of therapy sessions attended from highest to lowest, the fifth and sixth cases (the two middle ones), are both 7s. Either way, the median is 7 (had the two middle scores been different, we would consider their average as the median).

median

When you have an even number of cases, the median can fall between two different numbers. In that case, you use the average of the two. In the example of time to read ambiguous sentences, there are exactly 100 cases. The 50th highest case is 27.8, and the 51st highest case is 27.6. The median is therefore 27.7, the average of 27.8 and 27.6.

In certain cases, the median can be a more useful indicator of central tendency than the mean. Most commonly this is when there are a few extreme cases that would strongly affect the mean but would not affect the median. For example, suppose that among the 100 families on a banana plantation in Central America, 99 families have an annual income of $100 and 1 family (the owner's) has an annual income of $90,100. The mean family income on this plantation would be $1,000 (99 x 100 = 9,900; 9,900 + 90,100 = 100,000; 100,000/100 = 1,000). But no family has an income even close to $1,000, so this number is completely misleading. The median income in this case would be $100—a figure much more typical of whomever you would meet if you walked up to someone randomly on the plantation.

Reaction time results are another example of when the median might be preferred. Suppose that the times (in seconds) on five testings were .74, .86, 2.32, .79, and .81. The 2.32-s time may have occurred because the person was momentarily distracted. So using the median to describe the central tendency might be better, deemphasizing the one extreme time as probably appropriate.

The median is used occasionally in psychology as a descriptive statistic. Again, it is most likely to be used in situations where there are a few extreme cases (like the reaction time example), called **outliers,** that would make the mean unrepresentative of the main body of cases. There are even a few circumstances in which psychologists use the median as part of more complex statistical techniques. However, in practice, psychologists almost always use the mean as the measure of central tendency, and it serves as a fundamental building block for most other statistical techniques.

outliers

The Variance and the Standard Deviation

Besides a distribution's central tendency, a researcher wants to know how spread out it is. For example, suppose that you were asked, "How old are the students in your statistics class?" At a city-based university with many returning and part-time students, the mean age might turn out to be 38. So you could tell whoever asked you, "The average age is 38." But this would not tell the whole story. It would be possible, for example, to have a mean of

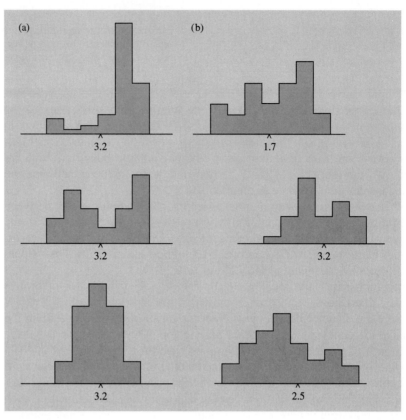

FIGURE 2-9
Examples of distributions with (a) the same mean but different amounts of spread and (b) different means but the same amount of spread.

38 because every student in the class was exactly 38 years old. Or you could have a mean of 38 because exactly half the class was 18 and the other half was 58. These would be two quite different situations.

Figure 2-9 shows three different frequency distributions with the same mean but different amounts of spread around the mean and three with different means but the same amount of spread.

Variance

variance

The **variance** of a distribution is a measure of how spread out the scores are around the mean in the distribution. It represents the average of each score's squared difference from the mean. To compute the variance, you would first subtract the mean of the distribution from each score in the distribution, thereby finding each score's **deviation score.** The deviation score tells you

deviation score

how far away the actual score is from the mean. (It also tells you whether the actual score is above or below the mean, according to whether the deviation score is positive or negative.) Next you square each of these deviation

squared deviation score

scores (multiply each by itself) to get each score's **squared deviation score.** Familiarize yourself well with this paragraph: This procedure is a fundamental step in a great many statistical processes.

Why square the score? When you square a number, whether it is initially positive or negative, it always comes out positive. Deviation scores for numbers below the mean are negative; deviation scores for numbers above the mean are positive. If you do not eliminate the plus and minus signs of the deviation scores, the pluses and minuses balance each other out, and you get an average deviation score of 0, no matter how spread out or clustered together the scores are.

Once you have the squared deviation scores, you add them up to get the **sum of squared deviations** and divide by the number of squared deviation scores to get the average or mean of squared deviations. This average of the squared deviations is the variance.[1]

Although this procedure may seem a bit cumbersome or hard to remember at first, it works quite well. If one distribution is more spread out than another, the larger distribution will of necessity have a larger variance because being spread out has the effect of making the deviation scores (and hence the squared deviation scores) bigger. For example, in the case of the class where everyone was exactly 38 years old, the variance would be exactly 0—that is, there would be no variance. (In terms of the numbers, each person's deviation score would be $38 - 38 = 0$; 0 squared is 0. The average of a bunch of zeros is 0.) By contrast, the class of half 18-year-olds and half 58-year-olds would have a rather large variance of 400. (The 18-year-olds would each have deviation scores of $18 - 38 = -20$. The 58-year-olds would have deviation scores of $58 - 38 = 20$. In both cases, the squared

---

[1]You may wonder why statisticians don't just use the deviation scores themselves, simply making all deviations positive, and use the average of these. This was actually done in the past, and the average of the deviation scores—treating all deviations as positive—is called the *average deviation* or *mean deviation*. Unfortunately, however, in spite of its conceptual and computational simplicity, the average deviation does not work out very well as part of more complicated statistical procedures because it is hard to do algebraic manipulations with a formula that ignores the signs of some of its numbers.

There is also another, deeper reason why statisticians use the squared approach. Using the squared deviations has the effect of giving more influence to large deviations (squaring a deviation of 4 gives a squared deviation of 16; squaring a deviation of 8 gives a squared deviation of 64). As you will learn in later chapters, deviation scores often represent "errors": The mean is expected, and deviations from it are errors or discrepancies from what is expected. Thus using squared scores has the effect of "penalizing" large errors to a greater extent than small errors.

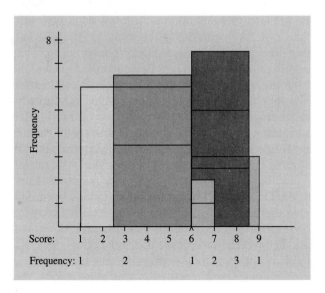

FIGURE 2-10
Illustration of the meaning of the variance by showing areas corresponding to squared deviation scores, using the fictional example of the number of therapy sessions attended.

deviation scores— –20 squared or 20 squared—would come out to 400. And the average of all 400s is 400.)

Now suppose that the class had equal numbers at ages 18, 28, 38, 48, and 58. The mean would in this case still be 38. The variance, however, would be 200. (The calculation of this example is not important at the moment; but if you are interested, it works out to 200 because you would be averaging cases in which the squared deviation scores for the 18-year-olds were 400; for the 28-year-olds, 100; for the 38-year-olds, 0; for the 48-year-olds, 100; and for the 58-year-olds, 400.)

It may help to think of the variance in graphic terms. Figure 2-10 shows the therapy session scores from our earlier example as a histogram. Consider the lowest number, the person who attended only one session. This person has a deviation score of –5 sessions (1 minus the mean of 6 equals –5). Squaring the deviation score makes 25 squared units. This is shown in the figure as an area. The figure shows the squared deviation areas for all 10 patients. The average of these areas is the variance.

The variance plays an important role in many other statistical procedures. However, the variance is used only occasionally as a descriptive statistic because it is scaled in squared units, a metric that is not very intuitively direct for giving a sense of just how spread out the distribution is. For example, it is clear that a class with a variance of 400 has a more spread-out distribution than one whose variance is 200. However, the actual number 400 does not give an obvious insight into the actual variation among the ages, none of which are anywhere near 400.

Standard Deviation

standard deviation

The statistic most widely used for describing the spread of a distribution is the **standard deviation.** The standard deviation is the square root of the variance: To find the standard deviation of a distribution, you first compute the variance and then take its square root. If the variance of a distribution is 400, the standard deviation is 20. If the variance is 9, the standard deviation is 3; if the variance is 100, the standard deviation is 10; and so on.

Because the variance is an indicator of the average amount of squared deviation from the mean, the standard deviation is in terms of direct, ordinary, not-squared distance from the mean. Roughly speaking, the standard deviation is the average amount by which scores differ from the mean. Thus in a class with an age distribution with a standard deviation of 20 years, the ages are spread out, on the average, about 20 years in each direction from the mean. In a distribution of the number of children among families in a particular country, the mean might be 4 and the standard deviation 1. That would mean that the distribution is such that for every family with exactly four children (0 deviation from the mean), you might well find one with six or two children (deviations of 2 children from the mean). But it might not work that way, since it could be that half the families have exactly five and the other half exactly three. Or it might be that most have four, but a few have none and a few have eight (see Figure 2-11). Nevertheless, knowing the standard deviation gives you a general sense of the degree of spread, even if it does not tell you the precise shape of the distribution.

Note that the standard deviation is not *exactly* the average extent to which scores in the distribution differ from the mean. To be precise, the

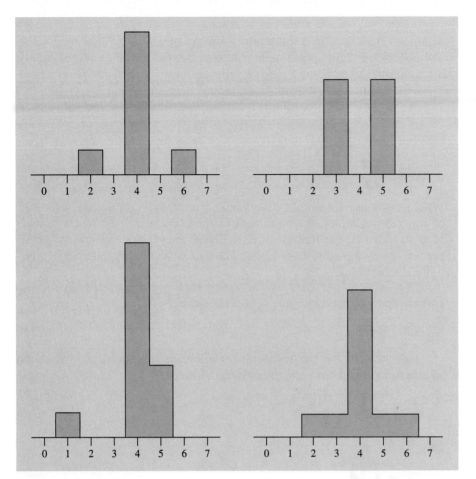

standard deviation is the square root of the average of the scores' squared deviations from the mean. This squaring, averaging, and then taking the square root produces a slightly different result from simply averaging the scores' deviations from the mean. Nevertheless, the result of this approach has sufficient mathematical and statistical advantages to outweigh the slight disadvantage of giving only an approximate description of the average variation from the mean.

Formulas for the Variance and the Standard Deviation

The variance, in words, is the average squared deviation from the mean. In symbols, this is how it looks:

$$SD^2 = \frac{\Sigma(X - M)^2}{N} \tag{2-2}$$

SD^2 is the symbol for the variance. (Later you will learn its other symbols, S^2 and σ^2—the lowercase Greek letter "sigma" squared. The different symbols correspond to different circumstances in which the variance is used and, in some cases, even slightly different calculations.) *SD* is short for *standard deviation*, emphasizing that the variance is the standard deviation squared.

SD^2

The top part of the formula describes the sum of squared deviations. *X* refers to each score in the distribution, and *M* refers to the mean of the distribution. Thus, $X - M$ is the score minus the mean, or the deviation score. The superscript 2, of course, tells you to square the deviation score. Finally, the sum sign (Σ) tells you to add together all these squared deviation scores.

Because the sum of squared deviations is an important calculation in a number of statistical procedures, it has its own symbol, *SS*, and the formula for the variance is sometimes written using this symbol in the numerator instead of $\Sigma(X - M)^2$:

$$SD^2 = \frac{SS}{N} \tag{2-3}$$

Whether you use the simplified symbol *SS* or the full description of the sum of squared deviations, the bottom part of the formula is just N, the number of cases. That is, the formula says to divide the sum of the squared deviation scores by the number of squared deviation scores (the number of cases in the distribution).

The standard deviation is the square root of the variance. So, if you already know the variance, the formula is simply

$$SD = \sqrt{SD^2} \tag{2-4}$$

The formula for the standard deviation starting from scratch is the square root of what you calculate for the variance:

$$SD = \sqrt{\frac{\Sigma(X - M)^2}{N}} \tag{2-5}$$

or

$$SD = \sqrt{\frac{SS}{N}} \tag{2-6}$$

Steps for Computing the Variance and the Standard Deviation

1. Compute the mean: Add up all the scores and divide by the number of scores.
2. Compute the deviation scores: Subtract the mean from each score.
3. Compute the squared deviations scores: Multiply each deviation score times itself.
4. Compute the sum of the squared deviation scores (*SS*): Add up all the squared deviation scores.
5. Compute the average of the squared deviation scores (SD^2): Divide the sum of the squared deviation scores by the number of scores. This is the variance.
6. Compute the square root of the average of the squared deviation scores (*SD*): Find the square root of the number computed in Step 5. This is the standard deviation.

Applying these steps to the therapy session example, we saw earlier that the mean number of sessions was 6: 60 (the sum of all the scores) divided by 10 (the number of scores). The rest of the steps are best carried out as shown in Table 2-1. In general, you will find it easiest to perform your computations using a calculator, especially one with a square root key.

SS

TABLE 2-2
Computation of Variance and Standard Deviation for Children's Attitudes Toward Achievement

Attitude Score	–	Attitude Score Mean	=	Deviation Score	Squared Deviation Score	Attitude Score	–	Attitude Score Mean	=	Deviation Score	Squared Deviation Score
77		87.36		–10.36	107.33	65		87.36		–22.36	499.97
78		87.36		– 9.36	87.61	84		87.36		– 3.36	11.29
98		87.36		10.64	113.21	80		87.36		– 7.36	54.17
85		87.36		– 2.36	5.57	115		87.36		27.64	763.97
59		87.36		–28.36	804.29	44		87.36		–43.36	1,880.08
59		87.36		–28.36	804.29	32		87.36		–55.36	3,064.73
59		87.36		–28.36	804.29	107		87.36		19.64	385.73
108		87.36		20.64	426.01	57		87.36		–30.36	921.73
86		87.36		– 1.36	1.85	118		87.36		30.64	938.81
104		87.36		16.64	276.89	107		87.36		19.64	385.73
111		87.36		23.64	558.85	30		87.36		–57.36	3,290.17
67		87.36		–20.36	414.53	50		87.36		–37.36	1,395.77
77		87.36		–10.36	107.33	63		87.36		–24.36	593.41
66		87.36		–21.36	456.25	74		87.36		–13.36	178.49
70		87.36		–17.36	301.37	76		87.36		–11.36	129.05
74		87.36		–13.36	178.49	43		87.36		–44.36	1,967.81
65		87.36		–22.36	499.97	25		87.36		–62.36	3,888.77
108		87.36		20.64	426.01	73		87.36		–14.36	206.21
92		87.36		4.64	21.53	115		87.36		27.64	763.97
68		87.36		–19.36	374.81	40		87.36		–47.36	2,242.97
95		87.36		7.64	58.37	45		87.36		–42.36	1,794.37
56		87.36		–31.36	983.45	86		87.36		– 1.36	1.85
87		87.36		– .36	.13	113		87.36		25.64	657.41
92		87.36		4.64	21.53	115		87.36		27.64	763.97
73		87.36		–14.36	206.21	111		87.36		23.64	558.85
92		87.36		4.64	21.53	114		87.36		26.64	709.69
106		87.36		18.64	347.45	94		87.36		6.64	44.09
74		87.36		–13.36	178.49	110		87.36		22.64	512.57
97		87.36		9.69	92.93	96		87.36		8.64	74.65
109		87.36		21.64	468.29	90		87.36		2.64	6.97
69		87.36		–18.36	337.09	112		87.36		24.64	607.13
103		87.36		15.64	244.61	103		87.36		15.64	244.61
113		87.36		25.64	657.41	108		87.36		20.64	426.01
119		87.36		31.64	1,001.09	110		87.36		22.64	512.57
45		87.36		–42.36	1,794.37	82		87.36		– 5.36	28.73
99		87.36		11.64	135.49	73		87.36		–14.36	206.21
111		87.36		23.64	558.85	101		87.36		13.64	186.05
78		87.36		– 9.36	87.61	72		87.36		–15.36	235.93
95		87.36		7.64	58.37	61		87.36		–26.36	694.85
54		87.36		–33.36	1,112.89	75		87.36		–12.36	152.77
68		87.36		–19.36	374.81	67		87.36		–20.36	414.53
42		87.36		–45.36	2,057.53	74		87.36		–13.36	178.49

TABLE 2-1
Computation of Variance and Standard Deviation in the Number of Therapy Session Example

Score (Number of Sessions)	−	Mean Score (Mean Number of Sessions)	=	Deviation Score	Squared Deviation Score
7		6		1	1
8		6		2	4
8		6		2	4
7		6		1	1
3		6		−3	9
1		6		−5	25
6		6		0	0
9		6		3	9
3		6		−3	9
8		6		2	4
			Σ:	0	66

$$\text{Variance} = SD^2 = \frac{\Sigma(X - M)^2}{N} = \frac{SS}{N} = \frac{66}{10} = 6.6$$

$$\text{Standard deviation} = SD = \sqrt{SD^2} = \sqrt{6.6} = 2.57$$

Additional Examples of Computing the Variance and the Standard Deviation

The computation of the variance and standard deviation for the teachers' ratings of grade school students' attitudes toward achievement is shown in Table 2-2. Notice that in this example, as in the previous ones, we added up the actual deviations to be sure that they summed to 0, to check our arithmetic.

We can interpret this result as saying, roughly speaking, that a student's attitude toward achievement varies from the mean by an average of 22.55 points. This can also be described graphically on the histogram, as shown in Figure 2-12.

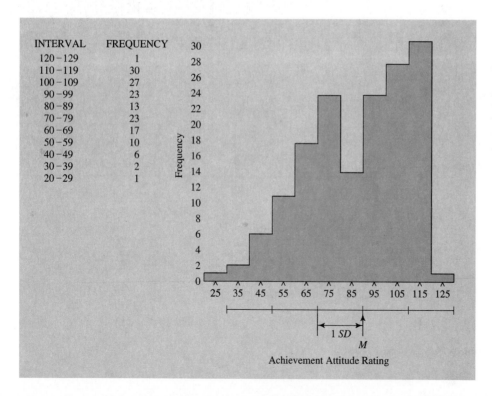

INTERVAL	FREQUENCY
120–129	1
110–119	30
100–109	27
90–99	23
80–89	13
70–79	23
60–69	17
50–59	10
40–49	6
30–39	2
20–29	1

FIGURE 2-12
Graphic description o[f] standard deviation as [a] distance along the bas[e of] a histogram, using tea[ch]ers' ratings of grade school students' attitu[des] toward achievement. (Data from Moorehou[se] & Sanders, 1992.)

TABLE 2-2 *(cont.)*

Attitude Score	–	Attitude Score Mean	=	Deviation Score	Squared Deviation Score	Attitude Score	–	Attitude Score Mean	=	Deviation Score	Squared Deviation Score
55		87.36		−32.36	1,047.17	88		87.36		.64	.41
74		87.36		−13.36	178.49	94		87.36		6.64	44.09
69		87.36		−18.36	337.09	104		87.36		16.64	276.89
109		87.36		21.64	468.29	95		87.36		7.64	58.37
87		87.36		− .36	.13	62		87.36		−25.36	643.13
74		87.36		−13.36	178.49	104		87.36		16.64	276.89
112		87.36		24.64	607.13	70		87.36		−17.36	301.37
97		87.36		9.69	92.93	64		87.36		−23.36	545.69
91		87.36		3.64	13.25	117		87.36		29.64	878.53
101		87.36		13.64	186.05	116		87.36		28.64	820.25
105		87.36		17.64	311.17	65		87.36		−22.36	499.97
97		87.36		9.69	92.93	82		87.36		− 5.36	28.73
107		87.36		19.64	385.73	119		87.36		31.64	1,001.09
92		87.36		4.64	21.53	115		87.36		27.64	763.97
100		87.36		12.64	159.77	81		87.36		− 6.36	40.45
109		87.36		21.64	468.29	107		87.36		19.64	385.73
114		87.36		26.64	709.69	111		87.36		23.64	558.85
103		87.36		15.64	244.61	118		87.36		30.64	938.81
107		87.36		19.64	385.73	63		87.36		−24.36	593.41
100		87.36		12.64	159.77	53		87.36		−34.36	1,180.61
117		87.36		29.64	878.53	104		87.36		16.64	276.89
74		87.36		−13.36	178.49	112		87.36		24.64	607.13
120		87.36		32.64	1,065.37	90		87.36		2.64	6.97
86		87.36		− 1.36	1.85	74		87.36		−13.36	178.49
105		87.36		17.64	311.17	65		87.36		−22.36	499.97
108		87.36		20.64	426.01	79		87.36		− 8.36	69.89
115		87.36		27.64	763.97	53		87.36		−34.36	1,180.61
96		87.36		8.64	74.65	115		87.36		27.64	763.97
97		87.36		9.69	92.93	84		87.36		− 3.36	11.29
106		87.36		18.64	347.45	93		87.36		5.64	31.81
110		87.36		22.64	512.57	68		87.36		−19.36	374.81
112		87.36		24.64	607.13	70		87.36		−17.36	301.37
95		87.36		7.64	58.37	114		87.36		26.64	709.69
113		87.36		25.64	657.41	91		87.36		3.64	13.25
71		87.36		−16.36	267.65					Σ: 0.00	77,807.84

$$\text{Variance} = SD^2 = \frac{\Sigma(X-M)^2}{N} = \frac{SS}{N} = \frac{77,807.84}{153} = 508.55$$

$$\text{Standard deviation} = SD = \sqrt{SD^2} = \sqrt{508.55} = 22.55$$

Note. Data from Moorehouse & Sanders (1992).

TABLE 2-3
Computation of Variance and Standard Deviation for the Fictional Study of Sentence Reading Time

Score (Reading Time)	Mean Score (Reading Time Mean)	= Deviation Score	Squared Deviation Score	Score (Reading Time)	Mean Score (Reading Time Mean)	= Deviation Score	Squared Deviation Score
27.2	27.55	− .35	.12	29.3	27.55	1.75	3.06
28.4	27.55	.85	.72	26.4	27.55	−1.15	1.32
26.3	27.55	−1.25	1.56	28.5	27.55	.95	.90
25.1	27.55	−2.45	6.00	27.0	27.55	− .55	.30
25.4	27.55	−2.15	4.62	25.6	27.55	−1.95	3.80
29.8	27.55	2.25	5.06	25.1	27.55	−2.45	6.00
26.1	27.55	−1.45	2.10	28.3	27.55	.75	.56
29.3	27.55	1.75	3.06	27.9	27.55	.35	.12
28.7	27.55	1.15	1.32	27.6	27.55	.05	.002
27.6	27.55	.05	.002	27.5	27.55	− .05	.003
25.8	27.55	−1.75	3.06	28.6	27.55	1.05	1.10
26.6	27.55	− .95	.90	25.8	27.55	−1.75	3.06
28.6	27.55	1.05	1.10	28.7	27.55	1.15	1.32
28.6	27.55	1.05	1.10	28.9	27.55	1.35	1.82
25.8	27.55	−1.75	3.06	28.9	27.55	1.35	1.82
26.0	27.55	−1.55	2.40	25.2	27.55	−2.35	5.52
26.3	27.55	−1.25	1.56	25.9	27.55	−1.65	2.72
26.2	27.55	−1.35	1.82	25.4	27.55	−2.15	4.62
27.3	27.55	− .25	.06	25.4	27.55	−2.15	4.62
28.0	27.55	.45	.20	28.5	27.55	.95	.90
27.9	27.55	.35	.12	28.3	27.55	.75	.56
29.6	27.55	2.05	4.20	29.6	27.55	2.05	4.20
25.8	27.55	−1.75	3.06	29.3	27.55	1.75	3.06
25.0	27.55	−2.55	6.50	28.9	27.55	1.35	1.82
28.2	27.55	.65	.42	29.2	27.55	1.65	2.72
28.3	27.55	.75	.56	29.8	27.55	2.25	5.06
29.0	27.55	1.45	2.10	25.9	27.55	−1.65	2.72
29.1	27.55	1.55	2.40	28.1	27.55	.55	.30
28.7	27.55	1.15	1.32	27.8	27.55	.25	.06
28.7	27.55	1.15	1.32	29.5	27.55	1.95	3.80
27.4	27.55	− .15	.02	29.6	27.55	2.05	4.20
27.0	27.55	− .55	.30	29.5	27.55	1.95	3.80
25.2	27.55	−2.35	5.52	25.6	27.55	−1.95	3.80
27.5	27.55	− .05	.003	25.9	27.55	−1.65	2.72
29.9	27.55	2.35	5.52	28.7	27.55	1.15	1.32
26.6	27.55	− .95	.90	28.4	27.55	.85	.72
25.8	27.55	−1.75	3.06	28.4	27.55	.85	.72
27.1	27.55	− .45	.20	28.0	27.55	.45	.20
25.1	27.55	−2.45	6.00	26.5	27.55	−1.05	1.10
28.7	27.55	1.15	1.32	27.0	27.55	− .55	.30
28.7	27.55	1.15	1.32	26.1	27.55	−1.45	2.10
27.5	27.55	− .05	.003	28.9	27.55	1.35	1.82
28.5	27.55	.95	.90	28.3	27.55	.75	.56
26.1	27.55	−1.45	2.10	28.5	27.55	.95	.90
25.4	27.55	−2.15	4.62	25.2	27.55	−2.35	5.52
27.3	27.55	− .25	.06	26.6	27.55	− .95	.90
29.6	27.55	2.05	4.20	27.4	27.55	− .15	.02
29.0	27.55	1.45	2.10	27.3	27.55	− .25	.06
27.5	27.55	− .05	.003	28.8	27.55	1.25	1.56
27.6	27.55	.05	.002	28.5	27.55	.95	.90
					Σ:	0.00	203.30

$$\text{Variance} = SD^2 = \frac{\Sigma(X-M)^2}{N} = \frac{SS}{N} = \frac{203.3}{100} = 2.03$$

$$\text{Standard deviation} = SD = \sqrt{SD^2} = \sqrt{2.03} = 1.42$$

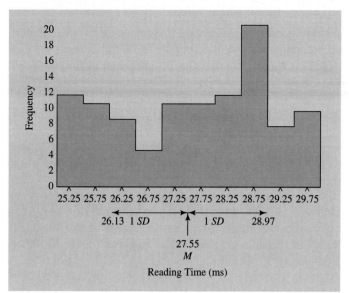

FIGURE 2-13
Graphic description of the standard deviation as the distance along the base of a histogram, using time (in milliseconds) needed to read ambiguous sentences (fictional data).

Finally, consider the example of the study of the time required to read ambiguous sentences. The computation for these data is shown in Table 2-3. Speaking in approximate terms, the average subject's time to read an ambiguous sentence varies by 1.42 ms from the mean of 27.55 ms. This is illustrated in Figure 2-13.

Computational Formulas for the Variance and the Standard Deviation

In actual research situations—as in these last two examples—psychologists must often compute the variance and the standard deviation for distributions with a great many cases, often involving decimals or large numbers. In these circumstances, the steps described can be quite tedious, even with a calculator. Luckily, over the years, a number of shortcuts have been developed to simplify the computation. Any such shortcut we will call a **computational formula.** Computational formulas for the variance and standard deviation are given in the appendix to this chapter.

computational formula

However, today most psychologists compute the variance and the standard deviation (as well as other statistical indices) by computer, meaning that the computational formulas are rarely used by researchers anymore. In fact, in the cases of the variance and the standard deviation, even many calculators are set up so that you need only enter the scores and press a button or two to get the variance and the standard deviation.

In this book, we emphasize using the ordinary formulas—what we call **definitional formulas**—because they correspond to the definition of the statistic. Usually when we have you try to work something out by hand, we have you use standard definitional formulas. The work may be more tedious, but it reinforces the underlying understanding of what you are doing. The purpose of this book is to help you understand statistical procedures, not to turn you into a computer by having you memorize and use computational formulas you will rarely, if ever, employ again. (To make the actual calculations not too complicated, however, our practice problems generally use small groups of whole numbers. For students who have access

definitional formulas

to a computer, the study guide accompanying this textbook includes material designed to give you experience doing statistics as psychologists normally would, working with standardized statistics programs on a computer.)

The Variance as the Sum of Squared Deviations Divided by $N-1$

You should be aware that psychologists often use a slightly different formula for the variance, whether defining it or calculating it. We have defined the variance as the average of the squared deviation scores. That means dividing the sum of squared deviation scores by the number of scores—SS/N. But you learn in Chapter 9 that for many purposes it is instead correct to define the variance as the sum of squared deviation scores divided by *1 less than the number of scores*—in these cases, the variances is $SS/(N-1)$. In fact, the number given in research articles for the variance (or for its square root, the standard deviation) is often figured using the $SS/(N-1)$ definition. Also, when calculators or computers give the variance or the standard deviation automatically, the number may be figured in this way. But don't worry. The approach you are learning in this chapter—variance = SS/N—is entirely correct for the purposes for which we have been using it (describing the variation in a group of scores), for the material covered in the rest of this chapter (Z scores), and for the material you learn in Chapters 3 through 8. We mention this other approach—variance = $SS/(N-1)$—here only to avoid any confusion that might arise when you read about variance or standard deviation in other places or if your calculator or a computer program produces a figure for the standard deviation that does not seem to make sense. To keep things simple, we wait to discuss the rationale and use of the $N-1$ approach until it is needed, starting in Chapter 9.

Z Scores

So far you have learned about describing a distribution of scores in terms of its mean and variation. In this section, you learn how to describe a particular score in terms of its location in a distribution.

Suppose that you were told that someone named Alan had seen the psychotherapist (the one we have been considering in this chapter) for 9 sessions. If we did not know the distribution of sessions, it would be hard to tell whether Alan had attended a lot or a few sessions in relation to other clients. However, if we know that the mean is 6 and the standard deviation is 2.57, it is clear not only that Alan attended an above-average number of sessions but also that the extent by which Alan exceeded the average (3 sessions more than average) was a bit more than the therapist's patients typically vary from the average. This is all illustrated in Figure 2-14.

FIGURE 2-14
Relation of the number of sessions attended by a client named Alan to the overall distribution of number of sessions attended by all clients of a particular (fictional) therapist.

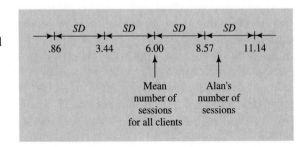

BOX 2-1

The Sheer Joy (Yes, Joy) of Statistical Analysis

You are learning statistics for the fun of it, right? No? Or maybe so after all. Because if you become a psychologist, at some time or other you will form a hypothesis, gather some data, and analyze them. (Even if you plan a career as a psychotherapist, you will probably eventually wish to test an idea about the nature of your clients and their difficulties.) That hypothesis, your own original idea, and the data you gather to test it are going to be very important to you. Your heart may well be pounding with excitement as you analyze the statistics.

Consider some of the comments of social psychologists we interviewed for our book *The Heart of Social Psychology* (Aron & Aron, 1989). Deborah Richardson, who studies interpersonal relationships, confided that her favorite part of being a social psychologist is looking at the statistical output of the computer analyses:

> It's like putting together a puzzle. . . . It's a highly arousing, positive experience for me. I often go through periods of euphoria. Even when the data don't do what I want them to do . . . [there's a] physiological response. . . . It's exciting to see the numbers come off—Is it actually the way I thought it would be?—then thinking about the alternatives.

Harry Reis, former editor of the Group Process and Interpersonal Relations section of the *Journal of Personality and Social Psychology*, sees his profession the same way:

> By far the most rewarding part is when you get a new data set and start analyzing it and things pop out, partly a confirmation of what led you into the study in the first place, but then also other things. . . . "Why is that?" Trying to make sense of it. The kind of ideas that come from data. . . . I love analyzing data.

Bibb Latane, an eminent psychologist known for, among other things, his work on why people don't always intervene to help others who are in trouble, reports eagerly awaiting

> the first glimmerings of what came out . . . [and] using them to shape what the next question should be. . . . You need to use everything you've got, . . . every bit of your experience and intuition. It's where you have the biggest effect, it's the least routine. You're in the room with the tiger, face to face with the core of what you are doing, at the moment of truth.

Bill Graziano, whose work integrates developmental and social psychology, calls the analysis of his data "great fun, just great fun." And in the same vein, Peggy Clark, who studies emotion and cognition, declares that "the most fun of all is getting the data and looking at them."

So you see? Statistics in the service of your own creative ideas can be a pleasure indeed.

What Is a Z Score?

A **Z score** is an ordinary score transformed so that it better describes that score's location in a distribution. Specifically, a Z score is the number of standard deviations the score is above the mean (if it is positive) or below the mean (if it is negative). Thus the standard deviation now becomes a kind of yardstick, a unit of measure in its own right. In the therapy example, Alan, who attended 9 sessions, has a Z score of +1.17 because he was 1.17 standard deviations above the mean (a little more than 1 standard deviation of 2.57 sessions above the mean). Another client, Sarah, who had seen the therapist for 6 sessions, would have a Z score of 0 because her score was exactly the mean—that is, it was 0 standard deviations above or below the mean. And a client who had attended only 1 session, 5 less than average, would be nearly 2 standard deviations below the mean (a Z score of −1.95)—this patient would be about twice as much below average as clients of this therapist typically vary from average in the number of sessions they attend.

Z score

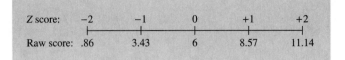

Z score:	−2	−1	0	+1	+2
Raw score:	.86	3.43	6	8.57	11.14

Z Scores as a Scale

raw scores

Figure 2-15 shows, for the therapy session example, a scale of Z scores lined up against a scale of **raw scores**, much as a ruler might have inches lined up on one side and the corresponding centimeters on the other or a thermometer might have the Fahrenheit scale on one side and the Celsius scale on the other. (A raw score is an ordinary measurement before it has been made into a Z score.)

Additional Examples

Z scores have many practical uses and are crucial to many of the statistical procedures you learn in the rest of this book. So it is important that you become very familiar with them and how to work with them.

Let us take another example. Suppose that a developmental psychologist observed 3-year-old Peter in a standardized laboratory situation playing with other children of the same age, and the psychologist counted the number of times Peter spoke to the other children. The result, over several observations, was that Peter spoke to other children about 8 times per hour of play. Without any standard of comparison, it would be hard to draw any conclusions from this. Suppose, however, that it was known from previous research that under similar conditions, the mean number of times children speak was 12, with a standard deviation of 4. Then clearly Peter spoke less often than other children in general, but not extremely less often. Peter would have a Z score of −1 (if $M = 12$ and $SD = 4$, a score of 8 is 1 SD below M). If Ian was observed speaking to other children 20 times in an hour, Ian would clearly be unusually talkative, with a Z score of +2. Ian would speak not merely more than the average but more by twice as much as children tend to vary from the average! (See Figure 2-16.)

Z Scores as Providing a Generalized Standard of Comparison

Another advantage of Z scores is that all kinds of scores with different ranges can be converted to Z scores and compared. If the same children in our example were also measured on a test of language skill, we could directly compare the Z scores on language skill to the Z scores on speaking to other children. Suppose that Peter had a score of 100 on the language

FIGURE 2-16
Number of times each hour that two children spoke, expressed as raw scores and Z scores (fictional data).

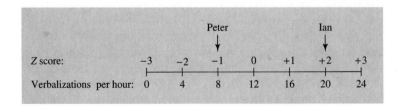

Z score:	−3	−2	−1	0	+1	+2	+3
Verbalizations per hour:	0	4	8	12	16	20	24

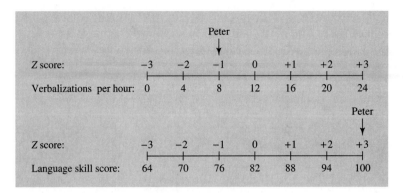

FIGURE 2-17
Scales of Z scores and raw scores for verbalizations per hour and language skill, showing the first child's score on each (fictional data).

skill test. If the mean on that test was 82 and the standard deviation was 6, then clearly Peter is much better than average at language skill, with a Z score of +3. Hence it seems unlikely that Peter's less than usual amount of speaking to other children is due to poorer than usual language skill (see Figure 2-17).

What is important to notice in this latest example is that by using Z scores, in effect we put the results of both observation of verbalization and the language skill test on the same scale. This is almost as wonderful as being able to compare apples and oranges! Converting a number to a Z score is a bit like converting the terms and quantities for measurement in various obscure languages into one language that everyone can understand—cubits and inches, for example, into centimeters. It is a very valuable tool.

Formulas for Converting a Raw Score to a Z Score

An ordinary measurement (or any other number in a distribution before it has been made into a Z score) is called a raw score. As we noted, a Z score is the number of standard deviations the raw score falls above (or, if negative, below) its mean. To compute a Z score, you subtract the mean from the raw score, giving the deviation score. You then divide the deviation score by the standard deviation. In symbols, the formula is

$$Z = \frac{X - M}{SD} \tag{2-7}$$

For example, using the formula for the child who scored 100 on the language test,

$$Z = \frac{X - M}{SD} = \frac{100 - 82}{6} = \frac{18}{6} = 3$$

Formula for Converting a Z Score to a Raw Score

To change a Z score back to a raw score, the process is reversed: You multiply the Z score by the standard deviation and then add the mean. The formula is

$$X = (Z)(SD) + M \tag{2-8}$$

For example, if a child has a Z score of −1.5 on the language ability test, then the child is 1.5 standard deviations below the mean. Since a standard deviation in this example is 6 raw score points, the child is 9 raw score points below the mean. The mean is 82, so 9 points below this is 73. Using the formula,

$$X = (Z)(SD) + M = (-1.5)(6) + 82 = -9 + 82 = 73$$

Steps to Convert a Raw Score to a Z Score

To convert a raw score to a Z score:
1. Compute the deviation score: Subtract the mean from the raw score.
2. Compute the Z score: Divide the deviation score by the standard deviation.

Steps to Convert a Z score to a Raw Score

To convert a Z score to a raw score:
1. Compute the deviation score: Multiply the Z score by the standard deviation.
2. Compute the raw score: Add the mean to the deviation score.

Examples of Computing Z Scores from Raw Scores and Vice Versa

Consider the first example we used in Chapter 1 of the stress ratings of 151 statistics students. The mean of that distribution was 6.46, and the standard deviation was 2.30 (SS =797.5; SD^2 = 797.5/151 = 5.28; SD = $\sqrt{5.28}$ = 2.30). Figure 2-18 shows the relationship of the raw score and Z score scales. If a student's stress raw score was 9, the student is clearly above the mean. Specifically, using the formula,

$$Z = \frac{X - M}{SD} = \frac{9 - 6.46}{2.3} = \frac{2.54}{2.3} = 1.10$$

In comparison, a student with a Z score of –2.5 has a stress raw score well below the mean. Using the formula, the exact raw stress score is computed as

$$X = (Z)(SD) + M = (-2.5)(2.3) + 6.46 = -5.75 + 6.46 = .71$$

Consider some examples from the study of students' attitudes toward achievement (Moorehouse & Sanders, 1992). Recall that the mean was 87.36 and the standard deviation was 22.55. Thus the person who scored 87 had a deviation score of –.36 (87 – 87.36). The Z score is then –.02 (–.36/22.55). This score is just under the mean. Similarly, the person who scored 120 had a deviation score of 32.64 (120 – 87.36). The Z score is 1.45 (32.64/22.55). This person is 1.45 standard deviations above the mean.

To go the other way, suppose that you knew that a person's Z score was 0.56. This person's raw score would be the Z score times the standard devia-

FIGURE 2-18
Raw score and Z score scales for 151 statistics students' ratings of their stress level (data from Aron et al., 1993), showing the scores of two sample cases.

Z score:	–3	–2	–1	0	+1	+2	+3
Stress rating:	–0.44	1.86	4.16	6.46	8.76	11.06	13.36

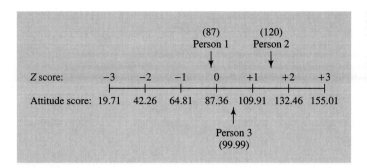

FIGURE 2-19
Raw score and Z score scales for teachers' ratings of 153 grade school students' attitudes toward achievement (Moorehouse & Sanders, 1992), showing scores of three sample cases.

tion, plus the mean: $(.56 \times 22.55) + 87.36 = 99.99$. These relationships are illustrated in Figure 2-19.

Finally, consider the example involving sentence reading time. In that study, recall that we computed the mean of the 100 subjects' reading times to be 27.55 ms and the standard deviation to be 1.43 ms. A person with a reading time of 28.8 ms has a Z score computed as follows:

$$Z = \frac{X - M}{SD} = \frac{28.8 - 27.55}{1.43} = \frac{1.25}{1.43} = .87$$

A person with a Z score of 2.0 has a reading time computed as follows:

$$X = (Z)(SD) + M = (2.0)(1.43) + 27.55 = 2.86 + 27.55 = 30.41$$

The reading time for a person with a Z score of -1.1 is

$$X = (Z)(SD) + M = (-1.1)(1.43) + 27.55 = -1.57 + 27.55 = 25.98$$

These relationships are illustrated in Figure 2-20.

Some Characteristics of Z Scores

The mean of a distribution of Z scores is always exactly 0. This is because converting to a Z score involves subtracting the mean from each raw score. To put this another way, the sum of the positive Z scores in a distribution must always equal the sum of the negative Z scores in that distribution.

The standard deviation of a distribution of Z scores is always exactly 1. This is because converting to a Z score involves dividing each raw score by the standard deviation. Also, because the standard deviation is 1, the variance, the standard deviation squared, is always 1. Table 2-4, shows the Z scores for the therapy session example, along with the computations for the mean and standard deviation of the Z scores. This example shows that with Z scores, the mean is 0 and the standard deviation (and variance) is 1.

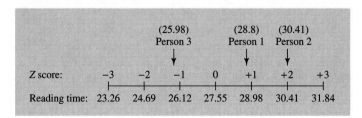

FIGURE 2-20
Raw score and Z score scales for 100 students' time (in milliseconds) to read ambiguous sentences (fictional data), showing scores of three sample cases.

TABLE 2-4

Computation of the Mean and the Standard Deviation of Z Scores in the Therapy Session Example

Number of Sessions (Raw Score)	Z Score for Number of Sessions	Z Score Mean	Z Score Deviation	Squared Z Score Deviation
7	.39	0	.39	.15
8	.78	0	.78	.61
8	.78	0	.78	.61
7	.39	0	.39	.15
3	−1.17	0	−1.17	1.37
1	−1.95	0	−1.95	3.80
6	0.00	0	0.00	0.00
9	1.17	0	1.17	1.37
3	−1.17	0	−1.17	1.37
8	.78	0	.78	.61
	Σ: 0.00			10.04[a]

$$M = \frac{\Sigma X}{N} = \frac{0}{10} = 0$$

$$SD^2 = \frac{\Sigma(X-M)^2}{N} = \frac{SS}{N} = \frac{10}{10} = 1$$

$$SD = \sqrt{1} = 1$$

[a]If there were no rounding error, this would equal exactly 10.

standard scores

Because Z scores have these standard values for the mean and the standard deviation and because, as we saw earlier, Z scores provide a kind of standard scale of measurement for any variable, Z scores are also sometimes called **standard scores.** (However, sometimes the term *standard score* is used only for a Z score for a distribution that is a normal curve. As you learn in Chapter 5, Z scores are even more useful when the distribution is a normal curve.)

Controversies and Limitations: The Tyranny of the Mean

Although the use of statistics is so widespread in psychology that it would seem to be the discipline's sole tool or language, it is important to know that there have been several rebellions against the reign of statistics. One of the most unexpected can be found at the heart of behaviorism.

Behaviorism is often portrayed as the school of psychology historically most dedicated to keeping the field strictly scientific. Behaviorism opposes the study of inner states because they are impossible to observe objectively; its best known advocate, B. F. Skinner, was also opposed to statistics. Skinner even said, "I would much rather see a graduate student in psychology taking a course in physical chemistry than in statistics. And I would include [presumably before statistics] other sciences, even poetry, music, and art" (Evans, 1976, p. 93).

Skinner held that observing behavior is the best way to understand it, and that meant observing individual cases. He did not categorically reject generalizing from one case alone—if one thought one had seen an important learning principle operating, it was of course necessary to observe it repeatedly. But he was constantly pointing to the information lost by averaging the results of a number of cases. For instance, Skinner (1956) cited the example of three overeating mice—one naturally obese, one poisoned with gold, and one whose hypothalamus had been altered. Each had a different curve for learning to press a bar for food, revealing much about the eating habits created by each condition. If these learning curves had been summed or merged statistically, the result would have represented no actual eating habits of any real mouse at all. As Skinner said, "These three individual curves contain more information than could probably ever be generated with measures requiring statistical treatment, yet they will be viewed with suspicion by many psychologists because they are single cases" (p. 232).

A different voice of caution was raised by humanistic psychology, which began in the 1950s as a "third force" in reaction to psychoanalysis (the only significant clinical psychology at the time) and behaviorism (the dominant experimental and theoretical psychology at the time). One of humanistic psychology's criticism of the rest of psychology as it then existed was that these two approaches were reducing us all to either unconscious instincts or a bundle of learned stimulus-response pairs, whereas humans are much more.

A humanistic psychology textbook by Tageson (1982) expresses the position very well. He described seeing a Berkeley student during the 1964 Free Speech movement wearing an IBM card pinned to her shirt, reading "Do not fold, spindle, or mutilate me!" To Tageson this image represented the human spirit's refusal to be buried under social forces, to have its consciousness denied.

> We are, it appears, the only self-conscious animals in any meaningful sense. . . .
> "I am here," she seemed to be saying, "and I will be dealt with. I refuse to be
> numbered and profiled and pigeonholed and objectified. I am a person, and you
> must deal with me, and you cannot do so by attempting to distill the richness
> and uniqueness of my existence into a few holes on a computer card." (pp. 1–2)

The point of humanistic psychology is that human consciousness should be studied intact, as a whole, as it is experienced by individuals. Although statistics can be usefully applied to ascertain the mathematical relationships between phenomena, including events in consciousness, human conscious experience can never be fully explained by reducing it to numbers (any more than it can be reduced to words). Each individual's experience is unique.

This viewpoint existed previously. In clinical psychology and the study of personality, voices were raised to argue that much more of what really matters in psychology can be learned from the in-depth study of one person than from averages of persons—the "idiographic" versus the "nomothetic" approaches, to use the terms Gordon Allport borrowed from Wilhelm Windelband (see Hilgard, 1987). And the philosophical underpinnings of the in-depth study of individuals can be found in phenomenology, which began in Europe after World War I (see Husserl, 1970).

Phenomenology is a philosophical position opposed to logical positivism. Logical positivism argues that there is an objective reality to be known; it is the philosophical position that traditionally underlies scientific efforts. Science is said to be objective and able to uncover this reality because it proceeds through experiments that anyone can observe or repeat to obtain the same results. Phenomenologists argue, however, that even these repeated observations are really private events in consciousness. When one person says or writes, "I saw the rat press the bar seven times," and another person claims to have seen the same thing, it is difficult or impossible to know that this event in fact occurred. Instead, each person has constructed a reality. And the supposedly more subjective experience of free will, for example, can also be constructed as easily as a rat's behavior, by listening to accounts by others and relating them to one's own experience until some picture of the human experience of free will emerges, not through quantitative methods of averaging large numbers, but through the qualitative study of the unique expressions of individuals about that experience.

Today the phenomenological viewpoint is represented less by humanistic, clinical, or personality psychologists than by proponents of qualitative research methodologies (e.g., McCracken, 1988). These methods were developed mainly in anthropology, where behaviorism and logical positivism never gained the hold that they did in psychology. The qualitative method typically involves long interviews or observations of a few subjects, with the highly skilled researcher deciding as the event is taking place what is important to remember, record, and pursue through more questions or observations. The mind of the researcher is the main tool because, according to this approach, only that mind can find the important relationships among the many categories of events arising in the respondent's speech.

Many people who favor qualitative methods (eg., McCracken and Tageson) do not suggest that quantitative methods should be dropped but rather that they should be blended with qualitative ones. We should first discover the important categories through a qualitative approach, then determine their incidence in the larger population through quantitative methods. Too often, these advocates would argue, quantitative researchers jump to conclusions about the important categories without first exploring the human experience of them through free-response interviews or observations.

Finally, let us note some thoughts about the "trouble with statistics" from the psychology of Carl Jung—what he called the "statistical mood" and its effect on a person's feeling of uniqueness. As the Jungian analyst Marie Louise von Franz (1979) noted, when we walk down a street and observe the hundreds of blank faces and begin to feel diminished or even glad that humans don't live forever, this is the statistical mood. We feel how much we are just part of the crowd, ordinary. Yet Franz points out that if some catastrophe were to happen, each person would respond uniquely. There is at least as much irregularity to life as ordinariness.

> The fact that this table does not levitate, but remains where it is, is only because the billions and billions and billions of electrons which constitute the table tend statistically to behave like that. But each electron in itself could do something else. (p. IV-17)

Likewise, when we are in love, we feel that the other person is unique and wonderful. Yet in a statistical mood, we realize that the other person is ordinary, like many others.

Franz argues that this "statistical mood" is damaging to love and life. "An act of loyalty is required towards one's own feelings" (p. IV-18). Feeling "makes your life and your relationships and deeds feel unique and gives them a definite value" (pp. IV-18–IV-19). In particular, feeling the importance of our single action makes immoral acts—war, and killing, for example—less possible. We cannot count the dead as numbers but must treat them as persons with emotions and purposes, like ourselves. In short, there are definite arguments for limiting our statistical thinking to its appropriate domains and leaving our heart free to rule in others.

The Mean, Variance, Standard Deviation, and Z Scores as Described in Research Articles

The mean and the standard deviation (and occasionally the variance) are commonly reported in research articles. Sometimes mean and standard deviation are included in the text of an article. For example, our fictional psychotherapist, in a research article about her practice, would write, "The mean number of sessions for the last 10 clients was 6.0 ($SD = 2.57$)."

More commonly, however, means and standard deviations are reported in tables. This is especially likely to be the case when there are several groups involved or when research participants are tested under several different conditions. For example, Christensen and Burrows (1991) included a table to describe the scores of several subgroups on the Christensen Dietary Distress Inventory (CDDI), a measure of the extent to which emotional distress is due to diet (see Table 2-5). Note, however, that in the majority of cases, tables in research articles report means but not standard deviations or variances.

Means of different groups in a study are also often reported in graphs. One common type of graph shows the mean of each group as the height of a bar, sometimes including marks indicating 1 standard deviation in each direction from the mean on the graph. For example, Figure 2-21 is from a study (Foa, Feske, Murdock, Kozak, & McCarthy, 1991) comparing three groups of women: (a) rape victims who were still suffering from posttraumatic stress

TABLE 2-5
Mean and Standard Deviation of CDDI Scores

Group	N	CDDI M	SD
Dietary Responders	41	20.20	4.87
Out-patient Sample			
Total	39	12.64	4.79
No Depression Symptoms	22	10.31	3.91
Depression Symptoms	17	15.00	4.47
College Students	144	10.05	4.28

Note. From Christensen L., & Burrows R., (1991), tab. 1. Criterion validity of the Christensen Dietary Distress Inventory. *Canadian Journal of Behavioral Science, 23,* 245–247. Copyright, 1991, by the Canadian Psychological Association. Reprinted by permission.

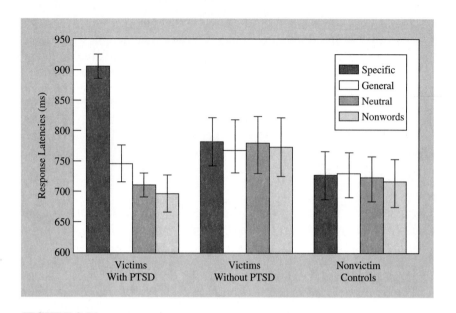

FIGURE 2-21
Graph in a research article showing means and standard deviations for time to determine the color of words of various types comparing rape victims who are or who are not suffering from posttraumatic stress disorder (PTSD) and women from a matched control group. (From Foa, E. B., Feske, U., Murdock, T. B., Kozak, M. J., & McCarthy, P. R. (1991), fig. 1. Processing of threat-related information in rape victims. *Journal of Abnormal Psychology, 100,* 156–162. Copyright © 1991 by the American Psychological Association. Reprinted by permission of the author.

disorder (PTSD, a common anxiety disorder resulting from a catastrophic event), (b) rape victims no longer suffering from PTSD, and (c) a control group of matched women who were not rape victims. Each woman was shown a series of words on a computer screen. The words were in different colors, and the task was to press a computer key as quickly as possible to indicate the color. The words themselves were of four types, presented in mixed order: (a) words specifically associated with rape, such as *assault* and *trapped*; (b) words that are generally upsetting to people, such as *cancer* or *coffin*; (c) neutral words; and (d) made-up nonwords. The measure was response latency—how many milliseconds it took each woman to press the key for the color. As can be seen from the figure, and as predicted by the researchers, the mean response latency for rape victims with PTSD was much slower on rape-specific words than for members of the other two groups. The standard deviation lines make it clear that this longer response time to rape-specific words was uniform among women in this group (that is, there was not a lot of variation in relation to how much higher this mean was).

Sometimes, instead of giving the standard deviation in a table or showing marks for it on a graph, researchers will report instead what is called the "standard error." The standard error of a group of scores will always be smaller than the standard deviation—usually much smaller. We describe it in some detail in Chapter 7 (where we usually refer to it as the *standard deviation of the distribution of means*).

TABLE 2-6
Means and Standard Deviations of Supervisors' and Incumbents' Job Evaluation Ratings

Compensable Factor	Supervisors		Incumbents	
	Points	*Z score*	*Points*	*Z score*
Skill				
M	217.78	.06	213.41	− .04
SD	76.01	.94	81.75	1.03
Problem Solving				
M	107.50	−.32	123.01	.17
SD	28.38	.88	32.96	.88
Impact				
M	103.13	−.13	111.12	.10
SD	29.63	.82	103.13	1.02
Environment				
M	60.92	−.20	66.50	.11
SD	16.51	.90	18.95	1.04
Supervision				
M	157.78	−.16	175.88	.09
SD	61.31	.95	67.11	1.02
Total				
M	647.10	−.14	689.93	.07
SD	157.79	.91	186.60	1.04

Note. From Huber, V. L. (1991), tab. 1. Comparison of supervisor-incumbent and female-male multidimensional job evaluation ratings. *Journal of Applied Psychology, 76,* 115–121. Copyright, 1991, by the American Psychological Association. Reprinted by permission of the author.

Finally, what about Z scores? Though widely used in the process of analyzing results of psychology studies, Z scores are only rarely reported in published research articles. Occasionally, however, if an article describes individual cases, comparisons to other individuals or to norms for the general population will be made using Z scores. Also, in studies in which several different measures are used, the various kinds of raw scores may be converted to Z scores so that comparisons between measures will be more readily understood. For example, Huber (1991) compared supervisors' and employees' ratings of five aspects of the various jobs performed at a major television station. The five aspects of the jobs were measured on different scales, with different means and different standard deviations. Thus, as shown in Table 2-6, in addition to using raw scores, Huber converted the scores for all subjects on each scale to Z scores and then computed the means and standard deviations of these Z scores separately for supervisors and employees ("incumbents" on her table). Notice that the two groups tended to give about the same ratings for skill (a fairly objective aspect of a job), but in the other categories, supervisors tended to rate the jobs considerably lower than the employees did. Z scores make such comparisons much easier.

Summary

The mean is the ordinary average—the sum of the scores divided by the number of scores. Expressed in symbols, $M = \Sigma X/N$.

Some less commonly used alternative descriptors of central tendency of a distribution are the mode—the most common single value—and the median—the value of the middle score if all the scores were lined up from highest to lowest.

The spread of the scores in a distribution can be described by the variance—the average of the squared deviation of each score from the mean. Expressed in symbols: $SD^2 = \Sigma(X - M)^2/N$. Also, the sum of squared deviations is symbolized as SS. Thus $SD^2 = SS/N$.

The standard deviation is the square root of the variance. In symbols, $SD = \sqrt{SD^2}$. It can be best understood as an approximate measure of the average amount by which scores differ from the mean.

A Z score is the number of standard deviations a raw score is above or below the mean of a distribution. Among other applications, Z scores permit comparisons of scores on different scales.

Some psychologists, especially those associated with behaviorism, humanistic psychology, phenomenology, and qualitative methods, mistrust statistical methodology because in the process of creating averages, knowledge about the individual case is lost. Many people holding these views, however, acknowledge that statistical analysis does play an important role but argue that when studying any particular topic, careful study of individuals should always come first.

Means and standard deviations are commonly reported in research articles in the text, in tables, or in graphs (in which the standard deviation may be shown as a line extending above and below the mean). Z scores are rarely reported in research articles.

Key Terms

central tendency	mode	standard score
computational formula	N	sum of squared deviations (SS)
definitional formula	outliers	variance (SD^2)
deviation score	raw score	Z score
mean (M)	squared deviation score	Σ
median	standard deviation (SD)	

Practice Problems

These problems involve computation (with the assistance of a calculator). Most real-life statistics problems are done on a computer. But even if you have a computer, do this by hand to ingrain the method in your mind.

For practice in using a computer to solve statistical problems, refer to the computer section of each chapter of the study guide that accompanies this text.

All data are fictional (unless an actual citation is given).

Answers to Set I are given at the back of the book.

SET I

1. For each data set, determine the following (be sure to show your work!): (a) mean, (b) median, (c) *SS* (sum of squared deviations), (d) variance, and (e) standard deviation.

Set A: 32, 28, 24, 28, 28, 31, 35, 29, 26

Set B: 6, 1, 4, 2, 3, 4, 6, 6

2. The temperature on December 26 in Montreal was measured, in degrees Celsius, at 10 random times. They were −5, −4, −1, −1, 0, −8,−5, −9, −13, and −24. Describe the typical temperature and the amount of variation to a person who has never had a course in statistics. Give three ways of describing the typical temperature and two ways of describing its variation, explaining the differences and how you computed each. (You will learn more if you try to write your own answer first, before reading our answer. Your own answer need not be quite so thorough as the sample answer in the book.)

3. A study is conducted of the number of dreams recounted over a 2-week period by 30 people in psychotherapy. In an article describing the results of the study, the authors report: "The mean number of dreams was 6.84 (*SD* = 3.18)." Explain what this means to a person who has never had a course in statistics.

4. On a measure of anxiety, the mean is 79 and the standard deviation is 12. What are the *Z* scores for each of the following actual scores? (a) 91, (b) 68, (c) 103.

5. On a particular intelligence test, the mean number of items correct is 231, and the standard deviation is 41. What are the actual or raw scores on this test for people with IQs of (a) 107, (b) 83, and (c) 100? (IQ is figured as 100, plus the *Z* score times 16. That is, an IQ score is set up to have a mean of 100 and a standard deviation of 16.) (*Note:* To do this problem, first compute the *Z* score corresponding to the IQ score; then use that *Z* score to find the raw score.)

6. Six months after a divorce, the former wife and husband each take a test that measures divorce adjustment. The wife's score is 63, and the husband's score is 59. Overall, the mean score for divorced women on this test is 60 (*SD* = 6); the mean score for divorced men is 55 (*SD* = 4). Which of the two has adjusted better to the divorce in relation to other divorced people of the same gender? Explain your answer to a person who has never had a course in statistics.

SET II

1. Define the mean, median, and mode. Cite an instance when the median would be the preferred measure of central tendency.

2. For each data set, determine the following (be sure to show your work!): (a) mean, (b) median, (c) *SS* (sum of squared deviations), (d) variance, and (e) standard deviation.

Set A: 2, 2, 0, 5, 1, 4, 1, 3, 0, 0, 1, 4, 4, 0, 1, 4, 3, 4, 2, 1, 0

Set B: 1,112, 1,245, 1,361, 1,372, 1,472

Set C: 3.0, 3.4, 2.6, 3.3, 3.5, 3.2

3. A psychologist interested in political behavior measured the square footage of the desks in the official office of four U.S. governors and of four chief executive officers (CEOs) of major U.S. corporations. The figures for the governors were 44, 36, 52, and 40. The figures for the CEOs were 32, 60, 48, and 36. Compute the mean and the standard deviation for the governors and for the CEOs, and explain what you have done to a person who has never had a course in statistics. Also note the ways in which the means and standard deviations differ, and speculate on the possible meaning of these differences, presuming that they are representative of U.S. governors and large corporations' CEOs in general.

4. A study involves measuring the number of days absent from work for 216 employees of a large company during the preceding year. As part of the results, the researcher reports, "The number of days absent during the preceding year (*M* = 9.21; *SD* = 7.34) was . . ." Explain the material in parentheses to a person who has never had a course in statistics.

5. On a standard measure of hearing ability, the mean is 300 and the standard deviation is 20. (a) Give the *Z* scores for persons who score 340, 310, and 260. (b) Give the raw scores for persons whose *Z* scores on this test were 2.4, 1.5, 0, and −4.5.

6. A person scores 81 on a test of verbal ability and 6.4 on a test of quantitative ability. For the verbal ability test, the mean for people in general is 50 and the standard deviation is 20. For the quantitative ability test, the mean for people in general is 0 and the standard deviation is 5. Which is this person's stronger ability, verbal or quantitative? Explain your answer to a person who has never had a course in statistics.

Chapter Appendix: Optional Computational Formulas for the Variance and the Standard Deviation

Alternative but mathematically equivalent forms of the formulas for the variance and the standard deviation have been developed to make it easier when these are computed by hand, as was necessary before the invention of the computer or the calculator with a standard deviation key.

Again, here is the definitional formula for the variance:

$$SD^2 = \frac{\Sigma(X - M)^2}{N} = \frac{SS}{N}$$

This is tedious to compute by hand because you must first find the deviation score for each case. However, the numerator of this equation, the sum of squared deviations, can be manipulated algebraically so that you need only use the sum of all the scores (something you will have already calculated to find the mean) and the sum of the squares of each actual score (which is much quicker to calculate than having first to find each deviation score and then to square it). This alternative formula is

$$SD^2 = \frac{\Sigma X^2 - (\Sigma X)^2/N}{N} \tag{2-9}$$

Note that ΣX^2 means that you square each score and then take the sum of these squared scores. However, $(\Sigma X)^2$ means that you first add up all the scores and then take the square of this sum.

The computational formula for the standard deviation is the square root of the computational formula for the variance:

$$SD^2 = \sqrt{\frac{\Sigma X^2 - (\Sigma X)^2/N}{N}}$$

Table 2-7 shows the calculation of the variance and standard deviation for the data in our therapy session example, using the computational formula. Compare this computation to the one in Table 2-1 for the same data using the definitional formula.

TABLE 2.7
Calculation of the Variance and Standard Deviation in the Therapy Session Example Using the Computational Formulas

Number of Sessions (X)	Number of Sessions Squared (X^2)
7	49
8	64
8	64
7	49
3	9
1	1
6	36
9	81
3	9
8	64
Σ: 60	426

$$SD^2 = \frac{\Sigma X^2 - (\Sigma X)^2/N}{N} = \frac{426 - 60^2/10}{10} = \frac{426 - 3,600/10}{10} = \frac{426 - 360}{10} = \frac{66}{10} = 6.6$$

$$SD = \sqrt{SD^2} = \sqrt{6.6} = 2.57$$

3 Correlation

I N a recent study (Aron, Aron, & Smollan, 1992), 208 college students were asked to describe their closest personal relationship and to answer a number of questions about it. One of the findings was that for male students, the longer they had been in a romantic relationship, the closer they felt to their partner. That is, in general, males who had high levels of length of time with their partner tended to report high levels of closeness with their partner; those males who had low levels of length of time with their partner tended to report low levels of closeness with their partner. (We will reveal the results for females later.)

You can also see this pattern visually. Figure 3-1 is a graph of the results of this study, with scores on the closeness measure on the vertical axis and scores on the length-of-relationship measure on the horizontal axis. Each subject's score is shown as a dot. The general pattern—with, of course, many exceptions—is that the dots go from the lower left corner to the upper right corner. That is, lower scores on one variable more often go with lower scores on the other variable, and higher with higher. Even though the pattern is far from one to one, it is a clear general trend.

The pattern of high scores on one variable going with high scores on the other variable, low scores going with low scores, and moderate with moderate, is an example of a **correlation.**

correlation

There are countless examples of correlation: In children, there is a correlation between age and coordination skills; among students, we usually assume that there is a correlation between amount of time studying and amount learned; in the marketplace, we often assume that a correlation exists between price and quality—that higher prices go with higher quality and lower with lower.

FIGURE 3-1
Scatter diagram showing the correlation for males between relationship length and closeness. (Data from Aron, Aron, & Smollan, 1992.)

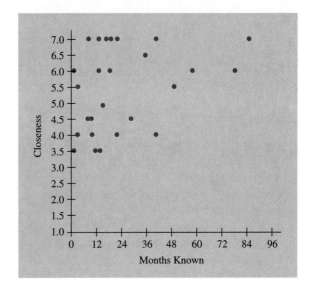

This chapter explores the nature of correlation, including how it is described graphically, different types of correlations, how a numerical index of correlation known as a *correlation coefficient* is computed, and how the correlation coefficient is interpreted. Chapter 4 discusses how you can use correlation to predict the level of one variable (such as college grades) from knowledge of a person's score on another correlated variable (such as high school grades). In considering the topic of correlation, we move on from the descriptive statistics of a single variable's distribution (Chapters 1 and 2) to describing the relationship between the distributions of two variables.

Independent or Predictor Variables and Dependent Variables

independent variable
dependent variable

Before going into correlation, however, we first need to introduce some important terminology. When considering two variables at a time, it is often the case that scores on one variable are thought of as a *cause* and scores on the other variable as an *effect*. For example, we might think of relationship length as causing the degree of closeness. The variable that is considered a cause is called the **independent variable,** and the one that is considered an effect is called the **dependent variable.** (The dependent variable has this name because its value depends on the value of the independent variable; the independent variable's score, by contrast, has this name because its value does not depend on the dependent variable. In this little world of only two variables, in which one is the cause of the other, one is independent and the other one depends on it.) In our example, relationship length would be the independent variable and closeness the dependent variable.

However, in this example, as in many examples in psychology, it is possible and even reasonable to reverse which variable is considered the cause and which the effect. Only in true experiments, where the experimenter controls the level of the independent variable (for example, by randomly assigning people to different levels of a variable), or in situations where one variable is not under anyone's control (for example, age) can we be fairly confident about which is cause and which is effect.

Hence psychologists are often a bit uncomfortable using the terms *independent variable* and *dependent variable* in studies in which two variables are simply measured as they exist in a group of people, as in our example of relationship length and closeness. Nevertheless, even if we cannot say with certainty what is cause and what is effect, it is still possible to use knowledge about one variable to *predict* scores on the other variable. For example, in daily life, we may assume that if people have been in a relationship a long time, they are probably closer than people who have been in a relationship only a short time. In this case, we are using relationship length to predict closeness. The underlying cause and effect do not really matter so long as relationship length and closeness consistently go together. Thus when examining two variables that go together, some psychologists prefer to call the one they are predicting from the **predictor variable.** However, the other one is usually still called the dependent variable. (The proper term for the predicted variable is the *criterion variable*, but this is almost never used in psychology except in some statistics textbooks.) Following custom, in this book we will usually refer to one of the two variables being correlated as the predictor variable and the other as the dependent variable.

predictor variable

We go into causality in more detail later in this chapter, and Chapter 4 is all about prediction. We bring these issues up briefly now because when discussing correlation, it is helpful to be able to use names for the two variables being correlated, and these are the conventional names. In fact, in many cases in psychology, we only really care about the extent to which two variables go together, without giving one any special status as the cause of the other or as the basis for making predictions about the other. Nevertheless, psychologists are often forced to make such distinctions, even if they have to do so arbitrarily, simply to follow standards used in graphing (as you will soon see), as well as for the more complex multiple correlation, which we consider in Chapter 4.

Graphing Correlations: The Scatter Diagram

Figure 3-1, showing the correlation between relationship length and closeness, is an example of a **scatter diagram.** A scatter diagram permits you to see at a glance the degree and pattern of relation of the two variables.

scatter diagram

How to Make a Scatter Diagram

There are three steps to making a scatter diagram:

1. Draw the axes, and determine which variable should go on which axis. The independent or predictor variable goes on the horizontal axis, the dependent variable on the vertical axis. In Figure 3-1, we put relationship length (months known) on the horizontal axis and closeness on the vertical axis because in the context of the study, we were interested in seeing if relationship length might be a cause of the degree of closeness.

2. Determine the range of values to use for each variable, and mark them on the axes. Your numbers should go upward on each axis, starting from where the axes meet. Ordinarily, begin with the lowest value your measure can possibly have (usually 0), and continue to the highest value your measure can possibly have. When there is no obvious or reasonable lowest or highest possible value, begin or end at a value that is as high or low as people ordinarily score in the group of people of interest for your study. (However, unlike the kinds of graphs described in Chapter 1, a scatter diagram is not drawn to the 1.5:1 width-to-height proportions. Scatter diagrams are square, with a 1:1 ratio of horizontal and vertical axes.)

In Figure 3-1, the horizontal axis starts at 0 months together and the vertical axis starts at 1, which is the lowest possible score on the closeness test used. The highest value on the horizontal axis is 96 months, which is a reasonable maximum length for most romantic relationships among college students. The highest value on the vertical axis is 7, which is the highest possible value on the closeness test.

3. Mark a dot for the pair of scores for each case. Locate the place on the horizontal axis for that person's score on the predictor variable. Then move up to the height on the vertical axis that represents the person's score on that variable, and mark a clear dot.

If there are two cases in one place, you can either put the number 2 in that place or locate a second dot as near as possible to the first—touching, if possible—but making it clear that there are in fact two dots in the one place.

An Example

Suppose that a company is considering increasing the number of people managed by each of its floor managers but is concerned about the stress that this might create for these managers. The company expects that the more people managed, the higher a manager's stress. To examine the question, a personnel psychologist suggests studying five managers randomly selected from all the company's floor managers. (In practice, a much larger group should be used, but we will use five cases for simplicity.) The five managers are given a stress questionnaire on which the possible scores range from 0 (no stress at all) to 10 (extreme stress). The results might look like those shown in Table 3-1.

1. Draw the axes, and determine which variable should go on which axis. Since the company is interested in the effect of number of employees supervised on stress level, we consider number of employees supervised the predictor variable and put it on the horizontal axis; stress level is the dependent variable and goes on the vertical axis (see Figure 3-2a).

TABLE 3-1
Employees Supervised and Stress Level (Fictional Data)

Employees Supervised	Stress Level on Questionnaire
6	7
8	8
3	1
10	8
8	6

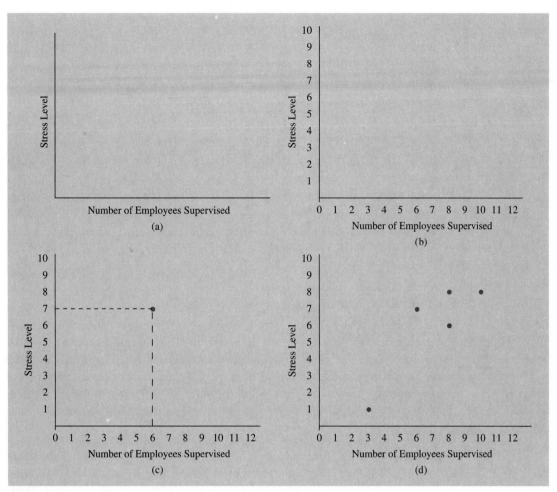

FIGURE 3-2
How to make a scatter diagram. (a) The axes are set up—the predictor variable (employees supervised) on the horizontal axis, the dependent variable (stress level) on the vertical axis. (b) The range of values has been determined and marked on the axes. (c) A dot has been placed for the pair of scores for the first case. (d) A dot has been placed for the pair of scores for all five cases.

2. Determine the range of values to use for each variable, and mark them on the axes. For the horizontal axis, we don't know the maximum possible, but let's assume that in this company no manager is permitted to supervise more than 12. Thus the horizontal axis goes from 0 to 12. The vertical axis goes from 0 to 10, the limits of the questionnaire in this example. (See Figure 3-2b.)

3. Mark a dot for the pair of scores for each case. For the first case, the number of employees supervised is 6. So you would move across to 6 on the horizontal axis. Then you would move up to the point corresponding to 7 (the stress level for the first manager) on the vertical axis. Place a dot at this location (see Figure 3-2c). Do the same for each of the remaining four cases. The result should look like Figure 3-2d.

FIGURE 3-3
The scatter diagram of Figure 3-1 with the line drawn in to show the general trend. (Data from Aron et al., 1992.)

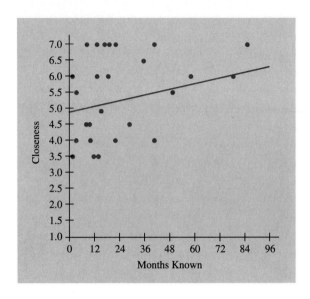

Patterns of Correlation

positive correlation
linear correlation

So far we have examined the situation in which highs go with highs, lows with lows, and mediums with mediums. This situations is called a **positive correlation.** And because the pattern in the scatter diagram roughly approximates a straight line, it is also an example of a **linear correlation.**

For example, in the scatter diagram of Figure 3-1, you could draw a line showing the general trend of the dots, as we have done in Figure 3-3. Similarly, you could draw such a line in our second example, as shown in Figure 3-4. (One reason why these examples of linear correlations are called "positive" is that in Cartesian geometry, the slope of a line is called "posi-

FIGURE 3-4
The scatter diagram of Figure 3-2d with the line drawn in to show the general trend.

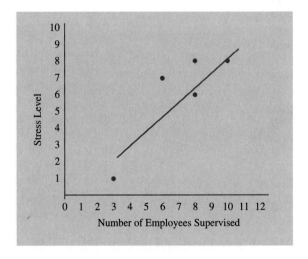

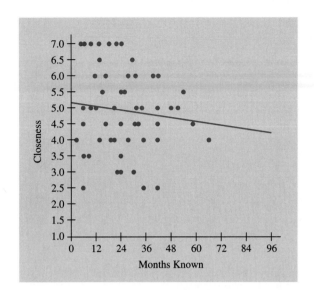

FIGURE 3-5
Scatter diagram with the line drawn in to show the general
trend for negative correlation between two variables—longer
length of relationship goes with less closeness for females.
(Data from Aron et al., 1992.)

tive" when it goes up and to the right on a graph like this. In Chapter 4, you
learn precise rules for drawing such lines and determining their slope.)

Negative Correlations

Sometimes the relationship between the variables of interest is not positive.
Instead, high scores go with low and low with high. This is called a **nega-**
tive correlation.

    For example, in the study of relationship length and closeness, the
researchers found that for females, in general, the longer they had been
together, the *less* close they felt to their partner—a result quite opposite that
found for males! (That result should provide you with a start for some interesting conversations—see, you can learn all sorts of interesting things in
your statistics course!) This pattern is shown in the scatter diagram in
Figure 3-5. We put a line in the figure to emphasize the general trend of the
dots—and you can see that as it goes from left to right, it slopes slightly
downward. (Compare this to the result for the males, shown in Figure 3-3,
which slopes upward.)

    A study by Mirvis and Lawler (1977), two organizational psychologists,
provides another example of a negative correlation. They found that absenteeism had a negative linear correlation with "intrinsic satisfaction" with the
job. That is, the higher the level of job satisfaction, the lower the level of
absenteeism. Put another way, the lower the level of job satisfaction, the
higher the absenteeism.

Curvilinear Correlations

Sometimes the relationship between two variables does not follow any kind
of straight line, positive or negative, but instead follows the more complex
pattern of a **curvilinear correlation.** For example, it is known that up to a

negative correlation

curvilinear correlation

FIGURE 3-6
Example of a curvilinear relationship—task performance and arousal.

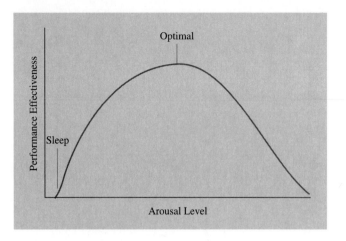

FIGURE 3-7
Examples of curvilinear relationships: (a) the way we feel and the complexity of a stimulus; (b) the number of people who remember an item and its position on a list; (c) children's rate of substituting digits for symbols and their motivation.

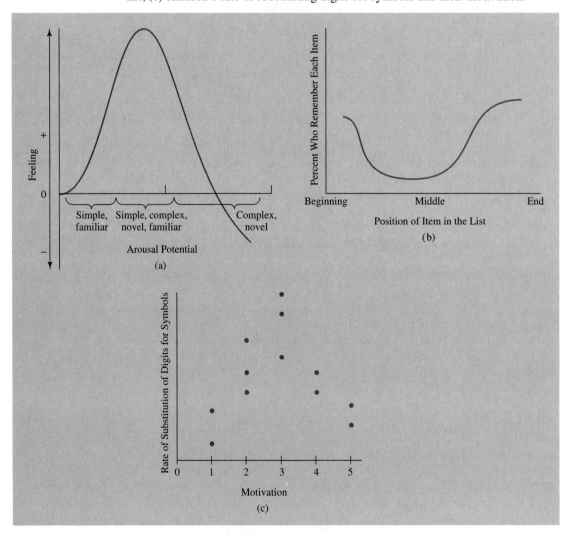

point, physiological arousal improves performance on a task, but beyond that point, still greater physiological arousal decreases performance. That is, going from being nearly asleep to a moderate level of arousal makes you more effective, but beyond that moderate level, further increases in arousal may make you too "keyed up" to perform well. This particular curvilinear pattern is illustrated in Figure 3-6. Notice that it would be impossible to draw any single straight line that would describe this relationship very well. Some other examples of curvilinear relationships are shown in Figure 3-7.

Not all curvilinear relationships are even simple curves. Occasionally they can be more complicated (and still they can be expressed mathematically, something you learn about in advanced statistics classes). It is really quite important to look at scatter diagrams to unearth these richer relationships rather than automatically carrying out correlations assuming that the only relationship is a straight line.

No Correlation

It is also possible for two variables to be completely unrelated to each other. For example, if you were to do a study of creativity and shoe size, your results might appear as shown in Figure 3-8. The dots are spread everywhere, and there is no line, straight or otherwise, that is any reasonable representation of a trend. There is simply **no correlation.**

no correlation

In actual research situations, sometimes a relationship between two variables exists, but it is not very strong and is consequently hard to see in a scatter diagram. This is particularly likely to be true in a study in which a large number of cases are studied and the relationship between the two variables is very small or subtle, yet there still might be reason for confidence that the relationship is more than a coincidence just because of its small but consistent presence in so many cases. Figure 3-9 presents a scatter diagram in which a small positive linear correlation was found to exist between the two variables. Can you see it?

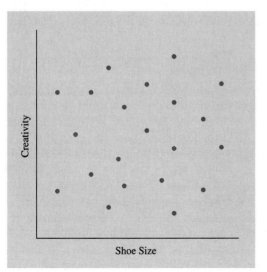

FIGURE 3-8
Two variables with no association with each other—creativity and shoe size.

FIGURE 3-9
A scatter diagram in which a small positive
linear correlation was found to exist between
the two variables.

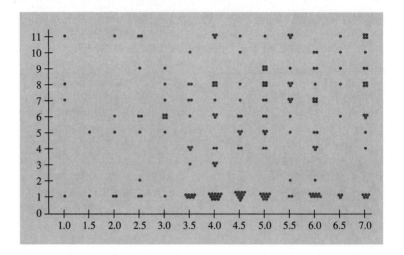

Computing an Index of Degree of Linear Correlation: The Pearson Correlation Coefficient

Although looking at a scatter diagram gives a rough indication of the type and degree of relationship between two variables, it is obviously not a very precise approach. A measure of the degree of correlation is needed.

Degree of Correlation

degree of correlation

What we mean by the **degree of correlation** is the extent to which there is a clear pattern of some particular relationship between the distributions of the two variables. For example, we described a positive linear correlation as the situation in which high scores go with highs, mediums with mediums, lows with lows. The degree of such a correlation, then, is the extent to which highs go with highs, and so on. Similarly, the degree of negative linear correlation between two variables is the extent to which highs on one variable go with lows on the other, and so forth. In terms of a scatter diagram, a high degree of linear correlation means that the dots all fall very close to a straight line (the line sloping up or down depending on whether the linear correlation is positive or negative).

Measuring the Degree of Linear Correlation

The first step in one approach to determining the degree of any linear correlation is to have some consistent way of deciding what is a high and what is a low score—and how high is a high and how low a low. (Another approach, described in Chapter 4, is to determine how far each dot falls from the line.) This means comparing scores on different measures, and this problem of comparing apples and oranges, as we saw in Chapter 2, is best solved by using Z scores.

A Z score, you will recall, is the number of standard deviations a score is from the mean. Whatever the scale on which you have measured something, if you convert your raw scores to Z scores, a raw score that is high compared to the other raw scores in its distribution (that is, above the mean) will always have a positive Z score, and a raw score that is low compared to the other raw

BOX 3-1

Galton: Gentleman Genius

Francis Galton is credited with inventing the statistic called correlation, although Karl Pearson and others worked out the formulas. In Chapter 14 (Box 14-1) you will learn about Pearson, and in Chapter 9 (Box 9-1) about William Gossett, another important early statistician, who invented the *t* test. Gossett was a student and colleague of the slightly older Karl Pearson. Pearson in turn saw himself as a student and colleague of the still older Galton (to whom Pearson gave all the credit for the discovery of correlation). In other words, statistics at this time was a tight little British club (see Box 16-1). (In fact, most of science was an only slightly larger club—Galton was also greatly influenced by his own cousin, Charles Darwin.)

Of the members of this club, Galton was typical, an eccentric, independently wealthy gentleman scientist. Aside from his work in statistics, he possessed a medical degree, had explored "darkest Africa," invented glasses for reading underwater, experimented with stereoscopic maps, dabbled in meteorology and anthropology, and wrote a paper about receiving intelligible signals from the stars.

Above all, Galton was a compulsive counter. Some of his counts are rather infamous. Once while attending a lecture, he counted the fidgets of an audience per minute, looking for variations with the boringness of the subject matter. While twice having his picture painted, he counted the artist's brush strokes per hour, concluding that each portrait required an average of 20,000 strokes. And while walking the streets of various towns in the British Isles, he classified the beauty of the female inhabitants by fingering a recording device in his pocket to register "good," "medium," or "bad."

Galton's consuming interest, however, was the counting of geniuses, criminals, and other types in families. He wanted to understand how each type was produced so that science could improve the human race by encouraging governments to enforce eugenics—selective breeding for intelligence, proper moral behavior, and other qualities—to be determined, of course, by the eugenicists. (Eugenics has since been generally discredited.) The concept of correlation came directly from his first simple efforts in this area, the study of the relation of the height of children to their parents.

Indeed, much of the science of statistics, or "biometrics," as Galton called it, arose as the application of mathematics to issues in biology and social science. And of all the statistics, correlation was an especially useful tool for these sciences, in which strict experiments, such as breeding experiments on humans, often could not be conducted. At first, Galton's method of exactly measuring the tendency for "one thing to go with another" seemed almost the same as proving the cause of something. For example, if it could be shown mathematically that most of the brightest people came from a few highborn British families and most of the least intelligent people came from poor families, that would prove that intelligence was caused by the inheritance of certain genes (provided that you were prejudiced enough to overlook the differences in educational opportunities). The same study might prove more convincingly that if you were a member of one of those better British families, history would make you a prime example of how easy it is to misinterpret the meaning of a correlation.

References: Peters (1987); Tankard (1984).

scores in its distribution (and thus below the mean) will always have a negative *Z* score. Furthermore, regardless of the particular measure used, *Z* scores give a standard indication of just how high or low each score is. A *Z* score of 1 is always exactly 1 standard deviation above the mean, and a *Z* score of 2 is twice as many standard deviations above the mean. *Z* scores on one variable are directly comparable to *Z* scores on another variable.

There is, however, an additional reason why Z scores are used for computing the degree of correlation. It has to do with what happens if you multiply a score on one variable times a score on the other variable—which is called a *cross-product*. When using Z scores, this is called a **cross-product of Z scores.** If you multiply a high by a high, with Z scores you will always get a positive cross-product (because no matter what the scale, scores above the mean become positive Z scores, and a positive times a positive is a positive). Further—and here is where it gets interesting—if you multiply a low by a low, with Z scores you will also always get a positive cross-product (because no matter what the scale, scores below the mean become negative Z scores, and a negative times a negative gives a positive). Thus if highs on one variable go with highs on the other and lows on one go with lows on the other, the cross-products of Z scores will always be positive. When considering a whole distribution of scores, if you take each subject's Z score on one variable and multiply it by that subject's Z score on the other variable, the result of doing this when highs go with highs and lows with lows is that all the multiplications will come out positive. And if you sum up these cross-products of Z scores, which are all positive, you will end up with a big positive number.

By contrast, with a negative linear correlation, highs go with lows and lows with highs. In terms of Z scores, this would mean positives with negatives and negatives with positives. Multiplied out, that gives all negative cross-products. If you add all these negative cross-products together, you get a large negative number.

Finally, if there is no linear correlation, then for some subjects highs on one variable would go with highs on the other variable or lows with lows, making positive cross-products, and for others highs on one variable would go with lows on the other variable and lows with highs, making negative cross-products. Adding up these cross-products for all the subjects in the study would result in the positive cross-products and the negative cross-products canceling out, giving a number around 0.

Thus by changing all your scores to Z scores, multiplying the two Z scores for each person times each other, and adding up the cross-products, you get a large positive number if there is a positive linear correlation, a large negative number if there is a negative linear correlation, and a number near 0 if there is no linear correlation.

However, you are still left with the problem of assessing the degree of a positive or negative linear correlation. Obviously, the larger the number, the bigger the correlation—but how large is large, and how large is not very large? You can't judge from the sum of the cross-products alone, which increases rapidly merely by adding the cross-products of more cases together. (That is, a study with 100 subjects would have a bigger sum of cross-products than the same study with only 25 subjects.)

The solution is to divide this sum of the cross-products of the Z scores by the number of cases. That is, you compute the *average* of the cross-products of Z scores. It turns out that this average can never be more than +1—a

positive linear **perfect correlation.** Its minimum is –1—a negative linear perfect correlation. In the case of no linear correlation, it will be 0.

For a positive linear correlation that is not perfect, which is the usual case, the average of the cross-products of Z scores will be between 0 and +1. To put it another way, if the general trend of the dots is upward and to the right, but they do not fall exactly on a single straight line, this number is between 0 and +1. The same rule holds for negative correlations: They fall between 0 and −1.

The Correlation Coefficient

The average of the cross-products of Z scores thus serves as an excellent measure of the degree of linear correlation and is called the **correlation coefficient.** It is also called the *Pearson correlation coefficient* (or the *Pearson product-moment correlation coefficient*, to be very traditional), after Karl Pearson (whom you meet in Box 14-1). Pearson, along with Francis Galton (see Box 3-1), played a major role in developing the technique. The correlation coefficient is abbreviated by the letter **r** (short for *regression*, a concept closely related to correlation; we discuss regression in Chapter 4).

r

Figure 3-10 shows scatter diagrams and the associated correlation coefficient for several examples with different degrees of linear correlation.

Formula for the Correlation Coefficient

The whole foregoing discussion can be summarized by a few symbols, the formula for the correlation coefficient:

$$r = \frac{\Sigma Z_X Z_Y}{N} \tag{3-1}$$

where r is the correlation coefficient, Z_X is the Z score for each case on the X variable, Z_Y is the Z score for each case on the Y variable, $Z_X Z_Y$ is Z_X times Z_Y (the cross-product of the Z scores) for each case, $\Sigma Z_X Z_Y$ is the sum of the cross-products over all the cases, and N is the number of cases.

Steps for Computing the Correlation Coefficient

The discussion can also be summarized as a series of steps:

1. **Convert all scores to Z scores.** This requires calculating the mean and the standard deviation of each raw variable, then computing the Z score for each raw score.
2. **Compute the cross-product of the Z scores for each case.** That is, for each case, multiply the Z score for one variable times the Z score for the other variable.
3. **Sum the cross-products of the Z scores.**
4. **Divide by the number of cases.** Be sure to use the number of cases, not the number of scores. That is, if you have 18 people with one score on each variable, you divide by 18, not 36.

Definitional Versus Computational Formulas for the Correlation Coefficient

The procedure just described, based on the definitional formula, elucidates the logic behind the computed correlation coefficient. Following these steps in the examples to come (and in the practice problems at the end of the chapter)

Computing an Index of Degree of Linear Correlation: The Pearson Correlation Coefficient   77

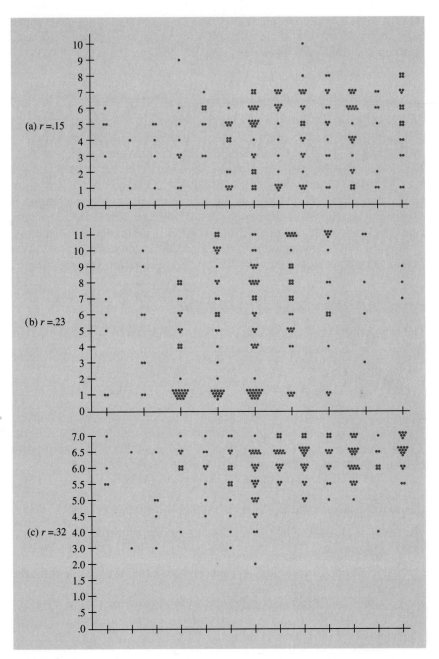

FIGURE 3-10
Scatter diagrams and the associated correlation coefficient for several cases with different degrees of linear correlation.

helps ingrain this logic in your mind. However, when computing a correlation coefficient for an actual study, you would almost always use a computer. If it is ever truly necessary to compute a correlation coefficient by hand (or with a calculator) for an actual study, the computational formula in Appendix I to this chapter will greatly speed up your work.

FIGURE 3-10 (*cont.*)

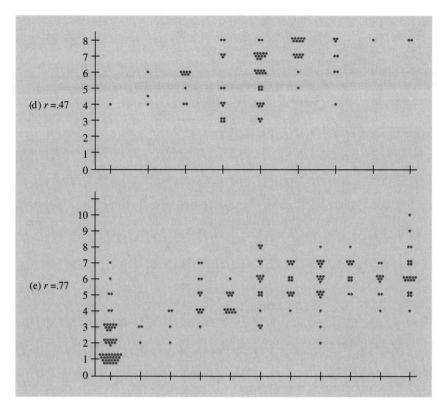

(d) r = .47

(e) r = .77

An Example

Let's try these steps with the managers' stress example.

1. Convert all scores to Z scores. Starting with the number of employees supervised, the mean is 7 (sum of 35 divided by 5 subjects), and the standard deviation is 2.37 (sum of squared deviations, 28, divided by 5 subjects, for a variance of 5.6, the square root of which is 2.37). For the first subject, then, a score of 6 is 1 below the mean of 7, and 1 divided by 2.37 is .42. Thus the first score is .42 standard deviations below the mean, or a Z score of −.42. We compute the rest of the Z scores in the same way and show them in the appropriate columns in Table 3-2.

TABLE 3-2
Calculations for the Correlation Coefficient for the Managers' Stress Study (Fictional Data)

Number of Employees Supervised (X)				Stress Level (Y)				Cross-Products
X	$X - M$	$(X - M)^2$	Z_X	Y	$Y - M$	$(Y - M)^2$	Z_Y	$Z_X Z_Y$
6	−1	1	− .42	7	1	1	.38	−.16
8	1	1	.42	8	2	4	.77	.32
3	−4	16	−1.69	1	−5	25	−1.92	3.24
10	3	9	1.27	8	2	4	.77	.98
8	1	1	.42	6	0	0	0.00	0.00

$\Sigma = 35$		$SS = 28$		$\Sigma = 30$		$SS = 34$		$\Sigma Z_X Z_Y = 4.38$
$M = 7$		$SD^2 = 5.60$		$M = 6$		$SD^2 = 6.80$		$r = .88$
		$SD = 2.37$				$SD = 2.61$		

2. Compute the cross-product of the Z scores for each case. For the first case, multiply $-.42$ times $.38$. This gives $-.16$. The cross-products for all the subjects are shown in the last column of Table 3-2.

3. Sum the cross-products of the Z scores. Adding up all the cross-products of Z scores, as shown in Table 3-2, gives a sum of 4.38.

4. Divide by the number of cases. Dividing 4.38 by 5 (the number of cases) gives a result of .876, rounded off to .88—the correlation coefficient. In terms of the correlation coefficient formula,

$$r = \frac{\Sigma Z_X Z_Y}{N} = \frac{4.38}{5} = .88$$

Since this correlation coefficient is positive and near 1, the highest possible value, this is a very strong positive linear correlation.

Integrating the Steps and Additional Examples

In general, when faced with a correlation problem, the proper approach is first to construct a scatter diagram and then, if the scatter diagram does not show a clear curvilinear pattern, to compute a correlation coefficient. If there is no curvilinear pattern, it is still a good idea to "eyeball" the scatter diagram a bit more and roughly estimate the degree and direction of linear correlation, if one is apparent, before doing any computations. This permits a check against errors in computing the correlation coefficient. Having done this, you go on to compute the correlation coefficient.

Summary of Steps in a Correlation Problem

Combining the various procedures covered in this chapter, the steps are as follows:

A. Construct a scatter diagram.
  1. Draw the axes, and determine which variable should go on which axis.
  2. Determine the range of values to use for each variable, and mark them on the axes.
  3. Mark a dot for the pair of scores for each case.
B. Determine if clearly curvilinear. If so, do not compute the correlation coefficient (or do so with the understanding that you are only describing the degree of linear relationship).
C. Estimate the direction and degree of linear correlation.
D. Compute the correlation coefficient.
  1. Convert all scores to Z scores.
  2. Compute the cross-product of the Z scores for each case.
  3. Sum the cross-products of the Z scores.
  4. Divide by the number of cases.
E. Check the sign and size of your computed correlation coefficient against your estimate from the scatter diagram.

TABLE 3-3
Effect of Number of Exposures to Words on the Number of Such Words Recalled (Fictional Data)

Subject ID Number	Number of Exposures (Independent Variable)	Number of Words Recalled (Dependent Variable)
1	1	4
2	1	3
3	2	3
4	2	5
5	3	6
6	3	4
7	4	4
8	4	6
9	5	5
10	5	2
11	6	7
12	6	9
13	7	6
14	7	8
15	8	9
16	8	8

As we noted earlier, in actual research practice the correlation coefficient would usually be calculated with a computer in an instant. Most computer packages can also make a scatter diagram (and the user has some say over how the axes and scales on them are set up). However, following the examples (and working through the practice problems at the end of the chapter), using all these rather tedious steps, is intended to help you understand the logic behind the output that so mindlessly streams out of the computer.

An Example

Suppose that a memory researcher conducted an experiment on a theory predicting that the number of exposures to a word increases the chance that the word will be remembered. Two subjects are randomly assigned to be exposed to a list of 10 words once, two subjects to be exposed twice, and so forth, up to a total of eight exposures to each word, for 16 subjects in all. Results of this fictional experiment are shown in Table 3-3.

A. Construct a scatter diagram.

1. Draw the axes, and determine which variables should go on which axis. Based on the design of the experiment, the number of exposures is the independent variable, so it will be on the horizontal axis, and the number of words recalled is the dependent variable, so it will be on the vertical axis (see Figure 3-11a).

2. Determine the range of values to use for each variable, and mark them on the axes. The number of exposures varies in the study from 1 to 8. The number of words remembered cannot be lower than 0 or more than 10, the total number on the list. (See Figure 3-11b.)

FIGURE 3-11
Steps for making a scatter diagram for the data in Table 3-3. (a) Set up the axes—the independent variable (number of exposures) on the horizontal axis, the dependent variable (number of words recalled) on the vertical axis. (b) Determine the range of values, and mark them on the axes. (c) Place a dot for the pair of scores for each of the 16 cases.

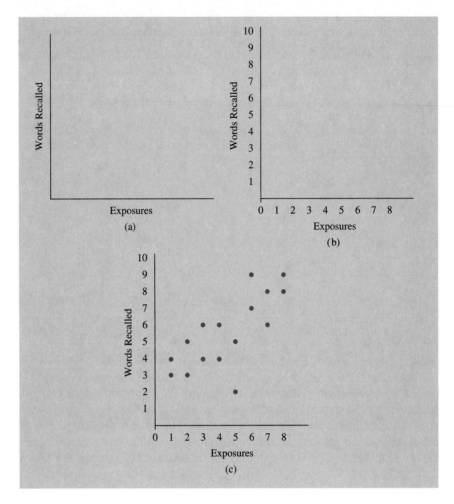

3. Mark a dot for the pair of scores for each case. The first dot is located at 1 on the horizontal axis and 4 on the vertical axis. Marking each dot in turn, in the same way, completes the scatter diagram (see Figure 3-11c).

B. Determine if clearly curvilinear. There seems to be a strong linear trend.

C. Estimate the direction and degree of linear correlation. The dots go up and to the right, and most fall tightly around an imaginary straight line. Thus there seems to be a fairly strong positive linear correlation.

D. Compute the correlation coefficient.

1. Convert all scores to Z scores. The mean of the number of exposures works out to 4.5, with a standard deviation of 2.29. Thus the first score of 1 is 3.5 exposures below the mean, which is 1.53 standard deviations below the mean, or $Z = -1.53$. Using the same procedure for all the other scores produces the Z scores shown in the appropriate columns of Table 3-4. (The table does not show the steps of computing the deviation and squared deviation scores used to figure the standard deviations.)

2. Compute the cross-product of the Z scores for each case. For example, the first cross-product is -1.53 times $-.74$, which equals $+1.13$. All of the cross-products are shown in the rightmost column of Table 3-4.

3. Sum the cross-products of the Z scores. This gives a result of 10.81.

TABLE 3-4
Computation of the Correlation Coefficient for the Effect of Number of Exposures to Each Word on the Number of Such Words Recalled (Fictional Data)

Subject ID Number	Number of Exposures (Independent Variable)		Number of Words Recalled (Dependent Variable)		Z-Score Cross-Product
	X	Z_X	Y	Z_Y	$Z_X Z_Y$
1	1	−1.53	4	− .74	1.13
2	1	−1.53	3	−1.21	1.85
3	2	−1.09	3	−1.21	1.32
4	2	−1.09	5	− .27	.29
5	3	− .65	6	.21	− .14
6	3	− .65	4	− .74	.48
7	4	− .22	4	− .74	.16
8	4	− .22	6	.21	− .05
9	5	.22	5	− .27	− .06
10	5	.22	7	.68	.15
11	6	.65	2	−1.68	−1.10
12	6	.65	9	1.62	1.06
13	7	1.09	6	.21	.23
14	7	1.09	8	1.15	1.25
15	8	1.53	9	1.62	2.48
16	8	1.53	8	1.15	1.76
Σ:	72		89		10.81
M:	4.5		5.6		$r = .68$
SD =	$\sqrt{84/16} = 2.29$		$\sqrt{72/16} = 2.1$		

4. Divide by the number of cases. Dividing the sum of the cross-products of Z scores, 10.81, by the number of cases, 16, gives .68, which is the correlation coefficient. That is, $r = .68$.

E. Check the sign and size of your computed correlation coefficient against your estimate from the scatter diagram. The obtained result of +.68 is, as expected, a fairly strong positive linear correlation.

Another Example

Suppose that an educational psychologist obtained information on average class size and average achievement test score from the five elementary schools in a particular small school district, as shown in Table 3-5. The question she then asks is, what is the relationship between these two variables?

TABLE 3-5
Average Class Size and Achievement Test Scores in Five Elementary Schools (Fictional Data)

Elementary School	Class Size	Achievement Test Score
Main Street	25	80
Casat	14	98
Harland	33	50
Shady Grove	28	82
Jefferson	20	90

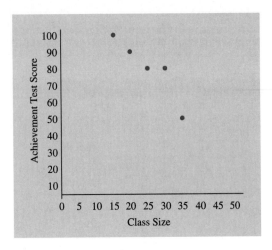

FIGURE 3-12
The last step in making a scatter diagram for the data in Table 3-5: A dot has been placed for each pair of scores for each of the five cases.

A. Construct a scatter diagram.

   1. Draw the axes, and determine which variable should go on which axis. Although the researcher does not explicitly state which variable is the predictor and which is predicted, it is probably most reasonable to think of class size as affecting achievement test scores rather than the reverse. The axes are thus drawn with class size along the bottom.

   2. Determine the range of values to use for each variable, and mark them on the axes. We will assume that the achievement test scores go from 0 to 100. Class size has a logical minimum of 1 (though school board policy surely makes it higher). We didn't know the maximum, so we guessed 50. In a real research situation, the actual maximum would be known.

   3. Mark a dot for the pair of scores for each case. The completed scatter diagram is shown in Figure 3-12.

B. Determine if clearly curvilinear. The correlation has a generally linear pattern. (However, with so few points it is harder to tell than it would be if we had a larger, more realistic number of cases.)

C. Estimate the direction and degree of linear correlation. The dots descend quite consistently from left to right, indicating a strong negative linear correlation.

D. Compute the correlation coefficient.

   1. Convert all scores to Z scores. The mean for class size is 24, and the standard deviation is 6.54. Thus the Z score for the first class size, of 25, is $(25 - 24)/6.54 = 0.15$. All of the Z scores are shown in the appropriate columns of Table 3-6.

   2. Compute the cross-product of the Z scores for each case. The first cross product is .15 times 0, which is 0. The second is -1.53 times 1.10, which equals -1.68. All of the cross-products of Z scores are shown in the rightmost column of Table 3-6.

   3. Sum the cross-products of the Z scores. The total is -4.52.

   4. Divide by the number of cases. The sum -4.52 divided by 5 is $-.90$; that is, $r = -.90$.

E. Check the sign and size of the computed correlation coefficient against your estimate from the scatter diagram. A coefficient of $-.90$ corresponds well to the original estimate of a strong negative linear correlation.

TABLE 3-6
Computation of the Correlation Coefficient for Average Class Size and Achievement Test Scores in Five Elementary Schools (Fictional Data)

School	Class Size		Achievement Test Score		Cross-Product
	X	Z_X	Y	Z_Y	$Z_X Z_Y$
Main Street	25	.15	80	0.00	0.00
Casat	14	−1.53	98	1.10	−1.68
Harland	33	1.38	50	−1.84	−2.53
Shady Grove	28	.61	82	.12	.08
Jefferson	20	− .61	90	.61	− .38
Σ:	120		400		−4.52
M:	24		80		$r = -.90$
	$SD = \sqrt{214/5} = 6.54$		$\sqrt{1{,}328/5} = 16.30$		

Testing the Statistical Significance of the Correlation Coefficient

The correlation coefficient, by itself, is a descriptive statistic. It describes the degree and direction of linear correlation in the particular group of people measured. However, when conducting research in psychology, we are often more interested in a particular set of scores as representative of the larger population that we have not studied directly. For example, the personnel psychologist gave the stress questionnaires to only five managers in the company, but with the intention that they would be typical of the managers of the company in general. (In practice, one would want a much larger group than five for this purpose—we have used small numbers in our examples to make them easier to follow.)

The problem, however, is that by studying only some of the cases, it is possible to pick by chance the ones in which highs happened to go with highs and lows with lows, even though, had we studied *all* the cases, there might really be no correlation. We say that a correlation is *significant* if it is unlikely that we could have obtained a correlation this big if in fact the overall group had no correlation. Specifically, we determine whether that likelihood is less than some small degree of probability (p), such as 5% or 1%. If it is that small, we say that the correlation is "statistically significant" with "$p < .05$" or "$p < .01$."

The process and underlying logic of determining **statistical significance** is the major focus of this book starting with Chapter 5, and we would be jumping ahead if we were to try to explain it now. However, by the time you have completed the later chapters, the details will be quite clear. (The needed information is in Appendix II to this chapter, but we suggest that you leave this material until you have completed Chapter 9.) We mention this now so that you will have a general idea of what is meant if you see references to statistical significance, "$p < .05$," or some such phrase when reading a research article that reports correlation coefficients.

statistical significance

Issues in Interpreting the Correlation Coefficient

A correlation coefficient describes the direction and degree of linear correlation between two variables. However, there are a number of subtle cautions in interpreting a correlation coefficient.

Causality and Correlation

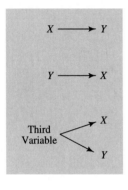

If two variables have a significant linear correlation, we normally assume that there is something causing that relationship. However, the **direction of causality** cannot be determined from the statistical result alone. For any particular correlation between variables X and Y, there are three possible directions of causality: X could be causing Y, Y could be causing X, or some third factor could be causing both X and Y. It is also possible (and often likely) that more than one direction of causality is operating at once.

For example, the positive linear correlation between relationship length (X) and closeness (Y) for males could be due to the length of time spent together causing greater closeness (X causing Y), it could be due to males who feel close to their partner choosing to stay with their partner longer (Y causing X), or it could be due to a process in which males who have more relationship skills are thus able both to feel close to their partner and to make the relationship last (third factor, relationship skills, causing both X and Y).

Now take the managers' stress example. The study began with the implicit idea that supervising more people (X) causes an increase in stress level (Y). The result of the study was a strong positive correlation between X and Y. This result is certainly consistent with the interpretation that X causes Y. But the result is equally consistent with the conclusion that Y causes X (perhaps managers who appear stressed are seen as working hard, and their superiors assign them more people to supervise). It is also possible that the significant correlation results from some third factor causing X and Y to go together. For example, certain sections of the factory may both need more people and generate more stress.

There is considerable confusion about this issue of correlation and causality. It is complicated by there being two uses of the word *correlation*. Sometimes the word is used to describe a statistical procedure (as we have used it in this chapter). At other times it is used to describe a type of research design in which two variables are measured in a group of people without randomly assigning subjects to particular values of one of the variables (see Appendix A). Ordinarily, correlational *research designs* are statistically analyzed using the correlation coefficient, and experimental research designs are analyzed using procedures that you will learn about in Chapters 9 through 13.

However, there are exceptions. We used an example earlier in the chapter in which subjects were randomly assigned to different numbers of exposures and then the number of words recalled was measured. Although we computed a correlation coefficient from these data, the study was not a correlational research design but rather a true experiment. So although by itself the correlation coefficient that we computed told us nothing about causality, it was clear from the research design that the only plausible causal direction is that the number of exposures caused the difference in recall.

Illusory Correlation: When You Know Perfectly Well That If It's Big, It's Fat—and You Are Perfectly Wrong

The concept of correlation was not really invented by statisticians. It is one of the most basic of human mental processes. The first humans must have thought in terms of correlation all the time—at least those who survived. "Every time it snows, the animals we hunt go away. Snow belongs with no animals. When the snow comes again, if we follow the animals, we may not starve."

In fact, correlation is such a typically human and highly successful thought process that we seem to be psychologically organized to see more correlation than is there—like the Aztecs, who thought that good crops correlated with human sacrifices (let's hope they were wrong), and like the following examples from social psychology of what is called *illusory correlation*.

Illusory correlation is the term for the overestimation of the strength of the relationship between two variables (the term has also had other special meanings in the past). Right away you may think of some harmful ethnic, racial, gender, and age-related illusory correlations. One source of illusory correlation is the tendency to link two infrequent and therefore highly memorable events. If Group B is smaller than Group A, and if in both groups one third of the people are known to commit certain infrequent but undesirable acts, research shows that Group B, whose members are less frequently encountered, will in fact be blamed for far more of these undesirable acts than Group A. This is true even though the odds are greater that a particular act was committed by one of the one third in Group A, since A has more members. The prob-

lem is that infrequent events stick together in memory—membership in the less frequent group and the occurrence of less frequent behaviors form an illusory correlation. One obvious consequence is that we remember anything unusual done by the member of a minority group better than we remember anything unusual done by a member of a majority group.

Most illusory correlations, however, occur simply because of prejudices. Prejudices are implicit, erroneous theories that we carry around with us. For example, we estimate that we have encountered more confirmation of an association between two social traits than we have actually seen: driving skills and a particular age group; level of academic achievement and a specific ethnic group; certain speech, dress, or social behaviors and residence in some region of the country. One especially interesting example is that most people in business believe that job satisfaction and job performance are closely linked, when in fact the correlation is quite low. People who do not like their job can still put in a good day's work; people who rave about their job can still be lazy about doing it.

The point is, next time you ask yourself why you are struggling to learn statistics, it might help to think of it as a quest to make ordinary thought processes more righteous. So again we assert that statistics can be downright romantic: It can be about conquering evil mistakes with the purity of numbers, subduing unholy prejudices with the honesty of data.

References: Hamilton (1981); Hamilton and Gifford (1976).

By contrast, it is possible to apply statistical procedures normally used to analyze experiments to a situation in which the underlying logic of the design is actually correlational. Such a case might be when people high in depression are compared to people low in depression on a measure of the number of conversations in a week. Whatever the statistical procedure used, and whatever its result, the interpretation of this study will always be ambiguous as to what caused what.

The Correlation Coefficient and the Proportionate Reduction in Error

A correlation coefficient indicates the strength or degree of a linear relationship, with larger values of r (values farther from 0) indicating a higher degree of correlation. That is, an r of .4 signifies a stronger linear correlation than an r of .2. However, an r of .4 is not twice as strong as an r of .2. To compare correlations with each other, the measure to use is r^2. This is called, for reasons you will learn in Chapter 4, the **proportionate reduction in error** (and also the *proportion of variance accounted for*).

A correlation of .2 is equivalent to an r^2 of .04, and a correlation of .4 is equivalent to an r^2 of .16. Thus a correlation of .4 actually signifies a relationship four times as strong as one of .2!

Restriction in Range

If a correlation is computed when only a limited range of the possible values on one variable is included in the group studied, the correlation cannot be properly extended to apply to the entire range of values the variable might have among people in general. This is called **restriction in range.**

For example, suppose that an educational psychologist is interested in the relation of grade level and knowledge of geography. If this researcher studied the entire range of school grade levels, the results might appear as shown in the scatter diagram in Figure 3-13a. That is, the researcher might well find a strong positive correlation. But suppose that the researcher had studied only the first three grades (where little geography is taught). The

r^2
proportionate reduction in error

restriction in range

FIGURE 3-13
An example of restriction in range comparing two scatter diagrams: (a) when the entire range is shown (of school grade level and knowledge of geography) and (b) when the range is restricted (to the first three grades).

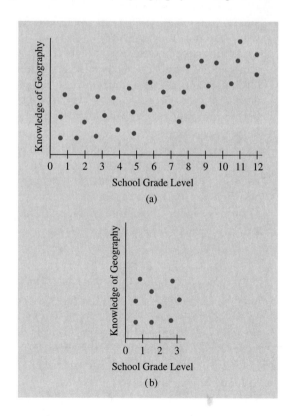

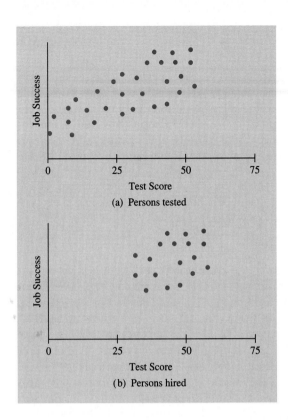

FIGURE 3-14
The effect of restriction in range on correlation.

(a) Persons tested

(b) Persons hired

scatter diagram (see Figure 3-13b) would show little, if any, correlation (and the computed correlation would be near 0), yet the researcher would be making a mistake by concluding that grade level is unrelated to geography over all grades.

It is easy to make such mistakes in interpreting correlations. You will occasionally see them even in published research articles and even more often hear them in informal discussions of research findings. For example, businesses sometimes try to determine whether their hiring tests reflect how successful the persons hired turn out on the job—and find very little relationship. What they fail to take into account is that they hired only people who did well on the tests. Their study of job success included only the subgroup of high scorers. This example is illustrated in Figure 3-14.

Unreliability of Measurement

The correlation coefficient, as we have noted, can be understood as describing how close the dots fall to a line through a scatter diagram. However, one of the reasons why dots may not fall close to the line is random error in measurement—for example, a questionnaire that includes some ambiguous items. Often in psychology our measures are not perfectly accurate or "reliable" (this concept is discussed in Appendix A and Chapter 17). The result is that a correlation computed between two measures—such as anxiety and self-criticism—is lower than it would be if we had perfect measures of these variables.

The reduction in a correlation due to unreliability of measures is called *attenuation*. More advanced statistics books and psychological measurement textbooks describe formulas for **correction for attenuation** if the degree of reliability of the measures can be determined. You will sometimes read in research articles that correlations have been "disattenuated" or "corrected for attenuation."

Although these procedures are beyond the scope of this book, you should remember the general rule that when measures have a lot of measurement error (as most questionnaires do), correlations reported in an article employing these measures may substantially underestimate the true correlation between the underlying variables that these imperfect measures are meant to reveal.

Controversies and Recent Developments: What Is a Large Correlation?

A lively current controversy about the correlation coefficient is what constitutes a "large" r. Traditionally, a large correlation is considered to be .50 or above, a moderate correlation to be about .30, and a small correlation to be about .10 (Cohen, 1988). In fact, in psychology it is rare to obtain correlations between two variables that are greater than .40. In part this is because in real life, things are not as simple as "A goes with B"—more than one predictor variable is probably associated with the dependent variable, so no one correlation could possibly tell the whole story. Low correlations are also due to the low reliability of many measures in psychology.

It is traditional to caution that a low correlation is not very important even if it is statistically significant. After all, a correlation of .10 is equivalent to only a 1% proportionate reduction in error. Furthermore, even experienced research psychologists tend to overestimate the degree of association that a correlation coefficient represents. Michael Oakes (1982) at the University of Sussex gave 30 research psychologists the two columns of numbers shown in Table 3-7 and asked them to estimate (without doing any calculations) the degree of correlation (r). What is your guess? The intuitions of the British researchers (who are as a group at least as well trained in statistics as psychologists anywhere in the world) ranged from $-.20$ to

TABLE 3-7
Table Presented to 30 Psychologists to Estimate r

X	Y
1	1
2	10
3	2
4	9
5	5
6	4
7	6
8	3
9	11
10	8
11	7
12	12

Note. Data from Oakes (1982).

+.60, with a mean of .24. You can calculate the true correlation for yourself—it comes out to .50! Similarly, Oakes gave another group of 30 researchers just the *X* column and asked them to fill in numbers in the *Y* column that would come out to a correlation of .50 (again, just using their intuition and without any calculations). When Oakes computed the actual correlations that their numbers represented, they averaged .68. In other words, even experienced researchers think of a correlation coefficient as representing a greater degree of association than it actually does.

By contrast, Ralph Rosnow of Temple University and Robert Rosenthal of Harvard (1989b) have argued that in many cases even very low correlations can have important practical implications and that when correlations are thought of in other ways, they seem large indeed. To explain their point, it is necessary to divide up the cases in a correlation analysis into two halves, a lower half and an upper half. If there was no correlation, then within each half of one variable there would be a 50–50 split on the other variable.

For example, consider the study with which we began the chapter, a correlation of relationship length with closeness. We could divide the males' length of relationships in half so that if we began at the top with longer relationships, the top half are in a long-term group and the bottom half in a short-term group. (In terms of numbers, this means giving all those in the upper half a score like +1 and all those in the lower half a score like −1.) We could also list the males according to their closeness so that the top half are in a close group and the bottom half in a nonclose group. (Again, in terms of numbers, this means giving all those in the top half one number such as +1 and those in the bottom half a different number, such as −1.) If there was no correlation, then among those in the upper long-term group, half would also be in the upper close group and an equal half would be in the lower, nonclose group. However, if there really is a correlation between these two variables, the split in either half of one variable will not be 50–50 but will show males high on one variable also high on the other.

What is striking in the Rosnow and Rosenthal argument is that when you split two variables into upper and lower halves, the difference in percentages between the two halves is exactly what you would get if you computed the correlation coefficient![1] That is, if the percentage breakdown is 45–55, a correlation computed between the variables (as split in halves) would come out to .10; if the split is 40–60, the correlation comes out to .20; if the split is 35–65, it comes out to .30; and so on.

For example, in the study showing a positive correlation for men of relationship length and closeness, splitting the subjects into halves gives the figures presented in Table 3-8 (known as a **binomial effect size display**), which shows that 69% of the long-term males fall into the close group and 31% of them into the nonclose group—and 69% minus 31% gives 38%. (Calculating the correlation coefficient from the usual formulas with the subjects divided in half in this way also gives a correlation of .38.) The point is that the difference between these percentages, 38%, sounds much larger than when one

binomial effect size display

[1]The correlation coefficient in this case is computed by giving all subjects in the upper half on a variable a score like +1 on that variable and all those in the lower half on that variable a score like −1. (Since everything is converted to *Z* scores when carrying out a correlation, it really doesn't matter what two numbers you use, so long as you are consistent in using them.) Because some information is lost with this process—the gradations among the high and low scores—the resulting correlations are usually somewhat lower than if calculated with the original data.

TABLE 3-8
Binomial Effect Size Display for Male's Closeness and Relationship Length

	Close	Nonclose
Long-term relationships	69%	31%
Short-term relationships	31%	69%

Note. Data from Aron et al. (1992).

speaks of the correlation of these two variables in terms of reducing the proportion of error, as we did in that study, by "only" 21%.

To demonstrate the practical importance of small correlations, Rosnow and Rosenthal (1989b) give an example of a now famous study in which doctors either did or did not take aspirin each day, with heart attacks the outcome of interest (Steering Committee of the Physicians Health Study Research Group, 1988). The results were that taking aspirin was correlated −.034 with heart attacks. That is, it produces about a 0.1% proportionate reduction in error. Still, this low correlation meant that 3.4% fewer of the doctors taking the aspirin had heart attacks. As shown in Table 3-9, among the more than 20,000 doctors who were in the study, this correlation represents 72 more heart attacks (and 13 more deaths) in the group that did not take aspirin. When we think of small differences as number of deaths, our whole attitude changes, doesn't it? A small reduction in error seems more worth attending to.

Correlation Coefficients as Described in Research Articles

Correlation coefficients are described either in the text of research articles or in tables. In the text, they are usually given with the letter r, an equal sign, and the correlation coefficient (e.g., $r = .31$). (Sometimes the "significance level," such as $p < .05$, will also be reported.) For example, the result

TABLE 3-9
Effect of Aspirin on Heart Attack

Condition	MI Absent	MI Present
Aspirin	10,933	104
Placebo	10,845	189
Binomial Effect Size Display of $r = .034$		
Aspirin	51.7	48.3
Placebo	48.3	51.7
Total	100.0	100.0
	Nonfatal MI	**Fatal MI**
Aspirin	99	5
Placebo	171	18

Note. MI = Myocardial infarction. Data from Steering Committee of the Physicians Health Study Research Group (1988).

TABLE 3-10
Pearson Correlations Among Measures

Measure	1	2	3	4	5	6
1. Dependency	—					
2. Self-criticism	.51***	—				
3. Internality	.48***	.53***	—			
4. Stability	.47***	.63***	.40*	—		
5. Globality	.45**	.62***	.44**	.77***	—	
6. BDI	.53***	.64***	.46**	.40*	.38*	—
SD	.39*	.61***	.44**	.38*	.47***	.71***

Note. $N = 60$. BDI = Beck Depression Inventory. SD = Semantic Differential. From Brown, J. D., & Silberschatz, G., (1989), tab. 1. Dependency, self-criticism, and depressive attributional style. *Journal of Abnormal Psychology*, *98*, 187–188. Copyright, 1989, by the American Psychological Association. Reprinted by permission of the author.
* $p < .01$. ** $p < .001$. *** $p < .0001$.

with which we started the chapter would be described as follows: "For males there was a positive correlation ($r = .46$) between length of relationship and closeness." (The sentence might also have included, in the parentheses, "$N = 41, p < .05$").

Tables of correlation are very common, especially when more than two variables are involved. In that case, a table is presented in which each variable is listed both at the top and at the left side, and the correlation of each pair of variables is shown inside the table. This is sometimes called a **correlation matrix.**

Table 3-10 is from a study of personality traits measured in a group of psychiatric patients (Brown & Silberschatz, 1989). Notice that the correlation of a variable with itself is not given. Also notice that only half of the table is filled in. That is because it would be repetitive to fill in the other half, since a correlation, for example, of depression with self-criticism is the same as a correlation of self-criticism with depression. (Also notice that significance levels are shown by means of asterisks, with a note at the bottom as to the probability level the asterisks represent.)

correlation matrix

Summary

A scatter diagram describes the relation between two variables. The lowest to highest possible values of the independent or predictor variable are marked on the horizontal axis, and the lowest to highest possible values of the dependent variable are marked on the vertical axis. Each individual pair of scores is represented as a dot on this two-dimensional graph.

When the dots in the scatter diagram generally follow a straight line, this is called a linear correlation. In a positive linear correlation, the line goes upward to the right (so that low scores go with low and high with high). In a negative linear correlation, the line goes downward to the right (so that low scores go with high and high with low). In a curvilinear correlation, the dots follow a line other than a simple straight line. No correlation exists when the dots do not follow any kind of line.

The correlation coefficient (r) is an index of the degree of linear correlation. It is the average of the cross-products of Z scores. The correlation coefficient is highly positive when there is a strong positive linear correlation, because positive Z scores are multiplied by positive and negative Z scores by negative. The coefficient is highly negative when there is a strong negative linear correlation, because positive Z scores are multiplied by negative and negative Z scores by positive. The coefficient is 0 when there is no linear correlation, because positive Z scores are sometimes multiplied by positive and negative Z scores by negative, but sometimes the reverse is true, so that positive and negative cross-products cancel each other out.

The maximum positive value of r, +1, arises when there is a perfect positive linear correlation. The maximum negative value of r, –1, arises when there is a perfect negative linear correlation.

A correlation is usually based on measures taken of a particular group that is intended to represent some larger group. When statistical procedures (to be taught later) applied to data support the hypothesis that a correlation does exist in the larger group, we say that the correlation is statistically significant.

Comparisons of the degree of linear correlation are considered most accurate in terms of the correlation coefficient squared (r^2), the proportionate reduction in error.

Correlation does not determine the direction of causation. If two variables, X and Y, are correlated, this could be because X is causing Y, Y is causing X, or a third factor is causing both X and Y.

A computed correlation coefficient can underrepresent the true correlation in the general group if the smaller group selected for study is restricted in range or if the scores are obtained with unreliable measures.

Many psychologists argue that the correlation coefficient is an overestimate of the importance of the association of two variables, and studies suggest that in fact psychologists tend to think of any particular correlation coefficient as representing a greater degree of association than actually exists. However, looking at the relationship of two variables by dividing each into an upper and lower half and examining the 2 x 2 table that results (called a *binomial effect size display*) suggests that even very small correlations, ignored in the past, can actually have great practical importance.

Correlational results are usually presented in research articles either in the text with the value of r (and sometimes the significance level) or in a special table (a correlation matrix) showing the correlations among several variables.

Key Terms

binomial effect size display
correction for attenuation
correlation
correlation coefficient (r)
correlation matrix
cross-product of Z scores
curvilinear correlation
degree of correlation

dependent variable
direction of causality
independent variable
linear correlation
negative correlation
no correlation
perfect correlation
positive correlation

predictor variable
proportionate reduction in
  error (r^2)
restriction in range
scatter diagram
statistical significance

Practice Problems

These problems involve computation (with the assistance of a calculator). Most real-life statistics problems are done on a computer. But even if you have a computer, do this by hand to ingrain the method in your mind.

For practice in using a computer to solve statistical problems, refer to the computer section of each chapter of the study guide that accompanies this text.

All data are fictional (unless an actual citation is given). Answers to Set I are given at the back of the book.

SET I

For Problems 1 and 2 do the following: (a) Make a scatter diagram of the raw scores; (b) describe in words the general pattern of association, if any; (c) compute the correlation coefficient; (d) explain the logic of what you have done, writing as if you were speaking to someone who has never had a statistics course (but who does understand the mean, standard deviation, and Z scores); and (e) describe three logically possible directions of causality.

1. A researcher was interested in the relation between psychotherapists' degree of empathy and their patients' satisfaction with therapy. As a pilot study, four patient-therapist pairs were studied. Here are the results:

Pair Number	Therapist Empathy	Patient Satisfaction
1	70	4
2	94	5
3	36	2
4	48	1

2. An instructor asked five students how many hours they had studied for an exam. Here are the number of hours studied and their grades:

Hours Studied	Test Grade
0	52
10	95
6	83
8	71
6	64

3. In a study of people first getting acquainted with each other, the amount of self-disclosure of one's partner and one's liking for one's partner were measured. Here are the results:

Partner's Self-Disclosure		Liking for Partner	
Actual score	Z score	Actual score	Z score
18	.37	8	1.10
17	.17	9	1.47
20	.80	6	.37
8	−1.72	1	−1.47
13	− .67	7	.74
24	1.63	1	−1.47
11	−1.09	3	− .74
12	− .88	5	0.00
18	.38	7	.74
21	1.00	3	− .74

In this problem, the Z scores are given to save you some computation time. (a) Make a scatter diagram of the raw scores; (b) describe in words the general pattern of association, if any; and (c) compute the correlation coefficient.

4. Pfeiffer and Wong (1989) developed what they call the Multidimensional Jealousy Scale. Their test included three subscales: "Cog," which measures cognitive jealousy (beliefs about the other person and the situation that are associated with being jealous); "Emo," which measures emotional jealousy (how jealous the person feels); and "Beh," which measures behavioral aspects of jealousy (things a person is doing that show jealousy).

To examine the test's usefulness and its relation to other variables, Pfeiffer and Wong administered this test and several other tests to 120 individuals ranging from 18 to 50 years old. The other measures they used were the Memorial University of Newfoundland Scale of Happiness (MUNSH), Rubin's Love Scale (which measures how much love a person feels for a partner), Rubin's Like Scale (which measures how much liking a person feels for a partner), and White's Relationship Jealousy Scale (WRJS).

Table 3-11 on page 96 presents the results of this comparison. Explain the results as if you were writing to a person who has never had a course in statistics; be sure to comment on possible directions of causality for each result.

5. For each of the following situations, indicate why the correlation coefficient might be a distorted estimate of the true relation (and what kind of distortion you would expect) between each of these pairs of variables:

(a) Scores on two questionnaire measures of personality are correlated.

(b) Comfort of living situation and happiness are correlated among a group of millionaires.

TABLE 3-11
Correlation Coefficients Involving Jealousy, Love, Liking, and Happiness

	Cog	Emo	Beh	MUNSH	Rubin Love	Rubin Like	WRJS
Cog		.14	.30***	−.08	−.20**	−.37***	.38**
Emo			.42***	−.24**	.20**	−.15*	.53***
Beh				−.17*	−.06	−.43***	.56***
MUNSH					−.02	.26**	−.03
Rubin Love						.45***	−.09
Rubin Like							−.30**

Note. Data reprinted with permission from Pfeiffer, S. M., & Wong, P. T. P. (1989), tab. 3. Multidimensional jealousy. *Journal of Social and Personal Relationships*, 6, 181–196. Copyright, 1989, by Sage Publications Ltd.
* $p < 0.05$. ** $p < 0.01$. *** $p < 0.001$.

6. The following have been prepared so that Data Sets B through D are slightly modified versions of Data Set A. Make scatter diagrams and compute the correlation coefficients for each data set. (Answers are provided for Data Sets A and B only.)

Data Set A		Data Set B		Data Set C		Data Set D	
X	Y	X	Y	X	Y	X	Y
1	1	1	1	1	5	1	1
2	2	2	2	2	2	2	4
3	3	3	3	3	3	3	3
4	4	4	5	4	4	4	2
5	5	5	4	5	1	5	5

7. A researcher is interested in whether a new drug affects whether or not a cold develops. Eight people are tested: Four take the drug and four do not. (Those who take it are rated 1, those who don't, 0.) Whether they get a cold (rated 1) or not (0) is recorded. Four possible results are shown. Compute the correlation coefficient in each case. (Answers are provided for possibilities A and B only.)

Possibility A		Possibility B		Possibility C		Possibility D	
Take drug	*Get cold*	*Take drug*	*Get cold*	*Take drug*	*Get cold*	*Take drug*	*Get cold*
0	1	0	1	0	1	0	1
0	1	0	1	0	1	0	1
0	1	0	1	0	0	0	1
0	1	0	0	0	0	0	0
1	0	1	1	1	1	1	0
1	0	1	0	1	1	1	0
1	0	1	0	1	0	1	0
1	0	1	0	1	0	1	0

SET II

For Problems 1 and 2 do the following: (a) Make a scatter diagram of the raw scores; (b) describe in words the general pattern of association, if any; (c) compute the correlation coefficient; (d) explain the logic of what you have done, writing as if you were speaking to someone who has never had a statistics course (but who does understand the mean, standard deviation, and Z scores); and (e) describe three logically possible directions of causality.

1. Four individuals are given a test in manual dexterity (high scores mean better dexterity) and an anxiety test (high scores mean more anxiety). The scores are as follows.

Person	Dexterity	Anxiety
1	1	10
2	1	8
3	2	4
4	4	−2

2. Four young children were monitored closely over a period of several weeks to measure their pattern of viewing violent television programs and their amount of violent behavior toward their playmates. The results were as follows:

Child's Code Number	Weekly Viewing of Violent TV (h)	Number of Violent or Aggressive Acts Toward Playmates
G3368	14	9
R8904	8	6
C9890	6	1
L8722	12	8

For Problems 3 and 4, follow the instructions for Problem 3 in Set I.

3. The Louvre Museum is interested in the relation of the age of a painting to public interest in it. The number of people stopping to look at each of 10 randomly selected paintings is observed over a week. The results are as shown:

Painting Title	Approximate Age (Years)		Number of People Stopping to Look	
	X	Z_x	Y	Z_y
The Entombment	465	1.39	68	− .69
Mys Mar Ste Catherine	515	1.71	71	− .59
The Bathers	240	− .09	123	1.19
The Toilette	107	− .96	112	.82
Portrait of Castiglione	376	.80	48	−1.38
Charles I of England	355	.67	84	− .14
Crispin and Scapin	140	− .75	66	− .76
Nude in the Sun	115	− .91	148	2.05
The Balcony	122	− .86	71	− .59
The Circus	99	−1.01	91	.10

4. A schoolteacher thought that he had observed that students who dressed more neatly were generally better students. To test this idea, the teacher had a friend rate each of the students for neatness of dress. Following are the ratings for neatness, along with each student's score on a standardized school achievement test.

Child	Neatness Rating		Score on Achievement Test	
	X	Z_x	Y	Z_y
Janet	18	− .52	60	− .66
Gareth	24	−1.43	58	−1.09
Grove	14	−1.82	70	1.47
Kevin	19	− .20	58	−1.09
Joshua	20	.13	66	.62

Child	Neatness Rating		Score on Achievement Test	
	X	Z_x	Y	Z_y
Nicole	23	1.11	68	1.04
Susan	20	.13	65	.40
Drew	22	.78	68	1.04
Marie	15	−1.50	56	−1.51
Chad	21	.46	62	− .23

5. Solano and Koester (1989) conducted a series of studies about the relationship of loneliness (as measured on the UCLA loneliness scale) with (a) how anxious people are about communicating with other people and (b) a measure of social skills. These tests were given to 321 undergraduates, consisting of 168 males and 153 females. They report their results as follows:

> The correlations between communication anxiety and the UCLA score were similar to those found [in a previous study]. The correlation for the total sample was .35, $p < .001$, for males .41, $p < .001$, for females .30, $p < .001$. The correlation for the social skill 5 ratings and loneliness for the total sample was −.15, for males −.16, $p < .05$, and for females −.10, *n.s.* (p. 130).

Explain the results as if you were writing to a person who has never had a course in statistics; be sure to comment on possible directions of causality for each result. You do not need to explain the meaning of the significance levels. (That is, you can ignore "$p < .001$," "$p < .05$," and "ns.")

6. Arbitrarily select eight full personal names, each from a different page of the telephone directory. Make a scatter diagram and compute the correlation coefficient and its statistical significance for the relation between number of letters in first and last name. Describe the result in words, and suggest a possible interpretation for your results.

Chapter Appendix I: Optional Computational Formula for the Correlation Coefficient

The steps for computing a correlation coefficient can be combined into a single formula for use when carrying out computations by hand (or with a calculator). Ordinarily, these steps are to compute (a) the Z scores for each raw score, (b) the cross-products of the Z scores, and (c) the average of the cross-product of the Z scores. (As you will have seen from the practice problems, computing the Z scores is particularly tedious when working by hand, especially if you must first compute the means and standard deviations.) Through quite a bit of algebraic manipulation, the formula can be simplified as follows:

$$r = \frac{N\Sigma XY - (\Sigma X)(\Sigma Y)}{[\sqrt{N\Sigma X^2 - (\Sigma X)^2}][\sqrt{N\Sigma Y^2 - (\Sigma Y)^2}]} \qquad (3\text{-}2)$$

When using this procedure, it is helpful to lay your data out in a five-column chart, consisting of columns for X, X^2, Y, Y^2, and the XY cross-products. Note that no Z scores are involved anywhere and that the cross-products you compute are based directly on raw scores. Also, as we reminded you in the appendix to Chapter 2, ΣX^2 is found by taking each X score and squaring it and then adding up these squared scores; $(\Sigma X)^2$, by contrast, is found by taking the sum of all the X scores (without squaring any of them) and then squaring this sum.

Table 3-12 shows the computation, using this formula for the managers' stress example. Compare this to Table 3-2.

TABLE 3-12
Calculations Using the Computational Formula for the Correlation Coefficient for the Managers' Stress Study (Fictional Data)

Employees Supervised		Stress Level		Cross-Products
X	X^2	Y	Y^2	XY
6	36	7	49	42
8	64	8	64	64
3	9	1	1	3
10	100	8	64	80
8	64	6	36	48
Σ: 35	273	30	214	237

$$r = \frac{N\Sigma XY - (\Sigma X)(\Sigma Y)}{[\sqrt{N\Sigma X^2 - (\Sigma X)^2}]\ \ [\sqrt{N\Sigma Y^2 - (\Sigma Y)^2}]}$$

$$r = \frac{(5)(237) - (35)(30)}{[\sqrt{(5)(273) - (35)^2}]\ \ [\sqrt{(5)(214) - (30)^2}]}$$

$$r = \frac{1{,}185 - 1{,}050}{(\sqrt{1{,}365 - 1{,}225})\ \ (\sqrt{1{,}070 - 900})}$$

$$r = \frac{135}{(\sqrt{140})(\sqrt{170})} = \frac{135}{(11.83)(13.04)} = \frac{135}{154.26} = .88$$

Chapter Appendix II: Hypothesis Tests and Power for the Correlation Coefficient

This material is for students who have completed Chapter 9.

Significance of a Correlation Coefficient

Hypothesis testing of a correlation coefficient follows the usual five-step process. However, there are three important points to note. First, usually the null hypothesis can be stated as that the correlation in a population like that observed is no different from a population in which the true correlation is zero. Second, if assumptions (explained in the next paragraph) are met, the comparison distribution is a t distribution with degrees of freedom equal to the number of subjects minus 2. Third, the correlation coefficient's score on that t distribution is computed using the formula

$$t = \frac{(r)(\sqrt{N-2})}{\sqrt{1-r^2}} \qquad (3\text{-}3)$$

Also note that the significance tests of a correlation, like a t test, can be either one-tailed or two-tailed. A one-tailed test means that the researcher has predicted the sign (positive or negative) of the correlation.

Assumptions for the significance test of a correlation coefficient are somewhat complex. Ordinarily, both variables should be normally distributed, and the distribution of each variable at each point of the other variable should have about equal variance. However, as with the t test and analysis of variance, moderate violations of these assumptions are not fatal.

Here is an example, using the manager's stress study. We will suppose that the researchers predicted a positive correlation between number of employees supervised and stress, to be tested at the .05 level.

1. Reframe the question into a research hypothesis and a null hypothesis about the populations. The populations of interest are these:

Population 1: Managers like those in this study
Population 2: Managers for whom there is no correlation between number of employees supervised and stress

The null hypothesis is that the two populations have the same correlation. The research hypothesis is that Population 1 has a higher correlation than Population 2. (That is, the prediction is for a population correlation greater than 0.)

2. Determine the characteristics of the comparison distribution. Assuming that we meet the assumptions (in practice, it would be hard to tell with only five cases), the comparison distribution is a t distribution with df = 3. (That is, df = $N - 2 = 5 - 2 = 3$.)

3. Determine the cutoff sample score on the comparison distribution at which the null hypothesis should be rejected. The t table (Table B-2 in Appendix B) shows that for a one-tailed test at the .05 level, with 3 degrees of freedom, we need a t of at least 2.353.

4. Determine the score of your sample on the comparison distribution. We computed a correlation of $r = .88$ and $N = 5$. Applying the formula to find the equivalent t, we get

$$t = \frac{(r)(\sqrt{N-2})}{\sqrt{1-r^2}} = \frac{(.88)(\sqrt{3})}{\sqrt{1-.77}} = \frac{(.88)(1.73)}{\sqrt{.23}} = \frac{1.52}{.48} = 3.17$$

5. Compare the scores obtained in Steps 3 and 4 to decide whether to reject the null hypothesis. The t score of 3.17 for our sample is more extreme than the minimum needed t score of 2.353. The null hypothesis can thus be rejected, and the research hypothesis is supported.

Effect Size and Power

The correlation coefficient itself is a measure of effect size. Cohen's (1988) conventions for the correlation coefficient are .10 for a small effect size, .30 for a medium effect size, and .50 for a large effect size. Table 3-13 gives approximate power, and Table 3-14 gives minimum sample size for 80% power. (More complete tables are provided in Cohen, 1988, pp. 84–95, 101–102.)

TABLE 3-13
Approximate Power of Studies Using the Correlation Coefficient (r) for Testing Hypotheses at the .05 Level of Significance

		Effect Size		
		Small ($r = .10$)	Medium ($r = .30$)	Large ($r = .50$)
Two-tailed				
Total N:	10	.06	.13	.33
	20	.07	.25	.64
	30	.08	.37	.83
	40	.09	.48	.92
	50	.11	.57	.97
	100	.17	.86	[a]
One-tailed				
Total N:	10	.08	.22	.46
	20	.11	.37	.75
	30	.13	.50	.90
	40	.15	.60	.96
	50	.17	.69	.98
	100	.26	.92	[a]

[a]Nearly 1.00.

TABLE 3-14
Approximate Number of Subjects Needed to Achieve 80% Power for a Study Using the Correlation Coefficient *(r)* for Testing a Hypothesis at the .05 Significance Level

	Effect Size		
	Small *(r = .10)*	*Medium* *(r = .30)*	*Large* *(r = .50)*
Two-tailed	783	85	28
One-tailed	617	68	22

4 Prediction

I N the first three chapters, we looked at methods for describing a group of scores, including, in Chapter 3, how to describe the relation between two distributions of scores. Now we turn to one of the major practical applications of statistical methods, making predictions. Psychologists of various kinds are called on to make informed (and precise) guesses about such things as how well a particular job applicant is likely to perform if hired, how much a reading program is likely to help a particular third grader, or how likely a potential parolee is to commit a violent crime if released. Learning the intricacies of statistical prediction also deepens your insight into other statistical topics and prepares you for central themes in more advanced statistics courses.

In this chapter, we consider procedures for making predictions about one variable (such as college grade point average) based on information about another variable (such as SAT scores). We then examine how to estimate the expected accuracy of the predictions we make using these procedures. Finally, we introduce situations in which predictions about one variable (such as college GPA) are made based on information about two or more other variables (such as using both SAT scores and high school GPA).

Terminology of Bivariate Prediction

In what is called **bivariate prediction** (*bivariate* means "of two variables") or **bivariate regression,** we use a person's score on one variable (for example, SAT scores) to make predictions about that person's score on another variable (for example, college GPA). Reviving the terminology we intro-

bivariate prediction
bivariate regression

TABLE 4-1
Terminology for Two Variables in Bivariate Prediction

	Variable Predicted From	Variable Predicted To
Name	Predictor variable	Dependent variable
Alternative name	Independent variable	Criterion variable
Symbol	X	Y
Example	SAT scores	College GPA

duced in Chapter 3, the variable you use to help make the prediction (such as SAT) is called the *predictor variable*. (The predictor variable is also often called the *independent variable*, especially if it is considered to be the cause of the other variable.) The variable you make predictions about (such as college GPA) is usually called the *dependent variable*. (The dependent variable in a prediction situation is technically called the *criterion variable*, but this usage is not common in most areas of psychology research.) Usually we label the predictor variable X and the dependent variable Y. That is, we use a person's score on X to help predict that person's score on Y. (For a summary, see Table 4-1.)

We referred to these two kinds of variables in our discussion of correlation in Chapter 3. However, in that context, it made relatively little difference which was which, since we cared only about the degree of relationship between the two. In the context of prediction, however, it is essential to keep straight which variable you are making predictions about and which one you are using to help in making the predictions.

The Bivariate Prediction Model With Z Scores

prediction model

regression coefficient

standardized regression coefficient, (β)

It simplifies learning bivariate prediction if we begin by restricting ourselves to using Z scores; later we proceed to prediction with raw scores. The **prediction model,** or formula, that we use to make predictions with Z scores is as follows: A person's predicted Z score on the dependent variable is found by multiplying a particular number, called a **regression coefficient,** times that person's Z score on the predictor variable. Because we are working with Z scores (which are also called *standard scores*), the regression coefficient in this case is called a **standardized regression coefficient;** it is symbolized by the Greek letter "beta" (**β**). (And because it is a kind of a measure of how much weight or importance to give the predictor variable, it is called the "beta weight" or simply the "beta.") In symbols,

$$\hat{Z}_Y = (\beta)(Z_X) \tag{4-1}$$

$\hat{Z}_Y$ is the predicted value of the Z score for the particular subject's score on the dependent variable Y. The caret or hat symbol means "predicted value of." β is the standardized regression coefficient. Z_X is the known Z score for the particular subject's score on the predictor variable X.

For example, suppose that for a particular university, the beta for predicting college GPA from SAT is .3. And suppose that a person has an SAT score that is 2 standard deviations above the mean (that is, a Z score of +2).

The predicted Z score for this person's college GPA would be $.3 \times 2 = .6$, or .6 standard deviations above the mean on college GPA. In symbols,

$$\hat{Z}_Y = (\beta)(Z_X) = (.3)(2) = .6$$

The Standardized Regression Coefficient (β) as r

It can be proved mathematically (using calculations that are beyond the level of this book) that in bivariate prediction with Z scores, the optimal number to use for beta is the correlation coefficient (which you learned about in Chapter 3). That is, in bivariate prediction, $\beta = r$.

To gain some insight into why this should be so, consider the two extreme situations in which there is either no correlation or a perfect correlation between predictor and dependent variables. In the first case, where $r = 0$, this means that knowing the person's score on the predictor variable does not help you in making predictions; it is simply irrelevant. Thus your best prediction is that the person will score average on the dependent variable. With Z scores, average is always 0 and a beta of 0 ensures that whatever the score on the independent variable, you always predict 0 (since 0 times any number is 0):

When $r = 0$: $\quad \hat{Z}_Y = (\beta)(Z_X) = (0)(Z_X) = 0$

By contrast, if $r = 1$, that means that there is a perfect correlation between predictor and dependent variables. When there is a perfect correlation, the Z score on the predictor variable is always the same as the Z score on the dependent variable. (Recall from Chapter 3 that a correlation means that highs go with highs and lows with lows. Highs and lows are precisely measured by Z scores, and a perfect correlation means that highs go perfectly with highs and lows perfectly with lows.) Any number times 1 is itself, and when there is a perfect positive correlation, beta is 1 (when there is a perfect negative correlation, beta $= -1$):

When $r = 1$: $\quad \hat{Z}_Y = (\beta)(Z_X) = (1)(Z_X) = Z_X$

Thus when the correlation between predictor and dependent variables is 0, the best number for beta is 0; when the correlation is 1, the best number for beta is 1. It is not surprising that in the intermediate cases, when r is between 0 and 1, the best number for beta is also between 0 and 1.

An Example

Consider again the managers' stress example from Chapter 3. Now it will be very important to remember that in this example, stress level is the dependent variable predicted by number of employees supervised, the predictor variable. The correlation coefficient between employees supervised and managers' stress level was .88. Thus $\beta = .88$, and the model for predicting a manager's Z score for stress is to multiply .88 times the Z score for the number of employees that the manager will supervise. For example, if a new manager were going to be supervising 10 employees, this would represent a Z score of $+1.27$ on employees supervised. (We converted 10 to a Z score using the procedure you learned in Chapter 2 for converting raw scores to Z scores: $Z = (X - M)/SD$.)

Thus we would predict a Z score on stress level by multiplying .88 times 1.27, which comes out to 1.12. This means that a manager who supervised 10 employees is predicted to have a stress level that is slightly more than 1 standard deviation above the mean. In terms of the formula,

$$\hat{Z}_Y = (\beta)(Z_X) = (.88)(1.27) = 1.12$$

By contrast, if the new manager were going to supervise only three employees, the model would predict a Z score stress level of .88 times −1.69 (the Z score when the number supervised is three), which is −1.49. That is,

$$\hat{Z}_Y = (\beta)(Z_X) = (.88)(-1.69) = -1.49$$

Why Prediction Is Sometimes Called Regression

Statisticians usually refer to bivariate prediction as "bivariate regression." The term *regression* comes from the fact that when there is less than a perfect correlation between two variables, the dependent variable Z score is some fraction (the value of r) of the predictor variable Z score. As a result, the dependent variable Z score is closer to its mean (that is, it regresses or returns toward a Z of 0).

For example, in the managers' stress example, the new manager who was going to supervise 10 employees has a Z score for employees to be supervised of 1.27, but the predicted stress level Z score has "regressed" to only 1.12.

Bivariate Prediction Using Raw Scores

We consider two ways of making predictions using raw scores.

Convert Raw to Z, Make Prediction, Convert Z to Raw

One way to make a prediction involving raw scores is as follows:

1. Convert the raw score on the predictor variable to a Z score.
2. Multiply beta times this Z score to get the predicted Z score on the dependent variable.
3. Convert the predicted Z score on the dependent variable to a raw score.

For example, in the managers' stress study, when we wanted to predict the stress level of a manager supervising 10 employees, we first converted 10 to a Z score (1.27). This was Step 1. Corresponding to Step 2, we then found the predicted stress-level Z score by multiplying beta times this Z score (.88 times 1.27 gave a predicted Z score of 1.12). Step 3 (which we did not do earlier) is to convert this predicted Z score of 1.12 to a raw score (which, using the formula from Chapter 2 for converting a Z score to a raw score, comes out to 8.92).

These steps, and the computations involved, are illustrated systematically in Table 4-2 for the other sample prediction we made earlier in this chapter for the manager who will be supervising three people.

In using these steps, be careful when making the conversions between raw and Z scores to use the mean and standard deviation for the correct

TABLE 4-2
Summary, Using Formulas, of Steps for Making Raw Score Predictions With Raw-to-Z and Z-to-Raw Conversions, With an Example

Step	Formula	Example
1	$Z_X = (X - M_X)/SD_X$	$Z_X = (3 - 7)/2.37 = -1.69$
2	$\hat{Z}_Y = (\beta)(Z_X)$	$\hat{Z}_Y = (.88)(-1.69) = -1.49$
3	$\hat{Y} = (SD_Y)(\hat{Z}_Y) + M_Y$	$\hat{Y} = (2.61)(-1.49) + 6 = 2.11$

variable. In Step 1, you are working exclusively with the score, mean, and standard deviation for the predictor variable (X); in Step 3, you are working exclusively with that information for the dependent variable (Y).

Direct Raw Score–to–Raw Score Prediction

An alternative procedure reduces the three-step process we used to a single formula that automatically takes into account the conversion into and from Z scores (Steps 1 and 3). That is, if you substitute the formulas for converting to and from Z scores into the prediction model and do some algebraic manipulation, you can get a single **raw score prediction formula:**

$$\hat{Y} = a + (b)(X) \tag{4-2}$$

This formula emphasizes two terms that we have not considered before, b and a. b is the **raw score regression coefficient.** b is similar to β, the standardized regression coefficient, but b is used only with raw scores and is not the same as the correlation coefficient. a is the **regression constant.** a gets added into the predicted value of the raw score dependent variable to take into account the means of the raw score distributions. (With Z scores, a regression constant is not needed because the variables always have mean Z scores of 0.)

The raw score regression coefficient (b) and the regression constant (a) can be calculated directly from knowing β (which in the case of bivariate prediction is r) and the means and standard deviations of the two variables:

$$b = (\beta)(SD_Y/SD_X) \tag{4-3}$$

$$a = M_Y - (b)(M_X) \tag{4-4}$$

In our managers' stress example, $\beta = .88$, $M_X = 7$, $SD_X = 2.37$, $M_Y = 6$, and $SD_Y = 2.61$. Thus

$$b = (\beta)(SD_Y/SD_X) = (.88)(2.61/2.37) = (.88)(1.10) = .97$$

$$a = M_Y - (b)(M_X) = 6 - (.97)(7) = 6 - 6.79 = -.79$$

$$\hat{Y} = a + (b)(X) = -.79 + (.97)(X)$$

If a potential manager will be supervising 10 individuals, the predicted stress level will be

$$\hat{Y} = -.79 + (.97)(X) = -.79 + (.97)(10) = -.79 + 9.7 = 8.91$$

If three people are to be supervised,

$$\hat{Y} = -.79 + (.97)(X) = -.79 + (.97)(3) = -.79 + 2.91 = 2.12$$

raw score prediction formula

raw score regression coefficient

regression constant

(Note that these results agree, within rounding error, with what we computed using the three-step approach of raw-to-Z, prediction, and Z-to-raw.)

More generally, consider the meaning of b and a as illustrated in the following example. The raw score regression coefficient (b) of .97 means that every increase of one person supervised is associated with an increase in .97 points on what you predict for the manager's stress level. If two are supervised, you multiply .97 by 2; if three, .97 by 3.

The regression constant (a) of −.79 means that, in addition, you adjust your prediction, for any number of employees, by subtracting .79 points on the stress scale. This is why it is a constant: You always use the same value.

The regression constant of −.79 also tells you that when X is 0, you would predict a stress score of −.79. (However, in this case, X is the number of employees supervised, and it seems unlikely for a manager to supervise no one. This is fortunate, since it is also unlikely that someone could have less than zero stress.)

The Regression Line

You can visualize a prediction model as a line on a graph in which the horizontal axis represents the predictor variable scores and the vertical axis represents the predicted scores on the dependent variable. (The graph is set up like the scatter diagrams you learned to make in Chapter 3.) The line is called a **regression line** and shows the relation between values of the predictor variable and the predicted values of the dependent variable. In the example of employees supervised (predictor) and managers' stress level (dependent), the regression line is shown on the graph in Figure 4-1. By following the regression line, you can find the level of stress that is predicted from any particular number of employees supervised. The dotted lines show the predictions we calculated for managers supervising 3 and 10 people.

regression line

FIGURE 4-1
The regression line for the managers' stress example using raw scores, showing predicted levels of stress for managers supervising 3 and 10 employees.

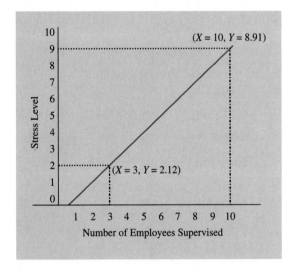

Slope of the Regression Line

slope

The steepness of the angle of the regression line, called its **slope,** is of particular interest. The slope is the amount the line moves up for every unit it moves across. In the example in Figure 4-1, the line moves up .97 stress points for every additional person supervised. In fact, the slope of the line is exactly b, the regression coefficient.

This equivalence of the slope of the regression line and b also emphasizes that a regression coefficient serves as a kind of *rate of exchange* between the predictor and dependent variables. That is, the regression coefficient tells you how many predicted units of the dependent variable you get for any given number of units of the predictor variable. It is like knowing that on a given day, one Canadian dollar buys five French francs. (However, don't carry the analogy too far. When exchanging money, we are making a relatively exact transaction. With prediction models, the exchange is of an actual amount in the predictor variable in relation to a predicted amount in the dependent variable. Except in the case of a perfect correlation, that prediction will have some error.)

How to Draw the Regression Line

The first steps are setting up the axes and labels of your graph—the same steps as you learned in Chapter 3 for setting up a scatter diagram. Then, since the regression line is a straight line, you need only calculate the location of any two points and draw the line that passes through them. Overall, there are four steps, which we will illustrate with the managers' stress example:

1. Draw and label the axes for a scatter diagram of the two variables, as described in Chapter 3, with the predictor variable on the horizontal axis. (You might use the mnemonic "what's known forms a stable *basis* for what's predicted or envisioned up *high*.") This is shown in Figure 4-2a for the managers' stress example.

2. Pick any value of the predictor variable, compute the corresponding predicted value on the dependent variable, and mark the point on the graph. If we select a predictor variable score of 2, the predicted dependent variable score in our example will be $-.79 + (.97 \times 2) = 1.15$. This point $(X = 2, Y = 1.15)$ is marked in Figure 4-2b.

3. Do the same thing again, starting with any other value of the predictor variable. (You will be able to draw the line more accurately if you pick a value for the predictor variable fairly different from the first.) In the example, if we select a predictor variable score of 8, the predicted dependent variable Z score will be $-.79 + (.97 \times 8) = 6.97$. This point $(X = 8, Y = 6.97)$ is marked in Figure 4-2c.

(Remember, to make a regression line, you select any two arbitrary values of X and find the predicted value of Y for each. Thus you can draw a regression line without being given any particular values of X.)

4. Draw a line that passes through the two marks. The line is shown in Figure 4-2d.

You can check the accuracy of your line by finding any third point. One easy point to locate is where the regression line crosses the vertical axis (a

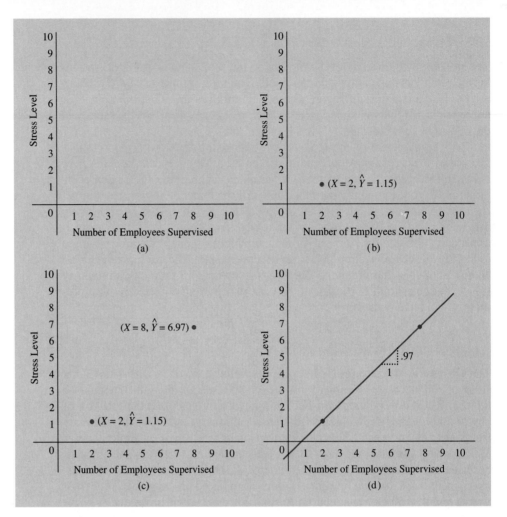

FIGURE 4-2
Steps in drawing a regression line using the managers' stress example. (a) Axes are drawn and labeled. (b) A point is marked for one value of the predictor variable (2) and its corresponding computed predicted value on the dependent variable (1.15). (c) A point is marked for another value of the predictor variable (8) and its corresponding computed predicted value on the dependent variable (6.97). (d) A line is drawn that passes through the two points. Also shown is how one unit across is equal to .97 units up.

point called the "Y intercept"). Since this is the point at which $X = 0$, its value on the Y axis will always equal a, the regression constant. (When $X = 0$, then $(b)(X) = 0$, so all that is left of the regression formula is a.)

As yet another check on the accuracy of your line, you can see if the slope corresponds to b—for each unit across, how much does it go up? In Figure 4-2d, the dotted lines show that the slope is .97: For each unit across, the line goes up .97 units.

Error and Proportionate Reduction in Error

How accurate are the predictions you make using the procedures we have described? If you are predicting the future, there is no way to know for sure in advance. However, you can make an estimate. This can be done by con-

TABLE 4-3
Calculation of Error and Squared Error Using Raw Scores for the Managers'
Stress Example (Fictional Data)

Employees Supervised	Stress Level		Error	Error^2
	Actual	*Predicted*		
X	*Y*	*$\hat{Y}$*	*$Y - \hat{Y}$*	*$(Y - \hat{Y})^2$*
6	7	5.03	1.97	3.88
8	8	6.97	1.03	1.06
3	1	2.12	−1.12	1.25
10	8	8.91	− .91	.83
8	6	6.97	− .97	.94
			Sum =	7.96

sidering how accurate your prediction model would have been if you had used it to make predictions for the scores you used to compute the correlation coefficient in the first place. You can then use that information to make a projection of how accurate your predictions would be in the future.

For example, in the case of our managers, there is no way of knowing for sure how accurate the predictions will be for the stress level of new managers. But you could ask, "Suppose I had used this model to predict the stress level for the managers I have already studied? How accurate would those predictions have been?" Consider the five managers we used in Chapter 3 to compute the correlation of .88. The first manager supervised 6 people and had a stress level of 7. If we had used our prediction model –.79 + (.97)(X)—we would have predicted a stress level for this manager of 5.03. The first three columns of Table 4-3 show the number of employees supervised, the actual stress levels, and the stress levels we would have predicted using the prediction model. Notice that the predicted stress scores are moderately close to the actual stress scores.

Error and Squared Error

To determine the accuracy of these predictions more precisely, we first calculate how much error we would have made—after all, the smaller the error, the greater the accuracy. **Error** is the actual score minus the predicted score. And because errors will offset each other (some will be negative and some positive), we square the errors. (Recall that we did the same thing in Chapter 2 when working with deviations from the mean.) Thus

error

$$\text{Error}^2 = (Y - \hat{Y})^2 \tag{4-5}$$

The errors and squared errors for our managers are shown in the two rightmost columns of Table 4-3.

Graphic Interpretation of Error

Figure 4-3 shows the scatter diagram for the managers' stress example with the regression line drawn in. In this graph, the five actual scores are shown as dots; predicted stress scores for all values of employees supervised are along the regression line. Thus the error for any particular manager—the difference between the manager's actual and predicted stress scores—is rep-

FIGURE 4-3
Scatter diagram for the managers' stress example, with the regression line drawn in and dotted lines indicating errors (vertical distance from actual score, indicated by a dot, and predicted value as shown by the location of the regression line).

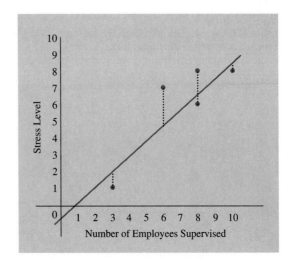

resented on the graph by the vertical distance between the dot for the manager's actual score and the regression line. We have drawn dotted lines to show the error for each case.

Proportionate Reduction in Error

Now, how is squared error useful? The most common way to think about the accuracy of our prediction model is to compare squared errors to see how much better our predictions are likely to be using this model than if we had to make predictions without the model. The strategy we follow is this: (a) Compute the amount of squared error we would make if we predicted using the prediction model, (b) compute the amount of squared error we would make predicting without the model, and (c) compute a comparison of the two amounts of squared error.

sum of the squared errors (SS_E)

The amount of squared error we would make if we predicted using the prediction model is the **sum of the squared errors** we just calculated from the last column in Table 4-3, namely, 7.96. This is labeled SS_{error} or SS_E. So $SS_E = 7.96$.

How do we compute the amount of squared error we would make predicting without the model? If we could not use the prediction model—in our example, if we could not obtain information about the number of employees supervised, the predictor variable—our best strategy would be to predict that a manager will have the average score on stress level, the dependent variable—namely, a mean stress score of 6.

To take another example, if we wanted to predict a person's college GPA and we were not able to use a model involving SAT or any other variable, our best bet would be to predict that the person's college GPA would be the average for students at that university.

total squared error when predicting from the mean (SS_T)

Thus the amount of squared error we would make predicting without a model is the amount of squared error we would make predicting from the average, the mean. Error when predicting from the mean is the difference between the actual score and the mean. Squared error is the square of this number. The sum of these squared errors is the **total squared error when predicting from the mean;** we call this number SS_T.

(By the way, what we are now calling SS_T is the same concept as what we called SS in Chapter 2, as part of computing the variance. We defined SS as the sum of squared deviations from the mean. A deviation from the mean is the difference between the score and the mean. This is exactly the same thing as the error that results when our prediction is the mean.)

The comparison we compute in determining the advantage of the prediction model over the situation when predicting from the mean is a comparison of SS_E with SS_T. This comparison is called the **proportionate reduction in error**. It is calculated by first finding the difference between the squared error created by using the mean (SS_T) and by using the prediction model (SS_E). That is, $SS_T - SS_E$. Then this number, the amount of squared error reduced by using the prediction model, is divided by the total amount that could be reduced (SS_T). That is, you could use the mean—not a very good method because it produces a lot of error—so now you are seeing how much better you can do. This is expressed as a proportion, called the "proportionate reduction in error."

proportionate reduction in error

$$\text{Proportionate reduction in error} = \frac{SS_T - SS_E}{SS_T} \qquad (4\text{-}6)$$

Consider the situation in which the prediction model was no improvement over predicting from the mean. That is, the worst situation is where SS_E equals SS_T (SS_E can never be worse than SS_T). In this case, the prediction model has reduced zero error ($SS_T - SS_E = 0$), and it has reduced 0% of the total error ($0/SS_T = 0$).

Now consider the situation in which the prediction model gives perfect predictions with no error whatsoever. In this case, the prediction model has reduced the error by 100%. (In terms of the equation, if $SS_E = 0$, then the numerator will be $SS_T - 0$, or SS_T; dividing SS_T by SS_E gives 1, or 100%.)

In most actual cases, the proportionate reduction in error will be somewhere between 0% and 100%.

An Example

Table 4-4 shows the raw score predictions, errors, squared errors, sums of squared errors, and proportionate reduction in error for the managers' stress example. As you can see, there is a 77% reduction in error from our prediction model over using the mean to predict.

TABLE 4-4
Calculation of Proportionate Reduction in Error for the Managers' Stress Example (Fictional Data)

Actual	Predicting Using Mean			Using Prediction Model		
Y	*Mean*	*Error*	*Error²*	$\hat{Y}$	*Error*	*Error²*
7	6	1	1	5.03	1.97	3.88
8	6	2	4	6.97	1.03	1.06
1	6	−5	25	2.12	−1.12	1.25
8	6	2	4	8.91	− .91	.83
6	6	0	0	6.97	− .97	.94
			$SS_T = \overline{34}$			$SS_E = \overline{7.96}$

$$\text{Proportionate reduction in error} = \frac{SS_T - SS_E}{SS_T} = \frac{34 - 7.96}{34} = \frac{26.04}{34} = .77$$

Proportionate Reduction in Error as r^2

The proportionate reduction in error always equals the correlation coefficient squared. That is,

$$\text{Proportionate reduction in error} = r^2 \qquad (4\text{-}7)$$

r^2

(Because of this equivalence, r^2 is used as the standard way of symbolizing the proportionate reduction in error.)

For example, in the managers' stress study, the correlation coefficient was .88, and .88 squared is .77—the same number as we just calculated so laboriously (by finding predicted scores, errors, squared errors, sums of squared errors, and proportionate reduction in squared error).

The point of calculating the proportionate reduction in error as we did was to help you understand this important concept. In an actual research situation, you would use the simpler procedure of squaring the correlation coefficient.

proportion of variance accounted for

You should also know that proportionate reduction in error is sometimes also called the **proportion of variance accounted for.** This name is used because SS_T, a kind of measure of variance from the dependent variable's mean, is closely related to the variance of the dependent variable. Proportionate reduction in error describes how much of SS_T is reduced, or accounted for, by the prediction model.

Graphic Interpretation of Proportionate Reduction in Error

If you were to predict each score by using the mean, a line on a graph representing these predictions would be a horizontal line—no matter what the score on the predictor variable, you are predicting the same thing, the mean, on the dependent variable.

Figure 4-4 shows the scatter diagram for the managers' stress example with the regression line from the prediction model and also with the horizontal line representing predictions from the mean. Notice that in nearly all cases, the regression line (which is based on the prediction model) falls closer to the

FIGURE 4-4
Scatter diagram for the managers' stress example showing both the regression line using the prediction model and the horizontal line representing predictions based on the mean. Note that dots representing actual scores are generally closer to the regression line than the horizontal line.

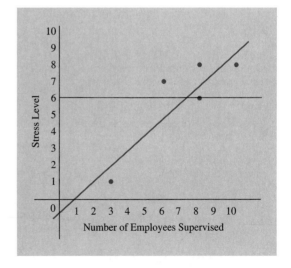

TABLE 4-5
Means and Standard Deviations from the Experiment on the Effect of Number of Exposures on Number of Words Recalled (Fictional Data)

	Number of Exposures (Predictor Variable)	Number Recalled (Dependent Variable)
Mean	4.5	5.6
Standard deviation	2.29	2.1
Correlation	$r = .68$	

dot than the horizontal line (which is based on predicting from the mean). The proportionate reduction in error can be thought of as the extent to which the regression line's accuracy is greater than the horizontal line's accuracy.[1]

Another Example of Bivariate Prediction

Now let's apply the various aspects of bivariate prediction to another example, the fictional memory experiment from Chapter 3. Table 4-5 shows the means and standard deviations for the two variables and also their correlation.

When using Z scores, our prediction model would be to multiply beta, which is .68 (the same as r), times the Z score for number of exposures:

$$\hat{Z}_Y = (\beta)(Z_X) = (.68)(Z_X)$$

For example, suppose that you knew that someone would receive seven exposures to each word, which is a Z score for exposures of 1.09. You could then predict that the Z score for words recalled would be the result of multiplying .68 times 1.09. This comes out to a predicted Z score for number of words recalled of .74. Similarly, if a person will be exposed to each word only four times (a Z score for exposure of $-.22$), you would predict a Z score number of words of $-.15$: .68 x $-.22 = -.15$. To restate these two examples in terms of formulas:

For $Z_X = 1.09$: $\quad \hat{Z}_Y = (\beta)(Z_X) = (.68)(1.09) = .74$

For $Z_X = -.22$: $\quad \hat{Z}_Y = (\beta)(Z_X) = (.68)(-.22) = -.15$

But recall that we have two methods available. First, we can do as we just did—convert the raw score on the predictor variable (seven exposures, four exposures) to a Z score, make the prediction, and convert the predicted Z score on the dependent variable to another raw score. Looking at our result for the first example, a predicted Z score of .74 on number of words recalled is equivalent to a raw score of 7.2 words recalled: the mean of 5.6 plus Z of 0.74 times the standard deviation of 2.1. And a predicted raw score of -.15 is equivalent to a raw score of 5.3 words: $5.6 + (2.1 \times -.15) = 5.3$.

[1]A less common measure of accuracy of a prediction model is the average of the squared errors (SS_E divided by the number of subjects), which is expressed in terms of the original scale of numbers by taking its square root. The number computed in this way (or using a slight variation of this approach) is called the *standard error of estimate*. The standard error of estimate indicates about how much actual scores typically vary from the values predicted for them using the regression model. (The entire procedure is parallel to using the standard deviation as an indicator of how much scores typically deviate from the mean.) However, because the standard error of estimate is rarely reported in psychology research articles, we will not focus on it in this book.

FIGURE 4-5
The regression line for the word recall example, showing predicted number of words recalled for individuals with four and with seven exposures to each word.

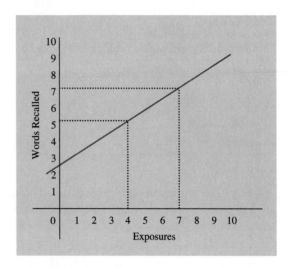

Alternatively, the raw score prediction model can be used to save some steps. This is how that would be computed:

$$b = (\beta)(SD_Y/SD_X) = (.68)(2.1/2.29) = (.68)(.92) = .63$$

$$a = M_Y - (b)(M_X) = 5.6 - (.63)(4.5) = 5.6 - 2.84 = 2.76$$

$$\hat{Y} = a + (b)(X) = 2.76 + (.63)(X)$$

If a person will receive seven exposures,

$$\hat{Y} = 2.76 + (.63)(X) = 2.76 + (.63)(7) = 2.76 + 4.41 = 7.17$$

If a person will receive four exposures,

$$\hat{Y} = 2.76 + (.63)(X) = 2.76 + (.63)(4) = 2.76 + 2.52 = 5.28$$

(These results agree with the more rounded-off figures we computed using the raw-to-Z, prediction, Z-to-raw approach.)

Figure 4-5 shows a graph of the two variables with the regression line for this model, along with dotted lines showing the two predictions we computed here.

What about accuracy of prediction? Table 4-6 shows, for each subject in the experiment, actual score, score that would have been predicted using the prediction model, errors (differences), and squared errors.

The sum of squared errors using the prediction model is 39.65 (SS_E). To compute the proportionate reduction in error, we also need the sum of squared error when predicting using the mean (SS_T). This comes out to 72. (You can compute this yourself to check. Remember, to get SS_T, you take each score minus the mean to get the error, square this error, and then sum the squared errors. For example, for the first subject, the squared error when predicting from the mean is a score of 4 minus the mean of 5.6, which is an error of −1.6 and a squared error of 2.56.)

Thus we have reduced the squared error almost in half, from 72 to 39.65. To be precise, the reduction of 32.35, when divided by the SS_T of 72, makes a proportionate reduction in error of .45 (or 45%). In terms of the formula,

$$\text{Proportionate reduction in error} = \frac{SS_T - SS_E}{SS_T} = \frac{72 - 39.65}{72} = \frac{32.35}{72} = .45$$

TABLE 4-6
Observed and Predicted Scores and Errors for the Experiment on the Effect of Number of Exposures on Number of Words Recalled (Fictional Data)

Subject	Number of Exposures	Number of Words Recalled		Error	Error²
	X	Y	$\hat{Y}$		
1	1	4	3.4	.6	.36
2	1	3	3.4	− .4	.16
3	2	3	4.0	−1.0	1.00
4	2	5	4.0	1.0	1.00
5	3	6	4.6	1.4	1.96
6	3	4	4.6	− .6	.36
7	4	4	5.3	−1.3	1.69
8	4	6	5.3	.7	.49
9	5	5	5.9	− .9	.81
10	5	7	5.9	1.1	1.21
11	6	2	6.5	−4.5	20.25
12	6	9	6.5	2.5	6.25
13	7	6	7.1	−1.1	1.21
14	7	8	7.1	.9	.81
15	8	9	7.8	−1.3	1.69
16	8	8	7.8	.2	.40
				$SS_E =$	39.65

This figure also equals (within rounding error) the correlation coefficient squared:

Proportionate reduction in error $= r^2 = .68^2 = .46$

Finally, Figure 4-6 shows the scatter diagram with the regression line drawn in.

Extension to Multiple Regression and Correlation

So far we have considered the situation in which you predict the score on a dependent variable based on knowledge of a score on a single predictor variable. What if you could also use information about additional predictor

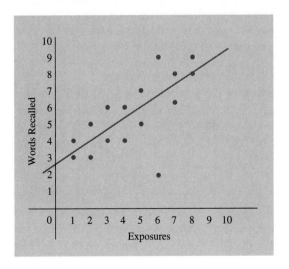

FIGURE 4-6
Scatter diagram for the word recall example, with the regression line drawn in.

variables? For example, in predicting managers' stress levels, all you knew was the number of employees to be supervised. But suppose that you also knew something about the working conditions, such as noise level and number of deadlines required to be met each month. This information might allow you to make a much more accurate prediction of stress level.

The association between a dependent variable and two or more predictor variables is called **multiple correlation;** making predictions in this situation is called **multiple regression.**

multiple correlation

multiple regression

We will explore the terminology and some of the key ideas involved in multiple regression and correlation. An examination of the logic and procedures of the computations and the fine points of using multiple regression are beyond the scope of an introductory book. However, we will discuss these topics in sufficient detail to permit you to understand in a general way research articles that employ this widely used approach. (Reis & Stiller, 1992, found that multiple regression was used in 3% of social psychology studies in 1968 and 21% in 1988.)

Z-Score Prediction Model in Multiple Regression

In multiple regression, each of the two or more predictor variables has its own regression coefficient in the prediction formula. The predicted Z score of the dependent variable is found by multiplying the Z score for each predictor variable times its beta (standardized regression coefficient) and then adding up the results of this multiplication for all the predictor variables. For example, the Z-score multiple regression formula with three predictor variables is as follows:

$$\hat{Z}_Y = (\beta_1)(Z_{X1}) + (\beta_2)(Z_{X2}) + (\beta_3)(Z_{X3}) \tag{4-8}$$

β_1 is the standardized regression coefficient for the first predictor variable. Similarly, β_2 and β_3 are the standardized regression coefficients for the second and third predictor variables (X_2 and X_3). Z_{X1} is the Z score for the first predictor variable. Similarly, Z_{X2} and Z_{X3} are the Z scores for the second and third predictor variables.

For example, in the managers' stress situation, if we had some data and worked the figures out as we did for bivariate regression, a multiple regression model for stress level (Y) employing the predictor variables of number of employees supervised (which we will now call X_1) and also noise level (X_2) and number of deadlines per month (X_3) might be

$$\hat{Z}_Y = (.51)(Z_{X1}) + (.11)(Z_{X2}) + (.33)(Z_{X3})$$

Thus suppose that you were asked to predict the stress level of a potential manager who had a Z score of 1.27 for number of employees to be supervised (a fairly high number), a Z score of -1.81 for noise of working conditions (a low level), and a Z score of .94 for number of deadlines per month (a somewhat high number). Your predicted Z score for stress level would be computed by multiplying .51 times the employees supervised Z score, .11 times the noise Z score, and .33 times the deadlines Z score and then adding up the results:

$$\hat{Z}_Y = (.51)(1.27) + (.11)(-1.81) + (.33)(.94) = .65 + -.20 + .31 = .76$$

So under these conditions, you would predict a stress-level Z score of .76, which means a stress level about three fourths of a standard deviation above the mean.

Relation of Betas in Multiple Regression to Ordinary Correlations of Predictor Variables With the Dependent Variable

Notice one important difference from bivariate regression. In multiple regression, the beta for a predictor variable is *not* the same as the ordinary correlation coefficient (r) of that predictor variable with the dependent variable. In most cases, the beta will be lower (closer to 0) than r. The reason for this is that usually part of what any one predictor variable measures will overlap with what the other predictor variables measure. And in multiple regression, beta is related to the unique, distinctive contribution of the variable, excluding any overlap with other predictor variables.[2]

Consider the managers' stress example. When we were using bivariate prediction from the number of employees supervised, we used a prediction model based on a correlation coefficient of .88, which was also beta. Now, with the multiple regression model, beta for employees supervised is only .51. It is less because part of what employees supervised measures overlaps with what noise and number of deadlines measure. (With more people to supervise, noise and deadlines increase automatically—each is not an unrelated additional difficulty.) To put it another way, the three predictor variables are correlated with each other. Since in the multiple regression model, the beta for employees supervised represents only what employees supervised measures after taking out what the other two predictors measure, it is less. Each of the betas for the other variables in the multiple regression model will usually also be less than their corresponding ordinary correlation with the dependent variable, as they are in this example.

Multiple Regression With Raw Scores

Just as with bivariate regression, it is possible with multiple regression to have a raw score prediction formula. With three predictor variables (and the regression constant—go back to bivariate regression with raw scores if you've forgotten about a),

$$\hat{Y} = a + (b_1)(X_1) + (b_2)(X_2) + (b_3)(X_3) \tag{4-9}$$

In the case of the managers' stress example, if we had some data and worked the figures out using a procedure similar to what we used for bivari-

---

[2]Technically, the unique contribution to the proportionate reduction in error of a predictor variable, in the context of the other predictor variables, is a statistic called the *squared semipartial correlation* (sr^2), a number that is occasionally reported in research articles. However, it is most common in psychology for researchers to report only the betas and then to talk about them as approximate indicators of the unique contribution of a variable. So long as the "approximate" is remembered, this is not unreasonable because beta and sr^2 are closely related: A large beta usually corresponds to a large sr^2, the sign (positive or negative) of a beta is always the same as the sign of the sr^2, and the significance of a beta is always the same as the significance of the sr^2. In any case, because of this common usage (and also because an adequate discussion of sr^2 is beyond the scope of an introductory book), in our discussion here we adopt this loose understanding of beta as indicating the unique contribution of a variable to the prediction.

ate regression with raw scores, the raw score prediction model might be

$$\hat{Y} = -4.70 + (.56)(X_1) + (.06)(X_2) + (.86)(X_3)$$

Suppose that a potential manager was going to supervise eight people at a very high noise level of 85 decibels and with 4 deadlines per month (which is higher than the average of 3). The expected stress level would be quite high:

$$\hat{Y} = -4.70 + (.56)(8) + (.06)(85) + (.86)(4) = -4.70 + 4.48 + 5.1 + 3.44 = 8.32$$

You would predict that this manager would have a stress level of 8.32.

Each raw score regression coefficient (b) gives you the raw score rate of exchange for its predictor variable in the context of the other predictor variables. Thus at a given level of number of employees supervised and noise, each additional deadline increases the predicted stress score by .86 points; at any given level of employees supervised and number of deadlines, each decibel of noise increases the predicted stress score by .06 points; and at any given level of noise and number of deadlines, each additional person supervised increases the predicted stress score by .56 points.

Multiple Correlation Coefficient

multiple correlation coefficient

The **multiple correlation coefficient** (usually symbolized as R) describes the overall correlation between the predictor variables, taken together, and the dependent variable.

Because all the predictor variables contribute to the correlation, R will be at least as high as the highest individual correlation of a predictor variable with the dependent variable. However, recall that each predictor variable usually overlaps with the others in its association with the dependent variable. Hence the multiple correlation coefficient is usually less than the sum of each predictor variable's correlation with the dependent variable.

In the managers' stress example, suppose that for the three predictors with the dependent variable, r is .88 (employees supervised with stress level), .38 (noise with stress level), and .63 (deadlines with stress level). In this case, the multiple correlation of the stress score with the three predictors taken together will have to be at least .88 (the highest of the correlations) because the correlation with all three variables together could not be less than with any of them alone. By contrast, R could not be higher than the sum of the r values, which in this case is 1.89 (.88 + .38 + .63). In fact, R, like r, can never be higher than 1, no matter how many predictor variables are involved. (R ranges from 0 to 1. Unlike r, it cannot be negative—for reasons you don't have to worry about. Remember, however, that a beta or a b, whether in bivariate or multiple regression, can be negative.) In the example, $R = .96$.

Proportionate Reduction in Error in Multiple Regression

Finally, as with bivariate prediction, you can compute the proportionate reduction in error. Error in multiple regression is the same as error in bivariate regression, so review that discussion if you need to. Error is calculated by taking the actual score minus the predicted score—this time obtained with a prediction model using multiple regression. Squared error, the sum of squared error (SS_E), and the proportionate reduction in squared error are also all calculated in exactly the same way. In multiple regression, as in bivariate regression, proportionate reduction in error compares SS_E to SS_T (SS_T, remember, is the sum of squared errors using the mean of the dependent variable to predict the dependent variable). And, as with bivariate prediction, the result comes out to be the correlation coefficient squared (in this case, R^2); in the example, if $R = .96$, $R^2 = .92$.

Finally, note that as with bivariate prediction, R^2 is also the proportion of variance accounted for. That is, R^2 tells you how much of the variation in the dependent variable is accounted for (predicted) by the set of predictor variables. In the example, 92% of the variation in manager stress is accounted for by number of employees supervised, noise level, and number of deadlines per month.

An Example of Multiple Regression and Correlation

Watts and Wright (1990) administered questionnaires about delinquency and substance use to male high school students and convicted male delinquents in residence at the Texas Youth Commission facility. Table 4-7 shows the results for one of the ethnic groups studied. You can see that there are sizable correlation coefficients between amount of violent delinquency and use of each type of substance. However, look what happens when the predictor variables are all considered together (in the multiple regression equation). The betas vary considerably. Stated as a Z-score multiple regression model, it would be

$$\hat{Z}_{\text{Delinquency}} = (-.007)(Z_{\text{Alcohol}}) + (.183)(Z_{\text{Tobacco}})$$
$$+ (-.046)(Z_{\text{Marijuana}}) + (.677)(Z_{\text{Other}})$$

When considered in combination, the main factor in making predictions of violent delinquency would seem to be the use of "other illegal drugs," and a secondary factor might be use of tobacco. That is, given that you know the usage of other drugs and tobacco, knowing about alcohol and marijuana use does not add to the ability to make predictions of delinquency. For example, alcohol predicts quite well on its own (.415) but predicts almost nothing (−.007) when there is knowledge of other drug use because whatever predictive information is provided by alcohol use is probably already provided by knowing that the person uses other drugs.

(Also remember that in making any interpretations based on a study like this that employed a correlational design, we cannot be certain what is cause

TABLE 4-7
Drug Use as Predictors of Delinquency

Drug Used	r	β
Alcohol	.415	−.007
Tobacco	.415	.183
Marijuana	.513	−.046
Other illegal drugs	.712	.677
	$R = .729$; $R^2 = .531$	

Note. Data from Watts, W., & Wright, L. (1990). The relationship of alcohol, tobacco, marijuana, and other illegal drug use to delinquency among Mexican-American, black, and white adolescent males. *Adolescence, 25,* 171–181. Reprinted by permission.

and what is effect. It could very well be that the drug use is the result and not the cause of the delinquency or that some third factor, such as the kind of environment in which the youths were raised, might be responsible for both the substance use and the delinquency.)

You could actually use our multiple regression formula to make predictions. For example, suppose that you were asked to predict the degree of violent delinquency of a youth who had a Z score of -1 on alcohol use, a Z of 0 (the mean) on tobacco use, a Z of $+1$ on marijuana use, and a Z of -2 on use of other illegal drugs. Using the Z-score multiple regression model, your prediction would be

$$\hat{Z}_{\text{Delinquency}} = (-.007)(-1) + (.183)(0) + (-.046)(1) + (.677)(-2)$$
$$= .007 + 0 + -.046 + -1.354 = -1.393$$

You would predict this youth to have a quite low score (1.393 standard deviations below the mean) on violent delinquency.

Suppose that another youth had exactly the same pattern except for having a high level of use of other illegal drugs—say, a Z score of $+2$.

$$\hat{Z}_{\text{Delinquency}} = (-.007)(-1) + (.183)(0) + (-.046)(1) + (.677)(2)$$
$$= .007 + 0 + -.046 + 1.354 = 1.315$$

This youth would be expected to have a quite high score on violent delinquency.

Finally, consider a youth who is the same as the first youth, the one with the low use of other illegal drugs and a predicted Z score of -1.477, except that this youth drinks heavily, having a Z score for alcohol use of $+2$.

$$\hat{Z}_{\text{Delinquency}} = (-.007)(2) + (.183)(0) + (-.046)(1) + (.677)(-2)$$
$$= -.014 + 0 + -.046 + -1.354 = -1.414$$

This youth would also be expected to have a low violent delinquency score. That might seem surprising, since one would associate heavy drinking with delinquency. And in most cases, high rates of drinking are associated with delinquency, as shown by the r of .415. However, young people who drink also usually use other illegal drugs (at least according to the data for this group in this particular setting), and that would seem to be why drinking when considered alone was associated with delinquency.

Time for an aside. Did your perception change as soon as the example involved making predictions about a person's potential for crime and possible imprisonment? We hope so. When we use large studies to make predictions about a single person, we should immediately sense the inherent stereotyping and potential for injustices. No wonder people often resent statistics. But they are merely a tool for looking into the future, like intuition or clinical experience—and they are only as compassionate as the person using them for making a decision. If a callous person cites "cold" numbers to justify a prejudiced decision, it is not the numbers that are cold. (For some discussion of these issues, see Box 4-1.)

Before leaving this sample study, it will be instructive to examine the R for these data. Notice that R of .729 is higher than the highest ordinary r (which was .712), but is certainly considerably less than the sum of the individual r values (in fact, the sum would add up to more than 1, which, as we noted earlier, is impossible). Finally, notice that R^2 is .531. This says that if you made predictions using this multiple regression model for every youth

BOX 4-1

Clinical Versus Statistical Prediction

In 1954, Paul Meehl wrote an unsettling little book called *Statistical Versus Clinical Prediction.* In it, he argued that when experts such as clinical psychologists (or business managers, economic forecasters, engineers, or doctors, among others) use the kinds of unspecified internal cognitive processes that are usually called "trained intuitions," on the average they are not nearly as accurate at making important, life-changing predictions as anybody at all could be by employing very simple, straightforward *formulas.* That is, in psychiatric diagnosing, a supposedly well-trained clinician's interview and diagnosis are less useful than a mere rule such as "if the person has been admitted to the hospital twice before, is over 50, and appears suicidal, then . . ."—the kind of rule generated by using multiple regression procedures.

In the first decade after Meehl's questioning of the accuracy of experts, considerable efforts were made to disprove him. But on the whole, according to a review by Kleinmuntz (1990), Meehl's discovery has held up: Unaided human cognition is, on the average, less accurate than the statistical method of regression analysis. Consequently, the focus has turned to how cognition operates, why it is flawed, and what, if anything, can be done to improve it.

The flaws are mainly that people make illusory correlations (see Box 3-2). Or they are overconfident; they do not keep a record of their successes and failures to check to see whether they are in fact accurate but instead put too much weight on their remembered successes and forget their failures. And sadly, overconfidence comes in part from experience, which in fact is seldom of much help because it does not provide feedback (clinicians may make hundreds of diagnoses without learning whether they were correct). Finally, human memory and cognition may not have the capacity to handle the information and operations required to make certain complex decisions.

A great deal of research has addressed how to "debias" human decision making and has found that it can indeed be improved. In particular, people can be shown when their intuition will be more accurate (for example, when rapid and therefore unconscious work is required or when simple averaging will suffice) and when a formula is preferable (when there is time for deliberation or when rules are more complicated). Finally, there is considerable work on combining human cognition with "decision aids," such as computer programs with built-in decision rules supplied by experts. The human component is used to input the necessary more subjective assessments ("this person's talk sounds suicidal"), and the formula is used to combine measurements *consistently* ("being suicidal should *always* carry a weight of .8, prior hospitalization a weight of .5, being over 50 a weight of .3," etc.).

Having summarized all of this, however, Kleinmuntz (1990) observes that in most decision-making situations, human judgments are still being used instead of the more accurate formulas or formulas in combination with cognition. The reasons are many. First, when the stakes are high, as when involving life and death, most people still have more faith in human decisions, perhaps because of the hope that inspired intuition can beat the odds in a particular case. Second, people believe, perhaps rightly, that the complex patterns presented by real-life situations are grasped better by human experts closest to and most used to those situations. Third, the decision-making formulas do not exist or are not available to the people who need them. Finally, the cost of creating and testing a decision formula is often prohibitive or is so complex a problem in itself that it also requires a decision formula!

Still, the use of "decision support systems" is on the rise. For example, expert chess players have developed such aids using their own expertise, and these aids can actually outwit their own creators sometimes, merely by being thoroughly consistent. Thus some chess players have become comfortable using decision support systems to keep themselves on track during a game. (Has their very public sort of competition forced them to be the first to forget pride and adopt formulas?) And we can expect doctors, clinical psychologists, engineers, and others also to adopt formulas employing self-generated rules—particularly to offset the effects of fatigue or emotional involvement—once the method becomes better known and more acceptable to their all-too-human egos.

in the group studied, the average squared error in predicting actual delinquency scores would be 53.1% less than if you had just used the mean of the delinquency scores as the best predictor of individual scores. In terms of proportion of variance accounted for, 53.1% of the variation in delinquency in this group is accounted for by the drug use variables.

Another Example

Consider another example. Singer (1990) was interested in the emotion people feel when recalling life events. He suggested that recalled events are often associated with particular life goals (such as blazing a new path, helping others, or being forceful) and that how positively we feel when recalling an event depends on (a) how desirable that goal is for us and (b) whether the event was helpful in achieving the goal. To examine this idea, Singer tested 30 students. The students were given sentences relating to various life goals and asked to recall some event earlier in their lives that each sentence stimulated. They also rated how desirable the goal was and how much the event helped them achieve the goal.

Table 4-8 shows Singer's results for one of the life goals, being forceful. Notice that the bivariate r values are substantial, supporting Singer's claim that the two predictor variables (goal desirability and goal achievement) are each related to how positively we feel when recalling a relevant memory. However, in order for Singer to be confident that each of the predictor variables was contributing independently of the other, it was necessary to carry out the multiple regression. In this case, you can see that the betas are smaller than the bivariate r values. This is because goal desirability and goal attainment are correlated. But also notice that each still contributes a considerable amount even in the context of the other. That is, although the betas are smaller than the r values, they are still substantial. Also notice that R is substantial, indicating that when taken together, goal desirability and goal attainment are quite strongly related to how positively

TABLE 4-8
Ordinary Correlations and Standardized Regression Coefficients for Multiple Regression of Goal Desirability and Goal Attainment as Predictors of Positivity of Emotions Experienced During Recall of Autobiographical Memories as Associated With Being Forceful

Life Goal	Ordinary Correlations		Multiple Regression			
	Goal Desirability	*Goal Attainment*	*Goal Desirability*	*Goal Attainment*	*R*	*R2*
	r	r	β	β		
Positivity of emotions when recalling event associated with being forceful	.46	.48	.35	.39	.59	.35

Note. From Singer, J. A. (1990). Affective responses to autobiographical memories and their relationship to long-term goals. *Journal of Personality, 58,* 535–549. Reprinted by permission.

we feel about a memory. Indeed, the information in these two variables reduces the squared error by 35% over the squared error that would be expected by predicting only from the mean of the emotion experienced. That is, 35% of the variation in positivity of emotion was accounted for by goal desirability and goal attainment.

The objective of Singer's study was not primarily prediction. However, for purposes of illustration, we will consider what the multiple regression model would be and make some sample predictions. The Z-score model would be

$$\hat{Z}_{\text{Positive emotions}} = (.35)(Z_{\text{Desirability}}) + (.39)(Z_{\text{Attainment}})$$

Suppose that a person considered being forceful a highly desirable goal, rating it with a score equivalent to a Z of +2.5, and also felt that the recalled event very much helped achieve that goal, rating it with a score equivalent to a Z of +2. Using the model,

$$\hat{Z}_{\text{Positive emotions}} = (.35)(Z_{\text{Desirability}}) + (.39)(Z_{\text{Attainment}})$$
$$= (.35)(+2.5) + (.39)(+2) = .88 + .78 = 1.66$$

Thus the person would be expected to feel a fair amount of positive emotion, an amount 1.66 standard deviations above the mean.

Now suppose that a person felt that being forceful was quite undesirable ($Z = -2.5$), but the event remembered had only an average effect on attaining the goal of being forceful ($Z = 0$). The result is a predicted Z score for emotion of $-.88$, indicating that you would expect the person to feel less positive than the average:

$$\hat{Z}_{\text{Positive emotions}} = (.35)(Z_{\text{Desirability}}) + (.39)(Z_{\text{Attainment}})$$
$$= (.35)(-2.5) + (.39)(0) = -.88 + 0 = -.88$$

Controversies and Limitations

All of the limitations we discussed in the context of correlation (Chapter 3) apply with equal or greater force to bivariate and multiple prediction: In regression models as they are ordinarily calculated, the degree of predictability will be underestimated if the underlying relationship is curvilinear, the sample is restricted in range, or the measures are less than perfectly reliable. Nor does the computation of a prediction model, which is essentially a process involving numbers, tell us anything about the underlying direction of causality, an issue that depends not on the numbers but on the experimental design (also see Appendix A). It is noteworthy, however, that in the process of developing regression models, especially in elaborate multiple regression models, these limitations are often overlooked in research reports.

One ongoing controversy of interest relates to a problem that arises only in multiple regression: How do you assess the relative importance of the several predictor variables in predicting the dependent variable? For purely predictive purposes, the regression coefficients (either standardized or raw score) serve well. But for a theoretical understanding of the relative importance of the different predictors, the regression coefficients are not necessarily the best indicators. The problem is that a regression coefficient is related to the unique contribution of the predictor variable to the prediction after considering all the other predictors. When predicting by itself, without considering the other predictors (that is, using its ordinary correlation with the dependent variable), it may appear to have a quite different importance relative to the other predictors. For example, in the delinquency and drug use example, the betas suggest that use of tobacco is more important in predicting delinquency than use of marijuana, but the ordinary correlations suggest exactly the opposite. Furthermore, if other predictor variables were added, such as use of other legal drugs, the entire pattern of betas might change again. What importance do you attach, then, to a predictor variable that shows so many different faces in so many different contexts (prediction models)?

multicollinearity

In general, as long as the predictor variables are correlated with each other—a condition called **multicollinearity** (which is the usual situation in multiple regression)—there is no agreed-on approach to the question of the relative importance of these sorts of predictor variables. Although a great many approaches to this problem have been considered over the years (see Cohen & Cohen, 1983), it is generally agreed that the best that can be done is to consider all the information available (such as the ordinary correlations and the regression coefficients) as giving an indication of different ways of looking at relative importance.

In addition to these and other controversies relating to the statistical aspects, there has been an ongoing controversy for many years about the superiority of statistical prediction over more intuitive, humanistic, or clinical approaches. This issue is addressed in Box 4-1.

Prediction Models as Described in Research Articles

It is actually fairly rare for bivariate prediction models to be cited in psychology research articles; in most cases, simple correlations are reported. Multiple regression models, however, are commonly reported (as in the delinquency and drug use example). Table 4-9 shows the results of a multiple regression analysis. This table is from a study (Bankston, Thompson, Jenkins, & Forsyth, 1990) of 1,177 drivers in Louisiana in which the dependent variable was whether or not the driver carried a firearm in his or her car. As can be seen from the table, the betas show an especially strong influence of gender and cultural factors (French-English ratio and location size). The "constant" noted at the bottom of the table is the regression constant (a in the raw score prediction equation). The table also includes, in addition to R^2 and the unstandardized and standardized regression coefficients, some other statistics (F, standard error and significance of t). These have to do with the statistical significance of the results; you will have a better understanding of these after you have read Chapters 5 through 11.

TABLE 4-9
Regression Results for State Sample ($N = 1,177$)

Variable	Unstandardized Coefficient	Standard Error	Beta	Significance of t
French-English ratio	−.061*	.018	−.099*	.001
Fear index	.014	.008	.049	.105
Income	.022	.012	.034	.304
Gender	−.256*	.060	−.126*	.000
Victim experience	.090	.060	.044	.133
Age	−.003	.002	−.047	.118
Location size	−.041*	.015	−.085*	.006
Education	−.027	.017	−.052	.113

Constant = 1.077
$R^2 = .034$
$F = 5.21$
Significance of $F = .000$

Note. *$p < .05$. Unstandardized coefficients that have an absolute value at least twice the standard error are significant at the .05 level. Data from Bankston, W., Thompson, C., Jenkins, Q., & Forsyth, C. (1990). The influence of fear of crime, gender, and southern culture on carrying firearms for protection. *Sociological Quarterly, 31,* 287–305. Copyright, 1990, by JAI Press, Inc. Reprinted by permission.

Summary

Bivariate prediction (or regression) makes predictions about a dependent variable based on knowledge of a person's score on a predictor variable. The best model for predicting a person's Z score on the dependent variable is to multiply a number called the standardized regression coefficient (beta) times the person's Z score on the predictor variable. The best number to use for the standardized regression coefficient in bivariate prediction is the correlation coefficient of the two variables.

Predictions with raw scores can be made by converting the person's score on the predictor variable to a Z score, multiplying it by beta, and then converting the resulting predicted Z score on the dependent variable to a raw score. It is also possible to combine these three steps into a single formula that permits predictions directly from a person's raw score on the predictor variable to a predicted raw score on the dependent variable. This formula has two main parts, a regression coefficient (called b) that is multiplied by the person's raw score on the predictor variable and a regression constant (called a) that is added to the result. Predicted values of the dependent variable using this formula, if drawn on a graph of the two variables, form the regression line. The slope of this line equals the raw score regression coefficient; the regression constant is where this line crosses the vertical axis.

The accuracy of prediction can be estimated by applying the prediction model to the data on which the original correlation was based. The difference between each actual score and what would have been predicted for that subject using the prediction model is called error. Squaring these errors and summing them gives the sum of squared errors (SS_E). You then compare SS_E

to the sum of squared error when using just the mean of the dependent variable as your predicted score (SS_T). The reduction in squared error gained by using the model ($SS_T - SS_E$), divided by the squared error when predicting from the dependent variable's mean (SS_T), is called the proportionate reduction in error or proportion of variance accounted for; it equals the correlation coefficient squared.

In multiple regression, a dependent variable is predicted using two or more predictor variables. In a multiple regression model, each predictor variable is multiplied by its own regression coefficient, and the results are added up to make the prediction. (When raw scores are used, a regression constant is also added in once.) Each regression coefficient indicates the relation of the predictor to the dependent variable in the context of the other predictor variables. The multiple correlation coefficient describes the overall degree of association between the dependent variable and the predictor variables taken together.

Bivariate and multiple regression have all the same limitations as bivariate regression. In addition, in multiple regression there is ordinarily considerable ambiguity in interpreting the relative importance of the predictor variables.

Key Terms

bivariate prediction
bivariate regression
error
multicollinearity
multiple correlation
multiple correlation
  coefficient (R)
multiple regression
prediction model

proportionate reduction in
  error (r^2)
proportion of variance
  accounted for (r^2)
raw score prediction formula
raw score regression
  coefficient (b)
regression coefficient

regression constant (a)
regression line
slope
standardized regression
  coefficient (β)
sum of squared errors (SS_E)
total squared error when predicting from the mean (SS_T)

Practice Problems

These problems involve computation (with the assistance of a calculator). Most real-life statistical problems are done on a computer. But even if you have a computer, do these by hand to ingrain the method in your mind.

For practice in using a computer to solve statistical problems, refer to the computer section of each chapter of the study guide that accompanies this text.

All data are fictional (unless an actual citation is given).

Answers to Set I are given at the back of the book.

SET I

1. A sports psychologist working with athletes in a particular sport has found that the score on a test of knowledge of physiology correlates .4 with number of injuries received over the subsequent year. The psychologist now plans to test all new athletes and use this information to predict the number of injuries they are likely to receive. (a) Indicate the predictor variable, dependent variable, and beta; (b) write the Z-score prediction model; and (c) indicate the predicted Z scores for number of injuries for athletes whose Z scores on the physiology test are –2, –1, 0, +1 and +2.

2. For each of the following, (a) through (g), determine the raw score prediction model. Then make a single graph showing all the regression lines, labeling each by its letter. (Be sure to make your graph large enough so that the lines are clearly separate.)

	Dependent Variable (Y)		Predictor Variable (X)		
	M	SD	M	SD	r
(a)	10	2.0	10	2.0	.4
(b)	20	2.0	10	2.0	.4
(c)	10	2.0	20	2.0	.4
(d)	10	2.0	10	4.0	.4
(e)	10	4.0	10	2.0	.4
(f)	10	2.0	10	2.0	−.4
(g)	10	2.0	10	2.0	.8

3. A professor has found that scores on the midterm exam predict scores on the final exam. The raw score prediction formula is

Final exam score = 40 + (.5)(midterm exam score).

Compute the predicted final exam scores for each of eight students whose scores on the midterm were 30, 40, 50, 60, 70, 80, 90, and 100.

4. In Chapter 3, Set I, Problem 1, we described a study in which a researcher was interested in the relation between psychotherapists' degree of empathy and their patients' satisfaction with therapy. As a pilot study, four patient-therapist pairs were studied. The results are presented here, including the means and standard deviations. The correlation coefficient was .90, and the SS_T for patient satisfaction was 10.

Pair Number	Therapist Empathy (X)	Patient Satisfaction (Y)
1	70	4
2	94	5
3	36	2
4	48	1
M	62	3
SD	22.14	1.58

(a) Determine the raw score prediction formula for predicting satisfaction from empathy, (b) use this formula to find the predicted satisfaction scores for each of the four patient-therapist pairs, (c) compute the error and squared error for each of the four predictions, (d) draw the scatter diagram and put the regression line into it, (e) find the proportionate reduction in error (using SS_E and SS_T), (f) take the square root of the proportionate reduction in error you calculated to see if it matches the correlation coefficient, and (g) explain what you have done to someone who understands mean, standard deviation, Z scores, and correlation coefficient, but does not know any more about statistics.

5. In Chapter 3, Problem 2 in Set I was about an instructor who asked five students how many hours they

had studied for an exam. The number of hours studied and their grades, along with means and standard deviations, are shown here. The correlation was .84, and SS_T for test grade was 1,110. Complete steps (a) though (g) as described in Problem 4 for predicting test grade from hours studied.

Hours Studied (X)	Test Grade (Y)
0	52
10	95
6	83
8	71
6	64
M 6	73
SD 3.35	14.90

6. Deluga (1991) studied the relation of managers' performance to the kinds of influence attempts made by subordinates in a nonprofit community hospital in the northeastern United States. The 80 subordinates studied completed a standard questionnaire about the ways in which they try to influence their bosses. The questionnaires produced scores in terms of three types of strategies: "hard" (going to higher authorities, making forceful demands, and forming coalitions with other organization members), "soft" (relying on friendliness, ingratiation, flattery), or "rational" (bargaining and using facts and data to support a rational argument). The managers were also rated for their performance in terms of how satisfied the subordinate was with the manager, the manager's overall effectiveness, and the effectiveness of the work unit.

Deluga's main findings are presented in Table 4-10 (p. 130). Explain the results of the analysis for manager effectiveness (the middle row) as if you were writing to a person who understands correlation but has never had any exposure to regression or multiple regression analysis.

7. Based on Table 4-10, determine the regression equation (for Z scores), and then calculate the predicted manager effectiveness for the manager of each of the following subordinates (figures are Z scores):

Subordinate	Hard	Soft	Rational
A	−1	−1	−1
B	0	0	0
C	1	1	1
D	1	0	0
E	0	1	0
F	0	0	1
G	3	1	1
H	1	3	1
I	3	1	3

TABLE 4-10
Results of Multiple Regression Analysis of Health Care Manager Performance Variables on Subordinate Upward Influence Behavior

Performance Variables	Adjusted R^2	Subordinate-Influencing Behavior		
		Hard β	*Soft* β	*Rational* β
Subordinate satisfaction with manager	.25	−.54*	−.04	.04
Manager effectiveness	.23	−.66**	.14	.09
Work unit effectiveness	−.01	−.23	.21	.11

Note. Data from Deluga, R. J. (1991), tab. 1. The relationship of subordinate upward-influencing behavior, health care manager interpersonal stress, and performance. *Journal of Applied Social Psychology*, *21*, 78–88. Copyright, 1991, by V. H. Winston & Son, Inc. Reprinted by permission. *$p < .01$. **$p < .001$.

SET II

1. Think of something that you would like to be able to predict and what information would be useful in predicting it. (Both should be things that can be measured on a numerical scale.) Then write a prediction model, noting the name of the predictor variable and the name of the dependent variable. Also estimate a number for beta that you think makes some sense based on what you know about the things you are making predictions about. Finally, explain why you picked the beta size you did.

2. For each of the following, determine the Z-score prediction model and the raw score prediction model. Also make a single graph showing all the (raw score) regression lines, labeling each by its letter, (a) through (e), and making your graph large enough so that the lines are clearly separated.

	Dependent Variable (*Y*)		Predictor Variable (*X*)		
	M	*SD*	*M*	*SD*	*r*
(a)	0	1.0	0	1.0	.3
(b)	5	1.0	5	1.0	.3
(c)	0	5.0	0	5.0	.3
(d)	0	1.0	5	5.0	.3
(e)	0	1.0	0	1.0	.0

3. In Chapter 3, Set II, Problem 1, four individuals were given a test of manual dexterity (high scores mean better dexterity) and an anxiety test (high scores mean more anxiety). The scores, means, and standard deviations are given here. First compute the correlation between dexterity and anxiety (or refer to your answer from Chapter 3). SS_T for anxiety was 84. Complete (a) though (g) as described in Problem 4, Set I, in this chapter for predicting anxiety from dexterity.

Person	Dexterity	Anxiety
1	1	10
2	1	8
3	2	4
4	4	−2
M	2	4
SD	1.22	4.58

4. Repeat Problem 3, doing parts (a) though (f), but this time predicting dexterity from anxiety. Then indicate which results are different and which are the same as you obtained in Problem 3. (Note: SS_T for dexterity is 6.)

5. Maliphant, Hume, and Furnham (1990) measured base heart rates (BHR) and personality traits in 44 girls aged 12 and 13. The personality traits, measured with the Junior Eysenck Personality Inventory (JEPI), included extroversion (E), neuroticism (N), and psychoticism (P). Part of their results section (edited slightly) reads as follows:

> Multiple regression of heart rate on the combined E, N, and P scores of the JEPI indicate that 32.9% of the variance is accounted for in the BHR measure (Table 4). N and E scores provided the best combination of variables in relation to BHR. Further investigation of the relationship of these JEPI measures with heart rate is indicated. (p. 623)

The most important part of their Table 4, for purposes of this problem, is that they give the raw score regression equation, as

$$BHR = 115 − (1.35)(N) − (1.23)(P) − (0.769)(E)$$

Explain these results as if you were writing to a person who understands correlation but has never had any exposure to regression or multiple regression analysis.

6. Using the regression equation in Problem 5, determine the predicted heart rate for each of the girls whose scores on the JEPI are as follows:

Girl	N	P	E
A	10	10	10
B	12	12	12
C	14	14	14
D	16	10	10
E	10	16	10
F	10	10	16

7. Ask five other students of the same gender as yourself to give you their own height and also their mother's height. Compute the correlation coefficient, determine the raw score prediction model for predicting a person's height from his or her mother's height, and make a graph showing the regression line. Finally, based on your prediction model, predict the height of a person of your gender whose mother's height is (a) 5 feet, (b) 5 feet 6 inches, and (c) 6 feet. (Note: Either convert inches to decimals of feet or do the whole problem using inches.)

5 Some Key Ingredients for Inferential Statistics
The Normal Curve, Probability, and Population Versus Sample

ORDINARILY, psychologists conduct research in order to test the adequacy of some theoretical principle or the effectiveness of some practical procedure. For example, a psychophysiologist might measure changes in heart rate from before to after solving a difficult problem in order to test the adequacy of a theory that predicts that heart rate should change following successful problem solving. An applied social psychologist might examine the effectiveness of a program of neighborhood meetings designed to encourage water conservation. Such research efforts, and virtually all other studies conducted in psychology, aim to use the results of the experiment to shed light on the acceptability of the theory or the usefulness of the procedure. These goals are accomplished through inferential statistical procedures.

This and the next three chapters introduce the logic of inferential statistics, which is the foundation for the rest of what you learn in this book. In this chapter, we consider three topics: the normal curve, probability, and population versus sample. This is a comparatively short chapter, preparing the way for the next ones, which will be more difficult.

The Normal Distribution

We noted in Chapter 1 that the graphs of many of the distributions of variables that psychologists measure (as well as many other distributions in nature) follow a unimodal, roughly symmetrical, bell-shaped distribution. These bell-shaped histograms or frequency polygons approximate a precise

FIGURE 5-1
A normal curve.

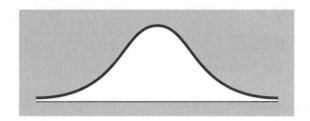

normal distribution
normal curve

and important mathematical distribution called the **normal distribution,** or more simply, the **normal curve.**[1] (It is also often called a *Gaussian distribution* after the astronomer Karl Friedrich Gauss. However, if its discovery can be attributed to anyone, it should really be to Abraham De Moivre—see Box 5-1. An example of the normal curve is shown in Figure 5-1.

Why the Normal Curve Is So Common in Nature

Take, for example, the number of digits a particular person can remember accurately on various testings. On some testings the number may be high, on others low, and on most somewhere in between. That is, the number of digits a person can recall on various testings probably approximately follows a normal curve. Suppose that the person has a basic underlying ability to recall, say, seven digits in this kind of memory task. Nevertheless, on any particular testing, the actual number recalled will be affected by various influences (noisiness of the room, the person's mood at the moment, a combination of digits unwittingly confused with a familiar phone number, a sequence of digits that happens to be all the same number, etc.). These various influences will add up to make the person do better than seven on some testings and worse than seven on others. But if the particular combination of such influences that occur at any testing is essentially random, on most testings positive and negative influences should cancel out. The chances of all the negative influences happening to come together on a testing when none of the positive influences show up is not very good. Thus, in general, the person remembers a middle amount, an amount in which all the opposing influences cancel each other out. Very high or very low scores are much less common.

This creates a unimodal distribution (most of the cases near the middle and fewer at the extremes) that is symmetrical (because a score is as likely to be above as below the middle). Being a unimodal symmetrical curve does not guarantee that it will be close to a normal curve; it could be too flat or too peaked. However, it can be shown mathematically that in the long run, if the influences are truly random, a precise normal curve will result. (The proof can be found in a mathematical statistics text.)

---

[1]The formula for the normal curve (when the mean is 0 and the standard deviation is 1) is

$$f(x) = \frac{1}{\sqrt{2\pi}} e^{-x^2/2}$$

where $f(x)$ is the height of the curve at point x and π and e are the usual mathematical constants (approximately 3.14 and 2.72, respectively). However, psychology researchers almost never use this formula because it is built into the various computer programs that do statistical calculations involving normal curves. And when work must be done by hand, any needed information about the normal curve is provided in tables in statistics books.

BOX 5-1

De Moivre, the Eccentric Stranger Who Invented the Normal Curve

The normal curve is central to statistics, the foundation of most statistical theories and procedures. If any one person can be said to have discovered this fundamental of the field, it was Abraham De Moivre. He was a French Protestant who came to England at the age of 21 because of religious persecution in France, which in 1685 denied Protestants all their civil liberties. In England, De Moivre became a friend of Isaac Newton, who was supposed to have often answered questions by saying, "Ask Mr. De Moivre—he knows all that better than I do." Yet because he was a foreigner, De Moivre was never able to rise to the same heights of fame as the British-born mathematicians he worked among and who respected him so greatly.

De Moivre was mainly an expert on chance. In 1733, he wrote a "method of approximating the sum of the terms of the binomial expanded into a series, from whence are deduced some practical rules to estimate the degree of assent which is to be given to experiments." His paper essentially described the normal curve. The description was only in the form of a law, however; De Moivre never actually drew the curve itself. In fact, he was not very interested in it.

His ideas on the normal distribution were only a tool he developed for figuring out odds on two-possibility events, such as a coin toss, when the number of cases is very large. Up to then, a sort of chart called the "arithmetic triangle" was used to approximate the outcome. But the chart had to be very large for, say, 1,000 coin tosses or 1,000 measurements that were or were not accurate (these problems were faced first in astronomy and psychophysics). De Moivre solved that difficulty with his "method of approximating."

Credit for discovering the normal curve is often given to Pierre Laplace, a Frenchman who stayed home, or Karl Friedrich Gauss, a German, or Thomas Simpson, an Englishman. All worked on the problem of the distribution of errors around a mean, even going so far as describing the curve or drawing approximations of it. But De Moivre, even without drawing it,

was the first to compute the areas under the normal curve at 1, 2, and 3 standard deviations, and Karl Pearson (discussed in Box 14-1), an important later statistician, felt strongly that De Moivre was the true discoverer of this important concept.

In England, De Moivre was highly esteemed as a man of letters as well as of numbers, being familiar with all the classics and able to recite whole scenes from his beloved Molière's *Misanthropist*. But for all his feelings for his native France, the French Academy elected him a *foreign* member of the Academy of Sciences just before his death. While in England, he was ineligible for a university position because he was a foreigner there as well. He remained in poverty, unable even to marry. In his earlier years, he worked as a traveling teacher of mathematics. Later, he was famous for his daily sittings in Slaughter's Coffee House in Long Acre, making himself available to gamblers and insurance underwriters (a profession equally uncertain and hazardous before statistics were refined), who paid him a small sum for figuring odds for them.

De Moivre's death was rather interesting. He worked a great deal with infinite series, which always converge to a certain limit. One story has it that De Moivre began sleeping 15 more minutes each night until he was asleep all the time, then died. Another version claims that his work at the coffeehouse so drove him to despair that he simply went to sleep until he died. Probably the most accurate version is that he had some illness that caused him to sleep more and more. At any rate, in his eighties he could stay awake only 4 hours a day, although he was said to be as keenly intellectual in those hours as ever. Then his wakefulness was reduced to 1 hour, then none at all. At the age of 87, after 8 days in bed, he failed to wake and was declared dead from "somnolence"—a man clever enough not only to invent the normal curve but to rest his way out of this world as well.

References: Pearson (1978); Tankard (1984).

FIGURE 5-2
Normal curve with approximate percentages of cases
between the mean and 1 and 2 standard deviations
above and below the mean.

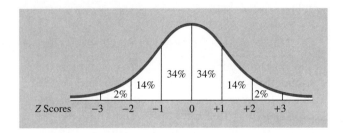

The Normal Curve and Percentage of Cases Between
the Mean and 1 and 2 Standard Deviations from the Mean

Because this shape is standard, there is a known percentage of cases below
or above any particular point. For example, exactly 50% of the cases fall
below the mean, since in any symmetrical distribution, half the cases are
below the mean. But also, more interestingly, as shown in Figure 5-2,
approximately 34% of the cases fall between the mean and 1 standard deviation from the mean. (Notice, incidentally, that in Figure 5-2 the 1 *SD* point
on the normal curve represents the curve's flux point, the place on the curve
where it starts going more out than down.)

To illustrate the usefulness of the regularity of the normal curve, consider IQ scores. On many widely used intelligence tests, the mean IQ is 100,
the standard deviation is 16, and the distribution of IQs is considered to be
normal (see Figure 5-3). Knowing about the normal curve and the percentages of cases between the mean and 1 standard deviation above the mean
allows us to know that about 34% of people have IQs between 100, the
mean, and 116, the IQ score 1 standard deviation above the mean. Similarly,
because the normal curve is symmetrical, about 34% of people have IQs
between 100 and 84 (the score 1 standard deviation below the mean), and
68% (34% + 34%) have IQs between 84 and 116.

As you can also see from looking at the normal curve, there are many
fewer cases between 1 and 2 standard deviations from the mean than there are
between the mean and 1 standard deviation from the mean. Indeed, this must
be so because if 50% of the cases fall above the mean and 34% of the cases
fall between the mean and 1 standard deviation above the mean, that leaves
only 16% of the cases higher than 1 standard deviation above the mean.

It turns out that about 14% of the cases fall between 1 and 2 standard
deviations above the mean (see Figure 5-2). The rest are even farther out.
(And because the normal curve is symmetrical, about 14% of the cases are
between 1 and 2 standard deviations below the mean.) Thus about 14% of

FIGURE 5-3
Distribution of IQ scores on many standard intelligence tests
(with *M* = 100 and *SD* = 16).

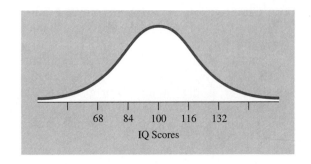

people have IQs between 116 (1 standard deviation above the mean) and 132 (2 standard deviations above the mean).

If you can remember the 50%, 34%, and 14% figures, you will have a good sense of the percentage of cases above and below a score if you know its number of standard deviations from the mean.

It is also possible to reverse this approach and figure out a person's number of standard deviations from the mean from a percentage. For example, if you are told that a person scored in the top 2% on a test (and if you can assume that scores on the test are approximately normally distributed), the person must have a score that is at least 2 standard deviations above the mean. Similarly, if you were selecting animals for study and needed to consider their visual acuity, if visual acuity was normally distributed and you wanted to use animals in the middle two thirds (a figure close to 68%) for visual acuity, you would select animals that scored between 1 standard deviation above and 1 standard deviation below the mean. If you knew the mean and the standard deviation of the visual acuity test, you could then go on to say what the lowest and highest acuity levels actually are in terms of raw scores.

The Normal Curve Table and Z scores

The 50%, 34%, and 14% figures are useful practical approximation rules for getting a sense of where a particular score stands on a distribution. However, in many research and applied situations, psychologists need more precise information. Because the normal curve is exactly defined, it is possible to compute the exact percentage of cases between any two points on the normal curve, not just those in which a score happens to be right at 1 or 2 standard deviations from the mean. That is, it is possible to determine the exact percentage of cases between any two Z scores: Exactly 68.59% of cases have a Z score between +.62 and −1.68, exactly 2.81% between +.79 and +.89, and so forth.

These percentages can be computed using the formula for the normal curve and integrating, using calculus. However, this can also be accomplished much more simply. Statisticians have worked out tables for the normal curve that give the percentage of cases between the mean (a Z score of 0) and any other Z score. If you want to know the percentage of cases between the mean and a Z score of .62, you simply look up .62 in the table, and it tells you that 23.24% of the cases, in a perfect normal distribution, fall between the mean and this Z score.

We have included such a **normal curve table** in Appendix B (Table B-1). As you can see, the table consists of two columns: The first column lists the Z score, and the column next to it the percentage of cases between the mean and that Z score. Notice also that the table repeats these two columns several times on the page, so be sure to look across only one column! Also notice that only positive Z scores appear on the table. This is because the normal curve is perfectly symmetrical, so the percentage of cases between the mean and, say, a Z of +2.38 is exactly the same as the percentage of cases between the mean and a Z of -2.38.

In our example, you would find .62 in the "Z" column and then, right next to it in the "% mean to Z" column, you would find 23.24.

You can also reverse the process (as we also saw with the 50%-34%-14% approximations) and find the Z scores corresponding to particular per-

normal curve table

centages of cases. For example, if you were told that Janice's creativity score was in the top 10% of people taking a test (assuming that creativity scores were normally distributed), you could figure out her Z score as follows: First you would reason that if she is in the top 10%, 40% of the cases fall between her score and the mean (since there are 50% above the mean and she is in the top 10% of cases overall, which leaves 40%). Then you would look at the "% mean to Z" column of the table until you found a percentage that was very close to 40%. In this case, the closest you could come would be 39.97%. Finally, you would then look at the "Z" column to the left of this percentage. In this case, 39.97% corresponds to a Z score of 1.28.

Rules for Computing the Percentages of Cases From Raw Scores and Z Scores Using a Normal Curve Table

If you are working with raw scores, first convert them to Z scores, using the procedures described in Chapter 2. Then proceed as follows.

To find the percentage of cases above a particular Z score, look up the Z score in the "Z" column, and find the percentage in the adjacent "% mean to Z" column. If the Z score is positive, subtract this percentage from 50%. If the Z score is negative, add 50% to it.

To find the percentage of cases below a particular Z score, look up the Z score in the "Z" column, and find the percentage in the adjacent "% mean to Z" column. If the Z score is positive, add 50% to this percentage. If the Z score is negative, subtract this percentage from 50%.

Examples

Consider a couple of examples involving IQ scores. If a person has an IQ of 125, the Z score is $+1.56$. In the normal curve table, 1.56 in the "Z" column corresponds to 44.06 in the "% mean to Z" column. Thus 44.06% of the cases fall between the mean IQ and an IQ of 125 (Z score of $+1.56$). Since 50% of the cases are above the mean and since 44.06% of the cases above the mean are below this person's IQ, that leaves 5.94% ($50\% - 44.06\%$) above this person's score; with a total of 100%, there are 94.06% with lower IQs. (This is all illustrated in Figure 5-4.)

Consider a person with an IQ of 95. The corresponding Z score is $-.31$. The normal curve table shows that 12.17% of the cases are between the mean and a Z score of .31. The percentage of cases above a Z score of $-.31$

FIGURE 5-4
Distributions of IQ scores showing percentages of cases above and below an IQ score of 125.

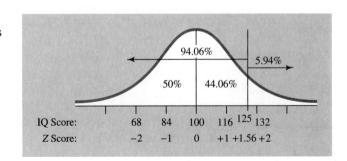

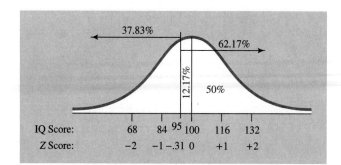

FIGURE 5-5
Distributions of IQ scores showing percentages of cases above and below an IQ score of 95.

are 12.17% plus the 50% above the mean, for a total of 62.17%. The percentage of cases below a Z score of −.31 are the total of 50% below the mean, less the 12.17% between the mean and −.31, leaving 37.83% (50% − 12.17%). (This is all illustrated in Figure 5-5.)

Rules for Computing Raw Scores and Z Scores From Percentages of Cases Using the Normal Curve Table

To find the raw score in any of these cases, first find the Z score, using one of the procedures described here, then convert it to a raw score using the steps outlined in Chapter 2.

To find the Z score corresponding to a score that has a particular percentage of cases higher than it, assuming that the percentage is less than 50%, first subtract the percentage from 50%, look up the closest percentage you can find to this difference in the "% mean to Z" column of the normal curve table, and find the Z score in the adjacent "Z" column. (If the percentage is greater than 50%, subtract the figure from 100% and then use the procedure that follows.)

To find the Z score corresponding to a score that has a particular percentage of cases lower than it, assuming that the percentage is less than 50%, first subtract it from 50%, look up the closest percentage you can find to this difference in the "% mean to Z" column of the normal curve table, and find the Z score in the adjacent "Z" column. Be sure to make it negative (put a minus sign in front of it). (If the percentage is more than 50%, subtract it from 100% and then use the procedure in the preceding paragraph.)

Most of you will find it easier to make a picture of the curve and think out these problems rather than trying to memorize and mechanically follow these rules. The rules are here mainly to help you if you get lost or if you wish to check your work.

Examples

Once again, we will use the distribution of IQ scores for our examples. What IQ score would a person need to be in the top 5%? Since 50% of people lie above the mean, at least 45% would score between this person and the mean (50% − 5% = 45%). Looking in the "% mean to Z" column of the normal curve table, the closest figure to 45% is 44.95% (or you could use 45.05%). This corresponds, in the adjacent "Z" column, to a Z score of 1.64. Using the formula from Chapter 2—$X = M + (Z)(SD)$—with a mean

FIGURE 5-6
Z score corresponding to the top 5%.

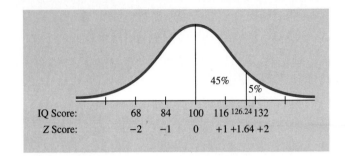

IQ of 100 and a standard deviation of 16, you could conclude that to be in the top 5%, a person would need an IQ of at least 126.24 (see Figure 5-6).

Now consider what IQ score corresponds to the point at which a person is in the bottom 2.5%. Being in the bottom 2.5% means that at least 47.5% of the cases fall between the mean and this score (50% – 2.5%). In the normal curve table, 47.5% in the "% mean to Z" column corresponds to a Z score of 1.96. Since we are below the mean, this becomes –1.96. Converting to a raw score, the IQ for the bottom 2.5% comes out to an IQ of 68.64 (see Figure 5-7).

FIGURE 5-7
Z score corresponding to the bottom 2.5%.

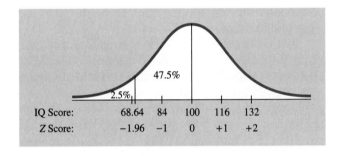

Probability

As in all of science, the purpose of psychological research is to ascertain the validity of a theory or the effectiveness of a procedure. But at best, our research can only make that validity or effectiveness seem more or less likely; it cannot give us the luxury of knowing for certain. Thus probability plays a central role in science and in particular in the procedures of inferential statistics that are used to move from results of experiments to conclusions about theories or applied procedures based on those results.

Probability has been studied for centuries by mathematicians and philosophers, yet even today it is rife with controversy. Fortunately, however, you need to know only a few key ideas to understand and conduct the inferential statistical procedures you will be learning in this book.[2] And these few key points are not very difficult—indeed, some students find them intuitively obvious.

[2]There are, of course, many areas of probability theory that are not directly relevant to statistics and even many areas relevant to statistics that are not central to the main themes of statistical inference as used in psychology. For example, computing joint and conditional probabilities, which is covered in many statistics books, is not covered here because it is rarely encountered in published research in psychology and is not necessary for an intuitive understanding of the logic of the major inferential statistical procedures covered in this book.

In statistics we usually define **probability** as "the expected relative fre- | probability
quency of a particular outcome." An **outcome** is the result of an experiment | outcome
(or virtually any event, such as a coin coming up heads or it raining tomorrow). *Frequency* indicates how many times something occurs. The *relative
frequency* is the number of times something occurs relative to the number of
times it could have occurred—that is, the proportion of times it occurs (a
coin coming up heads might come up heads 8 times out of 12 flips, for a
relative frequency of 8/12, or 2/3). **Expected relative frequency** indicates | expected relative frequency
what you would expect to get in the long run, if you were to repeat the
experiment many times (in the case of a fair coin, in the long run you would
expect to get 50%, or 1/2 heads). This is called the **long-run relative-fre-** | long-run relative-frequency
quency interpretation of probability. | interpretation of probability

We also use probability to convey how certain we are that a particular | subjective interpretation of
thing will happen. This is called the **subjective interpretation of probabil-** | probability
ity. Suppose that you say there is a 95% chance that your favorite restaurant
will be open tonight. You could be using a kind of relative frequency interpretation, implying that if you were to check whether this restaurant was
open many times on days like today, on 95% of those days you would find
it open. However, your statement more likely reflects a subjective interpretation: On a scale of 0% to 100%, you would rate your confidence that it is
open at 95%. To put it another way, you would feel that a bet was fair that
had odds based on a 95% chance of the restaurant's being open.

BOX 5-2

Pascal Begins Probability Theory at the Gambling Table, Then Learns to Bet on God

Whereas in England statistics were used to keep track of death rates and to prove the existence of God (see Box 1-1), the French and the Italians developed statistics at the gaming table. In partic- ular, there was the "problem of points"—the divi- sion of the stakes in a game after it has been interrupted. If a certain number of plays were planned, how much of the stakes should each player walk away with, given the percentage played so far?

The problem was discussed at least as early as 1494 by Luca Pacioli, a friend of Leonardo da Vinci. But it was unsolved until 1654, when it was presented to Blaise Pascal by the Chevalier de Méré. Pascal, a French child prodigy, attended meetings of the most famous adult French math- ematicians and at 15 proved an important theo- rem in geometry. In correspondence with Pierre Fermat, another famous French mathematician, Pascal solved the problem of points and in so

doing began the field of probability theory and the work that would lead to the normal curve.

By the way, not long after solving this prob- lem, Pascal suddenly became as religiously devout as the English statisticians. He was in a runaway coach on a bridge and was saved from drowning only by the traces of the team break- ing at the last possible moment. He took this as a warning to abandon his mathematical work in favor of religious writings and later formulated "Pascal's wager": that the value of a game is the value of the prize times the probability of win- ning it; therefore, even if the probability is low that God exists, we should gamble on the affir- mative because the value of the prize is infinite, whereas the value of not believing is only finite worldly pleasure.

Reference: Tankard (1984).

Which interpretation one adopts does not affect how probability is calculated. We introduced these concepts here for two reasons. First, we wanted to give you some deeper insight into the meaning of the term *probability*, which will be prominent throughout the rest of your learning about statistics, even if, as is so often the case, this deeper understanding does not take the form of set-in-stone dogma. Second, being familiar with two interpretations is crucial to understanding some of the deepest controversies in statistics—one of which we will introduce at the end of this chapter.

Calculating Probabilities

In statistical applications, probabilities are calculated as the proportion of successful outcomes expected in a given situation—the number of possible successful outcomes divided by the number of all possible outcomes.

Thus to calculate the probability of getting heads when flipping a coin, there is one possible successful outcome (getting heads) out of two possible outcomes (getting heads or getting tails), making a probability of 1/2, or .5. In a throw of a single die, the probability of a 2 (or any other particular side of the die) is 1/6, or .17, because there is one possible successful outcome out of six possible outcomes. The probability of throwing a die and getting a number 3 or lower is 3/6, or .5—there are three possible successful outcomes (a 1, a 2, or a 3) out of six possible outcomes.

To take a slightly more complicated example, suppose that a class has 200 people in it, and 30 are seniors. If you were to pick someone from the class at random, the probability of picking a senior would be 30/200, or .15. This is because there are 30 possible successful outcomes (getting a senior) out of 200 possible outcomes.

Range of Probabilities

Probabilities are proportions and therefore cannot be less than 0 or greater than 1 (in terms of percentages, they range from 0% to 100%). Something that has no chance of happening has a probability of 0, and something that is certain to happen has a probability of 1.

Probabilities Expressed as Symbols

p

Probability is usually symbolized by the letter **p**. The actual probability figure is usually given as a decimal, though occasionally fractions or percentages are used. Thus a 50–50 chance is ordinarily expressed as $p = .5$, but it could also be expressed as $p = 1/2$ or $p = 50\%$.

It is also common to express probabilities as inequalities, that is, in terms of a probability being "greater than" (symbolized >) or "less than" (<) some number. For example, the statement "the probability is less than 1%" might be symbolized as "$p < .01$."

Probability and the Normal Distribution

Until now we have considered probabilities mainly in terms of specific events that might or might not happen. But it is also possible to talk about a range of events that might or might not happen. The example of a throw of a die com-

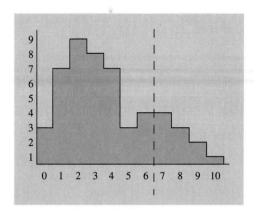

FIGURE 5-8
Frequency distribution (shown as a histogram) of 50 cases in which $p = .2$ (10/50) of randomly selecting a case with a score of 7 or higher.

ing out 3 or lower is one such case. Other examples would be the probability of selecting someone on a city street who is between the ages of 30 and 40 and the probability of the temperature tomorrow being lower than 50 °F.

If you think of probability in terms of proportion of cases, probability can be readily associated with frequency distributions (see Chapter 1). In the frequency distribution shown in Figure 5-8, 10 of the total of 50 cases scored 7 or higher. Thus if you were selecting cases at random, there would be 10 chances (possible successful outcomes) out of 50 (all possible outcomes) of selecting one that was 7 or higher, so $p = 10/50 = .2$.

The normal distribution can also be thought of as a probability distribution. The normal curve describes a frequency distribution in which the proportion of cases between any two Z scores is known. But as we are seeing, the proportion of cases between any two Z scores is the same as the probability of selecting a case between those two Z scores. For example, the probability of a case falling between the mean and a Z score of +1 (1 standard deviation above the mean) is about 34%; that is, $p = .34$.

What we are saying may have been obvious all along. In a sense it is merely a technical point that the normal curve can be seen as either a frequency distribution or a probability distribution. We mention this only so that you will not be surprised or confused when we refer later to the probability of a case coming from a particular region of the normal curve.

Sample and Population

We are going to introduce you to some important concepts by thinking beans. Suppose that you are cooking a pot of beans and taste a spoonful to see if they are done. In this example, the pot of beans is a **population,** the entire set of things of interest. The spoonful is a **sample,** the subset of the population about which you actually have information. This is illustrated in Figure 5-9.

population

sample

In psychology research, we typically study samples not of beans but of individuals to make inferences about some larger group to which information in the sample is relevant. Thus a sample might consist of 50 Canadian women who participate in a particular experiment, while the population might be intended to be all Canadian women. Or in a typical opinion survey, 1,000 people are selected from the voting-age population and asked for

FIGURE 5-9
Populations and samples: In (a), the entire pot of beans is the population, the spoonful a sample. In (b), the larger circle represents the population, the circle within it a sample. In (c), the frequency distribution represents the population, and the particular shaded cases together make up a sample.

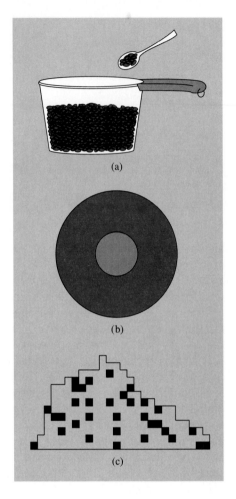

whom they plan to vote. The opinions of these 1,000 individuals are the sample. The opinions of the larger voting public, to which the pollsters hope to generalize their results, is the population (see Figure 5-10).[3]

Why Samples Are Studied Instead of Populations

Obviously, if researchers are going to be drawing conclusions about a population, the results would be most accurate if they could study the entire population, rather than a subgroup from that population. However, in most research situations this is simply impracticable or even impossible. Far more important, however, is that the whole point of research is to be able to make generalizations or predictions about events beyond our reach. We would not call it research if you tested your three cars to see which gets better gas mileage—unless you hoped to say something about the gas mileage

[3]Strictly speaking, *population* and *sample* refer to a set of scores (numbers or measurements), not to the subjects measured. Thus in the first example, the sample is really the scores of the 50 Canadian women, not the 50 women themselves, and the population is really what the scores would be if all Canadian women were measured.

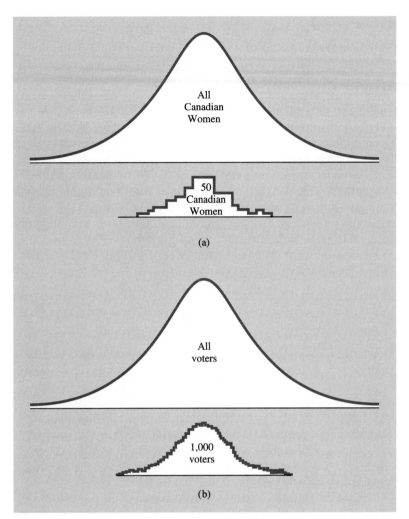

FIGURE 5-10
Additional examples of populations and samples. In (a), the population is the scores of all Canadian women, and a sample consists of the scores of the 50 particular Canadian women studied. In (b), the population is the voting preferences of the entire voting-age population, and a sample consists of the voting preferences of the 1,000 voting-age people who were surveyed.

of those models of cars in general. In other words, a researcher might conduct an experiment on the way in which people store words in short-term memory using 20 students as the subjects in the experiment. But the purpose of the experiment is not to find out how these particular 20 students respond to the experimental condition but rather to learn something about human cognition under these conditions in general.

Thus the strategy in almost all psychology research is to study a sample of individuals who are believed to be representative of the general population (or of some particular population of interest). More realistically, researchers try to study people who do not differ from the general population in any systematic way that would be expected to matter for that topic of research.

So in psychology research (and nearly all scientific research), the sample is what is studied, and the population is an unknown that researchers make inferences about on the basis of the sample. Most of what you will be learning about in the rest of this book relates to the issue of drawing conclusions about populations based on information from samples.

Methods of Sampling

random selection

There are so many ways of selecting a sample for a particular research project that we have provided a discussion of several of these methods in Appendix A (also see Box 5-3). Briefly, in most cases the ideal method of sampling is called **random selection.** The researcher obtains a complete list of all the members of a population and randomly selects some number of them to study. An example of a random method of selection would be to put each name on a table tennis ball, put all the balls in a big hopper, shake it up, and have someone blindfolded select as many as are needed. (In practice, most researchers use a computer-generated list of random numbers. Just how computers or persons can create a list of truly random numbers is an interesting question in its own right that we examine in Box 15-1.)

haphazard selection

It is important to distinguish truly random selection from what might be called **haphazard selection,** such as just taking whoever is available or happens to be first on a list. It is surprisingly easy to accidentally select a

---

BOX 5-3

Surveys, Polls, and 1948's Costly "Free Sample"

It is time to make you a more informed reader of poll or survey results in the media. Usually the results of properly done public polls will be accompanied, somewhere in fine print, by a statement like "From a telephone poll of 1,000 American adults taken on June 4–5. Sampling error ±3%." What does all this mean?

The Gallup poll is as good an example as any (Gallup, 1972), and there is no better place to begin than 1948, when all three of the major polling organizations—Gallup, Crossley (for Hearst papers), and Roper (for *Fortune*)—wrongly predicted Thomas Dewey's victory over Harry Truman for the U.S. presidency. Yet Gallup's prediction was based on 50,000 interviews and Roper's on 15,000. By contrast, to predict George Bush's 1988 victory Gallup used only 4,089. Since 1952, the pollsters have never used more than 8,144—but with very small error and no outright mistakes. What has changed?

The method used before 1948, and never repeated since, was called "quota sampling." Interviewers were assigned a fixed number of persons to interview, with strict quotas to fill in all the categories that seemed important, such as residence, sex, age, race, and economic status. Within these specifics, however, they were free to interview whomever they liked. In the good old days, before 1948's disaster, it was well known that the

polls favored Republicans. Republicans generally tended to be marginally easier to interview—they were more likely to have telephones and permanent addresses and to live in better houses and better neighborhoods. This slight bias had not mattered when the results still made it obvious that the Democrats were going to win, as was the case prior to 1948. In 1948, however, the election was very close, and the Republican bias produced the embarrassing mistake that changed survey methods forever.

Since 1948, Gallup and the other survey organizations have used what is called a "probability method." Simple random sampling is the purest case of the probability method. But simple random sampling for a survey about a U.S. presidential election would require drawing names from a list of all the eligible voters in the nation—a lot of people. Then each person selected would have to be found, in diversely scattered locales. So instead, "multistage cluster sampling" is used. To describe it roughly, the United States is divided into seven size-of-community strata, from large cities to rural open country; these groupings are divided into seven geographic regions (New England, Middle Atlantic, etc.), after which smaller equal-sized groups are zoned, and then blocks are drawn from the zones, with the probability of selection

---

sample that is a biased subset of the population as a whole. For example, a survey of attitudes about your statistics instructor taken only among people sitting near you would be affected by all the factors influencing choice of seat, some of which have to do with precisely what you are studying (how much they like the instructor or the class). And of course, asking people who sit near you would yield opinions more like your own than a truly random sample would.

Unfortunately, it is only occasionally possible in psychology research to study a truly random sample. Much of the time, in fact, studies are conducted with whoever is willing or available to be a research participant. At best, as noted, a researcher tries to study a sample of individuals who are not systematically unrepresentative of the population in any known way. For example, if a study is about a process that is likely to differ for people of different age groups, the researcher will attempt to include people of all age groups in the study or to draw conclusions only about the age groups that could be studied.

---

being proportional to the size of the population or number of dwelling units. Finally, an interviewer is given a randomly selected starting point on the map and is required to follow a given direction, take households in sequence, and ask for the youngest man 18 or older or, if no man is at home, the oldest woman 18 or older (this has been found to compensate best for the tendencies for young men, and then all men, and then older women, in that order, to be not at home and hence underrepresented).

Two points are true of all samples constituted by the probability method: The interviewers have no choice at all about whom they interview, and there is a formal procedure for selecting the sample that involves the planned use of chance. Ideally, each individual in the population (in this case, eligible voters) has an equal chance of being selected. However, the Gallup procedure is biased against people who live in large households, as only one person is ever interviewed per household, so any given person in a large household is less likely to be polled. But this is adjusted for statistically.

Since phone surveys cost about one third of door-to-door polls and most persons now own phones, making this method less biased in favor of the rich than in Truman's time, telephoning is often the favored method for polling today.

Phoning also allows computers randomly to dial phone numbers through a complicated system called random digit dialing (RDD), which, unlike telephone directories, includes unlisted numbers. RDD also sorts out business phones by automatically checking the Yellow Pages and eliminating numbers listed there.

Whether the survey is taken by telephone or face to face, there will be about 35% nonrespondents after three attempts to make contact. This creates yet another bias to be reckoned with, through questions about how much time a person spends at home, so that a slight extra weight can be given to the responses of those who were reached but usually are at home less, to make up for those missed entirely. Indeed, many of the questions in both phone and face-to-face surveys are asked only to identify potential biases in the representativeness of the sample of the population of interest (for example, questions of eligible voters to check whether they are likely to actually vote, an important matter in predicting election results).

So now you know quite a bit about opinion polls. But we have left two important questions unanswered: Why are only 1,000 included in a poll meant to describe all U.S. adults, and what does the term *sampling error* mean? For these answers, you must wait for Chapter 7 (Box 7-1).

TABLE 5-1
Population Parameters and Sample Statistics

	Population Parameter	**Sample Statistic**
Basis:	Scores of entire population	Scores of sample only
Specificity:	Usually unknown	Computed from known data
Symbols:		
Mean	μ	M
Standard deviation	σ	SD
Variance	σ^2	SD^2

Statistical Terminology for Samples and Populations

population parameters

The mean, variance, and standard deviation of a population are called **population parameters.** A population parameter is usually an unknown that is estimated from sample information. You don't taste all the beans, just the spoonful. "They're done" is an estimation of the whole pot.

μ
σ^2
σ

To keep this distinction in mind, population parameters are usually symbolized by Greek letters. The symbol for the mean of a population is μ**,** the Greek letter "mu"; the symbol for its variance is σ^2**,** and the symbol for its standard deviation is σ**,** the squared and unsquared versions, respectively, of the lowercase Greek letter "sigma." You won't see these symbols often, except while learning statistics, because, again, you seldom know the population parameters or expect to.

sample statistics

The mean, variance, and standard deviation you calculate to describe a sample are **sample statistics.** A sample statistic is computed from known information. Generally, the symbols for sample statistics are ordinary letters, as we have used so far. (However, as you learn in Chapter 9, we often use yet another kind of standard deviation or variance when estimating a population parameter using information in a sample.) These various symbols are summarized in Table 5-1.

Relation of Normal Curve, Probability, and Sample Versus Population

In most research situations, as noted, we do not know the population parameters. However, we usually do assume that the shape of the population is roughly a normal curve. So researchers generally collect information from a sample in order to make probabilistic inferences about the parameters of a normally distributed population.

Consider an experiment to examine whether students learn more when studying all at once or when their studying is spread over a period of time. Sixty students are randomly selected to participate in the study, with half randomly assigned to study all at once and half to study the same number of hours spread out over several weeks. At the end of the several weeks, both groups are given a test, and there is a difference between the two groups in their mean scores on this test.

Now let's consider this experiment in terms of the language we have been using in this chapter. The group that studied all at once is a sample intended to represent how students in the general population would perform if they were assigned to study all at once; the group that studied over time is a sample intended to represent how the population of students in general would perform if assigned to study over time. The mean of each group is a sample statistic computed from the results of the experiment. The populations represented by these samples do not even really exist (as no students other than those in the experiment have been assigned to these conditions), but if they did exist, it is presumed that the population would be normally distributed. However, we have no basis prior to this study for presuming anything about the means or variances of these populations, the population parameters. (Even when we study samples from populations that really exist, such as a comparison of test performance between a sample of psychiatric patients with schizophrenia and a sample with bipolar disorder, we will usually assume that the populations represented by our two samples are normally distributed, but we do not know anything about what the test performance of these populations would be beyond what we can infer from our samples or from previous research with other samples.)

Finally, the question of interest is a question about probability: Suppose that the means of the two populations (population parameters) are in fact the same, and thus how students study really doesn't matter. What then is the probability that the means of our two samples (sample statistics) could be as different as they actually are?

The way we stated this question may seem rather convoluted; however, it is just such thinking about probabilities, samples, and populations that is the foundation of most inferential statistics in psychology. It is, in a nutshell, the logic of what is called "hypothesis testing," which we explore step by step in Chapter 6. You needn't ponder it now—we only introduced the ideas here to give you an idea of how the various elements covered in this chapter fit together in the kinds of statistical problems faced in real-life psychology research.

Controversies and Limitations

The three topics we have introduced in this chapter—the normal curve, probability, and sample and population—are actually the subjects of considerable controversy, basic as they are. We shall explore a major controversy associated with each.

Is the Normal Curve Really So Normal?

We have said that real distributions in the world often approximate the normal curve very closely. The extent to which this is true is very important, and not merely because assuming a normal curve makes Z scores easier to interpret. As you will see in later chapters, most of the statistical techniques that psychologists use assume that their samples come from populations that are normally distributed. The extent to which this is a reasonable assumption has been a long-standing source of debate. But the predominant view has been that given the way psychological measures are developed, a bell-shaped distribution "is almost guaranteed" (Walberg, Strykowski, Rovai, & Hung, 1984, p. 107). Or as Hopkins and Glass (1978) put it, measurements in all disciplines are such good approximations to it that one might think "God loves the normal curve!"

However, there has been a persistent line of criticism about whether nature really packages itself so neatly. Micceri (1989) has recently presented strong evidence that the measures most commonly used in psychology—achievement or ability tests (such as the SAT and the GRE) and psychometric tests (such as the MMPI)—often do not yield scores that are normally distributed "in nature." Micceri obtained data sets and examined the distributions of scores of 440 psychological and educational measures that had been used on very large samples. All of his data sets had samples of over 190 individuals, and the majority had samples of over 1,000 (14.3% even had samples of 5,000 to 10,293). Yet large samples were of no help— no distribution investigated passed all tests of normality (mostly Micceri looked for asymmetry or "lumpiness" and "heavy tails"). Few measures yielded distributions that even came reasonably close to looking like the normal curve. Nor were these variations predictable: "The distributions studied here exhibited almost every conceivable type of contamination" (p. 162), although some were more common with certain types of tests. Micceri discusses many obvious reasons for this nonnormality, such as "ceiling" or "floor" effects (e.g., biology students taking a biology achievement test will score toward the middle or high end—few will be ignorant of the topic).

The question is, how much has it mattered that the distributions for these measures were so nonnormal? According to Micceri, it is just not known. Although computer simulations (called Monte Carlo studies, discussed in Box 10-1) have been done for the purpose of ascertaining the impact of violating the assumptions of the major statistical methods, there are some good reasons to think that the real world produces certain kinds of violations (mainly "lumpiness" and multimodality), whereas Monte Carlo studies look at others (mainly smooth curves with extreme tail weights or asymmetry). Micceri's study is one of the first to look at real data, but it does not test how well any statistical method holds up when the assumption of the normal curve is violated; it seeks only to demonstrate the commonness of those violations within psychology's standard measures and to provide a better understanding of typical violations.

Until more is known, the general opinion among psychologists will no doubt remain supportive of the traditional statistical techniques, with the underlying mathematics based on the assumption of normal population distributions. The reason for this nonchalance in the face of findings such as Micceri's is that under most conditions in which they are used, the traditional techniques seem to give results that are reasonably accurate even when the formal requirement of a normal population distribution is not met. (In fact, a recent study by Sawilowsky & Blair, 1992, which looked specifically at some of the particular distributions Micceri had identified, suggests that this conclusion holds for these particular distributions as well.) In this book, we generally adopt this majority position favoring the use of the traditional techniques in all but the most extreme cases. But you should be aware that a vocal minority of psychologists would disagree. Some of the alternative statistical techniques they favor (ones that do not rely on assuming a normal distribution in the population) are presented in Chapter 15.

Galton, one of the major pioneers of statistical methods (recall Box 3-1), said of the normal curve, "I know of scarcely anything so apt to impress the imagination. . . . [It] would have been personified by the Greeks and deified, if they had known of it. It reigns with serenity and in complete self-efface-ment amidst the wild confusion" (1889, p. 66). Ironically, it may be true that in psychology, at least, it truly reigns in pure and austere isolation, with no even close-to-perfect real-life imitators.

What Does Probability Really Mean?

We have already introduced the major controversy in the area of probability theory as it is applied to statistics in psychology, the dispute between the long-term relative-frequency interpretation and the subjective degree-of-belief interpretation. In most cases, though, it really does not much matter which interpretation is used—the statistics are the same. But among the minority of theorists who favor the subjective interpretation, some hold a rather critical view of the mainstream of statistical thinking. In particular, they have advocated what has come to be called the "Bayesian approach" (for example, see Phillips, 1973). The approach is named after Thomas Bayes, an early-18th-century Nonconformist English clergyman who devel-oped a probability theorem appropriately known as "Bayes' theorem."

Bayes' theorem itself can be proved mathematically and is not contro-versial. However, its applications in statistics are hotly debated. The details of the approach are beyond the scope of this text, but the main point of dis-pute can be made clear here: The Bayesians say that what science is about is conducting research in order to adjust our preexisting beliefs in light of evi-dence we collect. Thus conclusions drawn from an experiment are always in the context of what we believed about the world before doing the experi-ment. The mainstream view, by contrast, says that it is better not to make any assumptions about prior beliefs. We should just look at the evidence as it is, judging whether the experiment has shown any reliable effects at all (or no effect whatsoever). Some statisticians in the mainstream do acknowl-edge that the Bayesian description of science may be more accurate. But they also point out that accepting the Bayesian method in our statistical computations would mean that the conclusion drawn from each study would depend too heavily on the subjective belief of the particular scientist conducting the study. Thus the same experimental results from different sci-entists could lead to different conclusions.

The Bayesian approach represented a lively (though never majority) movement in psychological statistics during the 1960s and 1970s. Since then it has become much less prominent as a movement, at least under this banner. Nevertheless, many of the issues raised by this dispute remain important in new guises (Games, 1988; Gigerenzer & Murray, 1987). We will see examples of this in our discussion of the controversy over one-tailed versus two-tailed tests of significance in Chapter 6 and in a number of contexts in Chapter 8 on power and effect size.

Sample and Population

Most of the statistical procedures you learn in the rest of this book are based on the assumption that the sample studied is a random sample of the popula-tion. As we pointed out, however, this is rarely the case in psychology research. Most often, our samples represent whatever subjects are available to participate in our experiment—meaning that most studies are done with college students, volunteers, convenient laboratory animals, and the like. Further, our samples tend to be quite small, so that even if it is reasonable to believe that the kinds of subjects studied are typical of the population in general, there are often too few to make valid generalizations.

Some psychologists are concerned about this problem and have suggested that researchers need to use different statistical approaches that make generalizations only to the kinds of people that are actually being used in the study. (For example, if our sample has a particular nonnormal distribution, we should assume that we can generalize only to a population with the same particular nonnormal distribution.) We will have more to say about their suggested solutions in Chapter 15.

Sociologists, as compared to psychologists, are much more concerned about the representativeness of the groups they study, and studies reported in sociology journals (or in sociologically oriented social psychology journals) are much more likely to use formal methods of random selection and large samples or at least to address the issue in their articles.

The main reason that psychologists are more comfortable with using not clearly random samples is that they are mainly interested in the *relationships* among variables. If in one population an increase in X is associated with an increase in Y, this relationship should probably hold in other populations, even if the actual levels of X and Y differ from population to population. For example, suppose that a researcher conducts the experiment we used as an example in Chapters 3 and 4, testing the relation of number of exposures to a list of words to number of words remembered. Suppose further that this study is done with college students and that the result is that the greater the number of exposures, the greater the number of words remembered, with $r = .68$. It is quite likely true that the actual number of words remembered from the list would on the average be different for other kinds of people—chess masters (who probably have highly developed memories) may recall more words; people who have just been upset may recall fewer words. But even in these groups, we would expect that the more times exposed to the list, the more words will be remembered, and it is reasonable, in fact, to assume that the correlation will be about the same in these groups. That is, even if the mean number of words recalled differs from group to group, the *relation* of number recalled to number of exposures will probably not change. (Stated in terms of our discussion of correlation in Chapter 3, when everything is converted to Z scores, the relation among the Z scores on different variables is probably the same in all groups.)

In sociology, representativeness of samples is much more important because the interest is more likely to be in the actual mean and variance of a variable in a particular society—things that psychologists are rarely in a position to examine (and rarely seek to do).

Normal Curves, Probabilities, Samples, and Populations in Research Articles

The material covered in this chapter is primarily used as a foundation for understanding the topics covered in subsequent chapters. It is rarely discussed explicitly in research articles (except articles about methods or statistics). Occasionally, you will see the normal curve mentioned, in the context of describing the scores on a particular variable. (We say more about this, and give some examples from published articles, in Chapter 15, where we consider circumstances in which the scores do not follow a normal curve.)

Probability is also rarely discussed directly, except in the context of statistical significance, a topic we mentioned briefly in Chapter 3. In almost any article you look at, the Results section will be strewn with descriptions of various methods associated with statistical significance, followed by some expression such as "$p < .05$" or "$p < .01$." The p refers to probability, but the probability of what? That is the main topic of our discussion of statistical significance in Chapter 6.

Finally, you will occasionally see a brief mention of the method of selecting the sample from the population. For example, Hunsley and Lefebvre (1990) conducted a survey of clinical psychologists in Canada. In the Methods section of their article, they wrote, "The questionnaire was sent . . . to a random sample of 300 members of CRHSPP [Canadian Register of Health Service Providers in Psychology] who were listed in the 1988 membership directory" (p. 351). Thus Hunsley and Lefebvre specified both the listing they used for the population and the method they used (random selection) to obtain their sample. As is sometimes the case in surveys of this kind, the actual return rate was fairly low (in this case only 29.3%). So even though they used random selection to contact potential members of their sample, the sample itself was not random, in that it overrepresented whatever characteristics make a clinical psychologist likely to respond to such a survey. The researchers were well aware of this problem and discussed it in some length in the article. One approach they used was to check whether the clinicians who responded had distributions similar to the population as a whole on the demographic (background) characteristics that were known about the population (CRHSPP members) as a whole, such as gender, region of the country, and degree held. They concluded that "with the possible exception of an underrepresentation of female psychologists"—21.6% of their respondents were female, versus 33% of CRHSPP—"the demographic information we have on the respondents indicates that the sample of psychologists is likely to be representative of the CRHSPP membership" (p. 355).

Summary

Many distributions of variables in psychology research approximately follow a bell-shaped, symmetrical, unimodal distribution called the normal curve. Because it is precisely mathematically defined, a known percentage of cases fall between any two points on a normal curve.

A useful approximation for working with normal curves is that 50% of the cases fall above the mean, 34% between the mean and 1 standard deviation above the mean, and 14% between 1 and 2 standard deviations above the mean.

A normal curve table gives the percentage of cases between the mean and any particular positive Z score. Using this table, and knowing that the curve is symmetrical and that 50% of the cases fall above the mean, it is possible to determine the percentage of cases above or below any particular

Z score and also the Z score corresponding to the point at which a particular percentage of cases begins.

Most psychologists consider the probability of an event to be its expected relative frequency, though some treat it as the subjective degree of belief that the event will happen. Probability is usually calculated as the proportion of successful outcomes to total possible outcomes. It is symbolized by p and has a range from 0 (event is impossible) to 1 (event is certain). The normal distribution can be thought of as providing a way to know the probabilities of scores' being within particular ranges of values.

A sample is an individual or group that is studied—usually as representative of a larger group, or population, that cannot be examined in its entirety. Ideally, the sample is selected from a population using a strictly random procedure. The mean, variance, and so forth of a sample are called sample statistics; when of a population, they are called population parameters and are symbolized by Greek letters—μ for mean, σ^2 for variance, and σ for standard deviation.

Most of the techniques you learn in the rest of this book make probabilistic inferences to draw conclusions about populations based on information from samples. In this process, populations are usually assumed to be normally distributed.

There are controversies relating to each of the major topics. One question is about whether normal distributions are truly typical of the populations of scores for the variables we study in psychology. Another debate, raised by advocates of a "Bayesian" approach to statistics, is whether we should explicitly construct our statistical procedures to take the researcher's initial subjective expectations into account. Finally, the representativeness of the samples that psychologists use, which are typically not obtained through strict random selection, has been contested—though there are also reasons to think that for the topics most psychologists study, this may not matter very much.

Research articles rarely discuss normal curves (except briefly when the distribution at hand seems not to be normal) or probability (except in the context of significance testing, described in Chapter 6). However, procedures of sampling, particularly when the study is a survey, are usually described, and the representativeness of a sample when random sampling could not be used may be discussed.

Key Terms

expected relative frequency	outcome	subjective interpretation
haphazard selection	population	of probability
long-run relative-frequency	population parameters	μ
interpretation of probability	probability (p)	σ
normal curve	random selection	σ^2
normal curve table	sample	
normal distribution	sample statistics	

Practice Problems

These problems involve computation (with the assistance of a calculator). Most real-life statistics problems are done on a computer. But even if you have a computer, do this by hand to ingrain the method in your mind.

For practice in using a computer to solve statistical problems, refer to the computer section of each chapter of the study guide that accompanies this text.

All data are fictional (unless an actual citation is given).

Answers to Set I are given at the back of the book.

SET I

1. Suppose that the population of a particular city was found to have a mean score of 40 and a standard deviation of 5 on a measure of concern about the environment and that these attitude scores are normally distributed. Approximately what percentage of cases has a score (a) above 40, (b) above 45, (c) above 30, (d) above 35, (e) below 40, (f) below 45, (g) below 30, (h) below 35? What is the minimum score a person has to have to be in the top (i) 2%, (j) 16%, (k) 50%, (l) 84%, (m) 98%? (Use the 50%-34%-14% approximations for these problems.)

2. Suppose that it is known that on a particular measure of eye fatigue, the distribution for college students, after 1 h writing on a computer, has a normal distribution. What percentage of students has Z scores (a) below 1.5, (b) above 1.5, (c) below −1.5, (d) above −1.5, (e) above 2.10, (f) below 2.10, (g) above .45, (h) below −1.78, (i) above 1.68?

3. Assuming a normal curve, (a) if a person is in the top 10% of the country on mathematics ability, what is that person's Z score? (b) If the person was in the top 1%, what would be the Z score?

4. How high a score would a person need to be in the top 5% on a test of coordination that has a normal distribution with a mean of 50 and a standard deviation of 10? Explain your answer to someone who has never had a course in statistics.

5. The following numbers of individuals in a company received special assistance from the personnel department last year:

Drug/alcohol	10
Family crisis counseling	20
Other	20
Total	50

If you were to select a case at random from the records for last year, what is the probability that it would be (a) drug/alcohol, (b) family, (c) drug/alcohol or family, (d) any category except "Other," (e) any of the three categories?

6. A research article describing the level of self-esteem of U.S. high school students emphasizes that it surveyed a "random sample" of high school students. Explain to a person who has never had a course in statistics or research methods what this means and why it is important.

SET II

1. The amount of time it takes to recover physiologically from a particular stimulus is found to be normally distributed with a mean of 80 s and a standard deviation of 10 s. Approximately what percentage of cases has a score (a) above 100, (b) below 100, (c) above 90, (d) below 90, (e) above 80, (f) below 80, (g) above 70, (h) below 70, (i) above 60, (j) below 60? What is the highest score a person can have and still be in the bottom (k) 2%, (l) 16%, (m) 50%, (n) 84%, (o) 98%? (Use the 50%-34%-14% approximations for this problem.)

2. Suppose that on a test of creativity, the scores of architects are normally distributed. What percentage of architects has Z scores (a) above .10, (b) below .10, (b) above .20, (d) below .20, (e) above 1.10, (f) below 1.10, (g) above −.10, (h) below −.10?

3. In the example in Problem 2, what is the minimum Z score an architect can have to be in the (a) top 50%, (b) top 40%, (c) top 60%, (d) top 30%, (e) top 20%?

4. Suppose that you are designing an instrument panel for a large industrial machine that requires one to reach 2 ft from a particular position. The reach from this position for adult women is known to have a mean of 2.8 ft with a standard deviation of .5, and the reach for adult men is known to have a mean of 3.1 ft with a standard deviation of .6. Both men's and women's reach from this position is normally distributed. If this design is implemented, what percentage of women and what percentage of men will not be able to work on this instrument panel? Explain your answer to a person who has never had a course in statistics.

5. You are conducting a survey at a college with 800 students, 50 faculty members, and 150 administrative staffers. Each of these 1,000 individuals has a single listing in the campus phone directory. If you were to cut up the directory and pull out a listing at random to contact, what is the probability it would be (a) a student, (b) a faculty member, (c) an administrative staffer, (d) a faculty member or administrative staffer, (e) anyone except staff or administration?

6. Suppose that you were going to conduct a survey of visitors to your campus and you wanted the survey to be as representative as possible. How would you select the people to survey, and why would that be your best method?

6

Introduction to Hypothesis Testing

I N Chapter 5, you learned about the normal curve, probability, and the distinction between a sample and a population. In this chapter, we introduce the crucial topic of **hypothesis testing.** Hypothesis testing is a systematic procedure for determining whether the results of an experiment (which studies a sample) provide support for a particular theory or practical innovation (which is thought to be applicable to a population). Hypothesis testing is the central theme in all of the remaining chapters of this book, as it will be in virtually all the research you are likely to encounter in psychology.

hypothesis testing

We should warn you at this point that many students find the most difficult part of the course to be mastering the basic logic of this chapter and the two that follow. This chapter in particular requires some mental gymnastics, and even if you follow everything the first time through, you will be wise to review it thoroughly. Hypothesis testing involves a cluster of ideas that make little sense covered in isolation. So in this chapter you will learn a comparatively large number of ideas all at once. On the positive side, once you have a good grasp of the material in this chapter and the two that follow, your mind will be accustomed to this sort of thing, and the rest of the course should seem easier.

At the same time, we have kept this introduction as simple as possible, putting off what we could to later chapters. For example, real-life psychology research almost always involves samples of many—sometimes a great many—individuals. But in the interest of simplifying the number of ideas you must learn at the outset, all of the examples in this chapter are about studies in which the sample is a single individual. To accomplish that, we have had to create some rather odd examples. Just remember that we are building a foundation that will, by Chapter 9, prepare you to understand hypothesis testing as it is actually carried out.

157

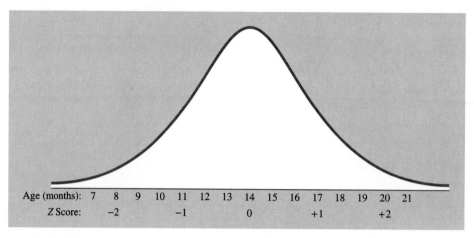

FIGURE 6-1
Distribution of when North American babies begin to walk (fictional data).

A Hypothesis-Testing Example

Here is your first necessarily odd, fictional example. A large research project has been going on for several years in which new babies are given a special vitamin and then their development is monitored during the first 2 years of life. The distribution of ages at which North American babies start to walk is shown in Figure 6-1. Notice that the mean is 14 months, the standard deviation is 3 months, and the ages are normally distributed. Thus, for example, it can be seen that less than 2% (babies who fall 2 standard deviations below the mean) start walking before 8 months of age. (This fictional distribution is actually close to the true distribution psychologists have found for European babies, although that true distribution is slightly skewed to the right; Hindley, Filliozat, Klackenberg, Nicolet-Meister, & Sand, 1966.)

Based on some new theories, one of the researchers working on the project reasons that if the vitamin the babies are taking could be more highly refined, the effect of the vitamin would be dramatically greater—babies taking the highly purified version should start walking much earlier than other babies. (We will assume that it was absolutely clear that the purification process could not possibly make the vitamin harmful.) However, refining the vitamin in this way is enormously expensive for each dose. So the research team decides to try the procedure with enough doses to serve only one baby. A baby in the project is then randomly selected to take the highly purified version of the vitamin, and its progress is followed along with that of all the other babies in the project. What kind of result should lead the researchers to conclude that the highly purified vitamin allows babies to walk earlier?

This is an example of a hypothesis-testing problem. The researchers want to draw a general conclusion about the theory that the purified vitamin permits babies to walk earlier, based on information from a sample (in this strange example, a sample of one baby.)

The Core Logic of Hypothesis Testing

There is a standard way to approach a hypothesis-testing problem. (We will oversimplify in order to emphasize the core logic of how this is done.) The researcher will employ the following reasoning. Ordinarily, the chances of a baby's starting to walk at age 8 months or earlier would be less than 2%. This is highly unlikely. So if the baby in our study starts walking by 8 months, we will be able to *reject* the idea that the specially purified vitamin has *no* effect. And if we reject the idea that the specially purified vitamin has no effect, we must *accept* the idea that it *does* have an effect. (You may want to read this paragraph again.)

Having laid out the conditions under which they can decide whether the special purification procedure makes a difference, the researchers can then proceed to observe how early the baby who takes the specially purified vitamins starts walking and then draw the appropriate conclusions.

This kind of opposite-of-what-you-predict, roundabout reasoning is at the heart of inferential statistics in psychology. It is not unlike a double negative. One reason for this approach is that the hypothesis of no difference is one for which we may have the information needed. In the case of our purified vitamin example, the researchers know what the probabilities of babies' walking at different ages are if the special purification process does not have an effect—it is simply the probability of a baby's walking at various ages that is already known from examining babies who have not received the specially purified vitamin (the distribution shown in Figure 6-1).

It turns out, however, that without such an admittedly tortuous way of going at the problem, in most cases the problem simply can't be solved at all. In our example, it would be very difficult, with the information available, to draw any meaningful conclusions about whether the vitamin purified by the special process does cause babies to walk early. And, as you will see in later chapters, this is not something unique to this bizarre example.

In virtually all cases of research in psychology, whether involving experiments, surveys, or whatever, we draw conclusions by evaluating the probability of getting our research results if the opposite of what we are predicting were true.

The Hypothesis-Testing Process

Next we will again examine the solution to our sample problem, considering each step in some detail as well as introducing you to the special terminology used.

Step 1: Reframing the Questions Into a Research Hypothesis and a Null Hypothesis About the Populations

First, note that the researchers are interested in the effects on babies in general (not just this individual case), so it will be useful to frame the question in terms of populations. That is, for purposes of analyzing the present situation, we can think of babies as falling into two groups:

Population 1: Babies who take the specially purified vitamin
Population 2: Babies who do not take the specially purified vitamin

(Note that although there is only one real-life case of Population 1, it represents an as-yet-unborn future group of many babies to whom the researchers want to apply their results.)

The prediction of the psychologist, based on theory, is that Population 1 babies (those who take the specially purified vitamin) will generally walk earlier than Population 2 babies (those who do not take the specially purified vitamin). A statement like this, about the relation between populations predicted by a theory (or based on practical experience), is called a **research hypothesis.**

research hypothesis

If the prediction is wrong, however, then an opposite situation holds: Population 1 babies (those who take the specially purified vitamin) will generally *not* walk earlier than Population 2 babies (those who do not take the specially purified vitamin). This opposite prediction is that there is no difference in when Population 1 and Population 2 babies start walking—they start at the same time. A statement like this, about a relation between populations that represents the crucial *opposite* of the research hypothesis, is called a **null hypothesis.** The null hypothesis has this name because it is usually used to indicate a situation in which there is no difference (the difference is null) between two populations.[1]

null hypothesis

Note that the research hypothesis and the null hypothesis are opposites and mutually exclusive—if one is true, the other cannot be true. This oppositeness is at the heart of the hypothesis-testing process. In fact, because this oppositeness and the whole idea of the null hypothesis are so central to the hypothesis-testing logic, the research hypothesis, which holds that there is a difference between groups and is thus the opposite of the null hypothesis, is often called the "alternative hypothesis." The situation is actually a bit ironic. From the standpoint of our interest in the issues, it is the research hypothesis we care most about. But from the point of view of hypothesis testing, the chief role of the research hypothesis has become its status as the alternative to the null hypothesis.

Step 2: Determining the Characteristics of the Comparison Distribution

Now that the question has been framed in terms of a choice between a research hypothesis and a null hypothesis, the next step is to consider how the information we can obtain about a sample might relate to these hypotheses. The question we ask is this: Given a particular sample value (in this case, one score), what is the probability of obtaining it if the null hypothesis is true?

[1]Considering that the research hypothesis is that Population 1 babies would walk earlier than Population 2 babies, the null hypothesis is actually that Population 1 babies will walk either at the same time as *or later than* Population 2 babies. This subtlety of oppositeness will be considered at the end of the chapter. For now, to simplify learning, we will sometimes act as if the null hypothesis implies that the two populations are essentially the same and sometimes as if it implies that the one population is the same as *or* in the opposite direction of the research hypothesis.

The answer lies in assuming that the sample was selected from the distribution that represents the situation in which the null hypothesis is true. And in this case, the characteristics of that distribution are known: It has a particular mean and standard deviation, and in our example, as is assumed in most cases, it is an approximately normal distribution. Thus we can calculate the probability that any particular sample could have been drawn randomly from such a distribution.

In the purified-vitamin example, if the null hypothesis is true, the baby we test comes from a population that follows a normal curve with a mean of 14 months and a standard deviation of 3 months. This is the case because if the null hypothesis is true, Populations 1 and 2 are the same and thus have the characteristics already known to be true of Population 2 (which was shown in Figure 6-1). Knowing that this distribution follows a normal curve with a mean of 14 and a standard deviation of 3 allows us to determine the precise probability of getting a sample in any particular section of this distribution. For example, the probability of getting a baby who starts walking at 14 months or earlier is 50%, the probability of getting a baby who walks before 11 months (that is, has a Z score of -1 or less) is 16% (50% minus the 34% between the mean and 1 standard deviation below the mean), and so forth.

In this book, the distribution representing the situation if the null hypothesis is true—the distribution to which you compare your sample—will be called the **comparison distribution.** (It is also sometimes called a "statistical model" and in most cases also corresponds to what is called a "sampling distribution," a distribution of a characteristic of samples—an idea we discuss in Chapter 7.) In the present example, the comparison distribution is simply the same as the distribution of cases in Population 2, the population in which the experimental procedure has not been applied. The general principle is that after stating the null hypothesis (in Step 1), the next step (Step 2) is to determine the distribution to which you can compare your sample under the assumption that the null hypothesis is true.

comparison distribution

Step 3: Determining the Cutoff Sample Score on the Comparison Distribution at Which the Null Hypothesis Should Be Rejected

Ideally, well before making an observation, researchers consider what kind of observation would be sufficiently extreme to reject the null hypothesis. In the present case, the researchers might decide, for example, that if the null hypothesis were true (meaning that it doesn't matter whether a baby is fed the specially purified vitamin or not), observing a baby who walks at 8 months or earlier would be very unlikely. That is, being 2 standard deviations below the mean, walking at 8 months could occur less than 2% of the time. Thus by examining the comparison distribution, the researchers can decide, even before making their observation of a baby who takes the specially purified vitamin, that *if* the result of their observation is a baby who walks before 8 months, they will reject the null hypothesis.

However, if the baby the researchers study does not start walking until after 8 months, they *cannot* feel confident in accepting the null hypothesis. Such a result—failing to get a result sufficiently extreme to reject the null hypothesis—only makes the experiment inconclusive. It doesn't prove anything. We will have more to say about this later.

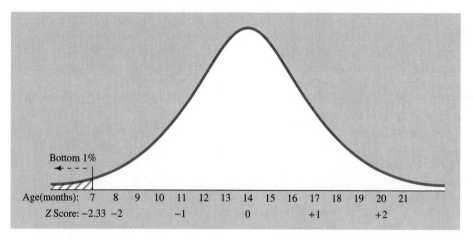

FIGURE 6-2
Distribution of when North American babies begin to walk, with bottom 1% indicated (fictional data).

In practice, researchers do not generally use an actual number of units on the direct scale of measurement (in this case, months); instead, they state how extreme a score should be in terms of a probability value and its associated Z score. In this case, the researchers might decide that if a result were less likely than 2%, they would reject the null hypothesis. Since 2% corresponds to a Z score of about –2, they would set –2 as their Z score cutoff point on the comparison distribution for deciding that a result is sufficiently extreme to reject the null hypothesis. (The **cutoff sample score** is also known as the "critical value.")

Suppose that the researchers are even more cautious than this and decide that they will reject the null hypothesis only if they get a result that could occur by chance 1% of the time or less. They could then figure out, using the normal curve table, that to have a score in the lower 1% of a normal curve, one needs a Z score of –2.33 or less. (In our example, a Z score of –2.33 corresponds to 7 months.) In Figure 6-2, we have shaded the 1% of the comparison distribution in which a sample would be considered so extreme that the possibility that it came from a distribution like this would be rejected.

In general, psychology researchers use a cutoff on the comparison distribution that corresponds to a probability of 5% that a score will be at least that extreme. That is, the null hypothesis is rejected if the probability of obtaining one's result—if the null hypothesis were true—is less than 5%. This probability is usually written as "$p < .05$." However, in some areas of research, or when researchers want to be especially cautious, they use a cutoff of 1% ($p < .01$).

These are called **conventional levels of significance** and are described as the .05 significance level or the .01 significance level. When a sample value is so extreme that the null hypothesis is rejected, the result is said to have attained **statistical significance.** We discuss the issues in deciding on the significance level to use in more detail in Chapters 7 and 8.

cutoff sample score

conventional levels of significance

statistical significance

Step 4: Determining Your Sample's Score on the Comparison Distribution

Once the researcher has determined the Z score that a sample would have to reach on the comparison distribution in order for the null hypothesis to be rejected, the next step is to conduct the study and observe the actual sample's raw score result. The researcher then determines what that score's Z score would be on the comparison distribution.

Let us assume that the researchers followed the baby's progress, and it turns out that the baby starts walking at 6 months. Recall that the mean of the comparison distribution to which we are comparing these results is 14 months and the standard deviation is 3 months. Thus a baby who walks at 6 months is 8 months below the mean, which is $2\frac{2}{3}$ standard deviations below the mean. Thus the Z score for the sample baby on the comparison distribution is -2.67. Figure 6-3 shows the location of our sample baby on the comparison distribution.

Step 5: Deciding Whether or Not to Reject the Null Hypothesis

This step is entirely mechanical once it is clear (a) what Z score the sample must have on the comparison distribution to reject the null hypothesis and (b) the actual Z score of the sample. To determine whether or not to reject the null hypothesis, you compare the needed Z score to the actual Z score. In this case, suppose that the researchers determined that the null hypothesis would be rejected if the Z score of the sample was lower than -2. Since the actual result was -2.67, which is lower than -2, the null hypothesis is rejected.

FIGURE 6-3
Distribution of when North American babies begin to walk, indicating both the bottom 1% and the single case of the baby representing the sample (fictional data).

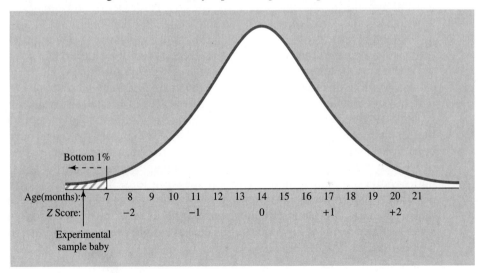

(Had they chosen to use the more conservative 1% significance level, the needed Z score would have been −2.33. Since the actual Z was −2.67, even with this more conservative rule, the null hypothesis would still be rejected.)

If the null hypothesis is rejected, what remains is the research hypothesis. Thus the team of psychologists can conclude that the results of the study *support the research hypothesis.*

Implications of Rejecting or Failing to Reject the Null Hypothesis

Two points should be emphasized about interpreting conclusions from the hypothesis-testing process. First, note that even if the null hypothesis is rejected and the research hypothesis is supported (as in our example), researchers would not say that the result "proves" the research hypothesis or that the results show that the research hypothesis is "true." These conclusions are too strong, since results always involve probabilities based on samples in order to support conclusions about populations. *Proven* and *true* are reserved for logic and mathematics; to use these words in a description of conclusions drawn from scientific research is thoroughly unprofessional. (It is okay to use *true* when speaking hypothetically—for example, "*if* this hypothesis were true, then . . ."—but not when speaking of an actual result.)

Second, when results are *not* sufficiently extreme to reject the null hypothesis, we do not say that the results "support the null hypothesis." Such results mean only that the experiment was inconclusive. Although the results may not be extreme enough to reject the null hypothesis, the null hypothesis might still be false (and conversely, the research hypothesis true). Suppose, for example, that in our example the specially purified vitamin had only a slight but still real effect. In that case, we would not expect to find any single baby given the purified vitamin to walk a lot earlier than other babies. The best way for the researchers to check out this possibility of a slight effect would be to do a study involving many babies receiving the purified vitamin. If most of those began walking even slightly earlier than the average for babies in general, we might begin to be convinced that the null hypothesis was untenable. (We consider the logic of these situations in which samples involve more than a single case in Chapter 7.)

The point is that to demonstrate that the null hypothesis is true requires evidence supporting the proposition that there is really no difference (or a difference in the opposite direction) between the populations. But it is always possible that there is a difference much smaller than what the particular study was able to detect. Therefore, when a result fails to be sufficiently extreme to reject the null hypothesis, researchers generally say only that the results are inconclusive. Sometimes, however, if many studies have been done using large numbers and accurate measuring procedures, evidence may build up in support of the approximate accuracy of a particular null hypothesis. And sometimes, when speaking loosely, researchers will describe a failure to reject a null hypothesis as a result that "supports the null hypothesis." Technically, however, this is usually much too strong a statement as a result of any one study. (We have more to say on this issue in Box 6-1 and in Chapter 8.)

BOX 6-1

"Nothing Happened—It Worked!"

The null hypothesis states that there is no difference between populations represented by different groups or experimental conditions. And as Anthony Greenwald (1975) points out, there are some long-standing assumptions about the null hypothesis: that no real conclusion can be drawn from a failure to reject the null hypothesis; that little knowledge is gained from a finding that fails to reject the null hypothesis because science advances by finding differences, not by finding a lack of them; and that if the null hypothesis appears true, the odds are that the experiment was not done properly—the number of subjects was not large enough, or random "noise" got in.

But there is always a possibility that the null hypothesis represents a correct picture of reality. Of course, it is not likely that a difference is exactly zero or null. But neither is it likely that the difference is any other exact value. If it falls somewhere around zero, however, it may mean that the reality is that what difference there is is largely trivial. This is important knowledge.

Yet, according to Greenwald, null results are systematically underrepresented in the psychology research literature for several reasons. First, researchers pursue only nonnull hypotheses to begin with. Second, if they obtain null results, they do not write them up for publication but may keep fiddling with measures and conducting new studies in the hope of eventually obtaining significance, rarely considering that there may be no significant difference, which is interesting in itself. Third, editors of psychology journals in which scientific reports are published seem more likely to reject papers submitted to them if the researchers failed to reject the null hypothesis. Such findings are considered dull and perhaps reflective of researcher inexperience. And once a paper has been rejected for publication at one such journal, if it contained null results a researcher is much less likely to try to publish it elsewhere.

Greenwald cites several examples of research topics in social psychology that at first seemed to show real differences but eventually proved to be null. For example, between 1939 and 1958, at least 10 studies found that subjects exposed to information on a controversial topic would learn it more easily if the information agreed somewhat with their existing attitude—and this "fact" was reported in many psychology textbooks. But the idea failed to be supported in the next decade, with more in-depth study, and it was finally abandoned. Its embarrassingly long life was apparently due to the fact that in the first studies, the finding was only near significance (such as $p < .10$) but was reported as a side issue in other studies. Once the phenomenon was in print, researchers continued to report and editors to print results rejecting the null hypothesis and unintentionally paid less attention to null results when they were found.

Greenwald's advice is that researchers should be open to any outcome of their research. When planning a study, they should think ahead about the possibility of obtaining a result that fails to reject the null hypothesis and what information that would add to psychology. Also, if a null result arises from well-planned research, it should not be construed as a failure. Instead, it should prompt further research to see if there may indeed be little or no difference. (In fact, as we will see in Chapter 8, it is sometimes possible to provide fairly good evidence in favor of something like the null hypothesis, even in a single study.)

Greenwald wrote his article in the 1970s. Is his advice being taken in the 1990s? The answer seems to be no. Although new controversies continue about the null hypothesis (see Chapter 8), it is still rare to see a research article in a major journal in which the main result is that there is no significant difference between groups.

Summary of the Steps of Hypothesis Testing

Here is a summary of the five steps of hypothesis testing:

1. Reframe the question into a research hypothesis and a null hypothesis about the populations.
2. Determine the characteristics of the comparison distribution.
3. Determine the cutoff sample score on the comparison distribution at which the null hypothesis should be rejected.
4. Determine the score of your sample on the comparison distribution.
5. Compare the scores obtained in Steps 3 and 4 to decide whether to reject the null hypothesis.

Another Example of Hypothesis Testing

Here is another fictional example. Two happy-go-lucky personality psychologists are examining the theory that happiness arises from positive experiences. In particular, these researchers argue that if people have something very fortunate happen to them, they will become very happy and stay happy for a long time. So the researchers plan the following experiment: A person will be randomly selected from the North American adult public and given $1 million. Six months later, this person's happiness will be measured. It is already known (in this fictional example) what the distribution of happiness is like in the general population of North American adults, and this is shown in Figure 6-4. On the test being used, the mean happiness score is 70, the standard deviation is 10, and the distribution is approximately normal.

The psychologists now proceed following the same hypothesis-testing procedure illustrated in the purified-vitamin example. The researchers will consider how happy the person would have to be before they can confidently reject the null hypothesis (that receiving that much money does not make people happier 6 months later). If the result that the researchers obtain shows a very high level of happiness at that time, the psychologists would

FIGURE 6-4
Distribution of happiness scores (fictional data).

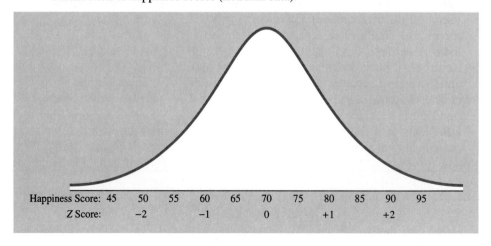

reject the null hypothesis and conclude that getting $1 million probably does make people happier 6 months later. But if the result is not very extreme, these researchers would conclude that there is not sufficient evidence to reject the null hypothesis, and the results of the experiment are therefore inconclusive.

Now let us examine the hypothesis-testing procedure in more detail in this example, following the steps summarized earlier.

1. Reframe the question into a research hypothesis and a null hypothesis about the populations. The populations of interest are these:

Population 1: People who 6 months ago received $1 million
Population 2: People who 6 months ago did not receive $1 million

The prediction of the personality psychologists, based on this theory of happiness, is that Population 1 people will generally be happier than Population 2 people. The null hypothesis is that Population 1 people (those who get $1 million) will not be happier than Population 2 people (those who do not get $1 million).

2. Determine the characteristics of the comparison distribution. Eventually we want to compare our score to the situation that would arise if the null hypothesis is true (to see if we can reject that scenario). If the null hypothesis is true, the distributions of both Populations 1 and 2 are the same. We know what Population 2's distribution is, so it can serve as the comparison distribution.

3. Determine the cutoff sample score on the comparison distribution at which the null hypothesis should be rejected. What kind of observation would be sufficiently convincing to reject the null hypothesis? In the present case, let's assume that the researchers decided in advance to reject the null hypothesis as too unlikely if the results obtained could occur less than 5% of the time if this null hypothesis were true. Because we know that the comparison distribution is a normal curve, we can find from the normal curve table that the top 5% of cases begin at a Z score of about 1.64. So the researchers might set as the cutoff point for rejecting the null hypothesis a result in which the sample's Z score on the comparison distribution is at or above +1.64. (Since the mean of the comparison distribution is 70 and the standard deviation is 10, the null hypothesis would be rejected if the sample result was at or above 86.4. That is, following the usual rule for converting a Z score to a raw score, $1.64 \times 10 = 16.4$, which when added to the mean of 70 gives 86.4.)

50% - 5% = 45% => Z = 1.64

4. Determine the score of your sample on the comparison distribution. Now for the results: Six months after giving this randomly selected person $1 million, the researchers give their now wealthy subject the happiness test. The person's score is 80. As can be seen from Figure 6-4, a score of 80 has a Z score of +1 on the comparison distribution.

5. Compare the scores obtained in Steps 3 and 4 to decide whether to reject the null hypothesis. Since the minimum Z score needed to reject the null hypothesis has been set at +1.64 (the Z score appropriate to the 5% significance level) and since the Z score of our sample case is only +1, our sample is not extreme enough to provide grounds for rejecting the null hypothesis. Thus the null hypothesis cannot be rejected, and the results of the experiment are inconclusive. Researchers might also say the same thing

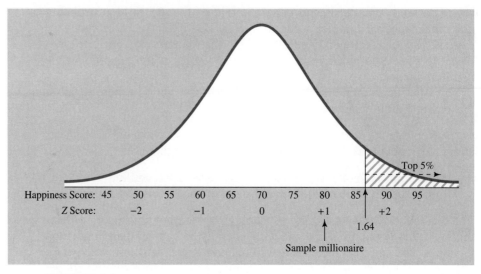

FIGURE 6-5
Distribution of of happiness scores with upper 5% shaded and showing the location of the sample millionaire (fictional data).

by noting that the results were "not statistically significant." Figure 6-5 shows the comparison distribution with the top 5% shaded and the location of our sample millionaire indicated.

You may be interested to know that Brickman, Coates, and Janoff-Bulman (1978) conducted a more elaborate study based on the same question, in which they studied lottery winners as examples of people suddenly having a very good event happen to them. Their results were similar to those in our fictional example, with the group winning the money being not much happier 6 months later than people who did not win the money. Also, another group they studied, people who had become paraplegics through a random accident, were found to be not much less happy than other people 6 months later. Because these researchers used comparatively large numbers of subjects and studied the issue in several different ways, their results suggest that if a major event does have a lasting effect on happiness, it is probably not a very big one. So it looks like the lottery isn't the answer.

One-Tailed and Two-Tailed Hypothesis Tests

In the examples of hypothesis testing considered so far, the research hypotheses have been about situations in which there was a clear expectation about whether the population of interest would have higher or lower values than the population to which it was being compared. In the purified-vitamin example, the researchers were interested in whether the baby would walk *earlier* than other babies. In the happiness example, the personality psychologists expected the person who received the $1 million to be *happier* than other people. The researchers in these studies were really not primarily interested in the possibility that giving the specially purified vitamins would cause babies to start walking later or that people getting $1 million might actually become less happy.

Directional Hypotheses and One-Tailed Tests

These studies are examples of **directional hypotheses** because in each case, the researchers proposed a specific direction of the effect. Most research conducted in psychology involves directional hypotheses.

directional hypotheses

It is important to notice that when a researcher puts forward a directional hypothesis, the appropriate null hypothesis is also, in a sense, directional. If the research hypothesis is that getting $1 million will make a person happier, the null hypothesis is that the money will either have no effect or make the person less happy. Thus, as was shown, for example, in Figure 6-5, for the null hypothesis to be rejected, the sample had to have a score in the top 5%—the upper extreme or tail of the comparison distribution. (A score at the other tail would be considered the same as a score in the middle for purposes of rejecting the null hypothesis or not.) For this reason, tests of directional hypotheses are called **one-tailed tests.**

one-tailed tests

Nondirectional Hypotheses and Two-Tailed Tests

Sometimes, however, a research hypothesis is simply that one population will differ from the other, without specifying whether it will differ by having higher scores or lower scores. For example, an industrial psychologist may be interested in the impact of a social skills program on productivity. It is possible that the program will improve productivity by making the working environment more pleasant. But it is also possible that it will hurt productivity by encouraging people to socialize instead of work. Thus the research hypothesis would simply be that the skills program changes the level of productivity. The null hypothesis would be that the program does not affect productivity one way or the other.

Whenever a hypothesis specifies a difference, without predicting the direction of that difference, it is called a **nondirectional hypothesis.** To test the significance of a nondirectional hypothesis, one must examine whether a score is extreme at either tail of the comparison distribution. Hence this is called a **two-tailed test.**

nondirectional hypothesis

two-tailed test

Determining Cutoff Points With Two-Tailed Tests

There is a special complication in a two-tailed test. Suppose that the researcher selects the 5% significance level. With a one-tailed test, the null hypothesis would be rejected if the sample fell in a particular extreme 5% of the comparison distribution. But with a two-tailed test, if the top 5% is used when the score is extreme in the high direction and the bottom 5% is used when a score is extreme in the low direction, there is a total of 10% of the comparison distribution in which the null hypothesis could be rejected. The significance level is really 10%, which most researchers would find too high.

The solution to this problem is that when conducting a two-tailed test, you divide the significance percentage between the two tails. With a 5% significance level, for example, you would reject a null hypothesis only if the sample was so extreme that it was in either the top 2½% or the bottom 2½%. In this way, the chance of the null hypothesis's being true is kept at a total of 5%.

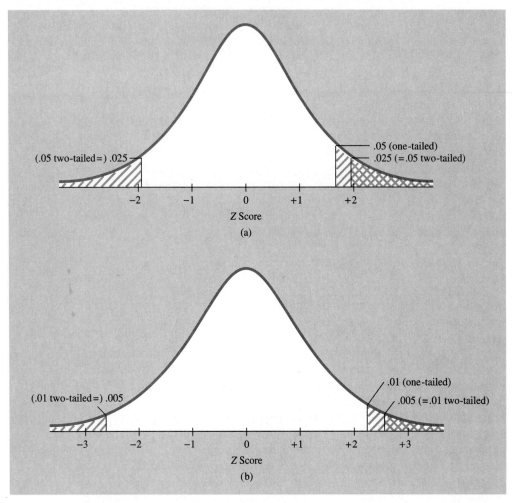

FIGURE 6-6
Comparison of significance level cutoffs for one- and two-tailed tests: (a) .05 significance level; (b) .01 significance level. (The one-tailed tests in these examples assume the prediction was for a high score.)

Note that if the comparison distribution is a normal curve, conducting a two-tailed test makes the cutoff Z scores for the 5% level +1.96 or –1.96. But for a one-tailed test, the cutoff was not so extreme—only +1.64 or –1.64—but only one side of the distribution was considered. These situations are illustrated in Figure 6-6a. Using the 1% significance level, a two-tailed test (.5% at each tail) has cutoffs of +2.58 and –2.58, while a one-tailed test's cutoff is either +2.33 or –2.33 (see Figure 6-6b).

When to Use One-Tailed or Two-Tailed Tests

It is easier to reject the null hypothesis with a one-tailed test, in the sense that a sample result need not be so extreme before an experimental result is significant. But there is a price: With a one-tailed test, if the result is extreme in the other direction, no matter how extreme, the null hypothesis cannot be rejected.

In principle, you plan to use a one-tailed test when you have a clearly directional hypothesis and a two-tailed test when you have a clearly nondirectional hypothesis. In practice, the situation is not so simple. Even when a theory clearly predicts a particular result, we sometimes find that the result is just the opposite of what we expected and that this result may actually be more interesting. (What if, as in all the fairy tales about wish-granting genies and fish, receiving $1 million and being able to fulfill almost any wish had made that one subject miserable? That might have been very interesting indeed.) By using one-tailed tests, we run the risk of having to ignore possibly important results.

Because of these considerations, there is debate as to whether one-tailed tests should be used, even when there is a clearly directional hypothesis. To be safe, many researchers use two-tailed tests for both nondirectional and directional hypotheses. In fact, in most psychology articles, unless the researcher specifically notes that a one-tailed test was used, it is usually assumed that it was a two-tailed test.

You should remember, however, that in most cases, the final conclusion is not really affected by whether a one- or two-tailed test is used. It is our experience that a result is either so extreme that it will be significant by any reasonable standard or so far from extreme that it would not be significant no matter what procedure was used.

What happens when a result yields less certain conclusions? The researcher's decision about one- or two-tailed tests takes on added importance, and the researcher attempts to use the approach that under the circumstances of the research will yield the most accurate (and noncontroversial) conclusion. The idea is to let nature—and not a researcher's decisions—determine the conclusion as much as possible. Furthermore, in any such case where a result is less than completely clear one way or the other, most researchers will not be comfortable drawing strong conclusions until further research is done.

An Example of Hypothesis Testing Using a Two-Tailed Test

Here is one more fictional example, this time using a two-tailed test. Clinical psychologists at a private psychiatric residential treatment center believe that they have developed a new type of therapy that will relieve depression in patients to a greater degree than the therapy now given. However, as with any treatment, one cannot rule out the possibility that a patient might do worse. So the researchers will make a nondirectional hypothesis.

The psychologists will proceed in the following fashion: An incoming patient will be randomly selected to be given the new form of therapy instead of the usual. (In a real study, of course, more than one patient would be selected, but let's assume that only one person has been trained to do the new therapy and she has time to treat only one patient.) The patient's depression will be measured using the Minnesota Multiphasic Personality Inventory (MMPI), which is administered automatically to all patients after 4 weeks. The MMPI has been given at this treatment center for a long time. So it is possible to determine in advance the distribution of scores on the MMPI Depression scale at 4 weeks after entry for patients who have been diagnosed at entry as depressed and who receive the usual therapy. In our fic-

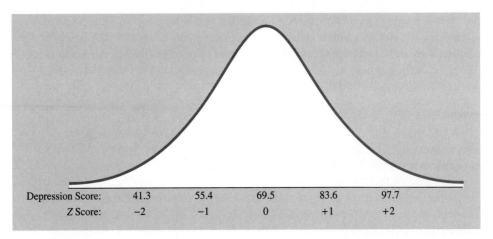

| Depression Score: | 41.3 | 55.4 | 69.5 | 83.6 | 97.7 |
| Z Score: | −2 | −1 | 0 | +1 | +2 |

FIGURE 6-7
Distribution of MMPI Depression scale scores at 4 months after admission for diagnosed depressed psychiatric patients receiving the standard therapy (fictional data).

tional example, that distribution follows a normal curve with a mean of 69.5 and a standard deviation of 14.1 (these figures correspond roughly to those obtained in a national survey of 75,000 psychiatric patients; Dahlstrom, Larbar, & Dahlstrom, 1986). This distribution is shown in Figure 6-7.

The hypothesis-testing procedure is then conducted as follows:

1. Reframe the question into a research hypothesis and a null hypothesis about the populations. The two populations of interest are these:

Population 1: Patients diagnosed as depressed who receive the new therapy
Population 2: Patients diagnosed as depressed who receive the standard therapy

The research hypothesis is that when measured on Depression 4 weeks after admission, patients who receive the new therapy (Population 1) will score differently from patients who receive the current therapy (Population 2). The opposite of the research hypothesis, the null hypothesis, is that patients who receive the new therapy will have the same depression level as the patients who receive the usual therapy. (That is, the null hypothesis is that the depression level measured 4 weeks later is the same for Populations 1 and 2.)

2. Determine the characteristics of the comparison distribution. If the null hypothesis is true, the distributions for Populations 1 and 2 will be the same. We know the distribution of Population 2, so it can serve as our comparison distribution. As noted, it is normally distributed with $\mu = 69.5$ and $\sigma = 14.1$.

3. Determine the cutoff sample score on the comparison distribution at which the null hypothesis should be rejected. The clinical psychologist team selects the 5% significance level. We noted at the outset that the researchers have made a nondirectional hypothesis, so a two-tailed test must be used. This means that the null hypothesis will be rejected only if the patient's Depression score on the comparison distribution is in either the top or bot-

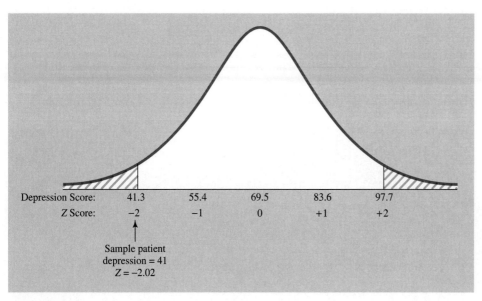

FIGURE 6-8
Distribution of MMPI Depression scale scores with upper and lower $2\frac{1}{2}\%$ shaded and showing the sample patient who received the new therapy (fictional data).

tom $2^{1}/_{2}\%$ of the comparison distribution. In terms of Z scores, these cutoffs are thus +1.96 and –1.96 (see Figure 6-8).

4. Determine the score of your sample on the comparison distribution. The patient who received the new therapy was measured 4 weeks after admission. The patient's score on the MMPI Depression scale was 41. This corresponds to a Z score on the comparison distribution of –2.02.

5. Compare the scores obtained in Steps 3 and 4 to decide whether to reject the null hypothesis. A Z score of –2.02 is just below the Z score of –1.96, which is where the lower $2^{1}/_{2}\%$ of the comparison distribution begins. This is a result so extreme that it is unlikely to have occurred if this patient represented a population no different from Population 2. Therefore, the clinical psychologists reject the null hypothesis. This result supports their research hypothesis that the new therapy does indeed change patients' depression level as measured by the MMPI.

Controversies and Limitations

We have already noted that there is some debate about whether one- or two-tailed tests should be preferred. Everyone agrees that two-tailed tests should be used in exploratory research or in studies in which there are equally good reasons to expect results in either direction. But when there is a clear basis for predicting a result in a given direction, some psychologists prefer the one-tailed test. After all, it fits with the logic of the situation: A theory is being tested, and if results come out opposite to the theory, that adds no more information than if the results simply fail to come out in the predicted direction. In either case, the theory is not supported. However, when a result opposite to what is expected does come about, the unexpected result may be

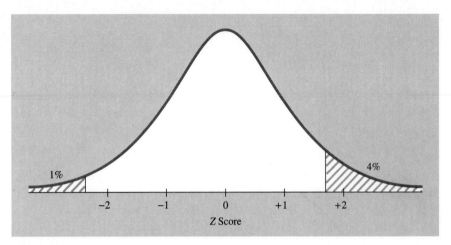

FIGURE 6-9
Normal curve with significance levels suggested by Aron and Gilmore (1992).

of considerable scientific interest, and it may be quite useful to be able to determine whether that unexpected result is more extreme than would have been expected if the null hypothesis were true.

You might think that a good solution is to use one-tailed tests, and if the result comes out in the reverse direction from what was expected, then use a two-tailed test. But this sets up a situation in which the null hypothesis can be rejected too often—if you were using the 5% level, it could be rejected 5% of the time if it was extreme in the originally expected direction and $2^1/2\%$ of the time if it were extreme in the reverse direction, making a total of $7^1/2\%$.

Aron and Gilmore (1992) have suggested that psychologists use a compromise procedure. In this approach, illustrated in Figure 6-9, the null hypothesis is rejected if the result falls in the extreme 4% in the predicted direction or in the extreme 1% in the reverse direction. (This idea was suggested in seed form by Kaiser, 1960, and was discussed by Cohen, 1962.) This makes a total 5% significance level but still gives "credit" for having a theory predicting a directional effect. Furthermore, it makes sure that an unexpected result is quite extreme before it is taken seriously (with a two-tailed test, it would be considered significant if it was in the extreme $2^1/2\%$, but with the 4% and 1% approach, the unexpected result would have to be in the extreme 1%). This proposal, however, is new and has not yet been adopted by other researchers.

Hypothesis Tests as Reported in Research Articles

In general, hypothesis testing is reported in research articles in the context of one of the specific statistical procedures you learn in later chapters. For each result of interest, the researcher usually first notes whether the result was "statistically significant." Next the researcher usually gives the name of the specific technique used in determining the probabilities, such as a t test or an F test (covered in Chapters 9–13). Finally, there will be an indication of the significance level, such as "$p < .05$" or "$p < .01$." For example, Biner

(1991), who conducted a study of the effect of lighting on the evaluation of potentially aversive (unpleasant) events, reported one result as follows: "Subjects exposed to the bright lighting evaluated the potential outcome . . . as much more aversive than those exposed to the dim lighting, $t(18) = 2.38$, $p < .05$" (p. 222).

When researchers write "$p < .05$," they mean that the probability of their results if the null hypothesis were true is less than .05 (5%). If the result was close but did not reach the significance level chosen, it may be reported anyway as a "near significant trend," with "$p < .10$," for example. If the result is not significant, sometimes the actual p level will be given (for example, "$p = .27$"), or the abbreviation ns, for "not significant," will be used. In addition, if a one-tailed test was used, that will usually also be noted. Again, when reading research articles, assume a two-tailed test if nothing is said otherwise.

Even though a researcher has chosen a significance level in advance, such as .05, results that meet more rigorous standards may be noted as such. (You are supposed to be impressed.) Thus in the same article you may see results in which some are noted as "$p < .05$," others as "$p < .01$," and still others as "$p < .001$," for example.

Finally, in many cases the results of hypothesis testing are shown simply as asterisks in a table of results, in which a result with an asterisk has attained significance and one without one has not. For example, Table 6-1 presents the results of a study by Abrams and Balota (1991) in which subjects were shown a series of letters and had to move a handle a few inches in one direction or its opposite, as quickly as possible, to indicate whether it was or was not a word. Sometimes the series of letters was not a word (a "nonword" in the table), and sometimes it was an actual word that was either commonly used ("high-frequency") or rarely used ("low-frequency"). The

TABLE 6-1
Results of Experiment 1

Dependent Measure	Nonword	Word	
		Low-Frequency	*High-Frequency*
Reaction time (ms)***	626.6	613.1	499.2
Percent correct***	93.0	86.0	98.0
Movement duration (ms)**	136.3	131.8	128.0
Final velocity (cm/s)**	79.5	78.0	80.6
Peak acceleration (cm/s/s)**	151.6	152.9	159.8
20 ms after movement onset			
Position (cm)	.21	.20	.22
Velocity (cm/s)	15.6	15.7	16.3
Acceleration (cm/s/s)**	96.9	96.8	101.6
50 ms after movement onset			
Position (cm)*	1.17	1.17	1.23
Velocity (cm/s)**	47.4	48.4	50.3
Acceleration (cm/s/s)	106.0	108.5	111.0

$*p < .05$. $**p < .005$. $***p < .001$. All comparisons are between high- and low-frequency words using a t test with 19 degrees of freedom and are in the predicted direction. Movement duration is the time interval from movement onset until the handle passed a target location 5.3 cm from the starting location; final velocity is the velocity of the handle at the end of that interval; acceleration is proportional to force. From Abrams, R. A., & Balota, D. A. (1991), tab. 1. Mental chronometry: Beyond reaction time. *Psychological Science*, 2, 153–157. Copyright, 1991, by the American Psychological Society. Reprinted by permission.

point of the study was to replicate earlier studies showing that widely used words are recognized more quickly and also to show that it is not just the initial reaction but also the physical follow-through (in this case, finishing the handle move) that is faster, as shown in the table by the results 20 ms and 50 ms after the decision. The important thing to note in the table for purposes of the present discussion are the asterisks (and the corresponding notes at the bottom of the table) indicating significance levels for the various measures.

Notice that in all of these cases, researchers generally do not make the research hypothesis or the null hypothesis explicit or describe any of the other steps of the process in any detail. It is assumed that the reader understands all of this very well.

Summary

The basic idea of hypothesis testing is to examine the probability that the outcome of a study could have arisen even if the actual situation was that the experimental treatment or comparison made no difference. If this probability is low, the scenario is rejected, and the theory from which the treatment or comparison was proposed is supported. The expectation of a difference or an effect is the research hypothesis, and the hypothetical situation in which there is no difference or effect is the null hypothesis. When an obtained result would be extremely unlikely if the null hypothesis were true, the null hypothesis is said to be rejected and the research hypothesis supported. If the obtained results are not very extreme, the study is said to be inconclusive.

Psychologists usually consider a result too extreme if it is less likely than 5%, though a more stringent 1% cutoff is sometimes used. These percentages may apply to the probability of the result's being extreme in a predicted direction, a directional or one-tailed test, or to the probability of its being extreme in either direction, a nondirection or two-tailed test.

The hypothesis-testing process involves five steps:

1. Reframe the question into a research hypothesis and a null hypothesis about the populations.
2. Determine the characteristics of the comparison distribution.
3. Determine the cutoff sample score on the comparison distribution at which the null hypothesis should be rejected.
4. Determine the score of your sample on the comparison distribution.
5. Compare the scores obtained in Steps 3 and 4 to decide whether to reject the null hypothesis.

A continuing controversy is about when it is appropriate to use a one-tailed test, a two-tailed test, or possibly a combination in which there is more of the percentage at one tail.

Research articles typically report the results of hypothesis testing by noting that a result was or was not significant and giving the probability level cutoff (usually 5% or 1%) at which the decision was made.

Key Terms

comparison distribution
conventional levels of significance ($p < .05$, $p < .01$)
cutoff sample score

directional hypothesis
hypothesis testing
nondirectional hypothesis
null hypothesis

one-tailed test
research hypothesis
statistical significance
two-tailed test

Practice Problems

These problems involve computation (with the assistance of a calculator). Most real-life statistics problems are done on a computer. But even if you have a computer, do this by hand to ingrain the method in your mind.

For practice in using a computer to solve statistical problems, refer to the computer section of each chapter of the study guide that accompanies this text.

All data are fictional (unless an actual citation is given). Answers to Set I are given at the back of the book.

Study	Population		Sample Score	p	Tails of Test
	μ	σ			
A	10	2	14	.05	1 (high predicted)
B	10	2	14	.05	2
C	10	2	14	.01	1 (high predicted)
D	10	2	14	.01	2
E	10	4	14	.05	1 (high predicted)
F	10	1	14	.01	2
G	10	2	16	.01	2
H	12	2	16	.01	2
I	12	2	8	.05	1 (low predicted)

SET I

1. Define the following terms in your own words: (a) research hypothesis, (b) null hypothesis, (c) hypothesis testing procedure, (d) comparison distribution, (e) .05 significance level, (f) one-tailed test.

2. For each of the following, (a) indicate what two populations are being compared, (b) state the research hypothesis, (c) state the null hypothesis, and (d) say whether you should use a one-tailed or two-tailed test and why.

(i) Do Canadian children whose parents are librarians do better than Canadian children in general on reading ability?

(ii) Is the level of income for residents of a particular city different from the level of income for people in the region?

(iii) Do people who have experienced an earthquake have more or less self-confidence than the general population?

3. Based on the information given for each of the following studies, determine whether or not to reject the null hypothesis. In each case, give the Z-score cutoff on the comparison distribution at which the null hypothesis should be rejected, the Z score on the comparison distribution for the sample score, and the conclusion. (Assume that all populations are normally distributed.)

4. A psychologist interested in the senses of taste and smell has conducted an extensive set of studies in which individuals are given each of 20 different foods (apricot, chocolate, cherry, coffee, garlic, etc.), each in the form of a liquid dropped on the tongue. Over the entire student population at her university, the mean number that students can identify correctly is 14, with a standard deviation of 4. (Let's assume that somehow all the students at this college had been tested—perhaps as a part of a medical screening at the start of each year). The psychologist has reason to believe that people's success has more to do with smell than with taste. So she sets up special procedures that keep the person from being able to use the sense of smell during the test. The psychologist then tries the procedure on one randomly selected student. This student is able to identify only 5 correctly. Using the .05 significance level, what should the researcher conclude? Explain your answer to someone who has never had a course in statistics.

5. A psychologist working with people who have undergone a particular type of major surgery proposed that people will recover from the operation more quickly if friends and family are in the room with them for the first 48 hours after the operation. It is known (in this fictional example) that time to recover is normally distributed with a mean of 12 days and a standard deviation of 5 days. The procedure is tried with a randomly selected patient, and this patient recovers in 18 days. Using the .01 significance level, what should the researcher conclude? Explain your answer to someone who is familiar with mean, standard deviation, Z scores, and the normal curve but doesn't know anything else about statistics or hypothesis testing.

6. Pecukonis (1990), as part of a larger study, measured ego development (a measure of overall maturity) and ability to empathize with others among a group of 24 aggressive adolescent girls in a residential treatment center. The girls were divided into high and low ego development groups, and the empathy ("cognitive empathy") scores of these two groups were compared. In his Results section, Pecukonis reported, "The average score on cognitive empathy for subjects scoring high on ego development was 22.1 as compared with 16.3 for low scorers, . . . $p < .005$" (p. 68). Explain this result to a person who has never had a course in statistics. (Focus on the meaning of this result in terms of the general logic of hypothesis testing and statistical significance.)

SET II

1. List the steps of the hypothesis-testing process, and explain the procedure and rationale of each.

2. For each of the following, (a) indicate what two populations are being compared, (b) state the research hypothesis, (c) state the null hypothesis, and (d) say whether you should use a one-tailed or two-tailed test and why.

(i) In an experiment, people are instructed to solve a problem by focusing on the details. Is the speed of solving the problem different for people who get such instructions compared to people who are given no special instructions?

(ii) Based on anthropological reports in which the status of women is scored on a 10-point scale, the mean and standard deviation across many cultures are known. A new culture is found in which there is an unusual family arrangement. The status of women is also rated in this culture. Do cultures with the unusual family arrangement provide higher status to women than cultures in general?

(iii) Do people who live in big cities develop more stress-related conditions than people in general?

3. Based on the information for each of the following studies, determine whether or not to reject the null hypothesis.

Study	Population		Sample Score	p	Tails of Test
	μ	σ			
A	100.0	10.0	80	.05	1 (low predicted)
B	74.3	11.8	80	.01	2
C	16.9	1.2	80	.05	1 (low predicted)
D	88.1	12.7	80	.05	2

4. A researcher has discovered that certain sounds will make rats much more aggressive and predicts that the sounds will also make them do worse on learning tasks. Assume that it is known that an ordinary, average rat can learn to run a particular maze correctly on 18 trials, with a standard deviation of 6. The researcher now tries an ordinary rat on the maze, but with the sound. The rat takes 38 trials to learn the maze. Using the .05 level, what should the researcher conclude? Explain your answer to someone who is familiar with mean, standard deviation and Z scores but doesn't know anything else about statistics or hypothesis testing.

5. A family psychologist has developed an elaborate training program to help the adjustment of men who marry women with adolescent children. Assume that it is known from previous research that such men, 1 month after moving in with a new wife and her children, have a stress level of 85 with a standard deviation of 15. As a pilot experiment, the training program is tried on one man randomly selected from all those in a particular city who during the preceding month have married a woman with an adolescent child. After the training program this man's stress level is 60. Using the .05 level, what should the researcher conclude? Explain your answer to someone who has never had a course in statistics.

6. Dykman, Horowitz, Abramson, and Usher (1991), as part of a larger study, compared the social competence self-ratings of 60 college students who scored low on a standard depression scale to 60 who scored high on that scale. They reported the results of this comparison in the first line of a table (see Table 6-2) which also includes comparisons on a number of other measures. Focusing just on this first line, and also ignoring the numbers—but not the stars—in the "$t(118)$" column, explain what this result means to a person who has never had a course in statistics. (Focus on the meaning of this result in terms of the general logic of hypothesis testing and statistical significance.)

TABLE 6-2
Group Means on Major Variables

Variable	Nondepressed		Depressed		
	M	SD	M	SD	t(118)
Social competence self-rating	1.62	0.69	2.88	1.09	−7.60**
Importance rating	2.13	0.95	2.07	1.05	0.72
Self-ranking of performance	2.48	0.70	3.07	0.71	−4.53**
Peers' ranking of performance	2.12	1.02	2.69	1.06	−3.01*
Confederates' ranking of performance	2.30	0.80	2.70	0.80	−2.68*
Interpretation of ambiguous feedback pairs	2.82	0.15	3.00	0.20	−5.38**
Interpretation of written feedback	4.58	2.22	3.25	2.44	3.13*

Note. Except for interpretation of written feedback, lower numbers indicate more positive ratings. For self-, peers', and confederates' rankings of performance, the possible range of rankings is 1–4, wherein lower numbers indicate higher rankings. For interpretation of ambiguous feedback pairs, the possible range of mean values is 2.50–3.50, wherein 3.00 represents the unbiased mean value. *p < .01. **p < .001. Data from Dykman, B. M., Abramson, L. Y., Horowitz, L. M., & Usher, M. (1991), tab. 1. Schematic and situational determinants of depressed and nondepressed students' interpretation of feedback. *Journal of Abnormal Psychology*, *100*, 45–55. Copyright, 1991, by The American Psychological Association. Reprinted by permission of the author.

7

Hypothesis Tests With Means of Samples

IN Chapter 6, we introduced the basic logic of hypothesis testing, illustrating the principles with examples of studies in which the sample was a single individual. As we noted, however, in actual practice, psychology research usually involves a sample of many. In this chapter, we build on what you have learned so far and consider the central ideas associated with hypothesis testing involving a sample of more than one. Mainly this requires examining in some detail what we call a distribution of means.

The Distribution of Means

The procedure of hypothesis testing in the usual research situation, where we are studying a sample of many individuals, is exactly the same as you learned in Chapter 6—with an important exception. When you have more than one subject in your sample, there is a special problem with Step 2, determining the characteristics of the comparison distribution. The problem is that the score of interest in your sample is the mean of the group of scores. But the comparison distributions we have been considering so far have been distributions of populations of individual subjects (such as the population of ages when individual babies start walking or the population of individual scores on a happiness questionnaire). Comparing the mean of a sample of, say, 50 subjects to a distribution of a population of individual scores is a mismatch—like comparing apples and oranges. Instead, when you are interested in the mean of a sample of 50 subjects, you need a comparison distribution that is a distribution of all possible means of samples of 50 subjects. (Read that again.) Such a comparison distribution we will call a **distribution of means.**

distribution of means

181

Put more formally, a distribution of means is a distribution of the means computed on each of a very large number of samples of the same size, randomly drawn from a particular population of individual cases. (Statisticians also call this distribution of means a "sampling distribution of the mean." In this book, however, we use the term *distribution of means* to make it clear that we are discussing populations, not samples or distributions of samples.)

Because the distribution of means is the proper comparison distribution when there is more than one subject in a sample, determining its characteristics is a crucial additional procedure that is necessary in most research situations in order to carry out hypothesis testing.

Constructing a Distribution of Means

The idea of a distribution of means can be understood by considering how one could construct such a distribution from an ordinary population distribution of individual cases. Suppose that our population was of the grade levels of the 90,000 elementary and junior high school children in a particular U.S. state. And suppose further (to keep the example simple) that there are exactly 10,000 children at each grade level, from first through ninth grade. This population distribution would be rectangular, with a mean of 5, a variance of 6.67, and a standard deviation of 2.58 (see Figure 7-1).

Next suppose that you wrote each child's grade level on a table tennis ball and put all 90,000 plastic balls into a giant vat. The vat would contain 10,000 balls with a 1 on them, 10,000 with a 2 on them, and so forth. Stir up the balls in the vat, and then take two of them out. You have taken a random sample of two cases. Suppose that the balls bear a 2 and a 9, respectively. In that case, the mean grade level of your sample of two subjects is 5.5, the average of 2 and 9. Now you put the balls back, mix up all the balls, and select two balls again. Maybe this time you get two 4s, making the mean of your second sample 4. Then you try again; this time you get a 2 and a 7, making your mean 4.5. So far you have three means: 5.5, 4, and 4.5.

These three numbers (each a mean of a sample of grade levels of two schoolchildren) can be described as a distribution, with its own mean (the mean of 5.5, 4, and 4.5, which is 14/3 = 4.67), variance (the variance of 5.5,

FIGURE 7-1
Distribution of grade levels among 90,000 elementary and junior high school students (fictional data).

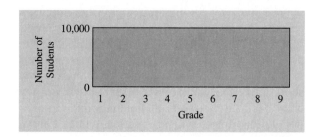

FIGURE 7-2
Distribution of the means of three randomly drawn samples of two cases each from a population of 90,000 elementary and junior high school students (fictional data).

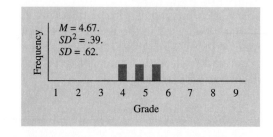

4, and 4.5, which is .39), standard deviation ($\sqrt{.39} = .62$), and shape. A histogram of this distribution of three means is shown in Figure 7-2.

If you continued the process, the histogram of means would continue to grow. An example after 10 random samples of two balls each is shown in Figure 7-3a. Figure 7-3b shows the histogram of the distribution of means after 20 random samples of two each. After 100 random samples, the histogram of the distribution of the means might look like Figure 7-3c; after

FIGURE 7-3
Distributions of the means of randomly selected samples of two cases each from a population of 90,000 balls, consisting of 10,000 bearing each of the numbers from 1 through 9. Numbers of sample means in each distribution shown are (a) 10 sample means, (b) 20 sample means, (c) 100 sample means, and (d) 1,000 sample means. (Actual sampling simulated using computer-generated pseudorandom numbers.)

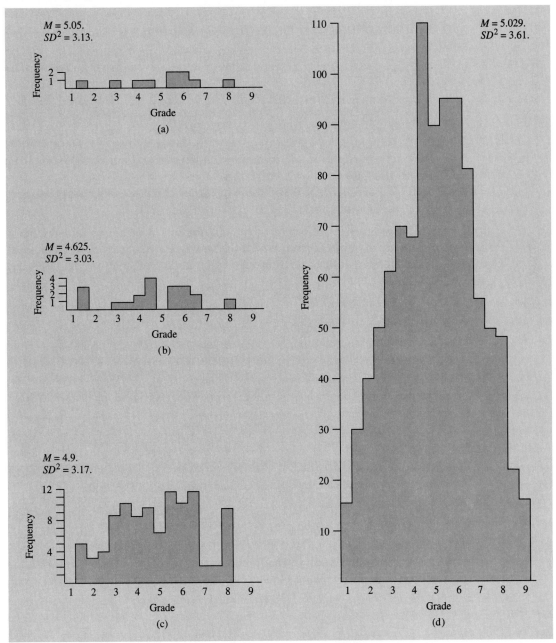

183

1,000, like Figure 7-3d. (We actually constructed the histograms shown in Figure 7-3 by using a computer to make the random selections—instead of using 90,000 table tennis balls and a giant vat.)

In practice, researchers almost never have the opportunity to draw many different samples from a population—it takes considerable effort to obtain a single sample and measure the individuals in it. Fortunately, however, as you will soon see, the characteristics of a distribution of means can be determined directly, using some simple rules, without drawing a single sample. The only knowledge needed is the characteristics of the population distribution of individual cases and the number of cases in each sample. (Don't worry for now about how you could know the characteristics of the population of individual cases.) But although you get the same result, thinking of it in terms of drawing a large number of random samples and computing the mean of each makes it easier to understand what a distribution of means is.

Characteristics of the Distribution of Means

Notice three things about the distribution of means we constructed in our example:

1. The mean of the distribution of means came out to be about the same as the mean of the original population of individual grade levels from which the samples were drawn (5 in both cases).
2. The spread of the distribution of means came out to be less than the spread of the distribution of the population of individual cases from which the samples were drawn.
3. The shape of the distribution of means came out to be approximately normal (or at least unimodal and symmetrical).

These three relationships of the distribution of means to the population of individual subjects from which the samples are drawn are not unique to this example. All three relationships apply in the vast majority of cases, and the first two apply in every case.

These relationships are the foundation for a set of simple mathematical rules that allow you to determine the mean, variance, and shape of a distribution of means without having to write on plastic balls and draw endless samples. As we noted earlier, all you need to know are the characteristics (mean, variance, shape) of the population of individual subjects and the number of subjects in each sample in the distribution of means (in our example there were two subjects in each sample). Let's look more closely at these simple rules.

Determining the Mean of a Distribution of Means

mean of a distribution of means

The **mean of a distribution of means** is the same as the mean of the population of individual cases from which the samples are taken. Because each sample is based on randomly selected values from the population of individual cases, sometimes the mean of a sample will be higher and sometimes lower than the mean of the whole population of individuals. However, there is no *systematic* reason for the means of these samples to tend to be higher or lower than the mean of the population. If enough samples are taken, the high values and low values balance each other out.

Determining the Variance of a Distribution of Means

As we said, a distribution of means will be less spread out than the population of individual cases from which the samples are taken. The reason for this is as follows: Any one score, even an extreme score, has some chance of being selected in a random sample. But the chance is less of two extreme scores being selected in the same random sample, particularly since to create an extreme sample mean, they would have to be two scores that were extreme in the same direction. So there is a moderating effect of increasing numbers. In any one sample, the deviants tend to be balanced out by middle cases or by deviants in the opposite direction, making each sample tend toward the middle and away from extreme values. With fewer extreme values for the means, the variance of the means is less.

Consider our example. There were plenty of 1s and 9s in the population, making a fair amount of spread. That is, about a ninth of the time, if you were taking samples of single scores, you would get a 1, and about a ninth of the time you would get a 9. But if you are taking samples of two at a time, you would get a sample with a mean of 1 (that is, in which *both* balls were 1s) or a mean of 9 (both balls being 9s) much less often. The chances of getting two balls that average out to a middle value such as 5 is much more likely (since several combinations could give this result—a 1 and a 9, a 2 and an 8, a 3 and a 7, a 4 and a 6, and two 5s).

The more cases in each sample, the less spread out the distribution of means of that sample size. This is because with a larger number of cases in each sample, it is even rarer for extreme cases in that sample not to be balanced out by middle cases or extremes in the other direction in the same sample. In terms of the plastic balls, we saw that it was fairly unlikely to get a mean of 1 when taking samples of two balls at a time. If we were taking three balls at a time, getting a sample with a mean of 1 (all three balls would have to be 1s) is even less likely, and getting middle values becomes more likely.

Using samples of two balls at a time, the variance of the distribution of means came out to about 3.33. This is half of the variance of the population of individual cases, which was 6.67. If we had constructed a distribution of means using samples of three balls each, the variance of the distribution of means would have been 2.22, which is one third of the variance of the population of individual cases. Had we randomly selected five balls for each sample, the variance of the distribution of means would have been one fifth of the variance of the population of individual cases.

These examples follow a general rule: The **variance of a distribution of means** is the variance of the distribution of the population of individual cases divided by the number of cases in the samples being selected. This rule holds in all situations and can be mathematically derived. (The proof can be found in any mathematically oriented statistics text.)

variance of a distribution of means

Formula for the Variance of a Distribution of Means

Stated as a formula, here is the rule for determining the variance of the distribution of means:

$$\sigma_M^2 = \frac{\sigma^2}{N} \qquad\qquad (7\text{-}1)$$

where σ_M^2 is the variance of the distribution of means, σ^2 is the variance of the population of individual cases, and N is the number of subjects in each sample.

In our example, the variance of the population of individual grade levels was 6.67, and there were two subjects in each sample. Thus the variance of the distribution of means is computed as follows:

$$\sigma_M^2 = \frac{\sigma^2}{N} = \frac{6.67}{2} = 3.34$$

To use a different example, suppose that the population of interest had a variance of 400 and you wanted to know the variance of a distribution of means of 25 cases each:

$$\sigma_M^2 = \frac{\sigma^2}{N} = \frac{400}{25} = 16$$

Determining the Standard Deviation of a Distribution of Means

standard deviation of a distribution of means

The **standard deviation of a distribution of means** is the square root of the variance of the distribution of means. Stated as a formula,

$$\sigma_M = \sqrt{\sigma_M^2} = \sqrt{\frac{\sigma^2}{N}} \qquad (7\text{-}2)$$

where σ_M is the standard deviation of the distribution of means.

Sometimes this formula is algebraically manipulated to emphasize the relation between standard deviations of the population and of the distribution of means:

$$\sigma_M = \sigma/\sqrt{N} \qquad (7\text{-}3)$$

Because of its importance in hypothesis testing (as you will soon see), the standard deviation of the distribution of means is sometimes called by a special name of its own, the *standard error of the mean*, or the *standard error*, for short. It has this name because it represents the degree to which particular means of samples are typically "in error" as estimates of the mean of the population of individual cases. That is, the standard error of the mean tells you how much the particular means in the distribution of means deviate from the mean of the population (remember, the mean of the population and the mean of the distribution of means are the same). (This idea is applied in estimating error in the results of opinion polls, as described in Box 7-1 on pp. 190–191.)

The Shape of a Distribution of Means

shape of the distribution of means

In general, a distribution of means will tend to be unimodal and symmetrical. In the grade-level example, the population distribution of students at individual grade levels was rectangular (having an equal number of cases at each value). Nevertheless, the **shape of the distribution of means** was roughly that of a bell unimodal and symmetrical—had we taken many more than 1,000 samples, the curve would have been much more clearly unimodal and symmetrical.

A distribution of means tends to be unimodal due to the same basic process of extremes balancing each other out that we noted in the discussion of the variance: Middle values are more likely, and extreme values are less likely. It tends to be symmetrical for the same reason: Because skew is caused primarily by extreme scores, if there are fewer extreme scores, there is less skew. In the grade-level example, the distribution of means we created came out so clearly symmetrical because the population distribution of individual grade levels was symmetrical. But even had the population distribution of individual cases been skewed to one side, the distribution of means would have been closer to symmetrical.

As the number of subjects in each sample gets larger, the distribution of means of all possible samples of that number of subjects is a better and better approximation to the normal curve. In fact, with samples of 30 or more subjects, even with a nonnormal population of individual cases, the approximation of the distribution of means to a normal curve is so close that the percentages in the normal curve table will be extremely accurate.[1,2]

Finally, note that whenever the population distribution of individual cases is normal, a distribution of means, regardless of the number of cases in each sample, will always be normal.

Summary of the Rules for Determining the Characteristics of a Distribution of Means

The foregoing discussion provides the rules for determining the characteristics of a distribution of means based on the characteristics of the population distribution of individual cases and the number of subjects in each sample:

1. The mean of a distribution of means is the same as the mean of the distribution of the population of individual cases.
2. The variance of a distribution of means is the variance of the distribution of the population of individual cases divided by the number of subjects in each sample ($\sigma_M^2 = \sigma^2/N$). And its standard deviation is the square root of its variance ($\sigma_M = \sqrt{\sigma_M^2}$).
3. The shape of a distribution of means is at least approximately normal if either the size of each sample is greater than 30 or the distribution of the population of individual cases is normal. Otherwise, it will at least tend to be unimodal and roughly symmetrical.

These principles are shown graphically in Figure 7-4.

[1]In this discussion, we have ignored the issue that a normal curve is a smooth theoretical distribution, whereas in most real-life examples, scores fall at specific intervals. So one difference between the sample distribution of table tennis balls' means and a normal curve is that the normal curve is smooth. In psychology research, we usually assume that even though our measurements are at specific intervals, the underlying thing being measured is continuous and well approximated by a normal curve.

[2]Actually, we have considered this principle of a distribution of means tending toward a normal curve before, in Chapter 5, where we used it to explain why so many things in nature are distributed as a normal curve. In that chapter, we explained it as the various influences balancing each other out, to make an averaged influence come out with most of the cases near the center and a few at each extreme. Now we have made the same point using the terminology of a distribution of means. If you think of any distribution of individual cases in nature as representing a situation in which each case is actually an average of a random set of influences on that individual case, that is saying that the distribution in nature is actually a distribution of means.

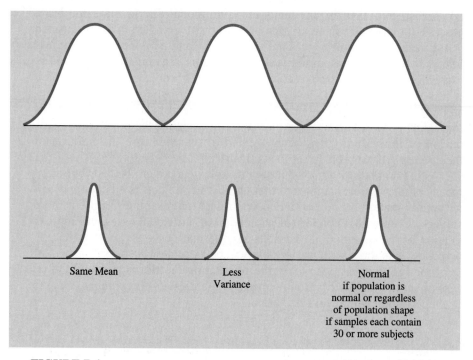

Same Mean

Less Variance

Normal if population is normal or regardless of population shape if samples each contain 30 or more subjects

FIGURE 7-4
Illustration of the principles of the relation of the distribution of means (lower curves) to the distribution of the population of individual cases (upper curves).

Example of Determining the Characteristics of a Distribution of Means

Consider the distribution of scores of the population of students who have taken the Graduate Record Examinations (GRE): It is approximately a normal distribution with a mean of 500 and a standard deviation of 100. What will be the characteristics of a distribution of all possible means for samples of 50 students each taken from this population?

1. Since the mean of the population is 500, the mean of the distribution of means will also be 500.

2. The variance of the distribution of means is the variance of the population of individual cases divided by the number of subjects in each sample. Since the standard deviation is 100, the variance is 10,000. Thus the variance of the distribution of means is 10,000 divided by 50, which is 200. In terms of the formula,

$$\sigma_M^2 = \frac{\sigma^2}{N} = \frac{10,000}{50} = 200$$

The standard deviation of the distribution of means is the square root of the variance of the distribution of means: $\sqrt{200} = 14.14$.

3. The shape of the distribution of means will be normal because both of our criteria are met: The population distribution of individual cases is normal, and the number of subjects in each sample is 30 or more.

Another Example of Determining the Characteristics of a Distribution of Means

The Adjective Check List (Gough & Heilbrun, 1983) is a widely used personality test. The test consists of a list of adjectives—*able, active, athletic*, and so forth—each of which is checked off by test takers if it applies to them. One of the subtests of the Adjective Check List focuses on aggression (adjectives such as *aggressive, argumentative*, and *assertive*). The test has been given to large numbers of people in the past, and it is known that scores on the Aggression scale have a skewed distribution with a mean of 51 and a variance of 93 (rounded off). What will be the characteristics of a distribution of means of all possible samples from this population of individual cases if the samples each contain 10 individuals?

1. The mean of the distribution of means will be 51, the same as the mean of the population of individual cases.

2. The variance of the distribution of means is the population variance, 93, divided by the number of subjects in each sample, which is 10. The result is 9.3. Using the formula,

$$\sigma_M^2 = \frac{\sigma^2}{N} = \frac{93}{10} = 9.3$$

The standard deviation of the distribution of means is the square root of 9.3, or 3.05.

3. The distribution of means will not be normal because the population distribution of individual cases is not normal and the number in each sample is only 10. However, like any distribution of means, it will tend to be unimodal and closer to symmetrical than the population distribution of individual cases.

Review of the Differences and Relationship Among These Distributions

We have now considered three different kinds of distributions: (a) the distribution of a population (that is, of individual cases), (b) the distribution of a particular sample drawn from that population, and (c) the distribution of all possible means of samples that could be drawn from that population of individual cases. Figure 7-5 illustrates these three distributions and Table 7-1 describes the comparisons.

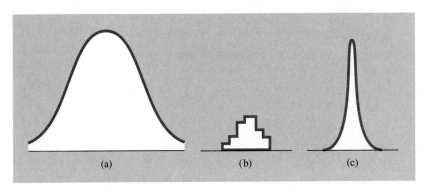

(a)   (b)   (c)

FIGURE 7-5
Comparison of three types of distributions: (a) the distribution of a population of individual cases, (b) the distribution of a particular sample drawn from that population, and (c) the distribution of means of all possible samples of a particular size drawn from that population.

BOX 7-1

More About Polls: Sampling Errors and Errors in Thinking About Samples

If you think back to Box 5-3 on surveys and the Gallup poll, you will recall that we left two important questions unanswered about the sort of fine print you find near the results of a poll, saying something like "From a telephone poll of 1,000 American adults taken on June 4–5. Sampling error ±3%." We said that you might wonder how such small numbers, like 1,000 (but rarely much less), can be used to predict the opinion of the entire U.S. public. And after plowing through this chapter, you may wonder what a "sampling error" means when a sample is not randomly sampled but rather selected by the complicated probability method described in Chapter 5.

To begin with the question of sample size, you know from this chapter that when sample sizes are large, like 1,000, the standard deviation of the distribution of means is greatly reduced. That is, the curve becomes very high and narrow, gathered all around the population mean. Thus the mean of any sample of that size is very close to being the population mean. To put it another way, the variance of the distribution of means of all possible samples—which reflects how much any sample's mean tends to differ from the population's mean—is the variance of the population divided by the sample size. The size of the population (of individual cases) itself or the relation of the sample's size to the population's does not play any role in this formula.

Still, you might persist in an intuitive feeling that the number required to represent all of the huge U.S. public might need to be larger than just 1,000. But if you think about it, when a sample is only a small part of a very large population, the sample's absolute size is the only determiner of accuracy. This absolute size determines the impact of the random errors of measurement and selection. A sample's size relative to the population does sometimes matter—if the population is so small that "removing" or interviewing some would increase the odds of the remaining ones' being interviewed. But when the population is in the millions, removing a thousand or two will have almost no impact on the odds of others' being interviewed. A survey of 1,000 out of 1 million voters or out of 10 million or 100 million will have essentially the same chance error. What is important is reducing bias or systematic error, which can be done only by careful planning.

Now we should return to this idea of sampling error, because in the context of polls,

TABLE 7-1
Comparison of Three Types of Distributions

	Particular Sample's Distribution	Distribution of Means	Population's Distribution
Content	The subjects' scores in a single sample	Means of samples randomly drawn from the population	All individuals' scores in the population
Shape	Could be any shape	Normal if population is normal, approximately normal if samples contain ≥ 30 cases each	Could be any shape, often normal
Mean	$M = \Sigma X/N$, calculated from scores of those in the sample	$\mu_M = \mu$	μ
Variance	$SD^2 = \Sigma(X - M)^2/N$, calculated from scores of those in the sample	$\sigma_M^2 = \sigma^2/N$	σ^2
Standard deviation	$SD = \sqrt{SD^2}$	$\sigma_M = \sqrt{\sigma_M^2} = \sigma/\sqrt{N}$	σ

where a simple random sampling is not used, a sampling error is not quite the same as the standard deviation of a distribution of means, as described in this chapter. Instead, the sampling error for polls is worked out according to past experience with the sampling procedures used. It is expressed in tables for different sample sizes (usually below 1,000, because that is where error increases dramatically). Sample size would be one heading, and percentage of subjects sharing the same opinion and responding in the same particular way (from, say, near 10% to near 90%), would be the other dimension of the table. The table would then provide an array of numbers representing the percentage points by which the results would vary (either plus or minus that number) 95% of the time if the sampling were repeated in the same time period, with the same procedures and interviewers. (In other words, sometimes there might be a bigger mistake made, which would be caught only if the poll were repeated, but this would not happen more than 5% of the time.)

Another table can be constructed for the percentage points at this same "95% confidence level" for ascertaining the likely error when predicting a difference between groups, such as men versus women on an issue.

Typical polling sampling errors might be anywhere from ±2% with a sample of 1,000 and shared opinions accounting for a low percentage to ±11% with a sample of 100 and a high percentage of shared opinions. Looking at the example we began with, which ended with "Sampling error ±3%," this means that given the 1,000 respondents (one dimension of the table) and the range of answers to the poll (the other dimension—and assuming, say, that there were never more than 70% of the respondents agreeing with any question), the statement is saying that 95% of the time, the results of a new sample of 1,000 would not vary by more than 3% from the ones obtained.

So now you understand opinion polls even better. The number of people polled is not very important (provided that it is at least 1,000 or so). What matters very much, however, is the method of sampling and estimating error, which will not be reported even in the fine print in the necessary detail to judge if the results are reliable. The reputation of the organization doing the survey is probably the best criterion. But if the sampling and error-estimating approach is not revealed, be cautious.

Hypothesis Testing Involving a Distribution of Means

Now we turn to the actual task of hypothesis testing when there is more than one case in the sample.

The Distribution of Means as the Comparison Distribution in Hypothesis Testing

In this new situation, the distribution of means can serve as the crucial intermediary between the sample and the null hypothesis. That is, the distribution of means can serve as what we have called the *comparison distribution*, whose characteristics are determined in Step 2 of the hypothesis-testing process. The distribution of means is the distribution to which the sample mean can be compared to see how likely it is that such a sample mean could have been selected if the null hypothesis is true.

Thus when a particular sample mean is obtained in a study, the researcher compares it to the distribution of the means that would arise if the null hypothesis were true. If the particular sample mean obtained in the study seems unlikely to have been selected from this distribution, the researcher can reject the null hypothesis.

Finding the *Z* Score of a Sample Mean on a Distribution of Means

A slight complication arises in the hypothesis-testing process when a sample of more than one subject is involved. The slight complication is that in determining the location of your sample on the comparison distribution, you are finding a *Z* score of your sample's mean on a distribution of means (instead of the *Z* score of a single subject on a distribution of a population of single subjects). Conceptually, converting the sample mean to a *Z* score is no different from what you have been doing all along when converting a raw score to a *Z* score. However, there can be some confusion because of the fact that more than one mean is involved. What is important to remember is that you are treating the sample mean like a single score and finding its *Z* score on the distribution that happens to be a distribution of means. To put it another way, the ordinary formula (from Chapter 2) for converting a raw score to a *Z* score is $Z = (X - M)/SD$. In the present situation, you are actually using the following formula,

$$Z = (M - \mu_M) / \sigma_M \qquad (7\text{-}4)$$

For example, if your sample mean is 18 and the distribution of means has a mean of 10 and a standard deviation of 4, the *Z* score of this sample mean is +2. Solving this using the formula,

$$Z = \frac{M - \mu_M}{\sigma_M} = \frac{18 - 10}{4} = \frac{8}{4} = 2$$

This is illustrated in Figure 7-6.

FIGURE 7-6
Z score for the mean of a particular sample on the distribution of means.

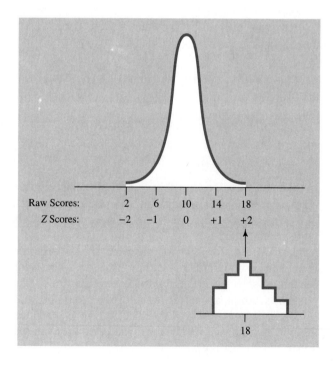

Example of Hypothesis Testing With a Sample of More Than One Subject

Recall from Chapter 1 the fictional experiment involving the reading of ambiguous and nonambiguous sentences. Let's suppose that the researchers had found that it takes people longer to read ambiguous sentences and are now interested in why this should be the case. One possibility is that in the studies conducted so far, the ambiguous sentences had no context. Thus the researchers conduct an experiment in which subjects are first given a context for the ambiguous sentence, one that ought to make it less ambiguous and thus speed up reading time. Of course, it is also possible that providing a context slows reading down by making the situation more complicated.

Based on the previous studies, the researchers know that reading times for ambiguous sentences without any context are roughly normally distributed with a mean of 27.5 ms and a variance of 1.96 ms ($\sigma = 1.40$ ms). This population distribution is shown in Figure 7-7a.

In this study, 40 subjects are tested using ambiguous sentences with a context. Their mean reading time was 27.1 ms. (The variance of the sample is not used in any way in the hypothesis-testing process when we know the population variance, as we do here.) The sample's distribution is shown in Figure 7-7c.[3]

What should the researchers conclude? Let's follow the steps of hypothesis testing.

1. Reframe the question into a research hypothesis and a null hypothesis about the populations. The two populations of interest are these:

Population 1: Subjects who read ambiguous sentences with a context
Population 2: Subjects who read ambiguous sentences without a context

The research hypothesis is that there is a difference in reading time between the population reading with a context and the population reading without a context. The null hypothesis is that there is no difference in reading time between the two populations. (These hypotheses are nondirectional: Although the researchers expect reading time to be faster with a context, the possibility that the context will slow it down cannot be ruled out, and such an outcome might be of considerable interest.)

2. Determine the characteristics of the comparison distribution. Now we must determine the characteristics of the distribution of means taken from the population of individual subjects who do not read the sentence in a context (Population 2). This population is the one that, if the null hypothesis is true, is no different from the population that reads with a context. In particular, we need to know the characteristics of a distribution of means of samples of 40 subjects each from this population.

---

[3]Actually, this study would be much better if the researchers also had another group of subjects who were randomly assigned to be tested for reading speed of ambiguous sentences without a context. Relying on the information from previous studies is a bit hazardous, since the circumstances of testing from one study to another may not be identical. However, for purposes of introducing the hypothesis-testing process one step at a time, in this example and the others in this chapter, we use situations in which a single sample is contrasted with a "known" population. Starting in Chapter 9, we extend the hypothesis-testing procedure to be applicable to more realistic research situations, those involving more than one group of subjects and those involving populations whose characteristics are not known.

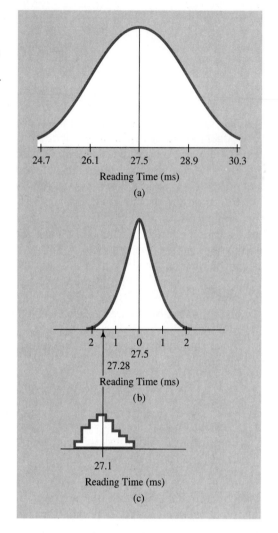

FIGURE 7-7
For the fictional experiment from Chapter 1 involving reading ambiguous sentences, (a) the distribution of the population of individual cases, (b) the distribution of means, and (c) the sample's distribution.

Now you follow the rules for determining the characteristics of a distribution of means: (a) Its mean is the same as the population mean, in this case, 27.5 ms. (b) Its variance is the population variance divided by the number of cases in each sample. Using the formula,

$$\sigma_M^2 = \frac{\sigma^2}{N} = \frac{1.96}{40} = .049$$

The standard deviation is the square root of this, .22. (c) The shape of the distribution will be close to a normal curve because the samples have more than 30 subjects each. This distribution of means is illustrated in Figure 7-7b.

3. Determine the cutoff sample score on the comparison distribution at which the null hypothesis should be rejected. Assume that the researchers decided on the 5% significance level. And, as we noted in Step 1, they have made a nondirectional hypothesis. Thus a two-tailed test is required. Because our comparison distribution (the distribution of means whose characteristics we just determined) is normal, we can now consult the normal curve table to find the Z score needed for the top and bottom $2\frac{1}{2}\%$. The table shows that to reject the null hypothesis at the 5% level, we need a Z score either at or above +1.96 or at or below −1.96. These two $2\frac{1}{2}\%$ regions in which the null hypothesis would be rejected are shown as shaded areas in the two tails of the distribution of means illustrated in Figure 7-7b.

4. Determine the score of your sample on the comparison distribution. The mean of the sample was 27.1 (see Figure 7-7c). The comparison distribution (our distribution of means), as we found in Step 2, has a mean of 27.5 and a standard deviation of .22. Using the formula,

$$Z = \frac{M - \mu_M}{\sigma_M} = \frac{27.1 - 27.5}{.22} = \frac{-.4}{.22} = -1.82$$

In Figure 7-7b, the location of the sample's mean on the distribution of means is shown with an arrow.

5. Compare the scores obtained in Steps 3 and 4 to decide whether or not to reject the null hypothesis. The Z score needed to reject the null hypothesis was ±1.96, and our obtained Z score was only −1.82; therefore, we cannot reject the null hypothesis, and the experiment is inconclusive. This can be seen graphically in Figure 7-7b, in which the location of our sample mean on the distribution of means is not so extreme as to be clearly unlikely to be drawn from this distribution.

This result, however, is nearly extreme enough to reject the null hypothesis. Thus the researchers might note that the result was "near significant" or "approached significance," perhaps adding "$p < .10$." (For significance at the .10 level, two-tailed, you only need a score of at least ±1.64.) But with a borderline result like this, the best advice is to run the experiment again, perhaps with more subjects (Chapter 8 contains a discussion of the effects of increasing subjects on the probability that your experiment will produce a significant result).

Another Example of Hypothesis Testing With a Sample of More Than One Subject

Here is another fictional example. Two educational psychologists studying the effects of instructions on timed scholastic achievement tests have a theory that if test takers are told to answer each question with the first response that comes into their head, they will do better. To examine this proposal, the researchers arrange to have 64 randomly selected fifth-grade schoolchildren take a standard school achievement test. The test is given in the usual way, except that the instructions have an additional sentence saying that the students should answer each question with the first response that comes into their head. The test, when given in the usual way, has an approximately normal distribution, with a mean of 200 and a standard deviation of 48, as shown in Figure 7-8a.

What kind of result should lead the educational psychologists to conclude that the procedure makes a difference?

1. Reframe the question into a research hypothesis and a null hypothesis about the populations. The two populations of interest are these:

Population 1: Fifth graders who get the special instructions
Population 2: Fifth graders who do not get the special instructions

The research hypothesis is that the population of fifth graders who take the test with the special instructions will have higher scores than the population of children who take the test in the normal way. The null hypothesis is that Population 1's scores will not be higher than Population 2's. (Note that these are directional hypotheses.)

FIGURE 7-8
For the fictional study of performance on a standard school achievement test, (a) the distribution of the population of individual cases, (b) the distribution of means, and (c) the sample's distribution

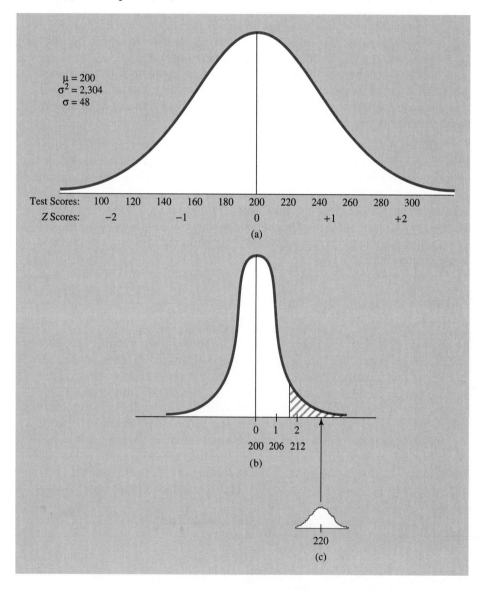

2. Determine the characteristics of the comparison distribution. Because our study gives us a mean of a sample of 64 cases, the comparison distribution has to be the distribution of means of all possible samples of 64 subjects each. This distribution will have a mean of 200 (the same as the population mean). Its variance will be the population variance divided by the number of subjects in the sample. The population variance is 2,304 (the population standard deviation of 48 squared); the sample size is 64; so the variance of the distribution of means will be 2,304/64, or 36. The standard deviation of the distribution of means is the square root of 36, or 6. Finally, since there are more than 30 subjects in the sample, the shape of the distribution of means will be approximately normal. Figure 7-8b shows the distribution of means.

3. Determine the cutoff sample score on the comparison distribution at which the null hypothesis should be rejected. Again, assume that the researchers decide to use the conventional 5% significance level. However, in this study they have a clear directional prediction and are not really interested in any effect in the opposite direction. (If the special instructions do not improve test scores, they would not be used in the future. Any possible results showing a negative effect are irrelevant.) Hence the null hypothesis will be rejected if the result falls in the upper 5% of the comparison distribution. Since it is a normal curve, the top 5% can be found from the normal curve table to start at a Z score of +1.64. This is shown as the shaded area in Figure 7-8b.

4. Determine the score of your sample on the comparison distribution. When the educational psychologists tested the 64 fifth graders, they had a mean of 220. (This sample's distribution is shown in Figure 7-8c.) This is 3.33 standard deviations above the mean of the distribution of means:

$$Z = \frac{M - \mu_M}{\sigma_M} = \frac{220 - 200}{6} = \frac{20}{6} = 3.33$$

5. Compare the scores obtained in Steps 3 and 4 to decide whether or not to reject the null hypothesis. The minimum Z score needed to reject the null hypothesis has been set at +1.64, and the Z score of the sample is +3.33. Thus the educational psychologists can reject the null hypothesis and conclude that the research hypothesis is tenable and that the result is statistically significant at the $p < .05$ level. This can be seen in Figure 7-8b by noting how extreme the sample mean is on the distribution of means (the distribution that would apply if the null hypothesis were true). The final conclusion is that among people like those studied, the special instructions do improve test scores.

Levels of Significance

A central issue in hypothesis testing arises in Step 3, where you determine the probability level at which a null hypothesis will be considered so unlikely that it should be rejected. In Chapter 6, we noted that psychologists generally use 5%, or sometimes 1%, as a cutoff point. Let us examine why.

Type I Error

Type I error

Setting the significance level cutoff at a large probability level, such as 20%, would mean that the null hypothesis would be rejected very easily. You would often be deciding to consider the research hypothesis supported when you should not. This is called a **Type I error.** For example, suppose that in the testing example, the special instructions in reality made no difference—the researcher just happened to pick 64 children who were unusually good at this test. In that case, deciding to reject the null hypothesis and concluding that the special instructions make a difference would be a Type I error.

Type I errors are of serious concern to scientists, who might construct entire theories and research programs, not to mention practical applications, based on a result that is in fact fallacious. (It is because these errors are of such serious concern that they are called Type I.) Thus the conservative approach is to set a very stringent significance level, such as 1% (.01), or even .1% (.001), so that the results have to be quite extreme before the null hypothesis is rejected.

Type II Error

If you set a very stringent significance level, such as .1%, however, you run a different kind of risk. In this case, you may fail to reject the null hypothesis—that is, you may fail to decide that the research hypothesis is supported by the evidence of the sample—when in fact the research hypothesis is true. This is called a **Type II error.** For example, consider the fictional study of reading ambiguous sentences with or without a context that we examined earlier in the chapter. Suppose that, in fact, providing a context for ambiguous sentences does permit people to read sentences faster, but the random sample that the researchers selected for study just happened to include people who are unusually slow at reading. In this case, having decided not to reject the null hypothesis, and thus refusing to draw a conclusion, would be a Type II error.

Type II error

Type II errors concern scientists, especially those interested in applications of psychological knowledge, because a Type II error could mean that a good theory or a useful practical procedure is not used. (Also see Box 6-1 on prejudice against the null hypothesis.)

Relation of Type I and Type II Errors

Avoiding one kind of error increases the chance of making the other. For example, setting the significance level at a stringent level (such as .1%) makes a Type I error less likely but a Type II error more likely; setting the significance level at a liberal level (such as 20%) makes a Type I error more likely but a Type II error less likely. The trade-off between these two conflicting concerns is usually resolved by compromise, hence the conventional 5% and 1% significance levels.

TABLE 7-2
Possible Correct and Erroneous Decisions in Hypothesis Testing

		Real Status of the Research Hypothesis (in practice, unknown)	
		True	*False*
Decision Using Hypothesis-testing Procedure	*Research hypothesis tenable (reject null hypothesis)*	Correct decision	Error (Type I)
	Study is inconclusive (fail to reject null hypothesis)	Error (Type II)	Correct decision

Summary of Possible Outcomes of Hypothesis Testing

The entire issue of possible correct and erroneous decisions in hypothesis testing can be diagrammed as shown in Table 7-2. Along the top of this table are the two possibilities about whether the research hypothesis is or is not actually true (something in practice you would never actually know). Along the side is whether your decision after hypothesis testing is to reject the null hypothesis (decide that the research hypothesis is tenable) or not to reject the null hypothesis (decide that the results are inconclusive regarding the research hypothesis). Table 7-2 shows that there are two ways to be correct and two ways to be in error in any hypothesis-testing situation. We have more to say about these issues in Chapter 8.

Controversies and Limitations

This chapter represents a step along the way in understanding the hypothesis-testing process as it is actually employed in psychological research. Though highly standardized and almost universally used by psychology researchers, the process has many aspects that have generated controversy. Some of these we have already considered in Chapters 5 and 6: the normalness of the normal curve, Bayesian statistical techniques, the appropriateness of using nonrandom samples, and issues relating to one- and two-tailed tests. We consider two of the other major controversies in this area in Chapter 8: emphasizing effect size versus statistical significance and the possibility of "proving" the null hypothesis (an issue we already broached in Box 6-1).

One controversy related to the material covered in this chapter has to do with the notion of a "known" population mean and standard deviation—a situation that, as we noted at the outset, arises only rarely in practice. The situation does arise, however, in a few situations, including what are called **norms** for standardized tests. For example, the average score for job applicants on the Anxiety subscale of the Multiple Affect Adjective Checklist

norms

(Zuckerman & Lubin, 1965) is 5.8, and the average score for recently divorced women on the Feelings of Self-Worth subscale of the Fisher (1978) Divorce Adjustment Scale is 97.0. Of course, these norms are not actually based on testing the entire population of job applicants or the entire population of divorced women; rather, they are based on samples of subjects that are so large that they are thought to be reasonably representative of the larger population.

The issue, however, is not that too few have been sampled or even that they may not be representative of the population at large. The most serious problem is that the meaning of a test may change when administered to specific subgroups of the population. For example, in some ethnic groups, where the emphasis is strongly on reputation in the community, the scores on a particular test may tell more about the person's opinion as to what will make a good impression than about anxiety or divorce adjustment. So if a comparison of the scores of such a group to the "general population" shows a significant difference, this may not necessarily mean that the group's underlying anxiety or divorce adjustment is really different, just that the way its members approach this test is different.

This problem is especially acute when ability or intelligence tests are used to compare various groups and conclusions are drawn (incorrectly) about differences in abilities or intelligence. In Chapter 14, one of the examples we use (Pugh & Boer, 1991) is a study in which some of the items on a widely used intelligence test were based on information that only U.S. citizens would be likely to know, such as names of presidents and details of the Civil War. Canadians, as you might expect, performed significantly worse on this part of the test (even though on other items, which were not biased in this way, they did as well as or better than U.S. citizens).

Hypothesis Tests About Means of Samples as Described in Research Articles

As we have noted several times, research in which there is a known population mean and standard deviation are quite rare in psychology, and we have asked you to learn about this situation mainly because it is a necessary building block for understanding hypothesis testing in common research situations. In the rare case in which research with a known population distribution is conducted, it is often described as involving a **Z test,** since it is the Z score that is checked against the normal curve.

Of the topics we have covered in this chapter, the one you are most likely to see discussed in a research article is the standard deviation of the distribution of means, used as an indication of the amount of variation that might be expected among means of samples of a given size from this population. In this context, it is usually identified as the **standard error,** abbreviated *SE*. Often the lines that go above and below the tops of the bars in a bar graph refer to standard error (instead of standard deviation).

For example, the chart in Figure 7-9 appears in an article by Introini-Collison and McGaugh (1986) in which they are evaluating the role of epi-

Z test

standard error

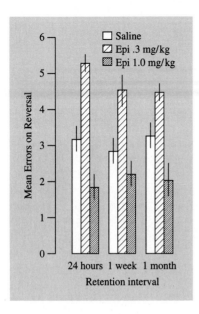

FIGURE 7-9
Effects of posttraining epinephrine (Epi) on discrimination reversal training 1 day, 1 week, and 1 month following original training (Means ± *SE*). *N* = 18 per group for 1-day group, 12 per group for 1-week and 1-month groups. From Introini-Collison, I. B., & McGaugh, J. L. (1986). Epinephrine modulates long-term retention of an aversively motivated discrimination. *Behavioral and Neural Biology, 45,* 358-365. Copyright, 1986, by Academic Press, Inc. Reprinted by permission.

nephrine (adrenaline) on retaining material that has just been learned. This graph shows results of a study in which mice were given either saline (salt water, a neutral control condition) or low or high dosages of epinephrine right after learning to identify the correct path in a particular maze. The bars show the number of errors the mice made 1 day, 1 week, and 1 month later. As can be seen from the graph, at all periods, the mice who had received the high dose of epinephrine made many fewer errors (indicating retention of learning), whereas those with the low dose of epinephrine actually did worse than those given only saline. The extent to which the distributions do not overlap is suggested by the extent to which the lines above and below the bars, which represent the standard deviation of the distribution of means, are small in comparison to the differences in the heights of the bars, which represent the means of the groups. The fact that the bars represent the means and the lines the standard error is described cryptically in the figure caption as "(Means ± *SE*)."

Figure 7-10 features an interesting graphic use of the standard error to show the degree of variation at each of several points in time. This figure is from a study by Gariepy, Hood, and Cairns (1988) that examined several generations of mice specifically bred to be either very unaggressive or very aggressive. (Not all studies using standard errors use mice; we just happened to find two good examples that did.) The point (either a solid box or an open circle) for each generation of each breed or "line" of mice shows the mean number of attacks for that group. The shading around the lines connecting the dots indicates the standard error associated with each mean (each point).

FIGURE 7-10
Generational changes in rates of
attacks for the high-aggressive
(NC-900) and low-aggressive
(NC-100) lines *(SE in gray)*. [From
Gariepy, J., Hood, K. E., & Cairns,
R. B. (1988). A developmental-
genetic analysis of aggressive
behavior in mice (*Mus musculus*):
III. Behavioral mediation by
heightened reactivity or immobil-
ity? *Journal of Comparative
Psychology, 102*, 392-399.
Copyright, 1988, by the American
Psychological Association.
Reprinted by permission of the
author.]

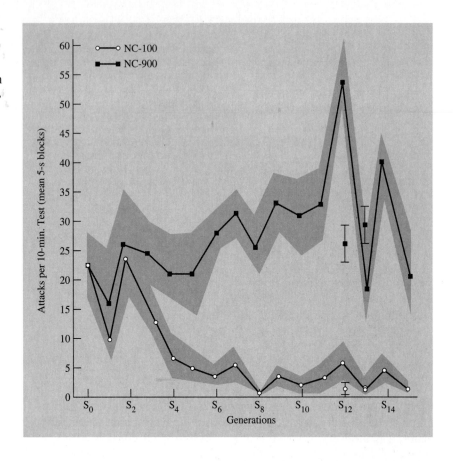

Summary

When studying a sample of more than one individual, the comparison distribution in the hypothesis-testing process is a distribution of means of all possible samples of the number of cases being studied. It can be thought of as
describing what the result would be of taking a very large number of samples of the same size, each drawn randomly from the population of individual cases, and making a distribution of the means of these samples.

The distribution of means has the same mean as the population of individual cases. However, it has a smaller variance because the means of samples are less likely to be extreme than individual cases are (extreme cases
drawn in any one sample are likely to be balanced by middle cases or
extremes in the other direction). Specifically, its variance is the variance of
the population of individual cases divided by the size of the sample. (Its
standard deviation is the square root of its variance.) The shape of the distribution of means approximates a normal curve if either (a) the population of
individual cases is normally distributed or (b) the sample size is 30 or more.

Hypothesis tests involving a single sample of more than one individual
and a known population are conducted in exactly the same way as the
hypothesis tests of Chapter 6 (where there was a single sample of a single
individual and a known population), except that the comparison distribution
is a distribution of means of samples of that size.

In hypothesis testing in general, there are two kinds of correct outcomes: (a) The null hypothesis is rejected and the research hypothesis is actually true, or (b) the null hypothesis is not rejected, and the research hypothesis is actually false. There are also two kinds of errors. A Type I error is when the null hypothesis is rejected but the research hypothesis is actually false. A Type II error is when the null hypothesis is not rejected but the research hypothesis is actually true.

A controversy that relates to known populations is the use of norms based on large-scale administrations of standardized tests to assess individuals who may come from a group that is not represented by the population studied.

The kind of hypothesis test described in this chapter is rarely used in research practice (you have learned it as a steppingstone), but the standard deviation of the distribution of means, often referred to as the "standard error" (SE), is occasionally used to describe the expected variability of means, particularly in bar graphs in which the standard error (instead of the more common standard deviation) may be shown as the length of a line above and below the top of each bar.

Key Terms

distribution of means
mean of a distribution
   of means (μ_M)
norms
shape of a distribution
   of means

standard deviation of a
   distribution of means (σ_M)
standard error (SE)
Type I error

Type II error
variance of a distribution
   of means (σ_M^2)
Z test

Practice Problems

These problems involve computation (with the assistance of a calculator). Most real-life statistics problems are done on a computer. But even if you have a computer, do this by hand to ingrain the method in your mind.

For practice in using a computer to solve statistical problems, refer to the computer section of each chapter of the study guide that accompanies this text.

All data are fictional (unless an actual citation is given). Answers to Set I are given at the back of the book.

SET I

1. Explain why the standard deviation of the distribution of means is generally smaller than the standard deviation of the distribution of the population of individuals.

2. For a population of individual cases that has a standard deviation of 10, what is the standard deviation of the distribution of means for samples of size (a) 2, (b) 3, (c) 4, (d) 5, (e) 10, (f) 20, (g) 100?

3. Given that a normally distributed population has a mean of 40 and a standard deviation of 6, which of the following samples would be less likely than 5% to be randomly selected from this population: (a) sample of 10 with a mean of 44, (b) sample of 1 with a mean of 48, (c) sample of 81 with a mean of 42, (d) sample of 16 with a mean of 42? Show how you arrived at your answer, including a diagram of the distributions involved.

4. Twenty-five women between the ages of 70 and 80 are randomly selected from the general population of women their age and take a special program to decrease their reaction time. After the course, the women had an average reaction time of 1.5 s. Assume that the mean reaction time for the general population of women of this age group is 1.8, with a standard deviation of .5 s. (Assume also that the population is approximately normal.) What should you conclude about the efficacy of the course? (Use the .01 level.) Explain your answer to someone who is familiar with the general logic of hypothesis testing, the normal curve, Z scores, and probability but is not familiar with the idea of a distribution of means.

5. A large number of people have seen a particular film of an automobile collision between a moving car and a stopped car and responded to a standard questionnaire about how likely it was that the driver of the moving car was at fault. The distribution of ratings (on a scale from *not at fault* = 0 and *completely at fault* = 10) under ordinary conditions is thus known and turns out to be normally distributed with μ = 5.5 and σ = .8. Sixteen randomly selected individuals are tested under conditions in which the wording of the question is changed so that instead of calling them just Car A and Car B, the question asks, "How likely is it that the driver of the car that crashed into the other was at fault?" Using this instruction, these 16 subjects gave a mean at-fault rating of 5.9. Using the 5% significance level, did the changed instructions significantly increase the rating of being at fault? Explain your answer to someone who has never taken statistics.

6. For each of the following studies, make a chart of the four possible correct and erroneous conclusions, and explain what each would mean.

(a) Schoolchildren are studied to see if increasing the amount of recess time improves in-class behavior.

(b) A study is done of whether colorblind individuals can distinguish gray shades better than the population at large.

(c) Individuals who have ever been in psychotherapy are compared to the general public to see if they are more tolerant of other people's upsets than the general population is.

7. Cut up 100 small slips of paper, and write each number from 0 to 9 on 10 slips each. Put the slips in a bowl or a hat, and mix them up. Now draw out a slip, write down the number on it, and put it back. Do this 20 times; then make a histogram, and compute the mean and the variance of the result. You should get an approximately rectangular distribution. Then take two slips out, figure out their mean, write it down, and put the slips back. Repeat this process about 20 times. Make a histogram, and compute the mean and the variance of this distribution of means. The variance should be about half of the variance of the distribution of samples of individual cases. Finally, repeat the process again, this time taking three slips at a time. This distribution of means of three cases each should have a variance of about a third of the distribution of samples of individual cases. Also note that as the sample size increases, your distributions are getting closer to normal. (Had you begun with a normally distributed distribution of slips, your distributions of means would have been fairly close to normal regardless of the number in each sample.)

(Technically, when taking the samples of two slips, this should be done by taking one, writing it down, putting it back, taking the next and writing it down, and

then considering these two scores as one sample for which you compute a mean. The same applies for samples of three slips. This is called "sampling with replacement." However, taking two or three slips at a time and putting them back will be a close enough approximation for this exercise and will save you some time.)

SET II

1. Under what conditions is it reasonable to assume that a distribution of means will follow a normal curve?

2. Indicate the mean and the standard deviation of the distribution of means for each of the following situations.

	Population		Sample Size
	Mean	*Variance*	
(a)	100	40	10
(b)	100	30	10
(c)	100	20	10
(d)	100	10	10
(e)	50	10	10
(f)	100	40	20
(g)	100	10	20

3. Based on the information given, state your conclusion for each study. (Be sure to indicate the characteristics of the comparison distribution, the cutoff, the score of your sample's mean on the comparison distribution, and your conclusion about whether or not to reject the null hypothesis. All hypothesis tests are two-tailed.)

	Population		Sample Size	Sample Mean	Significance Level
	μ	σ			
(a)	36	8	16	38	.05
(b)	36	6	16	38	.05
(c)	36	4	16	38	.05
(d)	36	4	16	38	.01
(e)	34	4	16	38	.01

4. A researcher is interested in whether people are able to identify emotions correctly in people from other cultures. It is known that, using a particular method of measurement, the accuracy ratings of adult North Americans in general are normally distributed with a mean of 82 (out of 100) and a variance of 20. But this distribution is based on ratings made of emotions expressed by members of their own culture. In this study, the researcher arranges to test 50 adult North Americans rating emotions of individuals from Indonesia. The mean accuracy for these 50 subjects was 78. Using the .05 level, what should the researcher conclude? Explain your answer to a person who has never taken a course in statistics.

5. A psychologist who studies dreams is investigating whether the number of dreams per month that people report in which they are alone is greater for those who have recently experienced a traumatic event than the number of dreams per month in which one is alone typically occurring in the general population. Suppose that the number of dreams people have in which they are alone is normally distributed in the population with a mean of 5 and a standard deviation of 4. The psychologist studies 36 individuals who have recently experienced a traumatic event, and their mean number of dreams, over a month, in which they are alone is 8. Using the .05 level, should you conclude that people who have recently had a traumatic experience have a significantly different number of dreams in which they are alone? Explain your answer to someone who is familiar with the general logic of hypoth-esis testing, the normal curve, Z scores, and probability but is not familiar with the idea of a distribution of means.

6. In each of the following studies, make a chart of the four possible correct and mistaken conclusions, and explain what each would mean.

(a) A study of whether infants born prematurely begin to recognize faces later than infants in general.

(b) A study of whether high school students who receive an AIDS prevention program in their school are more likely to practice safe sex than other high school students.

(c) A study of whether memory for abstract ideas is reduced if the information is presented in distracting colors.

8 Statistical Power and Effect Size

POWER is the ability to achieve your goals. So a reasonable measure of power in any given case would be the probability of achieving some particular goal. The goal of a psychological experiment is to attain significant results (reject the null hypothesis) if the research hypothesis really is true. The **statistical power** of a psychology experiment is the probability that the study will yield a significant result if the research hypothesis is true.

statistical power

As you learn about statistical power in this chapter, you will see that it is important for several reasons. For example, computing power when planning an experiment helps determine how many subjects to use. And understanding power is extremely important to anyone who reads psychological research—for example, in making sense of experimental results that are not significant or results that are statistically but not practically significant.

In this chapter, we systematically examine the concept of statistical power: What it is, how to compute it, what influences it, and why it is important. In the process, we also introduce the notion of effect size, which is a topic of considerable importance in its own right. However, we want especially to alert you to the need to attend closely to the discussion of power; sometimes this material may feel particularly difficult to grasp, so be patient with yourself, and take your time. You'll get it.

What Is Statistical Power?

We said that the statistical power of an experiment is the probability that the study will yield significant results if the research hypothesis is true. Notice that the power of an experiment is about the situation *if* the research hypothesis is true. If the research hypothesis is false, we do not want to get significant results (that would be a Type I error).

Now you may ask, "If the research hypothesis is true won't the experiment necessarily give significant results?" The answer is no. The particular sample that happens to be selected from the population studied may not turn out to be extreme enough to provide a clear case for rejecting the null hypothesis.

An Example

Consider the fictional example from Chapter 7 in which educational psychologists studied the effects of giving special instructions to a group of 64 fifth graders taking a standard achievement test. In the hypothesis-testing process for this example, we compared two populations:

Population 1: Fifth graders receiving special instructions
Population 2: Fifth graders not receiving special instructions

The research hypothesis was that Population 1 would score higher than Population 2.

Figure 8-1 illustrates the situation in which this research hypothesis is true. The distribution in the lower part of the figure is the distribution of means of all possible samples of 64 test scores for Population 2. This is also the comparison distribution, the distribution of means that you would expect if the null hypothesis were true. The shaded area on the right tail of this distribution is the region in which, should a mean of a sample fall here, the null hypothesis will be rejected. In the example, this shaded area begins at 209.84 (a Z score of 1.64), occupying 5% of this comparison distribution.

The distribution in the top part of the figure is the distribution of means of all possible samples of 64 test scores from Population 1; this is the distribution of means that the researchers predict for the population receiving special instructions. In Chapter 7, we never talked about this distribution, partly because this population is quite imaginary, *unless* the research hypothesis is true. If the null hypothesis is true, this upper distribution would have the same mean—and indeed be the same—as the distribution based on Population 2. However, for the purpose of examining power, we are now in this chapter explicitly considering the situation in which the research hypothesis is true, so we have drawn this distribution. And its mean is farther to the right on the scale than the mean of the comparison distribution shown below it. Specifically, the upper distribution of means is shown with a mean of 208 (whereas the comparison distribution's mean is only 200). This is to show that the population receiving the special instructions is expected to have, on the average, higher scores. (We will discuss later how a researcher decides just how much higher to expect this upper distribution's mean to be.)

Now suppose that the educational psychologists conduct the experiment. They give the special instructions to a group of 64 fifth graders and find their mean score on the test. If the research hypothesis is true, this amounts to saying that they randomly selected a mean from the upper distribution of means. The hypothesized population on which the upper distribution is based actually exists.

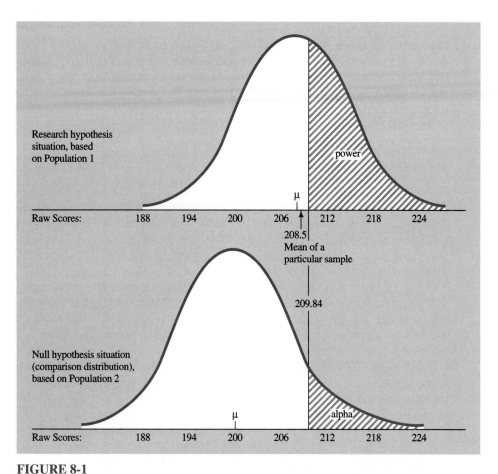

FIGURE 8-1
Distributions of means of 64 cases from a fictional study of fifth graders receiving special instructions prior to taking a standard achievement test. The lower distribution of means is based on a known distribution of individual test scores of fifth graders who do not receive any special instructions (Population 2). The upper distribution of means is based on a hypothesized distribution of individual test scores of fifth graders who receive the special instructions for which the researchers predict a mean of 208 (Population 1). Shaded sections of both distributions represent the area in which the null hypothesis will be rejected (representing the region in which a Type I error would occur in the lower distribution, power in the upper).

In this example, however, this upper distribution of means (from Population 1) is only slightly to the right of the comparison distribution. So chances are that any mean selected from this upper distribution will not be far enough to the right on the lower distribution (the comparison distribution, based on Population 2) to allow the researchers to reject the null hypothesis.

For example, the particular sample of 64 fifth graders studied might have a mean of 208.5, as shown by the arrow in the figure. Since a mean of at least 209.84 is needed to reject the null hypothesis, the result of this experiment would not be significant, even though we have said, for the purpose of determining power, that the research hypothesis really is true.

It is possible that the researchers would happen to select a sample from Population 1 with a mean sufficiently far to the right (that is, with a sufficiently high average test score) that they could reject the null hypothesis. But given the way we have set up the example, there is a better than even chance that the experiment will not turn out to be significant even if the research hypothesis is true. This is the essence of power, so you might want to think this through again.

Alpha, Beta, and Power

Recall from Chapter 7 that when testing a hypothesis, there are two kinds of errors we can make. A Type I error occurs when we decide that the experiment worked (reject the null hypothesis) when in fact the null hypothesis is true. The apparently significant result is just an accident. It is unlikely, given our 5% or 1% rejection rule, but accidents can happen (and, indeed, we expect them 5% or 1% of the time).

A Type II error occurs when we decide that the experiment is inconclusive (we do not reject the null hypothesis) when in fact our research hypothesis was true. In this case, the experiment failed to support the research hypothesis when it should have. This is the situation shown in Figure 8-1 when $M = 208.5$. In that example, there was a Type II error.

alpha

The probability of a Type I error is called **alpha** (the Greek letter α). It is the same as the level of probability used in determining the significance cutoff score and is fixed in advance of the study (in Step 3 of the hypothesis-testing process). It is usually set at 5%. In Figure 8-1, alpha is the shaded area in the right tail of the lower distribution (the comparison distribution representing the null hypothesis situation).

beta

The probability of a Type II error is called **beta** (the Greek letter β). (Do not confuse this beta with the beta that is the standardized regression coefficient discussed in Chapter 4.) Beta is the probability that even if the research hypothesis is true, our experiment would still fail to support it (fail to reject the null hypothesis). In Figure 8-1, beta is the unshaded area of the upper distribution (the distribution based on the research hypothesis prediction about Population 1). This is the area where, even though the research hypothesis is true, a mean would not be extreme enough to permit rejection of the null hypothesis. It is the area of the upper distribution to the left of the point at which the alpha area begins on the lower (comparison) distribution.

The *power* of an experiment is the probability that if the research hypothesis is true the experiment will support it (will reject the null hypothesis). That is, power is the probability of *not* making a Type II error. Numerically, it is 1 minus beta. In Figure 8-1, power is the shaded portion of the upper distribution. Its proportion of the distribution in this example is less than 50%.

Review of Possible Outcomes of Hypothesis Testing in Light of Alpha, Beta, and Power

As we saw in Chapter 7, the entire issue of possible correct and erroneous decisions in hypothesis testing can be diagrammed as shown here in Table 8-1 (which is similar to Table 7-2). The columns of this little table hold the two

TABLE 8-1
Possible Outcomes of Hypothesis Testing

		Real Status of the Research Hypothesis (in Practice, Unknown)	
		True	*False*
Decision Using Hypothesis-Testing Procedure	*Research hypothesis tenable (reject null hypothesis)*	Correct decision; p = power	Type I error; p = alpha
	Study is inconclusive (fail to reject null hypothesis)	Type II error; p = beta	Correct decision; p = 1 – alpha

possibilities about whether the research hypothesis is or is not actually true and the two rows state whether your decision after hypothesis testing is that the research hypothesis is tenable or not. We have also included this time a notation as to which part of the chart corresponds to alpha, beta, and power.

Calculating Statistical Power

The power of an experiment can be computed. In a case like the one we have been considering, computing power involves figuring out the area of the shaded portion of the upper distribution in Figure 8-1. Since distributions of means are usually approximately normal, and this is clearly the case in our example, our computations of power will use Z scores. First we figure out the Z score for the point at which the shaded area begins on the upper distribution; then we determine its area from a normal curve table.

An Example

Consider again Figure 8-1, showing the distributions of means for the fifth-grade testing example. In the example, the population of individual cases not receiving special instructions had a mean of 200 and a standard deviation of 48 (a variance of 2,304). Since we are interested in a sample of 64, in Chapter 7 we computed the standard deviation of the distribution of means of samples of that size to be 6 ($\sqrt{2,304/64} = 6$). And in this chapter, we said that we would be omniscient (for the purpose of computing power) and declare that the effect of the special instructions will be enough to raise the mean to 208. Based on these figures—*different* means and same standard deviations[1]—we have shown the Z scores for both distributions in Figure 8-2.

[1]Normally, we assume that regardless of whether the null hypothesis is true (that is, whether the means of the two populations are the same), the variances of both populations will be the same. Since the distributions of means for both populations are also based on the same number of cases in each sample (64 in this case), the standard deviations of these two distributions of means will also be the same.

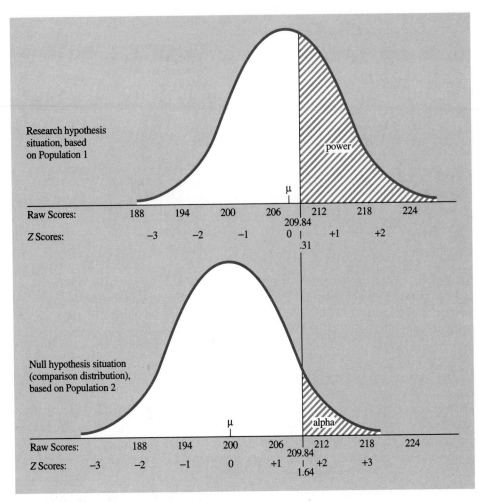

FIGURE 8-2
Distributions of means of 64 cases based on hypothesized (upper) and known (lower) distributions of populations of individual cases in a fictional study of fifth graders receiving special instructions prior to taking a standard achievement test. Z scores and raw scores are shown on both distributions corresponding to the significance cutoff on the lower distribution (significance cutoff based on $p < .05$, one-tailed).

In Chapter 7, we determined that using the 5% significance level, one-tailed, you need a Z score for the mean of your sample of at least 1.64 to reject the null hypothesis. Using the formula for converting Z scores to raw scores, this corresponds to a raw score of 200 + (1.64 **x** 6), or 209.84 (the figure we noted in the earlier discussions of this example).

Our prediction is that the distribution of means that could be created from the population in which fifth graders do receive special instructions (Population 1) has a mean of 208. Thus 209.84 on that population's distribution of means is 1.84 test points above the overall mean of 208 for that distribution, for a Z score of 1.84/6, or .31.

The normal curve table shows that 12% of a normal curve falls between the mean and a Z of .31, so 38% remains beyond a Z of .31. Thus in our example, 38% of the means drawn from Population 1 can be expected to have a Z score of .31 or above; 38% of the means can be expected to be above a raw score of 209.84.

Here is the conclusion: If the research hypothesis that the true mean of the population of students who get the special instructions is 208, the chance of getting a sample of 64 from this population that will yield a significant result (that is, the chance of getting a sample of 64 in which the mean is greater than 209.84) is 38%. Hence we say that the power of this experiment is 38%. Beta, the chance of making a Type II error, is 62% (100% − 38% = 62%).

Notice that the computation of power has nothing to do with the actual outcome of the experiment. In fact, it is ordinarily computed before conducting the study to help determine whether the study has enough power to be worth conducting (or whether the procedures of the proposed study should first be adjusted in some way to make it more powerful).

Summary of the Steps in Computing Power

Computing power for a study involving a mean of an actual sample compared to a known population involves four steps:

1. Gather the needed information. You need (a) the mean and standard deviation of the comparison distribution and (b) the predicted mean of the population that receives the experimental intervention (we discuss how to determine this mean shortly). You will also find it very helpful to make a diagram of the two distributions similar to Figure 8-2.

2. Determine the cutoff point, in raw score terms, needed on the comparison distribution to reject the null hypothesis.

3. Determine the Z score on the distribution of means for the population that receives the experimental manipulation that corresponds to the raw score found in Step 2.

4. Using the normal curve table, determine the probability of getting a score more extreme than that Z score.[2]

Another Example

Let's consider another fictional example. A large organization is concerned about the health of its employees and is considering instituting a policy under which employees are individually assessed and given needed training and advice on various health-related behaviors (exercise, diet, smoking, etc.). To test the effectiveness of the policy, the following study is planned: 80 employees will be randomly selected to participate and will be measured at the end of a year on a standard test of their overall health. We will assume that this organization does extensive testing of its employees, and it is known that in the organization as a whole (which is the population in this study), the mean score on the standard health test is 58, the standard deviation is 14, and the scores are normally distributed. For the program to be worth implementing, there must be an improvement of at least 5 points (that

---

[2]In this chapter, and whenever using this method of computing power—the only computational method you will learn in this book—you always assume a normal distribution of the distributions of means.

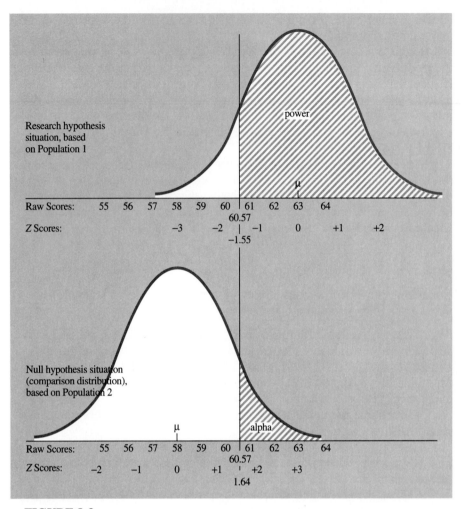

FIGURE 8-3
Distributions of means of 80 cases based on hypothesized (upper) and known (lower) distributions of populations of individual cases in a fictional study of employees receiving a health promotion program. Z scores and raw scores are shown on both distributions corresponding to the significance cutoff on the lower distribution (significance cutoff based on $p < .05$, one-tailed).

is, the predicted mean is 63). The .05 significance level will be used. The distributions of means for the two populations are shown in Figure 8-3.

What is the power of this experiment?

1. Gather the needed information. In our example, the mean of the comparison distribution is 58, and the predicted mean of the population that receives the experimental intervention is 63. The variance of the population is 196 ($14^2 = 196$). Thus the variance of the distribution of means, the comparison distribution, is 196/80, which is 2.45, and so it has a standard deviation of 1.57.

2. Determine the cutoff point, in raw score terms, needed on the comparison distribution to reject the null hypothesis. Using a one-tailed test (the organization is interested only in whether the program increases health) and the 5% significance level, the Z score cutoff is +1.64. And a Z of +1.64 equals a raw score of 60.57: $58 + (1.64 \times 1.57) = 60.57$. That is why in the lower distribution in Figure 8-3, we have shaded the area in the tail above 60.57. This is the alpha region.

3. Determine the Z score on the distribution for the population that receives the experimental manipulation for the raw score found in Step 2. A raw score of 60.57 is equivalent to a Z score of –1.55 on this distribution: $(60.57 - 63)/1.57 = -1.55$. We have shaded the area in the upper distribution to the right of –1.55 to indicate the power because that is the area in which a mean of an actual sample would turn out to be significant on the comparison distribution.

4. Using the normal curve table, determine the probability of getting a score beyond that Z score. The normal curve table shows about 44% between the mean and a Z of 1.55. Since the area in which we are interested is all of the area to the right of –1.55, there is a total of 44% plus the 50% above the mean, adding up to 94%. The power of this experiment is 94%.

Power Tables

The procedures we have described for computing power apply when we have a known population and a single sample representing a population being compared to it. In more complex cases—the kinds of experimental situations we consider in the next several chapters—computing power directly in this way becomes considerably more difficult. Fortunately, however, it is possible to determine the power of an experiment directly, using standard **power tables** (such tables have been prepared by Cohen, 1988, and Kraemer & Thiemann, 1987, among others).

power tables

The fundamental logic on which these tables are based is exactly what you have learned here, and using the tables requires exactly the same information that is needed to compute power directly. (Interestingly, power calculations are not directly available in standard computerized statistical packages.) Our purpose in this chapter, however, is to introduce you to the conceptual underpinnings of power. We want you to understand what influences it and how all this is applied in planning experiments and interpreting research results. In later chapters, whenever you learn a new hypothesis-testing procedure, we will also furnish power tables and discuss how to use them. (An index of these tables is provided as Table B-5 in Appendix B.)

What Determines Power

Power depends on two substantive issues plus some technical points. The two substantive issues are (a) how big an effect the research hypothesis predicts and (b) how many subjects are used in the experiment. The technical points are the significance level chosen, whether a one- or two-tailed test is used, and the kind of hypothesis-testing procedure employed.

Effect Size

If you look at Figs. 8-2 and 8-3, you can see that it is more likely that an experiment will yield a significant result if the two distributions being compared have little overlap. If the two distributions did not cover the same area at all, any mean of a sample drawn from the distribution in which the experimental manipulation has been applied would be extreme enough on the comparison distribution to yield a significant result.

Two distributions might have little overlap either because there is a large difference between their means (as in Figure 8-4a) or because they have so little variance that even with a small mean difference they do not overlap much (Figure 8-4b).

effect size The extent to which the two populations do not overlap (due to the combined impact of difference in means and low population variance) is called the **effect size** because it describes the degree to which the experimental manipulation has an effect of separating the two populations.

FIGURE 8-4
The hypothesized and comparison distributions of means might have little overlap (and hence the study have high power) because either (a) the two means are very different or (b) the variance is very small.

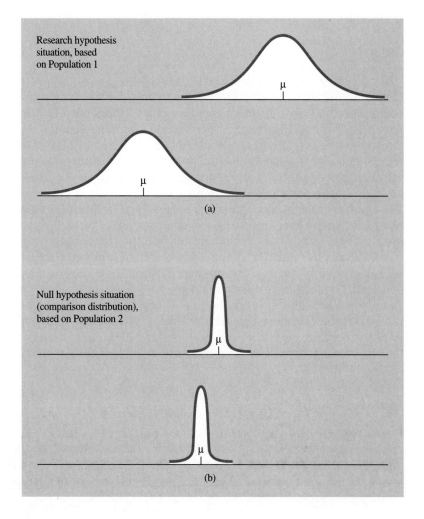

Example of How Power Is Affected by the Size of the Difference Between Means

As noted, the farther apart the means of the two populations, the less overlap of the two populations and therefore the bigger the effect size. Consider the fifth-grade testing example. Suppose that we had reason to hypothesize that the group receiving the special instructions would have a mean of 216. In this case, we would be hypothesizing a much bigger effect size than for the 208 prediction we used previously. Notice in Figure 8-5 that with the affected population having a hypothesized mean of 216, there is much less overlap in the distributions of means, so the power should be greater. Let's compute it. (We will follow systematically through all the steps once again, as another full example of the procedure.)

FIGURE 8-5
Distributions of means of 64 cases based on hypothesized (upper) and known (lower) distributions of populations of individual cases in a fictional study of fifth graders receiving special instructions prior to taking a standard achievement test. Z scores and raw scores are shown on both distributions corresponding to the significance cutoff on the lower distribution (significance cutoff based on $p < .05$, one-tailed). In this example, the hypothesized mean (of the upper distribution) is 216.

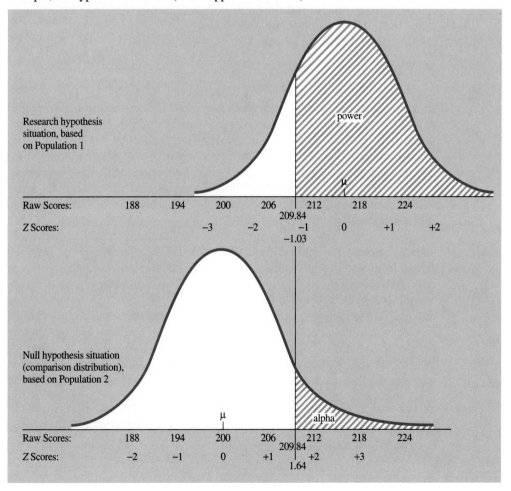

1. Gather the needed information. The mean of the comparison distribution is 200, and its standard deviation is 6; the predicted mean of the population that receives the experimental intervention is 216, and its standard deviation and hence the standard deviation of the distribution of means based on it is assumed to be the same. The distributions (as well as the shading of the alpha and power areas) are shown in Figure 8-5.

2. Determine the cutoff point, in raw score terms, needed on the comparison distribution to reject the null hypothesis. As when we used this example earlier in the chapter, the needed raw score mean for significance is +209.84.

3. Determine the Z score on the distribution for the population that receives the experimental manipulation for the raw score found in Step 2. A raw score of 209.84 is 6.16 below the hypothesized mean of 216, or a Z score of −1.03 on this distribution.

4. Determine the probability of getting a score beyond that Z score. According to the normal curve table, the chance of getting a sample with a Z score of −1.03 or higher is 85% (that is, 35% between this Z score and the mean and another 50% above the mean).

Compare when we hypothesize a large, 16-point difference between the two populations—a power of 85%—to the power of 38% when we hypothesized a much smaller difference of only 8 points between the two populations. (Similarly, compare Figures 8-5 and 8-2.)

Minimum Meaningful Difference

minimum meaningful difference

In actual practice, we rarely know how big a difference the experimental manipulation will make. Sometimes we can estimate it from similar prior research or based on some precise theory. But more often we are reduced to simply making a rough guess. One approach is to ask what is the smallest difference that would matter—that would contribute useful knowledge or have a practical impact—and then use that to figure our hypothesized mean when computing power. This is called the method of the **minimum meaningful difference.**

In the case of the fifth graders, for example, the researchers might reason that unless the special instructions made a difference of at least 10 points in test scores, it would not be worth the trouble to use them. In that case, power would be computed using a hypothesized mean of 210 (a figure 10 points higher than the known mean for fifth graders who do not receive the special instructions). The two distributions are shown in Figure 8-6. In this case, the needed score for significance of 209.84 is .16 test points below the hypothesized mean of 210. This gives a Z of −.03 on the distribution of means for the hypothesized affected population. Using the normal curve table, this gives a power of 51%. So if in fact the true difference is at least as large as the minimum meaningful difference, this experiment has at least a 51% chance of producing a significant result. (Is that enough to make the study worthwhile? We consider the question of how much power to require later in the chapter.)

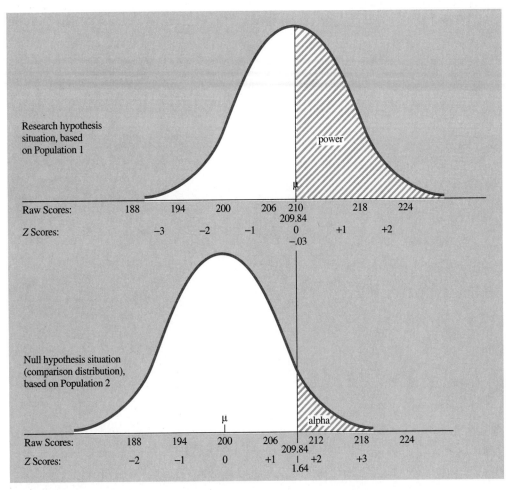

FIGURE 8-6
Distributions of means of 64 cases based on hypothesized (upper) and known (lower) distributions of populations of individual cases in a fictional study of fifth graders receiving special instructions prior to taking a standard achievement test. Z scores and raw scores are shown on both distributions corresponding to the significance cutoff on the lower distribution (significance cutoff based on $p < .05$, one-tailed). In this example, the hypothesized mean (of the upper distribution) is 210, based on a minimal meaningful difference from the comparison distribution of 10 points.

How Power Is Affected by Standard Deviation

As noted earlier, the amount of overlap between the two distributions is affected both by how far apart their means are and also by how spread out each population is. This was illustrated in Figure 8-4. In our fifth-grade testing example, suppose that instead of a population standard deviation of 48 ($\sigma^2 = 2,304$), the population standard deviation was 24 ($\sigma^2 = 576$). This would result in a standard deviation of 3 for a distribution of means of samples of 64 cases each ($\sigma_M = \sqrt{576/64} = 3$). As shown in Figure 8-7, this

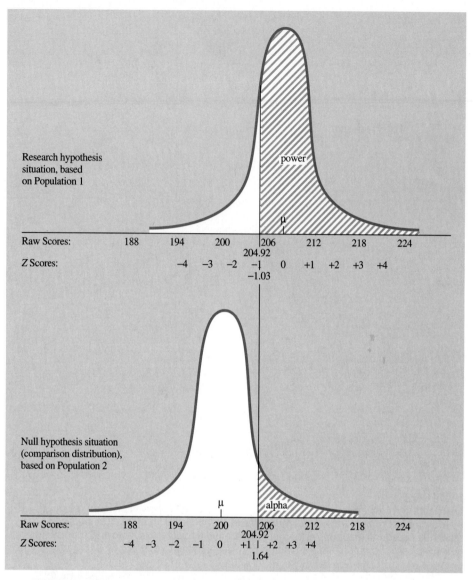

FIGURE 8-7
Distributions of means of 64 cases based on hypothesized (upper) and known (lower) distributions of populations of individual cases in a fictional study of fifth graders receiving special instructions prior to taking a standard achievement test. Z scores and raw scores are shown on both distributions corresponding to the significance cutoff on the lower distribution (significance cutoff based on $p < .05$, one-tailed). But this time the population standard deviation is half as large as that shown in Figure 8-2 (and used in the previous examples for this study).

makes the two populations have very little overlap (compare this to the situation with the original standard deviation shown in Figure 8-2.)

The needed score for significance at the 5% level, one-tailed, would be 200 plus the product of 3 (the standard deviation of the distribution of means) times 1.64, or 204.92. As you can see in Figure 8-7, this cutoff level is created on the lower distribution; when you follow the line up to the corresponding 204.92 on the upper distribution (the distribution of means for the hypothesized population receiving the special instructions), it falls below its hypothesized mean of 208. Numerically, it is 3.08 below its mean (208 − 204.92 = 3.08), or a Z score of −1.03 (minus because it is below the mean). Using the normal curve table, this corresponds to a power of 85%. Now we are doing better.

Computing Effect Size

From the examples it should be clear that effect size (and hence power) varies with either the difference between means or the standard deviation. In fact, in the examples, the result of halving the population standard deviation (from 48 to 24) gave exactly the same power (85%) as doubling the expected difference between the means (from 8 to 16 test points).

Effect size is calculated by taking into account both the best guess of a difference between the means and the population standard deviation (with the standard deviations assumed to be the same for both populations, remember). Here is the rule: Divide the hypothesized difference between the means by the standard deviation of the original population of individual cases. In terms of a formula, it is

$$d = \frac{\mu_1 - \mu_2}{\sigma} \qquad (8\text{-}1)$$

where d is the symbol for effect size (also known as "Cohen's d") of the type that is appropriate to the kind of hypothesis testing you have learned so far (in later chapters, you learn of other measures of effect size that are appropriate to different situations), μ_1 is the mean of Population 1 (the hypothesized mean for the population that is subjected to the experimental manipulation), μ_2 is the mean of Population 2 (which is also the mean of the comparison distribution), and σ is the standard deviation of Population 2 (again, assumed to be the standard deviation of both populations). Notice that when calculating effect size, we do not use the standard deviation of the distribution of means (σ_M) but rather that of the original population of individual cases (σ); we'll explain why shortly.

In our first example in this chapter, in which the difference between the means was 8 and the standard deviation of the original populations of individual cases was 48, the effect size was 8/48, or .17. In terms of the formula,

$$d = \frac{\mu_1 - \mu_2}{\sigma} = \frac{208 - 200}{48} = \frac{8}{48} = .17$$

In the example in which the mean difference was 16 test points and the population standard deviation was still 48, the effect size was doubled: 16/48, or .33. And when we used a mean difference of 8 with a population standard deviation of 24 the effect size was 8/24, which was also .33.

A More General Importance of Effect Size

When computing effect size, dividing the mean difference by the standard deviation of the population of individual cases standardizes the difference in the same way that a Z score gives a standard metric for comparison to other scores, even scores on different scales. Especially by using the standard deviation of the population of individual cases, we bypass the dissimilarity from study to study of different sample sizes, making comparison even easier and effect size even more of a standard metric.

Thus knowing the effect size of a study permits us to compare results with effect sizes found in other studies, even those using different sample sizes. Equally important, knowing effect size can permit us to compare studies using different measures that may have scales with quite different means and variances. And even within a particular study, our general knowledge of what is a small or a large effect size helps us evaluate the overall importance of a result. For example, a result may be significant but not very large. Or a result that is not significant (perhaps due to a small sample) may have just as large an effect size as was found in another study (perhaps one with a larger sample) in which the result was significant. Knowing the effect sizes of the studies help us make better sense of such outcomes. We examine both of these important implications of effect size in later sections of this chapter.

Effect Size Conventions

Obviously, it is usually difficult to know how big an effect to expect from a given experiment. If we knew, we would not need to do the research. But Jacob Cohen (1988), a psychologist who has done a great deal of work in developing the statistics of power, has suggested some **effect size conventions** based on the effects observed in psychology research in general.

Recall that we computed effect size as the predicted difference between the means of the two populations of interest, divided by the population standard deviation: $d = (\mu_1 - \mu_2)/\sigma$.

Cohen suggests that for comparing means, the kind of problem we are doing in this chapter, a "small effect size" is about .2. Cohen notes that with an effect size of .2, the populations of individual cases have an overlap of about 85%, and this is the effect size, for example, of the difference in height between 15- and 16-year-old girls (see Figure 8-8a), which is about a $\frac{1}{2}$-inch difference with a standard deviation of about 2.1 inches. (When we speak of percentage overlap in these examples, we are referring to the overlap of the populations of individual cases. The amount of overlap of the distributions of means will be less, depending on the sample size.)

Cohen considers a medium effect size to be .5, which means an overlap of about 67%. It is exemplified by the difference in heights between 14- and 18-year-old girls (see Figure 8-8b).

Finally, Cohen defines a large effect size as .8—only about 53% overlap and corresponding to the difference in height between 13- and 18-year-old girls (see Figure 8-8c). These three effect sizes are summarized in Table 8-2.

These conventions have proved immensely valuable to researchers in planning and evaluating research, so it will be worth considering a couple of additional examples of small, medium, and large effect size. First, consider IQ. As we noted earlier in the book, IQ tests typically have a standard deviation of 16 points. So an intervention that had a small effect size would imply an increase in IQ of 3.2 IQ points. (A difference of 3.2 IQ points between the mean of the group that received the intervention and the population that did not, divided by the population standard deviation of 16,

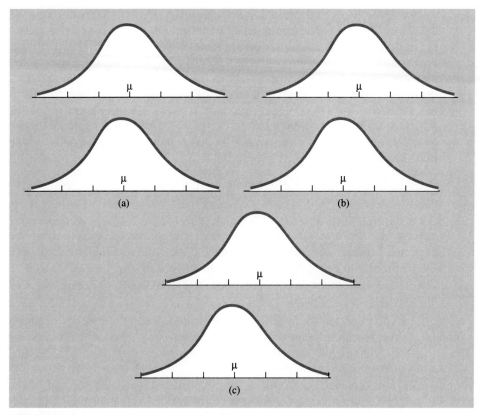

FIGURE 8-8
Comparisons of pairs of raw score population distributions illustrating conventions for effect size: (a) small effect size ($d = .2$), (b) medium effect size ($d = .5$), (c) large effect size ($d = .8$).

comes out to .2, a small effect size.) An intervention with a medium effect size would increase IQ by 8 points, and an intervention with a large effect size would increase IQ by 12.8 points. As another example, consider SAT scores ($\sigma = 100$). In a population with a mean SAT score of 500, individuals exposed to an intervention with a small effect size would score 520; those exposed to an intervention with a medium effect size would score 550, and those exposed to an intervention with a large effect size would score 580.

One other point should be made about Cohen's effect size conventions. Once you have chosen an expected effect size using these rules, if you also know the population standard deviation (as we do in our example), you can

TABLE 8-2
Summary of Cohen's Effect Size Conventions for Mean Differences

Verbal Description	Effect Size (d)
Small	.2
Medium	.5
Large	.8

compute the predicted mean for Population 1. We won't go through the details of doing this because once an expected effect size is set, it is possible to figure out power directly (using tables). Nevertheless, it may help you understand these conventions to consider their implications for the expected mean of Population 1 in our example (in which the population standard deviation is 48, Population 2's mean is 200, and there are 64 individuals in the sample). For a medium effect size ($d = .5$), the predicted mean for Population 1 would be 224 with a power of 99%. And for a small effect size ($d = .2$), the predicted mean would be 209.6 with a power of 52%. These two situations are illustrated in Figure 8-9.

Summary of Ways of Determining Expected Effect Size

A crucial step in the process of computing power, as we have seen, is determining the information associated with the expected effect size—the expected mean difference and the population standard deviation. Determining the expected mean difference is usually the part of effect size that raises the greatest difficulty, and we have addressed two ways of approaching this problem:

1. The expected mean difference is estimated based on theory or previous research findings. This is the preferred method, when it is possible. Often, however, research is breaking new ground, and the needed information is simply not available.
2. The expected mean difference is estimated using the method of the minimum meaningful difference. In applied research, this is usually the preferred method, as it focuses on the practical question of whether a difference is large enough to matter.

In addition, we have seen that it is possible to estimate effect size directly, without considering its parts, using Cohen's conventions. This approach is very widely used in theoretically based research. It has the advantage of not requiring highly specific information from prior research or very precise theories, while at the same time allowing the psychologist familiar with the research literature in the field to make general use of related findings or of the kind of relatively inexact theories that characterize the early stages of work in a particular research area.

Sample Size

The number of subjects in the sample has a profound effect on power. Remember, this influence is entirely separate from effect size, which we have just talked about. Sample size is one of the *two* main influences on power; the other is effect size.

The influence of sample size on power can be seen by considering that the larger the sample size, the smaller the standard deviation of the distribution of means (while, of course, there is no change in the standard deviation of the distribution of the population of individual cases). Thus the same distance between the means of two populations of individual cases represents less overlap in the distribution of means when sample size is larger because the two distributions of means are narrower (have less variation). To put it simply, for a given effect size, the more subjects, the more power.

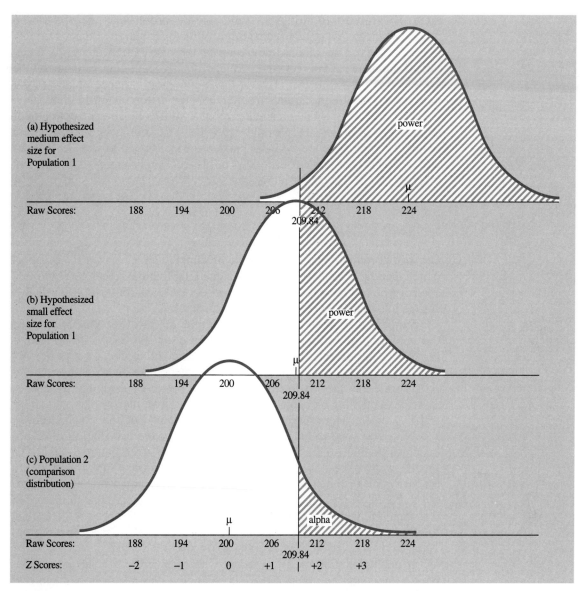

FIGURE 8-9
Distributions of means of 64 cases based on hypothesized (a, b) and known (c) distributions of populations of individual cases in a fictional study of fifth graders receiving special instructions prior to taking a standard achievement test. Z scores are shown on both distributions corresponding to the significance cutoff on the lower distribution (significance cutoff based on $p < .05$, one-tailed). (a) Hypothesized distribution with medium effect size. (b) Hypothesized distribution with small effect size.

Don't get mixed up. When the standard deviation of the population of individual cases is low, this also makes power high—ultimately because this makes the standard deviations of the distributions of means low, making these two distributions narrower and thus more separated. When the sample size is high (the sample contains many subjects), power is also high—also, ultimately, for the same reason. This makes the standard deviations of the distribution of means low, making their distributions more separated. But these two situations (and two different ways of influencing power) result in low standard deviations of the distribution of means for different reasons. The standard deviation of the distribution of means is the square root of what you get when you divide the population variance by the sample size ($\sigma_M = \sqrt{\sigma^2/N}$). Thus a low population variance decreases the numerator. But a high sample size increases the denominator. In both cases, the result of the division is a smaller number. But population standard deviation is part of effect size. Sample size is *not* part of effect size. Thus effect size and sample size are two independent influences on power. And as we will see shortly, these two different influences imply completely different kinds of practical steps for increasing power when designing a study.

Computing Power With Different Numbers of Subjects

One of the reasons that the influence of sample size on power is so important is that the number of subjects is something that the researcher can often control prior to the experiment. (The effect size, by contrast, is much less susceptible to substantial researcher influence.)

Suppose that, as in our original example, the most reasonable estimate of the effect size yielded a hypothesized mean of 208 for the group receiving the special instructions. However, after computing the power to be only 38% (as we did at the beginning of the chapter), the educational psychologists decide that they had better increase the power by using more subjects. So instead of using 64 subjects, they arrange to give the special instructions to 100 subjects. More subjects means more power—but how much more?

With 100 subjects, the standard deviation of the distribution of means becomes smaller, so these distributions overlap less (see Figure 8-10). To be precise, with a population standard deviation of 48 ($\sigma^2 = 2{,}304$) and a sample size of 100, the standard deviation of the distribution of means comes out to be 4.8 ($\sigma_M = \sqrt{2304/100} = \sqrt{23.04} = 4.8$). (Compare this to the previous standard deviation of 6 when using 64 subjects.) To get significance at the 5% level, one-tailed, you still need a Z score of 1.64, but this now converts to a raw score of 207.87: $200 + (1.64 \times 4.8) = 207.87$.

If our population of fifth graders who receive the special instructions have a mean of 208, then 207.87 is .13 below the mean, or a Z score of $-.03$. Based on the normal curve table, the chance of getting a sample with a mean that has a Z score of $-.03$ or above is about 51%. This is shown in Figure 8-10.

Still, even 51% is pretty low power given the investment that the researchers plan to put into the project. So they consider what would happen if they used a really large sample—say, 500. Now the standard deviation of the two distributions of means becomes only 2.15 ($\sqrt{2{,}304/500} = \sqrt{4.61} = 2.15$). The resulting distributions are shown in Figure 8-11. The needed significance Z score cutoff of 1.64 now converts to a raw score of 203.53: $200 + (1.64 \times 2.15) = 203.53$. This is 4.47 below the mean of 208, or a Z score of -2.08. The chance of getting a sample with a mean (power) that is -2.08 or higher, based on the normal curve table, is 98%!

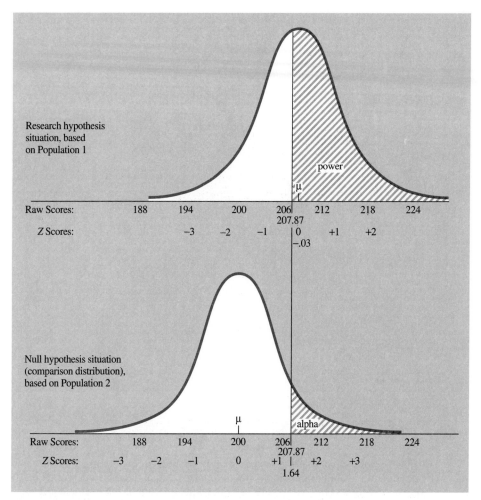

FIGURE 8-10
Distributions of means of 100 cases based on hypothesized (upper) and known (lower) distributions of populations of individual cases in a fictional study of fifth graders receiving special instructions prior to taking a standard achievement test. Z scores and raw scores are shown on both distributions corresponding to the significance cutoff on the lower distribution (significance cutoff based on $p < .05$, one-tailed).

Figuring Needed Sample Size for a Given Level of Power

In actual practice, the usual reason for computing power before conducting a study is to determine how many subjects are needed to achieve a reasonable level of power. This can be done by turning the steps of computing power on their head, beginning with a desired level of power—say, 80%—and then calculating how many subjects are needed to get that level of power. In the present example, with a predicted mean difference of 8 and a standard deviation of 48 (and using the 5% level, one-tailed), the researcher would need 222 subjects to obtain a power of 80%. We won't go into the computational details here because in practice, researchers would use a

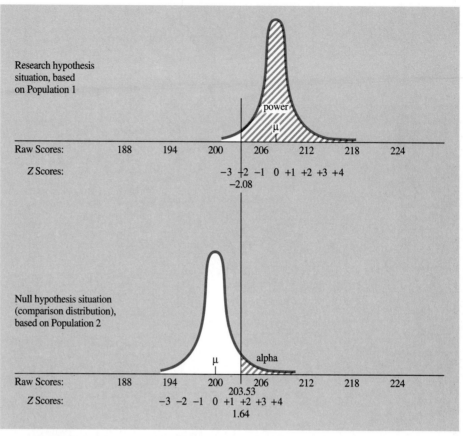

FIGURE 8-11
Distributions of means of 500 cases based on hypothesized (upper) and known (lower) distributions of populations of individual cases in a fictional study of fifth graders receiving special instructions prior to taking a standard achievement test. Z scores and raw scores are shown on both distributions corresponding to the significance cutoff on the lower distribution (significance cutoff based on $p < .05$, one-tailed).

table. Indeed, in subsequent chapters, each time we cover a new hypothesis-testing technique, in addition to providing power tables, we also provide a table giving the minimum number of subjects needed to achieve 80% power with small, medium, and large effect sizes.

Other Influences on Power

Three other factors play a role in determining power: significance level (alpha), number of tails used in testing (one or two), and statistical procedure.

Influence of Significance Level on Power

As we noted in Chapter 7, if you set a stringent significance level, such as .01, you are less likely to make a Type I error (the chance is only 1% instead of the usual 5%). But the trade-off is that it then becomes more likely that

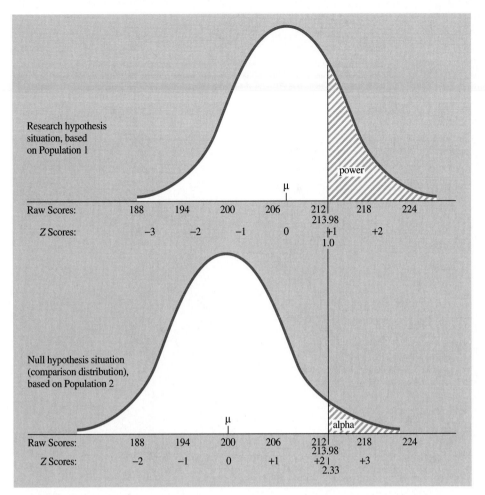

Research hypothesis
situation, based
on Population 1

power

Raw Scores:	188	194	200	206	212 213.98	218	224
Z Scores:		−3	−2	−1	0	+1 1.0	+2

Null hypothesis situation
(comparison distribution),
based on Population 2

alpha

Raw Scores:	188	194	200	206	212 213.98	218	224
Z Scores:		−2	−1	0	+1	+2 2.33	+3

FIGURE 8-12
Distributions of means of 64 cases based on hypothesized (upper) and known (lower)
distributions of populations of individual cases in a fictional study of fifth graders
receiving special instructions prior to taking a standard achievement test. Z scores and
raw scores are shown on both distributions corresponding to the significance cutoff
on the lower distribution, now using $p < .01$, one-tailed.

you will make a Type II error. That is, if nothing else is changed, alpha and
beta are complementary: Increase one, and you decrease the other.

In our original example, suppose that instead of using the 5% significance level, you wanted to use the 1% level (still one-tailed). In this case, to
get significance, the mean of your sample would have to have a Z score of
at least 2.33. As shown in Figure 8-12, for our original example using a
sample size of 64 and a standard deviation of 6 for the distribution of
means, at the 1% level, a raw score mean of at least 213.98 is needed for
significance. This is 5.98 test points above the mean of Population 1, or a Z
score of about 1. Only about 16% of the means will be above this number;
that is, power is only 16%. (This is much lower than even the original low
38% power at the 5% significance level, as shown in Fig. 8-2.)

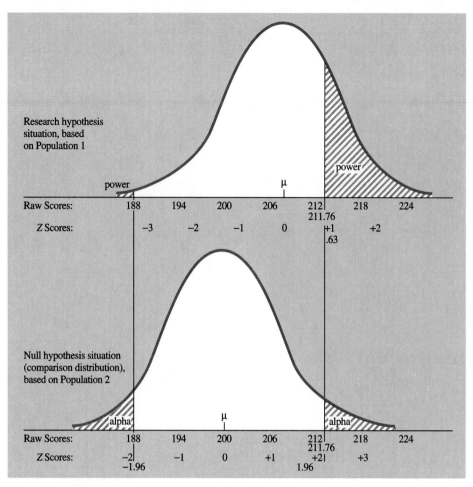

FIGURE 8-13
Distributions of means of 64 cases based on hypothesized (upper) and known (lower) distributions of populations of individual cases in a fictional study of fifth graders receiving special instructions prior to taking a standard achievement test. Z scores and raw scores are shown on both distributions corresponding to the significance cutoff on the lower distribution, using $p < .05$, but now two-tailed.

Effect of Using Two-Tailed Versus One-Tailed Tests

Similarly, using a two-tailed test makes it harder to get significance on any one tail, simultaneously making a Type I error less likely and a Type II error more likely. That is, keeping everything else the same, power is less with a two-tailed test than with a one-tailed test.

Suppose that we had used a two-tailed test instead of a one-tailed test (but still using the 5% level overall) in our fifth-grade testing example. In this situation, for significance we need a mean on the predicted positive side with a Z score of at least 1.96 (2.5% at each tail), which equals a raw score in our original example of 211.76. This figure is 3.76 above the hypothesized mean of 208, or a Z score of .63, giving a power of 26%. This is all illustrated in Figure 8-13. (It is true that you gain something in power from the small chance that the result will be extreme in the direction opposite the prediction. But as can be seen in the figure, this area is typically so small that it can be ignored in the computations.)

Other Hypothesis-Testing Procedures

Finally, there are cases where the researcher has a choice of more than one statistical procedure to apply to a given set of results. (Or there may be more than one type of research design available, such as between-subjects versus within-subjects; see Appendix A.) We have not considered any such cases so far in this book. However, you should know that when such choices are made, researchers will often consider how the different alternatives available will affect the power of the experiment they plan.

Summary of Influences on Power

Table 8-3 summarizes the effects of various factors on the power of an experiment. Note that power is greatest when the mean difference is large, the population standard deviation is small, the sample size is large, a not very stringent significance level is used (such as .05 as opposed to .01), and a one-tailed test is employed. Power is least when the opposites to these conditions hold. Also note that each of these influences is independent of the others, so that high levels of one can offset low levels of another.

TABLE 8-3
Influences on Power

Feature of the Study	Increases Power	Decreases Power
Effect size (d) $(d = [\mu_1 - \mu_2]/\sigma)$	Large d	Small d
Effect size combines the following two features:		
Hypothesized difference between population means $(\mu_1 - \mu_2)$	Large differences	Small differences
Population standard deviation (σ)	Small σ	Large σ
Sample size (N)	Large N	Small N
Significance level α	Lenient, high α (such as 5% or 10%)	Stringent, low α (such as 1% or .1%)
One-tailed versus two-tailed test	One-tailed	Two-tailed
Type of hypothesis-testing procedure used	Varies	Varies

Role of Power When Designing an Experiment

Power calculations play an important role when designing an experiment. If the power of a planned experiment is low, this means that even if the research hypothesis is true, this study is not likely to yield significant results in support of it. In such a case, the time and expense of carrying out the study are rarely worthwhile. So when the power of a planned experiment is found to be low, researchers attempt to find practical ways to increase the power to an acceptable level. (Many psychology researchers fail to think about power as much as they should when planning experiments; see Box 8-1.)

What Is an Acceptable Level of Power?

An increasingly used convention, suggested by Cohen (1988), is that a study should have 80% power to be worth conducting. However, if a study is very difficult or costly to conduct, a researcher might want even higher levels (such as 90% or even 95%) before undertaking the project.

BOX 8-1

The Power of Typical Psychology Experiments

More than three decades ago, Jacob Cohen (1962), a psychologist specializing in statistical methods, published a now well known analysis of the statistical power of studies described in articles published in the 1960 volume of the *Journal of Abnormal and Social Psychology*. He had observed that great attention is given to significance, or the issue of whether a Type I error has been made (that the null hypothesis was mistakenly rejected and some effect was being assumed from the results that in fact did not exist). But essentially no attention was given to the possibility of a Type II error (that the null hypothesis had been mistakenly accepted and a real effect was being dismissed as nonexistent). Power was not even discussed in these studies.

Cohen computed the power for the results in these articles. Not being familiar with the many content areas involved, he looked at power under three assumptions of effect size: small, medium, and large. If small, he found, the studies published had only one chance in six of detecting an effect. Not one had a better than 50-50 chance. If he assumed a medium effect in the population, the studies had a slightly better than 50-50 chance of detecting this effect. One quar-

ter still had less than one chance in three. Only assuming large effects gave the studies as they were designed a good chance of rejecting the null hypothesis. As Cohen put it, "A generation of researchers could be suitably employed in repeating interesting studies which originally used inadequate sample sizes. Unfortunately, the ones most deserving such repetition are least likely to have appeared in print" (p. 153).

In the last sentence, Cohen refers to the fact that many more studies that would have been appropriate for this journal were probably never written up because the researchers obtained nonsignificant results that the odds clearly showed they were doomed to obtain, given the low power of most studies in that field. These "experiments that failed" when in fact their hypotheses were never adequately tested represent tremendous knowledge that may have been lost, perhaps never to be explored again. And this loss is only because of a failure to be concerned about power—most often a failure to calculate, through a consideration of effect size, significance level, and power, the sample size that would best test the hypothesis.

Several other similar analyses of the power of

Conversely, if a study is very easy and inexpensive to conduct, a researcher might be willing to take a chance with a somewhat lower level of power (such as 60% or 70%).

The level of power that a researcher settles on also depends on how difficult and costly it is to increase power. Circumstances might make possible a quick and cheap study with power of 65%, but increasing power to even 70% might be nearly impossible. In other cases, even when a study is a major project, increasing the power might not involve much additional effort.

How to Increase the Power of a Planned Study

The power of a planned study can, in principle, be increased by changing any of the features summarized in Table 8-3—increasing the predicted mean difference, decreasing the population standard deviation, and so forth. In practice, however, all but one or two of the possibilities are ruled out in any given situation. Let's consider each in turn.

studies in a given journal have been conducted since Cohen's (e.g., Brewer's 1972 analysis of the *American Educational Research Journal* and Chase & Chase's 1976 study of the *Journal of Applied Psychology*). Meanwhile, Cohen published a handbook for analyzing power in the social sciences in 1969, and his revision of it appeared in 1988. Still, in an article published in 1989, Sedlmeier and Gigerenzer observed that Cohen's admonitions apparently had no effect during the intervening years. In fact, the power of studies in the same journal that Cohen had studied (now the *Journal of Abnormal Psychology*) had actually decreased over those years. And low power still went unnoticed. Only 2 of 64 experiments even discussed power, and these two had not estimated it. Meanwhile, in 11% of the studies published in that issue, nonsignificance was considered a confirmation of the null hypothesis, perhaps in an attempt to adhere to the traditional admonitions we questioned in Box 6-1. Yet Sedlmeier and Gigerenzer found that the median power in these particular studies was only .25. Certainly, if we are to consider it valuable information in itself when results favor the null hypothesis (again, see Box

6-1), it can only be taken that way when power is high enough so that if the research hypothesis was true, the study would at least have an even chance of showing it.

This stubborn failure by researchers to consider power is a bit shocking. It means that more often than not, researchers are going through all their work for nothing. The odds are against their finding what they seek, even if it is true. And it seems that methodology in psychology is so monolithic and fixed that it cannot be budged. But in an article in *American Psychologist* titled "Things I Have Learned (So Far)," Jacob Cohen (1990) looked back over the decades philosophically:

> I do not despair. I remember that W. S. Gossett, the fellow who worked in a brewery and appeared in print modestly as "Student," published the *t* test a decade before we entered World War I, and the test didn't get into the psychological statistics textbooks until after World War II.
>
> These things take time. So, if you publish something that you think is really good, and a year or a decade or two go by and hardly anyone seems to have taken notice, remember the *t* test, and take heart. (p. 1311)

Increasing the Expected Difference Between Population Means

The predicted mean difference is usually based on theory or previous research, on what will be a meaningful practical effect, or simply on Cohen's effect size conventions. Thus changing the prediction, though it might increase power, would undermine the point of the power calculation. For example, suppose that you had reason to believe that what you were studying has only a small, subtle effect. In that case, if you arbitrarily decided to consider it to have a large effect size, you would increase the power, but you would be calculating the power for a situation that does not represent what you really have reason to expect.

In some cases, however, it is possible to change the way the experiment is being conducted so that you have reason to expect a larger mean difference. For example, consider again our example of the experiment about the impact of special instructions on fifth graders. One way to increase the expected mean difference might be to make the instructions more elaborate, spending more time explaining them to the subjects, perhaps allowing time for practice, and so forth. Disadvantages of this approach are that it can be difficult or costly to implement or can create circumstances implementing the experimental treatment that are unrepresentative of those to which you want to generalize your results.

Decreasing the Population Standard Deviation

It is possible to decrease the population standard deviation in a planned experiment in at least two ways. One way is to conduct the study using a population that is less diverse than the one originally planned. For example, with the fifth-grade testing example, you might only use fifth graders in a particular suburban school system. (This assumes that the standard deviation for this more specific population is in fact smaller than for fifth graders in general.) A disadvantage of this approach is that the results apply only to the more limited population.

Another way to decrease the population standard deviation is to use conditions of testing that are more constant and measures that are more precise. For example, testing subjects under a standardized situation or in a controlled laboratory setting usually produces smaller overall variation among subjects in results (meaning a smaller standard deviation). Similarly, using tests with clear instructions and clear procedures for marking answers (that is, using highly reliable measures—covered in Chapter 17 and Appendix A) also tends to reduce the amount of overall variation. If more standardized testing conditions or more accurate measurement procedures are practical to implement, this is a highly recommended way to increase the power of an experiment.

Increasing Sample Size

The most straightforward way to increase power in a study is to use more subjects. Of course, if your subjects are astronauts who have walked on the moon, there is a limit to how many are available. But in most practical cases, sample size is the main way to modify a study to bring it up to sufficient power.

Using a Less Stringent Level of Significance or a One-Tailed Test

Ordinarily, the level of significance used should be the least stringent that gives adequate protection against Type I error; normally, this will be 5%. And whether you use a one- or a two-tailed test depends on the logic of the hypothesis being studied. Thus it is only in exceptional cases in which significance level and number of tails are factors to be modified to increase the power of a planned experiment.

Using a More Sensitive Hypothesis-Testing Procedure

So far, you have not learned any options for carrying out the hypothesis-testing procedure. However, in Chapter 15 you will see that there are circumstances in which there is more than one way to analyze the results of a study and that the relative power of the different methods is in fact a major consideration in making your choice of method.

Summary of Practical Ways of Increasing Power in a Planned Experiment

Table 8-4 summarizes some of the practical procedures a researcher can apply to increase the power of a planned experiment.

TABLE 8-4
Summary of Practical Ways of Increasing the Power of a Planned Experiment

Feature of the Study	Practical Way of Raising Power	Disadvantages
Hypothesized difference between population means $(\mu_1 - \mu_2)$	Increase the intensity of experimental manipulation.	May not be practical or may distort study's meaning.
Standard deviation (σ)	Use a less diverse population.	May not be available; decreases generalizability.
	Use standardized, controlled circumstances of testing or more precise measurement.	Not always practical.
Sample size (N)	Use a larger sample size.	Not always practical; can be costly.
Significance level (α)	Use a more lenient level of significance.	Raises alpha, the probability of Type I error.
One-tailed versus two-tailed test	Use a one-tailed test.	May not be appropriate to the logic of the study.
Type of hypothesis-testing procedure	Use a more sensitive procedure.	None may be available or appropriate.

Role of Power in Evaluating the Results of a Study

As we noted at the outset of this chapter, understanding statistical power and what influences it is of considerable importance in interpreting the results of psychology research. Here we consider the implications of what you have learned in this chapter as it applies in two situations: (a) when a result is significant and (b) when a result is not significant.

Role of Power When a Result Is Significant: Statistical Significance Versus Practical or Theoretical Significance

When evaluating the result of a study, statistical significance is considered first. If the result is not significant (and not even near to significant), the study is inconclusive, and ordinarily no inferences should be made based on patterns or trends in the data. Thus statistical significance is a necessary prerequisite to considering a result important, as either theoretically or practically significant.

For a result to be practically significant, however, in addition to statistical significance, it should be of a reasonable effect size. That is, even if a result is statistically significant, it could be a very slight effect that is not of any practical use.

We have learned that a study with a larger effect size is more likely to come out significant. But it is also possible for a study with a very small effect size to come out significant if the study has reasonable power due to other factors, especially a large sample size. Consider a study in which among all students who take the SAT in a particular year, a sample of 10,000 whose first name begins with a particular letter are randomly selected. And suppose that their mean SAT is 504, compared to the mean SAT of 500 ($SD = 100$) for the entire population. This result would be significant at the .001 level. But its effect size is a minuscule .04. That is, the significance test tells us that we can be quite confident that the population of students whose first name begins with this letter have higher SAT scores than the general population of students. But the effect size (or just looking at the mean difference) makes it clear that this difference is not very important; the distributions of the two populations overlap so much that it would be of little use in any individual case to know what letter a person's first name begins with.

The message of all this is that in evaluating a study, you must consider first whether the result is statistically significant. If it is, and if the study has any potential practical implications, you must then also consider whether the effect size is sufficiently large to make the result useful or interesting. If the sample was small, you can assume that a significant result is probably also practically significant. But if the sample size is very large, you must consider the effect size directly, as it is quite possible in such a case that it is too small to be useful.

Note that the implications are a bit paradoxical in light of what most people believe about sample size. Most people assume that the more subjects in a study that produced a significant result, the more important the result. In a sense, just the reverse is the case. All other things being equal, if a study with only a few subjects manages to attain significance, that significance must be due to a large effect size. A study with a large number of subjects that attains statistical significance may or may not have a large effect size.

Also notice that one should not just compare the significance level of two studies to see which has the more important result. A study with a small number of subjects that attains the .05 significance level might well have a larger effect size than a study with a large number of subjects that attains the .01 significance level.

Overall, then, the rule to remember is that obtaining significance in a study is based on both the effect size and the number of subjects. If one is large, the other can still be small. We have more to say on this topic later in this chapter.

Role of Power When a Result Is Not Significant

We saw in Chapter 6 that a result that is not significant is inconclusive. Often, however, we really would like to conclude that if the result is not significant, there is little or no difference between the population that did undergo the experimental manipulation and the one that did not. That is, if the result is not significant, we may want to say that the experimental manipulation did essentially nothing, that the research hypothesis was false. But the logic of hypothesis testing does not permit this kind of conclusion when the result is not significant. There is always the risk of a Type II error, and with low power, that risk is always higher.

Consider the relation of power to a nonsignificant result. If the power of the experiment was low, failing to get a significant result is simply inconclusive. The failure to find a significant result may have been because the research hypothesis was false (and no Type II error was in fact made). Or it may have been because the experiment had too little power for other reasons—for example, because it had too few subjects. Hence a real difference did not show up as statistically significant; a Type II error was made.

Conversely, if the power of the experiment was high, a nonsignificant result is fairly unlikely if the particular mean difference hypothesized is accurate. In this case, a nonsignificant result is a fairly strong argument that the research hypothesis (as specified with a specific mean difference) is false. This does not mean that all versions of the research hypothesis are false. For example, it is possible that the experimental manipulation does make a difference, but a much smaller one than was hypothesized when computing power.

In sum, a nonsignificant result from a study with low power is truly inconclusive. But a nonsignificant result from a study with high power does allow us to suggest, if not conclude, that either the research hypothesis is false or that there is less of an effect than was predicted when computing power. We have more to say about this topic later also.

Summary of the Role of Significance
and Sample Size in Interpreting Experimental Results

Table 8-5 summarizes the role of significance and sample size in interpreting experimental results.

TABLE 8-5
Role of Significance and Sample Size in Interpreting Experimental Results

Outcome Statistically Significant	Sample Size	Conclusion
Yes	Small	Important result
Yes	Large	Might or might not have practical importance
No	Small	Inconclusive
No	Large	Research hypothesis probably false

Controversies and Limitations

We now examine three current controversies that relate to the role of power and effect size in psychological research: (a) the possibility of "proving" the null hypothesis, (b) the importance of effect size versus statistical significance in interpreting results of experiments, and (c) the use of effect sizes to combine results from independent experiments.

Possibility of "Proving" the Null Hypothesis

It used to be an axiom taught in every introductory statistics textbook that "you can't prove the null hypothesis." What was meant by this is a point that we have emphasized throughout these chapters on hypothesis testing: When the results are not strong enough to reject the null hypothesis, the implication is that the results are inconclusive, not that the null hypothesis is true. As we noted earlier in this chapter, the failure to reject the null hypothesis could be due either to the research hypothesis's being false (that is, to the null hypothesis's being true) or to the experiment's having insufficient power. In fact, no matter how much power an experiment has, it is always possible that there is a real effect, but one that is so small that still more power would be necessary for it to show up. Put another way, no matter what the experimental results, it is always possible that the null hypothesis is not quite true, that there is some small difference between Populations 1 and 2. Some psychologists even emphasize that since the null hypothesis is that there is absolutely no difference between Populations 1 and 2, it is almost certainly false in every case.

The problem is that researchers are often in a position of being interested in a theoretical or practical question in which the prediction is that two groups or two experimental conditions will *not* produce different results—that the groups are the same or the experimental manipulation does not have any effect.

Strictly speaking, the conventional advice is correct: A study designed to show no difference is doomed to failure. The best you can hope for is a failure to reject the null hypothesis, which is only an inconclusive result. Hence textbooks on statistics and research methods warn students not to attempt research of this kind. (This is another "prejudice against the null hypothesis" as we discussed in Box 6-1.)

Cohen (1990) and others have offered a kind of solution. Yes, they say, you cannot strictly demonstrate the null hypothesis. But you can do something almost as good. You can use statistical results to make a convincing case that whatever difference exists must be very small. All you need to do is stipulate a specific small amount of difference. Then you (a) use that small difference as your predicted effect size, (b) set up an experiment that would have, say, 95% power of getting a significant result if that effect size actually exists in the world, and (c) conduct your study. If the study fails to achieve significance even with this amount of power, you have what amounts to a .05 (the leftover from the 95% power) significance level, which tells you that there is less than a 5% chance that your data came from a population with a difference larger than what you specified. However, conducting an experiment for a small effect size with 95% power will usually require an extremely large number of subjects, very often making the process impractical.

Effect Size Versus Statistical Significance

Recently, some psychologists (including Cohen, 1990) have argued that significance tests can be misleading and that it is more important to look at effect size in evaluating the outcome of an experiment. They argue, as we also noted earlier, that whether an experiment is or is not significant is as much a function of the number of subjects as it is of the underlying effect size. In other words, a study can fail to be significant simply due to too small a sample. And of course, it can easily be significant with a large sample even though the effect is very small. Further, they note, significance tests give an all-or-nothing outcome, whereas in reality a result may be near or far from the arbitrary cutoff of .05 or .01. (Worse still, they note, the emphasis on significance encourages the all-too-common error of confusing significance level with effect size—for example, considering a .05 result as "less significant" than a .01 result when in fact significance is a yes-no indication.) Finally, they argue that providing effect size gives information that can be compared to other studies and used in accumulating information over independent studies as research in a field progresses.

Of course, few psychologists would say that we should eliminate significance tests altogether. They recognize that when sample size is small, it is still possible to obtain a large effect size by chance, so significance tests protect against taking such results too seriously. Similarly, there are times when a very small effect size is nevertheless important (refer to the discussion of the binomial effect size display in Chapter 3), and it is crucial to know whether such a result should be trusted as not due to chance. But these observers feel that significance has been overemphasized. Most hold that significance should always be computed and reported but that effect size should also be computed and should be given the major emphasis in the discussion of results.

Others hold a quite different view. Chow (1988), for example, makes a distinction between applied and theoretically oriented research. In the context of applied research, where we are actually interested in how big a difference there is between two groups or how much a particular program changes things, effect sizes provide useful information. But when doing theoretical research, the situation is different—effect sizes are irrelevant and even misleading. Consider one of the experiments we mentioned in an earlier chapter (Abrams & Balota, 1991) involving speed of recognizing that a string of letters formed a word. Part of that study was intended to show that we process this kind of information faster when the words are familiar than when they are unfamiliar. This was a prediction based on theory (and in this case also on previous research). The result was significant. But the actual effect size would depend on all sorts of details that relate only to this particular experiment, such as the size and shape of the lever, the particular degree of familiarity of the words used, the size and distance and colors used in presenting the words on the computer screen, and so forth. Knowing the effect size actually gives very little information that would be worth having in interpreting the results of the study. What matters in a study like this, Chow says, is that the prediction of a difference in reaction time to familiar versus unfamiliar words was generated from theory, the results were consistent with what was predicted (as shown by the statistical significance), and thus the theory is supported.

And it is not only in cognitive psychology that research is primarily theoretical in this way. Experimental studies of motivations for interpersonal attraction, of how neural processes are influenced by chemical changes, of how infants develop language, or of how memory differs for emotional and nonemotional events are all examples of primarily theoretical research of the type that Chow emphasizes.

In fact, the current balance of the use of significance tests and effect sizes is probably just what one might expect from the points that Chow makes. In applied areas of psychology, there is an increasing emphasis on effect size. But in more theoretical areas of psychology, it is much rarer to see explicit mentions of effect size. Our own view is that even in theoretically oriented research, the potential loss (due to misplaced emphasis) by including effect size is probably offset by, among other benefits, the usefulness to future researchers of having such information to help them in computing power when planning their own studies.

Meta-Analysis

meta-analysis

A major development in recent decades has been the introduction of **meta-analysis,** a statistical method for combining the results of independent studies (*meta* is Greek for "beyond" or "above," so a meta-analysis is a kind of higher-order analysis, beyond or above the analysis of a single study). Meta-analysis is used primarily in articles that review the experiments conducted in a particular area of research.

Basically, a meta-analytic review of the literature involves (a) finding all the studies conducted on a given topic (such as the effectiveness of short-term cognitive psychotherapy or differences between girls and boys on arithmetic skills) and (b) statistically combining the results of these studies. The details of the combining process can be quite sophisticated, but it basically involves averaging the effect sizes while taking such things as the number of subjects in each study into account. The process leads to an overall average effect size and an overall significance test (for all studies taken together), plus, in many cases, effect sizes for various subgroups of studies (such as those using different methods of short-term cognitive therapy or those using different measures of arithmetic skill or different ages of girls

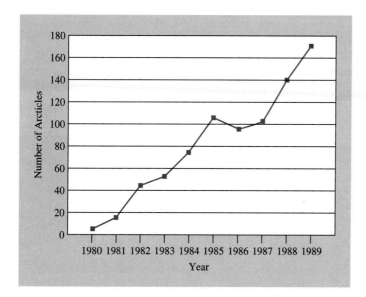

FIGURE 8-14
Number of psychology journal articles during the years 1980–1989 with *meta-analysis* (or other word with the same root) in the title. [Data from Myers, D. G. (1991). Union is strength: A consumer's view of meta-analysis. *Personality and Social Psychology Bulletin, 17,* 265–266. © 1991, by the Society for Personality and Social Psychology, Inc. Reprinted by permission of Sage Publications, Inc.]

and boys), as well as taking into account in various ways (some of them statistical) the methodological strengths and weaknesses of the studies (issues such as random assignment to conditions or quality of the measurements). An example of a recent meta-analysis that examined the relative impact of various meditation and relaxation techniques on reducing anxiety is described in Box 8-2.

Reviews of the research literature that use meta-analysis are an alternative to the traditional "narrative" literature review article that describes and evaluates each study and then attempts to draw some overall conclusion. As shown in Figure 8-14, the number of articles using meta-analysis increased dramatically during the 1980s. In recent years, even meta-analyses of meta-analyses have been published. However, as shown in Table 8-6, these articles are more common in the more applied areas of psychology, less common in more theoretical areas—a difference due in part to the issues noted in our discussion of the importance of effect size (which is at the heart of meta-analysis) in applied versus theoretical research.

TABLE 8-6
Number of Meta-Analytic Articles Published in Various Fields of Psychology (Through Mid-1987)

Subdiscipline	Frequency
Education	115
Psychological therapy	100
Industrial/organizational psychology	44
Social psychology	43
Sex differences	28
Health psychology	27
Mental health	26
Personality	16
Experimental psychology	13
Developmental psychology	8

Note. From Cooper, H. M., & Lemke, K. M. (1991), tab. 1. On the role of meta-analysis in personality and social psychology. *Personality and Social Psychology Bulletin*, *17,* 245–251. Copyright, 1991, by the Society for Personality and Social Psychology, Inc. Reprinted by permission of Sage Publications Inc.

BOX 8-2

Effect Sizes for Relaxation and Meditation: A Restful Meta-Analysis

The results of research on meditation and relaxation have been the subject of considerable controversy. Several traditional narrative reviews of the literature in these areas have drawn contradictory conclusions about whether any of these techniques are beneficial and, if so, which ones. Eppley, Abrams, and Shear (1989) decided to look at the issue systematically and conducted a meta-analysis of the effects of various relaxation techniques on trait anxiety (that is, ongoing anxiety as opposed to a temporary state). Eppley and colleagues chose trait anxiety for their meta-analysis because it is a definite problem related to many other mental health issues yet in itself is fairly consistent from test to test with the same measure and from one measure to another measure of it. That the anxiety part of the analysis be stable was important because the researchers were interested instead in the variation in the method of relaxation techniques: progressive relaxation (PR, the most commonly researched relaxation procedure), other forms of relaxation, Transcendental Meditation (TM, the most commonly researched meditation instruction), and other forms of meditation.

First the researchers culled the literature for articles, reading not only journals but also books and unpublished doctoral dissertations. An interesting side note was the question of whether dissertation studies are done as competently as journal articles; if analyzed separately, would they produce different results? They did not. And Eppley and colleagues noted that besides being generally very well supervised, dissertations have the advantage of including more null results (yet again, remember Box 6-1), whereas graduated researchers are not likely to try to publish null results, leaving dissertations as the most common way for null findings to reach the literature.

As for the bottom line, Eppley and colleagues compared effect sizes for each of the four main methods, using the difference between the posttest score for the experimental group (the group that received the treatment) minus the posttest score of the control group, divided by the standard deviation—this is a version of d as

defined by Cohen (1988) that we have considered in some detail in this chapter. The result was that the average effect size for the 35 TM studies was .70 (meaning an average difference of .70 standard deviation on the anxiety measure). This effect size was significantly larger than the effect sizes for any of the other groups: The average effect size for the 44 studies on all other types of meditation was .28, for the 30 PR studies it was .38, and for the 37 studies on other forms of relaxation it was .40.

But the meta-analysis had really just begun. There were many subvariables of interest: For example, looking at different subject populations, people who were screened to be highly anxious contributed more to the effect size, and prison populations and younger subjects seemed to gain more from TM. There was no impact on effect size of the skill of the instructors, expectations of the subjects, whether subjects had volunteered or been randomly assigned to conditions, experimenter bias (the TM results were actually stronger when the apparently pro-TM researchers' data were eliminated), the various measures of anxiety, and the research designs.

One clue to TM's high performance seemed to lie in the fact that techniques involving concentration produced a significantly smaller effect, whereas TM makes a special point of teaching an "effortless, spontaneous" process. The researchers thought the other difference might be the mantras, or sounds, used in TM, which are said to come from a very old tradition and are also selected for each student by the instructor. There is some research indicating that different sounds do produce different effects. And in this meta-analysis, methods of meditation employing randomly selected Sanskrit sounds or personally selected English words did not obtain the same strong results.

Whatever the reasons, the authors conclude that there are "grounds for optimism that at least some current treatment procedures can effectively reduce trait anxiety" (p. 973). So if you are prone to worry about little matters like statistics exams, consider these results.

Many psychologists believe that meta-analysis is a dramatic improvement over the traditional approach to reviewing literature, noting that it is more objective, enforces greater rigor on the reviewer, and gives precise information never before available. Critics argue that meta-analysis is mechanical, tends to give equal weight to well-done and poorly done studies, and is highly dependent on the studies the researcher was able to find. An often-raised point regarding this last issue is called the "file drawer problem," referring to the fact that studies that do not show significant effects are rarely published and end up in the researcher's file drawer (as you'll recall from Box 6-1). The problem is that when a reviewer collects all the available studies, generally only published studies are found, so that the effectiveness of, say, a popular form of psychotherapy is overemphasized by combining results from only easily available studies.

The proponents of meta-analysis, however, argue back that narrative reviews are also likely to be overinfluenced by the studies that are available. They also note that in meta-analysis, there are statistical techniques for taking into account how well a study was conducted (in terms of objective features of the study—how subjects were assigned to groups, reliability of measures, etc.), and these techniques are superior to the subjective, impressionistic method of the usual literature review. In part, as one proponent of meta-analysis (Beaman, 1991) noted, the issue is reminiscent of the debate over clinical versus statistical prediction that we described in Box 4-1.

Currently, both meta-analytic and traditional narrative reviews of the literature continue to be published in major psychology journals, but meta-analysis seems to be on the upswing.

Power and Effect Size as Discussed in Research Articles

Power is not often mentioned directly in research articles. Its greater role is in the planning of research and in interpreting research results. But occasionally it will be mentioned as justification for the number of subjects used. For example, Freund, Russell, and Schweitzer (1991) conducted a study on the impact of the delay between intake and first counseling session on the effectiveness of the counseling. The first paragraph of their Results section addressed the issue of whether their sample was large enough. The paragraph was headed "Power Analyses" and reads as follows:

> Power analyses (Cohen, 1977) were conducted to determine whether the available sample size was adequate to detect medium-sized effects. . . . We projected the median effect size (h^2) for research reported in the *Journal of Counseling Psychology* in 1985 (the year our study was completed) to be .15, which corresponds to Cohen's effect size (d) of .84. Power to detect such an effect size in the comparison of continuers and no-shows was .89, and power for the tests of correlations involving length of delay was .83. ([Footnote:] Power calculations were based on an alpha level of .05 for a directional hypothesis. Directional hypotheses were appropriate here because all previous reported effects of lengthy delays were either nonsignificant or in a negative direction.) These values signify that if a true effect exists in the population from which our sample was drawn, then our statistical tests would yield significant results 89% and 83% of the time, respectively. (p. 5)

Articles also occasionally mention effect size when comparing results of studies or parts of studies. For example, in part of a recent study of ours (Aron, Aron, Tudor, & Nelson, 1991), people made a series of decisions involving allocating small amounts of money to themselves or another person under anonymous conditions. In light of our theoretical model, we had predicted, and found, that the difference between what people allocate to their best friend versus a stranger is much greater than the difference between what they allocate to a stranger versus the person they know whom they most dislike. (That is, more money is given to the friend than is held back from the enemy.) In commenting on the statistical result, we noted:

> The magnitude of the difference is particularly evident if one compares effect sizes. . . . Using the mean difference divided by the standard deviation . . . gives an effect size of 1.31 for the friend-versus-stranger comparison and an effect size of .37 for the disliked-other-versus-stranger comparison. (p. 245)

Effect size is most commonly reported in meta-analyses, in which results from different articles are being combined and compared. We have given several examples of such meta-analytic studies, including one in Box 8-2. As an example of how these studies actually describe results in terms of effect size, consider a famous meta-analysis conducted by Shapiro and Shapiro (1983). They reviewed 143 studies of the effects of psychotherapy that used reasonably sound methods. Among their results was a comparison of the effectiveness of therapies in general on different types of patients (which they called the "target class"). Table 8-7 shows the number of studies (*N*), the percentage that this number represents of all the studies reviewed, the average effect size, and the standard deviation of the effect sizes. From this table you can see that the largest benefit from psychotherapy was found in studies focusing on people with phobias and the smallest benefit in studies focusing on people with anxiety and depression. Based on Cohen's conventions, however, even the smallest effect size was still large.

TABLE 8-7
Target Classes and Effect Size

Target Class	N	%	Mean Effect Size	SD
Anxiety and depression	30	7	.67	.62
Phobias	76	18	1.28	.88
Physical and habit problems	106	26	1.10	.85
Social and sexual problems	76	18	.95	.75
Performance anxieties	126	30	.80	.71

Note. From Shapiro, D. A., & Shapiro, D. (1983), tab. 5. Comparative therapy outcome research: Methodological implications of meta-analysis. *Journal of Consulting and Clinical Psychology, 51,* 42–53. Copyright, 1983, by the American Psychological Association. Reprinted by permission of the author.

Summary

The statistical power of a study is the probability that it will yield a significant result if the research hypothesis is true. The probability of not obtaining a significant result even though the research hypothesis is true (i.e., the probability of a Type II error) is called beta. Power is 1 – beta.

To calculate power (in the situation of a known population and a single sample), first determine the cutoff point for significance, in raw score terms, on the comparison distribution. Power is the probability of obtaining a mean at least this large on the distribution of Population 1 (the population exposed to the experimental treatment). Based on a specific hypothesized mean for Population 1 (and assuming a normal curve with the same known variance as Population 2), the Z score corresponding to this cutoff score on the comparison distribution can be determined, and the probability of exceeding it (which is the power of the study) can be found from the normal curve table.

There are two main ways to increase power: Increase the number of subjects, or increase the effect size. Effect size consists of both the size of the predicted difference between means (the greater the difference, the larger the effect size) and the population variance (the smaller this is, the larger the effect size). Power is also greatest when the significance level is least stringent and when a one-tailed test is used.

Effect size can be determined in advance of a study based on (a) theory or previous research findings, (b) determining the minimum difference between population means that would be meaningful, or (c) using conventions of .2 for a small effect, .5 for a medium effect, and .8 for a large effect.

The main practical ways to increase the power of a planned experiment are, again, increasing sample size or increasing effect size—by, for example, reducing variance with a less diverse population or more reliable measures or increasing the intensity of the experimental treatment.

Significant experimental findings with low power may not have practical importance, and nonsignificant experimental results with low power make it possible that important, significant results might show up if power were increased.

It is not possible to "prove" the null hypothesis, but with sufficient power, a nonsignificant finding may suggest that any true effect is extremely small.

Psychologists disagree over the relative importance of significance versus effect size in interpreting experimental results; theoretically oriented psychologists seem to emphasize significance, whereas applied researchers emphasize effect size.

Meta-analysis is a recently developed procedure for systematically combining effects of independent studies, primarily on the basis of effect sizes.

Key Terms

alpha (α)
beta (β)
effect size (*d*)

effect size conventions
meta-analysis
minimum meaningful difference

power tables
statistical power

Practice Problems

These problems involve computation (with the assistance of a calculator). Most real-life statistics problems are done on a computer. But even if you have a computer, do this by hand to ingrain the method in your mind.

For practice in using a computer to solve statistical problems, refer to the computer section of each chapter of the study guide that accompanies this text.

All data are fictional (unless an actual citation is given).

Answers to Set I are given at the back of the book.

SET I

1. Define *alpha* and *beta*.

2. Here is information about several possible versions of a planned experiment, each involving a single sample. Assuming that all populations are normally distributed, determine beta, power, and effect size for each; then make a diagram of the overlapping distributions on which you show the area representing alpha, beta, and power.

	Population		Pre-dicted Mean	N	Signif-icance Level	One or Two Tailed
	Mean	*SD*				
(a)	90	4	91	100	.05	1
(b)	90	4	92	100	.05	1
(c)	90	2	91	100	.05	1
(d)	90	4	91	16	.05	1
(e)	90	4	91	100	.01	1
(f)	90	4	91	100	.05	2

3. A psychologist, based on a particular theory of creativity, predicts that artists will be greater risk takers than the general population. The general population is normally distributed with a mean of 50 and a standard deviation of 12 on the risk-taking questionnaire this psychologist plans to use. The psychologist expects that artists will score, on the average, 55 on this questionnaire. If the psychologist plans to study 36 artists and test the hypothesis at the .05 level, what is the power of this study? Explain your answer to someone who understands hypothesis testing involving means of samples but has never learned about power.

4. You read a study in which the result is just barely significant at the .05 level. You then look at the size of

the sample. If the sample is very large (rather than very small), how should this affect your interpretation of (a) the probability that the null hypothesis is actually true and (b) the practical importance of the result?

5. What is the effect of each of the following on the power of a study?

(a) A larger predicted difference between the means of the populations

(b) A larger population standard deviation

(c) A larger sample size

(d) Using a more stringent significance level (e.g., .01 instead of .05)

(e) Using a two-tailed test instead of a one-tailed test

6. List two circumstances under which it is useful to employ power analysis procedures, indicating what the use is for each.

SET II

1. What is meant by the statistical power of an experiment?

2. Here is information about several possible versions of a planned experiment, each involving a single sample. Assuming that all populations are normally distributed, determine beta, power, and effect size for each, and then make a diagram of the overlapping distributions on which you show the area representing alpha, beta, and power.

	Population		Pre-dicted Mean	N	Signif-icance Level	One or Two Tailed
	Mean	*SD*				
(a)	0	.5	.1	50	.05	1
(b)	0	.5	.5	50	.05	1
(c)	0	.5	1.0	50	.05	1
(d)	0	.5	.5	100	.05	1
(e)	0	.5	.5	200	.05	1
(f)	0	.5	.5	400	.05	1

3. A psychologist is planning a study on the effect of motivation on performance on an attention task (identifying target letters in a stream of letters passing by at a rapid rate). The researcher knows from long experience that under ordinary experimental conditions, the population of students who participate in this task identify a mean of 71 of the key letters (of 100 that are presented), with a standard deviation of 10 (the distribution is approximately normal). The psychologist predicts that if the subject is paid a dollar for each letter identified correctly, the number correctly identified will increase to 74. If the psychologist plans to test 20 subjects under these conditions, using the .05 level, what is the power of this study? Explain your answer to someone who understands hypothesis testing involving means of samples but has never learned about power.

4. You read a study that just barely fails to be significant at the .05 level. You then look at the size of the sample. If the sample is very large (rather than very small),

how should this affect your interpretation of (a) the probability that the null hypothesis is actually true and (b) the probability that the null hypothesis is actually false?

5. You are planning a study that you compute as having quite low power. Name six things that you might do to increase power.

6. In a planned study, the population is normally distributed with a mean of 50 and a standard deviation of 8. Determine the predicted mean if the researcher expects the study to have (a) a medium effect size, (b) a small effect size, (c) a large effect size, (d) a minimum effect size of .1, (e) an effect size of .9.

9

The *t* Test for Dependent Means

A̲ᴛ this point, you may think you know all about hypothesis testing. But here's a surprise: What you know will not help you much as a psychologist because the procedures for testing hypotheses described up to now (which were, of course, absolutely necessary prerequisites for what you will now learn) involved comparing a group of scores to a known population. In real research practice, you are often comparing two or more groups of scores to each other, without any direct information about populations. For example, you may have sets of two scores for each of several people—such as scores on an anxiety test before and after psychotherapy or number of familiar versus unfamiliar words recalled in a memory experiment. Or you might have one score per person for two groups of people—such as an experimental group and a control group in a study of the effect of sleep loss. In both kinds of cases—which are among the most common in psychology—the only information available is from the samples. Nothing is known about the populations that the samples are supposed to represent. In particular, the researcher does not know the variance of the populations involved, which is a crucial ingredient in Step 2 of the hypothesis-testing process (determining the characteristics of the comparison distribution).

In this chapter, we examine the solution to the problem of not knowing the population variance by first focusing on a special situation, the comparison of the mean of a single sample to a population with a known mean but an unknown variance. Then, having seen how this problem is handled—with methods that are a slight extension of what you learned in Chapter 7—we extend the principles one more step, to the more common situation in which not only is the population variance unknown but we are not even making a comparison to any particular population; all we have are two scores for each of several subjects.

These two hypothesis-testing procedures in which the population variance is unknown are examples of what are called **t tests.** The *t* test is sometimes called "Student's t" because its main principles were originally developed by William S. Gosset, who published his articles under the name "Student" (see Box 9-1).

Introduction to the *t* Test: The *t* Test for a Single Sample

Hypothesis testing in our next situation—in which you have a single sample and a population for which the mean is known but not the variance—works in fundamentally the same way as you learned in Chapter 7. The only substantial differences are in procedures: You have to use a method to estimate the variance of the population (needed in Step 2), and you use a different table, not the normal curve table, to determine the cutoff point for rejecting the null hypothesis (for Step 3). However, as you will also see, there are a couple of interesting new wrinkles in the logic.

An Example

Suppose that your college newspaper reports an informal survey showing that students at your school spend an average of 2.5 h studying each day. Suppose further that you think that the students in your dormitory are studying much more. You randomly pick 16 students from your dorm and ask them how much they study each day. (We'll assume that they are all honest and accurate.) Your result is that these 16 students study an average of 3.2 h per day. What should you conclude? Do the students in your dorm study more than the college average? Or should you conclude that your results are so close to the college average that the small difference of .7 h (3.2 h – 2.5 h) is merely because you happened to pick 16 of the more studious students in your dorm?

Step 1 of the hypothesis-testing process is to reframe the problem. In this case the two populations are these:

Population 1: The kind of people who live in your dorm
Population 2: The kind of people at your college generally

The research hypothesis is that Population 1 people study more than Population 2 people; the null hypothesis is that Population 1 people do not study more than Population 2 people. So far the problem is no different from the ones covered in Chapter 7.

However, Step 2, determining the characteristics of the comparison distribution, raises a difficulty that we have not confronted before: You do not have the information necessary to determine the variance of the comparison distribution.

The comparison distribution, as in the cases we considered in Chapter 7, is a distribution of means—in this case, the distribution of all possible means of samples of 16 cases each drawn from the population of individual cases. Also as usual, the mean of the comparison distribution (the mean of this distribution of means) is the same as the mean of Population 2, which in this case you know from the newspaper survey to be 2.5 h. But you also need to know the variance of that distribution, and let's say that the variance

BOX 9-1

William S. Gosset, Alias "Student": Not a Mathematician, but a "Practical Man"

When William S. Gosset graduated from Oxford in 1899 with a degree in mathematics and chemistry, the Guinness brewers in Dublin, Ireland, were looking for a few young scientists to take a scientific look at beer making for the first time. Gosset took one of these jobs and soon had immersed himself in barley, hops, and vats of brew.

The problem was how to make beer less variable, to find the cause of bad batches. A proper scientist would say, "Conduct experiments!" But a business such as brewery could not afford to waste money on experiments involving large numbers of vats, some of which any brewer worth his hops knew would fail. So Gosset was forced to contemplate the probability of, say, a certain strain of barley producing terrible beer when the experiment could consist of only a few batches of each strain. Adding to the problem was that he had no idea of the variability of a given strain of barley—perhaps some fields of it were better than others. (Does this sound familiar? Poor Gosset, like today's psychologists, had no idea of his population's variance.)

But Gosset was up to the task. To his colleagues at the brewery he was a professor of mathematics. To his statistical colleagues, mainly at the Biometric Laboratory at University College in London, he was a mere brewer. In short, Gosset was the sort of scientist who was not above applying his talents to real life.

In fact, he seemed to revel in real life: raising pears, fishing, golfing, building boats, skiing, cycling (and lawn bowling, after he broke his leg by driving his car, a two-seater Model T Ford that he called "The Flying Bedstead," into a lamppost). And especially he reveled in simple tools that could be applied to anything, simple formulas that he could compute in his head. (A friend described him as an expert carpenter but claimed that Gosset did almost all of his finer woodwork with nothing but a penknife!)

So Gosset discovered the t distribution and invented the t test—simplicity itself—for situations when samples are small and the variability of the larger population is unknown. Most of his work was done on the backs of envelopes, with plenty of minor errors in arithmetic that he had to weed out later. Characteristically, he published his paper on his "brewery methods" only when editors of scientific journals demanded it. To this day, most statisticians call the t distribution "Student's t" because Gosset wrote under the anonymous name "Student" so that the Guinness brewery would not have to admit publicly that it sometimes brewed a bad batch!

References: Peters (1987); Stigler (1986); Tankard (1984).

---

of number of hours studied for the college (the Population 2 students) was not reported in the newspaper article. So you phone the paper. Unfortunately, the reporter who conducted the survey did not calculate the variance, and the original survey results are no longer available, so it cannot be determined. What to do?

Basic Principle of the t Test: Estimating the Population Variance from the Sample Information

If you don't know the population variance, you can estimate it from what you do know: the information in your sample.

How is this crucial estimation process possible? In the logic of hypothesis testing, the group of subjects we study are considered to be a random sample from a particular population. The variance of this sample ought to reflect the variance of that population. If the population has a lot of spread, a sample randomly selected from that population should have a lot of spread; if the population is very compact, with little spread, there should not be much spread in the sample either. Thus it should be possible to use the numbers in the sample to make an informed guess about the variance in the population.

There is, however, one small hitch. It can be shown mathematically that the variance of a random sample, on the average, will be slightly smaller than the variance of the population from which the sample is taken. For this reason, the variance of the sample is said to be a **biased estimate** of the population variance—biased in the sense that it tends to produce too small an estimate. To oversimplify a little, the reason that a sample's variance will tend to be smaller than the population's is that it is less likely to include extreme scores.[1]

Fortunately, you can compute an **unbiased estimate of the population variance** by using a slightly modified version of the ordinary variance formula. Instead of the ordinary process of dividing the sum of the squared deviations by the number of cases, you instead divide the sum of the squared deviations by the number of cases *minus 1*. Dividing by a smaller number makes the result bigger—in this case, just enough bigger to make it an unbiased estimate of the population variance. (Note that unbiased does not mean that any one estimate will be exactly correct. It only means that an estimate is equally likely to be too high as it is to be too low.) Here is the formula for the unbiased estimate of the population variance:

$$S^2 = \frac{\Sigma(X-M)^2}{N-1} = \frac{SS}{N-1}, \tag{9-1}$$

where S^2 is the unbiased estimate of the population variance, $\Sigma(X-M)^2$ or SS is the sum of squared deviations from the mean of the sample, and N is the number of cases in the sample. The estimated population standard deviation is the square root of the estimated population variance:

$$S = \sqrt{S^2} \tag{9-2}$$

In our example of hours spent studying, now we'll compute the estimated variance of the population from the sample's 16 scores. First compute the sum of squared deviations (subtract the mean from each of your scores, square those deviation scores, and add them all up). Let's presume in our example that this comes out to 9.6. To get the estimated population variance, you divide this sum of squared deviations by the number of subjects minus 1. The result of 9.6 divided by 15 is .64. In terms of the formula,

$$S^2 = \frac{\Sigma(X-M)^2}{N-1} = \frac{SS}{N-1} = \frac{9.6}{16-1} = \frac{9.6}{15} = .64$$

[1]If you are interested, a more precise explanation is as follows: Recall that the variance is based on deviations from the mean, and hence a population's variance is based on deviations from its mean. However, in calculating the variance of a sample, the deviations are figured from the sample's mean. Because the sample's mean is the optimal balance point for its scores, the average squared deviations from it will be less than from any other number, such as the population's mean. Indeed, if you knew the true population mean and used it to compute the deviation scores for each score in the sample, the variance calculated from the sample's scores in this way would not be a biased estimate of the population variance. One way to think of the correction for bias discussed in the next paragraph is that it exactly accounts for the degree to which a sample's mean tends to vary from the true population mean.

biased estimate

unbiased estimate of the population variance

Degrees of Freedom

The divisor you use to compute the estimated population variance—the number of cases minus 1—has a special name. It is called the **degrees of freedom.** It has this name because it refers to the amount of information in a sample that is "free to vary." This is a somewhat complicated notion, but basically the idea is that when calculating the variance, you first have to know the mean. And if you know the mean and all the numbers in the sample but one, you can figure out what the last number has to be with a little arithmetic. (If you are mathematically adventurous, try this out with some examples to see how it works.) Thus once you know the mean, one of the numbers in the sample is not free to take on any possible value. So the degrees of freedom is the number of cases minus 1. In terms of a formula,

$$df = N - 1 \tag{9-3}$$

where *df* is the degrees of freedom. In our example, $df = 16 - 1 = 15$. (In some situations considered in later chapters, there will be more restrictions, and the degrees of freedom will be even less. But for all the cases in this chapter at least, the degrees of freedom will always be the number of cases minus 1.)

The formula for computing the estimated population variance is often written using *df* instead of $N - 1$ in the denominator:

$$S^2 = \frac{\Sigma(X - M)^2}{df} = \frac{SS}{df} \tag{9-4}$$

Determining the Standard Deviation of the Distribution of Means From an Estimated Population Variance

Once you know the estimated population variance, computing the standard deviation of the comparison distribution involves the same procedures as we followed in Chapter 7. That is, we can think of the comparison distribution as a distribution of means. And as before, we can compute its variance as the variance of the population of individual cases (in this case an estimated population variance) divided by the sample size:

$$S_M^2 = \frac{S^2}{N} \tag{9-5}$$

The standard deviation of the distribution of means will be the square root of its variance:

$$S_M = \sqrt{S_M^2} \tag{9-6}$$

Note, however, that the symbol for the standard deviation of the distribution of means, when we are using an estimated population variance, is S_M, instead of σ_M, which is used when the population variance is known. That is, S_M is a statistic, calculated entirely from information in the known sample; σ_M is a population parameter.

In our example, the sample size was 16, and the estimated population variance that we just worked out was .64. Thus the estimated variance of the distribution of means will be .64 divided by 16, or .04. The corresponding standard deviation, as usual, is the square root of the variance, in this case, .2. In terms of the formulas,

$$S_M^2 = \frac{S^2}{N} = \frac{.64}{16} = .04$$

$$S_M = \sqrt{S_M^2} = \sqrt{.04} = .2$$

(Be careful. To find the variance of a distribution of means, you always divide the population variance, regardless of whether it is known or only estimated, by the sample size. In our example, you divided it by 16. It is only in the process of making the estimate of the population variance that you divide by the sample size minus 1.)

We have now almost completed Step 2 of the hypothesis-testing process, determining the characteristics of the comparison distribution, for our example in which we have had to estimate the population variance. We have seen that the distribution of means has a mean of 2.5 (the known population mean) and an estimated standard deviation (S_M) of .2. What we still do not know is the shape of the comparison distribution.

The Shape of the Comparison Distribution When Using an Estimated Population Variance: The *t* Distribution

In Chapter 7, where we knew the variance of the population, we saw that so long as it is reasonable to assume that the population distribution follows a normal curve, the shape of the distribution of means that we use as our comparison distribution will also be a normal curve. However, when carrying out the hypothesis-testing process using an estimated population variance (that is, when doing a *t* test), there is less true information and more room for error. The mathematical effect is that when using an estimated population variance, extreme means are slightly more likely to occur than would be found in a normal curve. Further, the smaller your sample size, the bigger this discrepancy, since you are estimating the population variance on the basis of less information.

The result of all this is that when doing hypothesis testing using an estimated variance, instead of your comparison distribution being the same as a distribution of means following a normal curve, the comparison distribution follows instead a mathematically defined curve called a *t* **distribution.**

t distribution

Actually, there are many *t* distributions. They vary in shape according to the degrees of freedom involved in estimating the population variance. (But given a particular number of degrees of freedom, the *t* distribution is defined mathematically.) Generally, a *t* distribution looks to the eye like a normal curve—bell-shaped, completely symmetrical, and unimodal. But a *t* distribution differs subtly in having fatter tails (that is, room for slightly more cases at the extremes). This contrast of the *t* distribution to the normal curve is shown in Figure 9-1. With a larger proportion of the area of the curve in the tails of the comparison distribution, to reject the null hypothesis (for example, to be in the top 5%), you need a sample with a mean that is farther out on the distribution. That is, it takes a more extreme sample mean to achieve significance when using a *t* distribution than when using a normal curve.

Just how much the *t* distribution differs from the normal curve depends on how little information is available for estimating the population variance.

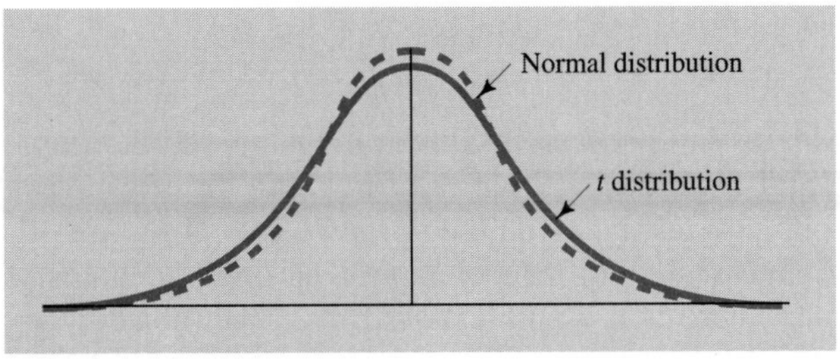

FIGURE 9-1
The t distribution compared to the normal curve.

If the estimate is based on a very small sample, so that the degrees of freedom are low, the t distribution is moderately different from the normal curve. For example, recall from Chapter 7 that the cutoff for a one-tailed test at the 5% level, using the normal curve, is 1.64. On a t distribution based on an estimated variance computed with 7 degrees of freedom (that is, with a sample size of 8), the one-tailed, 5% cutoff is 1.895. Conversely, if the estimate is based on a larger sample, for example, a sample of 25 (so that $df = 24$), the cutoff is 1.711, a figure much closer to that for the normal curve. In fact, mathematically, if your sample size is infinite, the t distribution is the same as the normal curve. (Of course, if your sample size were infinite, it would include all the cases in the population!) But even with sample sizes of 30 or more, the t distribution becomes virtually indistinguishable from a normal curve. (Notice that a sample size of 30 is once again an important transition point.)

In sum, there is a slightly different t distribution corresponding to the degrees of freedom involved in estimating the population variance. A t distribution with high degrees of freedom (even 30 or more) is very close to a normal curve. But a t distribution with lower numbers of degrees of freedom differs moderately from the normal curve, the important effect being that the significance cutoff points are higher (farther out on the tails).

We will see shortly how you can actually determine the cutoff point for a t distribution with any particular degrees of freedom. However, let us first return briefly to our example of the number of hours that students at your college study each night. We finally have everything we need to complete Step 2 of the hypothesis-testing process, which is determining the characteristics of the comparison distribution. We have already seen that the distribution of means will have a mean of 2.5 h and a standard deviation of .2. Based on what we have just considered, we can now add that the shape of the comparison distribution will be a t distribution with 15 degrees of freedom.[2]

[2]Statisticians make a subtle distinction in this situation between the comparison distribution and the distribution of means. We have avoided this distinction here and in subsequent chapters so as greatly to simplify the discussion of what is already fairly difficult. If you are interested, the distinction can be understood as follows: The general procedure of hypothesis testing, as we introduced it in Chapter 7, can be described as computing a Z score for your sample's mean, where $Z = (M - \mu)/\sigma_M$, where $\sigma_M = \sqrt{\sigma^2/N}$, and then comparing this Z score to a cutoff Z score from the normal curve table. We described this process as using the distribution of means as your comparison distribution.

Statisticians would say that actually you are comparing your computed Z score to a distribution of Z scores (which is simply a standard normal curve). Similarly, in the case of a t test, statisticians think of the procedure as computing a t score—which we will see shortly is the same as a Z score, but using S instead of σ, that is, $t = (M - \mu)/S_M$, where $S_M = \sqrt{S^2/N}$—and then comparing your computed t score to a cutoff t score from a t distribution table. Thus according to the formal statistical logic, the comparison distribution is a distribution of t scores, not of means, computed for all possible samples (of a given size) drawn from the population of individual cases.

Determining the Cutoff Sample Score for Rejecting the Null Hypothesis: Using the *t* Table

Step 3 of the hypothesis-testing process is determining the cutoff sample score for rejecting the null hypothesis. From the foregoing discussion you can see that, unlike hypothesis testing using the normal curve, there are different cutoff points for statistical significance, depending on the degrees of freedom in your sample. There is a whole different *t* distribution for any particular number of degrees of freedom. However, in order to avoid taking up pages and pages with tables for each possible *t* distribution, a simplified table is used that gives only the crucial cutoff points. We have included such a ***t* table** in Appendix B (Table B-2).

t table

In the present example, you have a one-tailed test (you are interested in whether students in your dorm study *more* than students in general at your college), and you will probably want to use the 5% significance level because the cost of a Type I error (mistakenly rejecting the null hypothesis) is not great. You have 16 subjects, making 15 degrees of freedom on which your population variance estimate was based.

Table 9-1 shows a portion of a *t* table like Table B-2. In the table, find the column for the .05 significance level for one-tailed tests, and move down it to the row for 15 degrees of freedom. The crucial cutoff number is 1.753. This means that you will reject the null hypothesis if your sample's mean is 1.753 or more standard deviations above the mean on the comparison distribution. (If you were using a known variance, the *Z* score needed to reject the null hypothesis based on the normal curve would have been 1.645.)

TABLE 9-1
Cutoff Scores for *t* Distributions with 1 Through 17 Degrees of Freedom

df	One-Tailed Tests			Two-Tailed Tests		
	.10	*.05*	*.01*	*.10*	*.05*	*.01*
1	3.078	6.314	31.821	6.314	12.706	63.657
2	1.886	2.920	6.965	2.920	4.303	9.925
3	1.638	2.353	4.541	2.353	3.182	5.841
4	1.533	2.132	3.747	2.132	2.776	4.604
5	1.476	2.015	3.365	2.015	2.571	4.032
6	1.440	1.943	3.143	1.943	2.447	3.708
7	1.415	1.895	2.998	1.895	2.365	3.500
8	1.397	1.860	2.897	1.860	2.306	3.356
9	1.383	1.833	2.822	1.833	2.262	3.250
10	1.372	1.813	2.764	1.813	2.228	3.170
11	1.364	1.796	2.718	1.796	2.201	3.106
12	1.356	1.783	2.681	1.783	2.179	3.055
13	1.350	1.771	2.651	1.771	2.161	3.013
14	1.345	1.762	2.625	1.762	2.145	2.977
15	1.341	1.753	2.603	1.753	2.132	2.947
16	1.337	1.746	2.584	1.746	2.120	2.921
17	1.334	1.740	2.567	1.740	2.110	2.898

Determining the Score of the Sample Mean on the Comparison Distribution: The t Score

Step 4 of the hypothesis-testing process is determining the score of your sample's mean on the comparison distribution. In previous chapters, this has meant finding the Z score on the comparison distribution—the number of standard deviations it is from the mean on the distribution of means. The exact same procedure is followed when using a t distribution. The only difference is that in the past, when the distribution of means we were using was a normal curve, we called the score we computed on it a Z score. Now, when we are using a t distribution, we call this score a **t score.** In terms of a formula,

$$t = \frac{M - \mu}{S_M} \tag{9-7}$$

t score

In our example, your sample's mean of 3.2 is .7 h from the mean of the distribution of means, which amounts to 3.5 standard deviations from the mean (.7 h divided by the standard deviation of .2 h). That is, the t score in the example is 3.5. In terms of the formula,

$$t = \frac{M - \mu}{S_M} = \frac{3.2 - 2.5}{.2} = \frac{.7}{.2} = 3.5$$

Determining Whether to Reject the Null Hypothesis

Step 5 of the hypothesis-testing procedure is determining whether or not to reject the null hypothesis. This step is exactly the same with a t test as it was in the situations we considered in Chapters 6 and 7. You compare the number in Step 3 (the cutoff score) with the number in Step 4 (the actual sample mean's score on this distribution). In the case of our example, the cutoff t score was 1.753 and the actual t score for our sample was 3.5. Conclusion: Reject the null hypothesis; the research hypothesis that students in your dorm study more than students in the rest of the college is supported.

Figure 9-2 illustrates the various distributions involved in this sample problem.

Summary of Hypothesis Testing When the Population Variance Is Not Known

The hypothesis-testing process when the population variance is not known is exactly the same as you used in Chapter 7, with four exceptions: (a) Instead of the population variance being known in advance, it is estimated from the sample (using the formula for the unbiased estimate, $S^2 = SS/df$); (b) instead of the comparison distribution following a normal curve, it is a t distribution with degrees of freedom equal to the number of subjects in your sample minus 1; (c) instead of looking up the cutoff point for significance on a normal curve table, a t table is used; and (d) the score of your sample on the comparison distribution, instead of being called a Z score, is called a t score. Table 9-2 systematically compares the steps of hypothesis testing in the two situations.

FIGURE 9-2
Distributions involved in the sample problem.

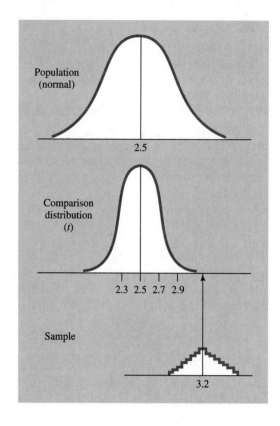

TABLE 9-2
Hypothesis Testing Involving a Single Sample Mean When Population Variance Is Unknown (*t* Test) Compared to When Population Variance Is Known

Step in Hypothesis Testing	Difference From When Population Variance Is Known
1. Reframe the question into a research hypothesis and a null hypothesis about the populations.	No difference in method.
2. Determine the characteristics of the comparison distribution:	
Population mean	No difference in method.
Population variance	Estimate from the sample.
Standard deviation of the distribution of sample means	No difference in method (but based on estimated population variance).
Shape of the comparison distribution	Use the *t* distribution with $df = N - 1$.
3. Determine the significance cutoff.	Use the *t* table.
4. Determine score of your sample on the comparison distribution.	No difference in method (but called a *t* score).
5. Compare Steps 3 and 4 to determine whether to reject the null hypothesis.	No difference in method.

TABLE 9-3
Data and Analysis for a Single-Sample t-Test for a Study of 10 People's Ratings of Hopefulness Following a Devastating Flood (Fictional Data)

Rating	Difference From the Mean	Squared Difference From the Mean
(X)	$(X - M)$	$(X - M)^2$
5	.3	.09
3	−1.7	2.89
6	1.3	1.69
2	−2.7	7.29
7	2.3	5.29
6	1.3	1.69
7	2.3	5.29
4	− .7	.49
2	−2.7	7.29
5	.3	.09
Σ: 47	0	32.10

$M + \Sigma X/N = 47/10 = 4.7.$
$df = N - 1 = 10 - 1 = 9.$
$\mu = 4.0.$
$S^2 = SS/df = 32.10/(10 - 1) = 32.10/9 = 3.57.$
$S_M^2 = S^2/N = 3.57/10 = .36.$
$S_M = \sqrt{S_M^2} = \sqrt{.36} = .60.$
t with $df = 9$ needed for 1% significance level, two-tailed $= \pm 3.250.$
Actual sample $t = (M - \mu)/S_M = (4.7 - 4)/.6 = .7/.6 = 1.17.$

Decision: Do not reject the null hypothesis.

Another Example of a Single-Sample t Test

In the following fictional study, a researcher was interested in whether people felt more or less hopeful following a devastating flood in a small rural community. Ten people randomly selected from the town rated how hopeful they felt using a 7-point scale from *extremely hopeful* (1) to *neutral* (4) to *extremely unhopeful* (7). Table 9-3 and Figure 9-3 show the results (as well as other information associated with the hypothesis test for this problem).

The researcher was interested in whether the responses would be consistently above or below the midpoint on the scale (4). Here is how the result would be arrived at.

1. Reframe the question into a research hypothesis and a null hypothesis about the populations. The two populations of interest are these:

Population 1: People who experienced the flood
Population 2: People who are neither hopeful nor unhopeful

The research hypothesis is that the two populations will score differently. The null hypothesis is that they will score the same.

2. Determine the characteristics of the comparison distribution. If the null hypothesis is true, the mean of both population distributions is 4. The variance of these population distributions, however, is not known. It must be estimated from the sample. As shown in Table 9-3, the sum of the squared deviations from the sample's mean is 32.10. Thus the estimated

FIGURE 9-3
Distributions involved in the
second sample problem.

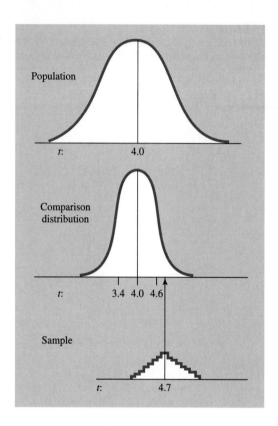

population variance is 32.10 divided by 9 degrees of freedom (10 – 1), making 3.57.

The distribution of means will have a mean of 4 (the same as the population mean). Its variance is determined in the usual way, except that the estimated population variance (instead of a known population variance) is divided by the sample size. This comes out to 3.57 divided by 10, giving .36. The square root of this, the standard deviation of the distribution of means, is .60.

3. Determine the cutoff sample score on the comparison distribution at which the null hypothesis should be rejected. The researcher, wanting to be very cautious about mistakenly concluding that the flood made a difference, decides to test the hypothesis at the .01 level. The hypothesis was nondirectional (that is, no specific direction of difference from the mean of 4 was specified; either result would have been of interest), so a two-tailed test is required. Using Table 9-1 (or Table B-2 in Appendix B, for 9 degrees of freedom, a t of 3.250 or higher or a t of –3.250 or lower is needed to reject the null hypothesis.

4. Determine the score of your sample on the comparison distribution. In the case of a t test, you need a t score. The mean of the sample (4.7) is .7 scale points from the null hypothesis mean of 4.0. That makes it 1.17 standard deviations on the comparison distribution from that distribution's mean (.7/.6 = 1.17). So $t = 1.17$.

5. Compare the scores obtained in Steps 3 and 4 to decide whether to reject the null hypothesis. The obtained t is not as extreme as the needed t,

TABLE 9-4
Steps for Conducting a *t*-Test for a Single Sample

1. Reframe the question into a research hypothesis and a null hypothesis about the populations.

2. Determine the characteristics of the comparison distribution.

   a. The mean is the same as the known population mean.

   b. The standard deviation is computed as follows:

      i. Compute the estimated population variance: $S^2 = SS/df$.

      ii. Compute the variance of the distribution of means: $S_M^2 = S^2/N$.

      iii. Compute the standard deviation: $S_M = \sqrt{S_M^2}$.

   c. The shape will be a *t* distribution with $N - 1$ degrees of freedom.

3. Determine the cutoff sample score on the comparison distribution at which the null hypothesis should be rejected.

   a. Determine the degrees of freedom, desired significance level, and number of tails in the test (one or two).

   b. Look up the appropriate cutoff in a *t* table.

4. Determine the score of your sample on the comparison distribution: $t = (M - \mu)/S_M$.

5. Compare the scores obtained in Steps 3 and 4 to decide whether or not to reject the null hypothesis.

so the null hypothesis cannot be rejected. The study is inconclusive. (Of course, had the researcher used a larger sample, giving more power, the result might have been quite different.)

Summary of Steps for Conducting a *t* Test for a Single Sample

Table 9-4 summarizes the steps of hypothesis testing when you have scores from a single sample and a population with a known mean but an unknown variance.

The *t* Test for Dependent Means

The type of situation just described, when you know the population mean but not its variance, is obviously very rare. Occasionally, you know both; usually, you know neither. This is a very common research situation, an intentional research design for many studies, and we will consider it now. At last we have built up to a real, very usable statistical method.

This situation, which we mentioned at the start of the chapter, involves studies in which there are two scores for each of several subjects. For example, a psychophysiologist might measure the amount of alpha waves in the EEG ("brain waves"), comparing measures taken for each person while doing abstract tasks against measures taken while doing concrete tasks. This kind of research setup is called a **repeated-measures design** (also known as a "within-subjects design"). (See Appendix A for a summary of the major types of research designs.) One widely used type of repeated-measures

repeated-measures design

design involves measuring the same subjects before and after some psychological or social intervention. For example, an industrial psychologist might measure days missed from work for 80 workers before and after a new health promotion program was introduced.

In this common situation of a repeated-measures design, where each subject is measured twice, the hypothesis-testing procedure used is a **_t_ test for dependent means.** It has the name "dependent means" because the means for each set of scores (for example, a set of before and after scores) are not independent in that they have been obtained from the same individuals. (In Chapter 10, we consider the case where scores from two different groups of subjects are compared, a research design analyzed by a "_t_ test for independent means.")[3]

t test for dependent means

A *t* test for dependent means is conducted in exactly the same way as the *t* test for a single sample, except that (a) we use difference scores and (b) we assume that the population mean is 0.

Difference Scores

The key problem in this situation of a repeated-measures design is that our sample consists of two sets of scores for each individual instead of just one. The solution is to convert the two scores per individual to one score per individual. This magic is done by creating **difference scores:** For each subject, subtract one score from the other.

difference scores

For example, in the EEG study, for each person the psychophysiologist would compute the level of EEG alpha waves during abstract tasks minus the level of EEG alpha waves during concrete tasks. This provides a single abstract-minus-concrete difference score for each person. Similarly, in the absence-from-work example, the industrial psychologist would subtract the number of days missed after the program from the number of days missed before the program, providing an after-minus-before difference score (really a change score) for each person. (Which number you subtract from which may be implied, as when you expect change, or may not matter as long as you are consistent and remember what the difference score means about the relationship of your variables.)

Once the difference score has been computed for each subject, the entire hypothesis-testing procedure is carried out using difference scores. That is, the situation is treated as a situation involving one sample of scores, a sample of difference scores.

---

[3]There is yet another situation, in which subjects are in matched pairs. An example would be a social interaction experiment in which two subjects are run at a time, one functioning as a leader and one a follower, and the enjoyment of the interaction is compared. In such a study, you can think of each experimental session as a subject with the follower's enjoyment, for example, functioning as the before score and the leader's enjoyment functioning as the after score. These kinds of studies, called "matched-pair designs," are analyzed using a *t* test for dependent means. They are completely different from the usual situation of a two-group experiment (which is analyzed with a *t* test for independent means), in which one group is tested under one set of conditions and the other group under different conditions, and there is no straightforward way to match subjects into one-to-one pairs.

Population of Difference Scores With a Mean of 0

The next problem that arises in the typical research situation involving a repeated-measures design is that the population mean is not specified. We merely have two sets of scores, such as a set of before scores and a set of after scores, which we have converted into a set of after-minus-before differences scores. To carry out hypothesis testing, we need to know the mean of the comparison distribution—the mean of the population in which there was no effect, the null hypothesis situation. In the situations we have encountered so far in this book, this population mean was known—for example, in the college dorm survey of hours studied, this was 2.5 hours, and in the flood study it was considered to be the middle of the scale, or 4. In the situation involving difference scores, however, the mean of the scores in the population is usually not known.

The solution is as follows: Ordinarily, the null hypothesis in a repeated-measures design is that there is no difference between the two sets of scores—that the level of EEG alpha waves is the same when doing abstract or concrete tasks or that the absentee rate will be the same before and after the health promotion program is introduced. (Notice that this null hypothesis situation of no difference represents a situation that may not even exist in reality. It is a kind of straw man, a hypothetical stance, against which we compare our actual sample information.) The research hypothesis of a difference is thus compared to a null hypothesis of no difference.

And here is the key point: Saying that in the population there is no difference between the two sets of scores is the same as saying that the mean of the population of the difference scores is 0. (You may want to read that sentence twice.) Thus when working with difference scores, we simply assume, for the purposes of hypothesis testing, an artificial comparison population of difference scores in which there is no difference and which thus has a population mean of 0.

Example of a *t* Test for Dependent Means

Olthoff and Aron (1993) gave a communication quality questionnaire to a number of engaged couples 3 months before and again 3 months after marriage. One group they studied consisted of 19 couples who had received typical premarital counseling from the ministers who were going to marry them (that is, the premarital counseling did not include any extensive focus on communication skills). (To keep the example simple, we will focus on just this one group, and on only the husbands in the group; scores for wives were similar, though the numbers were somewhat more varied, making it a poorer illustration for purposes of teaching the *t*-test procedure.)

The scores for the 19 husbands are listed in the "Before" and "After" columns in Table 9-5, followed by the entire *t*-test analysis. The mean of the before scores was 116.316, and the mean of the after scores was 104.263.

More important, however, we have also calculated the difference scores. The mean of the difference scores is −12.05, meaning that on the average, these husbands' communication quality decreased by about 12

TABLE 9-5
Data and *t*-Test Analysis for Communication Quality Scores Before and After Marriage for 19 Husbands Who Received No Special Communication Training

Husband	Communication Quality		Difference (After – Before)	Deviation of Differences From the Mean of Differences	Squared Deviation
	Before	After			
A	126	115	− 11	1.05	1.1
B	133	125	− 8	4.05	16.4
C	126	96	− 30	−17.95	322.2
D	115	115	0	12.05	145.2
E	108	119	11	23.05	531.3
F	109	82	− 27	−14.95	233.5
G	124	93	− 31	−18.95	359.1
H	98	109	11	23.05	531.3
I	95	72	− 23	−10.95	119.9
J	120	104	− 16	− 3.95	15.6
K	118	107	− 11	1.05	1.1
L	126	118	− 8	4.05	16.4
M	121	102	− 19	− 6.95	48.3
N	116	115	− 1	11.05	122.1
O	94	83	− 11	1.05	1.1
P	105	87	− 18	− 5.95	35.4
Q	123	121	− 2	10.05	101.0
R	125	100	− 25	−12.95	167.7
S	128	118	− 10	2.05	4.2
Σ:	2,210	1,981	−229	− .05	2,772.9

For difference scores:

$M = -229/19 = -12.05$.

$\mu = 0$ (assumed as a no-change baseline of comparison).

$S^2 = SS/df = 2{,}772.9/(19 - 1) = 154.05$.

$S_M^2 = S^2/N = 154.05/19 = 8.11$.

$S_M = \sqrt{S_M^2} = \sqrt{8.11} = 2.85$.

t with $df = 18$ needed for 5% level, two-tailed $= \pm 2.101$.

$t = (M - \mu)/S_M = (-12.05 - 0)/2.85 = -4.23$.

Decision: Reject the null hypothesis.

Note. Data from Olthoff & Aron (1993).

points. Is this decrease significant? In other words, how likely is it that this sample of change scores is a random sample from a population of change scores whose mean is 0?

Let's carry out the hypothesis-testing procedure summarized in Table 9-4.

1. Reframe the question into a research hypothesis and a null hypothesis about the populations. The two populations in this case are these:

Population 1: Husbands of the kind included in this study
Population 2: Husbands whose communication quality does not change after marriage

The research hypothesis is that Population 1 is different from Population 2. The null hypothesis is that the populations are the same.

Notice that we are attempting to test these hypotheses with no actual information about Population 2 husbands; indeed, if the research hypothesis is correct, such husbands do not even really exist. We simply assume, for the purposes of hypothesis testing, a comparison group of husbands who, if measured before and after marriage, would show no change. Population 1, by contrast, consists of real husbands, of which our particular sample is intended to be representative. If the null hypothesis is true, real husbands like those we have studied are the same as the theoretical husbands who don't change. That is, if the null hypothesis is true, real husbands don't change. But if the null hypothesis is false, real husbands do change.

2. Determine the characteristics of the comparison distribution. Assuming that the null hypothesis is true, the population mean (of difference scores) is 0. Its variance can be estimated from the sample of difference scores. As shown in Table 9-5, the sum of squared deviations of the difference scores from the mean of the difference scores is 2,772.9. With 19 subjects, there are 18 degrees of freedom, yielding an estimate of the population variance of 154.05.

The distribution of means will have a mean of 0 (the same as the population mean). Its variance will be the estimated population variance (154.05) divided by the sample size (19), which gives 8.11. The standard deviation is thus the square root of 8.11, which is 2.85. Finally, because Olthoff was working with an estimated population variance based on 18 degrees of freedom, the comparison distribution is a t distribution for 18 degrees of freedom.

3. Determine the cutoff sample score on the comparison distribution at which the null hypothesis should be rejected. We use a two-tailed test because there was no unambiguous basis for predicting either an increase or a decrease in communication quality. Using the 5% significance level and 18 degrees of freedom, Table B-2 shows that a t score at or above +2.101 or at or below −2.101 is needed to reject the null hypothesis.

4. Determine the score of your sample on the comparison distribution. Olthoff and Aron's sample had a mean difference score of −12.05—that is, it was 12.05 points below the mean of 0 on the distribution of means. Using the standard deviation of the distribution of means that we computed (2.85), the mean of the difference scores of −12.05 is 4.23 standard deviations below the mean of the distribution of means. So Olthoff's sample of difference scores has a t score of −4.23.

5. Compare the scores obtained in Steps 3 and 4 to decide whether to reject the null hypothesis. The t of −4.23 for the sample of difference scores is more extreme than the needed t of ±2.101, so the null hypothesis can be rejected. This suggests that Olthoff and Aron's subjects represent a population in which husbands' communication quality is different after marriage from what it was before.

Olthoff and Aron's actual study was considerably more complex than we have described. You may be interested to know that they found that the wives of these same subjects also showed this pattern of decreases after marriage. But in a group of otherwise similar engaged couples who received

FIGURE 9-4
Communication skills of wives given premarital
communications training and wives not given such
training. (Based on Olthoff & Aron, 1993.)

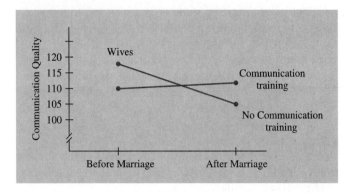

a substantial communication training program as part of the premarital
counseling from their minister, there was *no* significant decline in marital
communication quality after marriage (see Figure 9-4).

Another Example of a *t* Test for Dependent Means

Suppose that a researcher conducted a study of hand-eye coordination in
which each of nine surgeons was tested (not while doing surgery, of course)
under both quiet and noisy conditions. The prediction was that surgeons'
coordination would be better under quiet conditions. (Ideally, any possible
effects of practice or fatigue by doing the tasks twice would be equalized by
testing half the surgeons under noisy conditions first, then quiet, and half
under quiet conditions first, then noisy—see Appendix A for a discussion of
such "counterbalancing.")

The fictional results, along with the calculation of difference scores and
subsequent calculations, are shown in Table 9-6. The *t* test is conducted as
follows:

1. Reframe the question into a research hypothesis and a null hypothesis about the populations. The populations involved are these:

Population 1: Surgeons like those tested in this study
Population 2: Surgeons whose coordination is the same under quiet
and noisy conditions

The research hypothesis is that Population 1's mean difference scores
(quiet minus noisy) is greater than Population 2's. That is, the research
hypothesis is that surgeons perform better under quiet conditions. The null
hypothesis is that Population 1's difference in performance is not higher
than Population 2's. That is, the null hypothesis is that surgeons do no better
under quiet conditions.

2. Determine the characteristics of the comparison distribution. Under
the null hypothesis, the mean of the population of difference scores is 0.
The population variance estimated from the sample of difference scores—
the sum of the squared deviations of the difference scores from the mean of
the difference scores, divided by the degrees of freedom—is shown in Table
9-6 to be 7.5.

The comparison distribution will be a *t* distribution for 8 degrees of
freedom (since it is based on a population variance estimated with 8 degrees

TABLE 9-6
Results of a Study of Hand-Eye Coordination in Which Nine Surgeons Are Measured Under Noisy and Quiet Conditions (Fictional Data)

Surgeon	Conditions		Difference	Deviation	Squared Deviation
	Quiet	Noisy			
1	18	12	6	6 − 2 = 4	16
2	21	21	0	−2	4
3	19	16	3	1	1
4	21	16	5	3	9
5	17	19	−2	−4	16
6	20	19	1	−1	1
7	18	16	2	0	0
8	16	17	−1	−3	9
9	20	16	4	2	4
Σ:	170	152	18	0	60

For difference scores:

$M = 18/9 = 2.0$.

$\mu = 0$ (assumed as a no-change baseline of comparison).

$S^2 = SS/df = 60/(9 - 1) = 60/8 = 7.5$.

$S_M^2 = S^2/N = 7.50/9 = .83$.

$S_M = \sqrt{S_M^2} = \sqrt{.83} = .91$.

t for $df = 8$ needed for 1% significance level, one-tailed = 2.897.

$t = (M - \mu)/S_M = (2.00 - 0)/.91 = 2.20$.

Decision: Do not reject the null hypothesis.

---

of freedom) with a mean of 0 (same as the null hypothesis population) and a standard deviation of .91 (the square root of the estimated population variance divided by the sample size).

3. Determine the cutoff sample score on the comparison distribution at which the null hypothesis should be rejected. This is a one-tailed test (because there was a reasonable basis for predicting the direction of the difference). And we will assume that the researchers wanted to be conservative by using the 1% significance level. With 8 degrees of freedom, Table B-2 shows that a t score of at least 2.897 is needed to reject the null hypothesis.

4. Determine the location of your sample on the comparison distribution. The sample's mean difference of 2 is 2.20 standard deviations (of .91 each) on the distribution of means above that distribution's mean of 0.

5. Compare the scores obtained in Steps 3 and 4 to decide whether to reject the null hypothesis. The sample's t score of 2.20 is less extreme than the cutoff t of 2.897. Thus the null hypothesis cannot be rejected. The experiment is inconclusive.

A Third Example of a t Test for Dependent Means

A psychologist is interested in the development of responsiveness to strangers, using a new type of measure. He is able to measure 10 infants at 3 months of age and then again at 4 months. His prediction is that there will be an increase. The fictional results, along with the calculation of difference

TABLE 9-7
Results of a Study of Responsiveness to Strangers of 10 Infants Measured at 3 and 4 Months of Age (Fictional Data)

Infant	Age		Difference	Deviation	Squared Deviation
	3 months	*4 months*			
1	10.4	10.8	.4	.26	.07
2	12.6	12.1	−.5	−.64	.41
3	11.2	12.1	.9	.76	.58
4	10.9	11.4	.5	.36	.13
5	14.3	13.9	−.4	−.54	.29
6	13.2	13.5	.3	.16	.03
7	9.7	10.9	1.2	1.06	1.12
8	11.5	11.5	0.0	−.14	.02
9	10.8	10.4	−.4	−.54	.29
10	13.1	12.5	−.6	−.74	.55
Σ:	117.7	119.1	1.4	0	3.49

For difference scores:

$M = 1.4/10 = .14.$

$\mu = 0.$

$S^2 = SS/df = 3.49/(10 - 1) = 3.49/9 = .39.$

$S_M^2 = S^2/N = .39/10 = .039.$

$S_M = \sqrt{S_M^2} = \sqrt{.039} = .20.$

t for $df = 9$ needed for 5% significance level, one-tailed = 1.833.

$t = (M - \mu)/S_M = (.14 - 0)/.20 = .70.$

Decision: Do not reject the null hypothesis.

---

scores and subsequent calculations, are shown in Table 9-7. Here are the steps of hypothesis testing:

1. Reframe the question into a research hypothesis and a null hypothesis about the populations. The two populations of interest are these:

Population 1: Infants like those in this study
Population 2: Infants whose responsiveness to strangers is the same at 3 months and at 4 months of age

The research hypothesis is that Population 1's mean difference score (of responsiveness to strangers at 4 months minus responsiveness at 3 months) is greater than Population 2's. The null hypothesis is that Population 1's mean difference score is not greater than Population 2's.

2. Determine the characteristics of the comparison distribution. Its population mean is 0 difference. The estimated population variance is shown in Table 9-7 to be .39. The comparison distribution will be a t distribution for 9 degrees of freedom with a mean of 0 and a standard deviation of .20.

3. Determine the cutoff sample score on the comparison distribution at which the null hypothesis should be rejected. This is a one-tailed test (because there was a reasonable basis for predicting the direction of the difference). Using the 5% significance level and 9 degrees of freedom, Table B-2 shows that a t score of at least 1.833 is needed to reject the null hypothesis.

4. Determine the score of your sample on the comparison distribution. The sample's mean change of .14 is .70 standard deviations (of .20 each) on the distribution of means above that distribution's mean of 0.

TABLE 9-8
Steps for Conducting a *t* Test for Dependent Means

1. Reframe the question into a research hypothesis and a null hypothesis about the populations.

2. Determine the characteristics of the comparison distribution.

   a. Convert each subject's two scores into a difference score. Carry out the remaining steps using these difference scores.

   b. Compute the mean of the difference scores.

   c. Assume a population mean of 0: $\mu = 0$.

   d. Compute the estimated population variance of difference scores: $S^2 = SS/df$.

   e. Compute the variance of the distribution of means of difference scores: $S_M^2 = S^2/N$.

   f. Compute the standard deviation of the distribution of means of difference scores: $S_M = \sqrt{S_M^2}$.

   g. Note that it will be a *t* distribution with $df = N - 1$.

3. Determine the cutoff sample score on the comparison distribution at which the null hypothesis should be rejected.

   a. Determine the desired significance level and whether to use a one-tailed or a two-tailed test.

   b. Look up the appropriate cutoff in a *t* table.

4. Determine the score of your sample on the comparison distribution: $t = (M - \mu)/S_M$.

5. Compare the scores obtained in Steps 3 and 4 to decide whether to reject the null hypothesis.

5. Compare the scores obtained in Steps 3 and 4 to decide whether to reject the null hypothesis. The sample's *t* of .70 is considerably less extreme than the needed *t* of 1.833. Thus the null hypothesis cannot be rejected. The study is inconclusive.

Summary of Steps for Conducting a *t* Test for Dependent Means

Table 9-8 summarizes the steps in conducting a *t* test for dependent means.

Optional computational formulas for carrying out a *t* test for dependent means by hand are given in the Chapter Appendix.

Assumptions of the *t* Test

We noted earlier that when using an estimated population variance, the comparison distribution will be a *t* distribution. However, this can be assumed only if we think that the distribution of the population of individual cases from which we drew our sample follows a normal curve. Otherwise, the appropriate comparison distribution will follow some other shape (which usually cannot be determined).

So strictly speaking, a normal population distribution is a requirement within the logic and mathematics of the *t* test. Such a requirement for a hypothesis-testing procedure is called an **assumption:** A normal population distribution is said to be an assumption of the *t* test. The effect of this assumption is that if the population distribution is not normal, it is inappropriate to use the *t* test.

Unfortunately, it is rarely possible to tell whether the population is normal on the basis of the information in your sample—which, when doing a *t* test, is usually all you have to go on. But fortunately, as we saw in Chapter 5, distributions that arise in psychology research (and in nature generally) are thought to approximate a normal curve. (This also applies to distributions of difference scores.) Also fortunately, statisticians have found that in practice, applying the *t* test gives reasonably accurate results even when the population is rather far from normal. That is, the *t* test is said to be "robust" over moderate violations of the assumption of a normal population distribution. (How statisticians figure out the **robustness** of a test is an interesting topic, which is described in Box 10-1 in Chapter 10.)

Only one circumstance that arises with any frequency creates a serious problem when using the *t* test for dependent means. This is when the population is highly skewed (is very asymmetrical, with a much longer tail on one side than the other) and you are using a one-tailed test.

So it is wise when doing a *t* test to consider whether there is any indication that the population of difference scores is highly skewed, particularly if you are conducting a one-tailed test. One indication that the *population* distribution of difference scores might be highly skewed would be if your *sample's* distribution of difference scores is extremely skewed. Also, as noted in Chapter 5, the kinds of measures or experimental procedures you are using can create a skewed distribution. For example, if you are using measures that have a maximum score, and subjects scored near the maximum on the first test, then scores on a later test, after some experimental intervention, may be skewed because there will be a limit to how much increase is possible. More important, this would create a skewed distribution of difference scores.

When the assumption of a normal distribution of the population of difference scores is severely violated, several alternatives to the *t* test are available. Those alternatives are described in Chapter 15.

Effect Size and Power for the *t* Test for Dependent Means

Effect Size

Effect size for the *t* test for dependent means is computed in the same way as we did in Chapter 8:

$$d = \frac{\mu_1 - \mu_2}{\sigma} \tag{9-8}$$

(This *d* does not stand for dependent means or difference scores. Remember that when discussing effect size, *d* is for the difference among populations—it is an educated guess about parameters and is used for calculating effect size in many more situations than *t* tests for dependent means using difference scores.) When applying this rule, keep in mind that when using difference scores, the mean of Population 2 (μ_2) will be assumed to be 0 and the standard deviation (σ) is of the populations of difference scores. Thus the formula reduces to

$$d = \frac{\mu_1}{\sigma} \qquad\qquad (9\text{-}9)$$

with both terms relating to difference scores. Also note that you divide by the standard deviation of the population of individual difference scores σ, *not* by the standard deviation of the distribution of means of difference scores (σ_M). The key difference is that the computation of the standard deviation of the distribution of means involves dividing by the size of your particular sample. As we emphasized in Chapter 8, the point of effect size estimates is that they indicate the amount of difference between means in a way that is unaffected by sample size, thus permitting comparisons between studies that use different numbers of subjects. In the case of t tests for dependent means, the conventions for effect sizes are the same as you learned for the situation we considered in Chapter 8: A small effect size is .20, a medium effect size is .50, and a large effect size is .80.

As an example of computing this kind of effect size, suppose that a sports psychologist plans a study in which she will administer a questionnaire about attitudes toward teammates both before and after winning a championship. She is interested in a minimum meaningful difference from before to after of 4 points on the questionnaire and has reason to think that the standard deviation of difference scores on this attitude questionnaire is 8 points. In this case, $\mu_1 = 4$ and $\sigma = 8$. Thus $d = \mu_1/\sigma = 4/8 = .50$. In terms of the conventions, her planned study has a medium effect size.

If you are estimating the effect size based on a completed study,

$$d = \frac{M}{S} \qquad\qquad (9\text{-}10)$$

again with both M and S referring to difference scores. For our first example of a t test for dependent means (the Olthoff and Aron study of husbands' change in communication quality), the mean of the difference scores was -12.05, and the estimated population standard deviation of the difference scores was 12.41 (that is, since S^2 was 154.05, $\sqrt{S^2} = 12.41$). Thus the effect size is computed as $d = M/S = -12.05/12.41 = -.97$. This was clearly a large effect. (The sign of the effect, in this case negative, only means that the large effect was a decrease.)

Power

Table 9-9 gives the approximate power at the .05 significance level for small, medium, and large effect sizes and one- or two-tailed tests. For example, in the sports psychology example, where the researcher expected a medium effect size ($d = .50$), if she planned to conduct the study using the .05 level, two-tailed, with 20 subjects, the study would have a power of .59. This means that if the research hypothesis is in fact true, and has a medium effect size, there is a 59% chance that this study will come out significant.

The power table (Table 9-9) is especially useful when interpreting the practical importance of a nonsignificant result in a published study. For example, suppose that a study using a t test for dependent means failed to

TABLE 9-9
Approximate Power for Studies Using the _t_ Test for Dependent Means in Testing Hypotheses at the .05 Significance Level

Scores in Sample (_N_)	Effect Size		
	Small (d = .20)	_Medium (d = .50)_	_Large (d = .80)_
Two-tailed test			
10	.09	.32	.66
20	.14	.59	.93
30	.19	.77	.99
40	.24	.88	*
50	.29	.94	*
100	.25	*	*
One-tailed test			
10	.15	.46	.78
20	.22	.71	.96
30	.29	.86	*
40	.35	.93	*
50	.40	.97	*
100	.63	*	*

*Power is nearly 1.

find significance at the .05 level, two-tailed, using 10 subjects. Should you conclude that there is in fact no difference at all in the populations? Probably not. Even assuming a medium effect size, Table 9-9 indicates that there is only a 32% chance of obtaining a significant result (two-tailed) with only 10 subjects. Now consider a situation in which a study failed to find significance (again at the .05 level), one-tailed, using 100 subjects. In this case, Table 9-9 tells you that even assuming a small effect size, if the research hypothesis were true, there would be a 63% chance of the study's coming out significant. If there were a medium effect size in the population, the table indicates that there is almost a 100% chance that this study would have come out significant. Thus we can conclude from the results of this study that if there is a true difference in the populations, it is almost surely at most a rather small one.

To keep the table simple, we have given power figures for only a few different numbers of subjects (10, 20, 30, 40, 50, and 100). This should be sufficient for the kinds of rough evaluations you are called on to make when evaluating results of research articles.[4]

Planning Sample Size

Table 9-10 gives the approximate number of subjects needed to achieve 80% power for estimated small, medium, and large effect sizes using one- and two-tailed tests, for the .05 significance levels. (Eighty percent is a

[4]More detailed tables, in terms of numbers of subjects, levels of effect size, and significance levels, are provided by Cohen (1988, pp. 28–39). If you use his tables, note that the _d_ referred to is actually based on a _t_ test for independent means (the situation we consider in Chapter 10). For a _t_ test for dependent means, as you have learned to do in this chapter, first multiply your desired effect size by 1.4. For example, if your effect size is .30, you would consider it to be .42 (.30 × 1.4 = .42) for purposes of this table. The only other difference from our table is that Cohen describes the significance level by the letter _a_ (for "alpha level"), with a subscript of either 1 or 2, referring to a one- or two-tailed test. For example, a table that refers to "$a_1 = .05$" at the top means that this is the table for $p < .05$, one-tailed.

TABLE 9-10
Approximate Number of Subjects Needed to Achieve 80% Power for the *t* Test for Dependent Means in Testing Hypotheses at the .05 Significance Level

	Effect Size		
	Small (d = .20)	*Medium* (d = .50)	*Large* (d = .80)
Two-tailed	196	33	14
One-tailed	156	26	12

common figure used by researchers for the minimum power needed to make a study worth conducting.) For example, if you are planning a study in which you expect a large effect size and will use the .05 significance level, two-tailed, you only need 14 subjects to be assured of 80% power. By contrast, a study using the same significance level but in which you expect only a small effect size would require 196 subjects to achieve 80% power.[5]

The Power of Studies Employing the *t* Test for Dependent Means

Studies using difference scores often have considerably larger effect sizes for a given amount of expected difference than other kinds of research designs (for example, a study in which scores from two separate groups of individuals, each measured once, are compared). This is because the standard deviation of difference scores—what you divide by to get the effect size when using difference scores—is usually quite low. The only variation is within each subject over the tests. Variation among baselines of different subjects is ruled out because difference scores are all comparing subjects to themselves. The impact of this is that studies using difference scores may have comparatively high power even with small numbers of subjects. William S. Gosset, who essentially invented the *t* test (see Box 9-1), made much of this point in a historically interesting controversy over an experiment about milk. This controversy is described in Box 9-2.

Controversies and Limitations

The main controversies about the *t* test (and several related procedures covered in the next few chapters) have to do with its relative advantages and disadvantages in comparison to various alternatives—alternatives that we discuss in some detail in Chapter 15. There is, however, one consideration that we want to comment on now. It relates to all research designs in which the same subjects are tested before and after some experimental intervention. (This is the kind of situation that the *t* test for dependent means is often used to analyze.)

Simply measuring a group of people before and after an experimental procedure, without any kind of control group that does not undergo the procedure, is a weak research design (Cook & Campbell, 1979). As described in more detail in Appendix A, even if such a study produces a significant difference, it leaves many alternative explanations for why that difference

[5]Fuller tables, indicating needed numbers of subjects for levels of power other than 80% (and also for effect sizes other than .20, .50, and .80 and for other significance levels) are provided in Cohen (1988, pp. 54–55). However, see footnote 4 in this chapter about using these tables.

BOX 9-2

The Power of Studies Using Difference Scores:
How the Lanarkshire Milk Experiment Could Have Been Milked for More

In 1930, a major health experiment was conducted in Scotland involving 20,000 schoolchildren. Its main purpose was to compare the growth of a group of children who were assigned to drink milk regularly to those who were in a control group. The results were that those who drank milk showed more growth.

However, William Gosset, a contemporary statistician (see Box 9-1), was appalled at the way the experiment was done. It had cost about £7,500, which in 1930 was a huge amount of money, and was done wrong! Large studies such as this were very popular among statisticians in those days because they seemed to imitate the large numbers found in nature. Gosset, by contrast, being a brewer, was forced to use very small numbers in his studies—experimental batches of beer were too costly. And he was often chided by the "real statisticians" for his small sample sizes. But Gosset argued that no number of subjects was large enough when strict random assignment was not followed. And in this study, teachers were permitted to switch children from group to group if they took pity on a child whom they felt would benefit from receiving milk! (See Appendix A for a discussion of random assignment to groups.)

However, what is more interesting in light of the present chapter, Gosset demonstrated that the researchers could have obtained the same result with 50 pairs of identical twins, flipping a coin to determine which of each pair was in the milk group (and sticking to it). Of course, the statistic you would use is the t test as taught in this chapter—the t test for dependent means.

More recently, the development of power analysis, which we introduced in Chapter 8, has thoroughly vindicated Gosset. It is now clear just how surprisingly few subjects are needed when a researcher can find a way to set up a repeated-measures design in which difference scores are the basic unit of analysis. (In this case, each *pair* of twins would be one "subject.") As Gosset could have told them, studies that use the t test for dependent means can be extremely sensitive.

References: Peters (1987); Tankard (1984).

occurred—for example, the people might have matured or improved during that period anyway, or perhaps other events happened in between, or the subjects not getting benefits may have dropped out. It is even possible that the initial test itself caused changes that otherwise might not have occurred.

Note, however, that the difficulties of research that tests people before and after some intervention are shared only slightly with the kind of study in which subjects are tested under two conditions, such as noisy versus quiet, with half tested first under one condition and half tested first under the other condition.

t Tests as Described in Research Articles

Research articles typically describe t tests in one of two ways. First, they may be described in the text of the article. The description usually follows a standard format of t, the degrees of freedom in parentheses, an equal sign, the t score, and then the significance level—for example, "$t(24) = 2.80, p < .05$." Whether a one- or two-tailed test was used may also be noted (if not, assume that it was two-tailed). Usually the means, and sometimes the standard deviations, are given for each testing. Rarely is the standard deviation of the difference scores reported.

Here is an example. Pollard, Pollard, and Corn (1989) conducted a study of whether stressful life events tend to precede panic attacks in agoraphobics (people afraid of open or public places). As part of this study, 50 agoraphobics completed questionnaires about stressful life events occurring during the year just before the panic attack and about stressful life events occurring during a comparable period of time 4 years earlier. Their result was reported as follows: "There was a significant difference between the mean number of total stressful life events reported during the . . . panic onset period and . . . [four years earlier], $t(49) = 5.51, p < .001$" (p. 319). The actual means for the two periods were reported separately in a table.

Similarly, Olthoff and Aron (1993) might have reported their result in the example we used in this way: "There was a significant decline in communication quality, dropping from 116.32 before marriage to 104.26 after marriage, $t(18) = 2.76, p < .05$, two-tailed." The researcher in the surgeon study could have written the following: "The mean performance for the quiet group was 18.89, while the performance for the noisy group was 16.89. This difference was not statistically significant at the .01 level, even with a one-tailed test, $t(8) = 2.20$."

Second, the researcher may present the means of the groups in a table. For example, Harris, Thomas, and Booth (1990) examined the response of 12 infants to salted versus unsalted cereal (each infant was tested twice over 2 days with each type of cereal, with order counterbalanced). The infants were all 4 to 6 months old, the age when solid food is usually first introduced. Previous research was unclear about whether infants at this age would show any behavioral signs of food preferences, an issue that is important in deciding at what age solid food should be introduced. The responses of the infants to preferred and nonpreferred cereals were observed, and dependent-means t tests were conducted to compare the responses under the two conditions. As you can see from Table 9-11, the infants showed significant mean differences on a number of key behaviors, such as lower levels of refusal for the preferred cereal. Notice, incidentally, the method of using stars to indicate the level of significance. This is a common procedure—in fact, sometimes the t value itself is not given, just the stars (with the note at the bottom as to the exact p levels to which they refer).

TABLE 9-11
Percentage of Infant Behaviors Shown With Preferred and Nonpreferred Cereals

Behavioral Categories	Preferred Cereal		Nonpreferred Cereal		Paired Difference
	M	*SD*	*M*	*SD*	*t(11)*
Positive food acceptance	13.1	13.3	8.4	13.8	2.3*
Positive body movements	31.3	28.9	10.0	12.6	3.2***
Neutral food acceptance	63.6	20.9	54.6	25.1	2.1
Refusal	22.6	22.2	31.8	25.6	−2.6*
Crying	3.7	5.4	22.4	23.9	−3.0**
Negative body movements	34.4	22.3	46.2	25.1	−2.2*
Gaze at mother	41.5	32.8	38.2	31.8	0.4
Maternal vocalization	27.7	20.6	42.3	30.2	−1.9

$*p < .05. **p < .02. ***p < .01.$ All two-tailed.

From Harris, G., Thomas, A., Booth, D. A. (1990), tab. 1. Development of salt taste in infancy. *Developmental Psychology, 26,* 534–538. Copyright, 1990, by the American Psychological Association. Reprinted by permission of the author.

Summary

The same five steps of hypothesis testing described in Chapter 7 apply when the variance of the population is not known, except that (a) the population variance is estimated from the information in the sample using a formula that divides the sum of squared deviations (*SS*) by the degrees of freedom ($df = N - 1$), $S^2 = SS/df$; (b) the comparison distribution of means will have the shape of a *t* distribution (for which cutoffs are found in a *t* table), which has more area at the extremes than a normal curve (just how much more depends on how few degrees of freedom were used in estimating the population variance); and (c) the number of standard deviations from the mean that a sample's mean falls on the *t* distribution is called a *t* score, $t = (M - \mu)/S_M$.

Studies in which there is a group of subjects each having two scores, such as a before score and an after score, are often analyzed using a *t* test for dependent means. In this *t* test, you first compute a difference score for each subject, then proceed with the five-step hypothesis-testing procedure in the same way as if you had a single sample with an unknown variance and assuming that the null hypothesis is about a population of difference scores with a mean of 0 (no difference).

An assumption of the *t* test is that the population distribution is normal. However, even when the population distribution departs substantially from normal, the *t* test is usually sufficiently accurate. The major exception in the case of a *t* test for dependent means is when the population of difference scores appears to be highly skewed and a one-tailed test is being used.

The effect size of a study using a *t* test for dependent means is the mean of the difference scores divided by the standard deviation of the difference scores. Power and needed sample size for a given level of power can be determined from special tables. The power of studies using difference scores is typically much higher than that of studies using other designs with the same number of subjects.

Research methodologists point out that research involving a single group tested before and after some intervening event, without a control group, is a weak approach that permits many alternative explanations of any observed changes.

t tests are reported in research articles using a standard format—for example, "$t(24) = 2.80, p < .05$"—or in tables with the significance level indicated by asterisks.

Key Terms

assumption	robustness	*t* test for dependent means
biased estimate	*t* distribution	unbiased estimate of the population variance (S^2)
degrees of freedom (*df*)	*t* score	
difference scores	*t* table	
repeated-measures design	*t* test	

Practice Problems

These problems involve computation (with the assistance of a calculator). Most real-life statistics problems are done on a computer. But even if you have a computer, do this by hand to ingrain the method in your mind.

For practice in using a computer to solve statistical problems, refer to the computer section of each chapter of the study guide that accompanies this text.

All data are fictional (unless an actual citation is given). Answers to Set I are given at the back of the book.

SET I

1. The following sets of data are about situations in which, in each case, a single sample's mean is being compared to a population with a known mean but an unknown variance. For each data set, determine if the difference between the sample's mean and the population mean is significant. (If df is not given in the table, use the t for the nearest lower df value.)

	Sample Size (N)	Population Mean (μ)	Estimated Population Variance (S^2)	Sample Mean (M)	Tails	Significance Level (α)
(a)	64	12.40	9.00	11.00	1 (low predicted)	.05
(b)	49	1,006.35	317.91	1,009.72	2	.01
(c)	400	52.00	7.02	52.41	1 (high predicted)	.01

2. Suppose that a candidate running for sheriff claims that she will reduce the average speed of emergency response to less than $\frac{1}{2}$ h, which is thought to be the average response time under the incumbent sheriff. There are no past records, so the actual standard deviation of such response times cannot be determined. Thanks to this campaign, she is elected sheriff, and careful records are now kept. The response times for the first month are 26, 30, 28, 29, 25, 28, 32, 35, 24, and 23 min.

Using the 5% level of significance, did she keep her promise? Illustrate your answer with a histogram of the distribution of the sample and sketches of the population distribution and the distribution of means, showing the t score and cutoff points for significance. Explain your answer to someone who has never taken a course in statistics.

3. For each of the following sets of data about difference scores, determine if the mean difference is significantly greater than 0. Also compute the effect size. (If df is not given in the table, use the t for the nearest lower df value.)

Number of Difference Scores in Sample	Mean of Difference Scores in Sample	Estimated Population Variance of Difference Scores	Tails	Significance Level
(a) 20	1.7	8.29	1 (high predicted)	.05
(b) 164	2.3	414.53	2	.05
(c) 15	−2.2	4.00	1 (low predicted)	.01

4. A program to decrease littering was implemented in four cities in California's Central Valley starting in August 1992. The amount of litter in the streets (average pounds of litter collected per block per day) was measured during the July before the program was started and then the next July, after the program had been in effect for a year. The results were as follows:

City	July 1992	July 1993
Fresno	9	2 = 7
Merced	10	4 = 6
Bakersfield	8	9 = -1
Stockton	9	1 = 8

Using the 1% level of significance, was there a significant decrease in the amount of litter? Illustrate your answer with a histogram of each distribution and of the difference scores and sketches of the population distribution and distribution of means, showing the t score and cutoff points for significance. Explain your answer to someone who understands mean, standard deviation, and variance but knows nothing else about statistics.

5. Determine the power of each of the following studies (based on the .05 significance level):

	Effect Size	N	Tails
(a)	Small	20	1
(b)	Medium	20	1
(c)	Medium	30	1
(d)	Medium	30	2
(e)	Large	30	2

6. In a study of perceptual illusions made under two different lighting conditions, 20 subjects were each tested under the two different conditions. The experimenter reported: "Mean number of effective illusions was 6.72 under the bright conditions and 6.85 under the dimly lit conditions, a difference that was not significant, $t(19) = 1.62$." Explain this result to a person who had never had a course in statistics; be sure to use sketches of the distributions in your answer.

7. A study was done of personality characteristics of 150 students who were tested at the beginning and end of their first year of college. The researchers reported the results in the following table:

Personality Scale	Fall		Spring		Difference	
	M	*SD*	*M*	*SD*	*M*	*SD*
Anxiety	16.82	4.21	15.32	3.84	1.50**	1.85
Depression	89.32	8.39	86.24	8.91	3.08**	4.23
Introversion	59.89	6.87	60.12	7.11	.23	2.22
Neuroticism	38.11	5.39	37.32	6.02	.89*	4.21

$*p < .05. **p < .01.$

(a) Compute the t values for each personality scale (assume that *SD* in the table corresponds to what we have labeled *S*, the unbiased estimate of the population standard deviation). (b) Explain to a person who has never had a course in statistics what this table means.

SET II

1. The following sets of data are about situations in which, in each case, a single sample's mean is being compared to a population with a known mean but an unknown variance. For each data set, determine if the difference between the sample's mean and the population mean is significant.

	Sample Size	Population Mean	Estimated Standard Deviation	Sample Mean	Tails	Significance Level
	(*N*)	(μ)	(*S*)	(*M*)		(α)
(a)	16	100.31	2.00	100.98	1 (high predicted)	.05
(b)	16	.47	4.00	.00	2	.05
(c)	16	68.90	9.00	34.00	1 (low predicted)	.01

2. A biological theory asserts that humans have adapted to their physical environment and should therefore spontaneously follow a 24-h cycle of sleeping and waking even if they were not exposed to the usual pattern of sunlight. To test this notion, eight paid volunteers were placed (individually) in a room in which there was no light from the outside and no clocks or other indications of time. They could turn the lights on and off as they wished. After a month in the room, each individual tended to develop a steady cycle. Their cycles at the end of the study were as follows: 25, 27, 25, 23, 24, 25, 26, and 25.

Using the 5% level of significance, what should we conclude about the theory that 24 h is the natural cycle? Illustrate your answer with a histogram of the distribution of the sample and sketches of the population distribution and the distribution of means, showing the t score and

cutoff points for significance. Explain your answer to someone who has never taken a course in statistics.

3. Four individuals with high levels of cholesterol went on a special crash diet, avoiding high-cholesterol foods and eating oat bran. Their cholesterol levels before and after the diet were as follows:

Subject	Before	After
J.K.	287	255
L.M.M	305	269
A.K.	243	245
R.O.S.	309	247

Using the 5% level of significance, was there a significant change in cholesterol level? What was the effect size? Explain your answer to someone who has never taken a course in statistics. Use illustrations in addition to words.

4. Five individuals who had attended a mandatory workshop on speeding recorded their maximum driving speed for 2 weeks before and after the workshop. The results are shown in the table.

Subject	Before	After
L.B.	65	58
J.K.	62	65
R.C.	60	56
R.T.	70	66
J.M.	68	60

Using the 5% significance level, should we conclude that people are likely to drive more slowly after such a workshop? Give the effect size of your result.

5. The amount of oxygen consumption was measured in six individuals over two 10-min periods while sitting with their eyes closed. During one 10-min period, they listened to an exciting adventure story. During the other, they heard restful music. (Order of conditions was reversed for half of the subjects.) Based on the results shown, is oxygen consumption less when listening to the music? Use the 1% significance level.

Subject	Story	Music
1	6.12	5.39
2	7.25	6.72
3	5.70	5.42
4	6.40	6.16
5	5.82	5.96
6	6.24	6.08

6. Five sophomores were given an English achievement test before and after receiving instruction in basic grammar. Based on their scores, is it reasonable to conclude that future students would show higher scores after instruction? Use the 5% significance level.

Student	Before	After
A	20	18
B	18	22
C	17	15
D	16	17
E	12	9

7. A study was done comparing union activity of employees in 10 plants during two different decades. The researchers reported "a significant increase in union activity, $t(9) = 3.28$, $p < .01$." Explain this result to a person who has never had a course in statistics. Be sure to use sketches of the distributions in your answer. Also indicate the approximate power of this study.

Chapter Appendix: Optional Computational Formula for the t Test for Dependent Means

The usual steps of conducting a t test for dependent means, after converting to difference scores, are to compute (a) the mean of the difference scores, (b) the sum of squared deviations of the difference scores from the mean of difference scores, (c) the estimated variance of the distribution of the population of individual difference scores (S^2), (d) the estimated standard deviation of the distribution of means of difference scores (S_M), and (e) the t score. Combining some of these steps and applying some algebraic manipulation, once you have converted everything to difference scores, you can use the following computational formulas to find S and t.

$$S = \sqrt{\frac{\Sigma X^2 - (\Sigma X)^2/N}{N - 1}} \qquad (9\text{-}11)$$

$$t = \frac{\Sigma X/N}{S/\sqrt{N}} \qquad (9\text{-}12)$$

Table 9-12 shows the calculation of the t test for dependent means for our second example (the fictional study of surgeons' hand-eye coordination), using these computational formulas. Compare these computations to the ones in Table 9-6 for the same data but using the definitional formulas.

TABLE 9-12
Calculation of the t Test for Dependent Means for the Surgeons' Hand-Eye Coordination Example, Using the Computational Formulas (Fictional Data)

Surgeon	Conditions		Difference	Squared Difference
	Quiet	*Noisy*	*(X)*	*(X²)*
1	18	12	6	36
2	21	21	0	0
3	19	16	3	9
4	21	16	5	25
5	17	19	−2	4
6	20	19	1	1
7	18	16	2	4
8	16	17	−1	1
9	20	16	4	16
Σ:	170	152	18	96

$$S = \sqrt{\frac{\Sigma X^2 - (\Sigma X)^2/N}{N - 1}} = \sqrt{\frac{96 - 18^2/9}{9 - 1}} = \sqrt{\frac{96 - 324/9}{8}} = \sqrt{\frac{96 - 36}{8}} = \sqrt{\frac{60}{8}} = \sqrt{7.5} = 2.74$$

$$t = \frac{\Sigma X/N}{S/\sqrt{N}} = \frac{18/9}{2.74/\sqrt{9}} = \frac{2}{2.74/3} = \frac{2}{.91} = 2.20$$

10 | The *t* Test for Independent Means

THIS chapter examines the procedure for hypothesis testing in the very common situation in which a researcher is comparing two samples of subjects, such as an experimental group and a control group. Because the variances of the population distributions are not known and must be estimated, these situations require a *t* test. And this time it is called a ***t* test for independent means** because it compares the means of two entirely separate groups of people whose scores are independent of each other. This is in contrast to the *t* test for dependent means, considered in Chapter 9, in which there were two groups of scores, but both were for the same individuals (such as the same people measured before and after a counseling program).

t test for independent means

Basic Strategy of the *t* Test for Independent Means: The Distribution of Differences Between Means

The *t* test for independent means works in the same way as the hypothesis-testing procedures you have already learned, with one main exception: The key result is a difference between the means of two samples. Thus the comparison distribution must be a **distribution of differences between means.**

distribution of differences between means

Content of a Distribution of Differences Between Means

This special distribution is, in a sense, two steps removed from the populations of individual cases: First there is a distribution of means from each population of individual cases, and then there is a distribution of differences between pairs of means (one member of each pair drawn from each of these

FIGURE 10-1
The steps in creating a distribution of differences between means.

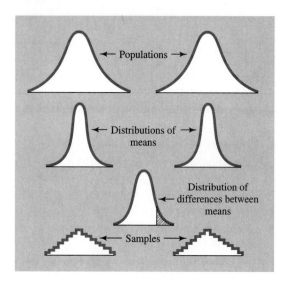

distributions of means). Think of this distribution of differences between means as arising by your randomly selecting one mean from the distribution of means for Population 1 and one mean from the distribution of means for Population 2 and then subtracting the mean selected from one distribution of means from the mean selected from the other. This gives a difference score between the two selected means. Then repeat the process. This creates a second difference, a difference between the two newly selected means. Repeating this process a large number of times creates a distribution of differences between means.

Illustration of the Overall Logic of the *t* Test for Independent Means

Figure 10-1 diagrams the entire logical construction involved in a distribution of differences between means. At the top are the two population distributions. We do not know the characteristics of these population distributions. But we do know that if the null hypothesis is true, the two population means are the same. That is, the null hypothesis is that $\mu_1 = \mu_2$. We can also estimate the variance of these populations, based on the sample information (these estimated variances will be S_1^2 and S_2^2).

In Figure 10-1, we have shown the two population distributions and, below each, the distribution of means for that population. Using the estimated population variance and knowing the size of each sample, we can determine the variance of each distribution of means in the usual way (it will have the variance of its parent population divided by the size of the samples).

Below these two distributions of means, and constructed from them, is the crucial distribution of differences between means. Because this distribution's variance is ultimately based on estimated population variances, we can think of it as a *t* distribution. The goal of a *t* test for independent means is to determine whether the difference between the two actual means falls beyond the cutoff (for example, the top 5%, which we have shaded in the figure) on this distribution of all possible differences between means drawn from the two populations. The two actual samples are shown (as histograms) at the bottom.

Remember, this whole procedure is really a kind of fabrication in the clouds that exists only as part of the reasoning process to help you draw conclusions based on the results of an experiment. The sole concrete reality in all of this is the actual scores in the two samples. The population variances are estimated on the basis of these sample scores, and the variances of the two distributions of means are based entirely on these estimated population variances (and the sample sizes). And as you will see shortly, the characteristics of the distribution of differences between means is based on these two distributions of means.

Nevertheless, the procedure is a powerful one—it has the power of mathematics and logic behind it—and it helps you develop general knowledge based on the specifics of a particular study.

With this overview of the basic logic, we now turn to five key details: (a) the mean of the distribution of differences between means, (b) the estimated population variance, (c) the variance and standard deviation of the distribution of differences between means, (d) the shape of the distribution of differences between means, and (e) the t score for the difference between the particular two means being compared.

Mean of the Distribution of Differences Between Means

In a t test for independent means, two populations are being considered— for example, one represented by the experimental group and one represented by the control group. In practice, a researcher does not know the true mean of either population. But the researcher does know that if the null hypothesis is true, these two populations have the same mean. Further, if these two populations have the same mean, the distribution of means for each of them will have the same mean. And if random samples are taken from two distributions with the same mean, the differences between the means of these random samples, in the long run, should balance out to 0.

Consequently, whatever the specifics of the study, the researcher knows that if the null hypothesis is true, the distribution of differences between means has a mean of 0.

Estimating the Population Variance

In Chapter 9, you learned to estimate the population variance on the basis of information in the sample. It is the sum of squared deviations divided by the degrees of freedom (the number in the sample minus 1): $S^2 = SS/df$.

To conduct a t test for independent means, it must be reasonable to assume that the populations that the two samples represent have the same variance. (If the null hypothesis is true, they also have the same mean.) So by making an estimate of that single common value of the population variance from each of the two samples, we are making two different estimates of what should be the same population variance. We have an embarrassment of riches. How we solve this problem depends on whether the number of scores in each sample is the same or different.

Estimated Population Variance When Sample Sizes Are Equal

When the number of cases in both samples is the same—that is, when we have equal sample sizes—the solution to this problem of having two samples from which to estimate the population variance is straightforward: Make an estimate from each sample, and average the two. Thus if the estimated population variance based on one sample is 60 and the estimated population variance based on the other sample is 80, the best overall estimate of the population variance would be 70 (the average of 60 and 80).

This procedure of averaging the two estimates gives what is called the **pooled estimate of the population variance** because it combines, or "pools," the information from the two samples. Stated as a formula, assuming equal sample sizes,

$$S_P^2 = \frac{S_1^2 + S_2^2}{2} \tag{10-1}$$

where S_P^2 is the pooled estimate of the population variance and S_1^2 is the estimated population variance based on the scores in the first sample (the sample that corresponds to Population 1). It is computed in the usual way—$S^2 = SS/df$—using the sum of squared deviations and degrees of freedom for this sample, as if no other sample existed. S_2^2 is the estimated population variance based on the scores in the second sample, computed the same way.

Applying the formula to our example in which the estimated variances are 60 and 80,

$$S_P^2 = \frac{S_1^2 + S_2^2}{2} = \frac{60 + 80}{2} = \frac{140}{2} = 70$$

Estimated Population Variance When Sample Sizes Are Not Equal

When one of the samples has more subjects than the other, finding the pooled estimate of the population variance by ordinary averaging is less than ideal. Ordinary averaging, in effect, gives equal weight to the two estimates. But if one estimate is based on more information, it should have more influence on the overall estimate. The solution is to use a **weighted average** based on the degrees of freedom (the number of cases minus 1) contributed by each sample. (Technically speaking, the amount of information on which each estimate is based is its degrees of freedom, not its sample size.)

A weighted average is computed by first figuring out the proportion that each sample's information contributes to the total information, then multiplying each sample's proportion times its estimate of the population variance. The two resulting products are summed. In terms of a formula,

$$S_P^2 = \frac{df_1}{df_1 + df_2}(S_1^2) + \frac{df_2}{df_1 + df_2}(S_2^2) \tag{10-2}$$

where df_1 is the degrees of freedom for the first sample (the number of subjects in the first sample minus 1) and df_2 is the degrees of freedom for the second sample.

Since $df_1 + df_2$ equals the total degrees of freedom, the formula can also be written as

$$S_P^2 = \frac{df_1}{df_T}(S_1^2) + \frac{df_2}{df_T}(S_2^2)$$ (10-3)

where df_T is the sum of the degrees of freedom in both samples $(df_T = df_1 + df_2)$.

For example, consider a study in which the population variance estimate based on an experimental group of 11 subjects is 60 and the population variance estimate based on a control group of 31 subjects is 80. The estimate from the experimental group is based on 10 degrees of freedom (11 subjects) and the estimate from the control group on 30 degrees of freedom (31 subjects). The total information on which the estimate is based is the total degrees of freedom—in this example, 40. Thus the experimental group provides one quarter (10/40 = 1/4) of the information, and the control group provides three quarters (30/40 = 3/4) of the information. The estimate from the experimental group of 60 is then multiplied by 1/4, making 15; the estimate from the control group of 80 is multiplied by 3/4, making 60; adding the two together gives an overall estimate of 15 plus 60, or 75.

Using the formula,

$$S_P^2 = \frac{df_1}{df_T}(S_1^2) + \frac{df_2}{df_T}(S_2^2) = \frac{10}{40}(60) + \frac{30}{40}(80)$$

$$= \frac{1}{4}(60) + \frac{3}{4}(80) = 15 + 60 = 75$$

Notice that this procedure does not give the same result, 70, as ordinary averaging (without weighting) of these two estimates would. This weighted, pooled estimate of 75 is closer to the estimate based on the control group alone than to the estimate based on the experimental group alone, which is appropriate because the control group estimate was based on more information.

But also note that this formula involving weighted averages actually works in all situations, whether the samples sizes are equal or not. The reason for this is that when sample sizes are equal (and thus degrees of freedom for each sample are also equal), the weighted-average formula reduces to the simple average. (If df_1 and df_2 are equal, they are each half of df_T. Multiplying 1/2 times each variance estimate and adding the two together is the same as taking the ordinary unweighted average.)

You may have also noticed that it would be possible to simplify the weighted-average formula by algebraic manipulation. However, we have left it in this form to emphasize the underlying logic. In practical applications, the computations are all done by computer. And in your own working of exercises, it is useful to keep the basic logic close at hand. Nevertheless, for the interested student, the appendix to this chapter provides an efficient formula for computing the t test for independent means by hand.

Calculating the Variance of Each of the Two Distributions of Means

Once you have determined the pooled estimate of the population variance, by whatever method, it is considered to be the best estimate for both populations. (As noted, to carry out a t test for independent means, we have to be able to assume that the two populations have the same variance.) The two distributions of means will not, however, necessarily have the same variance. The variance of a distribution of means, you will recall, is the variance of the population of individual cases divided by the sample size ($S_M^2 = S^2/N$). Thus only if the two distributions of means have the same sample size will they also have the same variance; otherwise, you must calculate the variance of each separately. In terms of formulas,

$$S_{M1}^2 = \frac{S_P^2}{N_1}$$

(10-4)

and

$$S_{M2}^2 = \frac{S_P^2}{N_2}$$

(10-5)

where S_{M1}^2 is the variance of the distribution of means based on the information in the first sample, S_{M2}^2 is the corresponding number for the second sample, N_1 is the number of subjects in the first sample, and N_2 is the number in the second sample.

Using the example of the study in which there were 11 in the experimental group and 31 in the control group, we found that the pooled estimate of the population variance is 75. So for the experimental group, the variance of the distribution of means would be 75/11, which is 6.82. For the control group, the variance would be 75/31, which is 2.42. (Remember that when figuring estimated variances, you divide by the degrees of freedom, but when figuring the variance of a distribution of means, which does not involve any additional estimation, you divide by the actual number of cases in the sample.) In terms of the formulas,

$$S_{M1}^2 = \frac{S_P^2}{N_1} = \frac{75}{11} = 6.82$$

$$S_{M2}^2 = \frac{S_P^2}{N_2} = \frac{75}{31} = 2.42$$

Variance and Standard Deviation of the Distribution of Differences Between Means

variance of the distribution of differences between means

The variance of each distribution of means contributes fully to the variance of the distribution of differences between means. Hence the **variance of the distribution of differences between means** will be the sum of the variances of the two distributions of means. In symbols,

$$S_{DIF}^2 = S_{M1}^2 + S_{M2}^2$$

(10-6)

where S_{DIF}^2 is the variance of the distribution of differences between means.

standard deviation of the
distribution of differences
between means

To obtain the **standard deviation of the distribution of differences between means** (S_{DIF}), we of course find the square root of the variance. The formula is

$$S_{\text{DIF}} = \sqrt{S_{\text{DIF}}^2}$$
(10-7)

(The standard deviation of the distribution of differences between means is also called the "standard error of the difference.")

Consider again the example of the study in which there were 11 in the experimental group and 31 in the control group. We found that the variance of the distribution of means for the experimental group was 6.82 and the variance of the distribution of means for the control group was 2.42. The variance of the distribution of the difference between means would thus be $6.82 + 2.42 = 9.24$. This makes the standard deviation of this distribution 3.04 (the square root of 9.24). In terms of the formulas,

$$S_{\text{DIF}}^2 = S_{M1}^2 + S_{M2}^2 = 6.82 + 2.42 = 9.24$$

$$S_{\text{DIF}} = \sqrt{S_{\text{DIF}}^2} = \sqrt{9.24} = 3.04$$

Shape of the Distribution of Differences Between Means

Because our distribution of differences between means is based on estimated population variances, our comparison distribution is a t distribution. And because it is based on estimates using information from two samples, the number of degrees of freedom for this t distribution is the sum of the degrees of freedom of the two samples. That is, as noted earlier in the chapter, $df_{\text{T}} = df_1 + df_2$. What is new is the understanding that df_{T}, the total degrees of freedom for both samples taken together, also represents the degrees of freedom on which our t distribution is based.

In the example with an experimental group of 11 and a control group of 31, the total degrees of freedom would be 40 ($11 - 1 = 10$; $31 - 1 = 30$; $10 + 30 = 40$).

Thus, in this example, to determine the t score needed for significance, you look up the cutoff point in the t table in the row with 40 degrees of freedom. If you were conducting a one-tailed test using the .05 significance level, the table shows that with 40 degrees of freedom, the difference between your means must be at least 1.684 standard deviations above the mean difference of 0 on the distribution of differences between means.

The t Score for the Difference Between the Two Actual Means

The t score that you compute in Step 4 of the hypothesis-testing procedure (determining the location of your sample on the comparison distribution) is found as follows: First determine the difference between the two means (that is, subtract one from the other). Then find the location of this difference on the distribution of differences between means by dividing your difference by the standard deviation of this distribution. In terms of a formula,

$$t = \frac{M_1 - M_2}{S_{DIF}}$$ (10-8)

where M_1 is the mean of the first sample and M_2 is the mean of the second sample.

For example, if the mean of the first sample is 198 and the mean of the second sample is 184, the difference between the two means is 14. If the standard deviation of the distribution of differences between means is 7, a difference of 14 is 2 standard deviations from the mean of 0 on this distribution. That is, the t score would be 2. In terms of the formula,

$$t = \frac{M_1 - M_2}{S_{DIF}} = \frac{198 - 184}{7} = \frac{14}{7} = 2$$

Steps of Hypothesis Testing With a t Test for Independent Means

The five steps of hypothesis testing that you learned in Chapter 6 and have continued to use since are the same when conducting a t test for independent means. There are only three changes from what you have done so far: (a) The comparison distribution is now a distribution of differences between means, (b) the degrees of freedom for finding the cutoff score on the t table is based on two samples, and (c) the score of your sample (needed in Step 4) will be based on the difference between your two means.

Example of a t Test for Independent Means

Seligman, Nolen-Hoeksema, Thornton, and Thornton (1990) conducted a study in which they administered the Attributional Style Questionnaire to 47 members of a nationally top-rated varsity college swim team. This questionnaire measures the way an individual tends to understand good and bad events and yields, among other information, an overall score that the researchers describe as a measure of optimism versus pessimism about good events. As part of this study, they compared these scores for the 26 women swimmers and the 21 men swimmers in their sample.

The results were that the women swimmers had a mean optimism score of 15.96 and an estimated population variance of 2.07. The men swimmers had a mean optimism score of 18.03 and an estimated population variance of 3.75. What should the researchers conclude?

Table 10-1 summarizes the calculations, and Figure 10-2 illustrates the various distributions involved. Let's take the problem step by step.

1. Reframe the question into a research hypothesis and a null hypothesis about the populations. The populations of interest are these:

Population 1: Women varsity swimmers
Population 2: Men varsity swimmers

The research hypothesis is that the two populations differ in their optimism. The null hypothesis is that the two populations have the same mean

TABLE 10-1
Computations for a t Test for Independent Means for a Study of Optimism Comparing Women and Men Varsity Swimmers

Women: $N_1 = 26$; $df_1 = N_1 - 1 = 25$; $M_1 = 15.96$; $S_1^2 = 2.07$
Men:　　$N_2 = 21$; $df_2 = N_2 - 1 = 20$; $M_2 = 18.03$; $S_2^2 = 3.75$

$df_T = df_1 + df_2 = 25 + 20 = 45$

$S_P^2 = \dfrac{df_1}{df_T}(S_1^2) + \dfrac{df_2}{df_T}(S_2^2) = \dfrac{25}{45}(2.07) + \dfrac{20}{45}(3.75) = .56(2.07) + .44(3.75) = 1.16 + 1.65 = 2.81$

$S_{M1}^2 = S_P^2/N_1 = 2.81/26 = .11$

$S_{M2}^2 = S_P^2/N_2 = 2.81/21 = .13$

$S_{DIF}^2 = S_{M1}^2 + S_{M2}^2 = .11 + .13 = .24$

$S_{DIF} = \sqrt{S_{DIF}^2} = \sqrt{.24} = .49$

Needed t with $df = 45$, 1% level, two-tailed $= \pm 2.690$

$t = (M_1 - M_2)/S_{DIF} = (15.96 - 18.03)/.49 = -2.07/.49 = -4.22$

Conclusion: Reject the null hypothesis; the results suggest that women swimmers are less optimistic than men swimmers.

Note. Data from Seligman, Nolen-Hoeksema, Thornton, & Thornton (1990).

FIGURE 10-2
The distributions involved in the example of a t test for independent means.

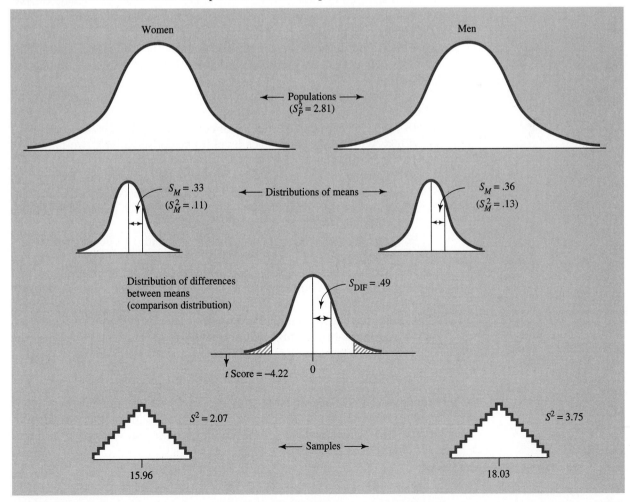

optimism. Although Seligman and associates were aware of previous research suggesting that women in general tend to be less optimistic than men (Nolen-Hoeksema, 1987), they were not sure that this difference would show up or even be in the same direction when comparing women and men who were all world-class athletes. So their hypothesis was nondirectional.

2. Determine the characteristics of the comparison distribution. The comparison distribution is a distribution of differences between means. Its mean is 0. Computing its standard deviation requires several steps. First we need to compute the pooled estimate of the population variance. Since we are working with unequal sample sizes, this requires using a weighted average. There are 25 degrees of freedom for the sample of women and 20 degrees of freedom for the sample of men, for a total of 45. Thus the women contribute 25/45, or 56%, and the men contribute 20/45, or 44%, of the total information. The weighted average is thus 56% of the population variance estimate from the women of 2.07 plus 44% of the population variance estimate for the men of 3.75. This comes out to 1.16 + 1.65 = 2.81.

After computing this pooled estimate of the population variance, we need to compute the variance of each of the two distributions of means. For the women, the variance of the distribution of means comes out to the pooled population (of individual cases) variance estimate of 2.81 divided by the sample size of 26, giving .11. For the men, the pooled population variance estimate of 2.81 divided by 21 gives a variance of .13 for its distribution of means. The variance of the distribution of differences between means is the sum of these two variances: .11 + .13 = .24. The standard deviation of the distribution of differences between means thus comes out to .49 (the square root of .24).

Finally, the shape of the comparison distribution (the distribution of differences between means) will be a t distribution with a total of 45 degrees of freedom.

3. Determine the cutoff sample score on the comparison distribution at which the null hypothesis should be rejected. Because Seligman and colleagues did not predict a particular direction of result, this will be a two-tailed test. With a 1% significance level (to be conservative), two-tailed, we need a t score of at least ± 2.690.

4. Determine the score of the sample on the comparison distribution. The t score is the mean difference (15.96 − 18.03) divided by .49, the standard deviation of the distribution of differences between means. This comes out to a t score of −4.22.

5. Compare the scores obtained in Steps 3 and 4 to decide whether to reject the null hypothesis. The t score of −4.22 for the difference between the two actual means is clearly more extreme than the minimum needed t score of ± 2.690. The null hypothesis can thus be rejected, and the research hypothesis is supported. As Seligman and co-workers (1990) concluded, "This suggests that women tend to be more pessimistic than men even when they have high status and high achievement" (p. 144).

Another Example of a t Test for Independent Means

Moorehouse and Sanders (1992) investigated whether an adolescent boy's sense of how well he is doing in school is related to his mother's work situation. The boys were all in seventh to ninth grade and were all from families in which the mother worked full-time. For purposes of this analysis, the boys were divided into two groups, those in which the mother's work gave her opportunities to solve problems (26 boys) and those in which the mother's work did not provide such opportunities (17 boys). The scores of these two groups of boys on a standard test of perceived academic competence (measuring the extent to which they see themselves as able to be successful at school) were then compared.

The results and the *t*-test analysis are illustrated in Figure 10-3; the raw data and computations are shown in Table 10-2. We will go through the analysis, following the hypothesis-testing procedure step by step.

1. Reframe the question into a research hypothesis and a null hypothesis about the populations. The populations of interest are these:

Population 1: Adolescent boys whose mothers' work involves solving problems

Population 2: Adolescent boys whose mothers' work does not involve solving problems

FIGURE 10-3
The distributions involved in the second example of a *t* test for independent means.

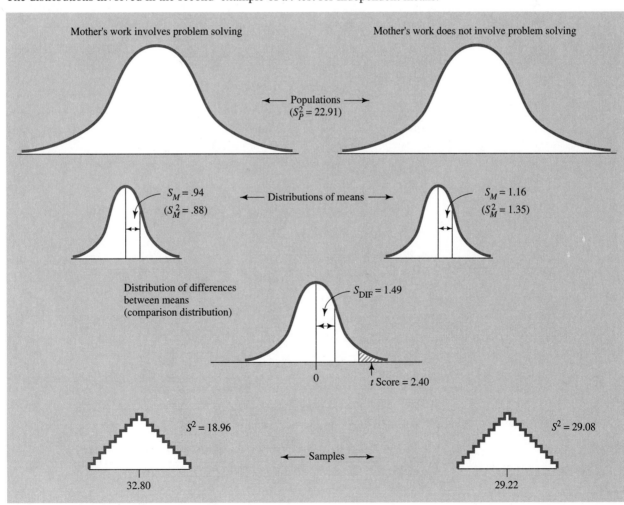

TABLE 10-2

Computations for a *t* Test for Independent Means for a Study of the Relation of the Work Situation of the Mothers of Adolescent Boys' to the Boys' Perceived Academic Competence

	Boys Whose Mothers' Work Involves Problem Solving			Boys Whose Mothers' Work Does Not Involve Problem Solving	
Score	*Deviation from mean*	*Squared deviation from mean*	*Score*	*Deviation from mean*	*Squared deviation from mean*
36.9	4.1	16.81	23.5	− 5.7	32.49
34.6	1.8	16.81	22.5	− 6.7	44.89
26.4	− 6.4	40.96	36.4	7.2	51.84
33.3	.5	.25	40.0	10.8	116.64
35.4	2.6	6.76	30.6	1.4	1.96
34.8	2.0	4.00	30.5	1.3	1.69
32.3	− .5	.25	34.5	5.3	28.09
34.5	1.7	2.89	31.3	2.1	4.41
36.0	3.2	10.24	19.4	− 9.8	96.04
24.5	− 8.3	68.89	29.6	.4	.16
31.6	− 1.2	1.44	24.8	− 4.4	19.36
36.1	3.3	10.89	25.0	− 4.2	17.64
36.8	4.0	16.00	28.8	− .4	.16
27.9	− 4.9	24.01	32.5	3.3	10.89
34.4	1.6	2.56	33.3	4.1	16.81
33.8	1.0	1.00	29.6	.4	.16
36.9	4.1	16.81	24.5	4.7	22.09
34.4	1.6	2.56			
31.7	− 1.1	1.21			
29.4	− 3.4	11.56			
34.1	1.3	1.69			
18.2	−14.6	213.16			
34.5	1.7	2.89			
35.3	2.5	6.25			
35.5	2.7	7.29			
33.4	.6	.36			
Σ: 852.7	0.0	473.97	496.8	0.0	465.32

$M_1 = 32.80$; $S_1^2 = 473.97/25 = 18.96$; $M_2 = 29.22$; $S_2^2 = 465.32/16 = 29.08$

$N_1 = 26$; $df_1 = N_1 - 1 = 25$; $N_2 = 17$; $df_2 = N_2 - 1 = 16$

$df_T = df_1 + df_2 = 25 + 16 = 41$

$S_P^2 = \dfrac{df_1}{df_T}(S_1^2) + \dfrac{df_2}{df_T}(S_2^2) = \dfrac{25}{41}(18.96) + \dfrac{16}{41}(29.08) = .61(18.96) + .39(29.08) = 11.57 + 11.34 = 22.91$

$S_{M1}^2 = S_P^2/N_1 = 22.91/26 = .88$

$S_{M2}^2 = S_P^2/N_2 = 22.91/17 = 1.35$

$S_{DIF}^2 = S_{M1}^2 + S_{M2}^2 = .88 + 1.35 = 2.23$

$S_{DIF} = \sqrt{S_{DIF}^2} = \sqrt{2.23} = 1.49$

Needed *t* with $df = 41$ (using $df = 40$ in table), 5% level, one-tailed = 1.684

$t = (M_1 - M_2)/S_{DIF} = (32.80 - 29.22)/1.49 = 3.58/1.49 = 2.40$

Conclusion: Reject the null hypothesis; the research hypothesis is supported.

Note. Data from Moorehouse & Sanders (1992).

Moorehouse and Sanders had grounds (from theory and previous research) to expect that boys whose mothers' work involves solving problems would have higher levels of perceived academic competence. Thus the research hypothesis was that Population 1 boys would score higher than Population 2 boys. The null hypothesis was that the Population 1 boys would not score higher than the Population 2 boys.

2. Determine the characteristics of the comparison distribution. The comparison distribution is a distribution of differences between means. Its mean is 0, as usual. The population variance estimated from the two samples comes out to 18.96 and 29.08, respectively. The pooled population variance estimate is thus the weighted average of these two: 25/41 times 18.96 and 16/41 times 29.08, which comes out to 22.91. The variance for each distribution of means, this pooled estimate divided by its sample size (22.91/26 and 22.91/17), comes out to .88 and 1.35. Summing the variance of these two gives the variance of the distribution of differences between means, 2.23—the square root of which, the standard deviation of this distribution, is 1.49. The shape of this comparison distribution will be a t distribution with a total of 41 degrees of freedom.

3. Determine the cutoff sample score on the comparison distribution at which the null hypothesis should be rejected. This requires a one-tailed test because a particular direction of difference between the two populations was predicted. Since the t table in Appendix B (Table B-2) does not have exactly 41 degrees of freedom, the next lowest (40) is used. (Since a lower df requires a higher t significance, using the t from the next lower df on the table ensures against exceeding the cutoff probability; even when the next higher df is nearer to the actual df, the next lower is still used because this is the more conservative procedure.) At the .05 level, a t of at least 1.684 is needed.

4. Determine the score of the sample on the comparison distribution. The t score—the mean difference (32.80 − 29.22) divided by the standard deviation of the distribution of differences between means (1.49)—comes out to 2.40.

5. Compare the scores obtained in Steps 3 and 4 to decide whether to reject the null hypothesis. Our t score of 2.40 for the difference between our two actual means is larger than the minimum needed t score of 1.684. The null hypothesis should be rejected. The research hypothesis is supported: Boys whose mothers' work involves solving problems see themselves as better at schoolwork than boys whose mothers' work does not involve solving problems. (Note that since random assignment to conditions was not used, nothing can be determined from the statistical results about whether the type of mother's work is actually causing greater perceived competence at schoolwork. The causality could be reversed, or some third variable might be causing the two to go together. For a discussion of this issue, see Chapter 3 and Appendix A.)

A Third Example of a t Test for Independent Means

Let's consider one more example. Suppose that a rehabilitation psychologist has developed a new job skills training program to help people who cannot hold a job. Fourteen such individuals who agree to be in the study are ran-

TABLE 10-3

Computations for a t Test for Independent Means for an Experiment Examining the Effectiveness (Using Employers' Ratings) of a New Job Skills Program for People Who Have Previously Not Been Able to Hold Jobs (Fictional Data)

	Experimental Group (Receiving Special Program)			Control Group (Receiving Standard Program)		
Score	Deviation from mean	Squared deviation from mean	Score	Deviation from mean	Squared deviation from mean	
6	0	0	6	3	9	
4	−2	4	1	−2	4	
9	3	9	5	2	4	
7	1	1	3	0	0	
7	1	1	1	−2	4	
3	−3	9	1	−2	4	
6	0	0	4	1	1	
Σ: 42	0	24	21	0	26	

$M_1 = 6; S_1^2 = 24/6 = 4; M_2 = 3; S_2^2 = 26/6 = 4.33$

$N_1 = 7; df_1 = N_1 - 1 = 6; N_2 = 7; df_2 = N_2 - 1 = 6$

$df_T = df_1 + df_2 = 6 + 6 = 12$

$S_P^2 = \dfrac{df_1}{df_T}(S_1^2) + \dfrac{df_2}{df_T}(S_2^2) = \dfrac{6}{12}(4) + \dfrac{6}{12}(4.33) = .5(4) + .5(4.33) = 2.00 + 2.17 = 4.17$

$S_{M1}^2 = S_P^2/N_1 = 4.17/7 = .60$

$S_{M2}^2 = S_P^2/N_2 = 4.17/7 = .60$

$S_{DIF}^2 = S_{M1}^2 + S_{M2}^2 = .60 + .60 = 1.20$

$S_{DIF} = \sqrt{S_{DIF}^2} = \sqrt{1.20} = 1.10$

Needed t with $df = 12$, 5% level, two-tailed $= \pm2.179$

$t = (M_1 - M_2)/S_{DIF} = (6.00 - 3.00)/1.10 = 3.00/1.10 = 2.73$

Conclusion: Reject the null hypothesis; the research hypothesis is supported.

domly assigned to either an experimental group, in which they receive the special program, or a control group, in which they are given an ordinary job skills program. At the end of the program, the psychologist arranges jobs for all the subjects. A month later, each employer is asked to rate how well the new employee is doing using a 9-point scale. The fictional results, along with the full t test analysis, are shown in Table 10-3 and illustrated in Figure 10-4. We also conduct the analysis, following the hypothesis-testing procedure step by step.

1. Reframe the question into a research hypothesis and a null hypothesis about the populations. The populations of interest are these:

Population 1: Individuals who could not hold a job who then participate in the special job skills program

Population 2: Individuals who could not hold a job who then participate in an ordinary job skills program

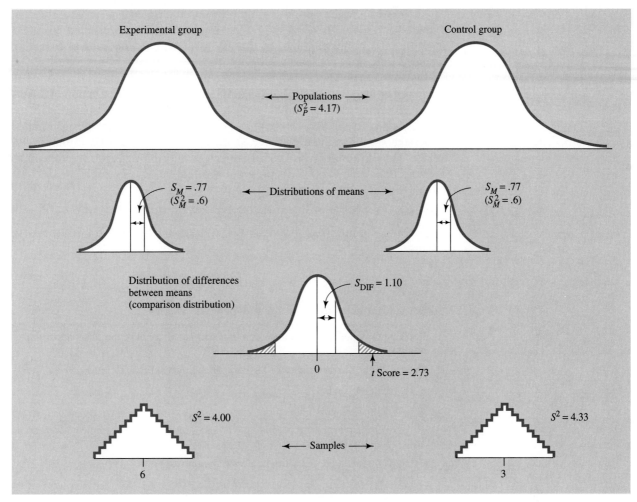

FIGURE 10-4
The distributions involved in the third example of a *t* test for independent means.

It is possible for the new program to have either a positive or a negative effect compared to the ordinary program, and either result would be of interest. Hence the research hypothesis, that the means of the two populations are different, is nondirectional. The null hypothesis is that the means of the two populations are the same.

2. Determine the characteristics of the comparison distribution. The distribution of differences between means will have a mean of 0. Its standard deviation is computed by finding the estimated population variance based on each sample, averaging these (since we have equal sample sizes, we can use either an ordinary or a weighted average) to get a pooled estimate, dividing the pooled estimate by the sample size to obtain the variance of each distribution of means, adding these together to get the variance of the distribution of differences between means, and then taking the square root of this variance. As shown in Table 10-3, this comes out to 1.10. The shape of the comparison distribution will be a *t* distribution with a total of 12 degrees of freedom.

3. Determine the cutoff sample score on the comparison distribution at which the null hypothesis should be rejected. For a two-tailed test (the hypothesis is nondirectional) at the .05 level with 12 degrees of freedom, we need a t score of at least ± 2.179.

4. Determine the score of the sample on the comparison distribution. The mean difference divided by the standard deviation of the distribution of differences between means, as shown in the table, comes out to a t score of 2.73.

5. Compare the scores obtained in Steps 3 and 4 to decide whether to reject the null hypothesis. Our t score of 2.73 exceeds the minimum of 2.179. Thus the null hypothesis is rejected, and the research hypothesis is supported: The new job skills program is effective.

Summary of Steps for Conducting a t Test for Independent Means

Table 10-4 summarizes the steps for conducting a t test for independent means.

TABLE 10-4
Steps for Conducting a t Test for Independent Means

1. Reframe the question into a research hypothesis and a null hypothesis about the populations.

2. Determine the characteristics of the comparison distribution.

   a. Its mean will be 0.

   b. Compute its standard deviation.

      i. Compute estimated population variances based on each sample (that is, compute two estimates).

      ii. Compute a pooled estimate of population variance:

$$S_P^2 = \frac{df_1}{df_T}(S_1^2) + \frac{df_2}{df_T}(S_2^2)$$

$$(df_1 = N_1 - 1 \text{ and } df_2 = N_2 - 1; df_T = df_1 + df_2)$$

      iii. Compute the variance of each distribution of means: $S_{M1}^2 = S_P^2/N_1$ and $S_{M2}^2 = S_P^2/N_2$.

      iv. Compute the variance of the distribution of differences between means: $S_{DIF}^2 = S_{M1}^2 + S_{M2}^2$.

      v. Compute the standard deviation of the distribution of differences between means: $S_{DIF} = \sqrt{S_{DIF}^2}$.

   c. Determine its shape: It will be a t distribution with df_T degrees of freedom.

3. Determine the cutoff sample score on the comparison distribution at which the null hypothesis should be rejected.

   a. Determine the degrees of freedom (df_T), desired significance level, and tails in the test (one or two).

   b. Look up the appropriate cutoff in a t table. If the exact df is not given, use the df below.

4. Determine the score of the sample on the comparison distribution: $t = (M_1 - M_2)/S_{DIF}$.

5. Compare the scores obtained in Steps 3 and 4 to decide whether to reject the null hypothesis.

Assumptions

The two major assumptions when conducting a t test for independent means are that the population distributions are normal and that they have the same variance. As was true of the t test for dependent means, the t test for independent means is generally robust over moderate violations of its assumptions. (How do we know this? See Box 10-1 on "Monte Carlo methods.")

Regarding the assumption of a normal population distribution, only if the two populations are thought to have dramatically skewed distributions, and in opposite directions, is there much of a problem. The t test is especially robust if a two-tailed test is used and if the sample sizes are not extremely small.

Likewise, regarding the assumption of equal population variances, even fairly substantial differences in the population variances estimated from the samples are usually acceptable, particularly if there are equal numbers in the two groups. However, if the two estimated population variances are quite different *and* if the samples have different numbers of cases, a modification of the usual t test procedure is sometimes used. This special procedure is called a "t test for independent means using separate variance estimates" and is described in most intermediate statistics texts.[1]

If *both* assumptions are violated—that is, if from the samples you can guess that the populations are clearly not normal *and* they clearly have different variances—the results of the t test for independent means is suspect. In this case—or in the case where the normality assumption alone is severely violated—you should use one of the alternative procedures described in Chapter 15. These various situations are summarized in Table 10-5.

[1] If you are interested, the special t test using separate variance estimates differs from the ordinary t test for independent means in two ways. First, the variance of each distribution of means is found in the usual way, by dividing the population variance estimate from that sample by its sample size. A pooled population variance estimate is not even computed. Second, the t score that results from this procedure does not quite follow the t distribution, so using the normal t table, without making special adjustments, gives too low a cutoff t score. These adjustments, which are done automatically by computer programs, are described in more advanced texts.

TABLE 10-5
Situations in Which the Ordinary t Test for Independent Means or Alternatives Should Be Used

	Populations Follow a Normal Curve	Populations Do Not Follow a Normal Curve
Population variances are equal ($\sigma_1^2 = \sigma_2^2$)	t test	t test if nonnormality is not extreme. If extreme, use Chapter 15 procedures.
Population variances are unequal ($\sigma_1^2 \neq \sigma_2^2$):		
Sample sizes are equal ($N_1 = N_2$)	t test if unequal σ^2 not extreme	Chapter 15 procedures
Sample sizes are unequal ($N_1 \neq N_2$)	Special separate variance estimates t test	Chapter 15 procedures

BOX 10-1

Monte Carlo Methods, or When Mathematics Becomes Just an Experiment And Statistics Depend on a Game of Chance

The name for the methods, *Monte Carlo* (after the famous Monegasque casino resort city), has been adopted only in recent years, but the approach itself dates back at least a few centuries, to when mathematicians would set down their pens or chalk and go out and try an actual experiment to test a particular understanding of a probability problem. For example, in 1777, Buffon, described, in his *Essai d'Arithmétique morale*, a method of computing the ratio of the diameter of a circle to its circumference by tossing a needle onto a flat surface containing parallel lines so that the needle fell randomly into any position and then computing the odds of its taking certain positions, such as touching the lines or not and lying at certain angles. The term *Monte Carlo* no doubt reflects the early understanding of mathematicians and statisticians that many of their problems were like ones involving games of chance. (Recall Pascal and the problem of points from Box 5-2.)

Wide use of Monte Carlo methods by statisticians became possible with the advent of computers. This is because the essence of Monte Carlo studies is the interaction of randomness and probabilities, which means testing out a great many possibilities. Indeed, the first application of Monte Carlo methods was in neutron physics, since the behavior of particles when scattered by a neutron beam is so complicated and so close to random that solving the problem mathematically from equations was practically impossible. But by artificially simulating the statistical conditions of what were essentially physical experiments, the physical world could be understood—or at least approximated in a good enough way.

Do you remember being shown Brownian motion in your chemistry or physics class in high school? Its study is a good example of a Monte Carlo problem. Here are atomic particles, more or less, this time in fluids, free to do an almost limitless number of almost random things. In fact, Brownian motion has been likened to a "random walk" of a drunkard. At any moment, the drunkard could move in any direction. But the problem is simplified by limiting the drunkard (or particle) to an imaginary grid.

Picture the grid of a city's streets. Further imagine that there is a wall around the city that the drunkard cannot escape (just as all particles must come to a limit—they cannot go on forever). At the limit, the wall, the drunkard must pay a fine, which also varies randomly. The point of this example is how very much is random—all the movements and also all the ultimate consequences. So the number of possible paths is enormous.

The random walk example brings us to the main feature of Monte Carlo methods: They require the use of random numbers. And for an explanation of them, you can look forward to Box 15-1.

Now let's return to what interests us here—

The hardest part about applying these rules is determining whether or not the assumptions hold. Remember that the issues of normality and equality of variances are about the populations and not about the samples. Now and then a normal population could easily produce a particular sample that was not normal. Likewise, two populations with equal variance could now and then produce two samples that yielded somewhat different estimates of the population variance. That is why we average the estimates. Hence we should be concerned that the assumptions might not apply only if the samples depart substantially from being normally distributed and having equal variances.

There are, in fact, hypothesis-testing procedures for checking whether assumptions are met. But they are not very widely employed. Some computerized statistical packages do report tests of whether the difference in the use of Monte Carlo studies to check out what will be the result of the violations of certain assumptions of statistical tests. For example, the computer may set up two populations with identical means, but the other parameters are supplied by the statistical researcher so that these violate some important assumption—perhaps the populations are skewed a certain way, or the two populations have different variances.

Then samples are randomly selected from each of these two offbeat populations (remember, they were invented by the computer). The means of these samples are compared using the usual t-test procedure with the usual t tables with all their assumptions. A large number, often around 1,000, of such pairs of samples are selected, and a t test is computed for each. The question is, how many of these 1,000 t tests will come out significant at the 5% significance level? Ideally, the result would be about 5%, or 50 of the 1,000. But what if 10% (100) of these supposedly 5%-level tests come out significant? What if only 1% do? If these kinds of results arise, then this particular violation of the assumptions of the t test cannot be tolerated. But in fact, most violations (except for very extreme ones) checked with these methods do not create very large changes in the p values.

Monte Carlo methods are a boon to statistics, but like everything else, they have their drawbacks as well and consequently their critics. One problem is that the ways in which populations can violate assumptions are almost limitless in their variations.

But even computers have their limits—Monte Carlo studies are tried on only a representative set of those variations. A more specific problem is that there is good reason to think that some of the variations that are not studied are far more like the real world than those that have been studied (see the discussion in Chapter 5 of the controversy about how common the normal curve really is). Finally, when we are deciding whether to use a particular statistic in any specific situation, we have no idea about the population our sample came from—is it like any on which there has been a Monte Carlo study performed or not? Simply knowing that Monte Carlo studies have proved some statistic to be robust in many situations does not prove that it is so in a given situation. We can only hope that it increases the chances that using the statistic is safe and justifiable.

At any rate, Monte Carlo studies are a perfect example of how the computer has changed science. As Shreider (1966) expressed it:

> Computers have led to a novel revolution in mathematics. Whereas previously an investigation of a random process was regarded as complete as soon as it was reduced to an analytic description, nowadays it is convenient in many cases to solve an analytic problem by reducing it to a corresponding random process and then simulating that process. (p. vii)

In other words, instead of math helping us analyze experiments, experiments are helping us analyze math.

variances between two samples suggests that the populations have different variances, and these tests are described in more advanced textbooks.

Effect Size and Power for the t Test for Independent Means

Effect Size

Effect size for the t test for independent means is computed using

$$d = \frac{\mu_1 - \mu_2}{\sigma} \tag{10-9}$$

Remember that because effect size is computed without taking the number of subjects in the samples into account, you divide by the standard deviation of the population of individual scores (σ), *not* by the standard deviation of the distribution of differences between means (σ_{DIF}). Cohen's (1988) conventions for the t test for independent means is $d = .20$ for a small effect size, $.50$ for a medium effect size, and $.80$ for a large effect size. (These are the same conventions for d as we have been using for the hypothesis-testing situations we considered in Chapters 8 and 9.)

Consider an example of computing this kind of effect size. Suppose that an environmental psychologist is working in a city with high levels of air pollution. This psychologist plans a study of number of problems completed (in a series of creativity tasks) over a 1-h period. The study compares performance by an experimental group of subjects who each take the test in a room with a special air purifier versus a control group of subjects who each take the test alone in the same room without the air purifier. The researcher expects that the control group will probably perform like others who have carried out this series of tasks in this city, which is a mean of 21. But the researcher expects that the experimental group, the subjects taking the test with the air purified, to perform better, completing about 29. This test is known in previous research to have a standard deviation of about 10. Thus $\mu_1 = 29$, $\mu_2 = 21$, and $\sigma = 10$. Given these figures, $d = (\mu_1 - \mu_2)/\sigma = (29 - 21)/10 = .80$, a large effect size.

When calculating the effect size of a completed study, we estimate effect size as

$$d = \frac{M_1 - M_2}{S_P} \tag{10-10}$$

For our first example of a t test for independent means (the Seligman et al., 1990, study comparing the optimism of women and men college swimmers), the mean of the sample of women was 15.96 and the mean of the sample of men was 18.03. We calculated the pooled estimate of the population variance to be 2.81; the standard deviation is thus 1.68. So $d = (M_1 - M_2)/S_P = (15.96 - 18.03)/1.68 = -1.23$, a very large effect size. (The sign of the effect size, negative in this case, only reflects the direction of the effect, not its magnitude.)

Power

Table 10-6 gives the approximate power for the .05 significance level for small, medium, and large effect sizes and one- or two-tailed tests. In the environmental psychology example, where the researchers expected a large effect size ($d = .80$), if they plan to conduct the study using the .05 level, one-tailed, with 10 subjects, they would have a power of .53. This means that even if the research hypothesis is in fact true and has a large effect size, there is only a 53% chance that the study will come out significant.

As we have noted in previous chapters, determining power is especially useful when interpreting the practical implication of a nonsignificant result. For example, suppose that you have read a study using a t test for independent means that failed to find significance at the .05 level, two-tailed, using 50 subjects in each group. Should you conclude that there is in fact no dif-

TABLE 10-6
Approximate Power for Studies Using the *t* Test for Independent Means
Testing Hypotheses at the .05 Significance Level

Number of Subjects (*N*)	Effect Size		
	Small (*d* = .20)	*Medium* (*d* = .50)	*Large* (*d* = .80)
One-tailed test			
10	.11	.29	.53
20	.15	.46	.80
30	.19	.61	.92
40	.22	.72	.97
50	.26	.80	.99
100	.41	.97	*
Two-tailed test			
10	.07	.18	.39
20	.09	.33	.69
30	.12	.47	.86
40	.14	.60	.94
50	.17	.70	.98
100	.29	.94	*

*Nearly 1.
Note. Based on Cohen (1988), pp. 28–39.

ference at all in the populations? This conclusion seems quite unjustified—Table 10-6 shows a power of only .17 for a small effect size, suggesting that if such a small effect does indeed exist in the populations, this study would not show it. Conversely, we can conclude that if there is a true difference in the populations, it is probably not large—Table 10-6 shows a power of .98 for a large effect size, suggesting that if such an effect exists, it almost surely would have shown up in this study.

Power When Sample Sizes Are Not Equal

For any given number of subjects, power is greatest when subjects are divided into two equal groups. For example, an experiment with 10 subjects in the control group and 30 in the experimental group is much less powerful than one with 20 in both groups. There is also a practical problem determining power from tables when sample sizes are not equal. Table 10-6 (like most power tables) is based on assuming equal numbers of subjects in each of the two groups.

When sample sizes are unequal, the **harmonic mean** of the two unequal **harmonic mean** sample sizes is equivalent (in terms of power) to the sample size when both are equal. The harmonic mean sample size (N') is given by this formula:

$$N' = \frac{(2)(N_1)(N_2)}{N_1 + N_2} \qquad (10\text{-}11)$$

Consider an extreme example in which there are 6 subjects in one group and 34 in the other. The harmonic mean comes out to about 10:

$$N' = \frac{(2)(N_1)(N_2)}{N_1 + N_2} = \frac{(2)(6)(34)}{6 + 34} = \frac{408}{40} = 10.2$$

TABLE 10-7
Approximate Number of Subjects Needed in Each Group (Assuming Equal Sample Sizes) to Achieve 80% Power for the *t* Test for Independent Means, Testing Hypotheses at the .05 Significance Level

| | Effect Size | | |
	Small (d = .20)	Medium (d = .50)	Large (d = .80)
One-tailed	310	50	20
Two-tailed	393	64	26

So even though you have a total of 40 subjects, the study has the power of a study with equal sample sizes of only about 10 each (which means that a study with a total of 20 subjects evenly divided would have served equally well). If the researcher is using the .05 level, two-tailed, and expects a large effect size, Table 10-6 indicates that this study would have a power of less than .39 (the figure for using 10 subjects). Had the researcher been able to set up the study by dividing the 40 subjects into 20 per group, the power would have been a much better .69.

Planning Sample Size

Table 10-7 gives the approximate number of subjects needed to achieve 80% power for estimated small, medium, and large effect sizes using one- and two-tailed tests, all using the .05 significance level.[2] For example, if you are planning a study in which you expect a medium effect size and will use the .05 significance level, one-tailed, you need 50 subjects in each group (100 total) to be assured of 80% power. By contrast, a study using the same significance level but in which you expect a large effect size would require only 20 subjects per group (40 total) for 80% power.

Controversies and Limitations

The *t* test for independent means has been subjected to all of the various critiques we have considered with regard to hypothesis testing more generally, including questions about the likelihood of really meeting the normal curve assumption, the alternative of Bayesian methods, and the suggestion that effect size is more important. Another controversy that applies to all hypothesis-testing procedures arises when conducting a large number of hypothesis tests in the same study. We introduce the controversy in this particular chapter because the issue was originally emphasized as the problem of "too many *t* tests."

If you conduct a large number of *t* tests, the chance of any one of them coming out significant at, say, the 5% level is really greater than 5%. In fact, if you make 100 independent comparisons, on the average 5 of them will come out significant at the 5% level even if there is no true difference at all between the populations that the two conditions of your experiment

---

[2]Cohen (1988, pp. 54–55) provides fuller tables, indicating needed numbers of subjects for levels of power other than 80%; for effect sizes other than .20, .50, and .80; and for other significance levels.

represent. Something like this kind of situation arises fairly often—for example, when two groups are compared on a large number of different measures, such as different measures of memory or different observed behaviors in mother-child interaction.

The fundamental issue is not controversial: Everyone agrees that in a study involving a large number of comparisons, if only a few results come out significant, these differences should be viewed very cautiously. The controversy is about how cautiously and about how few is "only a few." One reason there is room for controversy is that in most cases, the many comparisons being made are not independent—the chance of one coming out significant is related to the chance of another coming out significant.

Consider an example. A study compares a sample of lawyers to a sample of doctors on 100 personality traits. If the researcher simply conducts 100 t tests and if these 100 t tests were truly independent, we would expect that on the average, 5 would come out significant just by chance. In fact, tables exist for calculating quite precisely the chance of any particular number of t tests coming out significant. The problem, however, is that in practice these 100 t tests are *not* independent. Many of the various personality traits are probably correlated, such as scales measuring assertiveness and self-confidence—if doctors and lawyers differ on assertiveness, they probably also differ on self-confidence. Thus certain sets of comparisons may be more or less likely all to come out significant by chance, so that in some cases even more than 5 in 100 could be a chance result.

Another complication is that in most cases, differences on some of the variables are more important than on others in terms of the theory being tested or the practical application toward which the study is directed. Taking this complication together with the problem of nonindependence has created a variety of contending solutions. We will introduce some of the solutions in Chapter 12 when we consider the related problem of multiple comparisons—a situation arising when there are more than two groups being compared in the same study.

The t Test for Independent Means as Described in Research Articles

In most cases, the result of a t test for independent means is reported in research articles by giving the means (and sometimes also the standard deviations) of the two samples, plus the same sort of expression as you saw in Chapter 9, in which the letter t is followed by the degrees of freedom in parentheses, then the actual t value, followed by the significance level—for example, "$t(38) = 4.72, p < .01$."

Thus the result of the Moorehouse and Sanders (1992) study that we examined earlier might be reported as follows: "The mean perceived academic competence for the boys whose mothers' work involved problem solving was 32.8 ($SD = 4.27$), and the mean for the boys whose mothers' work did not involve problem solving was 29.2 ($SD = 5.23$); $t(41) = 2.42, p < .05$, one-tailed." Variations on this form are common. For example, in the swimmers' optimism example, Seligman et al. (1990) described their result as follows: "The men's composite score . . . was much more optimistic than the women's (men $\overline{X} = 18.03, SD = 3.15$; women $\overline{X} = 15.96, SD = 1.4$; $t =$

4.3, $p < .0001$)" (p. 144). Notice that these researchers used the $\overline{X}$ symbol for the mean and that they did not give the degrees of freedom (which the reader could figure out from the sample sizes, which were given elsewhere in the article).

Also as you saw in Chapter 9, the details of the hypothesis-testing process are usually not stated, and sometimes the entire hypothesis-testing result is indicated merely by whether a number in a table is or is not starred. Table 10-8 shows a very complete table of t tests taken from a study conducted by Heatherton, Polivy, and Herman (1991). In this study, 24 college women volunteers were weighed several times over a 6-month period. The t tests compared weight *changes* (from before to after a period of time) and weight *fluctuations* (ups and downs within a period of time) between those who were often on a diet (the "Restrained" group in the table) versus those who rarely dieted ("Unrestrained").

Note that many of these results were not significant. What should be concluded about these? In this study, the number of subjects is indicated to have been 9 in one group and 15 in the other. The formula for the harmonic mean indicates that for purposes of computing power, there are about 11 subjects per group. That is,

$$N' = \frac{(2)(N_1)(N_2)}{N_1 + N_2} = \frac{(2)(9)(15)}{9 + 15} = \frac{270}{24} = 11.25$$

Using the nearest number of subjects in Table 10-6 (10 subjects) and a two-tailed test at the .05 level, the power of this study to find significance even for a large effect size is only .39; if in fact there is only a medium effect size, the power is about .18. So in spite of the failure to find significant differences, there may well be true, large differences in the population.

TABLE 10-8
Weight Change and Weight Variability in Pounds as Function of Restraint Status

Measure	Restrained		Unrestrained		t	df	p
	M	SD	M	SD			
Weight change							
Month	−2.17	5.47	0.29	1.52	1.66	22	.11
Six weeks	−2.19	7.18	−0.55	2.16	0.84	22	.41
Six months[a]	0.50	4.23	1.12	2.95	0.38	18	.71
Weight fluctuation							
Daily average	1.13	0.24	0.94	0.32	1.56	22	.13
Largest within week	2.22	0.34	1.77	0.34	3.12	22	.005
Weekly average	1.81	0.93	1.13	0.45	2.41	22	.025
Monthly average[b]	2.99	4.40	1.33	0.68	1.45	22	.16
Weight suppression index	4.61	6.18	0.94	2.80	2.00	22	.06
Weight over personal ideal	17.42	12.40	6.67	6.49	2.81	22	.01

Note. Cell sample sizes were 9 restrained and 15 unrestrained subjects.
[a]Cell sample sizes were 7 restrained and 13 unrestrained subjects for this comparison only.
[b]Monthly fluctuation obtained by the average of the absolute difference between the Tuesdays of Weeks 1 and 4, Weeks 2 and 5, and Weeks 3 and 6.

From Heatherton, T. F., Polivy, J., & Herman, C. P. (1991), tab. 1. Restraint, weight loss, and variability of body weight. *Journal of Abnormal Psychology, 100,* 78–83. Copyright, 1991, by the American Psychological Association. Reprinted by permission of the author.

Summary

A t test for independent means is used for hypothesis testing involving two samples of scores. The main difference from a t test for a single sample is that the comparison distribution is a distribution of differences between means of samples. This distribution can be thought of as arising in two steps: Each population of individual cases produces a distribution of means, and then a new distribution is created consisting of differences between pairs of means selected from these two distributions of means.

The distribution of differences between means has a mean of 0 and will be a t distribution with degrees of freedom equal to the total degrees of freedom contributed by the two samples. Its standard deviation is determined in several steps: (a) Each sample is used to estimate the population variance; (b) since the populations are assumed to have the same variance, a pooled estimate is computed by simple averaging of the two estimates if the numbers in each sample are equal or by a weighted average if they are not (multiplying each estimate by the proportion of the total degrees of freedom its sample contributes and adding up the products); (c) the pooled estimate is divided by each sample's number of cases to determine the variances of their associated distribution of means; (d) these two variances are added to produce the variance of the distribution of differences between means; and (e) the square root is taken.

The assumptions of the t test for independent means are that the two populations should have the same variance and be normally distributed, although the procedure seems to be robust to moderate violations of these assumptions.

Effect size for a t test for independent means is the difference between the means divided by the standard deviation. For a given number of subjects, power is greatest when sample sizes of the two groups are equal.

When many significance tests are conducted in the same study, such as a series of t tests comparing two groups on various measures, the possibility that any one of the comparisons may turn out significant by chance is greater than .05 (or whatever level is being used to test each comparison). There is considerable controversy about just how to adjust for this problem, though all observers agree that results should be interpreted cautiously in a situation of this kind.

When t tests for independent means are reported in research articles, commonly indicated are the t score, the degrees of freedom, and the significance level attained. Results may also be reported in a table where each significant difference is indicated merely by an asterisk.

Key Terms

Practice Problems

These problems involve computation (with the assistance of a calculator). Most real-life statistics problems are done on a computer. But even if you have a computer, do these by hand to ingrain the method in your mind.

For practice in using a computer to solve statistical problems, refer to the computer section of each chapter of the study guide that accompanies this text.

All data are fictional (unless an actual citation is given).

Answers to Set I are given at the back of the book.

SET I

1. Explain when you would use a t test for dependent means and when you would use a t test for independent means.

2. For each of the following experiments, determine if the difference between conditions is statistically significant at the .05 level (two-tailed). Also determine the effect size and approximate power (from Table 10-6).

	Experimental Group			**Control Group**		
	N	*M*	S^2	*N*	*M*	S^2
(a)	30	12.0	2.4	30	11.1	2.8
(b)	20	12.0	2.4	40	11.1	2.8
(c)	30	12.0	2.2	30	11.1	3.0

3. A social psychologist interested in mass communications randomly assigned (from a group of 82 volunteers) 61 people to get their news for a month only from television and 21 people to get their news for a month only from the radio. (Why the researcher didn't assign equal numbers to the two conditions is a mystery!) In any case, after the month was up, all subjects were tested on their knowledge of several political issues. The researcher did not have a prediction as to which news source would make people more knowledgeable but simply predicted that there is some kind of difference. These were the results of the study. TV group: $M = 24$, $S^2 = 4$; radio group: $M = 26$, $S^2 = 6$. Using the .01 level, what should the researcher conclude? Explain your answer to someone who has never had a course in statistics.

4. A teacher was interested in how much difference using the student's own name in a story made in terms of children's attention span while reading. Six children were randomly assigned to read a story under normal conditions (using names like Dick and Jane). The children were surreptitiously observed while reading. Five other children read versions of the same story, but with each child's own name substituted for one of the children in the story. Using the .05 level, does including the child's name make any difference? Explain your answer to a person who understands the t test for dependent means but does not know anything about the t test for independent means.

Normal Story		**Own-Name Story**	
Student	*Reading Time*	*Student*	*Reading Time*
A	2	G	4
B	5	H	16
C	7	I	11
D	9	J	9
E	6	K	8
F	7		

5. Frodi, Grolnick, Bridges, and Berko (1990) studied the play behavior of 63 infants that were 13 months old, 33 of them born to adult mothers and 30 to teenage mothers. (The adult mothers, in addition to being older, were also more likely to be middle-class.) Using a standard laboratory procedure, the infants were videotaped playing with a set of toys that involved problem solving under structured and unstructured-play conditions. The tapes were later rated for the degree to which the infant showed persistence, competence at solving the problems the toys presented, and positive mood. The results presented here apply to the structured-play situation. Explain what these results mean to a person who has never had a course in statistics. (You need not try actually to compute the effect size; just discuss the issues of power and such in general, considering the sample sizes.)

	Infants of Teenage Mothers	Infants of Adult Mothers	t	p
Persistence	231	171	2.78	.007
Affect	3.0	3.3	3.21	.002
Competence	58	53	.81	n.s.

6. Calculate an estimated effect size for the results in Problems 2 through 4.

SET II

1. (a) What is the "pooled estimate of the population variance"? (b) How do you determine the variance of the distribution of differences between means?

2. For each of the following experiments, (a) determine if the difference between conditions is statistically significant at the .05 level (one-tailed—in each case the prediction is for lower scores for the experimental group); (b) compute the effect size; and (c) determine approximate power.

	Experimental Group			Control Group		
	N	M	S^2	N	M	S^2
(i)	10	604	60	10	607	50
(ii)	40	604	60	40	607	50
(iii)	10	604	20	10	607	16

3. A psychologist theorized that people can hear better when they have just eaten a large meal. Six individuals were randomly assigned to eat either a large meal or a small meal and then have their hearing tested. The hearing ability scores (high numbers indicate greater ability) are given here. Using the .05 level, do the results support the psychologist's theory? Explain your answer to a person who has never had a course in statistics.

Big Meal		Small Meal	
Subject	Hearing	Subject	Hearing
A	22	D	19
B	25	E	23
C	25	F	21

4. Twenty students randomly assigned to an experimental group receive an instructional program; 30 in a control group do not. After 6 months, both groups are tested on their knowledge. The experimental group has a mean of 38 on the test (with an estimated population standard deviation of 3), and the control group has a mean of 35 (with an estimated population standard deviation of 5). Using the .05 level, what should the experimenter conclude? Explain your answer to a person who understands the t test for dependent means but does not know anything about the t test for independent means.

5. A pilot study of the effects of color on easing anxiety compared anxiety test scores of subjects who completed the test printed on either soft yellow paper or on harsh green paper. The scores for five subjects who completed the test printed on the yellow paper were 17, 19, 28, 21, and 18. The scores for four subjects who completed the test on the green paper were 20, 26, 17, and 24. Using the .05 level, one-tailed (predicting lower anxiety scores for the yellow paper), what should the researcher conclude?

6. Do men or women have longer first names? Take out a phone book and use the random numbers given here to select a page (if your phone book has closer to 100 pages, use just the first two digits). On the first page, look for the first clearly female name, and write down how many letters it has. Do the same thing (find the page for the number, etc.) 16 times. Then continue, getting lengths for 16 male names. (You will have to exclude names for which you cannot tell the gender.) Compute a t test for independent means using these two samples.

121, 798, 107, 971, 534, 740, 156, 55, 741, 128, 571, 939, 946, 731, 682, 516, 609, 569, 72, 932, 435, 912, 573, 581, 381, 120, 514, 338, 571, 743, 982, 471, 385, 663, 201, 323, 609, 430, 788, 296, 398, 174, 314, 120, 612, 100, 801, 352, 312, 993, 226

Chapter Appendix: Optional Computational Formulas for the t Test for Independent Means

The procedure described in this chapter, based on definitional formulas, involves computing (a) the mean (M) of each sample, (b) an estimated population variance (S^2) based on the data in each sample, (c) the pooled population variance estimate (S_P^2), (d) the variance of the distribution of means (S_M^2) corresponding to each population, (e) the variance and standard deviation of the distribution of differences between means (S_{DIF}^2 and S_{DIF}), and (f) the t score.

The first two steps (computing M and S^2 for each sample) can be computed using calculational formulas we have considered in Chapters 2 and 9, often available directly on calculators. A special computational formula is available, however, that combines Steps (c) through (e) to provide the standard deviation of the distribution of differences between means (S_{DIF}):

$$S_{DIF} = \sqrt{\frac{(N_1 - 1)(S_1^2) + (N_2 - 1)(S_2^2)}{N_1 + N_2 - 2}\left(\frac{1}{N_1} + \frac{1}{N_2}\right)} \qquad (10\text{-}12)$$

t is then calculated in the usual way as $(M_1 - M_2)/S_{DIF}$.

Table 10-9 shows the computation of S_{DIF} (and t) using Eq. (10-12) for the study of the optimism of women versus men varsity swimmers. Compare these computations to those in Table 10-1.

TABLE 10-9
Computations for a t Test for Independent Means for a Study of Optimism Comparing Women and Men Varsity Swimmers, Using the Calculational Formula for S_{DIF}

Women: $N_1 = 26$; $df_1 = N_1 - 1 = 25$; $M_1 = 15.96$; $S_1^2 = 2.07$.
Men: $\quad N_2 = 21$; $df_2 = N_2 - 1 = 20$; $M_2 = 18.03$; $S_2^2 = 3.75$.

$$S_{DIF} = \sqrt{\frac{(N_1 - 1)(S_1^2) + (N_2 - 1)(S_2^2)}{N_1 + N_2 - 2} \left(\frac{1}{N_1} + \frac{1}{N_2}\right)}$$

$$= \sqrt{\frac{(26 - 1)(2.07) + (21 - 1)(3.75)}{26 + 21 - 2} \left(\frac{1}{26} + \frac{1}{21}\right)}$$

$$= \sqrt{\frac{(25)(2.07) + (20)(3.75)}{45} (.038 + .048)}$$

$$= \sqrt{\frac{51.75 + 75}{45} (.086)}$$

$$= \sqrt{\frac{126.75}{45} (.086)} \quad = \sqrt{(2.82)(.086)} = \sqrt{.24} = .49$$

$df_T = df_1 + df_2 = 25 + 20 = 45$.

Needed t with $df = 45$, 1% level, two-tailed $= \pm 2.690$.

$t = (M_1 - M_2)/S_{DIF} = (15.96 - 18.03)/.49 = -2.07/.49 = -4.22$.

Conclusion: Reject the null hypothesis; the results suggest that women swimmers are less optimistic than men swimmers.

Note. Data from Seligman, Nolen-Hoeksema, Thornton, & Thornton (1990).

11

Introduction to the Analysis of Variance

CINDY Hazan and Philip Shaver (1987) arranged to have the *Rocky Mountain News*, a large Denver area newspaper, print a mail-in survey. In this survey, readers answered questions that permitted the researchers to compare, among other things, the amount of jealousy experienced by individuals with three different attachment styles: secure, anxious, and avoidant. (These attachment styles are thought to represent different ways of behaving and thinking, in close relationships, that develop from one's experience with early caretakers.)

With a *t* test, Hazan and Shaver could have compared the mean jealousy scores of any two of the attachment styles. But they were interested in differences among all three attachment styles. The statistical procedure for testing variation among the means of three or more groups is called the **analysis of variance,** sometimes abbreviated as **ANOVA.** (You could use the analysis of variance for a study with two groups, but the *t* test, which gives the same result in that case, is simpler.)

analysis of variance
ANOVA

In this chapter, we introduce the analysis of variance, focusing on the situation in which the different groups being compared each have the same number of scores. The more complicated situation, in which analysis of variance is applied when group sizes are not equal, is considered in Chapter 12. In Chapter 13, we complete our survey of analysis of variance by considering situations in which the different groups are arrayed across more than one dimension—for example, in the same analysis we might consider both gender and attachment style, making six groups in all (female secure, male secure, female anxious, etc.), but arrayed across the two dimensions of gender and attachment style. This latter situation is known as a "factorial analysis of variance." To emphasize the contrast with factorial analysis of variance, what you learn in this chapter and the next is often referred to as "one-way analysis of variance." (If this notion of dimension is confusing, don't worry. We will go through it slowly and systematically in Chapter 13. We only mention this now so that if you hear these terms, you will not be surprised.)

Basic Logic of the Analysis of Variance

The analysis of variance follows the same five steps of hypothesis testing we have been using all along. However, there are important differences from what you have learned so far in how each step is carried out.

The Null Hypothesis in the Analysis of Variance

Central to these differences from what you have learned already is that the null hypothesis in an analysis of variance is that the three or more populations being compared all have the same mean. (And it must be reasonable to assume, as for the *t* test, that whether or not the null hypothesis is true, the populations being compared all have the same variance.) For example, in the Hazan and Shaver study, the null hypothesis would be that the populations of securely attached, anxiously attached, and avoidant people all have the same degree of jealousy—that the mean jealousy is the same in these three populations. The research hypothesis would be that the degree of jealousy differs among these three populations—that their means are not all the same.

This basic question of hypothesis testing in analysis of variance is whether the means of the samples differ more than you would expect if the null hypothesis were true. This basic question about means is answered, surprisingly, by analyzing the different variances involved in the situation (hence the name *analysis of variance*). Thus much of our discussion focuses on variances—in particular, on two different ways of estimating population variances.

Estimating Population Variance From Variation Within Each Sample

In the analysis of variance, as in the *t* test, we do not know the population variances. But the variance of each of the populations that the samples represent can be estimated in the usual way from these same samples. And because we assume in the analysis of variance that all populations being compared have the same variance, these estimates can be pooled (we will deal with the arithmetic details later). The resulting pooled estimate is called the **within-group estimate of the population variance** because the estimates are based entirely on the variance *within* each of the samples.

The most important thing about this within-group estimate is that it is unaffected by whether or not the null hypothesis is true. In either case, it has to be reasonable to assume that the populations have the same variance, or we cannot conduct an analysis of variance at all (at least not using standard procedures).

within-group estimate of the population variance

Variance Between Means of Samples When the Null Hypothesis Is True

If you think of each sample mean as a number in its own right, you can think of the amount of variation among these numbers. What determines the amount of variation among these numbers? The logic is a bit tricky, so follow the next paragraph closely.

First, consider the variance among means that we expect when the null hypothesis is true. In this case, the samples represent identical populations, each such population having the same mean and also the same variance. The effect of this is that the variance of the means of these samples can only be due to the variance within each population. To understand this, note that since all samples are taken from identical populations, it is the same as taking all samples from a single population. So any differences among the means of these samples can arise only from variation among the scores that are being sampled. And any variation among the scores that are being sampled is entirely *within* the population—or, more precisely, within each of the several identical populations. And the higher the variance of each population the more variance there will be among the means of samples drawn from them. For example, if you were taking samples of six children from each of three large classrooms, each containing children of ages 5 through 10, the means of those three samples would be more various (have a higher variance) than if you had taken three samples from classrooms of children all aged 9 or 10.

Look at our example of the populations of secure, anxious, and avoidant attachment types studied by Hazan and Shaver. There will, of course, be some variance in the degree of jealousy of different people within each of these populations. Even if we suppose that these three populations all have the same mean degree of jealousy (as they would if the null hypothesis is true), a sample drawn from one population will probably not have exactly the same mean as a sample drawn from the second, and a sample drawn from the third will likely be a little different from the other two. And the more each of these populations varies within itself, the more the means of samples drawn from these populations will be expected to vary. Two examples are illustrated in Figure 11-1, one with a small variance (a) and one with a large one (b). But in both examples, the means of the three populations are the same, even as the means of the samples vary more or less, according to the variances within each of the three populations.

We have now seen that the variation of the means of samples taken from populations with the same mean reflects the variation of the scores within each population. This has a very important implication: If the variance among means of samples reflects the variance within each population, it should be possible to estimate the variance within each population in a second way. The first was pooling, or averaging, the three variances. But we could also estimate it by looking at the variance among the means of our samples. Such an estimate (which involves an intermediary step we consider later) is called a **between-group estimate of the population variance** (it is based on the variation between the means of the samples, the "groups"). (Grammatically, it ought to be *among* groups.) Notice that the between-group estimate has nothing to do with variation among *populations* if the null hypothesis is true—in that case, there is no variation among populations.

between-group estimate of the population variance

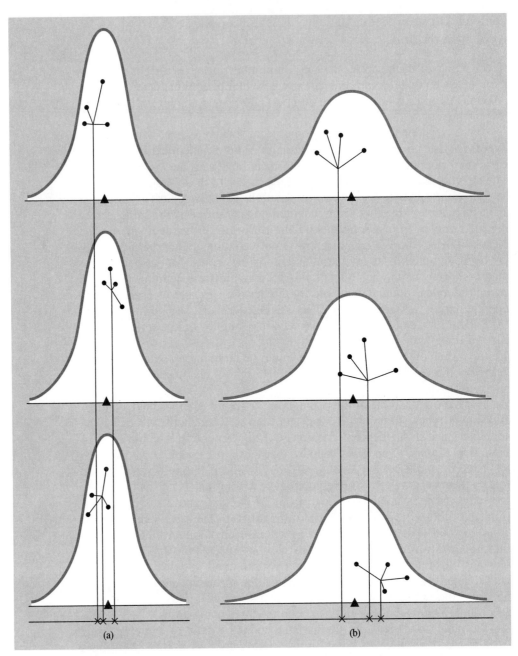

FIGURE 11-1
Illustration that means of samples from identical populations will not be identical.
Sample means from populations with less variation will vary less (a). Sample
means from populations with more variation will vary more (b). Population means
are indicated by a triangle, sample means by an X.

Variance Between Means of Samples When the Research Hypothesis Is True

Here's the important part: If the research hypothesis is true, the populations
themselves have different means. In this case, the variation among means of
samples taken from these populations still reflects the variation within the

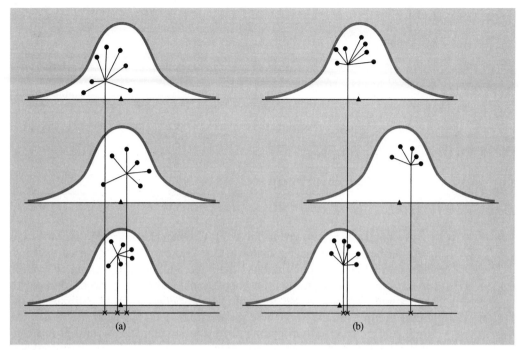

FIGURE 11-2
Illustration that means of samples from populations whose means differ will vary
more than sample means taken from populations whose means are the same.
Population means are indicated by a triangle, sample means by an X.

populations, but it also reflects the variation between the population means. That is, the means of the groups are spread out, but not because of variance alone within the populations. If the research hypothesis is true, these three populations have different means. Figure 11-2a shows three populations with the same means and the means of samples taken from them (this is the same situation as in Figure 11-1). Figure 11-2b shows three populations with different means (the situation we have just been discussing) and the means of samples taken from them.

Comparing the Within-Group and Between-Group Estimates of Population Variance

Table 11-1 summarizes what we have seen so far about the within-group and between-group estimates of population variance when the null hypothesis is true versus when the research hypothesis is true. When the null hypothesis is true, the two estimates are based on the same thing—literally, they are estimates of the same population variance—and should be about the same. (But only *about* the same—the two are estimates and are not perfectly accurate.) Another way of describing this relationship of the between-group estimate to the within-group estimate is that when the null hypothesis is true, it should be approximately 1:1. For example, if the within-group estimate is 107.5, the between-group estimate should be around 107.5, so that the ratio would be about 1. (A ratio is found by dividing one number by the other.)

TABLE 11-1
Sources of Variation Reflected in Within- and Between-Group Variance Estimates

	Variation Within Populations	Variation Between Populations
Null hypothesis is true		
Within-group estimate reflects	X	
Between-group estimate reflects	X	
Research hypothesis is true		
Within-group estimate reflects	X	
Between-group estimate reflects	X	X

By contrast, as shown in Table 11-1, when the research hypothesis is true, the between-group estimate reflects more sources of variation (both within and between populations) than the within-group estimate (which reflects only the variation within populations). Thus the between-group estimate should be larger, and the ratio of the between-group estimate to the within-group estimate should be greater than 1. (That is, if we divide the larger, the between-group estimate, by the smaller, the within-group estimate, we get not 1 but more than 1.)

This is the key principle of the analysis of variance: When the null hypothesis is true, the ratio of the between-group variance estimate to the within-group variance estimate should be about 1; but when the research hypothesis is true, this ratio should be greater than 1.

The F Ratio

F ratio

This crucial ratio of the between-group to the within-group variance estimate is called an **F ratio.** (The F is for Sir Ronald Fisher, an eminent statistician who developed the analysis of variance; see Box 11-1.)

The F Distribution and the F Table

F distribution
F table

The next question is just how much greater than 1 the F ratio must be before we are confident that the between-group estimate reflects real differences between populations so that we can reject the null hypothesis. As you might have guessed by now, statisticians have developed the mathematics of an **F distribution** and have prepared tables of F ratios. For any given situation, you merely look up in an **F table** how extreme an F ratio is needed to reject the null hypothesis at, say, the .05 level.

Let's return to our example of the Hazan and Shaver (1987) attachment style study. The results of that study, for jealousy, were as follows: The estimated variance of the population based on the differences among the means of the three attachment style samples (of 2.17, 2.88, and 2.57) was 23.19. The estimated variance of the population based on the variation of the scores within each of the attachment style samples, a pool of their variance, was .53. The ratio of the between-group to the within-group variance estimates

(23.19/.53) came out to 43.91. This ratio is considerably larger than 1. In fact, in this case the F ratio needed to reject the null hypothesis at the .05 level is only 3.01. Hazan and Shaver confidently rejected the null hypothesis and concluded that amount of jealousy varies according to attachment style.

An Analogy

Some students find an analogy helpful in understanding the analysis of variance. The analogy is to what engineers call the *signal-to-noise ratio*. For example, your ability to make out the words in a shortwave radio broadcast depends on the strength of the signal versus the amount of random noise. In the case of the F ratio in the analysis of variance, the difference among the means of the samples is like the signal—it is the information of interest. The variation within the samples is like the noise. When the variation among the samples is sufficiently great in comparison to the variation within the samples, you conclude that there is a significant effect.

Analysis of Variance Procedures

Having outlined the basic logic of the analysis of variance, we will go through an example to illustrate the details. (We use a fictional study to keep the numbers simple.)

Suppose that a social psychologist is interested in the influence of knowledge of previous criminal record on juries' perception of the guilt or innocence of a defendant. In the study, 15 volunteers who have been selected for jury duty (but have not yet served at a trial) are each shown a videotape of a 4-h trial. In the trial, a woman is accused of passing bad checks. Prior to viewing the tape, however, all subjects are given a "background sheet" with age, marital status, education, and other such information about the accused woman. The sheet is the same for all 15 subjects, except that for one third of the subjects, the last section says that she has been convicted three times before of passing bad checks (these subjects make up the "criminal record group"); for a third of the subjects, the last section says that she has a completely clean criminal record (the "clean record group"); and for a third of the subjects, there is no last section (the "no information group").

The subjects are randomly assigned to the version of the background sheet they read. After viewing the tape, all 15 participants make a rating on a 10-point scale which runs from *completely sure she is innocent* (1) to *completely sure she is guilty* (10). The results of this fictional study are shown in Table 11-2. As can be seen from the table, the means of the three groups are different (8, 4, and 5), but there is also quite a bit of variation within each of the three groups (variance estimates are 4.5, 5.0, and 6.5). Three computations are needed to test the hypothesis that the three populations are different: (a) a population variance estimate based on the variation of the scores within each of the samples, (b) a population variance estimate based on the differences among the group means, and (c) the ratio of the two, the F ratio. (In addition, the needed ratio for significance must be determined from an F table.) We shall consider each of these calculations in turn.

BOX 11-1

Sir Ronald Fisher, Caustic Genius of Statistics

Ronald A. Fisher, a contemporary of William Gosset (see Box 9-1) and Karl Pearson (see Box 14-1), was probably the brightest and certainly the most productive of this close-knit group of British statisticians. In the process of writing 300 papers and 7 books, he developed many of the modern field's key concepts: variance, analysis of variance, statistics (in the sense of describing a sample, as opposed to parameters of a population), significance levels, the null hypothesis, and almost all of our basic ideas of research design, including the fundamental importance of randomization.

It is one of those family legends that little Ronald, born in 1890 in East Finchley, a northern suburb of London, was so fascinated by math that one day, at age 3, when put into his high chair for breakfast, he asked his nurse, "What is a half of a half?" Told it was a quarter, he asked, "What's half of a quarter?" To that answer he wanted to know what was half of an eighth. At the next answer he purportedly thought a moment and said, "Then I suppose that a half of a sixteenth must be a thirty-toof." Ah, baby stories.

As a grown man, however, Fisher seems to have been anything but darling. Some observers ascribe this to a cold and unemotional mother, but whatever the reason, throughout his life the man was embroiled in bitter feuds, even with scholars who had previously been his closest allies and who certainly ought to have been comrades in research. When he was teased, apparently he responded with deadly seriousness; when others were anxious, he joked. William G. Cochran (a well-known statistician in his own right) reported a tale of their crossing a street together at a moment that was obviously unsafe. When Cochran hesitated, Fisher supposedly chided him: "Oh come on, a spot of natural selection won't hurt us." And Cochran sheepishly risked his neck.

Fisher's thin ration of compassion extended to his readers as well—not only was his writing hopelessly obscure, but it often simply failed to supply important assumptions and proofs. Gosset said that when Fisher began a sentence with *Evidently*, it meant two hours of hard work before one could hope to see why the point was evident. Another statistician sought to excuse him, however, saying that "Fisher was talking on a plane barely understood by the rest of humanity." And it is true that he was invariably

TABLE 11-2
Results of the Criminal Record Study (Fictional Data)

	Criminal Record Group			Clean Record Group			No Information Group		
	Rating	Deviation from Mean	Squared Deviation from Mean	Rating	Deviation from Mean	Squared Deviation from Mean	Rating	Deviation from Mean	Squared Deviation from Mean
	10	2	4	5	1	1	4	−1	1
	7	−1	1	1	−3	9	6	1	1
	5	−3	9	3	−1	1	9	4	16
	10	2	4	7	3	9	3	−2	4
	8	0	0	4	0	0	3	−2	4
Σ:	40	0	18	20	0	20	25	0	26

$M = 40/5 = 8.$
$S^2 = 18/4 = 4.5.$

$M = 20/5 = 4.$
$S^2 = 20/4 = 5.0.$

$M = 25/5 = 5.$
$S^2 = 26/4 = 6.5.$

admired and respected for his work, if not for his manners.

Indeed, his lack of empathy extended to all of humankind. Like Galton, Fisher was fond of eugenics, favoring anything that might increase the birthrate of the upper and professional classes and skilled artisans. Not only did he see contraception as a poor idea—fearing that the least desirable persons would use it least—but he defended infanticide as serving an evolutionary function. It was probably just as well that his opportunities to experiment with breeding never extended beyond the raising of his own children and some crops of potatoes and wheat.

The greatest influence on Fisher was probably his 14 years working at an agricultural experimental station called Rothamsted, in Hertfordshire, 25 miles north of London. At Rothamsted, Fisher, like Gosset at his brewery in Dublin, faced all sorts of practical problems, such as whether yearly applications of manure improved the yield of a field in the long run or was the cause of mysterious declines in production after many decades. Perhaps it was even this isolation from the personality disputes among London academics and this closeness to real issues that helped Fisher concentrate on developing statistics as a powerful methodological tool.

Although Fisher eventually became the Galton Professor of Eugenics at University College, his most influential appointment probably came when he was invited to Iowa State College in Ames for the summers of 1931 and 1936 (where he was said to be so put out with the terrible heat that he stored his sheets in the refrigerator all day). At Ames, Fisher greatly impressed George Snedecor, an American professor of mathematics also working on agricultural problems. Consequently Snedecor wrote a textbook of statistics for agriculture that borrowed heavily from Fisher's work at Rothamsted. The book so popularized Fisher's ideas about statistics and research design that its second edition sold 100,000 copies.

More important for psychology, while Fisher was at Ames, he also won over E. F. Lindquist, professor of education at the University of Iowa in Iowa City. Lindquist filled his next textbook with Fisher's ideas, introducing them to the fields of education and psychology, where they have played a major role to this day.

Estimating Population Variance on the Basis of Variation Within Each Group

The population variance can be estimated from any one group (that is, sample) by using the standard procedure for estimating a population variance from a sample: Compute the sum of the squared deviations (from that group's mean), and divide by that group's degrees of freedom (the number of cases in the group minus 1)—that is, $S^2 = SS/df$. For the example, as shown in Table 11-2, this yields an estimated population variance of 4.5 based on the criminal record group, an estimate of 5.0 based on the clean record group, and an estimate of 6.5 based on the no information group.

Because these estimates are all of populations assumed to have the same variance, we can pool the information into a single estimate. And because the sample sizes are equal, each group represents an estimate based on an equal amount of information, so we can pool these variance estimates by straight averaging. This yields an overall estimate of the population variance based on the variation within groups of 5.33 (4.5 + 5.0 + 6.5 = 16; 16/3 = 5.33).

The estimated variance based on the variation of the scores within each of the groups is the within-group variance estimate and is symbolized as S_W^2 or MS_W. MS_W is short for **mean squares within.** The term *mean squares* is another name for the variance because the variance is the mean of the squared deviations. S_W^2 or MS_W is also sometimes called the "error variance" and symbolized as S_E^2 or MS_E.)

The formula for the within-group variance estimate when sample sizes are equal is

$$S_W^2 \text{ or } MS_W = \frac{S_1^2 + S_2^2 + \ldots + S_{\text{Last}}^2}{N_G} \tag{11-1}$$

where S_W^2 or MS_W is the pooled estimate of the population variance based on the variation within the groups, S_1^2 is the estimated population variance based on the scores in the first group (the one associated with Population 1), S_2^2 is the estimated population variance based on the scores in the second group, S_{Last}^2 is the estimated population variance based on the scores in the last group (the dots, or ellipses, in the formula show that you are to fill in the population variance estimate for as many other groups as there are in the analysis), and N_G is the number of groups.

Using this formula for our computations, we get

$$S_W^2 \text{ or } MS_W = \frac{S_1^2 + S_2^2 + \ldots + S_{\text{Last}}^2}{N_G} = \frac{4.5 + 5.0 + 6.5}{3} = \frac{16.3}{3} = 5.33$$

Estimating Population Variance on the Basis of Differences Between Group Means

Determining the between-group estimate of the population variance involves two steps: (a) estimating from a few means the variance of a distribution of all possible means of samples of a given size and (b) extrapolating from the variance of this distribution of means to the population variance.

Estimating the Variance of the Distribution of Means. Treating each mean as a number, you can use the usual procedure to estimate from this sample of means the variance of the population of all possible means of samples of this size. First find the sum of squared deviations (find the mean of these numbers, the deviation of each number from this mean, the square of each of these deviations, and then the sum of these squared deviations); then divide this sum of squared deviations by the degrees of freedom (the number of means minus 1). Again, these numbers are means, and the distribution whose variance is being estimated is a distribution of a population of means. When estimating a population variance from sample data, you use the degrees of freedom, the number in the sample (of means) minus 1. In terms of a formula,

$$S_M^2 = \frac{\Sigma(M - GM)^2}{df_B} \tag{11-2}$$

where S_M^2 is the variance estimate of the distribution of means estimated from the particular means in your study; M is the mean of each of your samples; GM is the **grand mean,** the overall mean of all your scores, which is also the

TABLE 11-3
Computation of the Estimated Variance of the Distribution of Means Based on Means of the Three Experimental Groups in the Criminal Record Study (Fictional Data)

	Sample Means	Deviation from Grand Mean	Squared Deviation from Grand Mean
	(M)	$(M - GM)$	$(M - GM)^2$
	4	−1.67	2.79
	8	2.33	5.43
	5	− .67	.45
Σ:	17	−0.01	8.67

$GM = \Sigma M / N_G = 17/3 = 5.67$; $S_M^2 = \Sigma (M - GM)^2 / df_B = 8.67/2 = 4.34$.

mean of your means; and df_B is the degrees of freedom in the between-group estimate, the number of groups minus 1 (that is, $df_B = N_G - 1$).

In our jury example, the three means are 8, 4, and 5. The computations are shown in Table 11-3.

Extrapolating From the Estimated Variance of the Distribution of Means to an Estimated Variance of the Population of Individual Scores. What we have just calculated from a sample of a few means of a given size is the estimated variance of a distribution of all possible means of samples of a given size—in our example, samples of 5. From this we want to take a third step, by making a new estimation. This new estimation is of the variance of the population of individual scores. However, as we saw in Chapter 7, the variance of a distribution of means of samples will be smaller than the variance of the population of individual scores from which the samples are taken. This is because means are less likely to be extreme than individual scores are (because several scores that are extreme in the same direction are unlikely to be included in any one sample). Specifically, you learned in Chapter 7 that the variance of a distribution of means will be the variance of the parent distribution of individual scores divided by the number of cases in each sample.

Now, however, notice that we are going to do something different. In Chapter 7, we used an estimate of the variance of the population of individual cases to determine the variance of the distribution of means; now we have said that we are going to use an estimate of the variance of the distribution of means to determine the variance of the population of individual cases. That is, we are going to reverse the usual process. Therefore, instead of dividing by the size of the sample (in our example, 5), we do the reverse and *multiply* by the size of the sample. That is, to determine the variance of the population of individual scores, we multiply our estimate of the variance of the distribution of means times the sample size. The result of this process is the *between-group variance estimate*, also called **mean squares between.** Stated as a formula, when sample sizes are equal,

mean squares between

$$S_B^2 \text{ or } MS_B = (S_M^2)(n) \tag{11-3}$$

where S_B^2 or MS_B is the estimate of the population variance based on the variation between the means and n is the number of cases in each sample.

In terms of our example, in which there were 5 in each sample and an estimated variance of the distribution of means of 4.34, the population variance estimate using the between-group method comes out to 21.7. That is,

$$S_B^2 \text{ or } MS_B = (S_M^2)(n) = (4.34)(5) = 21.7$$

To summarize, the procedure of estimating the population variance based on the differences between group means is (a) to calculate the estimated variance of the distribution of means and then (b) to multiply that figure by the number of scores in each group.

Computing the F Ratio

The F ratio is the ratio of the between-group estimate of the population variance to the within-group estimate of the population variance. (Note that the potentially larger number, the between-group estimate, is always the numerator.) Stated as a formula,

$$F = \frac{S_B^2}{S_W^2} \qquad\qquad\qquad (11\text{-}4a)$$

or, using the mean squares symbols,

$$F = \frac{MS_B}{MS_W} \qquad\qquad\qquad (11\text{-}4b)$$

In the example, our ratio of between to within is 21.7: 5.33, which gives an F ratio of 4.07. Applying the formula to our example, $F = S_B^2/S_W^2$ or $MS_B/MS_W = 21.7/5.33 = 4.07$.

The F Distribution

During the hypothesis-testing process, in order to determine how extreme the F ratio in your study will have to be to reject the null hypothesis, you consult a table of F ratios. However, to understand exactly what this table represents, you should know how you would have constructed one on your own.

Suppose that you start with three large normal populations, all with the same mean and variance. Next you randomly select five cases from each. Then, on the basis of these three samples, you compute an F ratio (that is, you make a between-group estimate and a within-group estimate of the population variance and divide the first by the second). Let's say that this F ratio is 1.36. Now you select three new random samples of five cases each and compute a new F ratio. Perhaps this time it is .93. If you repeat this process many times, you will get an F distribution (the distribution of F ratios if the null hypothesis is true and you are selecting samples of five cases each from three different populations). The final result would look like the distribution shown in Figure 11-3.

Of course, in practice no one actually constructs an F distribution in this way. It is a mathematical distribution whose exact characteristics can be found from a formula. But the mathematics can also prove that if you had the patience to follow this procedure for a very long time, you would get the same result.

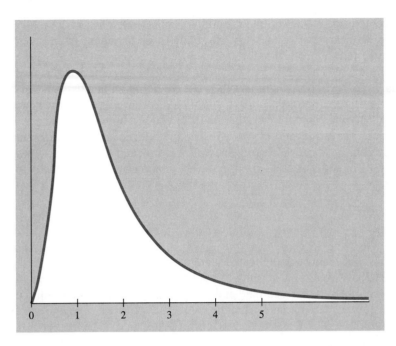

FIGURE 11-3
An F distribution.

As you can see in Figure 11-3, the F distribution is not symmetrical but is positively skewed. This is true of F distributions in general. The reason for the positive skew is that an F distribution is a distribution of ratios of variances. Variances are always positive numbers (a variance is an average of squared deviations, and anything squared is a positive number). And a ratio of positive numbers can never be less than 0 (if you are dividing one positive number by another, the result must be positive). But there's nothing to stop a ratio from being a very high number, although this is rare. Thus the F ratios' distribution cannot be lower than 0 and can rise quite high, but most F ratios pile up just on the positive side of 0.

Also notice that we use the F distribution as a comparison distribution for determining whether the between-group estimate of the population variance is sufficiently bigger (never smaller) than the within-group estimate of the population variance.[1] That is, we are always interested in the right-hand tail of the distribution, and all F tests in the analysis of variance are techni-

---

[1]It is possible, by chance, for F to be larger or smaller than 1 in any particular situation. Both the between-group and the within-group estimates are only estimates and can each vary a fair amount even when the null hypothesis is true. If F is considerably larger than 1, we reject the null hypothesis that in fact the populations all have the same mean. But what if F is substantially smaller than 1? This rarely happens. When it does, it could mean that there is *less* variation among the groups than would be expected by chance—something is restricting the variation between groups. One cause could be, when setting up the experiment, matching subjects across the groups on variables (such as age or intelligence) that turn out to be related to the variable being studied. One implication of this possibility is that matching groups in this way in advance of a study could actually work against getting significant results. Even if there are real differences among the population means, the influence of these differences on the between-group estimate can be offset by the effect of the matching. This issue is considered later in the chapter.

cally one-tailed tests. However, the meaning of a one-tailed test is not really the same as with a t test because in the analysis of variance, it does not make sense to talk about a direction of a difference, only of whether the variation among the means is greater than would be expected if the null hypothesis were true. Note also that when we are doing an analysis of variance involving three or more groups, a significant result tells us that we can reject the null hypothesis that there are no differences among the three population means, but it does not tell us which population means are different from which. It only says that overall they vary from each other. (We return to this issue of hypothesis tests about specific subpatterns of differences in Chapter 12.)

The F Table

The F table is a little more complicated than the t table. This is because there is a different F distribution according to both the degrees of freedom used in the between-group variance estimate and the degrees of freedom used in the within-group variance estimate. That is, you must consider two different **numerator degrees of freedom** to look up the needed cutoff point. One is the **numerator degrees of freedom**—the degrees of freedom used in the between-group variance estimate, the numerator of the F ratio. The other is the **denominator degrees of freedom**—the total degrees of freedom that go into figuring the within-group variance estimate, the denominator of the F ratio.

The numerator degrees of freedom is thus the number of groups minus 1 (since that is the degrees of freedom used in computing the between-groups variance estimate). Stated as a formula,

$$df_B = N_G - 1 \tag{11-5}$$

where df_B is the numerator degrees of freedom and N_G is the number of groups.

The denominator degrees of freedom is the sum of the degrees of freedom for all of the groups (since all of their estimates are included in the pooling). Stated as a formula,

$$df_W = df_1 + df_2 + \ldots + df_{Last} \tag{11-6}$$

where each df is the number of cases in its sample minus 1.

In the criminal record experiment example, the numerator degrees of freedom is 2—there are 3 means, minus 1 ($df_B = N_G - 1 = 3 - 1 = 2$). The denominator degrees of freedom is 12. This is because each of the groups has 4 degrees of freedom on which the estimate is based (5 scores minus 1) and there are 3 groups overall, making a total of 12 degrees of freedom: $df_W = df_1 + df_2 + \ldots + df_{Last} = (5-1) + (5-1) + (5-1) = 4 + 4 + 4 = 12$.

Thus you would look up the critical cutoff point for an F distribution "with 2 and 12" degrees of freedom. As shown in Table 11-4, this would indicate that for the .05 level, you would need an F ratio of at least 3.89 (or at the .01 level, one of at least 6.93) before you would reject the null hypothesis. The full F table appears as Table B-3 in Appendix B.

numerator degrees of freedom

denominator degrees of freedom

TABLE 11-4
Cutoff Scores for the *F* Distribution (Portion)

Denominator Degrees of Freedom	Significance Level	Numerator Degrees of Freedom					
		1	*2*	*3*	*4*	*5*	*6*
10	.01	10.05	7.56	6.55	6.00	5.64	5.39
	.05	4.97	4.10	3.71	3.48	3.33	3.22
	.10	3.29	2.93	2.73	2.61	2.52	2.46
11	.01	9.65	7.21	6.22	5.67	5.32	5.07
	.05	4.85	3.98	3.59	3.36	3.20	3.10
	.10	3.23	2.86	2.66	2.54	2.45	2.39
12	.01	9.33	6.93	5.95	5.41	5.07	4.82
	.05	4.75	3.89	3.49	3.26	3.11	3.00
	.10	3.18	2.81	2.61	2.48	2.40	2.33
13	.01	9.07	6.70	5.74	5.21	4.86	4.62
	.05	4.67	3.81	3.41	3.18	3.03	2.92
	.10	3.14	2.76	2.56	2.43	2.35	2.28

Hypothesis Testing with the Analysis of Variance

Hypothesis testing with the analysis of variance involves the same five steps as we have been using all along.

An Example

Let's consider how these steps work in the criminal record experiment.

1. Reframe the question into a research hypothesis and a null hypothesis about the populations. The populations of interest are these:

Population 1: Jurors told that the defendant has a criminal record
Population 2: Jurors told that the defendant has a clean record
Population 3: Jurors given no information on the defendant's record

The null hypothesis is that these three populations have the same mean. The research hypothesis is that their means differ.

2. Determine the characteristics of the comparison distribution. The comparison distribution will be an *F* distribution with 2 and 12 degrees of freedom.

3. Determine the cutoff sample score on the comparison distribution at which the null hypothesis should be rejected. Using the *F* table in Table 11-4 and assuming that we are using a .05 significance level, the needed *F* ratio is 3.89.

4. Determine the score of the sample on the comparison distribution. In the analysis of variance, the comparison distribution is an *F* distribution, and the sample's score on that distribution is thus its *F* ratio. In the example, the *F* ratio we computed was 4.07.

5. Compare the scores obtained in Steps 3 and 4 to decide whether to reject the null hypothesis. In the example, the computed F ratio is more extreme than the .05 significance level cutoff point. Thus the researcher would reject the null hypothesis that the three groups come from populations with the same mean. This suggests that they come from populations with different means: that people exposed to different kinds of information (or no information) about the criminal record of a defendant in a situation of this kind will differ in their ratings of the defendant's guilt.[2]

Another Example

Levenson (1990) conducted a study to help sort out whether risk taking involves a single underlying personality trait or whether different types of risk takers have different kinds of personalities. Specifically, Levenson studied three groups of risk takers: (a) residents in a drug treatment facility (whom he called "antisocial risk takers"), (b) rock climbers (whom he called "adventurous risk takers"), and (c) police and firefighters who had been decorated for bravery (whom he called "prosocial risk takers" or "heroes"). All of the subjects were administered a variety of personality tests. We will focus on a particular measure, the Thrill and Adventure Seeking Scale (Zuckerman, 1979).

The results (which have been modified slightly from the original study to simplify our discussion), along with the analysis of variance calculations, are shown in Table 11-5. The steps of the hypothesis-testing procedure follow.

1. Reframe the question into a research hypothesis and a null hypothesis about the populations. The populations of interest are these:

Population 1: Drug treatment facility residents
Population 2: Rock climbers
Population 3: Police and firefighters decorated for bravery

The null hypothesis is that these three populations have the same mean. The research hypothesis is that their means differ.

2. Determine the characteristics of the comparison distribution. The comparison distribution will be an F distribution. Its degrees of freedom are figured as follows: The between-group variance estimate is based on three groups, making 2 degrees of freedom. The within-group estimate is based on 17 degrees of freedom (18 subjects) in each of the three groups, making a total of 51 degrees of freedom.

3. Determine the cutoff sample score on the comparison distribution at which the null hypothesis should be rejected. Using Table B-3 in Appendix B, we look down the column for 2 degrees of freedom in the numerator and stop at the nearest row above our denominator degrees of freedom of 51, which is 50. We will use the .05 significance level. This means a cutoff F of 3.18.

4. Determine the score of the sample on the comparison distribution. This step requires determining our sample's F ratio. The numerator, which is the between-group variance estimate, is determined in two steps. First we

---

[2]Several real studies have looked at this issue of whether knowing a defendant's prior criminal record affects the likelihood of conviction. The overall conclusion seems to be reasonably consistent with that of the fictional study described here. For a review of this literature, see Dane and Wrightsman (1982).

TABLE 11-5
Thrill and Adventure Seeking Scale Scores of Three Groups of Risk Takers:
Results and Analysis of Variance

	Drug Treatment Residents	Rock Climbers	Police and Firefighters Decorated for Bravery
n	18	18	18
M	10.00	12.22	8.52
S	2.70	2.37	3.87
S^2	7.29	5.62	14.98

F distribution:

$$df_B = N_G - 1 = 3 - 1 = 2$$

$$df_W = df_1 + df_2 + \ldots + df_{Last} = (18 - 1) + (18 - 1) + (18 - 1) = 17 + 17 + 17 = 51$$

F needed for significance at .05 level from F table for $df = 2, 50$: 3.18.

Between-groups population variance estimate:
Table for finding S^2 for the three means

	M	Deviation	Squared Deviation
Drug users	10.00	− .25	.06
Climbers	12.22	1.97	3.88
Police and firefighters	8.52	−1.73	2.99
	Σ: 30.74		$\Sigma(M - GM)^2 = 6.93$
	GM: 10.25		

$$S_M^2 = \Sigma(M - GM)^2/df_B = 6.93/2 = 3.47$$
$$S_B^2 = (S_M^2)(n) = (3.47)(18) = 62.46$$

Within-groups population variance estimate:

$$S_W^2 = \frac{S_1^2 + S_2^2 + \ldots + S_{Last}^2}{N_G} = \frac{2.70^2 + 2.37^2 + 3.87^2}{3} = \frac{7.29 + 5.62 + 14.98}{3} = \frac{27.89}{3} = 9.30$$

F ratio: $F = S_B^2/S_W^2 = 62.46/9.30 = 6.72$

Conclusion: Reject the null hypothesis.

Note. Data from Levenson, M. R. (1990), slightly modified. Risk taking and personality. *Journal of Personality and Social Psychology, 58*, 1073–1080. Copyright, 1990, by the American Psychological Association. Reprinted by permission of the author.

estimated the variance of the distribution of means of all possible samples of 18 by using our three actual means as if they were individual numbers— we took the sum of their squared deviations from their mean, which comes out to 6.93, and divided this sum by the degrees of freedom, which is 2, giving 3.47. However, since this is an estimate of a variance of a distribution of means, we converted it to an estimate of the variance of the population of individual cases by multiplying it by the sample size, 18, which gives 62.46.

The denominator of the F ratio, the within-group variance estimate, is the average of the population variance estimates computed from each sample. (Be careful not to use estimates of the population standard deviation.) In this case, the average of 7.29, 5.62, and 14.98 comes out to 9.30.

The F ratio is the between-group estimate divided by the within-group estimate (62.46/9.30), which comes out to 6.72.

5. Compare the scores obtained in Steps 3 and 4 to decide whether to reject the null hypothesis. The computed F ratio of 6.72 is more extreme than the .05 significance level cutoff of 3.18. Thus Levenson rejected the null hypothesis and concluded that the three types of risk takers seem to be clearly different on their degree of thrill and adventure seeking. This outcome was consistent with Levenson's theory that risk taking does not represent a uniform, underlying personality trait.

Summary of Steps for Conducting an Analysis of Variance

Table 11-6 summarizes the steps involved in an analysis of variance of the kind we have been considering in this chapter.

Assumptions in the Analysis of Variance

The assumptions for the analysis of variance, as well as the various considerations about violation of those assumptions, are virtually the same as we considered for the t test for independent means in Chapter 10. That is, the mathematics hold only when the populations from which the samples come can be assumed to be normally distributed and to have equal variances.

But also as with the t test, in practice you obtain quite acceptable results even when these assumptions are moderately violated. The general opinion is that the assumption of a normal distribution is not critical unless you have reason to believe that your populations are strongly skewed in different directions or if your sample size is quite small. However, when this assumption is seriously violated, you should use one of the procedures described in Chapter 15, which is about dealing with situations in which population distributions cannot be assumed to follow a normal curve.

The assumption of equal population variances is also not a problem so long as you have no reason to believe that the variances are extremely disparate. As a rule, if the variance estimate of the group with the largest estimate is no more than 4 or 5 times that of the smallest and the sample sizes are equal, the conclusions should be acceptably accurate.

If the equal-variance assumption is severely violated, you can use special procedures that, in effect, set up a more stringent F ratio cutoff to determine if the result is significant at a given level (such as 5%). These procedures are described in advanced texts.

Effect Size and Power for the Analysis of Variance

Effect Size

Effect size for the analysis of variance is a little more complex to think about than in the case of the t test. With the t test, we divided the mean difference by the population standard deviation: $d = (\mu_1 - \mu_2)/\sigma$. In the analysis of variance, we can still divide by the population standard deviation (σ, or its estimate, S_w). But what is the equivalent to the difference between

TABLE 11-6
Steps for Conducting an Analysis of Variance (When Sample Sizes Are Equal)

1. Reframe the question into a research hypothesis and a null hypothesis about the populations.

2. Determine the characteristics of the comparison distribution.

    a. The comparison distribution will be an F distribution.
    b. The numerator degrees of freedom is the number of groups minus 1: $df_B = N_G - 1$.
    c. The denominator degrees of freedom is the sum of the degrees of freedom in each group (the number of cases in the group minus 1): $df_W = df_1 + df_2 + \ldots + df_{Last}$.

3. Determine the cutoff sample score on the comparison distribution at which the null hypothesis should be rejected.

    a. Determine the desired significance level.
    b. Look up the appropriate cutoff in an F table, using the degrees of freedom calculated in Step 2.

4. Determine the score of the sample on the comparison distribution. (This will be an F ratio.)

    a. Compute the between-group population variance estimate (S_B^2 or MS_b).

       i. Compute the means of each group.
      ii. Compute a variance estimate based on the means of the groups: $S_M^2 = \Sigma(M - GM)^2/df_B$.
      iii. Convert this estimate of the variance of a distribution of means to an estimate of the variance of a population of individual scores by multiplying by the number of cases in each group: S_B^2 or $MS_B = (S_M^2)(n)$.

    b. Compute the within-group population variance estimate S_W^2 or MS_W.

       i. Compute population variance estimates based on each group's scores: For each group, $S^2 = SS/df$.
      ii. Average these variance estimates: $S_W^2 = (S_1^2 + S_2^2 + \ldots + S_{Last}^2)/N_G$.

    c. Compute the F ratio: $F = S_B^2/S_W^2$ (or $F = MS_B/MS_W$).

5. Compare the scores obtained in Steps 3 and 4 to decide whether to reject the null hypothesis.

---

means, the numerator in figuring effect size? Cohen (1988) suggests that in the analysis of variance, we should think of the numerator for the effect size as the variation among the means—specifically, he recommends using the standard deviation of the distribution of means (σ_M or its estimate, S_M). Thus Cohen defines the **effect size for analysis of variance**, which he labels f, as follows:

effect size for analysis of variance

$$f = \frac{\sigma_M}{\sigma} \tag{11-7}$$

The important thing about this definition of effect size is that it gets larger due to either (a) a large difference among population means (the numerator of f) or (b) a small variance within the populations (the denominator of f). This is just what an effect size index ought to do.

In terms of estimated values from an actual study, we can estimate f, using

$$\text{estimated } f = S_M/S_W \tag{11-8}$$

As is always true of effect size calculations, the calculations do not take sample size into account—thus in the numerator we use S_M instead of S_B (which would be based on multiplying S_M^2 by the sample size). Cohen's conventions for f are .10 for a small effect size, .25 for a medium effect size, and .40 for a large effect size. In practice, it is often quite difficult to estimate effect size for an analysis of variance based on expectations about population values, and researchers are thus likely to rely mainly on the conventions when planning a study using analysis of variance.[3]

However, f can be computed easily from a completed study. Consider our first example, the fictional criminal record experiment. In that study, we computed S_M^2, the estimated variance of the distribution of means, based on the means of our three samples, to be 4.34; we computed S_w^2, the estimate of the variance of the populations of individual cases, based on the variance estimates using each group's scores, to be 5.33. Applying the formulas,

$$S_M = \sqrt{S_M^2} = \sqrt{4.34} = 2.08$$
$$S_W = \sqrt{S_W^2} = \sqrt{5.33} = 2.31$$
$$f = \frac{S_M}{S_W} = \frac{2.08}{2.31} = .90$$

This is a very large effect size (thanks to our made-up data). In our second example, the risk-taking study,

$$S_M = \sqrt{3.47} = 1.86$$
$$S_W = \sqrt{9.30} = 3.05$$
$$\text{estimated } f = \frac{S_M}{S_W} = .61$$

This is again a quite large effect size (also due to having made up the specific data, even if the overall means were real).

With a bit of algebraic manipulation, it turns out that the estimated f is the square root of F divided by the square root of the number of subjects in each group. That is,

$$\text{estimated } f = \frac{\sqrt{F}}{\sqrt{n}} \tag{11-9}$$

For example, in the criminal record study we had calculated F to be 4.07. Using the formula,

$$\text{estimated } f = \frac{\sqrt{F}}{\sqrt{n}} = \frac{\sqrt{4.07}}{\sqrt{5}} = \frac{2.02}{2.24} = .90.$$

This method is very helpful when evaluating the effect size of a completed study reported in a research article.

---

[3]In Chapter 12, after we have introduced the structural model approach to analysis of variance, you will learn how to compute another kind of effect size, the "proportion of variance accounted for." Because of its relation to the same concept in regression analysis (Chapter 4), this indicator of effect size has a more direct meaning for many researchers, and you will encounter it often. We discuss the relation of f to this effect size indicator in Chapter 12.

TABLE 11-7
Approximate Power for Studies Using the One-Way Analysis of Variance Testing Hypotheses at the .05 Significance Level

Subjects per Group (N)	Effect Size		
	Small *(f = .10)*	*Medium* *(f = .25)*	*Large* *(f = .40)*
Three groups (df_B = 2)			
10	.07	.20	.45
20	.09	.38	.78
30	.12	.55	.93
40	.15	.68	.98
50	.18	.79	.99
100	.32	.98	*
Four groups (df_B = 3)			
10	.07	.21	.51
20	.10	.43	.85
30	.13	.61	.96
40	.16	.76	.99
50	.19	.85	*
100	.36	.99	*
Five groups (df_B = 4)			
10	.07	.23	.56
20	.10	.47	.90
30	.13	.67	.98
40	.17	.81	*
50	.21	.90	*
100	.40	*	*

*Nearly 1.

Power

There are four determinants of the power of an analysis of variance of the kind we have considered in this chapter (a one-way analysis of variance). Three are the same as are found in any kind of study: effect size, sample size, and significance level. In addition, in the analysis of variance, we must consider the number of groups. Table 11-7 shows the approximate power for the .05 significance level for small, medium, and large effect sizes; sample size of 10, 20, 30, 40, 50, and 100 per group; and three, four, and five groups. These are the most common values of the various influences on power.[4]

For example, a planned study comparing five groups of 10 subjects each, with an expected large effect size ($f = .40$), to be carried out using the .05 level, would have power of .56. This means that even if the research hypothesis is in fact true and has a large effect size, there is only a little greater than even chance (56%) that the study will come out significant.

As we have noted in previous chapters, determining power is especially useful when interpreting the practical implication of a nonsignificant result. For example, suppose that you have read a study using an analysis of variance for four groups in which the researcher reports a nonsignificant result

[4]More detailed tables are provided in Cohen (1988, pp. 289–354). When using these tables, note that the value of u at the top of each table refers to df_B, which in the case of a one-way analysis of variance is 1 minus the number of groups, not the number of groups as used in our Table 11-7.

TABLE 11-8
Approximate Number of Subjects Needed in Each Group (Assuming Equal Sample Sizes) to Achieve 80% Power for the One-Way Analysis of Variance Testing Hypotheses at the .05 Significance Level

	Effect Size		
	Small *(f = .10)*	*Medium* *(f = .25)*	*Large* *(f = .40)*
Three groups ($df_B = 2$)	322	52	21
Four groups ($df_B = 3$)	274	45	18
Five groups ($df_B = 4$)	240	39	16

at the .05 level using 30 subjects per group. Table 11-7 shows a power of only .13 for a small effect size, suggesting that even if such a small effect exists in the population, this study would be very unlikely to have come out significant. But the table shows a power of .96 for a large effect size, suggesting that if a large effect existed in the population, it almost surely would have shown up in this study.

Planning Sample Size

Table 11-8 gives the approximate number of subjects needed to achieve 80% power at the .05 significance level for estimated small, medium, and large effect sizes for designs involving three, four, and five groups.[5] For example, if you are planning a study involving four groups in which you expect a small effect size (and will use the .05 significance level), you would need 274 subjects in each group—a total of 1,096 subjects in all—to be assured of 80% power. However, if you were able to modify the research plan (perhaps by using more accurate measures and a more powerful experimental manipulation) so that it was now reasonable to predict a large effect size, you would need only 18 subjects in each of the four groups, for a total of 72.

Controversy: Random Assignment Versus Systematic Selection

One controversy that has arisen in the context of analysis of variance has to do with the design of experiments. Ordinarily, the optimal way to set up an experiment is to use completely random assignment to experimental conditions (see Appendix A). However, to reduce random error, some researchers modify strict random assignment by setting up their study to make sure that the subjects in each experimental group are on the average the same on one or more variables that are relevant to the study. Consider a study in which fourth graders will be assigned to one of three different experimental math programs.

[5]More detailed tables are provided in Cohen (1988, pp. 381–389). If you use these, see footnote 4 in this chapter.

The researchers may want to make sure that the average IQ and average math skills are the same in each of the groups before the experiment begins.[6]

The controversy about the use of group matching to minimize average differences on relevant variables has to do with its effect on the power of the analysis of variance for testing the outcome of the study. Systematic selection artificially reduces the natural variation among samples (to the extent that the variables on which the matching is being done are related to the variable being studied). If you lower the random variation among the samples, the total variation among means—the numerator of the F ratio—should on the average be smaller. By contrast, the denominator of the F ratio, the within-group variance estimate, is unaffected by group matching versus ordinary random assignment. If you reduce the numerator and keep the denominator the same, the F ratio can only be smaller. And a smaller F ratio means a smaller chance of getting significance even if there is a true mean difference between the populations represented by your experimental conditions—that is, you lower power. (This is counterintuitive, since on the face of it, reducing "noise" should increase power. But the problem is that you are reducing noise unevenly, so the noise that would normally contribute to the between-group variance estimate is lost, while the noise in the within-group variance estimate remains.) Thus the traditional advice in most textbooks of experimental design is not to use group matching of this sort in setting up experiments.

Recently, however, Ross and Klein (1988) have questioned this traditional advice. They concede that with group matching, the numerator of the F ratio (and therefore the F ratio as a whole) should on the average be reduced. But they also point out that this applies *on the average* and that it is quite possible that in certain specifiable situations, the F ratio might actually be increased by this procedure.

Ross and Klein conducted a series of Monte Carlo studies (see Box 10-1) to determine the actual effect of group matching under various conditions. The result of their studies was that using group matching, as compared to ordinary random assignment, (a) is better if the null hypothesis is true, in that the chance of making a Type I error (mistakenly rejecting the null hypothesis) is reduced; (b) is worse when the research hypothesis is true but the true differences among group means are small, in that power is reduced in this case; and (c) is better when the research hypothesis is true and the true differences among group means are large, in that power is increased in this case. However, it turns

[6]One way of doing this would be to take all the subjects and randomly assign as many as are needed for the first group. Then you would assign additional students for each of the other groups, a few at a time, consistently adjusting who is included until the three groups have the same average IQ and math skills scores. In the kind of group matching we are discussing here, the resulting setup is still a true experiment in a sense, in that the group a subject is in is determined by the experimenter, not by naturally occurring groupings, and any given child has an equal chance of being in any of the three groups, given that assignment is determined by matching or not matching children in the first group, which was indeed randomly selected. Group matching of this kind—the kind that this section is about—should not be confused with matching done to try to equate preexisting groups because random assignment is not possible, such as a study comparing males and females or people of three different nationalities. That is a much less rigorous method. We are also not talking here about a sort of matching that is one to one—for example, sets of three students are created so that three members of each set are very similar and then, for each set, the three are randomly assigned across the three experimental conditions. This latter procedure of individual matching, which is not controversial, is almost always an advantage but is usually impracticable.

out that in all of these cases, the very best procedure is to use group matching but to analyze the results with a more sophisticated statistical procedure called the "analysis of covariance" (described briefly in Chapter 17). The analysis of covariance systematically takes into account each subject's scores on the variables on which matching is done. Unfortunately, however, in many cases this procedure cannot be used because either its stringent assumptions cannot be met or the needed data are not available. Thus when group matching is feasible in a study, it seems to be advisable in Ross and Klein's situations (a) and (c), even if the special analysis of covariance procedure cannot be used, and the good old standard analysis of variance will be.

Analyses of Variance as Described in Research Articles

An analysis of variance of the kind we have considered in this chapter is usually described in a research article by giving the F, the degrees of freedom, and the significance level—for example, "$F(3, 67) = 5.21, p < .01$." The means for the groups are usually given in a table, although if there are only a few groups and only one or a few measures, the means may be given in the text. Returning to the criminal record experiment example, we would probably describe the analysis of variance results this way: "The means for the criminal record, clean record, and no information groups were 7.0, 4.0, and 5.0, respectively, $F(2, 12) = 4.07, p < .05$."

Here is an example from a published article. Langlois and Roggman (1990) hypothesized that beautiful faces are those that represent the average. To test this idea, they photographed a large number of college students, then took a random selection of the photos and, using computer technology, converted the facial information to numeric data that were then averaged to produce composite faces. Subjects in the experiment simply viewed various computer-produced images of faces and rated their attractiveness. Some of the subjects rated faces that were from single individuals; others rated faces made of composites of 2, 4, 8, 16, or 32 faces. The idea was that if beauty is having all average features, then the faces made from composites of more people should be rated as more beautiful. For male faces, Langlois and Roggman reported, "The ANOVA comparing images of individual male faces with 2-, 4-, 8-, 16-, and 32-face images revealed a significant effect of the number of faces, $F(5, 95) = 2.90, p = .017$" (p. 118). Looking at the pattern of means, the clear tendency was, as predicted, for the composites involving more faces to be rated as more attractive. (The results were the same for female faces.)

In this study—as in most cases involving the analysis of variance—the researchers would ordinarily also like to conduct some systematic analysis of which means differ from which other means. That topic will be considered in Chapter 12.

Summary

The analysis of variance (ANOVA) is used to test hypotheses involving differences among means of several samples. The procedure compares two estimates of population variance. One, called the "within-group estimate," is determined by pooling the variance estimates from each of the samples. The other, called the "between-group estimate," is based on the variation among the means of the samples.

The F ratio is computed by dividing the between-group estimate by the within-group estimate. If the null hypothesis is true, meaning that all the samples come from populations with the same mean, the F ratio should be about 1, since the two population variance estimates are based on the same element, the variation within each of the populations. But if the research hypothesis is true, and the samples come from populations with different means, the F ratio should be larger than 1 because the between-group estimate is now influenced by the variation both within the populations and between them, while the within-group estimate is still affected only by the variation within each of the populations.

When the samples are of equal size, the within-group population variance estimate is the average of the estimates of the population variance computed from each sample; the between-group population variance estimate is computed by first finding the estimate of the variance of the distribution of means (computed by using the ordinary formula for S^2 but computing it with the means) and then multiplying this estimate by the sample size to make it comparable to the variance of a distribution of individual cases (which is what the within-group estimate is about).

The distribution of F ratios under the null hypothesis is known, and significance cutoff values are available in tables according to the degrees of freedom for each population variance estimate, the between-group (numerator) estimate being based on the number of groups minus 1 and the within-group (denominator) estimate being based on the sum of the degrees of freedom in each sample.

The assumptions for the analysis of variance are the same as for the t test—the populations must be normally distributed, with equal variances—and like the t test, the analysis of variance is considered robust to moderate violations of these assumptions.

Effect size in the analysis of variance can be computed for a completed study as the square root of F divided by the square root of the number of subjects in each group. Power depends on effect size, number of subjects, significance level, and number of groups.

Systematically assigning subjects to experimental groups to ensure similar averages on background variables generally reduces power because the procedure reduces the contribution of random variance to the between-group estimate but not to the within-group estimate. However, under certain conditions, this procedure can increase power.

Key Terms

analysis of variance (ANOVA)

between-group estimate of the population variance (S_B^2 or MS_B)

denominator degrees of freedom (df_W)

effect size for analysis of variance (f)

F distribution

F ratio

F table

grand mean (GM)

mean squares between (MS_B)

mean squares within (MS_W)

numerator degrees of freedom (df_B)

within-group estimate of the population variance (S_W^2 or MS_W)

Practice Problems

These problems involve computation (with the assistance of a calculator). Most real-life statistics problems are done on a computer. But even if you have a computer, do this by hand to ingrain the method in your mind.

For practice in using a computer to solve statistical problems, refer to the computer section of each chapter of the study guide that accompanies this text.

All data are fictional (unless an actual citation is given). Answers to Set I are given at the back of the book.

SET I

1. For each of the following summaries of data sets, determine if the null hypothesis (that the groups come from identical populations) can be rejected at the .05 level. Also compute the effect size and determine approximate power.

(a)

	Group 1	Group 2	Group 3
n	10	10	10
M	7.4	6.8	6.8
S^2	.82	.90	.80

GM = 7

(b)

	Group 1	Group 2	Group 3	Group 4
n	25	25	25	25
M	94	101	124	105
S	24	28	31	25

GM = 106

(c)

	Group 1	Group 2	Group 3	Group 4	Group 5
n	25	25	25	25	25
M	94	101	124	105	106
S	24	28	31	25	27

GM = 106

2. For each of the following data sets, determine if the null hypothesis (that the groups come from identical populations) can be rejected at the .01 level.

(a)

Group 1	Group 2	Group 3
8	6	4
8	6	4
7	5	3
9	7	5

(b)

Group 1	Group 2	Group 3
12	10	8
4	2	0
12	10	8
4	2	0

3. A psychologist at a private mental hospital was asked to determine whether there was any clear difference in the length of stay of patients with different categories of diagnosis. Looking at the last four clients in each of the three major categories, the results (in terms of weeks of stay) were as follows:

Diagnosis Category		
Affective Disorders	Cognitive Disorders	Drug-related Conditions
7	12	8
6	8	10
5	9	12
6	11	10

Using the .05 level, is there a significant difference in length of stay among diagnosis categories? Explain your answer to someone who understands everything involved in conducting a t test for independent means but who has never heard of the analysis of variance.

4. A study compared the felt intensity of unrequited love among three groups: (a) 50 subjects who were currently experiencing unrequited love—mean experienced intensity = 3.5, S^2 = 5.2; (b) 50 who had previously experienced unrequited love and described their experience retrospectively—M = 3.2, S^2 = 5.8; and (c) 50 who had never experienced unrequited love but described how they thought they would feel if they were to experience it—M = 3.8, S^2 = 4.8. Determine the significance of the difference among groups, using the 1% level, and explain your answer to a person who has never had a course in statistics.

5. A researcher is concerned that the level of need for mental health care among prisoners is different in different types of prison facilities. Thus the researcher randomly selects 40 prisoners from each of the three main types of prisons in a particular U.S. state and conducts interviews to determine their need for mental health care on a 10-point rating scale. In the article describing the results, the researcher reported the means for each group and then added: "The need for mental health care among prisoners in the three types of prison systems appeared to be clearly different, $F(2, 117) = 5.62$, $p < .01$." Explain what this means to a person who has never had a course in statistics.

6. Which type of English words are longer—nouns, verbs, or adjectives? Go to your dictionary, turn to random pages (using the random numbers listed here), and go down the column until you come to a noun. Note its length (in number of letters). Do this for 10 different nouns. Do the same for 10 verbs and then for 10 adjectives. Then conduct an analysis of variance comparing the three types of words. Also, assuming a large effect size, what is the power of this study (at the .05 level), and how many words of each type would be necessary for 80% power?

651, 73, 950, 320, 564, 666, 736, 768, 661, 484, 990, 379, 323, 219, 715, 472, 176, 811, 167, 612, 102, 452, 849, 615, 228, 352, 851, 981, 821, 834, 719, 525, 9

SET II

1. For each of the following summaries of data sets, determine if the null hypothesis (that the groups come from identical populations) can be rejected at the .05 level; also determine the effect size.

(a)	Group 1	Group 2	Group 3
n	5	5	5
M	10	12	14
S^2	4	6	5

(b)	Group 1	Group 2	Group 3
n	10	10	10
M	10	12	14
S^2	4	6	5

(c)	Group 1	Group 2	Group 3
n	5	5	5
M	10	14	18
S^2	4	6	5

(d)	Group 1	Group 2	Group 3
n	5	5	5
M	10	12	14
S^2	2	3	2.5

2. For each of the following data sets, determine if the null hypothesis (that the groups come from identical populations) can be rejected at the .05 level.

(a)	Group 1	Group 2	Group 3
	1	1	8
	2	2	7
	1	1	8
	2	2	7

(b)	Group 1	Group 2	Group 3
	1	4	8
	2	5	7
	1	4	8
	2	5	7

3. An industrial psychologist was interested in whether individuals working in different sectors of the company differed in their attitudes toward the company. The results for the three people surveyed in engineering were 10, 12, and 11; for the three in the marketing department, 6, 6, and 8; for the three in accounting, 7, 4, and 4; and for the three in production, 14, 16, and 13 (higher numbers mean more positive attitudes). Was there a significant difference in attitude toward the company among employees working in different sectors of the company at the .05 level? Explain your answer to a person who knows about hypothesis testing using the t test for independent means but is unfamiliar with the analysis of variance.

4. Do students at various colleges differ in how sociable they are? Twenty-five students were randomly selected from each of three colleges in a particular city and were asked to report on the amount of time they spent socializing each day with other students. The results for College X was a mean of 5 and an estimated population variance of 2; for College Y, $M = 4$, $S^2 = 1.5$; and for College Z, $M = 6$, $S^2 = 2.5$. What should you conclude? Use the .05 level, and explain your answer to a person who has never had a course in statistics.

5. An experiment is conducted in which 60 subjects each fill out a personality test, but not according to the way the subjects see themselves. Instead, 15 are randomly assigned to fill it out according to the way they think their mother sees them (that is, the way they think their mother would fill it out to describe the subject); 15 as their father would fill it out for them; 15 as their best friend would fill it out for them; and 15 as the professor they know best would fill it out for them. The main results appear in Table 11-9. Explain these results to a person who has never had a course in statistics.

6. Cut up 100 little pieces of paper of about the same size and write a 1 on 16, a 2 on 34, a 3 on 34, and a 4 on 16 of them (you are creating an approximately normal distribution). Put the slips into a bowl or hat, mix them up, draw out two, write the numbers on them down, and put them back. Then draw out another two, write down their numbers, and put them back, and finally another two, write down their numbers, and put them back. (Strictly speaking, you should sample "with replacement"—that means putting each *one*, not two, back after writing its number down—but we want to save you a little time, and it should not make very much difference in this case.) Then compute an analysis of variance for these three randomly selected groups of two each. Write down the F ratio, and repeat the entire drawing process and analysis of variance again. Do this entire process at least 20 times, and make a frequency polygon of your results. You are creating an F distribution for 2 (3 groups – 1) and 3 (2 – 1 in each of three groups) degrees of freedom. At what point do the top 5% of your F scores begin? Compare that to the 5% cutoff given on the F table in Appendix B for 2 and 3 degrees of freedom.

TABLE 11-9
Means for Main Personality Scales for Each Experimental Condition (Fictional Data)

Scale	Mother	Father	Friend	Professor	$F(3, 56)$
Conformity	24	21	12	16	4.21**
Extroversion	14	13	15	13	2.05
Maturity	15	15	22	19	3.11*
Self-confidence	38	42	27	32	3.58*

*$p < .05$. **$p < .01$.

12 The Structural Model in the Analysis of Variance

C HAPTER 11 introduced the basic logic of the analysis of variance. To review, the core principle is that we make two estimates of the population variance. One estimate, called the between-group population variance estimate (S_B^2 or MS_B), is based on the variation among the means of the groups. The other, called the within-group population variance estimate (S_W^2 or MS_W), is based on the variation of the scores within each of the groups. If the null hypothesis is true, these two estimates of the population variance should be about the same, and so the ratio of the between-group to the within-group estimate, the F ratio, should be about 1. But when the null hypothesis is false, the between-group estimate will be influenced by the differences among the means of the populations and hence will be larger than the within-group estimate, and the F ratio in this case will be greater than 1. In hypothesis testing, we compare our computed F ratio to a cutoff level (obtained from the F table) that indicates the point at which there is only a 5% (or 1%) or less chance of getting an F this extreme if the null hypothesis is true.

Building on this understanding, this chapter explores an alternative (but mathematically equivalent) way of understanding the analysis of variance, called the **structural model**. The core logic you learned in Chapter 11 still applies. However, the structural model provides a different and more flexible way of computing the two population variance estimates. This more flexible method makes it easier to handle the situation in which the number of subjects in each group are not equal, a major new situation we consider in this chapter. Further, understanding the structural model gives some deeper insights into the underlying logic of the analysis of variance. Finally, understanding the structural model approach will help you make sense of the way analysis of variance results are laid out in computer printouts and sometimes in research articles.

structural model

FIGURE 12-1

Example from the fictional criminal record study of the deviation of one subject's score from the grand mean being that subject's score's deviation from his or her group's mean plus that subject's group's mean's deviation from the grand mean.

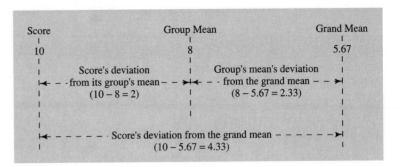

Principles of the Structural Model

Dividing Up the Deviation

The core idea of the structural model is to think of each score in terms of its overall deviation being divided into two parts. By the overall deviation, we are referring to the deviation of the score from the grand mean. The grand mean is the mean of *all* the scores, regardless of the group they are in. In the criminal record study example considered in Chapter 11, the grand mean of the 15 scores was 85/15 = 5.67. In the risk takers example from that chapter, the grand mean of the 54 scores was 10.25.

This deviation of each score from the grand mean can be divided into two parts: (a) the deviation of the score from the mean of its group and (b) the deviation of the mean of its group from the grand mean. (Before too long, rest assured, we will be using these to compute our two familiar population variance estimates, one based on within-group and the other on between-group variations. But for now, just follow along this new approach.)

Consider, for example, the subject in the criminal record study whose score was the first in the column for the criminal record group in Table 11-2. This subject rated the defendant's guilt as a 10. Since the grand mean of all subjects' guilt ratings was 5.67, this person's score has a total deviation of 4.33 (10 − 5.67 = 4.33). The mean of the criminal record group by itself was 8. Thus the deviation of this person's score from his or her group's mean is 2 (10 − 8 = 2), and the deviation of that group's mean from the grand mean is 2.33 (8 − 5.67 = 2.33). Note that these two deviations—2 and 2.33—add up to the total deviation of 4.33. This is illustrated in Figure 12-1. Study it until you grasp it well.

Summing Up the Squared Deviations

sum of squared deviations

It is possible to square each of these deviation scores and to add them up over all the subjects to get a **sum of squared deviations** for each type of deviation score. If you do so, it turns out that the sum of squared deviations of each score from the grand mean is equal to (a) the sum of the squared deviations of each score from its group's mean plus (b) the sum of the squared deviations of each score's group's mean from the grand mean. This principle can be stated as a formula:

$$\Sigma(X - GM)^2 = \Sigma(X - M)^2 + \Sigma(M - GM)^2 \quad \text{or} \quad SS_T = SS_W + SS_B \quad (12\text{-}1)$$

where $\Sigma(X - GM)^2$ or SS_T (T for total) is the sum of squared deviations of each score from the grand mean, completely ignoring the group a score is in; $\Sigma(X - M)^2$ or SS_W (W for within-group, as in Chapter 11) is the sum of squared deviations of each score from its group's mean, over all groups; and $\Sigma(M - GM)^2$ or SS_B (B for between-group, as in Chapter 11) is the sum of squared deviations of each score's group's mean from the grand mean, over all the groups.

(This rule applies only to the *sum* of all the scores. For each individual score, the deviations themselves always add up, but not the squared deviations.)

From the Sums of Squared Deviations to the Population Variance Estimates

Now we are ready to use these sums of squared deviations to compute our two needed population variance estimates. This is done by dividing each sum of squared deviations by an appropriate degrees of freedom. The between-group population variance estimate (S_B^2 or MS_B) is the sum of squared deviations of each score's group's mean from the grand mean (SS_B) divided by the degrees of freedom on which it is based (df_B, the number of groups minus 1). Stated as a formula,

$$S_B^2 = \frac{\Sigma(M - GM)^2}{df_B} \qquad \text{or} \qquad MS_B = \frac{SS_B}{df_B} \qquad (12\text{-}2)$$

The within-group population variance estimate (S_W^2 or MS_W) is the sum of squared deviations of each score from its group's mean (SS_W) divided by the total degrees of freedom on which this is based (df_W; the sum of the degrees of freedom over all the groups—the number of scores in the first group minus 1, plus the number in the second group minus 1, etc.). Stated as a formula,

$$S_W^2 = \frac{\Sigma(X - M)^2}{df_W} \qquad \text{or} \qquad MS_W = \frac{SS_W}{df_W} \qquad (12\text{-}3)$$

Note that in computing the population variance estimates, we have ignored the sum of squared deviations of each score from the grand mean (SS_T). This sum of squares is useful mainly for checking our arithmetic in computing the other two sums of squares (since these other two must add up to SS_T).

Figure 12-2 again shows the division of the deviation score into two parts, but this time emphasizing which deviations are associated with which population variance estimates.

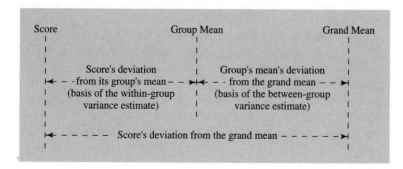

FIGURE 12-2
The score's deviations from its group's mean is the basis for the within-group population variance estimate; the group's mean's deviation from the grand mean is the basis for the between-group population variance estimate.

The logic of this structural model approach is that if the null hypothesis is true, all of the deviation of a score from the grand mean—both the part from differences between groups and the part from differences within groups—is due to the same sorts of utterly random variation. Sometimes there will be a little more variation among scores from their group mean and sometimes a little more variation among group means from the grand mean. But on the average, these two variations should be the same. (We need adjust only for our familiar principle that variation among means tends to be much less than variation among individual scores. In the case of the structural model, we make this adjustment when we divide the various sums of squares by their appropriate degrees of freedom.)

The result of all this is that, on the average, if the null hypothesis is true, we expect the between-group and the within-group population variance estimates to be about the same—to have a 1:1 ratio, an F of 1. Conversely, when the null hypothesis is false, meaning that the population means are different from each other, the deviation of a score's group's means from the grand mean is likely to take up a larger share of the overall deviation of the score from the grand mean. Thus when the research hypothesis is true, we expect the ratio of the between-group to the within-group population variance estimates based on these deviations, the F ratio, to be greater than 1.

Relation of the Structural Model Approach to the Chapter 11 Method

The methods we have just described for computing the within-group and between-group variance estimates using the structural model approach give exactly the same result as the methods you learned in Chapter 11 for calculating these two variance estimates. (If you enjoy algebra, you might see if you can derive the earlier formulas from the ones you have just learned.) The computational procedures, however, are quite different. For example, in this chapter's structural model approach, when figuring the within-group variance estimate method, you never actually compute the variance estimate for each group and average them. Similarly, for the between-group estimate, with this structural model approach, you never multiply anything by the number of cases in each sample. In any case, the point is that with either method, you get the ingredients (the within-group and between-group variance estimates) for computing an F ratio, and either way, the result comes out the same.

The deeper logic of the analysis of variance with the structural model is also essentially the same as what you learned in Chapter 11, with a twist. What is the same is that if the null hypothesis is true, the two population variance estimates should be about equal, and if the null hypothesis is false, the between-group estimate should be greater (because differences among population means contribute to it) than the within-group estimate. The twist is one of emphasis. The approach you learned in Chapter 11 emphasizes entire groups, comparing a variance based on differences among group means to a variance based on averaging variances of the groups. The structural model approach emphasizes individual scores, comparing a variance

BOX 12-1

Analysis of Variance as a Way of Thinking About the World

The analysis of variance is a wonderfully basic idea worth looking at a little more, not only because it is the way you will think more and more as you read or conduct research, but also because it is in fact the way you think already.

In conducting any research (or trying to decide on the quality of a study you are reading), you are interested in whether a certain variable really makes a difference. So you organize two (or more) groups between which you wish to show that any difference present is there purely because one group received the variable's influence and the other did not. For example, to see the effect of entering into conversations on friendship formation, you have one group converse with a stranger every day for a week and one group do nothing special and then look for a difference in number of new friendships. To be certain that the difference shows up if there is one, you equalize the impact on the two groups of anything else that might be able to cause that same difference: No one is to join any clubs or go to any parties that week. You also try to control any other "random" effects that could allow so much variation that it would be easy for one group to be different for extraneous reasons. For example, you do not enlist people who differ greatly from normal in their physical attractiveness or who do not speak English fluently. (This is not the same as group matching, discussed in Chapter 11, when the groups are systematically made the same on some variable.)

This sort of standard thinking about the research design itself parallels the logic of the analysis of variance, a purely statistical technique. As one of the classic textbooks on research design (Kerlinger, 1973) puts it, "The main technical function of research design is to control variance" (p. 306). That is, researchers want to maximize the variance of the variable or variables of the research hypothesis (the numerator, or between-group variance) and to control the extraneous variables not under study and other random or error variance (all of which contribute to the denominator, or within-group variance). So the analysis of variance is very similar to the way researchers think as they plan an experiment.

We also said, however, that the analysis of variance is similar to how you have always thought. Kelley (1971) has suggested that we are all scientists at heart, forming hypotheses and testing them, and that our method of making distinctions and deciding about causation uses analysis of variance reasoning. Suppose that we are new to a country, and as we travel, we observe a blond woman dropping letters into a bright blue domed box. If we see other blonde women dropping letters into green boxes, red bins, purple cylinders, and yellow canisters, we build up the data for the important variable being the hair color and gender of the person (we make the person the numerator, the between-group variance). The container can vary and is unimportant (we make it the denominator, the within-group variance). But if we see many other sorts of persons putting letters always into bright blue domed boxes, we know that the boxes are the between-group difference that matters, the persons just random stuff. (In Canada, they would be red boxes.)

Likewise, as naive psychologists, we may wonder about the concept called honesty. Is it a trait of certain people, or does everyone "have a price"? Doubtless you have observed people and situations throughout your life and have your own theory, which reflects which you think is larger, the numerator, the trait of honesty, or the denominator, the effect of situations (such as the size of a bribe, whether others will know if one was honest, etc.).

If you are familiar with the developmental psychologist Jean Piaget, you will recognize that analysis of variance–type thinking is part of what he called "formal operations," the style of abstract thinking normally acquired around age 14. So you should have no trouble grasping the analysis of variance—you have been innocently using it for years!

based on deviations of individual scores' groups' means from the grand mean to a variance based on deviations of individual scores from their group's mean. Also, the Chapter 11 method focuses directly on what contributes to the overall population variance estimate, whereas the structural model approach focuses directly on what contributes to the divisions of the deviations of scores from the grand mean.

These logical differences are fairly subtle, and in the end, they boil down to the same thing. So if the computations and logic are both about the same, why have we asked you to learn two different ways of thinking about this? We taught you the Chapter 11 method mainly because it is more intuitive. It is especially suitable for helping you grasp what the population variance estimates are about and why they should be the same when the null hypothesis is true and not the same when it isn't. In addition, with that method, an analysis of variance can be computed in a straightforward way from means and variances of groups, without needing to work directly with scores. However, as we said at the start of this chapter, it is important to introduce you to the structural model because (a) it has been the most widely used (in part because it is closer to the computational formulas that so long dominated everyone's thinking), (b) it is more flexible and thus easier for you to use when working with unequal-sized groups (as you will see in this chapter) and with factorial analysis of variance (introduced in Chapter 13), and (c) it is related to a fundamental mathematical approach to which we wanted to be sure to expose those of you who might be going on to more advanced statistics courses.

Using the Structural Model to Conduct an Analysis of Variance

This method of conducting an analysis of variance, by dividing up the overall deviation into parts, is illustrated for the criminal record example in Table 12-1. This table shows all three types of deviations and squared deviations for each score. For example, for the first person, the deviation from the grand mean is 4.33 (that is, the score of 10 minus the grand mean of 5.67), and this deviation squared is 18.74. The deviation of the score from its group's mean is 2, and this deviation squared is 4. Finally, the deviation of the score's group's mean from the grand mean is 2.33, and this deviation squared is 5.43. (Note that the deviations of each score's group's mean from the grand mean is the same number for all the scores in a group.) At the bottom of each row we have also summed the squared deviations of each type.

The bottom part of Table 12-1 shows the analysis of variance computations. After figuring out all three sums of squared deviations (SS_T, SS_W, and SS_B), the next step is to check for accuracy, following the principle that the sum of squared deviations of each score from the grand mean comes out to the sum of the other two kinds of squared deviation scores.

Computing the degrees of freedom, the next step shown in the table, is done the same way as we did in Chapter 11. Then the table shows the computations of the two crucial population variance estimates, computed by dividing the appropriate sum of squared deviations by its corresponding degrees of freedom. Finally, the table shows the computation of the F ratio in the usual way by dividing the between-group variance estimate by the

TABLE 12-1
Analysis of Variance for the Criminal Record Study Using the Structural Model Approach (Fictional Data)

Criminal Record Group

X	X – GM		X – M		M – GM	
	Deviation	Squared deviation	Deviation	Squared deviation	Deviation	Squared deviation
10	4.33	18.74	2	4	2.33	5.43
7	1.33	1.77	–1	1	2.33	5.43
5	– .67	.45	–3	9	2.33	5.43
10	4.33	18.74	2	4	2.33	5.43
8	2.33	5.43	0	0	2.33	5.43
$\overline{40}$		$\overline{45.13}$		$\overline{18}$		$\overline{27.14}$

$M = 40/5 = 8$

Clean Record Group

X	X – GM		X – M		M – GM	
	Deviation	Squared deviation	Deviation	Squared deviation	Deviation	Squared deviation
5	– .67	.45	1	1	–1.67	2.79
1	–4.67	21.81	–3	9	–1.67	2.79
3	–2.67	7.13	–1	1	–1.67	2.79
7	1.33	1.77	3	9	–1.67	2.79
4	–1.67	2.79	0	0	–1.67	2.79
$\overline{20}$		$\overline{33.95}$		$\overline{20}$		$\overline{13.95}$

$M = 20/5 = 4$

No Information Group

X	X – GM		X – M		M – GM	
	Deviation	Squared deviation	Deviation	Squared deviation	Deviation	Squared deviation
4	–1.67	2.79	–1	1	–.67	.45
6	.33	.11	1	1	–.67	.45
9	3.33	11.09	4	16	–.67	.45
3	–2.67	7.13	–2	4	–.67	.45
3	–2.67	7.13	–2	4	–.67	.45
$\overline{25}$		$\overline{28.25}$		$\overline{26}$		$\overline{2.25}$

$M = 25/5 = 5$

Sums of squared deviations:

$\Sigma(X - GM)^2$ or $SS_T = 45.13 + 33.95 + 28.25 = 107.33$

$\Sigma(X - M)^2$ or $SS_W = 18 + 20 + 26 = 64$

$\Sigma(M - GM)^2$ or $SS_B = 27.14 + 13.95 + 2.25 = 43.34$

Check ($SS_T = SS_W + SS_B$): $SS_T = 107.33$; $SS_W + SS_B = 64 + 43.34 = 107.34$
  (slight difference due to rounding error)

Degrees of freedom:

$df_T = N - 1 = 15 - 1 = 14$

$df_W = df_1 + df_2 + \ldots + df_{Last} = (5 - 1) + (5 - 1) + (5 - 1) = 4 + 4 + 4 = 12$

$df_B = N_G - 1 = 3 - 1 = 2$

Check ($df_T = df_W + df_B$): $14 = 12 + 2$

Population variance estimates:

S_W^2 or $MS_W = SS_W/df_W = 64/12 = 5.33$

S_B^2 or $MS_B = SS_B/df_B = 43.34/2 = 21.67$

F ratio: $F = S_B^2/S_W^2$ or $MS_B/MS_W = 21.67/5.33 = 4.07$

within-group variance estimate. All these figures—degrees of freedom, variance estimates, and F—come out to exactly the same figures (within rounding error) as we computed in Chapter 11.

Analysis of Variance Tables

analysis of variance table

An **analysis of variance table** is a chart produced by computers (originally by hand) in computing an analysis of variance. Its content reflects the structural model. It has columns for the *source* (the type of variance estimate or deviation score involved), *SS* (the sum of squared deviations), *df* (degrees of freedom), *MS* (mean squares—that is, *SS* divided by *df*, the variance estimate, which is also called S^2 but in an analysis of variance table is almost always referred to as *MS*), and *F* (the *F* ratio). Each row of the table refers to one of the variance estimates. The first row is for the between-group variance estimate and is usually identified (under "Source") as "Between" or "Group," although you will sometimes see it called "Model" or "Treatment." The second row is for the within-group variance estimate and is usually presented as "Within" or "Error." The final row is for the sum of squares based on the total deviation of each score from the grand mean and is usually called simply "Total." Table 12-2 is an analysis of variance table filled in for the criminal record study example.

When the results of an analysis of variance are displayed in a table in a research article, usually either *SS* or *MS* is given, but not both. Note also that the layout of this table emphasizes that you can check the accuracy of the computations of sums of squared deviations and degrees of freedom by seeing that the between and within figures add up to the total. (However, the total *MS*, if you were to compute it, would not ordinarily equal $MS_B + MS_W$.)

Analysis of Variance with Unequal-Sized Groups

Now we come to one reason why we have taught you this second approach. The analysis of variance may be easier to understand as we taught it in Chapter 11, but it is often easier to compute as we teach it in this chapter. One such case is when the groups are of unequal size. Of course, computers do most of the computing. But when the computer uses the method in this chapter and gives you output expressed in its terms, it is important that you be able to understand it all.

TABLE 12-2
Analysis of Variance Table for the Criminal Record Study (Fictional Data)

Source	SS	df	MS	F
Between	43.34	2	21.67	4.07
Within	64	12	5.33	
Total	107.33	14		

Whether groups have the same or different numbers of cases, the basic logic of the analysis of variance—the comparison of estimates of the population variance based on between-group versus within-group variation—is still always the same. But the procedures for computing the within- and between-group variance estimates you learned in Chapter 11 would require complex adjustments to give appropriate weighting to the information obtained from the different-sized groups.

The structural model approach works out so that it automatically makes these adjustments for unequal sample sizes. For example, in computing the within-group variance estimate, the influence of each group is automatically weighted proportionately because the number of deviations included in the sum of squared deviations from each group is precisely the number of cases in that group.[1]

An Example

Let's consider another analysis of variance example (again fictional, to keep things simple), but this time with unequal-sized groups. Suppose that a researcher at an alcohol treatment center decides to compare the effectiveness of three different treatment methods used at this center, which we will call Treatment A, Treatment B, and Treatment C. The researcher randomly assigns each of the available 10 clients to receive one of these treatments; 4 clients end up with Treatment A, 3 with Treatment B, and 3 with Treatment C. Now suppose further that 2 weeks later, client satisfaction with the three programs is measured on a scale that yields scores ranging from 1 to 20. Results, computations, and the analysis of variance table are shown in Table 12-3; the various distributions involved are illustrated in Figure 12-3. We will follow the usual hypothesis-testing procedure step by step.

[1]Another advantage of the approach to the analysis of variance that you learned in Chapter 11, besides its usefulness in clarifying the underlying logic, is that it permits you to compute an analysis of variance using only the means and estimated population variances. This can be useful when the raw data are not available—for example, in computing an analysis of variance based on means and standard deviations reported in a research article. So if the sample sizes were not equal, here is how you would determine the population variance estimates using Chapter 11's method.

The computation for S_W^2 with unequal sample sizes is a direct extension of the procedure you learned in Chapter 10 for computing S_P^2, the pooled estimate of the population variance. That is, S_W^2 is the sum of the weighted S^2 for each group, the weighting being the df for that group (its N minus 1) divided by the total df for all the groups. That is,

$$S_W^2 = \frac{df_1}{df_1 + df_2 + \ldots + df_{Last}}(S_1^2) + \frac{df_2}{df_1 + df_2 + \ldots + df_{Last}}(S_2^2) + \ldots + \frac{df_{Last}}{df_1 + df_2 + \ldots + df_{Last}}(S_{Last}^2)$$

Computing S_B^2 is a bit more complex. First you compute the overall grand mean (which is not just the mean of the means): Compute the product of the mean of each group multiplied by that group's N, add up these products, and divide by the total N:

$$GM = \frac{(M_1)(n_1) + (M_2)(n_2) + \ldots + (M_{Last})(n_{Last})}{n_1 + n_2 + \ldots + n_{Last}}$$

Then you find S_B^2: Compute the product of the squared deviation of each group mean (from the grand mean) multiplied by that group's N, add these products, and divide by the between-group degrees of freedom (df_B = number of groups minus 1):

$$S_B^2 = \frac{(M_1 - GM)^2(n_1) + (M_2 - GM)^2(n_2) + \ldots + (M_{Last} - GM)^2(n_{Last})}{df_B}$$

TABLE 12-3
Analysis of Variance for the Alcohol Treatment Study (Fictional Data)

Treatment A				Treatment B				Treatment C			
X	$X-GM$	$X-M$	$M-GM$	X	$X-GM$	$X-M$	$M-GM$	X	$X-GM$	$X-M$	$M-GM$
	Dev Dev²	Dev Dev²	Dev Dev²		Dev Dev²	Dev Dev²	Dev Dev²		Dev Dev²	Dev Dev²	Dev Dev²
8	1 1	−2 4	3 9	7	0 0	1 1	−1 1	6	−1 1	2 4	−3 9
13	6 36	3 9	3 9	3	−4 16	−3 9	−1 1	4	−3 9	0 0	−3 9
10	3 9	0 0	3 9	8	1 1	2 4	−1 1	2	−5 25	−2 4	−3 9
9	2 4	−1 1	3 9								
40	50	14	36	18	17	14	3	12	35	8	27

$M = 40/4 = 10$ $M = 18/3 = 6$ $M = 12/3 = 4$

Note. Dev = Deviation; Dev² = Squared deviation

$GM = (40 + 18 + 12)/10 = 70/10 = 7$

$df_T = N - 1 = 10 - 1 = 9$

$df_W = df_1 + df_2 + \ldots + df_{Last} = (4 - 1) + (3 - 1) + (3 - 1) = 3 + 2 + 2 = 7$

$df_B = N_G - 1 = 3 - 1 = 2$

F needed for $df = 2, 7$ at the .05 level $= 4.74$

$SS_T = 50 + 17 + 35 = 102$

$SS_W = 14 + 14 + 8 = 36$

$SS_B = 36 + 3 + 27 = 66$

ANALYSIS OF VARIANCE TABLE:

Source	SS	df	MS	F
Between	66	2	33	6.42
Within	36	7	5.14	
Total	102	9		

Conclusion: Reject the null hypothesis.

---

1. Reframe the question into a research hypothesis and a null hypothesis about the populations. The populations of interest are these:

Population 1: Alcoholics receiving Treatment A
Population 2: Alcoholics receiving Treatment B
Population 3: Alcoholics receiving Treatment C

The null hypothesis is that these three populations have the same mean. The research hypothesis is that they do not all have the same mean.

2. Determine the characteristics of the comparison distribution. The comparison distribution in an analysis of variance is always an F distribution. Its degrees of freedom are figured in the same way as we have all along: The within-group variance estimate is based on the number of cases minus 1 in each group, making 3 in the first group and 2 in each of the other groups, for a total of 7. The between-group variance estimate is based on three groups, making 2 degrees of freedom. Thus this will be an F distribution for 2 and 7 degrees of freedom.

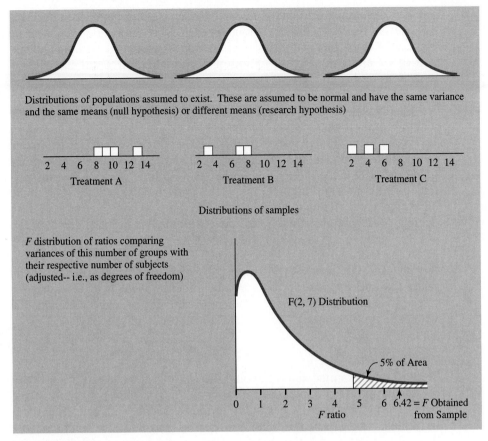

FIGURE 12-3
The distributions involved in the fictional alcohol treatment study.

3. Determine the cutoff sample score on the comparison distribution at which the null hypothesis should be rejected. Using the F table in Appendix B (Table B-3), we look down the column for 2 degrees of freedom in the numerator and stop at 7 degrees of freedom for the denominator. Using the .05 significance level (the middle figure), we find a cutoff F ratio of 4.74.

4. Determine the score of the sample on the comparison distribution. Because the comparison distribution is a distribution of F ratios, this step requires determining our sample's F ratio (using this chapter's method). The numerator, which is the between-group variance estimate, is based on the deviation of each score's group's mean from the grand mean. For example, the first score's group mean is 10 and the grand mean is 7, so this deviation is 3, making a squared deviation of 9. Summing all 10 squared deviations of this kind gives 66, as shown in the analysis of variance table ($SS_B = 66$). Next this sum of squared deviations is divided by the between-group degrees of freedom (df_B). The result, as shown in the analysis of variance table, comes out to 33. This, again, is the numerator, the between-group population variance estimate.

The denominator of the F ratio, the within-group population variance estimate, is based on the deviations of each score from its group's mean. For example, the first score is 8 and its group's mean is 10, making a deviation of –2 and a squared deviation of 4. Summing all 10 of the squared deviations of this kind gives 36. This is divided by the within-group degrees of freedom (df_W, which is 7), giving 5.14.

Finally, again, the F ratio is the between-group estimate divided by the within-group estimate, which comes out to 6.42.

When using this chapter's method and working by hand, it is wise at this point to compute the sum of squared deviations of each score from the grand mean, as done on the line in the table beginning with SS_T. This permits a check on your arithmetic, since this sum should equal the total of the other two sums of squared deviations. The same should also be done with degrees of freedom, as it was in the table with the line beginning with df_T.

5. Compare the scores obtained in Steps 3 and 4 to decide whether to reject the null hypothesis. The computed F ratio of 6.42 is more extreme than the .05 significance level cutoff point of 4.74. Thus the researcher can reject the null hypothesis and conclude (if these were real data) that the three kinds of treatments have different effects on the level of satisfaction with their treatment of alcoholic clients like those in this facility.

Another Example

We will now examine some fictional data based on results of a real study conducted by Ward, Leventhal, and Love (1988). These researchers were interested in the various coping styles used by people with cancer, particularly those who use a style that Ward and colleagues called "repression": "avoiding contact with the threat and repressing feelings and thoughts of danger." Volunteer cancer patients were given a personality test dividing them into four coping styles: (a) repression, (b) highly distressed, (c) not highly distressed (but also not repressing the distress), and (d) highly distressed and defensive about it. The researchers predicted that the repressors would differ from the other three groups in several ways, including the number of side effects they would experience from chemotherapy. Table 12-4 is based on the researchers' actual findings, somewhat simplified. The table also presents the key computations and the usual final analysis of variance table. The various distributions involved are illustrated in Figure 12-4. We analyze this example following the usual step-by-step hypothesis-testing procedure.

1. Reframe the question into a research hypothesis and a null hypothesis about the populations. These are the populations of interest:

Population 1: Cancer patients who are repressors
Population 2: Cancer patients who are highly distressed
Population 3: Cancer patients who are not highly distressed
Population 4: Cancer patients who are distressed and defensive

The null hypothesis is that these four populations have the same mean. The research hypothesis is that they do not all have the same mean.

2. Determine the characteristics of the comparison distribution. The

TABLE 12-4
Analysis of Variance Based on Ward, Levenson, and Love (1988) (Fictional Data)

Repressors				Highly Distressed Patients				Low-Distress Patients				Defensive Distressed Patients			
	Squared deviations				Squared deviations				Squared deviations				Squared deviations		
X	X − GM	X − M	M − GM	X	X − GM	X − M	M − GM	X	X − GM	X − M	M − GM	X	X − GM	X − M	M − GM
7	9	1	4	11	1	0	1	10	0	1	1	11	1	0	1
8	4	0	4	10	0	1	1	12	4	1	1	11	1	0	1
10	0	4	4	12	4	1	1					11	1	0	1
7	9	1	4												
32	22	6	16	33	5	2	3	22	4	2	2	33	3	0	3

$M = 32/4 = 8$ $\qquad$ $M = 33/3 = 11$ $\qquad$ $M = 22/2 = 11$ $\qquad$ $M = 33/3 = 11$

$GM = (32 + 33 + 22 + 33)/12 = 10$

$df_T = N - 1 = 12 - 1 = 11.$

$df_W = df_1 + df_2 + \ldots + df_{Last} = (4 - 1) + (3 - 1) + (2 - 1) + (3 - 1) = 3 + 2 + 1 + 2 = 8$

$df_B = N_G - 1 = 4 - 1 = 3$

F needed for $df = 3, 8$ at .05 level $= 4.07$

$SS_T = 22 + 5 + 4 + 3 = 34$

$SS_W = 6 + 2 + 2 + 0 = 10$

$SS_B = 16 + 3 + 2 + 3 = 24$

ANALYSIS OF VARIANCE TABLE:

Source	SS	df	MS	F
Between	24	3	8	6.4
Within	10	8	1.25	
Total	34	11		

Conclusion: Reject the null hypothesis.

comparison distribution is an F distribution with 3 and 8 degrees of freedom, as shown in Figure 12-4.

3. Determine the cutoff sample score on the comparison distribution at which the null hypothesis should be rejected. From Table B-3, with 3 degrees of freedom in the numerator and 8 in the denominator, we find a cutoff at the .05 level of 4.07 (see Figure 12-4).

4. Determine the score of your sample on the comparison distribution. Table 12-4 shows the computations of the sample's F ratio using this chapter's structural model–based method. The numerator, which is the between-group population variance estimate based on the deviations of each score's group's mean from the grand mean, comes out to 8. The denominator, the within-group population variance estimate based on the variation of each score from its group's mean, comes out to 1.25. Thus the F ratio is 6.4.

5. Compare the scores obtained in Steps 3 and 4 to decide whether to reject the null hypothesis. Because the sample's F of 6.4 exceeds the cutoff F of 4.07, we can reject the null hypothesis and conclude that the four kinds of coping styles are associated with different amounts of side effects from chemotherapy (see Figure 12-4).

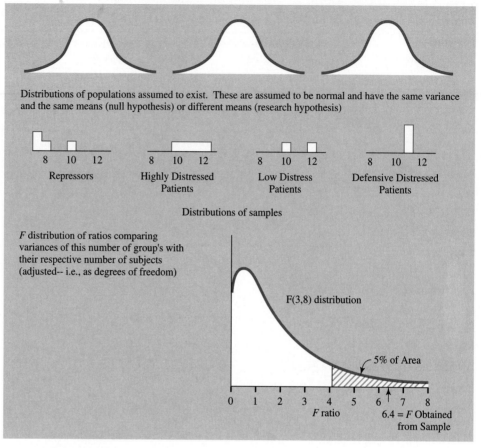

Distributions of populations assumed to exist. These are assumed to be normal and have the same variance and the same means (null hypothesis) or different means (research hypothesis)

8 10 12	8 10 12	8 10 12	8 10 12
Repressors	Highly Distressed Patients	Low Distress Patients	Defensive Distressed Patients

Distributions of samples

F distribution of ratios comparing variances of this number of group's with their respective number of subjects (adjusted-- i.e., as degrees of freedom)

F(3,8) distribution

5% of Area

0   1   2   3   4   5   6   7   8
F ratio

6.4 = F Obtained from Sample

FIGURE 12-4
The distributions involved in the analysis of variance for the fictional data based on Ward, Leventhal, and Love (1988).

Summary of Procedures for Computing an Analysis of Variance Using the Structural Model–Based Method

The top half of Table 12-5 summarizes the steps in conducting an analysis of variance using this chapter's method. The bottom half shows an analysis of variance table with the symbols for all the parts inserted in each section where the numbers would usually go, followed by the same style of analysis of variance table with the various formulas filled in where the numbers would usually go. Note that the only real difference from the procedure you learned in Chapter 11 is in Step 4, Substeps b through g. And remember, this is the method to use when groups are of different sizes.

Computational formulas for the analysis of variance based on the structural model approach (and thus suitable for use with unequal sample sizes) are given in the appendix to this chapter.

Multiple Comparisons

In an analysis of variance, when the null hypothesis is rejected, this implies that the population means are not all the same. What is not clear, however, is which population means differ from which. For example, in the criminal

TABLE 12-5
Steps, Symbols, and Formulas for Computing an Analysis of Variance Using the Structural Model–Based Method (Equal or Unequal Sample Sizes)

Hypothesis-Testing Steps

1. Reframe the question into a research hypothesis and a null hypothesis about the populations.
2. Determine the characteristics of the comparison distribution.
   a. The comparison distribution will be an F distribution.
   b. The numerator degrees of freedom is the number of groups minus 1: $df_B = N_G - 1$.
   c. The denominator degrees of freedom is the sum of the degrees of freedom in each group (the number of cases in the group minus 1): $df_W = df_1 + df_2 + \ldots + df_{Last}$.
   d. Check the accuracy of your computations by making sure that df_W and df_B sum to df_T (which is the total number of cases minus 1).
3. Determine the cutoff sample score on the comparison distribution at which the null hypothesis should be rejected.
   a. Determine the desired significance level.
   b. Look up the appropriate cutoff in an F table.
4. Determine the score of the sample on the comparison distribution. (This will be an F ratio.)
   a. Compute the mean of each group and the grand mean of all scores.
   b. Compute the following deviations for each score:
      i. Its deviation from the grand mean $(X - GM)$.
      ii. Its deviation from its group's mean $(X - M)$.
      iii. Its group's mean's deviation from the grand mean $(M - GM)$.
   c. Square each of these deviation scores.
   d. Compute the sums of each of these three types of deviation scores (SS_T, SS_W, and SS_B).
   e. Check the accuracy of your computations by making sure that $SS_W + SS_B = SS_T$.
   f. Compute the between-group variance estimate: SS_B/df_B.
   g. Compute the within-group variance estimate: SS_W/df_W.
   h. Compute the F ratio: $F = S_B^2/S_W^2$.
5. Compare the scores in Steps 3 and 4 to decide whether to reject the null hypothesis.

Symbols Corresponding to Each Part of an Analysis of Variance Table

Source	SS	df	MS	F
Between	SS_B	df_B	MS_B (or S_B^2)	F
Within	SS_W	df_W	MS_W (or S_W^2)	
Total	SS_T	df_T		

Formulas for Each Part of an Analysis of Variance Table

Source	SS	df	MS	F
Between	$\Sigma(M - GM)^2$	$N_G - 1$	SS_B/df_B	MS_B/MS_W
Within	$\Sigma(X - M)^2$	$df_1 + df_2 + \ldots + df_{Last}$	SS_W/df_W	
Total	$\Sigma(X - GM)^2$	$N - 1$		

Definitions of Basic Symbols

Σ = sum of the appropriate numbers for all cases
M = mean of a score's group
GM = grand mean
N_G = number of groups
X = each score
N = total number of cases in the study

record study, the sample of jurors in the criminal record group assigned the most guilt ($M = 8$), the no information jurors the second most guilt ($M = 5$), and the clean record jurors the least guilt ($M = 4$). From the analysis of variance results we concluded that the true means of the three populations these groups represent are not all the same. But it is not even guaranteed (though it is likely) that the two most extremely different groups—the criminal record and the clean record groups—do not represent populations with the same mean. It is certainly not clear whether or not the no information group's population mean should be considered to be different from either of the other two groups' population means.

multiple comparisons

The determination of which particular population means differ is called making **multiple comparisons** because there are usually several pairs of means being compared. Multiple comparisons is a complex topic that is usually covered in some detail in the intermediate statistics course. It is also an area with a great deal of controversy.

There is one thing, however, on which almost everyone agrees. It is usually *not* sufficient simply to compute a series of *t* tests, one for each possible pair of means. Without modification, this kind of procedure is too likely to yield what appears to be a significant result. For example, with three groups, there are three possible *t* tests (Group 1 versus 2, 2 versus 3, and 1 versus 3). If each of the three possible *t* tests has a .05 chance of being wrongly significant, the chance that at least one of the set of three *t* tests will be wrongly significant is close to 15%. With four groups, there could be six comparisons, which means that if you used the .05 level for each test, you would have an overall risk of nearly 30% that at least one will be significant just by chance.[2] Furthermore, a researcher may want to make additional comparisons that are not simply of one group to another—for example, an average of three groups compared to a fourth (perhaps the first three are different types of experimental groups and the fourth is a control group). Thus the number of comparisons, even with a fairly small number of groups, can be quite large.

The controversy comes in when statisticians try to agree on the best alternative to simply carrying out a bunch of *t* tests. The solutions available depend in part on the situation.

Planned Comparisons

planned comparisons

One kind of situation is when the researcher has decided in advance to look at some particular small number of comparisons that are directly related to the theory or to some practical application. These are called **planned comparisons** (or sometimes *a priori comparisons* or *planned contrasts*) because they have been planned in advance of the study. For example, in the criminal record study, the researcher may have decided in advance that the only

---

[2]Actually, the probability of getting at least one of three significant by chance at the .05 level is .143 and of getting at least one in six is .265. The formula for three tests is $1 - (1 - \alpha)(1 - \alpha)(1 - \alpha)$, with α representing the significance level—in this case, .05. With six possibilities, the formula is 1 minus what you get when you multiply out $(1 - \alpha)$ six times.

comparisons of interest are the criminal record group versus the clean record group and the criminal record group versus the no information condition. (Actually, with only two comparisons, it is often considered acceptable to do two *t* tests without any special adjustments—but we will use this example to illustrate the concepts in this discussion.)

One widely used approach to analyzing planned comparisons is the **Bonferroni procedure**. This approach requires the use of a more stringent significance level for each comparison so that the overall chance of any one of the comparisons being mistakenly significant is still reasonably low. For example, if each of two planned comparisons used the .025 significance level, the overall chance of any one of them being mistakenly significant would still be less than .05; with three planned comparisons, you could use the .017 level (3 times .017 gives .05); and so forth.

Bonferroni procedure

Post Hoc Comparisons

The other situation employing multiple comparisons occurs after the study is completed, when the researcher is simply fishing through the results to see which populations differ from each other. These are called **post hoc comparisons** (or *a posteriori comparisons*) because they are not planned in advance. For example, beforehand the researcher in the criminal record study may not have narrowed down the possible comparisons on the basis of specific hunches about which were important. The researcher is simply interested in which of the three groups differ from each other. So there are three possible comparisons (more if we consider such comparisons as those that compare one group to the combination of the other two).

post hoc comparisons

In post hoc comparisons, all possible comparisons have to be considered in evaluating the chance of any one of them turning out to be significant. For this reason, using the Bonferroni procedure for post hoc comparisons, though safe, would give very low power. The .05 level would be cut into so many pieces that getting any one comparison to come out significant would be a long shot. So statisticians have developed a variety of procedures to use in these fishing expeditions, procedures that attempt to keep the overall alpha at some level like .05 while at the same time not too drastically reducing power. You may see some of these referred to in articles you read, described by the names of their developers—the Scheffé, Tukey, and Neuman-Keuls methods are the most widely used. Which procedure is best under various conditions is still not settled and remains a topic of dispute. You will learn more about the possibilities and controversies if you take an intermediate statistics course.

Effect of Different Methods of Conducting Multiple Comparisons

Planned comparisons are almost always more powerful than post hoc comparisons, and the fewer planned comparisons, the more power. Thus when a researcher is genuinely in a position, in advance, to narrow down the number of comparisons that will be worth carrying out, using a solid rationale, it can make a real difference in the final conclusion.

However, in most real-life situations, the outcome is pretty much the same whatever planned comparison procedure is used. This is true for post hoc comparisons as well. If a result is so close that the method used matters, the result should probably be taken with some caution in any case. What does matter is that the researcher uses an appropriate method for dealing with the risks of multiple comparisons, whether planned or post hoc, and does not merely conduct a series of 50 t tests as if each were its own world.

Assumptions in the Analysis of Variance with Unequal Sample Sizes

We considered the assumptions for the analysis of variance in Chapter 11. However, when the sizes of the groups are not close to equal, the procedure is much more sensitive to violations of the equal-variance assumption. In fact, with unequal sample sizes, the analysis of variance becomes suspect when the most extremely different population variance estimates (among those from the different samples) are even as much as $1\frac{1}{2}$ times the other.

Effect Size and Power

In Chapter 11, we introduced f, an indicator of effect size for the analysis of variance based on the standard deviation of the means of the populations divided by the average variance within each of the populations. In terms of estimated values, $f = S_M/S_W$. We also mentioned that you could manipulate the formula so that when evaluating the effect size in a completed experiment, you could estimate f directly from knowing the F value and number of subjects per cell: $f = \sqrt{F}/\sqrt{n}$. In addition, we noted Cohen's (1988) conventions for f: for a small effect size, $f = .10$; for a medium effect size, $f = .25$; and for a large effect size, $f = .40$. Finally, we provided power tables and minimum sample size tables for the analysis of variance, based on these conventions for small, medium, and large effect sizes, all as defined by f. And f remains a completely appropriate effect size to use, whether the analysis of variance is computed using the method of Chapter 11 or the structural model approach of this chapter.

However, as we also noted in Chapter 11, a disadvantage of f as a measure of effect size is that its magnitude is not intuitively meaningful even to most experienced researchers—when using f, the researcher is forced to rely primarily on the conventions for a sense of just how important an effect is indicated by a given size of f.

There is, however, another measure commonly used as an indicator of effect size in analysis of variance, whichever method is used. (We could not introduce this alternative measure until now because it is computed using elements in the structural model approach.) We will first describe this measure and how it is computed, then turn to how it is interpreted and why it gives a more intuitively meaningful indication of effect size than f.

Proportion of Variance Accounted For

proportion of variance accounted for (R^2)

An indicator of effect size in analysis of variance, besides f, is the **proportion of variance accounted for (R^2).**[3] Note that we use the same symbol, R^2, for the proportion of variance accounted for in an analysis of variance as we do for the proportion of variance accounted for in multiple correlation and regression (see Chapter 4). This is because, in both cases, the proportion of variance accounted for describes the extent to which variation in the dependent variable can be accounted for (predicted or explained) by the independent variable. In the context of the analysis of variance, the independent variable refers to the group that a subject is in. So the degree to which variation in the dependent variable is explained by the independent variable is the degree to which a subject's particular score is related to or determined by the group the subject is in. (We will have more to say in Chapter 16 about the many links between the analysis of variance and multiple regression and correlation.)

To be precise, R^2 is the proportion of the total variation of scores from the grand mean that is accounted for by the variation between the means of the groups. It is computed using the sums of squares in the sample data—the between-group sum of squares (SS_B) divided by the total sum of squares (SS_T). In terms of a formula,

$$R^2 = \frac{SS_B}{SS_T} \tag{12-4}$$

Consider the criminal record study. In that example, the sum of squared deviations of the scores from the grand mean was 107.33, and the sum of squared deviations of the scores' groups' means from the grand mean was 43.44. Thus the proportion of the total variation accounted for by the variation between groups is 43.44/107.33, or 40%. In terms of the formula,

$$R^2 = \frac{SS_B}{SS_T} = \frac{43.44}{107.33} = .40$$

In situations in which the sums of squares are not available (as is often true in published studies), it is also possible to compute R^2 directly from F and the degrees of freedom. The formula is

$$R^2 = \frac{(F)(df_B)}{(F)(df_B) + df_W} \tag{12-5}$$

For example, in the criminal record study,

$$R^2 = \frac{(F)(df_B)}{(F)(df_B) + df_W} = \frac{(4.07)(2)}{(4.07)(2) + 12} = \frac{8.14}{8.14 + 12} = \frac{8.14}{20.14} = .40$$

Interpreting the Proportion of Variance Accounted For

The proportion of variance accounted for is a useful indicator of effect size because it has the direct meaning embraced in its name. Further, researchers

---

[3]The proportion of variance accounted for is also occasionally referred to as the *correlation ratio*. At other times, you may see it symbolized as η^2, the Greek letter "eta" squared.

TABLE 12-6
Cohen's Conventions for Effect Sizes in a One-Way Analysis of Variance

	Effect Size		
	Small	*Medium*	*Large*
f	.10	.25	.40
R	.10	.24	.37
R^2	.01	.06	.14

are familiar with R^2 and what its various magnitudes mean from its use in correlation and regression analysis. Finally, the proportion of variance accounted for is useful because its square root, R, is a kind of correlation coefficient (see Chapters 3 and 4) that is very familiar to most researchers.

R^2, being a proportion of two positive numbers (SS_B/SS_T), has a minimum of 0 and a maximum of 1. (This is also true of its square root, R.) However, in practice it is rare for an analysis of variance to have an R^2 even as high as .50. Table 12-6 gives Cohen's (1988) conventions for effect size for R^2, along with comparable values for f and R. (With these values, when you have R or R^2 instead of f, you can still use the power and sample size tables in Chapter 11.) Note that even a large effect size for R^2 is only about 14%. Also note that at the three effect size levels shown, f and R are quite similar.[4] However, at very high levels they would not be so close—for example, an f of 1. corresponds to an R of .71. Nevertheless, at the levels of effect size common in the analysis of variance, it can be quite useful to think of f as very roughly corresponding to a correlation coefficient.

Finally, although it is common to use R^2, the proportion of variance accounted for, as an indicator of effect size, effect size is technically supposed to refer to real differences among population means, and R^2, strictly speaking, is a descriptive statistic that refers entirely to the sample situation. Its computations make no adjustments for extrapolating to the population. On the average, R^2 tends to overestimate the true proportion of variance accounted for in the population. However, so long as there is a reasonable number of subjects per group or R^2 is being used only as a rough estimate (usually the case when figuring power), the slight degree of bias is not a practical problem. So even though less biased measures are introduced in more advanced texts, R^2 will suffice in most actual research situations.

Controversies, Limitations, and Recent Developments

The implication of the analysis of variance is that we are often in a situation of comparing three or more groups (if we are comparing two groups, we could use a t test). However, Rosnow and Rosenthal (1989b) argue that such

---

[4]The exact relation between R^2 and f is $R^2 = f^2/(1 + f^2)$ and $f = \sqrt{R^2/(1 - R^2)}$. However, if you try to compute one from the other using data from an actual study, the results will not agree exactly with what you get when calculating each directly. This is because f is based on estimated population standard deviations and R^2 is a description of sample data.

"diffuse" tests are rarely very valuable. They say that in almost all cases, when we test the overall difference among three or more groups, "we have tested a question in which we almost surely are not interested" (p. 1281). In which questions *are* we interested? Comparisons between specific pairs—whether between two groups or one against a combination of groups.

Rosnow and Rosenthal are advocating that when calculating the analysis of variance, we should analyze only planned comparisons. These should replace entirely the overall F test for whether we can reject the hypothesis of no difference among population means. Traditionally, planned comparisons, when used at all, are a supplement to the overall F test. So this is a rather revolutionary idea.

Consider an example. Reissman, Aron, and Bergen (1993) randomly assigned volunteer married couples to one of three groups: (a) a group in which each couple was asked to spend 1.5 h each week doing one of several activities that the couple had previously listed as exciting, (b) a group in which the 1.5 h each week was spent doing activities previously listed as pleasant, and (c) a control group doing no special extra activities. Before and after these 10 weeks, all couples were tested on their marital satisfaction. Reissman and colleagues were not really interested in the overall comparison among the three groups. From the point of view of the theories they were examining, there were two interesting planned comparisons: the exciting group versus the pleasant group and both of these groups taken together versus the control group. (In this study, the result was that the exciting group had a significantly greater improvement in marital satisfaction than the pleasant group, but the difference between both activity groups combined versus the control group was not significant.)

Sometimes when we are testing an overall variation among groups, what we are really interested in is an even more specific relationship—for example, one group is expected to have a large effect, a second group the next largest effect, and so forth. In fact, the researcher may not just order the groups according to their expected influence but actually assign numerical weights to each group in proportion to its relative predicted degree of effect. In this situation, the researcher can carry out a special kind of planned comparison called a **linear contrast**. In essence, it is like conducting a correlation in which, for each subject, one variable is the predicted influence of the group the subject is in and the other variable is the score on what is being measured. Linear contrasts are much more powerful than an overall diffuse analysis of variance—provided that the groups really are ordered in the predicted way.

linear contrast

Let's consider an example of a study using a planned linear contrast. Alexander, Langer, Newman, Chandler, and Davies (1989) randomly assigned elderly nursing home patient volunteers to learn and practice daily one of four mental practices: (a) a general mental relaxation technique, (b) mindfulness training (a guided attention technique), (c) transcendental meditation (TM), or (d) a no-treatment control. In addition to other less dramatic measures, the groups were compared 3 years later on how many were still alive. Based on previous research and theory, Alexander and colleagues predicted a specific pattern of outcome, with TM having the most effect, mindfulness next greatest, and the other two conditions about the same and least.

(Specific relative weights were assigned as well.) Then they carried out a planned linear contrast. In fact, Alexander and associates actually cited the Rosnow and Rosenthal paper and commented that "contrasts of this type are considered preferable to using unfocused, omnibus F tests" (p. 955). (The result did support the hypothesis—the linear contrast was significant, with the most still alive in the TM condition, the next most still alive in the mindfulness condition, and the least still alive in the other two conditions. It should be noted, however, that in this particular case the result would probably have been significant using an ordinary analysis of variance.)

The Reissman and Alexander studies exemplify Rosnow and Rosenthal's advice to use planned comparisons instead of an overall analysis of variance. But this approach has not yet been widely adopted and is still controversial. The main concern about the procedure is much like the issue we considered in Chapter 7 regarding one- and two-tailed tests. If we adopt the highly targeted, planned comparisons recommended by Rosnow and Rosenthal, we lose out on finding unexpected differences not initially planned.

Multiple Comparisons as Described in Research Articles

When reporting analyses of variance, results will also commonly be presented for any multiple comparisons. Sometimes these will be described in the text of the article. Thus the results might mention that "planned comparisons were carried out between Groups A and C and between Groups C and D. Both were significant."

TABLE 12-7
Love Subscale Means for the Three Attachment Types (Newspaper Sample)

Scale Name	Avoidant	Anxious/ Ambivalent	Secure	$F(2, 571)$
Happiness	3.19_a	3.31_a	3.51_b	14.21***
Friendship	3.18_a	3.19_a	3.50_b	22.96***
Trust	3.11_a	3.13_a	3.43_b	16.21***
Fear of closeness	2.30_a	2.15_a	1.88_b	22.65***
Acceptance	2.86_a	3.03_b	3.01_b	4.66**
Emotional extremes	2.75_a	3.05_b	2.36_c	27.54***
Jealousy	2.57_a	2.88_b	2.17_c	43.91***
Obsessive preoccupation	3.01_a	3.29_b	3.01_a	9.47***
Sexual attraction	3.27_a	3.43_b	3.27_a	4.08*
Desire for union	2.81_a	3.25_b	2.69_a	22.67***
Desire for reciprocation	3.24_a	3.55_b	3.22_a	14.90***
Love at first sight	2.91_a	3.17_b	2.97_a	6.00**

Note. Within each row, means with different subscripts differ at the .05 level of significance according to a Scheffé test.
*$p < .05$.
**$p < .01$.
***$p < .001$.
From Hazan, C., & Shaver, P. (1987), tab. 3. Romantic love conceptualized as an attachment process. *Journal of Personality and Social Psychology, 52,* 511–524. Copyright, 1987, by the American Psychological Association. Reprinted by permission of the author.

For post hoc comparisons, particularly when there are a large number of groups, resulting in a very large number of comparisons, a procedure is often used in which small letters are put by the means in the tables. This indicates that the means with the same letter are not significantly different from each other; those with different letters are. (If there is no letter, that mean is not significantly different from any of the others.) For example, Table 12-7 presents the actual results on the love experience measures in the Hazan and Shaver (1987) study (our first example in Chapter 11). Consider the first row (the Happiness results). The avoidant and anxious/ambivalent groups are not significantly different from each other since they have the same letter (*a*). But both are significantly different on Happiness compared to the secure group, which has a different letter (*b*). In the Jealousy row, however, all three groups differ from one another.

When reading results of post hoc comparisons, as mentioned earlier, you will see many different procedures named, including "Neuman-Keuls," "Tukey HSD," and "Scheffé." But as we also noted, these procedures are just various approaches to testing differences in a way that attempts to make sure that the probability that any one of them will wrongly turn out significant is not unacceptably large.

For example, consider a study by Kupfersmid and Fiala (1991) comparing graduates of different kinds of applied psychology doctoral programs on their scores on the U.S. nationwide Examination for the Professional Practice of Psychology (EPPP). Kupfersmid and Fiala reported their results as follows:

> An analysis of variance was applied to EPPP scores across four program specialties: clinical, school, counseling, and PsyD [a less research-oriented doctoral degree]. The results were statistically significant $F(3, 84) = 7.52$, $p < .0001$. Post hoc testing using the Scheffé method . . . found one pairwise comparison to be statistically significant ($p < .05$). Candidates for clinical psychology programs had EPPP scores ($M = 154.99$, $SD = 8.6$) higher than those of candidates graduating from school psychology programs ($M = 144.65$, $SD = 6.33$). (p. 534)

Summary

Another approach to the analysis of variance is called the structural model. In this approach, the deviation of each score from the grand mean is divided into two parts: (a) the score's difference from its group's mean and (b) its group's mean's difference from the grand mean. These deviations, when squared, summed, and divided by the appropriate degrees of freedom, yield the same within- and between-group estimates as were obtained using the method described in Chapter 11. However, the structural model is more flexible and can be applied to situations that involve unequal numbers of subjects.

Computations using the structural model are usually summarized in an analysis of variance table, with columns for source of variation (between and within), sums of squared deviations (*SS*), degrees of freedom (*df*), population variance estimates (*MS*, which equals SS/df), and *F* (which equals MS_B/MS_W).

Assumptions are the same as for any analysis of variance, though the procedure is less robust with unequal sample sizes.

An analysis of variance is usually followed up by multiple comparisons, either planned or post hoc, that examine differences between specific pairs or subgroups of means. Such comparisons have to protect against the possibility of getting some significant results just by chance because a great many comparisons can be made.

The proportion of variance accounted for (R^2) is a readily calculable measure of analysis of variance effect size.

Some experts recommend that instead of using an analysis of variance to make diffuse, overall comparisons among several means, researchers should plan in advance to conduct specific planned comparisons, targeted directly to their theoretical questions.

Key Terms

analysis of variance table
Bonferroni procedure
linear contrast
multiple comparisons

planned comparisons
post hoc comparisons
proportion of variance accounted
  for (R^2)

structural model
sum of squared deviations
  (SS_B, SS_W, SS_T)

Practice Problems

These problems involve computation (with the assistance of a calculator). Most real-life statistics problems are done on a computer. But even if you have a computer, do this by hand to ingrain the method in your mind.

For practice in using a computer to solve statistical problems, refer to the computer section of each chapter of the study guide that accompanies this text.

All data are fictional (unless an actual citation is given). Answers to Set I are given at the back of the book.

SET I

1. The data here are the same as for Problem 2a of Set I in Chapter 11. Work out the same problem using the structural model approach, and compare your answer to what you found in Chapter 11 (use the .01 level).

Group 1	Group 2	Group 3
8	6	4
8	6	4
7	5	3
9	7	5

2. Compute an analysis of variance for the following data (at the 1% significance level):

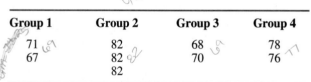
GM = 75.11

Group 1	Group 2	Group 3	Group 4
71	82	68	78
67	82	70	76
	82		

3. For each of the following data sets, compute (a) the means of each group, (b) an analysis of variance using the structural model approach (at the 5% significance level), and (c) R^2.

(i)

Group 1	Group 2	Group 3
3	0	1
4	1	2
5	2	3

(ii)

Group 1	Group 2	Group 3
3	0	1
5	0	3
	1	
	2	
	2	

4. A researcher is interested in the self-esteem levels of teachers of three different subjects. The levels of self-

TABLE 12-8
Study 1: Means for Enjoyment, Perceived Competence, and Task Characteristics Ratings by Activity Condition

Measure	Activity Condition		
	Hidden words *(n = 31)*	*Copying* *(n = 30)*	*Lettering* *(n = 29)*
Enjoyment	14.59_a	9.08_b	11.17_c
Perceived competence	9.72_a	9.89_a	7.65_b
Characteristics ratings			
Puzzle	4.59_a	1.86_b	2.31_b
Vocabulary skills	3.19_a	1.48_b	1.21_b
Eye-hand coordination	2.53_a	3.69_b	4.03_b
Compete against self	3.59_a	3.14_a	2.17_b
Artistic activity	1.97_a	1.41_a	3.66_b
Writing and drawing skills	1.78_a	2.66_a	3.86_b

Note. Possible scores range from 3 to 21 for enjoyment (midpoint = 10.5), from 2 to 14 for perceived competence (midpoint = 7), and from 1 to 5 for description ratings. Means with different subscripts differ significantly at $p < .05$.

From Sansone, C., Weir, C., Harpster, L., & Morgan, C. (1992), tab. 1. Once a boring task, always a boring task? Interest as a self-regulatory mechanism. *Journal of Personality and Social Psychology*, *63*, 379–390. Copyright 1992 by the American Psychological Association. Reprinted by permission of the author.

esteem for the four English teachers studied were 2, 2, 3, and 5. For the three math teachers studied, the self-esteem levels were 6, 4, and 5. And for the five social studies teachers studied, the levels were 9, 6, 7, 10, and 13. Do the results support a difference in the mean self-esteem levels for the three types of teachers (at the .05 level)?

Explain your answer to someone who has never taken a course in statistics but does understand mean, variance, and estimated population variance (including the notions of sample, population, and degrees of freedom).

5. A study compared the effectiveness of drug abuse prevention programs. Around North America there are four programs using Method A; their overall ratings are 13, 8, 10, and 9. Three programs use Method B; their ratings are 5, 7, and 6. And three programs use method C; their ratings are 4, 6, and 2. On the basis of these samples, should we conclude that programs using different methods have different degrees of effectiveness? Use the .05 level. Write a report to a government committee explaining your conclusions. The report should be written so that it will be understood by officials who may have never had a course in statistics.

6. Sansone, Weir, Harpster, and Morgan (1992) conducted an experiment to examine how people manage to keep up interest when carrying out boring tasks. Subjects were given a matrix of letters and randomly assigned to one of three conditions: (a) locating *hidden words* in the matrix, (b) *copying* the matrix using their own handwriting, and (c) *lettering* by trying to imitate the matrix type style exactly. After working on their task for several min-

utes, subjects answered a questionnaire about their enjoyment and about how competent they felt ("perceived competence") while doing the activity. (They also answered several other questions.) These results appear in the first two lines of Table 12-8. (Higher scores represent more enjoyment, perceived competence, and descriptiveness.) Explain the pattern of findings on Enjoyment and Perceived Competence to someone who has never had a course in statistics.

SET II

1. Problem 3 of Set II in Chapter 11 was an analysis of variance problem investigating whether individuals working in different areas of a company differed in their attitudes toward the company. The results, in terms of positiveness of attitudes, for the three people surveyed in engineering were 10, 12, and 11; for the three in the marketing department, 6, 6, and 8; for the three in accounting, 7, 4, and 4; and for the three in production, 14, 16, and 13. Work out the same problem using the structural model approach, and compare your answer to what you found in Chapter 11.

2. Compute an analysis of variance for the following data (at the 5% significance level):

Group 1	Group 2	Group 3	Group 4	Group 5
1	3	2	2	4
7	11	12	8	10
		6		8

3. Compute an analysis of variance for each of the following data sets, using the structural model approach for each (at the 5% significance level). Also compute R^2.

(a)	Group 1	Group 2	Group 3
	0	0	4
	2	2	6
		0	
		2	

(b)	Group 1	Group 2	Group 3
	0	0	4
	2	2	6
			5
			6

4. A sleep researcher compared the effect of three types of sleep disturbance (being woken at various intervals) on alertness the next morning. Originally, there were 12 subjects who were randomly assigned to one of the three conditions, making 4 per condition. However, one of the subjects in the Disturbance Schedule I condition did not follow the instructions, and this subject's data could not be used in the analysis, making unequal sample sizes. The results on the alertness measure were as follows: Disturbance Schedule I: 120, 140, 140; Disturbance Schedule II: 130, 150, 120, 140; Disturbance Schedule III: 100, 90, 110, 120. Do the results support a differential effect on alertness for the three types of disturbance schedules (at the .05 level)? Explain your answer to someone who has never taken a course in statistics but does understand mean, variance, and estimated population variance (including the notions of sample, population, and degrees of freedom).

5. Problem 5 of Set II in Chapter 10 was a t test for independent means for a pilot study of the effects of color on easing anxiety. It compared anxiety test scores of subjects who completed the test printed on either soft yellow paper or harsh green paper. The scores for five subjects who completed the test printed on yellow paper were 17, 19, 28, 21, and 18. The scores for four subjects who completed the test on the green paper were 20, 26, 17, and 24. Compute an analysis of variance for these same data. If you take the square root of the F ratio, it should come out the same (within rounding error) as the t score you computed using the t test for independent means. (We discuss this link between the t test and the analysis of variance in Chapter 16.)

6. Anderson and Ford (1986) randomly assigned 60 undergraduates to one of three experimental conditions: (a) playing a highly aggressive video game, (b) playing a mildly aggressive video game, or (c) no game. Afterward all subjects completed a questionnaire that included a measure of how hostile the subject felt at the moment. An analysis of variance showed that "the effect of the game manipulation was highly significant, $F(2, 54) = 8.45$, $p < .001$" (p. 397). Anderson and Ford continue:

Specific contrasts revealed that subjects in either of the video game conditions were reliably more hostile than those in the no-game condition, $ts(54) > 2.8$, $ps < .02$. The highly aggressive game led to slightly more hostility than did the mildly aggressive game, but not significantly so, $t = 1.1$. (p. 397)

Explain these results to a person who has never taken a course in statistics.

Chapter Appendix: Optional Computational Formulas for the Sums of Squares in a One-Way Analysis of Variance

Computational formulas for the sums of squares are as follows:

$$SS_{\mathrm{T}} = \Sigma X^2 - \frac{(\Sigma X)^2}{N} \tag{12-6}$$

$$SS_{\mathrm{B}} = \frac{(\Sigma X_1)^2}{n_1} + \frac{(\Sigma X_2)^2}{n_2} + \ldots + \frac{(\Sigma X_{\mathrm{Last}})^2}{n_{\mathrm{Last}}} - \frac{(\Sigma X)^2}{N} \tag{12-7}$$

$$SS_{\mathrm{W}} = SS_{\mathrm{T}} - SS_{\mathrm{B}} \tag{12-8}$$

where $N_1, N_2, \ldots, n_{\mathrm{Last}}$ are the number of subjects in each group.

Table 12-9 shows the calculations using these formulas for the last full example in this chapter. Compare these calculations to those shown in Table 12-4 using the definitional formulas.

TABLE 12-9
Analysis of Variance Based on Ward, Levenson, & Love (1988) Using Computational Formulas for the Sums of Squared Deviations (Fictional Data)

Repressors		Highly Distressed Patients		Low-Distress Patients		Defensive Distressed Patients	
X	X^2	X	X^2	X	X^2	X	X^2
7	49	11	121	10	100	11	121
8	64	10	100	12	144	11	121
10	100	12	144			11	121
7	49						
Σ: 32	262	33	365	22	244	33	363

$\Sigma X = 32 + 33 + 22 + 33 = 120$

$\Sigma X^2 = 262 + 365 + 244 + 363 = 1{,}234$

$$SS_T = \Sigma X^2 - \frac{(\Sigma X)^2}{N} = 1{,}234 - \frac{120^2}{12} = 1{,}234 - \frac{14{,}400}{12} = 1{,}234 - 1{,}200 = 34$$

$$SS_B = \frac{(\Sigma X_1)^2}{n_1} + \frac{(\Sigma X_2)^2}{n_2} + \ldots + \frac{(\Sigma X_{Last})^2}{n_{Last}} - \frac{(\Sigma X)^2}{N} = \frac{32^2}{4} + \frac{33^2}{3} + \frac{22^2}{2} + \frac{33^2}{3} - \frac{120^2}{12}$$

$$= \frac{1{,}024}{4} + \frac{1{,}089}{3} + \frac{484}{2} + \frac{1{,}089}{3} - \frac{14{,}440}{12} = 256 + 363 + 242 + 363 - 1{,}200 = 24$$

$$SS_W = SS_T - SS_B = 34 - 24 = 10$$

13

Factorial Analysis
of Variance

THIS chapter introduces the **factorial analysis of variance,** an extension of the procedures you learned in Chapters 11 and 12. This method provides a highly flexible and efficient approach to analyzing results of certain types of complex experiments that are very widely used in psychology.

    We are going to begin this chapter by examining in depth the nature of these complex factorial research designs, then proceed to a briefer discussion of the logic and computational procedures for a factorial analysis of variance. Our reversal of things in this chapter is for a good reason. The logic and terminology of these experimental designs will probably be new for you, whereas the logic and computational procedures involved in conducting a factorial analysis of variance are a fairly straightforward extension of what you learned in Chapter 12.

factorial analysis of variance

Basic Logic of Factorial Designs and Interaction Effects

We will introduce the idea of factorial designs and interaction effects with an example. Hobfoll and Leiberman (1987), two Israeli researchers, were interested in how married women cope with the outcome of pregnancy (normal births, miscarriages). In one of their studies, they measured the degree of depression following the end of a pregnancy, comparing women who had high or low self-esteem. But they were also interested in whether depression was different for women who had high or low intimacy with their husbands. They could have conducted two studies, one comparing women with high versus low self-esteem, another comparing women with high versus low intimacy with their husband.

TABLE 13-1
Factorial Design Employed by Hobfoll and Leiberman (1987)

		Self-Esteem	
		High	*Low*
Intimacy	*High*	a	c
	Low	b	d

Instead, they looked at both self-esteem and intimacy in a single study. That is, they considered four groups of women (see Table 13-1): (a) with high self-esteem and high intimacy, (b) with high self-esteem and low intimacy, (c) with low self-esteem and high intimacy, and (d) with low self-esteem and low intimacy.

Factorial Design Defined

factorial design

The Hobfoll and Leiberman study is an example of a **factorial design.** This refers to a study in which the influence of two or more variables is studied at once by constructing groupings that include every combination of the levels of the variables. In this case, the self-esteem and intimacy variables each had two levels (high and low), making four possible combinations, all of which were included in the study.

Efficiency of Factorial Designs

A major advantage of a factorial design over conducting separate studies of each of two (or more) hypotheses is that a factorial design is more efficient. In the example, Hobfoll and Leiberman were able to use all the women to study each research question, thus involving twice as many women in the self-esteem comparison and twice as many in the intimacy comparison.

Interaction Effects

Another advantage of a factorial design is that it permits examination of the combined influences of the variables being studied. In the example, self-esteem and intimacy might be related to depression in a simple additive way—their combined influence is just the sum of their separate influences. Or it could be that only one, or neither, has an influence. In all these cases, looking at them in combination does not add any interesting information.

However, it is also possible that the mixture of the two changes the result. Perhaps high self-esteem and high intimacy combine in a synergistic way in which the whole is more than the sum of the parts, and together they are associated with a much bigger drop in depression than would be predicted by merely adding their separate influences. Or perhaps they cancel each other out somehow when both occur together. Or perhaps self-esteem makes a difference only in the low-intimacy group or only in the high-intimacy group.

TABLE 13-2
Mean Depression Scores in the Hobfoll and Leiberman (1987) Study

		Self-Esteem	
		High	*Low*
Intimacy	*High*	18.33	20.67
	Low	17.57	32.00

Situations in which the combination of variables has a special effect that could not be predicted from knowing about the effects of each of the two variables separately is called an **interaction effect.** An interaction effect occurs when the influence of one variable changes according to the level of another variable. In the Hobfoll and Leiberman study, there was an interaction effect. As can be seen from Table 13-2, the result was that the women in three of the four combinations had very little depression, and only the low-intimacy, low-self-esteem group had very much depression. The women managed well enough without intimacy or without self-esteem, but not without both.

interaction effect

If the study had looked at each variable separately, it would have concluded that each has a moderate effect. That conclusion is technically correct but in fact misleading. For example, the average depression for all low-self-esteem women was greater than the average for all high-self-esteem women—but most of that difference was contributed by those low on intimacy. Only this combination was associated with depression. Are you developing a feeling for the importance of uncovering interaction effects?

Terminology of Factorial Designs

We shall now examine the terms used to describe various aspects of factorial designs.

Dimensions in a Factorial Design

The Hobfoll and Leiberman (1987) study is an example of what is called a **two-way factorial design.** It is two-way because there are two **dimensions,** two main variables whose influence is being studied, and when diagrammed they form a two-dimensional chart. By contrast, the situations we considered in Chapters 11 and 12 each involved a **one-way design** because each was about the influence of only one variable (such as a person's attachment style or information about a defendant's criminal record), and it could be diagrammed along a line, as a single dimension.

two-way factorial design
dimensions

one-way design

Some studies investigate the influence of three or more variables at a time. For example, Hobfoll and Leiberman might also have been interested in whether age made a difference and might have divided each of their four groups into two subgroups, younger and older. This would create eight combinations: high self-esteem, high intimacy, younger; high self-esteem, high intimacy, older; high self-esteem, low intimacy, younger; and so forth. The

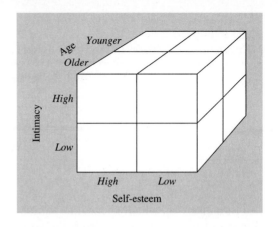

FIGURE 13-1
A three-way factorial design.

complete set of possibilities is diagrammed in Figure 13-1. Because they would be studying the influence of three variables at a time and it takes three dimensions to diagram such a study, this would be an example of a **three-way factorial design.** Although four-way and higher factorial designs cannot be diagrammed in any simple way, it is possible to conduct such studies. However, most psychology research is limited to two-way and occasionally three-way factorial designs.

three-way factorial design

Main Effects and Interaction Effects

main effect

Each variable or "way" (each dimension in the diagram) is a possible **main effect.** If the result for a variable, averaging across the other variable or variables, is significant, it is said to be a main effect. This is in contrast to the possibility of an interaction effect of the combination of variables. Thus in the Hobfoll and Leiberman study, there was a possibility of two main effects (one for self-esteem and one for intimacy) and one interaction effect (the combination of intimacy and self-esteem).

In a three-way design, there is the possibility of three main effects and four interactions. In the three-way design illustrated in Figure 13-1, there would be a possibility of one main effect for each variable: one for self-esteem, one for intimacy, and one for age. And there would be a possibility of an interaction effect for each combination of variables: one for self-esteem in combination with intimacy, one for self-esteem in combination with age, one for intimacy in combination with age, and one for intimacy in combination with self-esteem *and* age.

two-way interaction

In a two-way design, you are testing two main effects and one **two-way interaction.** In a three-way design, you are looking for three main effects, three two-way interactions, and one **three-way interaction.** (We will consider the interpretations of two- and three-way interactions shortly.) It is possible for any combination of main effects and interaction effects to be significant.

three-way interaction

Levels

levels

A factorial design is also often characterized by the number of divisions or **levels** of each variable. For example, in the Hobfoll and Leiberman study, self-esteem had two levels, high and low. Intimacy also had just two levels. Thus the Hobfoll and Leiberman study is a *2 × 2 factorial design* (the × is

TABLE 13-3
A 3 x 2 Factorial Design

	Self-Esteem		
	High	Medium	Low
Intimacy High			
Low			

read "by," so that you would pronounce *2 × 2* "two by two"). If the researchers had included younger versus older age to make a three-way factorial design, this would then be a *2 × 2 × 2 factorial design*.

Factorial experiments are not limited to two levels for each variable. For example, Hobfoll and Leiberman might have divided their subjects into high, medium, and low self-esteem (instead of just high and low). In that case (as shown in Table 13-3), they would have still had a two-way design, but with six groups (high self-esteem, high intimacy; medium self-esteem, high intimacy; low self-esteem, high intimacy; high self-esteem, low intimacy; medium self-esteem, low intimacy; and low self-esteem, low intimacy). This would then be a 3 × 2 factorial design. If they had used three levels of self-esteem and five levels of intimacy (for example, very high intimacy, high intimacy, medium intimacy, low intimacy, and very low intimacy), this would still be a two-way factorial design, but it would now be a 3 × 5 factorial design. If two levels of age were also included, it would become a three-way factorial design—a 3 × 5 × 2 factorial design.

Factorial designs with more than two levels of each variable are common in psychological research. Consider another example. Schachter, Christenfeld, Ravina, and Bilous (1991) conducted a study of the use of speech fillers (*uh, er, um*). Their theory was that people use speech fillers more when they have more options. Thus they conducted the following study. Number of fillers was counted in the speech of professors in the natural sciences, social sciences, and humanities, both when giving lectures and when being interviewed about their work with graduate students. Thus there were two variables: (a) field (natural science, social science, or humanities) and (b) situation (lecture and interview). The result was a 3 × 2 factorial design, as illustrated in Table 13-4.

Independent and Dependent Variables in Factorial Designs

Consistent with usage for experimental design generally (see Appendix A), in a factorial design the variables whose influence is being studied are *independent variables* and the variable supposedly being influenced is the

TABLE 13-4
Design of the Schachter, Christenfeld, Ravina, and Bilous (1991) Study of Speech Fillers

	Field		
	Natural science	Social science	Humanities
Situation Lecture			
Interview			

dependent variable. (Recall from Chapter 4 that when making predictions, we also call an independent variable a "predictor variable.") In the Hobfoll and Leiberman study, the independent variables were self-esteem and intimacy; the dependent variable was depression. In the Schachter study, the independent variables were field and situation; the dependent variable was number of speech fillers.

There can be two or more independent variables—the number of independent variables is the number of "ways" or dimensions of the factorial design. However, in all of the cases we consider in this book through Chapter 16, there is only one dependent variable, and it is not counted in determining the number of ways of the factorial design.

crossed

In a factorial design, the independent variables are said to be **crossed** because they are diagrammed with the levels of one crossing the levels of the other. (In the Hobfoll and Leiberman study, self-esteem is crossed with intimacy.)

Cell Means and Marginal Means

cell
cell means
marginal means

Each combination of levels of variables in a factorial design is called a **cell**. The results are usually reported as **cell means,** the mean score for the group of subjects representing a particular combination, and **marginal means** (sometimes called "marginals" for short), the mean score for all the subjects at a particular level of one of the independent variables. For example, in the Hobfoll and Leiberman study, there are four cells and four cell means—one for each combination of the self-esteem and intimacy levels.

In a 2 × 2 design such as the Hobfoll and Leiberman study, there are also four marginal means: one for *all* the high-self-esteem subjects (including both the low- and high-intimacy subjects who had high self-esteem), one for *all* the low-self-esteem subjects (whether low or high on intimacy), one for *all* the high-intimacy subjects (whether high or low on self-esteem), and one for *all* the low-intimacy subjects (you got the point). Marginal

row means, column means

means are also called **row means** and **column means,** corresponding to the dimension of the factorial design layout they represent. (Rows go across, columns up and down.) For example, as we laid out the Hobfoll and Leiberman study in Table 13-1, the two intimacy means are row means, and the two self-esteem means are column means.

To interpret a main effect, you look at the marginal means. (That is, to see which level of a variable had the higher score, you compare the mean for all subjects at one level of that variable with the mean for all subjects at the other level or levels of that variable.) To interpret an interaction effect, you look at the individual cell means, which represent the results for each combination of the independent variables.

Recognizing and Interpreting Interaction Effects

It is very important to gain a solid understanding of interaction effects. Not only are they an intrinsic part of interpreting the results of any factorial study, but also in many experiments the interaction effect is the main point of the research.

TABLE 13-5
Results of the Schachter, Christenfeld, Ravina, and Bilous (1991) Study of Speech Fillers

		Field		
		Natural science	*Social science*	*Humanities*
Situation	*Lecture*	1.45	4.09	4.85
	Interview	5.22	4.99	5.28

An interaction effect, as noted, occurs when the influence of one variable changes according to the level of another variable. In the Hobfoll and Leiberman (1987) study results (Table 13-2), there was an interaction effect because the relation of the level of self-esteem to depression changed according to the level of intimacy. If the level of intimacy was high, the level of self-esteem was unrelated to depression (both high- and low-self-esteem women had about the same levels of depression). But when the level of intimacy was low, the level of self-esteem made a huge difference on depression scores (low-self-esteem women were much more depressed).

In the study of speech fillers by Schachter and colleagues (1991), the prediction was for an interaction effect. The researchers reasoned that there are more options when lecturing in the humanities than in the social sciences and fewer options still in the natural sciences. But there should not be any difference in amount of options among these groups when they are being interviewed about their work with graduate students. The results of the study, shown in Table 13-5, confirmed this prediction. Specifically, there was an interaction such that the amount of speech fillers differed among the fields during lectures but did not differ much among the fields during interviews.

Verbal Description of Interaction Effects

An interaction effect can be made clear in three ways: verbally, numerically, and graphically. You can think out an interaction effect verbally as we have done in our examples, by saying that an interaction effect occurs whenever the influence of one independent variable changes according to the level of another independent variable. Notice also that interaction effects can be described from the point of view of either independent variable. (In a three-way factorial design, there are even more possibilities.) About our first example you can say that the relation of self-esteem to the dependent variable (depression) changes according to the level of intimacy, or you can say that the relation of level of intimacy to the dependent variable changes with the level of self-esteem. Similarly, about the number of speech fillers used, you can say that the influence of field on filler use depends on whether professors are giving lectures or being interviewed. Or you can say that professors' use of fillers when giving lectures versus when being interviewed depends on the field they are in.

Numerical Identification of Interaction Effects

You can see an interaction effect numerically by looking at the pattern of cell means. If there is an interaction effect, the differences in cell means across one row will not be the same as the differences in cell means across another row. Consider the Hobfoll and Leiberman example. The difference in the cell means across the high-intimacy row is such that the high self-esteemers (18.33) scored about the same as the low self-esteemers (20.67), the difference being only 2.34 points on the depression scale. But looking at the low-intimacy row, the cell means differ quite a bit—17.57 versus 32.00, making a difference of 14.43.

In the Schachter and associates example, in the lecture row the three kinds of professors differed quite a bit on their mean "uhs per minute"—4.85 for humanities, 4.09 for social science, and 1.45 for natural sciences, a difference between the two most extremely different means of 3.40 uhs per minute. But in the interview row, the three groups differed very much less—5.28 for humanities, 4.99 for social science, and 5.22 for natural science, a difference between the two most extremely different groups of only .29 uhs per minute.

Examples of Identifying and Verbally Describing Interaction Effects

Table 13-6 gives cell and marginal means for six possible results of a fictional 2 × 2 factorial study looking at the relation of age (younger, such as 25–29, versus older, such as 30–34) and education (high school versus college) to the dependent variable, income. These fictional results are exaggerated, to make clear when there are interactions and main effects. In real life, we often find small mean differences in the direction of an interaction or main effect that are not large enough to be statistically significant. These

TABLE 13-6
Possible Means for Results of a Study of the Relation of Age and Education to Income (Fictional Data, Thousands of Dollars)

	Outcome A				Outcome B				Outcome C		
	High School	*College*	*Overall*		*High School*	*College*	*Overall*		*High School*	*College*	*Overall*
Younger	20	20	20		30	20	25		10	30	20
Older	20	30	25		20	30	25		20	40	30
Overall	20	25			25	25			15	35	

	Outcome D				Outcome E				Outcome F		
	High School	*College*	*Overall*		*High School*	*College*	*Overall*		*High School*	*College*	*Overall*
Younger	10	10	10		20	30	25		20	30	25
Older	60	60	60		20	40	30		30	50	40
Overall	35	35			20	35			25	40	

usually represent variation due to random sampling. We will turn to significance testing later in the chapter.

In Outcome A, there is an interaction because in the "Younger" row, education makes no difference, but in the "Older" row, the college cell mean is much higher than the high school cell mean. One way to express this verbally would be to say that these results indicate that education is not related to income for the younger group, but for the older group, people with a college education earn much more than those with less education.

Fictional Outcome B is also an interaction, since in the "Younger" row the high school mean income is higher than the college mean income, but in the "Older" row the high school mean income is lower. Expressed verbally, this pattern indicates that among younger people, those with only a high school education make more money (perhaps because they entered the workplace earlier or the kinds of jobs they have start out at a higher level), but among older people those with a college education make more money.

Fictional Outcome C, interestingly, is not an interaction effect. In the "Younger" row, the high school mean is 20 lower than the college mean, and the same is true in the "Older" row. In words, whether young or old, people with college educations earn $20,000 more.

In fictional Outcome D, there is also no interaction—in neither row is there any difference. Regardless of education, older people earn $50,000 more.

Fictional Outcome E is an interaction because in the "Younger" row, the college mean is 10 higher, but in the "Older" row, the college mean is 20 higher. So among young people, college-educated people earn a little more, but among older people, those with a college education earn a lot more. (Or to put it in terms of the columns, this result is that age has no relation to income for people with only a high school education, but for those with a college education, the older they get, the more they earn.)

Finally, Outcome F is also an interaction effect because there is a smaller difference in the "Younger" row than in the "Older" row. As with Outcome E, this pattern indicates that for people with a college education, income increases more with age than it does for those with only a high school education.[1]

Table 13-7 shows possible results of another fictional study. In this 2 × 3 factorial experiment, the two independent variables are difficulty of the task (easy versus hard) and level of arousal (low, moderate, or high; in the fictional study, imagine that arousal refers to how anxious the subject is made to feel about the importance of doing well). The dependent variable is how well the subject performs a set of arithmetic tasks.

---

[1]Based on 1990 statistics from the U.S. Department of Education, the actual situation in the United States is closest to Outcome F, though not as extreme. People with a college education earn more than those with only a high school education in both age groups, but the difference is greater for the older group; for people aged 25–29, those with a college education earn about 45% more than those with only a high school education, but among people aged 30–34, those with a college education earn about 60% more than those with only a high school education. However, it is important to keep in mind that whether or not people receive a college education is also related to the social class of their parents and other factors that may affect income more than education does.

TABLE 13-7
Some Possible Outcomes of an Experiment on the Effect of Task Difficulty and Arousal Level on Performance (Fictional Data)

Outcome A

Task	Arousal Low	Moderate	High	Overall
Easy	10	10	10	10
Hard	20	20	20	20
Overall	15	15	15	

Outcome B

Task	Arousal Low	Moderate	High	Overall
Easy	10	20	30	20
Hard	10	20	30	20
Overall	10	20	30	

Outcome C

Task	Arousal Low	Moderate	High	Overall
Easy	10	20	30	20
Hard	20	30	40	30
Overall	15	25	35	

Outcome D

Task	Low	Moderate	High	Overall
Easy	10	20	30	20
Hard	10	20	60	30
Overall	10	20	45	

Outcome E

Task	Low	Moderate	High	Overall
Easy	10	20	10	13.3
Hard	20	10	20	16.7
Overall	15	15	15	

Outcome F

Task	Low	Moderate	High	Overall
Easy	10	20	30	20
Hard	30	20	10	20
Overall	20	20	20	

The interpretations of possible interactions are as follows:

Outcome A: No interaction—the cell means in the "Easy" row do not differ among themselves, and the cell means in the "Hard" row do not differ among themselves. But there is one main effect: Arousal has no impact on performance, but task difficulty does.

Outcome B: No interaction—the cell means in the "Easy" row increase by 10 from low to moderate and from moderate to high, and the cell means in the "Hard" row do the same. Again, there is only a main effect: Arousal has an impact on performance, but task difficulty does not.

Outcome C: No interaction—the cell means in the "Easy" row increase by 10 from low to moderate and from moderate to high, and the cell means in the "Hard" row do the same. Now there are two main effects: Arousal and task difficulty both affect task performance.

Outcome D: Interaction—the pattern of cell means in the "Easy" row, a difference of 10 from low to moderate and of 10 from moderate to high, is different from the pattern of cell means in the "Hard" row, a difference of 10 from low to moderate, as in the "Easy" row, but a difference of 40 from moderate to high. Thus performance on easy and hard tasks tends to improve with greater arousal, but the impact of high arousal is greater for hard than for easy tasks.

Outcome E: Interaction—the pattern of cell means in the "Easy" row is an increase of 10 and then a decrease of 10, whereas in the "Hard" row, it is a decrease of 10 and then an increase of 10. For easy tasks, performance is best under moderate arousal, but for hard tasks, performance is worst under moderate arousal.

Outcome F: Interaction—in the "Easy" row, the cell means increase as you go across, whereas in the "Hard" row, they decrease as you go across. For easy tasks, the more arousal, the better, but for hard tasks, arousal interferes with performance. (Outcome *F* is closest to a well-established finding in psychology known as the Yerkes-Dodson law.)

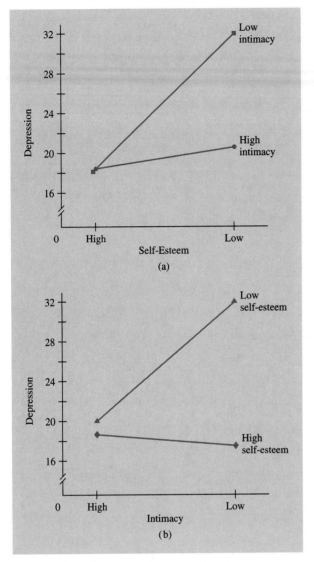

FIGURE 13-2
(a) Graph of Table 13-2 results as presented in the Hobfoll and Leiberman (1987) study. (b) Alternative version. [(a) From Hobfoll, S.E., & Leiberman, J. R. (1987). Personality and social resources in immediate and continued stress resistance among women. *Journal of Personality and Social Psychology*, 52, 18–26. Copyright, 1987, by the American Psychological Association. Used by permission of the author.]

Identifying Interaction Effects Graphically

Another common way of making sense of interaction effects is graphing them. It will really help you to understand these graphs if you read the next two sentences carefully several times. The graphs of interaction effects consist of putting the levels of one independent variable across the bottom of the graph, with height indicating mean score on the dependent variable. A line for each level of the other independent variable is then drawn in the graph.

Figure 13-2a is taken from the results graph that Hobfoll and Leiberman included in their article. The two self-esteem levels are across the bottom, and there is a line for each level of intimacy. Had they chosen, they could have drawn the graph the other way, with levels of intimacy across the bottom and a line for each level of self-esteem. This alternate graph is shown in Figure 13-2b.

FIGURE 13-3

(a) Graph of results for the Schachter, Christenfeld, Ravina, and Bilous (1991) study of speech fillers as it was printed. (b) Alternative version. [(a) From Schachter, S., Christenfeld, N., Ravina, B., & Bilous, F. (1991). Speech disfluency and the structure of knowledge. *Journal of Personality and Social Psychology*, *60*, 362–367. Copyright, 1991, by the American Psychological Association. Reprinted by permission of the author.]

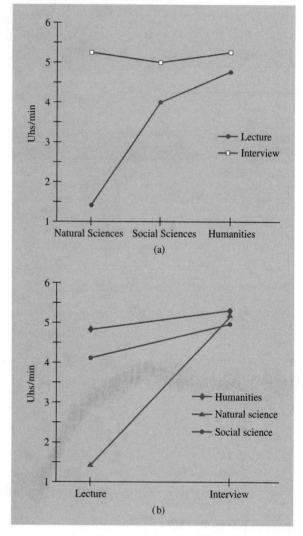

Figure 13-3a reproduces the graph from the Schachter et al. (1991) speech-filler study article. Figure 13-3b is an alternative version.[2]

The main thing to note about such graphs is this: Whenever there is an interaction, the lines in the graph will not be parallel. Being nonparallel is just a graphic way of saying that the pattern of differences between the cell means

[2]The use of lines, although common in psychology research articles, is somewhat controversial because they imply that the researcher has measured the dependent variable at each point along the scale. For example, in Figure 13-2a, which uses the data of Table 13-2, the implication of the graph seems to be that for the low-intimacy subjects, depression increases in a steady fashion from high to low self-esteem, when in fact nothing is known about what happens to depression in between high and low. (It is possible, for example, that had the in-between states been measured, this line would be curved, perhaps even taking a big jump or dive along the way.)

At least in this example, however, it makes sense to think of self-esteem as existing along a continuum, and it is possible to measure it this way even if it was not done in the study. The situation in Figure 13-3a, based on the Schachter study, is even more problematic. What is the meaning of the line that goes from natural sciences to social sciences? (Would psychology be in the middle somewhere?) Or in Figure 13-3b, how should we interpret the line from lecture to interview? (cont. on p. 379)

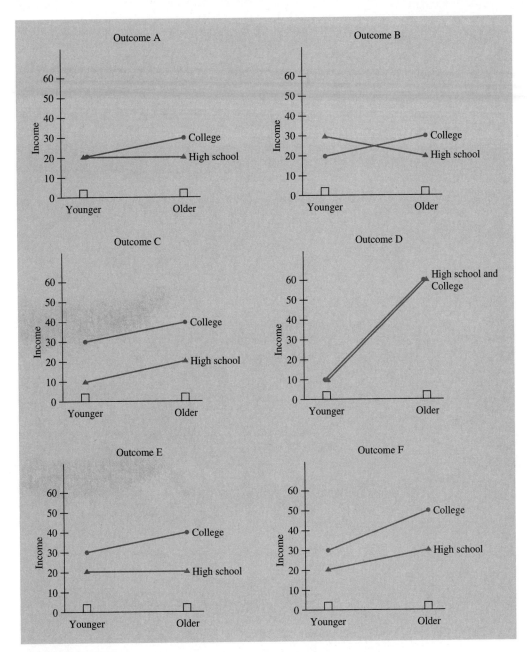

FIGURE 13-4
Graphs for the outcomes of the fictional data shown in Table 13-6.

from row to row is not the same. Figures 13-4 and 13-5 show the graphs for the same fictional outcomes shown as cell and marginal means in Tables 13-6 and 13-7, respectively. Notice that Outcomes C and D in Figure 13-4 and

The problem is that in the analysis of variance, the independent variables are always measured in categories, as opposed to continuous scales, so graphs with lines are necessarily misleading. Sometimes bar graphs are used instead—one bar per cell, with the bars for each row of cells lined up, in the same order, next to each other. But bar graphs do not make the interactions nearly as easy to see as line graphs do. In any case, because the line approach is the more common one in psychology, that is the approach we use here.

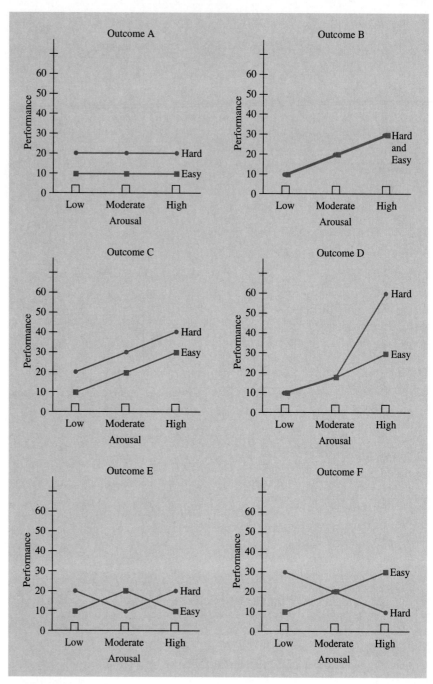

FIGURE 13-5
Graphs for the outcomes of the fictional data shown in Table 13-7.

Outcomes A, B, and C in Figure 13-5 have lines that are parallel. These were the examples that did not have interactions. All the other outcomes, which did have interactions, have lines that are not completely parallel.

Identifying and Interpreting Three-Way and Higher Interactions

In the foregoing examples, we have considered only two-way interactions. The same principles apply to three-way and higher interactions. For example, suppose that in the age and education example, the study had also included race. It might then turn out that there was a three-way interaction, such that the income of people with a college education increases faster with age for whites, but that among other racial groups, income increases at the same rate with age regardless of education. The graph for this fictional outcome is shown in Figure 13-6. Note that the simplicity of the chart and graphs of a two-way factorial design's outcome are largely lost with a three-way result.

Even psychology researchers must sometimes struggle to keep straight the meaning of a three-way interaction. Four-way and higher interactions can be extremely difficult to make sense of, particularly for a reader who is not as deeply entrenched in the terminology and methodology of the particular study as the researchers. Fortunately, even three-way interactions are only occasionally reported in the research literature, and four-way and higher interactions are very rare. (This is not necessarily because such high-order interactions do not occur. Rather, because they are so hard to make sense of when they do occur, researchers typically avoid looking for them.)

Relation of Interaction and Main Effects

We noted earlier that it is possible for any combination of main and interaction effects to be significant. For example, they may all be significant, as in the Hobfoll and Leiberman study. Or there can be an interaction effect with no main effects (a perfect crossover of effects), as in Outcome B in the age and education example. See how many possibilities you can identify in the two sets of fictional outcomes in Tables 13-6 and 13-7. (When examining the

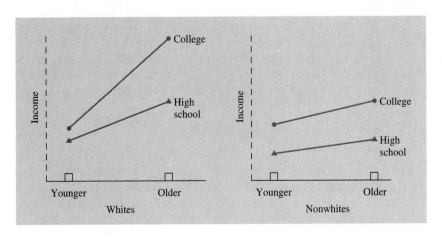

FIGURE 13-6
Graph for a three-way interaction: age, education, and race (fictional data).

corresponding graphs, Figures 13-4 and 13-5, notice that a main effect for the variable across the bottom appears as the lines averaging out to be not flat and that a main effect for the variable whose levels represent the different lines appears as one of the lines being generally higher than the other.)

When there is no interaction, a main effect has a clear and unqualified interpretation. However, when there is an interaction along with a main effect, you have to be cautious in drawing conclusions about the main effect. In the Hobfoll and Leiberman study, there were two main effects, along with the interaction. But an inspection of the cell means (or the graph) makes it clear that the main effects are entirely due to the low-self-esteem, low-intimacy cell. It would be misleading to make any statement about intimacy or self-esteem in general that was not qualified by the statement that the impact of one variable depends on the level of the other variable.

Sometimes the main effect clearly holds up over and above any interaction. For example, in Outcome F in the age and education example (Table 13-6), it seems clear that the main effect for age holds up over and above the interaction. That is, it is true for both people with and without a college education that older people earn more. (There is still an interaction, of course, because the extent to which older people earn more differs according to education.)

Basic Logic of the Two-Way Analysis of Variance

two-way analysis of variance
one-way analysis of variance

The statistical procedure for analyzing the results of a two-way factorial experiment is called a **two-way analysis of variance.** The basic logic is the same as you learned in Chapters 11 and 12, where the procedure was a **one-way analysis of variance.** The now familiar principle in any analysis of variance is this: You construct an F ratio of a population variance estimate based on the variation *between* the means of the groupings of interest to a population variance estimate based on variation *within* groups.

The Three F Ratios in a Two-Way Analysis of Variance

However, in a two-way analysis of variance, there are three F ratios: one for the column main effect, one for the row main effect, and one for the interaction effect. The numerator of each of these F ratios will be a between-group estimate corresponding to the means being compared for this particular main or interaction effect. But the within-group variance estimate is the same for all three F ratios—it is always the average of the population variance estimates made from the scores within each of the cells.

Logic of Determining the F Ratios for the Row and Column Main Effects

One way of understanding how the analysis is done for main effects is as follows. For the main effect over the columns, you compute an F ratio in which the numerator is a between-group variance estimate based on the variation between the column marginal means and the denominator is a within-group variance estimate based on averaging the variance estimates from each of the cells. In the Hobfoll and Leiberman (1987) study, this

BOX 13-1

Personality and Situational Influences on Behavior: An Interaction Effect

In Box 12-1, you saw that the analysis of variance mimics the way psychological researchers plan research and the way we all think. Knowing this parallel, whether researchers make the comparison consciously or not, they probably often use the crisp model of analysis of variance as a guide to their own logic. And they do this not only when analyzing data or even when designing research, but they probably use the analysis of variance as a metaphor when theorizing as well. The study of statistics is in a certain sense training in a style of seeing the world.

A clear example of statistics influencing the way psychologists think about their subject matter, not just their data, is in the study of personality. In the 1960s, the field of personality was forever changed by the work of Walter Mischel (1968), who appeared to have demonstrated that as a general rule, *situation* (a street signal turning red, for example, or a well-dressed person asking for help) is a far better predictor of behavior than any personality trait (for example, that a person is by nature cautious or altruistic). The embattled personality theorists, typically trained in psychodynamics, struggled to defend themselves within the rules of the game as Mischel had defined them—how much of the variance in behavior could really be predicted by their personality measures? That is, personality theorists were forced to think statistically.

One result of this challenge has been something called "interactionism" (e.g., Endler & Magnusson, 1976), the idea that behavior is best predicted by the interaction of person and situation. And you can instantly guess what statistical method has had its influence (you are studying it in this chapter).

For example, according to this model, neither the personality trait of anxiety nor the situation of taking the SAT is nearly as good a predictor of anxiety as knowing that a person with a given tendency toward anxiety perceives the taking of the SAT as an anxiety-producing situation. The emphasis is that behavior is being altered constantly by the individual's internal disposition interacting with his or her perception of the changing situation.

Let's follow an anxious man through some situations. He may feel even more or even less anxiety while proceeding from the testing situation to a dark, empty parking lot, depending again on the interaction of his trait of anxiety and his perception of this new situation. The same is true as he proceeds to drive home on the freeway, to open the garage door, to enter an empty house.

According to interactionism, the person is not a passive component but "an intentional active agent in this interaction process" (Endler & Magnusson, 1976, p. 968). The important part of the person aspect of the interaction is how a person thinks about a situation, and the important part of the situation is, again, its meaning for the person.

Interactionists admit that this sort of statistical model is still too mechanical and linear. In the real world, there is constant feedback between situation and person, something more like a transaction than an interaction. But they say that to test these models requires more complicated statistical tools—they can proceed only as fast as the development of statistical methodology and computer technology. So, as the experts in statistics produce more complicated methodologies, personality theorists will adopt them—not only as tools for data analysis but also as models in themselves of the mutual influence of the inner person and that person's outer world.

This same influence of statistics on theory is happening in cognition, perception, and learning (Gigerenzer & Murray, 1987), among many other fields of psychology. In a certain sense, we could say that pioneers in statistics are now determining not only the complexity of psychological research that is possible but also the depth of theorizing itself. They are carving out the channels through which psychologists' actual thinking patterns flow and therefore, at least for the present, are shaping and directing much of our understanding of psychology.

FIGURE 13-7
A diagram to help you understand a 2×2 factorial diagram: (a) the column between-group variance estimate as based on the difference between the mean of the subjects in the first (shaded) and second (unshaded) columns, (b) the row between-group estimate as based on the difference between the mean of the subjects in the top (shaded) and bottom (unshaded) row, and (c) the within-group variance estimate as based on the variation among scores in each cell.

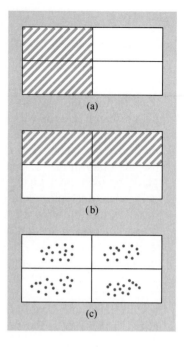

would mean that the F ratio for self-esteem (which is the columns variable as we have drawn the chart) would be a ratio of (a) a between-group variance estimate based on the difference between the high-self-esteem marginal mean and the low-self-esteem marginal mean and (b) a within-group variance estimate based on averaging the four population variance estimates corresponding to the four cells.

The procedure for the row main effect is the same, except, of course, that it would involve a between-group variance estimate based on the difference between the two row marginal means (the high-intimacy marginal mean versus the low-intimacy marginal mean in the example) but still using the same within-group estimate used in the F ratio for the column main effect.

Maybe you will find a two-way analysis of variance easier to understand if you see pictures of the comparisons. Figure 13-7a shows the column between-group variance estimate as based on the difference between the mean of the scores in the first column (the shaded area) and the mean of the scores in the second column (the unshaded area). Figure 13-7b shows the row between-group estimate as based on the difference between the mean of the scores in its top row (the shaded area) and the mean of the scores in the bottom row (the unshaded area). And Figure 13-7c shows the within-group variance estimate (used for all the F ratios) as based on the variation among the scores in each of the cells.

Logic of Determining the F Ratio for the Interaction Effect

The logic of the F ratio for the interaction effect is a bit more complex. It is also a ratio of a between-group estimate to a within-group estimate. And the within-group estimate is also the average of the population variance estimates made from all the individual cells—the same number that is used for the denominator of each of the main effect F ratios. What is not obvious is how to compute the between-group variance estimate for the interaction effect.

One approach is to think of the interaction effect as a description of the combinations left over after considering the row and column main effects. That is, in a 2 × 2 design, the main effects have grouped the four cells into rows and columns. But it is also possible to divide the cells into other kinds of groupings. As shown in Figure 13-8, in the Hobfoll and Leiberman study, a remaining possible organization of the four cells is as follows: (a) one grouping of two cells consisting of the upper left cell (high self-esteem, high intimacy) along with the lower right cell (low self-esteem, low intimacy) and (b) another grouping of two cells consisting of the lower left cell (high self-esteem, low intimacy) and the upper right cell (low self-esteem, high intimacy). The between-group variance estimate for the interaction effect can then be determined by using the means of these two groupings.

With a 2 × 2 design, as in the example, there is only one organization of pairs of cells that is not already accounted for by the row and column organizations—the grouping pattern shown in Figure 13-8. But with a larger two-way design, such as a 2 × 3, there is more than one way the groupings can be made, and all must be taken into account. Thus it can be quite complicated to compute the between-group variance estimate for the interaction effect using this kind of procedure when dealing with situations other than a 2 × 2 design. However, fortunately, it turns out that figuring the interaction between-group variance estimate is much more straightforward from the perspective of the structural model you learned in Chapter 12.

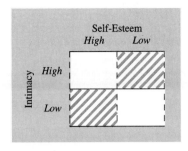

FIGURE 13-8
Interaction as a comparison of the mean of subjects in the shaded cells (high intimacy, low self-esteem and low intimacy, high self-esteem) to the mean of subjects in the unshaded cells (high intimacy, high self-esteem and low intimacy, low self-esteem) in the study by Hobfoll and Leiberman (1987).

Structural Model for the Two-Way Analysis of Variance

From the structural model perspective, each score's overall deviation from the grand mean can be divided into several components. In a two-way analysis, there are four components of this overall deviation:

1. The score's deviation from the mean of its cell. (This is used in the within-group population variance estimate.)
2. The deviation of the score's row's mean from the grand mean. (This is used in the between-group population variance estimate for the main effect for the variable spread across the rows.)
3. The deviation of the score's column's mean from the grand mean. (This is used in the between-group estimate for the main effect for the variable spread across the columns.)
4. A remaining deviation—what is left over after subtracting out the other three deviations from the overall deviation from the grand mean. (This is used in the between-group estimate for the interaction effect.)

These various deviation scores are illustrated in Figure 13-9. You might want to study this picture awhile—it is the best way to understand and remember what's going on.

Computations for the Two-Way Analysis of Variance

When conducting an analysis of variance using the structural model, the *F* ratios are found by (a) computing all the deviation scores of each type, (b) squaring them, (c) adding up the squared deviation scores of each type to

FIGURE 13-9
Partitioning of each score's deviation from the grand mean.

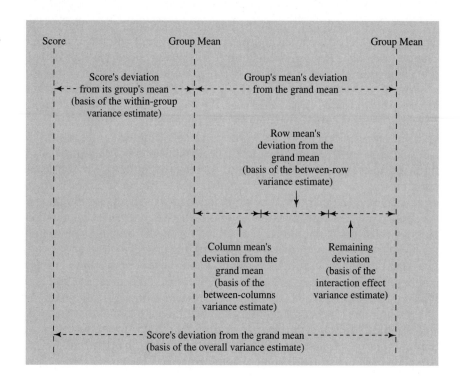

get the sums of squared deviations, (d) dividing each sum of squared deviations by its appropriate degrees of freedom to get the variance estimates, and (e) dividing the various between-group variance estimates by the within-group variance estimates.

In terms of formulas:

$$S_R^2 = \frac{\Sigma(M_R - GM)^2}{df_R} \text{ or } MS_R = \frac{SS_R}{df_R} \tag{13-1}$$

where S_R^2 or MS_R is the population variance estimate for rows, M_R is the mean of a score's row, SS_R is the sum of squared deviations for rows, and df_R is the degrees of freedom for rows.

$$S_C^2 = \frac{\Sigma(M_C - GM)^2}{df_C} \text{ or } MS_C = \frac{SS_C}{df_C} \tag{13-2}$$

where S_C^2 or MS_C is the population variance estimate for columns, M_C is the mean of a score's column, SS_C is the sum of squared deviations for columns, and df_C is the degrees of freedom for columns.

$$S_I^2 = \frac{\Sigma[(X - GM) - (X - M) - (M_R - GM) - (M_C - GM)]^2}{df_I}$$

or

$$MS_I = \frac{SS_I}{df_I} \tag{13-3}$$

where S_I^2 or MS_I is the population variance estimate for the interaction, SS_I is the sum of squared deviation for the interaction, and df_I is the degrees of freedom for the interaction.

$$S_W^2 = \frac{\Sigma(X - M)^2}{df_W} \text{ or } MS_W = \frac{SS_W}{df_W} \qquad (13\text{-}4)$$

where S_W^2 or MS_W is the within-group population variance estimate, M is the mean of a score's cell, SS_W is the sum of squared deviations within groups, and df_W is the within-group degrees of freedom.

$$F_R = \frac{S_R^2}{S_W^2} \text{ or } \frac{MS_R}{MS_W} \qquad (13\text{-}5)$$

where F_R is the F ratio for the row main effect.

$$F_C = \frac{S_C^2}{S_W^2} \text{ or } \frac{MS_C}{MS_W} \qquad (13\text{-}6)$$

where F_C is the F ratio for the column main effect.

$$F_I = \frac{S_I^2}{S_W^2} \text{ or } \frac{MS_I}{MS_W} \qquad (13\text{-}7)$$

where F_I is the F ratio for the interaction effect.

Before you can go ahead, you need to know how to figure the various degrees of freedom and how to lay out the analysis of variance table.

Degrees of Freedom for a Two-Way Analysis of Variance

Degrees of Freedom for Between-Group Variance Estimates for the Main Effects. The degrees of freedom for each main effect (each between-group variance estimate) is the number of levels of the variable minus 1. For example, if there are two levels, as in each main effect in the Hobfoll and Leiberman (1987) study, there is 1 degree of freedom. In the Schachter et al. (1991) speech filler study, the column main effect (field of study of the professors) had three levels. Thus there were 2 degrees of freedom for this main effect.

Stated as formulas,

$$df_C = N_C - 1 \qquad (13\text{-}8)$$

and

$$df_R = N_R - 1 \qquad (13\text{-}9)$$

where N_C = number of columns, and N_R = number of rows.

Degrees of Freedom for the Interaction Effect Variance Estimate. The degrees of freedom for the between-group variance estimate for the interaction effect is the total number of cells minus the number of degrees of freedom for both main effects, minus 1. In the Hobfoll and Leiberman study, there were four cells and 1 degree of freedom for each main effect—this leaves 2 degrees of freedom, minus 1 more, leaving 1 for the interaction. In the Schachter study, there were 6 cells and 2 degrees of freedom for the column effect and 1 for the row effect (lecture versus interview situation), leaving 3 degrees of freedom; when 1 more is subtracted, there are 2 left for the interaction.

Stated as a formula,

$$df_I = N_{Cells} - df_C - df_R - 1 \qquad (13\text{-}10)$$

TABLE 13-8
Layout of an Analysis of Variance Table for a Two-Way Analysis

Source	SS	df	MS	F
Between:				
Columns	SS_C	df_C	MS_C	F_C
Rows	SS_R	df_R	MS_R	F_R
Interaction	SS_I	df_I	MS_I	F_I
Within	SS_W	df_W	MS_W	
Total	SS_T	df_T		

where N_{Cells} = number of cells.
Applying the formula to the Hobfoll and Leiberman study,

$$df_I = N_{Cells} - df_C - df_R - 1 = 4 - 1 - 1 - 1 = 1$$

Applying the formula to the Schachter study,

$$df_I = N_{Cells} - df_C - df_R - 1 = 6 - 2 - 1 - 1 = 2$$

Degrees of Freedom for the Within-Group Population Variance Estimate. The within-group degrees of freedom is, as usual, the sum of the degrees of freedom for all the groups (in this case, all the cells). That is, for each cell, you take its number of cases minus 1, then add up what you get for all the cells. In terms of a formula,

$$df_W = df_1 + df_2 + \ldots + df_{Last} \tag{13-11}$$

where $df_1, df_2, \ldots, df_{Last}$ = the degrees of freedom for each cell (the number of cases in the cell minus 1), in succession, from the first cell to the last.

Table for a Two-Way Analysis of Variance

The analysis of variance table in a two-way analysis is like the ones in Chapter 12 (where we were conducting one-way analyses of variance), except that there is a row for each between-group effect. Table 13-8 shows the layout.

Example 1

Wong and Csikszentmihalyi (1991) conducted a study in which 170 high school students carried beepers for a week and filled out a form indicating what they were doing at random intervals (about every 2 waking hours) whenever beeped. The study was a 2×2 factorial design in which the independent variables were gender and student's score on a measure of desire to affiliate. The dependent variable was number of times (over the whole week) that the student was engaged in social activities when beeped. (There were other independent and dependent variables as well, but we will focus on these.)

The cell and marginal means for their results are shown in Table 13-9, exactly as reported by Wong and Csikszentmihalyi. However, to simplify our presentation of the material, we have made up scores that give the same cell and marginal means but include only 10 subjects per cell. These scores

TABLE 13-9
Cell and Marginal Means for Number of Times Engaged in Social Activities (Data from Wong & Csikszentmihalyi, 1991)

		Affiliation		
		Low	*High*	
Gender	*Boys*	10.30	9.22	9.76
	Girls	15.75	18.51	17.13
		13.03	13.87	13.45

and the computations for all the deviation scores are shown in Table 13-10. Table 13-11 shows the steps of computation using these deviation scores, including the analysis of variance table. Figure 13-10 graphs the results. We will explore the example following the usual step-by-step hypothesis-testing procedure.

1. Reframe the question into a research hypothesis and a null hypothesis about the populations for each main effect and the interaction effect. These are the populations of interest:

Population 1, 1: Girls who are low on desire for affiliation
Population 1, 2: Girls who are high on desire for affiliation
Population 2, 1: Boys who are low on desire for affiliation
Population 2, 2: Boys who are high on desire for affiliation

The first null hypothesis is that the combined populations for girls (Populations 1, 1 and 1, 2) have the same mean number of times engaged in social activities as the combined populations for boys (Populations 2, 1 and 2, 2). This is the null hypothesis for testing the main effect for gender (girls versus boys). The research hypothesis is that the populations of girls and boys have different means.

The second null hypothesis is that the combined populations for those low on desire for affiliation (Populations 1, 1 and 2, 1) have the same mean number of times engaged in social activities as the combined populations for those high on desire for affiliation (Populations 1, 2 and 2, 2). This is the null hypothesis for testing the main effect for desire for affiliation (low versus high). The research hypothesis is that populations high and low on desire to affiliate have different means.

The third null hypothesis is that the difference between the mean number of social activities of the two populations for girls (Population 1, 1 minus Population 1, 2) will be the same as the difference between the means of the two populations for boys (Population 2, 1 minus Population 2, 2). This is the null hypothesis for testing the interaction effect. (It could also be stated, with no change in meaning, as the difference between the two populations for lows equaling the difference between the two populations for highs.) The research hypothesis is that these differences will not be the same.

2. Determine the characteristics of the comparison distributions. The three comparison distributions will be F distributions with denominator degrees of freedom equal to the sum of the degrees of freedom in each of the cells (the number of cases in the cell minus 1). In this case, there are 10 subjects in each of the 4 cells, making 9 degrees of freedom for each, for a total

TABLE 13-10
Scores, Squared Deviations, and Sums of Squared Deviations for Fictional Data Based on the Wong and Csikszentmihalyi (1991) Study

	Low Affiliation						High Affiliation				
X	$(X-GM)^2$	$(X-M)^2$	$(M_R-GM)^2$	$(M_C-GM)^2$	INT^2	X	$(X-GM)^2$	$(X-M)^2$	$(M_R-GM)^2$	$(M_C-GM)^2$	INT^2
Boys											
12.1	1.82	3.24	13.62	.18	.92	11.1	5.52	3.53	13.62	.18	.92
11.4	4.20	1.21	13.62	.18	.92	10.4	9.30	1.39	13.62	.18	.92
11.2	5.06	.81	13.62	.18	.92	10.2	10.56	.96	13.62	.18	.92
10.9	6.50	.36	13.62	.18	.92	9.8	13.32	.34	13.62	.18	.92
10.3	9.92	0.00	13.62	.18	.92	9.2	18.06	0.00	13.62	.18	.92
9.8	13.32	.25	13.62	.18	.92	9.1	18.92	.01	13.62	.18	.92
9.7	14.06	.36	13.62	.18	.92	8.9	20.70	.10	13.62	.18	.92
9.5	15.60	.64	13.62	.18	.92	8.7	22.56	.27	13.62	.18	.92
9.3	17.22	1.00	13.62	.18	.92	8.2	27.56	1.04	13.62	.18	.92
8.8	21.62	2.25	13.62	.18	.92	6.6	46.92	6.86	13.62	.18	.92
103.0	109.32	10.12	136.20	1.80	9.20	92.2	193.42	14.50	136.20	1.80	9.20
Girls											
17.4	15.60	2.74	13.54	.18	.92	22.0	73.10	2.72	13.54	.18	.92
17.1	13.32	1.82	13.54	.18	.92	20.5	49.70	3.96	13.54	.18	.92
16.8	11.22	1.10	13.54	.18	.92	19.9	41.60	1.93	13.54	.18	.92
16.7	10.56	.90	13.54	.18	.92	19.1	31.92	.35	13.54	.18	.92
15.5	4.20	.06	13.54	.18	.92	18.5	25.50	0.00	13.54	.18	.92
15.3	3.42	.20	13.54	.18	.92	17.4	15.60	1.23	13.54	.18	.92
15.0	2.40	.56	13.54	.18	.92	17.0	12.60	2.28	13.54	.18	.92
15.4	3.80	.12	13.54	.18	.92	17.1	13.32	1.99	13.54	.18	.92
14.3	.72	2.10	13.54	.18	.92	17.1	13.32	1.99	13.54	.18	.92
14.0	.30	3.06	13.54	.18	.92	16.5	9.30	4.04	13.54	.18	.92
157.5	65.54	12.64	135.40	1.80	9.20	185.1	285.96	29.95	135.40	1.80	9.20

M = mean of the score's cell
M_R = mean of the score's row
M_C = mean of the score's column
INT = score's remaining deviation for the interaction

Example of computations of deviations, using the first score in the Low Boys cell:

$$(X-GM)^2 = (12.1-13.45)^2 = -1.35^2 = 1.82$$
$$(X-M)^2 = (12.1-10.30)^2 = 1.80^2 = 3.24$$
$$(M_R-GM)^2 = (9.76-13.45)^2 = -3.69^2 = 13.62$$
$$(M_C-GM)^2 = (13.03-13.45)^2 = -0.42^2 = .18$$
$$INT^2 = [(X-GM)-(X-M)-(M_R-GM)-(M_C-GM)]^2 = [(-1.35)-(1.80)-(-3.69)-(-.42)]^2$$
$$= (-1.35-1.80+3.69+.42)^2 = .96^2 = .92$$

$SS_T = 109.32 + 193.42 + 65.54 + 285.96 = 654.24$
$SS_W = 10.12 + 14.50 + 12.64 + 29.95 = 67.21$
$SS_R = 136.20 + 136.20 + 135.40 + 135.40 = 543.20$
$SS_C = 1.80 + 1.80 + 1.80 + 1.80 = 7.20$
$SS_I = 9.20 + 9.20 + 9.20 + 9.20 = 36.80$

Accuracy check: $SS_T = 654.24$; $SS_W + SS_R + SS_C + SS_I = 67.21 + 543.20 + 7.20 + 36.80 = 654.41$ (results are within rounding error).

TABLE 13-11
Computation of an Analysis of Variance Using Sums of Squares Based on the Wong and Csikszentmihalyi (1991) Study (Fictional Data)

F needed for Gender main effect ($df = 1, 36; p < .05$) = 4.12 ($df = 1, 35$ from table)
F needed for Affiliation main effect for ($df = 1, 36; p < .05$) = 4.12
F needed for interaction effect ($df = 1, 36; p < .05$) = 4.12

Source	SS	df	MS	F	
Gender	543.20	1	543.20	290.48	Reject the null hypothesis.
Affiliation	7.20	1	7.20	3.85	Do not reject the null hypothesis.
Gender × affiliation	36.80	1	36.80	19.68	Reject the null hypothesis.
Within cells	67.21	36	1.87		

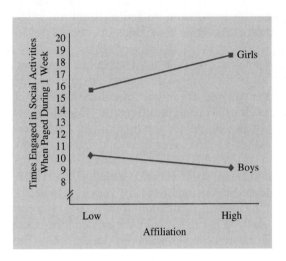

FIGURE 13-10
Graph of fictional (simplified) data based on the results of the Wong and Csikszentmihalyi (1991) study. [From Wong, M.M., & Csikszentmihalyi, M. (1991). Affiliation motivation and daily experience: Some issues on gender differences. *Journal of Personality and Social Psychology, 60,* 154–164. Copyright, 1991, by the American Psychological Association. Reprinted by permission of the author.]

of 36. The numerator for the comparison distribution for the gender main effect will have 1 degree of freedom (2 rows minus 1); the numerator for the desire for affiliation main effect also has 1 degree of freedom; and the numerator degrees of freedom for the interaction effect is, again, 1 (it is the number of cells, 4, minus the degrees of freedom for columns, minus the degrees of freedom for rows, minus 1). As a check of the accuracy of the degrees of freedom calculations, the three numerators plus the denominator degrees of freedom comes out to $1 + 1 + 1 + 36 = 39$; this is the same as the total degrees of freedom calculated as number of subjects minus 1 ($40 - 1 = 39$).

3. Determine the cutoff sample scores on the comparison distributions at which each null hypothesis should be rejected. Using the .05 significance level, Table B-3 indicates a cutoff for 1 and 35 degrees of freedom of 4.12 (the closest available on the table below 1 and 36). The degrees of freedom and the significance level are the same in this case for both main effects and the interaction, so the cutoff is the same for all three.

4. Determine the score of the sample on each comparison distribution. This step requires computing three F ratios. And these, as we have noted, require first computing various deviation scores, squaring each, and summing these squared deviations. The squared deviations for each subject are shown in Table 13-10. Notice that the table shows only the squared deviations.

Below the table of squared deviations, we show, as an example, how the squared deviations for the first score were calculated. When computing the deviation for the interaction effect, two tips will prove especially helpful: (a) Keep close track of the signs of the deviations you are subtracting, and (b) remember that this interaction deviation, prior to squaring, is computed from the original unsquared deviations, not the squared deviations.

Next, these individual squared deviations are summed to get SS_T and so on, as shown in the next portion of Table 13-10. Remember that the *sums* of the various squared deviations (SS_W, SS_R, SS_C, SS_I) add up. But within a single subject, the various squared deviations do not add up to the overall squared deviation of the score from the grand mean. Table 13-10 also shows the check for accuracy: The sum of the squared deviations from the grand mean equals the total of the sums of the other four kinds of squared deviations (within rounding error).

One other point in the computations in Table 13-10 requires comment. Ordinarily, in a 2×2 analysis, all of the squared deviations for rows are the same throughout (as are all of the squared deviations for columns and all of the squared deviations for interaction). The slight difference (136.20 versus 135.40) between the squared row deviations for the bottom-row cases versus the top-row cases is simply due to rounding error in calculating the row means.

The next steps are shown in the analysis of variance table in Table 13-11. First we entered the sum of squared deviations from the previous table for each variance estimate and also the degrees of freedom from Step 2. The rest of the table (the mean squares and the F values) were then calculated using these figures. You can see at the far right the conclusions drawn, which are discussed in Step 5.

5. Compare the scores obtained in Steps 3 and 4 to decide whether to reject the null hypotheses. The computed F ratio for the gender main effect of 290.48 is certainly more extreme than the cutoff of 4.12, so the null hypothesis that the girls' and boys' population have the same mean can be safely rejected; that is, the gender main effect (on what students were doing when beeped) is significant. The F of 3.85 for the need for affiliation main effect (on what students were doing when beeped) did not quite reach the needed 4.12 cutoff, so this effect could be said to have approached statistical significance but not to have achieved it. Finally, the interaction effect F of 19.68 exceeds 4.12, so the interaction effect is also significant. (In the actual study, the same basic pattern was found—the gender main effect and the interaction effect were significant, but the desire for affiliation main effect approached but did not quite reach significance.) Before reading further, you might try now to put into words what this interaction means.

Figure 13-10 shows the pattern of means graphically. As can be seen from the graph (and from the cell means in Table 13-9), the gender main effect is due to girls being engaged in more social activities than boys. And the interaction effect is due to desire for affiliation being associated with more social activities for girls but being essentially unrelated to number of social activities for boys. That is, there was a difference in number of activities between girls who were high and those who were low on desire for affiliation. But among boys, the difference was almost nonexistent (and even slightly in the opposite direction). This is why, overall, combining boys and girls, desire for affiliation appeared to have little or no influence on activities. You can see again how an analysis of variance to look at interaction effects uncovered an interesting relationship among these variables.

Example 2

Blanchard, Lilly, and Vaughn (1991) conducted a study of influences on the expression of reaction to racism. In this study, 72 white undergraduate women were approached while walking between classes and asked to participate in a survey. The survey asked what the college should do in response to anonymous racial notes. It was a 2×3 design. The two-level factor was whether students were asked to respond privately (on paper) or publicly (orally for the researcher and anyone else present to hear). The three-level factor was direction of influence. A third of the students were in a "no influence" condition, in which they simply completed the survey with no one other than the experimenter present. This is one level of the factor. For the other two thirds of the students, before they could begin answering, another student was invited to participate. This other student was actually a confederate of the experimenter, and it was arranged so that she always gave her responses to the questions first. Her opinions were either very antiracist or not at all antiracist, making the other two levels of the factor "antiracist influence" and "nonantiracist influence."

For purposes of clarity of exposition, we have once again constructed data that match the basic pattern of the actual findings of the study but involve many fewer subjects. We have also used whole number values. The results, using these scores, are graphed in Figure 13-11. The scores, the squared deviation scores, intermediate computations, and the analysis of variance table are all shown in Table 13-12. We shall follow the example through, step by step.

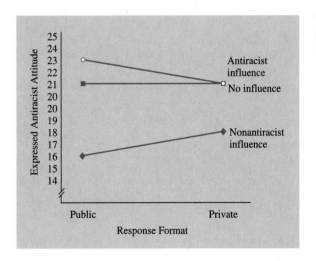

FIGURE 13-11
Graph of fictional (simplified) data based on the results of the Blanchard, Lilly, and Vaughn (1991) study.

TABLE 13-12
Analysis of Variance Computations for Fictional Data Based on Results of Blanchard, Lilly, and Vaughn (1991) study

Response Format

Public *Private*

		Public	Private	
	Antiracist influence	23	21	22
	No influence	21	21	21
	Nonantiracist influence	16	18	17
		20	20	20

Direction of Influence

F needed for main effect for response format ($df = 1, 18; p < .05) = 4.41$.
F needed for main effect for direction of influence ($df = 2, 18; p < .05) = 3.56$.
F needed for interaction effect ($df = 2, 18; p < .05) = 3.56$.

			Public Response Format						**Private Response Format**		
X	$(X-GM)^2$	$(X-M)^2$	$(M_R-GM)^2$	$(M_C-GM)^2$	INT	X	$(X-GM)^2$	$(X-M)^2$	$(M_R-GM)^2$	$(M_C-GM)^2$	INT^2

Antiracist influence

X	$(X-GM)^2$	$(X-M)^2$	$(M_R-GM)^2$	$(M_C-GM)^2$	INT	X	$(X-GM)^2$	$(X-M)^2$	$(M_R-GM)^2$	$(M_C-GM)^2$	INT^2
25	25	4	4	0	1	19	1	4	4	0	1
20	0	9	4	0	1	24	16	9	4	0	1
23	9	0	4	0	1	21	1	0	4	0	1
24	16	1	4	0	1	20	0	1	4	0	1
	50	14	16	0	4		18	14	16	0	4

No influence

22	4	1	1	0	0	24	16	9	1	0	0
19	1	4	1	0	0	18	4	9	1	0	0
22	4	1	1	0	0	22	4	1	1	0	0
21	1	0	1	0	0	20	0	1	1	0	0
	10	6	4	0	0		24	20	4	0	0

Nonantiracist influence

16	16	0	9	0	1	18	4	0	9	0	1
19	1	9	9	0	1	21	1	9	9	0	1
13	49	9	9	0	1	16	16	4	9	0	1
16	16	0	9	0	1	17	9	1	9	0	1
	82	18	36	0	4		30	14	36	0	4

M = mean of the score's cell
M_R = mean of the score's row
M_C = mean of the score's column
INT = score's remaining deviation for the interaction

Sample computations of deviations, using the first score in the Public Antiracist cell:

$$(X - GM)^2 = (25 - 20)^2 = 5^2 = 25.$$
$$(X - M)^2 = (25 - 23)^2 = 2^2 = 4.$$
$$(M_R - GM)^2 = (22 - 20)^2 = 2^2 = 4.$$
$$(M_C - GM)^2 = (20 - 20)^2 = 0^2 = 0.$$
$$INT^2 = [(X - GM) - (X - M) - (M_R - GM) - (M_C - GM)]^2 = (5 - 2 - 2 - 0)^2 = 1^2 = 1$$

$SS_T = 50 + 18 + 10 + 24 + 82 + 30 = 214$
$SS_W = 14 + 14 + 6 + 20 + 18 + 14 = 86$
$SS_C = 0 + 0 + 0 + 0 + 0 + 0 = 0$
$SS_R = 16 + 16 + 4 + 4 + 36 + 36 = 112$
$SS_I = 4 + 4 + 0 + 0 + 4 + 4 = 16$

Accuracy check: $SS_T = 214; SS_W + SS_R + SS_C + SS_I = 86 + 0 + 112 + 16 = 214$

Source	SS	df	MS	F	
Response format (columns)	0	1	0	0	Do not reject the null hypothesis.
Direction of influence (rows)	112	2	56	11.7	Reject the null hypothesis.
Interaction (columns × rows)	16	2	8	1.7	Do not reject the null hypothesis.
Within cells	86	18	4.8		

1. Reframe the question into a research hypothesis and a null hypothesis about the populations for each main effect and the interaction effect. These are the populations of interest:

Population 1, 1: Students responding publicly with antiracist influence
Population 1, 2: Students responding privately with antiracist influence
Population 2, 1: Students responding publicly with no influence
Population 2, 2: Students responding privately with no influence
Population 3, 1: Students responding publicly with nonantiracist influence
Population 3, 2: Students responding privately with nonantiracist influence

The first null hypothesis is that the combined populations of students responding publicly (Populations 1, 1; 2, 1; and 3, 1) have the same mean expression of antiracist attitudes as the combined populations of students responding privately (Populations 1, 2; 2, 2; and 3, 2). This is the null hypothesis for testing the main effect for Response Format (Public versus Private). The research hypothesis is that the populations of public and private responders have different mean expressions of antiracist attitudes.

The second null hypothesis is that there is no difference among the means of the combined populations exposed to antiracist influence (Populations 1, 1 and 1, 2), the combined populations exposed to no influence (Populations 2, 1 and 2, 2), and the combined populations exposed to nonantiracist influence (Populations 3, 1 and 3, 2). This is the null hypothesis for testing the main effect for Direction of Influence. The research hypothesis is that these three combined populations have different means.

The third null hypothesis is that the pattern of the means for the three populations responding in public (Populations 1, 1; 2, 1; and 3, 1) will be the same as the pattern of the means of the three populations responding in private (Populations 1, 2; 2, 2; and 3, 2). This is the null hypothesis for testing the interaction effect. (It could also be stated with no change in meaning as the hypothesis that the difference between the public and private response populations will be the same when comparing the two populations for antiracist influence, the two populations for no influence, and the two populations for nonantiracist influence.) The research hypothesis is that the pattern of the means of the three public response populations differs from the pattern of the means of the three private response populations.

2. Determine the characteristics of the comparison distributions. The three comparison distributions will be F distributions with denominator degrees of freedom equal to the sum of the degrees of freedom in each of the cells (the number of scores in the cell minus 1). In this case, there are 4 subjects in each of the six cells, making 3 degrees of freedom for each, for a total of 18. The numerator for the comparison distribution for the Response Format main effect will have 1 degree of freedom (2 columns minus 1); the numerator for the Direction of Influence main effect has 2 degrees of freedom (3 rows minus 1); and the numerator degrees of freedom for the interaction effect is also 2 (it is the number of cells, 6, minus the degrees of freedom for columns, 1, minus the degrees of freedom for rows, 2, minus 1). As a check for accuracy, the degrees of freedom for the three numerators plus the denominator degrees of freedom comes out to $1 + 2 + 2 + 18 = 23$; this is the same as the total degrees of freedom calculated as number of subjects minus 1 ($24 - 1 = 23$).

3. Determine the cutoff sample scores on the comparison distributions at which each null hypothesis should be rejected. Using the .05 significance level, Table B-3 gives the cutoffs shown just under the cell and marginal means at the top of Table 13-12.

4. Determine the score of the sample on each comparison distribution. This step requires computing three F ratios: computing all the deviation scores, squaring each, summing these squared deviations, dividing by the degrees of freedom to get the mean squares, and finally forming the ratios of the various between-group mean squares to the within-group mean squares, as shown in Table 13-12.

5. Compare the scores obtained in Steps 3 and 4 to decide whether to reject the null hypotheses. The computed F ratio for the Response Format main effect of 0 is certainly not significant. The F of 11.7 for the Direction of Influence main effect clearly is significant, since it far exceeds the needed F ratio of 3.56. And the interaction effect's F ratio of 1.7 did not reach the needed 3.56 cutoff, so the results remain inconclusive for this hypothesis.

Figure 13-11 shows the pattern of means graphically. As can be seen from the graph (and from the cell means at the top of Table 13-12), the Direction of Influence main effect seems to be due to the antiracist influence group expressing the most antiracist attitudes, the no direction of influence group expressing an intermediate degree of antiracist attitudes, and the nonantiracist influence group expressing the least antiracist attitudes. Note that the lines are not parallel, implying a possible interaction, but the interaction was not strong enough in this study to be significant. (It is rare to find completely parallel lines on such graphs, just as it is rare to have means exactly the same.)

Summary of Procedures for Computing a Two-Way Analysis of Variance

Table 13-13 summarizes the steps of hypothesis testing, and Table 13-14 shows the analysis of variance table and the formulas for a two-way analysis of variance. Calculational formulas and a worked-out example are given in the appendix to this chapter.

Assumptions in the Two-Way Analysis of Variance

The assumptions and the issues relating to their violation are virtually the same as those considered in Chapter 11. (In fact, as noted in that chapter, they are largely the same as for the t test for independent means.) But it should be noted that in the case of the factorial analysis of variance, the assumptions of population normality and equal variances apply to the populations corresponding to each cell.

TABLE 13-13
Steps of Hypothesis Testing for a Two-Way Analysis of Variance

1. Reframe the question into a research hypothesis and a null hypothesis about the populations for each main effect and the interaction effect.

2. Determine the characteristics of the comparison distributions.
   a. The comparison distributions will be F distributions with denominator degrees of freedom equal to the sum of the degrees of freedom in each of the cells (the number of cases in the cell minus 1): $df_W = df_1 + df_2 + \ldots + df_{Last}$.
   b. The numerator degrees of freedom for the F distribution for the columns main effect is the number of columns minus 1: $df_C = N_C - 1$.
   c. The numerator degrees of freedom for the F distribution for the rows main effect is the number of rows minus 1: $df_R = N_R - 1$.
   d. The numerator degrees of freedom for the F distribution for the interaction effect is the number of cells minus the degrees of freedom for columns, minus the degrees of freedom for rows, minus 1: $df_I = N_{Cells} - df_C - df_R - 1$.
   e. Check the accuracy of your computations by making sure that all of the degrees of freedom add up to the total degrees of freedom: $df_T = df_W + df_C + df_R + df_I$.

3. Determine the cutoff sample scores on the comparison distributions at which each null hypothesis should be rejected.
   a. Determine the desired significance levels.
   b. Look up the appropriate cutoffs in an F table.

4. Determine the score of the sample on each comparison distribution. (These will be F ratios.)
   a. Compute the mean of each cell, row, and column and the grand mean of all scores.
   b. Compute the following deviations for each score:
      i. Its deviation from the grand mean: $X - GM$.
      ii. Its deviation from its cell's mean: $X - M$.
      iii. Its row's mean's deviation from the grand mean: $M_R - GM$.
      iv. Its column's mean's deviation from the grand mean: $M_C - GM$.
      v. Its deviation from the grand mean minus all the other deviations: Interaction deviation $= (X - GM) - (X - M) - (M_R - GM) - (M_C - GM)$. (Be sure to compute this deviation using unsquared deviations and to pay close attention to signs.)
   c. Square each of these deviation scores.
   d. Compute the sums of each of these five types of squared deviation scores (SS_T, SS_W, SS_C, SS_R, and SS_I).
   e. Check the accuracy of your computations by making sure that the sum of squared deviations based on each score's deviation from the grand mean equals the sum of all the other sums of squared deviations: $SS_T = SS_W + SS_C + SS_R + SS_I$.
   f. Compute the between-group variance estimate for each main and interaction effect (MS_C or $S_C^2 = SS_C/df_C$; MS_R or $S_R^2 = SS_R/df_R$; MS_I or $S_I^2 = SS_I/df_I$).
   g. Compute the within-group variance estimate (MS_W or $S_W^2 = SS_W/df_W$).
   h. Compute the F ratios for each main and interaction effect ($F_C = S_C^2/S_W^2$ or MS_C/Ms_W; $F_R = S_R^2/S_W^2$ or MS_R/Ms_W; $F_I = S_I^2/S_W^2$ or MS_I/Ms_W).

5. Compare the scores obtained in Steps 3 and 4 to decide whether to reject the null hypotheses.

TABLE 13-14
Analysis of Variance Table and Formulas for a Two-Way Analysis of Variance

Analysis of variance table:

Source	SS	df	MS	F
Between:				
Columns	SS_C	df_C	MS_C (or S_C^2)	F_C
Rows	SS_R	df_R	MS_R (or S_R^2)	F_R
Interaction	SS_I	df_I	MS_I (or S_I^2)	F_I
Within	SS_W	df_W	MS_W (or S_W^2)	
Total	SS_T	df_T		

Formulas for each section of the analysis of variance table:

Source	SS	df	MS	F
Between:				
Columns	$\Sigma(M_C - GM)^2$	$N_C - 1$	SS_C/df_C	MS_C/MS_W
Rows	$\Sigma(M_R - GM)^2$	$N_R - 1$	SS_R/df_R	MS_R/MS_W
Interaction	$\Sigma[(X - GM)$ $- (X - M)$ $- (M_R - GM)$ $- (M_C - GM)]^2$	$N_{Cells} - N_C - N_R - 1$	SS_I/df_I	MS_I/MS_W
Within	$\Sigma(X - M)^2$	$df_1 + df_2 + \ldots + df_{Last}$	SS_W/df_W	
Total	$\Sigma(X - GM)^2$	$N - 1$		

Definitions of basic symbols:

$\Sigma =$ sum of the appropriate numbers for all *cases* (not all cells)
$M =$ mean of a score's cell
$M_R =$ mean of a score's row
$M_C =$ mean of a score's column
$GM =$ grand mean of all scores
$N_{Cells} =$ number of cells
$N_R =$ number of rows
$N_C =$ number of columns
$X =$ each score
$N =$ total number of cases in the study

Power and Effect Size in the Factorial Analysis of Variance

Power and effect size in a factorial analysis of variance are computed in about the same way as for a one-way analysis of variance (see Chapter 11), except that they must be figured separately for each main effect and interaction. It is quite possible, for example, for the power of one of the main effects to be much greater than for another main effect or for the interaction effect to have more or less power than the main effects. This means that when planning a study, to be safe, you may have to use enough subjects to attain adequate power for the effect with the smallest expected effect size. Similarly, when evaluating the results of a factorial experiment, the effect size of each main and interaction effect must be considered separately.

Effect Size

Effect size for each main and interaction effect can be computed either as f (as we did in Chapter 11) or as R^2, the proportion of variance accounted for (as we did in Chapter 12). However, in the context of the factorial analysis of variance, and especially when using the structural model approach as we have here, it is easier to work with the proportion of variance accounted for, with a small adjustment in the procedure you learned in Chapter 12.

In Chapter 12, you will recall, we described the proportion of variance accounted for as the proportion of the squared deviations of the scores from the grand mean that was accounted for by the deviations of the group means from the grand mean. That is, in a one-way analysis of variance, $R^2 = SS_B/SS_T$. However, consider the situation of the column effect in a two-way analysis of variance. We can certainly substitute SS_C for SS_B. That is, it makes sense to think of the numerator of this proportion as the sum of squared deviations of the column means from the grand mean, the variance created by the effect of the variable associated with the columns and otherwise not accounted for.

However, what about the denominator, the baseline, the variance that is to be accounted for in the proportion of variance accounted for? In a two-way analysis, the squared deviations of each score from the grand mean (SS_T—what would be the denominator for R^2 in a one-way analysis) are now partly accounted for by the row and interaction effects as well as by the column effect. But when evaluating the proportion of variance accounted for by the column effect, we are not interested in what the row effect or the interaction does—the column effect should not be held accountable for variance already accounted for by the row and interaction effects. Thus the squared deviations to be accounted for by columns should include only those squared deviations not already accounted for by rows or the interaction. To put this in terms of a formula,

$$R_C^2 = \frac{SS_C}{SS_T - SS_R - SS_I} \tag{13-12}$$

Similarly,

$$R_R^2 = \frac{SS_R}{SS_T - SS_C - SS_I} \tag{13-13}$$

$$R_I^2 = \frac{SS_I}{SS_T - SS_C - SS_R} \tag{13-14}$$

(Technically, each of these is a "partial" R^2 because it describes the proportion of variance accounted for by an effect after "partialing out" the other effects.)

In our example based on the Wong and Csikszentmihalyi (1991) beeper study, R^2 would be computed as follows:

$$R_C^2 \text{ (Affiliation)} = \frac{SS_C}{SS_T - SS_R - SS_I} = \frac{7.20}{654.24 - 543.20 - 36.80} = \frac{7.20}{74.24} = .10$$

$$R_R^2 \text{ (Gender)} = \frac{SS_R}{SS_T - SS_C - SS_I} = \frac{543.20}{654.24 - 7.20 - 36.80} = \frac{543.20}{610.24} = .89$$

$$R_I^2 \text{ (Interaction)} = \frac{SS_I}{SS_T - SS_C - SS_R} = \frac{36.80}{654.24 - 7.20 - 543.20} = \frac{36.80}{103.84} = .35$$

Thus based on the Cohen conventions for R_2 in the analysis of variance as presented in Chapter 12, there is an enormous effect size—a high R^2—for Gender and also a healthy effect size for the interaction. The nonsignificant effect for Affiliation had a medium to large effect size. (In the actual study, the effect sizes were much smaller. The effect sizes are so large in the example because we made up data with much less variance than in the study in order to show the patterns very clearly.)

If a study provides only the F values and degrees of freedom, the formula we gave in Chapter 12, $R^2 = (F)(df_B)/[(F)(df_B) + df_W]$, applies here—except that you substitute the particular effect's F and degrees of freedom. In terms of formulas,

$$R_R^2 = \frac{(F_R)(df_R)}{(F_R)(df_R) + df_W} \tag{13-15}$$

$$R_C^2 = \frac{(F_C)(df_C)}{(F_C)(df_C) + df_W} \tag{13-16}$$

$$R_I^2 = \frac{(F_I)(df_I)}{(F_I)(df_I) + df_W} \tag{13-17}$$

For example, in the beeper study, Affiliation was the column main effect. We computed F_C to be 3.85, degrees of freedom for this effect (df_C) was 1, and the degrees of freedom within cells (df_W) was 36. Thus,

$$R_C^2 = \frac{(F_C)(df_C)}{(F_C)(df_C) + df_W} = \frac{(3.85)(1)}{(3.85)(1) + 36} = \frac{3.85}{39.85} = .10$$

Power

In a factorial analysis of variance, the power of each effect is influenced by the overall structure of the design; for example, a three-level column effect will have different power if it is crossed with a two-level row effect than if it is crossed with a three-level row effect. Thus the power considerations are different for every number of levels of an effect and, for each of these levels, for the number of levels it is crossed with. However, to keep things simple, we present power figures for only the three most common two-way analysis of variance situations: all effects in a 2 × 2 design, a two-level (two-row or two-column) main effect in a 2 × 3 design, and a three-level (three-row or three-column) main effect in a 2 × 3 design. (The power of the interaction in a 2 × 3 design is the same as for the three-level main effect.) Table 13-15 presents approximate power at the .05 significance level for each of these situations for small, medium, and large effect sizes and for cell sizes of 10, 20, 30, 40, 50, and 100.[3]

For example, a planned 2 × 2 study with 30 subjects per cell and an expected medium effect size ($R^2 = .06$), to be carried out using the .05 level, would have power of .78. This means that if the research hypothesis is in fact true and has a medium effect size, the chance that the study will come out significant is about 78%. Or consider an example of a published study

[3]More detailed tables are provided in Cohen (1988, pp. 289–354). However, using these tables with a factorial design requires some preliminary computation, as explained by Cohen (pp. 364–379).

TABLE 13-15
Approximate Power for Studies Using 2×2 or 2×3 Analysis of Variance for Hypotheses Tested at the .05 Significance Level

N Per Cell	Effect Size		
	Small (f = .10) (R = .10) (R² = .01)	Medium (f = .25) (R = .24) (R² = .06)	Large (f = .40) (R = .37) (R² = .14)
All effects in a 2×2 analysis:			
10	.09	.33	.68
20	.13	.60	.94
30	.19	.78	.99
40	.24	.89	*
50	.29	.94	*
100	.52	*	*
Two-level main effect in a 2×3 analysis:			
10	.11	.46	.84
20	.18	.77	.99
30	.26	.92	*
40	.34	.97	*
50	.41	.99	*
100	.70	*	*
Three-level main effect and interaction effect in a 2×3 analysis:			
10	.09	.36	.76
20	.14	.67	.98
30	.21	.86	*
40	.27	.94	*
50	.32	.98	*
100	.59	*	*

*Nearly 1.

in which a nonsignificant result is found for an interaction effect in a 2×3 analysis of variance with 20 subjects per cell. Based on the table, power is only .14 for a small effect size, suggesting that even if such a small effect exists in the population, this study would be very unlikely to have come out significant. By contrast, the table shows a power of .98 for a large effect size, suggesting that if a large effect existed in the population, it would almost certainly have been significant in this study.

Planning Sample Size

Table 13-16 gives the approximate number of subjects per cell needed to achieve 80% power at the .05 significance level, for estimated small, medium, and large effect sizes for the same situations as were included in the power table.[4]

For example, suppose that you are planning a 2×3 analysis of variance in which you are predicting a large effect size for the main effect on the three-level variable and a medium effect size for the other main effect and interaction. To achieve 80% power (at the .05 significance level), you need 11 subjects per cell for the three-level main effect, 22 per cell for the two-level main

[4]More detailed tables are provided in Cohen (1988, pp. 381–389). If you use these, be sure to read Cohen's pages 396–403.

TABLE 13-16
Approximate Number of Subjects Needed in Each Cell (Assuming Equal Sample Sizes) to Achieve 80% Power for Studies Using a 2 × 2 or 2 × 3 Analysis of Variance, Testing Hypotheses at the .05 Significance Level

	Effect Size		
	Small *(f = .10)* *(R = .10)* *(R^2 = .01)*	*Medium* *(f = .25)* *(R = .24)* *(R^2 = .06)*	*Large* *(f = .40)* *(R = .37)* *(R^2 = .14)*
2 × 2: All effects	197	33	14
2 × 3: Two-level main effect	132	22	9
Three-level main effect and interaction	162	27	11

effect, and 27 per cell for the interaction effect. Since the whole experiment must be run at once, this means that you must have at least 27 per cell (unless you choose to risk lower power for the interaction effect). This would mean recruiting 162 subjects (27 for each of the six cells of the 2 × 3 design).

Extensions and Special Cases of the Factorial Analysis of Variance

The analysis of variance is an extremely versatile technique. Many research situations can be treated using the one-way and two-way analyses of variance just as described here and in Chapters 11 and 12. Others are more complex or have special considerations. We cannot, in this introductory book, go into the details of the statistical procedures for handling all the possibilities. (These are covered in "experimental design" textbooks—including Keppel, 1982; Kirk, 1982; or Maxwell & Delaney, 1990—or in the classic in the field, Winer, 1971.) However, it is possible to describe some of the variations and considerations and to provide some insight into the basic modifications that have to be made to what you have already learned.

Three-Way and Higher Analysis of Variance Designs

The most straightforward extension of the two-way analysis of variance is to experiments involving three-way or higher designs. In these cases, the analysis is conducted exactly as we have described in this chapter, except that there are additional main and interaction effects.

Sometimes an experiment involves variables that are of interest only if they interact with the major variables—examples of such variables are order of presentation or which of two experimenters conducted the study for each subject. In these cases, the researcher may begin with a multiway factorial analysis of variance. If these variables of secondary interest do not have significant interaction effects with the variables of primary interest, the analysis is then run again ignoring these secondary variables, and the design becomes a more manageable two- or three-way analysis of variance. The resulting analysis is said to be **collapsed** over the variables that are being ignored.

collapsed

Unequal Numbers of Subjects in the Cells

Conducting a factorial analysis of variance in the way we have described when there are unequal numbers of subjects in the cells generally turns out to give distorted results, even using the structural model approach. (With a *one-way* analysis of variance, using the structural model approach as we described it in Chapter 12 is not a problem when group sizes are unequal.)

There has been much controversy about how to deal with the issue. (One approach to which frustrated researchers sometimes resort is randomly to eliminate subjects from cells with too many—but such an approach is wasteful of power.) Now it is widely thought that a solution called the **least-squares analysis of variance** is the optimal approach, and most computer programs that compute the analysis of variance have this option available; some even use it automatically unless you indicate otherwise. (This approach is based on multiple regression analysis, which you learned something about in Chapter 4. Also note that when cell sizes are equal it gives the score result as the ordinary approach.) The result of using the least-squares approach is that each cell's influence on the main and interaction effects is equalized. This is usually what is desired. However, an influential paper (Milligan, Wong, & Thompson, 1987) suggested that this approach is not very robust to violations of the assumptions of normality or equal population variances (and other traditional approaches to the factorial analysis of variance with unequal cell sizes are just as nonrobust). Thus the best advice to researchers is to try to design studies that use equal cell sizes.

least-squares analysis of variance

Repeated-Measures Analysis of Variance

In all the cases we have considered in this chapter and Chapter 12, the different cells or groupings represented scores from different individuals. Sometimes, however, a researcher measures the same individual under several situations. (If there are only two such situations, such as before and after treatment, a dependent-means *t* test can be used, as described in Chapter 9.) For example, in a study of psychotherapy effects, patients may be measured before, right after, and again 3 months after therapy. This creates three groups of scores, but all on the same people. This would be an example of a **repeated-measures analysis of variance** design (because the same subjects are being measured repeatedly), and it would require a special analysis of variance. It is also sometimes called a "within-subject" design (because the variation is within, not between, the different subjects). Sometimes a repeated-measures variable is crossed in the same study with a between-subject variable—for example, in the therapy study, there might be a control group tested before, right after, and 3 months after undergoing some comparison procedure, such as attending an art class. This would be a mixed 2 (therapy versus control group) × 3 (before, after, 3 months after) design in which the first variable is the usual between-subject type we have been using all along and the second is a repeated-measures type. It is even possible to have two repeated-measures factors or even more complicated combinations.

repeated-measures analysis of variance

Such experimental designs involving one or more repeated-measures variables are fairly common. But there is a controversy over how they should be analyzed. One way involves a fairly straightforward extension of the procedures you have learned. However, the assumptions that must be made for this approach to give accurate results are quite stringent and are often not met in practice. Hence some researchers (e.g, Maxwell & Delaney, 1990) have argued forcefully that repeated-measures designs should always be analyzed using a much more complex "multivariate analysis of variance" procedure. Other researchers (e.g., Geisser & Greenhouse, 1958) argue for the modified normal procedure but make an adjustment to the degrees of freedom used to determine the cutoff F ratio. In any case, you should not be surprised to see repeated-measures analyses of variance reported in the research literature or discussion in such reports of the ways in which the researcher attempted to cope with the problem of not meeting special assumptions.

Limitations, Controversies, and Recent Developments

One recent development in the factorial analysis of variance is the observation by Rosnow and Rosenthal (1989a) that psychology researchers, even in articles published in the most prestigious journals, regularly and systematically demonstrate "confusion in thinking about interactions" (p. 143). This conclusion was based on a review of all the articles in the first and last issues in 1985 of nine major psychology journals. Of the 320 articles in these issues, 191 used some form of factorial analysis of variance. Of these, 37% had "clear-cut indications" of confused thinking, and in only 1% did the authors show that they had interpreted the interaction correctly. (The remainder either were ambiguous in the interpretation of their interaction effects or did not interpret them at all because they were not significant or not of theoretical interest.)

Before we consider the confusion that Rosnow and Rosenthal have emphasized, it will be worth briefly reviewing once again what we mean by an interaction effect. An interaction effect can be defined as arising when the influence of one variable changes according to the level of another variable. We have also seen that you can recognize an interaction effect if the difference between means within a column varies from one column to another. Similarly, you can recognize an interaction effect by noting whether the lines describing the means in a graph are not all parallel. Mathematically, this comes out to saying that there is a substantial amount of the between-group deviation left over in the cells when the row and column deviations are subtracted out. These ways of identifying an interaction effect are not what is in question.

Where the confusion arises, Rosnow and Rosenthal explain, is in the interpretation of an interaction effect once it has been identified. The most common method of making sense of an interaction effect is to look at the pattern of cell means. For example, when examining the results of the study of the relation of self-esteem and intimacy to depression, we noted that the level of depression was about the same in all conditions, except that it was much higher when both self-esteem and intimacy were low. Although this description is a correct interpretation of the overall result, it would not,

TABLE 13-17
Hobfoll and Leiberman (1987) Depression Scores: Original Uncorrected Cell Means and Cell Means After Subtracting Out Main Effects Following the Procedures of Rosnow & Rosenthal (1989a)

		Uncorrected Cell Means		Cell Means After Subtracting Out Main Effects	
		Self-Esteem		Self-Esteem	
		High	*Low*	*High*	*Low*
Intimacy	High	18.33	20.67	3.02	−3.02
	Low	17.57	32.00	−3.02	3.02

strictly speaking, be a correct interpretation of the interaction per se. That is, what we have interpreted when we speak in this way is the combined effect of the main and interaction effects. The interaction effect itself operates over and above the main effects. Thus an interpretation of the interaction effect itself should be of the cell means, after subtracting out the influence of the row and column effects. (Rosnow and Rosenthal call this the "residuals for the interaction.") In the case of the Hobfoll and Leiberman study, the pure interaction effect comes out to be an X. Table 13-17 shows this: The ordinary, "uncorrected" cell means (as described earlier in the chapter) do not make an obvious X, but the cell means representing the unique contribution of the interaction effect do.

In fact, in any 2 × 2 interaction effect, the pure interaction aspect always comes out as an X. There are no surprises if you use the Rosnow and Rosenthal method for a 2 × 2 experiment, except for the size of the scores that make up the X. However, with a larger than 2 × 2 design, the procedure, like peeling an onion, uncovers a pattern that is not necessarily obvious.

The point of all this is not so much that you should always go through this process of creating corrected cell means. Rather, the point is simply that you should be clear in your use of the word *interaction*. In most actual research situations, it is probably *not* really the interaction itself that is of interest. What is interesting, as it was in the Hobfoll and Leiberman study, is the pattern of the cell means, their specific expected order, and which ones are expected to be different from each other and which not. That is fine; Rosnow and Rosenthal just want to emphasize that if it is the pattern of cell means that is of interest, researchers should talk about the pattern of cell means (a pattern that is influenced by both main and interaction effects). They should not speak as if they are talking about the interaction only.

In some cases, however, it really is the interaction itself that is of main interest. This is most likely to be the case in highly theoretical studies in which the particular levels of the independent variable studied are arbitrary—as, for example, in an experiment in which the levels are high versus low intensity of a light stimulus, and just how high or how low is not really of interest. In such cases, we may really want to see what the interaction looks like over and above the influence of main effects.

Factorial Analysis of Variance Results as Reported in Research Articles

Factorial analysis of variance results are usually presented with a combination of a table and information in the text; if the interaction effect is of special interest, there will often be a graph as well. The table gives the cell means and sometimes also the marginal means. The F ratio (along with its degrees of freedom) and significance level for each main effect and interaction are written in the text of the article. The graph will usually be like those in this chapter. Sometimes, especially if the analysis was fairly complex (for example, involving more than two or three ways or within-subject), an abbreviated analysis of variance table may also be included.

Hobfoll and Leiberman (1987) described their primary result as follows:

> Mean depression scores for this analysis are presented in Table [13-2] and depicted in Figure [13-2a]. Self-Esteem, $F(1, 85) = 12.73$, $p < .001$, and Spouse Intimacy, $F(1, 85) = 5.06$, $p < .05$, and their interaction, $F(1, 85) = 6.63$, $p < .01$, were significant. Both high Self-Esteem and Spouse Intimacy resulted in lower depression at event occurrence. However, the interaction indicated that women possessing either one or both resources did equally well, whereas women having neither resource were significantly more depressed than those possessing either one or both. (p. 22)

Rosnow and Rosenthal (1989a) would probably question the final sentence's description of the pattern of means as being the interaction, but nevertheless, this is a clear, straightforward statement of results that you should be able to follow.

It might be useful also to imagine that you are seeing these results for the first time and want to compute the effect size of each main and interaction effect. This can be done using the F values and the degrees of freedom (which are reported in parentheses). For self-esteem, F is 12.73, degrees of freedom for the effect is 1, and within-cell degrees of freedom is 85. Using the formula for finding the proportion of variance accounted for from F and the degrees of freedom,

$$R_C^2 = \frac{(F_C)(df_C)}{(F)(df_C) + df_W} = \frac{(12.73)(1)}{(12.73)(1) + 85} = \frac{12.73}{97.73} = .13$$

This is a large effect size. Parallel computations (try them on your own) for the intimacy main effect and the interaction both yield medium effect sizes $R_R^2 = .06$, and $R_I^2 = .07$).

Wong and Csikszentmihalyi (1991) described their result as follows (note that their computed F ratios and degrees of freedom differ from those we used in the example, for which we used made-up data designed to approximate their final means):

> The percentage of episodes in which respondents indicated that they engaged in social interactions (such as talking, parties, going out with friends) was calculated for each person. We computed a two-way ANOVA with affiliation and gender as factors. Both the main effect for sex, $F(1, 166) = 26.39$, $p < .001$, and the Sex X Affiliation interaction, $F(1, 166) = 4.60$, $p < .05$, were significant. The main effect for affiliation was not, $F(1, 166) = 2.89$, $p = .09$. The results revealed an interesting pattern (see Table [13-9]). Highly affiliative girls more often reported engaging in social interactions with others than did

less affiliative girls. However, the difference between highly affiliative boys and less affiliative boys was much smaller and was in the opposite direction. Highly affiliative boys actually reported a slightly smaller percentage of social interaction episodes than did less affiliative boys. (p. 158)

Wong and Csikszentmihalyi did not provide a graph of their results.

Again, let's think about the effect size, even though these researchers did not discuss it. Based on the F values and degrees of freedom (calculating as we did in the Hobfoll and Leiberman study), the sex main effect accounted for 14% of the variance (that is, $R^2 = .14$), a large effect size. The R^2 for the interaction was .03, a smallish effect. It is also interesting to evaluate the nonsignificant result. Its effect size in this study was $R^2 = .02$, a small effect. We have all the information we need to find the power (from Table 13-15) for this study to have yielded a significant result at the .05 level if in fact there is a small effect in the population. Since the researchers had a total of 170 subjects (as we noted earlier in the chapter), there were about 40 in each of the four cells. Under these conditions, power for this effort was only 24%. Thus it would not be wise to conclude on the basis of this study that there was no main effect in the population for affiliation, although if there is one, it is probably small because there was an 89% chance that the result would have been significant if the true population effect size was of even medium magnitude.

Summary

A factorial research design distributes subjects into every combination of levels of two or more independent variables in order to permit the simultaneous study of the influence of these variables. Such designs are efficient and provide the opportunity to examine interactions among effects of different independent variables. An interaction effect occurs when the influence of one independent variable on the dependent variable differs according to the level of another independent variable. Factorial designs are described according to the number of independent variables or ways ("two-way," "three-way") and by numbers of levels ("2×2," "$3 \times 4 \times 3$").

Main and interaction effects can be identified (a) by inspection of means (main effects are indicated by differing marginal means, interactions by greater difference between cell means in one column or row than in another) or (b) graphically (main effects have different heights of lines or an average nonhorizontal slope of all lines; interaction effects are indicated when the lines are not parallel).

Computations for the two-way analysis of variance follow the structural model approach. Deviations are computed for each score from its cell mean (for the within-group population variance estimate), between row means and the grand mean (for the row main effect), between column means and the grand mean (for the column main effects), and the remainder of the deviation of the score from the grand mean (for the interaction effect). These deviations—squared, summed, and divided by their degrees of freedom—provide the respective population variance estimates for computing F ratios for testing the respective hypotheses. Each effect has its corresponding numerator population variance estimate, but all effects use the same within-group estimate as the denominator.

In the factorial analysis of variance, effect size and power are computed separately for each main and interaction effect. The most useful indicator of effect size is the proportion of variance accounted for.

The factorial analysis of variance can be extended beyond two-way designs and can also be used to handle repeated-measures studies and unequal sample sizes in the cells.

Key Terms

cell	interaction effect	repeated-measures analysis of variance
cell means	least-squares analysis of variance	row means
collapsed	levels	three-way factorial design
column means	main effect	three-way interaction
crossed	marginal means	two-way analysis of variance
dimensions	one-way analysis of variance	two-way factorial design
factorial analysis of variance	one-way design	two-way interaction
factorial design		

Practice Problems

These problems involve computation (with the assistance of a calculator). Most real-life statistics problems are done on a computer. But even if you have a computer, do these by hand to ingrain the method in your mind.

For practice in using a computer to solve statistical problems, refer to the computer section of each chapter of the study guide that accompanies this text.

All data are fictional (unless an actual citation is given). Answers to Set I are given at the back of the book.

SET I

1. Make up a fictional example for each of the following factorial designs, and draw the cell design: (a) a 2×5 design; (b) a $2 \times 2 \times 2$ design.

2. Each of the following represents a table of means in a factorial design. Assuming that any differences are statistically significant, for each table, (a) make two graphs showing the results; (b) indicate which effects (main and interaction), if any, are found; and (c) describe the meaning of the pattern of means and any main or interaction effects (or the lack thereof) in words. (All data are fictional.)

(i) Dependent variable: Income (thousands of dollars)

Age

	Young	Old
Class Lower		
Upper		

(ii) Dependent variable: Grade point average

Major

	Science	Arts
College Community	2.1	2.8
Liberal Arts	2.8	2.1

(iii) Dependent variable: Days sick per month

Gender

	Females	Males
Group Exercisers	2.0	2.5
Controls	3.1	3.6

(iv) Dependent variable: Rated restaurant quality (10 = high)

City

	New York	Chicago	Vancouver
Expensive	9	5	7
Cost Moderate	6	4	6
Inexpensive	4	3	5

3. A sports psychologist conducts a study of the effect of a motivational program on injuries among participants in three different sports. We present a chart showing the design. For each of the following possible outcomes, make up a set of cell means, and compute the marginal means: (a) a main effect for type of sport and no other main effect or interaction; (b) a main effect for program or not and no other main effect or interaction; (c) both main effects but no interaction; (d) a main effect for program or not and an interaction, but no main effect for type of sport; (e) both main effects and an interaction.

Dependent variable: Mean number of injuries per person over 10 weeks

	Sport		
Condition	**Baseball**	**Football**	**Basketball**
With motivational program			
Without motivational program			

4. (a) What would be the power of each of the effects in the study in Problem 3 if the researcher has 40 subjects per cell using the .05 level and assuming medium effect sizes for all effects? (b) How many subjects total would be needed to achieve 80% power if the researcher had reason to expect that all effects would be large?

5. A psychologist is interested in whether three different types of therapy have differential degrees of effectiveness according to the client's diagnosis. Patients with each of two kinds of problems were randomly assigned to one of three types of therapy. There were two patients per cell. Based on the data given, make a table of cell and marginal means, and draw a graph of them. Then compute the analysis of variance and effect sizes, and describe the results in words (indicate which effects are significant and, on the basis of the significant effects, how to understand the pattern of cell means). Use the .05 level.

	Therapy A	Therapy B	Therapy C
Diagnosis I	6	3	2
	2	1	4
Diagnosis II	11	7	8
	9	9	10

6. A psychologist who studies the legal system conducted a study of the effect on conviction of defendants' likability and nervousness. Each subject read the same transcript taken from an actual trial in which the guilt or innocence of a male defendant was quite ambiguous. All subjects also saw a brief videotape that supposedly showed the defendant on the witness stand. However, the way the actor played the part on the videotape differed for different subjects, including all the possibilities of likable versus not and nervous versus not. The dependent variable was the rating of the likelihood that the defendant is innocent (on a scale of 1, *very unlikely*, to 10, *very likely*). The results for the first 12 subjects of the study are as follows:

	Likable	Not Likable
Nervous	7	3
	8	4
	6	2
Not nervous	3	7
	3	5
	3	9

Make a table of cell and marginal means, and draw a graph of them. Then compute the analysis of variance, and explain the results and the way you arrived at them to someone who is familiar with the one-way analysis of variance (including the structural model approach) but not with the factorial analysis of variance.

7. In a study by Baron, Burgess, and Kao (1991), male and female subjects read accounts of stories that included a description of a sexist act perpetrated by either a male or a female against a female. The 193 subjects described the perpetrator in a way that could be scored for intensity of sexist behavior. Part of their Results section reads:

Perpetrator gender and subject gender main effects were both significant. Female subjects, compared with male subjects, gave more intense ratings to both male and female perpetrators . . .: $F(1, 189) = 5.06$, $p < .03$. . . . Furthermore, male perpetrators were seen as displaying more intense gender bias than female perpetrators: $F(1, 189) = 15.97$, $p < .0001$. The interaction between subject gender and perpetrator gender was nonsignificant in both analyses: $p < .34$. . . . These results can be seen in [the figure]. (p. 119).

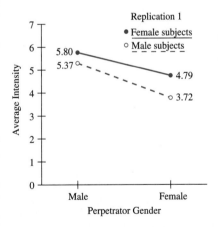

Average intensities of displayed sexist behavior (1 = *slightly displayed*, 7 = *extremely displayed*) seen in male and female perpetrators by male and female subjects. [Figure 1 from Baron, R.S., Burgess, M.L., & Kao, C.F. (1991). Detecting and labeling prejudice: Do female perpetrators go undetected? *Personality and Social Psychology Bulletin, 17,* 115–123. © 1991. Reprinted by permission of Sage Publications, Inc.]

Briefly describe the meaning of these results to a person who has never had a course in statistics. (Do not go into the computational details, just the basic logic of the pattern of means, the significant results, effect sizes, and issues of interpreting nonsignificant results.)

SET II

1. Make up a fictional example of each of the following factorial designs, and draw the cell design: (a) a 3×3 design; (b) a $3 \times 2 \times 2$ design.

2. Each of the following represents a table of means in a factorial design. Assuming that any differences are statistically significant, for each table, (a) make two graphs showing the results; (b) indicate which effects (main and interaction), if any, are found; and (c) describe the meaning of the pattern of means and any main or interaction effects (or the lack thereof) in words. (All data are fictional.)

(i) Dependent Variable: Intensity of attention

Program

		The Nutcracker	Modern
Type of Balletgoer	Regular	20	15
	Sometime	15	15
	Novice	10	5

(ii) Dependent variable: Approval rating for the president

Region

		West	East	Midwest	South
Class	Middle	70	45	55	50
	Lower	50	25	35	30

(iii) Dependent variable: Satisfaction with education

Gender

		Females	Males
Time After Obtaining BA	1 month	3	3
	1 year	4	4
	5 years	9	9

(iv) Dependent variable: Degree of jealousy of others' success

Degree of Success

		Great	Small
Status of Other	Friend	8	5
	Stranger	1	4

3. English-speaking subjects were instructed to try to read a paragraph for a half hour in one of three languages they did not understand, after either being told the main idea or not being told the main idea of what they were reading. They were given translations of some words. The dependent measure was how many of the other words they could correctly translate. The design is diagrammed here. For each of the following possible outcomes, make up a set of plausible means, compute the marginal means, and make a graph: (a) a main effect for language but no other main effect or interaction; (b) a main effect for being told or not told the main idea, no main effect for language, and an interaction effect; (c) both main effects but no interaction; (d) an interaction effect only.

Dependent variable: Number of words correctly translated

Language

		Dutch	Rumanian	Swedish
Told Main Idea	Yes			
	No			

4. (a) What would be the power of each of the effects in the study in Problem 3 if the researcher has 10 subjects per cell, using the .05 level, and assuming large effect sizes for the two main effects and a medium effect size for the interaction effect? (b) How many subjects would be needed to achieve 80% power in this case?

5. In a particular high school, three types of videotaped teaching programs were each tried for English, history, and math. The dependent measure was amount learned. There were two students per cell of this 3×3 design. (a) Based on the data given, make a table of cell and marginal means, and draw a graph of them. (b) Then compute the analysis of variance and describe the results in words (indicate which effects, if any, are significant and what any significant effects mean).

	English	History	Math
Program Type A	3	5	2
	3	4	3
Program Type B	6	8	6
	8	10	5
Program Type C	1	3	2
	3	4	0

6. For each of the following data sets, carry out an analysis of variance, including making a table of cell and marginal means and graphing the cell means.

(a)

	Experimental Condition	
	A	B
Group 1	0	3
	1	2
	1	3
Group 2	3	0
	2	1
	3	1

(b)

	Experimental Condition	
	A	B
Group 1	0	0
	1	1
	1	1
Group 2	3	3
	2	2
	3	3

(c)

	Experimental Condition	
	A	B
Group 1	0	3
	1	2
	1	3
Group 2	0	3
	1	2
	1	3

7. As part of a study by Gladue and Delaney (1990), men and women in a popular college-area bar were asked about the number and types of drinks they had had and their weight, and these data were used to compute the estimated blood alcohol concentration (EBAC). Patrons were interviewed at 9:00, 10:30, and midnight. They report their result as follows:

> A 2 (Gender) × 3 (Time) ANOVA for EBAC revealed a significant effect of time ($F[2, 95] = 26.35, p < .001$) but not of gender ($F[1, 95] = 1.10, p > .45$), nor was there any interaction (Time × Gender: $F[2, 95] = 1.89, p > .23$). (p. 382)

Estimates of Blood Alcohol Concentration (mg ethanol per 100 ml) by Time and Gender

Gender	Time					
	9:00 P.M.		*10:30 P.M.*		*12:00 A.M.*	
	M	*SD*	*M*	*SD*	*M*	*SD*
Males ($n = 58$)	50.7_a	6.3	105.9_b	9.3	153.7_c	13.6
Females ($n = 43$)	43.2_a	7.6	110.9_b	14.6	158.7_c	17.7

Note. Means having the same subscript did not significantly differ from each other.

From Gladue, B. A., & Delaney, H. I. (1990), tab. 1. Gender differences in perception of attractiveness of men and women in bars. *Personality and Social Psychology Bulletin, 16,* 378–391. Copyright, 1990, by the Society for Personality and Social Psychology, Inc. Reprinted by permission of Sage Publications, Inc.

Briefly describe the meaning of these results to a person who has never had a course in statistics. (Do not go into the computational details, just the basic logic of the pattern of means, the significant results, effect sizes, and issues of interpreting nonsignificant results.)

Chapter Appendix: Optional Computational Formulas

Calculational formulas for a two-way analysis of variance that do not require computing deviation scores for each individual are as follows:

The calculational formula for the overall sum of squared deviations is the same as in formula 12-6 (and the same as for *SS* in formula 2-9):

$$SS_T = \Sigma X^2 - \frac{(\Sigma X)^2}{N} \tag{13-18}$$

where ΣX^2 is the sum of each squared score, $(\Sigma X)^2$ is the square of the sum of all the scores, and N is the total number of scores.

The formula for the overall between-group effect is also the same as before (formula 12-7), except that the subscripts now refer to cells instead of groups.

$$SS_B = \frac{(\Sigma X_1)^2}{n} + \frac{(\Sigma X_2)^2}{n} + \ldots + \frac{(\Sigma X_{last})^2}{n} - \frac{(\Sigma X)^2}{N} \tag{13-19}$$

where $(\Sigma X_1)^2$, $(\Sigma X_2)^2$, $\ldots$, $(\Sigma X_{last})^2$ are the squares of the sums of all scores within each cell and n is the number of subjects in each cell.

Then, to compute the sum of squares within groups, $SS_W = SS_T - SS_B$.

The overall between-group formula is modified to calculate the sum of squares for rows, as follows:

$$SS_R = \frac{(\Sigma X_{R1})^2}{n_R} + \frac{(\Sigma X_{R2})^2}{n_R} + \ldots + \frac{(\Sigma X_{Rlast})^2}{n_R} - \frac{(\Sigma X)^2}{N} \qquad (13\text{-}20)$$

where $(\Sigma X_{R1})^2$, $(\Sigma X_{R2})^2$, . . . , $(\Sigma X_{Rlast})^2$ are the squares of the sums of all scores within each row and n_R is the number of subjects in each row.

The overall between-group formula for columns is thus

$$SS_C = \frac{(\Sigma X_{C1})^2}{n_C} + \frac{(\Sigma X_{C2})^2}{n_C} + \ldots + \frac{(\Sigma X_{Clast})^2}{n_C} - \frac{(\Sigma X)^2}{N} \qquad (13\text{-}21)$$

where $(\Sigma X_{C1})^2$, $(\Sigma X_{C2})^2$, . . . , $(\Sigma X_{Clast})^2$ are the squares of the sums of all scores within each column and n_C is the number of subjects in each column.

Finally, the sum of squares for interaction is computed as what remains after the row and column sums of squares are removed from the overall between-group sum of squares:

$$SS_I = SS_B - SS_R - SS_C \qquad (13\text{-}22)$$

Table 13-18 shows the calculations employing these formulas to compute the sums of squares for the example in the chapter in which we conducted a 2 × 3 analysis of variance on fictional data based on a study of reactions to racism conducted by Blanchard et al. (1991). Compare these results to those we obtained in Table 13-12 using the definitional formulas.

TABLE 13-18
Computation of Sums of Squares for a Two-Way Analysis of Variance Based on Blanchard et al. (1991), Using Calculational Formulas (Fictional Data)

Public Response Format		Private Response Format		Rows	
X	X^2	X	X^2		
Antiracist influence					
25	625	19	361		
20	400	24	576		**Antiracist Influence Row**	
23	529	21	441	ΣX	ΣX^2
24	576	20	400	176	3,908
Cell Σ: 92	2,130	84	1,778		
No influence					
22	484	24	576		
19	361	18	324	**No Influence Row**	
22	484	22	484	ΣX	ΣX^2
21	441	20	400	168	3,554
Cell Σ: 84	1,770	84	1,784		
Nonantiracist influence:					
16	256	18	324	**Nonantiracist**	
19	361	21	441	**Influence Row**	
13	169	16	256	ΣX	ΣX^2
16	256	17	289	136	2,352
Cell Σ: 64	1,042	72	1,310		
Column Σ: 240	4,942	240	4,872		

Overall $\Sigma X = 480$.
Overall $\Sigma X^2 = 9,814$.

$$SS_T = \Sigma X^2 - \frac{(\Sigma X)^2}{N} = 9,814 - \frac{480^2}{24} = 9,814 - \frac{230,400}{24} = 9,814 - 9,600 = 214$$

$$SS_B = \frac{92^2}{4} + \frac{84^2}{4} + \frac{84^2}{4} + \frac{84^2}{4} + \frac{64^2}{4} + \frac{72^2}{4} - \frac{480^2}{24}$$

$$= \frac{8,464}{4} + \frac{7,056}{4} + \frac{7,056}{4} + \frac{7,056}{4} + \frac{4,096}{4} + \frac{5,184}{4} - \frac{230,400}{24}$$

$$= 2,116 + 1,764 + 1,764 + 1,764 + 1,024 + 1,296 - 9,600 = 128$$

$$SS_W = SS_T - SS_B = 214 - 128 = 86$$

$$SS_R = \frac{(\Sigma X_{R1})^2}{n_R} + \frac{(\Sigma X_{R2})^2}{n_R} + \ldots + \frac{(\Sigma X_{Rlast})^2}{n_R} - \frac{(\Sigma X)^2}{N} = \frac{176^2}{8} + \frac{168^2}{8} + \frac{136^2}{8} - \frac{480^2}{24}$$

$$= \frac{30,976}{8} + \frac{28,224}{8} + \frac{18,496}{8} - \frac{230,400}{24} = 3,872 + 3,528 + 2,312 - 9,600 = 112$$

$$SS_C = \frac{(\Sigma X_{C1})^2}{n_C} + \frac{(\Sigma X_{C2})^2}{n_C} + \ldots + \frac{(\Sigma X_{Clast})^2}{n_C} - \frac{(\Sigma X)^2}{N}$$

$$= \frac{240^2}{12} + \frac{240^2}{12} - \frac{480^2}{24} = \frac{57,600}{12} + \frac{57,600}{12} - \frac{230,400}{24}$$

$$= 4,800 + 4,800 - 9,600 = 0$$

$$SS_I = SS_B - SS_R - SS_C = 128 - 112 - 0 = 16$$

14

Chi-Square Tests

T HIS chapter examines hypothesis-testing procedures that deal with variables whose values are categories—such as religious preference or hair color—rather than numbers, as is the case for most variables. These procedures focus on the number of cases in different categories rather than on mean scores on some dimension.[1] Consider an example.

Stasser, Taylor, and Hanna (1989) conducted a study comparing how small groups of different sizes and structures share information. The group discussions were about three candidates running for student body office. The descriptions of the three candidates had been designed by the researchers with the intention of making them equally preferred prior to the group discussion. So when the study was completed, one of the first steps in analyzing the results was to be sure that the three candidates were in fact equally preferred. Of the 531 subjects, 197 (37%) initially preferred Candidate A, 120 (23%) preferred Candidate B, and 214 (40%) preferred Candidate C. If the three candidates had been equally preferred, then about 177 ($33\frac{1}{3}$%) of the subjects should have preferred each. The second and third columns of Table 14-1 show the distribution of preferences over these three categories that Stasser and colleagues observed and the distribution that one would expect if they had been equally preferred. Clearly, there is a discrepancy. The question is, should we assume that this discrepancy from an equal distribution is no more than would be reasonably expected with a sample of this size?

---

[1]Actually, we *have* considered such variables already—as independent variables in the *t* test and the analysis of variance. In previous examples, some of these were gender, professor's field of study, and college-graduate status. However, we have not yet considered cases in which variables of this kind are *dependent* variables.

TABLE 14-1
Observed and Expected Frequencies of Preferences for Three Candidates

Candidate Preferred	Observed Frequency[a] (O)	Expected Frequency (E)	Difference $(O - E)$	Difference Squared $(O - E)^2$	Difference Squared Weighted by Expected Frequency $(O - E)^2/E$
A	197	177	20	400	2.26
B	120	177	−57	3,249	18.36
C	214	177	37	1,369	7.73

[a]Data from Stasser, Taylor, and Hanna (1989).

nominal variable
categorical variable

This example is quite different from the situations we have looked at previously, in which variables are numerical values on some dimension, such as score on a self-esteem questionnaire, length of time in a relationship, employer's ratings of an employee's job effectiveness on a 9-point scale, or speed of response in a reaction time test. Preference for a particular candidate, by contrast, is an example of a **nominal** or **categorical variable** in which the information we have is the number of cases in each category. These are called nominal variables because the different categories or levels of the variable have names instead of numbers. That is, nominal variables have no numerical relations among the different levels. Which candidate a subject prefers has three possible "levels," corresponding to the names of the three candidates. It makes no sense to label them 1, 2, and 3, except arbitrarily, since 3 is not higher than 2, nor is 2 intermediate between 1 and 3. Other examples of nominal variables are region of the brain involved in a task, gender, and occupation.

There are two main statistical techniques for hypothesis testing involving nominal variables. First we examine what are called chi-square tests for goodness of fit, and then we consider chi-square tests for independence.[2] The chi square tests were originally developed by Karl Pearson (see Box 14-1).

Chi-Square Test for Goodness of Fit

chi-square test for goodness of fit

The basic idea of a **chi-square test for goodness of fit** is that you test how well an observed frequency distribution (Chapter 1) fits some expected pattern of frequencies. This is done by computing a number that represents the degree to which the observed and expected patterns differ and then seeing whether that number represents a degree of divergence that is larger than you would expect by chance. We will examine the various steps involved in this process.

The Chi-Square Statistic

observed frequency
expected frequency

The degree of divergence between the **observed frequency** and the **expected frequency** for each category is simply the observed frequency minus the expected frequency. For example, in the Stasser et al. (1989)

[2]*Chi* is the Greek letter χ; it is pronounced /kī/, rhyming with *high* and *pie*.

BOX 14-1

Karl Pearson, Inventor of Chi-Square and Center of Controversy

Karl Pearson, sometimes hailed as the founder of the science of statistics, was born in 1857, the son of a Yorkshire barrister. Most of both his virtues and his vices are revealed in what he reported to his colleague Julia Bell as his earliest memory: He was sitting in his high chair, sucking his thumb, when he was told to stop or his thumb would wither away. Pearson looked at his two thumbs and silently concluded, "I can't see that the thumb I suck is any smaller than the other. I wonder if she could be lying to me." Here we see Pearson's faith in himself and in observational evidence and his rejection of authority. We also see his tendency to doubt the character of people with whom he disagreed.

Pearson studied mathematics on a scholarship at Cambridge. Soon after he arrived, he requested to be excused from compulsory divinity lectures and chapel. As soon as his request was granted, however, he appeared in chapel. The dean summoned him for an explanation, and Pearson declared that he had asked to be excused not from chapel "but from *compulsory* chapel."

After graduation, Pearson traveled and studied in Germany, becoming a socialist and a self-described "free-thinker." Returning to England, he wrote an attack on Christianity under a pen name and in 1885 founded a "Men and Women's Club" to promote discussion of the relations between the sexes. The club died out, but through it he met his wife, Maria Sharp.

Pearson eventually turned to statistics out of his interest in proving the theory of evolution, being especially influenced by Sir Francis Galton's work (see Box 3-1). Pearson, the better mathematician, saw in Galton's ideas of correlation the means to make fields such as psychology, anthropology, and sociology as scientific as physics and chemistry—he hoped to bypass the issue of causation through the use of this broader category of correlation, association, or contingency (ranging from 0, independence, to the "unity of causation" at 1). "No phenomena are causal," he said. "All phenomena are contingent, and the problem before us is to measure the degree of contingency."

Throughout his life, Pearson was controversial and strong-willed, especially when it came to "pseudoscience" and the masquerading of theology, metaphysics, or appeals to authority under the guise of science. He even thought physics should give up the use of words such as *atom, force, matter*, and *ether* because they were not observable phenomena.

Most of his research from 1893 to 1901 was on the laws of heredity and evolution, but he needed better statistical methods for his work. So he turned to other topics, eventually making his most famous contribution, the chi-square test. But Pearson also invented the method of computing correlation used today and coined the terms *histogram, skew*, and *spurious correlation*. When he felt that biology journals failed to appreciate his work properly, he founded the famous journal of statistics called *Biometrika*. In short, in Pearson's lifetime he led statistics from its early position as a matter largely ignored to one central to the scientific method, especially in the natural sciences.

Unfortunately, Pearson was a great fan of eugenics, the "improvement" of the human race through selective breeding, and his work was later used by the Nazis as justification for their treatment of Jews and other ethnic minorities. But as Pearson aged, his opinions met strong resistance and much discrediting evidence from other, younger statisticians—which only turned Pearson against more and more of his colleagues.

Indeed, throughout his life, Pearson was a man who evoked either devoted friendship or deep dislike. William S. Gosset (see Box 9-1), inventor of the *t* test, was one of his friends. Sir Ronald Fisher, inventor of the analysis of variance and a man associated with even more extreme attitudes (he is described in Box 11-1), was one of Pearson's worst enemies (and the kindly, peaceable Gosset, friends of both, was always trying to smooth matters between them). In 1933, Pearson finally retired, and Fisher, of all persons, took over his chair, the Galton Professorship of Eugenics at University College in London. In 1936, the two entered into their bitterest argument yet; Pearson died the same year.

References: Peters (1987); Stigler (1986); Tankard (1984).

study, for Candidate A the observed frequency of 197 is 20 less than the expected frequency of 177 (1/3 of 571). However, as usual, we need to square these differences (otherwise, the differences would always add up to 0 because differences in some categories in which the observed value is greater than the expected value would exactly balance out differences in other categories in which the expected numbers were greater than the observed numbers). The squared difference for Candidate A would be 20 squared, or 400. The observed and expected frequencies and the differences and squared differences for all three candidates are shown in Table 14-1.

In the Stasser example, the expected frequencies are the same in each category. But in many other research situations, expected frequencies differ considerably over the categories being considered. Hence to create a versatile index of divergence, you also need to weight each squared difference by the frequency expected in each category. For example, a divergence of 8 must be weighted more heavily if the expected frequency is 10 than if the expected frequency is 1,000. If the expected frequency is 10, a divergence of 8 is huge, but if the expected frequency is 1,000, a divergence of 8 is relatively minor.

To weight by the expected frequency, the squared difference between the observed and expected values is simply divided by the expected frequency. Thus for Candidate A in the Stasser example, you divide the squared difference of 400 by 177, giving a result of 2.26. The corresponding figures for Candidate B is 3,249/177 = 18.36, and for Candidate C it is 1,369/177 = 7.73.

The statistic we use to indicate the overall lack of fit between the expected and observed frequencies is called a **chi-square statistic.** It is defined as the sum, over all the categories, of the squared difference between the observed and expected frequencies divided by the expected frequency.

In terms of a formula,

$$\chi^2 = \Sigma \frac{(O - E)^2}{E} \qquad (14\text{-}1)$$

where χ^2 is chi-square; Σ is the summation sign, telling you to sum over all the different categories; O is the observed frequency for a category (the number of cases actually obtained in that category in the study); and E is the expected frequency for a category.

In the Stasser example, the chi-square statistic is $2.26 + 18.36 + 7.73 = 28.35$. Using the formula in Equation 14-1 yields this same result:

$$\chi^2 = \Sigma \frac{(O - E)^2}{E} = \frac{(197 - 177)^2}{177} + \frac{(120 - 177)^2}{177} + \frac{(214 - 177)^2}{177} = 28.35$$

Summary of Steps for Computing the Chi-Square Statistic

1. Determine the actual, observed frequencies in each category.
2. Determine the expected frequencies in each category.
3. In each category, compute observed minus expected frequencies, and square this difference.
4. Divide each squared difference by the expected frequency for its category.
5. Add up the results of Step 4 for the various categories.

chi-square statistic *(margin note)*

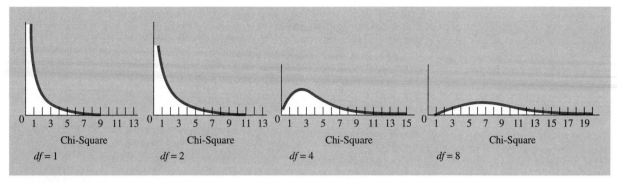

FIGURE 14-1
Examples of chi-square distributions for different degrees of freedom.

The Chi-Square Distribution

The next question is whether a chi-square of a given size represents a divergence between the observed and expected values that is larger than would be expected by chance. To answer that, we need to know the distribution of the chi-square statistic itself. Fortunately, it turns out that so long as we have a reasonable number of cases, the distribution of the chi-square statistic follows a known mathematical distribution quite closely. This distribution is called the **chi-square distribution.**

    The shape of the chi-square distribution depends only on the degrees of freedom available when determining the differences between observed and expected frequencies. In the chi-square test for goodness of fit, the numbers of degrees of freedom is the number of categories minus 1. This is the case because if you know the total and you know all but one of the observed frequencies, you can determine that last observed frequency by simple subtraction. (That is, the last observed frequency will be the total number of cases minus the observed frequency for all the other categories.) In the Stasser example, in which there are three categories, there are thus 2 degrees of freedom.

    The chi-square distributions for several different degrees of freedom are shown in Figure 14-1. Note that the distributions are all skewed to the right. This reflects the fact that the chi-square statistic cannot be less than 0 but can have very high values. (Chi-square must be positive because it is based on adding a group of fractions in which the numerator is a squared term—and thus must be positive—and the denominator is an expected frequency—which also has to be a positive number, as you cannot expect a negative number of cases in a category.)

chi-square distribution

The Chi-Square Table

The critical information when using the chi-square distribution for hypothesis testing is where the cutoffs fall for the desired significance level (usually 5%). A **chi-square table** provides the cutoff chi-square values for different significance levels for chi-square distributions of various degrees of freedom. For example, Table 14-2 shows a portion of a chi-square table like the one in Appendix B (Table B-4). The cutoff chi-square value for the .05 level

chi-square table

TABLE 14-2
Portion of a Chi-Square Table

	Significance Level		
df	*.10*	*.05*	*.01*
1	2.706	3.841	6.635
2	4.605	5.992	9.211
3	6.252	7.815	11.345
4	7.780	9.488	13.277
5	9.237	11.071	15.087

using a chi-square distribution with 2 degrees of freedom—the degrees of freedom for the Stasser example—is 5.992. Because the chi-square statistic computed in this study was much larger (28.35), the researchers concluded that it was not reasonable to assume that the observed values differed from a truly equal distribution simply due to sampling error. It seemed more reasonable to hold that the preferences for the candidates were truly different.

Steps of Hypothesis Testing: An Example

We have already carried out all the parts of a complete hypothesis test using the chi-square goodness of fit test in the Stasser example. However, it will be useful to review the process with the same example, this time following systematically our standard five steps. In the process we also consider some fine points.

1. Reframe the question into a research hypothesis and a null hypothesis about the populations. These are the two populations of interest:

Population 1: People like those in the experiment
Population 2: People who initially prefer each candidate equally

The research hypothesis is that the distribution of cases over categories in the two populations are different; the null hypothesis is that they are the same.

There are three points especially to notice about this step. First, as is often the case in hypothesis testing, one of the populations is hypothetical (in this case, Population 2) and may not actually exist.

Second, notice that in a chi-square situation, we are making a nondirectional hypothesis. We have not specified which of the candidates should be preferred by the greater number, only that the preferences will be different. Even though when we use the chi-square distribution we are examining extreme scores on a single tail, the underlying logic of the distribution is overall degrees of divergence, not divergence in any particular direction. (This is the same point we made in Chapter 11 about the analysis of variance and the *F* distribution.)

Finally, notice that the similarity or difference between distributions in which we are interested concerns the proportions of cases in each category. This is quite different from almost all our analyses in earlier chapters, in which the similarity or difference between the two populations was in terms of their means.

2. Determine the characteristics of the comparison distribution. The comparison distribution in this case is a chi-square distribution with 2 degrees of freedom (3 categories minus 1).

It is important not to be confused by the terminology here. The comparison distribution refers to the distribution of the statistic on which we will examine the probability of getting an extreme divergence. Thus it is the chi-square distribution itself. True, in the process of preparing to use the chi-square distribution we compared a distribution of observed frequencies to a distribution of expected frequencies. But the distribution of expected frequencies is not a comparison distribution in the sense in which we have been using the term comparison distribution in Step 2 of the hypothesis-testing process.

3. Determine the cutoff sample score on the comparison distribution at which the null hypothesis should be rejected. This is accomplished by looking up the figure in the chi-square table for the appropriate significance level and the appropriate degrees of freedom. In this case, we assumed that we wanted the .05 significance level, and we determined in Step 2 that there were 2 degrees of freedom. This yields a cutoff chi-square of 5.992.

4. Determine the score of your sample on the comparison distribution. Here is where you must do all the chi-square computation, including figuring out the expected frequencies for each category. For each category, you need to find the squared difference between the observed and expected frequencies and then divide that result by the expected value. Summing this figure over all the categories gives the chi-square statistic—in the example, 28.35.

5. Compare the scores obtained in Steps 3 and 4 to decide whether to reject the null hypothesis. Because the minimum chi-square needed to reject the null hypothesis has been set at 5.992 and the chi-square of our sample data is 28.35, the null hypothesis can be rejected. The research hypothesis that the two populations are different—that is, that the distribution of preferences is not equal—is supported.

Another Example

Consider another example. A fictional research team of clinical psychologists is interested in a theory that mental health is affected by the level of a certain mineral (mineral Q) in the diet, especially if levels of that mineral are high over many years. The research team has located a region of the country where mineral Q is found in very high concentrations in the soil and, as a result, in the water people drink and the food they eat that is grown locally. The researchers carry out a survey of people in this area, focusing on mental health disorders. Of the 1,000 people surveyed, 134 had anxiety disorders; 160 had suffered from alcohol or drug abuse, 97 from mood disorders (such as major chronic depression), and 12 from schizophrenia; and 597 did not report having experienced any of these problems.

The psychologists then compare their results to what they would have expected on the basis of data from large surveys of the U.S. public in general, in which it has been found that 14.6% of adults suffer at some point in life from anxiety, 16.4% from alcohol or drug abuse, 8.3% from mood disorders, and 1.5% from schizophrenia; and 59.2% do not experience any of

TABLE 14-3
Observed and Expected Frequencies for Types of Mental Health Disorders in a Region High in Mineral Q Compared to the General U.S. Population and the Chi-Square Goodness of Fit Test (Fictional Data)

Condition	Observed	Expected
Anxiety disorder	134	146 (14.6% × 1,000)
Alcohol and drug abuse	160	164 (16.4% × 1,000)
Mood disorders	97	83 (8.3% × 1,000)
Schizophrenia	12	15 (1.5% × 1,000)
None of these conditions	597	592 (59.2% × 1,000)

Degrees of freedom = 5 categories − 1 = 4

Chi-square needed, $df = 4$, .05 level: 9.488

$$\chi^2 = \Sigma \frac{(O-E)^2}{E} = \frac{(134-146)^2}{146} + \frac{(160-164)^2}{164} + \frac{(97-83)^2}{83} + \frac{(12-15)^2}{15} + \frac{(597-592)^2}{592}$$

$$= \frac{-12^2}{146} + \frac{-4^2}{164} + \frac{14^2}{83} + \frac{-3^2}{15} + \frac{5^2}{592} = \frac{144}{146} + \frac{16}{164} + \frac{196}{83} + \frac{9}{15} + \frac{25}{592}$$

$$= .99 + .10 + 2.36 + .60 + .04 = 4.09$$

Conclusion: Do not reject the null hypothesis.

these conditions (Regier et al., 1984). If their sample of 1,000 is not different from the general U.S. population, 14.6% of them (146) should have had anxiety disorders, 16.4% of them (164) should have suffered from alcohol and drug abuse, and so forth. The question the researchers posed is this: On the basis of the sample we have studied, can we conclude that the pattern of incidence of mental health problems among people in this region is different from that of the general U.S. population?

Table 14-3 shows the observed and expected frequencies and the computations for the chi-square test. We will consider the problem using the five-step hypothesis-testing procedure.

1. Reframe the question into a research hypothesis and a null hypothesis about the populations. The populations of interest are these:

Population 1: People in the region that has a high level of mineral Q
Population 2: The U.S. population

The research hypothesis is that the distribution of numbers of people over the five mental health categories is different in the two populations; the null hypothesis is that it is the same.

2. Determine the characteristics of the comparison distribution. The comparison distribution is a chi-square distribution with 4 degrees of freedom (5 categories − 1 = 4).

3. Determine the cutoff sample score on the comparison distribution at which the null hypothesis should be rejected. Using the standard 5% significance level, with 4 degrees of freedom, Table 14-2 (or Table B-4 in Appendix B) shows that the researchers need a chi-square of at least 9.488 to reject the null hypothesis. This is shown in Figure 14-2.

4. Determine the score of your sample on the comparison distribution. The computation of chi-square, as shown in Table 14-3, follows the usual

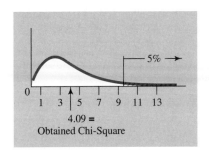

FIGURE 14-2
For the mineral Q example, the chi-square distribution ($df = 4$) showing the cutoff for rejecting the null hypothesis at the .05 level.

procedure of finding the difference between the observed and expected frequencies in each category, squaring these differences, dividing each by the expected number in its category, and then summing the results. In this case, we get a chi-square of 4.09.

5. Compare the scores obtained in Steps 3 and 4 to decide whether to reject the null hypothesis. The chi-square we computed of 4.09 is clearly less extreme than the cutoff score from the table of 9.488 (see Figure 14-2). The researchers cannot reject the null hypothesis; the study is inconclusive. (Having failed to reject the null hypothesis with such a large sample, it is reasonable to suppose that if there is any difference between the populations, it is quite small.)

A Third Example

Suppose that a professor at a large state university is teaching an introductory statistics course in which 200 students are enrolled. The class has just finished taking its midterm. In the past, the professor has always graded on a curve that approximates a normal distribution. This meant that the highest scoring 2.5% of the students received As, the next highest scoring 14% of the students received Bs, the next highest scoring 67% of the students received Cs, the next highest 14% of the students received Ds, and the lowest scoring 2.5% of the students received Fs.

This year, however, the professor has decided to assign grades according to percentages correct on the test (90% and up is an A, 80%–89% a B, and so forth). The question is, based on this sample of 200 midterm grades, is there any reason to think that the new system produces a different distribution of grades?

Table 14-4 shows the observed and expected frequencies and the computations for the chi-square test.

1. Reframe the question into a research hypothesis and a null hypothesis about the populations. There are two populations:

Population 1: Students who are graded according to the new system (which uses their score, regardless of how other students do in the class)

Population 2: Students who are graded using a curve following a normal distribution

The research hypothesis is that the populations are different; the null hypothesis is that the populations are the same.

TABLE 14-4
Observed and Expected Frequencies for Midterm Grades (Fictional Data)

Grade	Observed	Expected
A	10	5 (2.5% × 200)
B	34	28 (14.0% × 200)
C	140	134 (67.0% × 200)
D	10	28 (14.0% × 200)
F	6	5 (2.5% × 200)

Degrees of freedom = 5 categories − 1 = 4

Chi-square needed, $df = 4$, .01 level: 13.277

$$\chi^2 = \Sigma \frac{(O-E)^2}{E} = \frac{(10-5)^2}{5} + \frac{(34-28)^2}{28} + \frac{(140-134)^2}{134} + \frac{(10-28)^2}{28} + \frac{(6-5)^2}{5}$$

$$= \frac{5^2}{5} + \frac{6^2}{28} + \frac{6^2}{134} + \frac{-18^2}{28} + \frac{1^2}{5} = \frac{25}{5} + \frac{36}{28} + \frac{36}{134} + \frac{324}{28} + \frac{1}{5}$$

$$= 5 + 1.29 + .27 + 11.57 + .20 = 18.33.$$

Conclusion: Reject the null hypothesis.

2. Determine the characteristics of the comparison distribution. The comparison distribution is a chi-square distribution with 4 degrees of freedom (5 categories − 1 = 4).

3. Determine the cutoff sample score on the comparison distribution at which the null hypothesis should be rejected. The professor is conservative about statistical decisions and so chooses the .01 level. Using Table 14-2 (or Table B-4) for 4 degrees of freedom and the .01 level, a chi-square of at least 13.277 is needed to reject the null hypothesis.

4. Determine the score of your sample on the comparison distribution. To compute chi-square, it is first necessary to figure out the expected frequencies. This is done by multiplying the expected percentages times the number in the sample. For the first group (the As), the professor expected 2.5% on the basis of the normal curve system she used to use: 2.5% × 200 = 5. So, for the As, she had an expected value of 5. Fourteen percent would have gotten Bs under the old system, making an expected frequency, for her class of 200, of 28. These and the rest of the expected frequencies, plus the chi-square calculations, are shown in Table 14-4. The result is a chi-square of 18.33.

5. Compare the scores obtained in Steps 3 and 4 to determine whether to reject the null hypothesis. Because the critical chi-square value needed to reject the null hypothesis was 13.277 and the sample's chi-square value is 18.33, the professor can reject the null hypothesis and conclude that the populations are different (see Figure 14-3). The new grading method did not produce the same normal distribution of class grades. No direction of difference was predicted. However, an examination of the category values shows that with the point-grading method, more students received As, Bs, and Cs and fewer students received Ds and Fs than would have been expected with the previous grading method. (Although the professor was sorry to give up the elegance of the normal curve, she was delighted to have a basis for giving more good grades and fewer poor ones.)

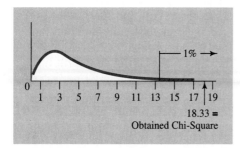

FIGURE 14-3
For the grading system example, chi-square distribution ($df = 4$) showing the cutoff for rejecting the null hypothesis at the .01 level.

Chi-Square Test for Independence

So far, we have looked at the distribution of one nominal variable over several levels or categories of itself—levels of grades, mental illness diagnoses—and compared obtained and expected distributions. In fact, this is a fairly uncommon analysis. Most of the time, chi-square is used to look for a relationship between two variables. In the mineral Q example, there was only one variable, diagnosis. Mineral Q was not a variable, in that it did not have two or more levels. Likewise, the grade example compared an obtained and an expected result—what all chi-squares do. But there was only one variable, grades.

In looking at two-variable chi-squares, we will employ an example to talk about (a) contingency tables—the way the numbers falling into the levels of the two nominal variables are laid out—and (b) the test of whether the two variables are independent versus in some way associated.

Consider the following fictional study. A survey is conducted at a large university in which 200 staff members who commute to work indicate the kind of transportation they use and whether they prefer to go to bed early and awaken early (these are "morning people") or go to bed late and awaken late ("night people"). The results are shown in Table 14-5. Notice the *two* nominal variables: type of transportation (with three levels) and sleep tendency (with two levels).

Contingency Tables

A table like Table 14-5, in which the distributions of two nominal variables are laid out so that you have the frequencies of their combinations as well as the totals, is called a **contingency table.** A contingency table is similar to tables used in factorial experiments (see Chapter 13) in that it is about the

contingency table

TABLE 14-5
Contingency Table of Observed Frequencies of Morning and Night People Using Different Types of Transportation (Fictional Data)

		Transportation			Total
		Bus	*Carpool*	*Own Car*	
Sleep Tendency	*Morning*	60	30	30	120 (60%)
	Night	20	20	40	80 (40%)
	Total	80	50	70	200 (100%)

relationship of two variables and includes both cell and marginal figures. One difference, however, is that in a contingency table, the numbers represent frequencies—numbers of cases—whereas in the tables used in the analysis of variance, the numbers in the cells and margins represent means. Also notice that in a contingency table, one variable might be an independent variable and one a dependent variable. In a factorial table used in a two-way analysis of variance, there are two independent variables, and the numbers in the cells (and margins) represent scores on a third, dependent variable.

A contingency table like Table 14-5 is called a 3×2 contingency table because it has three levels of one variable crossed with two levels of the other. (Which dimension is named first does not matter.) It is also possible to have larger contingency tables, such as a 4×7 or a 6×18 table, or to have a smaller table, a 2×2 contingency table. These are still two-dimensional but involve multiple levels of the two variables. It is possible to have a three-dimensional table too. However, the analysis of three-dimensional contingency tables requires statistical procedures somewhat different and more complex than the ones in this book.

Independence

The question of interest in this example is whether there is any link between the type of transportation people use and whether they are morning or night people. If there is no association, then whether a person is a night or a morning person has no relation to the type of transportation that person uses. Or to put it the other way, the proportion of morning and night people is the same among bus riders, carpoolers, and drivers of their own car. This situation of no relationship between the variables in a contingency table is called **independence.**

independence

Independence is usually used to refer to a lack of relationship between two nominal variables. But it is conceptually the same as the notion of no correlation or a 0 correlation coefficient (see Chapter 3), except that independence means no correlation of any kind, linear or otherwise. You may also be sensing that there's something here like an interaction in a two-way analysis of variance, and you are right. Think it through if you like, or be content that your intuition is correct.

Sample and Population

It is clear in the example that the proportions of night and morning people vary with different types of transportation. For example, the bus riders are split 60–20, so three fourths of the bus riders are morning people. Among people who drive their own car, the split is 30–40, so a slight majority are night people.

Still, the sample is only of 200. It is possible that in the larger population, the type of transportation a person uses is independent of the person's being a morning or a night person. Thus the question of interest is whether the variation from independence in the sample is sufficiently large to justify rejecting the hypothesis of independence in the population.

Applying Chi-Square to a Test of Independence

To test whether the divergence from independence in a sample is large enough to conclude that the population diverges from independence, two things are required: (a) a number that represents the degree to which a sample differs from independence and (b) knowledge of the distribution of that number in general. Both of these are accomplished with a slight modification of the chi-square test that you have already learned. This modified procedure is called a **chi-square test for independence.**

chi-square test for independence

Determining Expected Frequencies

The principle of applying chi-square to tests of independence rests on determining what frequencies would be expected in each cell of the contingency table if the two variables were independent. Once these expected frequencies are known, computing chi-square is a straightforward matter in which each cell represents a category and the number in that cell represents the observed frequency for that category.

Now look at Table 14-6, the original contingency table with the expected frequencies entered in parentheses next to the observed frequencies. Follow the logic of the next paragraph while looking at these numbers.

If the two variables, transportation and sleep tendency, are independent, the distributions of cases up and down each of the transportation columns (the cell for morning and the cell for night) should not differ. This distribution of morning and night people in each column should be the same as the overall distribution of cases, meaning that transportation method is not affecting the number. That overall morning and night distribution is shown in the total column at the right—60% morning and 40% night. Again, if morning versus night is independent of type of transportation used, this 60%–40% split should hold for each column (each transportation type). The 60%–40% overall split should hold for the bus group—making an expected frequency in the bus cell for morning people of 60% of 80, or 48, and an expected frequency of 32 (40% of 80) in the bus cell for night people. Similarly, the expected frequencies in the carpool column should break down its total of 50 people into a 60%–40% split of 30 (60% of 50) and 20 (40% of 50), respectively, and the expected frequencies in the own-car column should break down as 42 (60% of 70) and 28 (40% of 70).

TABLE 14-6
Contingency Table of Observed (and Expected) Frequencies of Morning and Night People Using Different Types of Transportation (Fictional Data)

		Transportation			Total
		Bus	Carpool	Own Car	
Sleep Tendency	Morning	60 (48)[a]	30 (30)	30 (42)	120 (60%)
	Night	20 (32)	20 (20)	40 (28)	80 (40%)
	Total	80	50	70	200 (100%)

[a] Expected frequencies are in parentheses.

Stated as a formula,

$$E = \left(\frac{R}{N}\right)\left(C\right)$$

(14-2)

where E = expected frequency for a particular cell, R = number of cases (observed) in this cell's row, N = number of cases total, and C = number of cases (observed) in this cell's column.

Applying the formula to the cell for morning persons who ride the bus,

$$E = \left(\frac{R}{N}\right)\left(C\right) = \left(\frac{120}{200}\right)\left(80\right) = (.60)(80) = 48$$

Notice that the expected frequencies add up to the same totals across columns and rows as the observed frequencies. (For example, in the first column, the expected frequencies of 32 and 48 add up to 80, just as the observed frequencies in that column of 60 and 20 do; similarly, in the top row, the expected frequencies of 48, 30, and 42 add up to 120, just as the observed frequencies of 60, 30, and 30 do.) This is necessarily true because the method of creating the expected frequencies involves redistributing the existing numbers within each column while keeping the distribution for the row totals the same. In any case, it is always a good idea to make sure that the expected frequencies do add up to the same row and column totals, as a check on your arithmetic.

Computing Chi-Square

Once the observed and expected frequencies are known, computing chi-square follows the same procedures as in the chi-square test for goodness of fit: Add up the results for each cell. We use the same formula as before, but now to compute the chi-square for our two-variable example:

$$\chi^2 = \Sigma = \frac{(O-E)^2}{E} = \frac{(60-48)^2}{48} + \frac{(30-30)^2}{30} + \frac{(30-42)^2}{42} + \frac{(20-32)^2}{32}$$

$$+ \frac{(20-20)^2}{20} + \frac{(40-28)^2}{28} = 3 + 0 + 3.43 + 4.5 + 0 + 5.14 = 16.07$$

Degrees of Freedom

As you have come to expect, before you can test for significance with most statistics, you must know the degrees of freedom. A rule for degrees of freedom in a chi-square contingency table is that it is the number of columns minus 1 times the number of rows minus 1. Put as a formula,

$$df = (N_C - 1)(N_R - 1)$$

(14-3)

where N_C is the number of columns and N_R is the number of rows. Using this formula for our example,

$$df = (N_C - 1)(N_R - 1) = (3 - 1)(2 - 1) = (2)(1) = 2$$

A contingency table with many cells may have relatively few degrees of freedom—in our example, six cells and 2 degrees of freedom. This is because in a chi-square test for independence, the degrees of freedom are

TABLE 14-7
Contingency Table Showing Marginal and Two Cells' Observed Frequencies to Illustrate Computation of Degrees of Freedom

		Transportation			Total
		Bus	Carpool	Own Car	
Sleep Tendency	Morning	60	30	——	120 (60%)
	Night	——	——	——	80 (40%)
	Total	80	50	70	200 (100%)

based on the number of cells in the contingency table in which the cell frequencies are free to vary once you have determined the **marginal frequencies**—the numbers at the ends of the rows and bottoms of the columns.

marginal frequencies

Consider the sleep tendency and transportation study. If you know the first two cell frequencies across the top, for example, and all the marginal frequencies, you could compute all the other cell frequencies. Table 14-7 shows the contingency table for this example with just the marginal frequencies and these two cell frequencies. You can complete the rest of the top row by figuring that if there is a total of 120 (the marginal frequency for that row) and the other two cells have 90 in them (60 + 30), then only 30 remain. These must go in the own-car cell. And if you know the cell frequencies for the morning people and the totals (column marginal frequencies) for morning and night, the night people are the numbers left over out of that total after subtracting out the morning people. (For example, if there are 80 bus riders and 60 are morning people, the remaining 20 must be night people.) So in this example, although there are six cells, there are only 2 degrees of freedom—only two cells whose frequencies are really free to vary.

Hypothesis Testing

With 2 degrees of freedom, Table 14-2 (or Table B-4) shows that the chi-square needed for significance at the .01 level is 9.211. Since our obtained chi-square of 16.07 is larger than this cutoff point, we can reject the null hypothesis that the two variables are independent in the population.

Steps of Hypothesis Testing and the Chi-Square Test for Independence: An Example

We have just conducted a complete hypothesis test using the chi-square test for independence (that is, for two variables). However, as we did when considering the chi-square test for goodness of fit (that is, for one variable), it will be useful to review the process, using the same example, but this time following systematically the five steps of hypothesis testing.

1. Reframe the question into a research hypothesis and a null hypothesis about the populations. These are the two populations of interest:

Population 1: People like those surveyed
Population 2: People for whom being a night or a morning person is independent of the kind of transportation used to commute to work

FIGURE 14-4
For the sleep tendency and transportation example, chi-square distribution (*df* = 2) showing the cutoff for rejecting the null hypothesis at the .01 level.

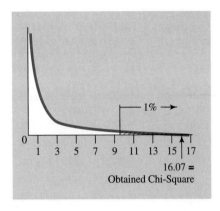

The null hypothesis is that the two populations are the same, that in general the breakdown of transportation types used is the same for morning and night people. The research hypothesis is that the two populations are different, that among people in general the breakdowns of frequencies over types of transportation are different for night and morning people.

Put another way, the null hypothesis is that the two variables are independent (that they are unrelated to each other); the research hypothesis is that they are not independent (that they are related to each other).

As was true when considering the chi-square test for goodness of fit, these are not directional hypotheses. We are not specifying any particular direction of relationship, just that there is nonindependence.

2. Determine the characteristics of the comparison distribution. The comparison distribution is a chi-square distribution with 2 degrees of freedom. If you know the number of cases in two cells and the marginals, all the others are fixed. Or, using the rule for contingency tables, the number of cells free to vary is the number of columns minus 1 times number of rows minus 1.

3. Determine the cutoff sample score on the comparison distribution at which the null hypothesis should be rejected. The sample score refers to its chi-square. You use the same table as for any chi-square test. In the example, setting a .01 significance level, with 2 degrees of freedom, a chi-square statistic of 9.211 or greater is needed to reject the null hypothesis.

4. Determine the score of your sample on the comparison distribution. Here is where you must do all the chi-square computation, following the steps listed earlier. In the example, the total chi-square statistic was 16.07.

5. Compare the scores obtained in Steps 3 and 4 to determine whether to reject the null hypothesis. Because the minimum chi-square needed to reject the null hypothesis has been set at 9.211 and the chi-square for our sample data is 16.07, the null hypothesis can be rejected (see Figure 14-4). The research hypothesis that the two variables are not independent in the population is supported.

Another Example

In connection with a paper on the nature of emotion, Russell (1991) conducted a small study to address a specific point of controversy. According to Russell, we do not recognize something as an emotion by applying clear-

TABLE 14-8
Is Pride an Emotion?

Definition	Response	
	Yes	*No*
Satisfaction or pleasure taken in one's work, achievements, or possessions	47	14
Sense of one's own proper dignity or value	36	20

Note. Subjects were university students who responded to a brief questionnaire during class time. Subjects were randomly assigned to condition, $\chi^2(1, N = 117) = 2.32$, n.s.

From Russell, J. A. (1991), tab. 2. In defense of a prototype approach to emotion concepts. *Journal of Personality and Social Psychology*, *60*, 37–47. Copyright, 1991, by the American Psychological Association. Reprinted by permission of the author.

cut criteria, as we would, for example, in recognizing something as a triangle (for which the criterion is having three sides). Instead, emotions are recognized by their similarity to a model case, what is called a *prototype*. Other researchers on emotion, however, have argued that people are fuzzy in identifying many emotions only because the words we use have more than one meaning. One such critic pointed out, for example, that the word *pride* can mean either (a) "pleasure or satisfaction taken in one's work, achievement, or possessions" or (b) "a sense of one's own proper dignity or value" (Johnson-Laird & Oatley, 1986; quoted in Russell, 1991, p. 43).

Russell met this critique head on by conducting a questionnaire survey in one of his classes. Students were given one or the other of the definitions of pride and asked whether pride was an emotion. Russell predicted that the definition of pride a student was given (one variable) would not make any difference in the proportion saying that it was or was not an emotion (the second variable). His results are shown in Table 14-8.

Russell gives the chi-square and the conclusion in his table. But as an illustration of the procedure for computing a chi-square test for independence, let us work it out fully and see if we get the same result.

Table 14-9 shows Russell's results, with the marginal totals and percentages for the two definitions along with the expected frequencies for each cell (in parentheses) based on these percentages. Also shown in the table are the computations for the chi-square test for independence.

1. Reframe the question into a research hypothesis and a null hypothesis about the populations. There are two populations of interest:

Population 1: People who are like those surveyed
Population 2: People whose belief that pride is or is not an emotion is independent of how pride is defined

The null hypothesis is that these two populations are the same—that the population represented by the people surveyed is identical to a hypothetical population in which the opinion as to whether pride is or is not an emotion is independent of the definition of pride these people are given. The research hypothesis is that these two populations are not the same—that the population this sample represents is *not* like a hypothetical population in which considering pride an emotion and definition given are independent. To put this another way, the null hypothesis says that there is no association between considering pride an emotion and definition given; the research

TABLE 14-9
Results and Computation of the Chi-Square Test for Independence Comparing Whether Subjects Rate Pride as an Emotion Differently According to the Definition of Pride Given

	Response		Total
	Yes	*No*	
Satisfaction	47 (43.3)	14 (17.7)	61 (52.14%)
Sense of dignity	36 (39.7)	20 (16.3)	56 (47.86%)
	83	34	117

(Row label at left: **Definition**)

Degrees of freedom = $(N_C - 1)(N_R - 1) = (2 - 1)(2 - 1) = (1)(1) = 1$.

Chi-square needed, $df = 1$, .05 level: 3.841.

$$\chi^2 = \Sigma \frac{(O - E)^2}{E} = \frac{(47 - 43.3)^2}{43.3} + \frac{(14 - 17.7)^2}{17.7} + \frac{(36 - 39.7)^2}{39.7} + \frac{(20 - 16.3)^2}{16.3}$$

$$= .32 + .77 + .34 + .84 = 2.27.$$

Conclusion: Do not reject the null hypothesis.

Note. Data from Russell (1991).

hypothesis is that there is such an association. (Note that Russell was actually predicting that there would be no difference. However, for consistency and to avoid confusion, we still refer to the no-difference situation as the null hypothesis and the situation in which the populations are different as the research hypothesis. It is just because of unusual situations like this that statisticians often prefer to use *null* and *alternative hypotheses* instead of *null* and *research hypotheses* as we do in this book.)

2. Determine the characteristics of the comparison distribution. This is a chi-square distribution with 1 degree of freedom, as shown in Table 14-9.

3. Determine the cutoff sample score on the comparison distribution at which the null hypothesis should be rejected. Using the .05 level and 1 degree of freedom, the chi-square table shows a cutoff of 3.841. (This is also illustrated in Figure 14-5.)

4. Determine the score of your sample on the comparison distribution. The expected frequencies for each cell are shown in parentheses in the contingency table at the top of Table 14-9. Each cell's expected frequency was calculated, as described earlier, by taking its row's percentage of all cases and multiplying that by the total number of cases in its column. Chi-square was then computed by taking for each cell the squared difference between observed and expected frequencies and then dividing this by the expected frequency. The total chi-square is shown in Table 14-9 to come out to 2.27. (This differs slightly from the 2.32 Russell reported due to rounding error; Russell probably used a computer program that maintains a large number of decimal places.)

5. Compare the scores obtained in Steps 3 and 4 to determine whether to reject the null hypothesis. The value of 2.27 is less extreme than the cutoff chi-square of 3.841 (see Figure 14-5). Thus we cannot reject the null hypothesis. The experiment is inconclusive as to whether or not people's feeling that pride is an emotion depends on the definition they are given.

FIGURE 14-5
For the example from Russell (1991), chi-square distribution ($df = 1$) showing the cutoff for rejecting the null hypothesis at the .05 level.

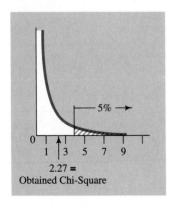

5%

2.27 =
Obtained Chi-Square

Russell actually drew a stronger conclusion from these data—he suggested that the failure to reject the null hypothesis was in support of the null hypothesis. (This was what Russell wanted to show; his position was that there is no relationship between pride's being seen as an emotion and the definition given.) In favor of Russell's conclusion about the null hypothesis being supported is the fact that the power of this study (with 117 subjects and using a .05 significance level) was relatively high. Thus one could argue that if there was a true association in the population, it was given a fair chance to show up in this study. However, the chi-square Russell obtained in his study was fairly high and not impossibly far from significance ($p = .13$). So one could also argue that there may well be a reasonable-sized association in the population that would have attained significance had the study been done with a slightly larger sample. We will have more to say about this issue later in the chapter when we discuss measures of effect size for chi-square.

A Third Example

Barglow, Vaughn, and Molitor (1987) conducted a study to examine the effect on the security of infants of mother's presence at home versus substitute care in the home during the day while the mother works. The 110 infants studied were all about 12 months old and were from middle-class two-parent families. In about half of the families the mother was at home, and in about half the mother had been working full time for at least the preceding 4 months. Based on observations of the infant's behavior in a standard "strange situation" procedure, each infant was classified as either "insecure-avoidant," "secure," or "insecure-resistant."

Table 14-10 shows the results of the study along with the percentages in the at-work and at-home groups and, in parentheses, the expected frequencies based on these percentages. Below the contingency table are the computations for the chi-square test of independence.

1. Reframe the question into a null hypothesis and a research hypothesis about the populations. There are two populations of interest:

Population 1: Infants like those surveyed
Population 2: Infants whose security or insecurity classification is independent of whether or not their mother works

The null hypothesis is that the two populations are the same, that in general the security or insecurity classification is independent of whether or not the mother works. The research hypothesis is that the populations are not the same—that infants like those surveyed are unlike the hypothetical population in which infant's security is independent of mother's working.

2. Determine the characteristics of the comparison distribution. This is a chi-square distribution with 2 degrees of freedom.

3. Determine the cutoff sample score on the comparison distribution at which the null hypothesis should be rejected. Using the .05 level and 2 degrees of freedom, the needed chi-square for significance is 5.991. This is illustrated in Figure 14-6.

4. Determine the score of your sample on the comparison distribution. The expected frequencies for each cell, calculated following the same pro-

TABLE 14-10
Results and Computation of the Chi-Square Test for the Study of Infant Security and Whether or Not Mother Works

	Insecure-Avoidant	Secure	Insecure-Resistant	Total
Mother Works	17 (10.80)	29 (33.88)	8 (9.33)	54 (49.1%)
At home	5 (11.20)	40 (35.12)	11 (9.67)	56 (50.9%)
Total	22	69	19	110 (100.0%)

Degrees of freedom = $(N_C - 1)(N_R - 1) = (3 - 1)(2 - 1) = (2)(1) = 2$.

Chi-square needed, $df = 2$, .05 level: 5.991.

$$\chi^2 = \Sigma \frac{(O - E)^2}{E} = \frac{(17 - 10.80)^2}{10.80} + \frac{(29 - 33.88)^2}{33.88} + \frac{(8 - 9.33)^2}{9.33}$$

$$+ \frac{(5 - 11.20)^2}{11.20} + \frac{(40 - 35.12)^2}{35.12} + \frac{(11 - 9.67)^2}{9.67}$$

$$= 3.559 + .703 + .190 + 3.432 + .678 + .183 = 8.74.$$

Conclusion: Reject the null hypothesis.

Note. Data from Barglow, Vaughn, & Molitor (1987).

cedures as in the previous examples, are shown in parentheses in the contingency table at the top of Table 14-10. Using these figures, the computations shown at the bottom of the table yield a chi-square of 8.74.

5. Compare the scores obtained in Steps 3 and 4 to determine whether to reject the null hypothesis. Because our value of 8.74 is larger than the cutoff chi-square of 5.991, the conclusion is to reject the null hypothesis (see Figure 14-6). So judging from a sample of infants from middle-class two-parent families, whether or not the mother works is associated with the infant's security or insecurity rating. (Remember, of course, that this is a correlational study in the sense that mothers were not randomly assigned to work or not, and thus the same issues we considered in Chapter 3 regarding causal interpretations apply here. For example, it is quite possible that some third factor, something that made some mothers work, might also account for the infants' security or insecurity. It is even possible that an infant's security or insecurity influenced the mother's decision about working.)

FIGURE 14-6
For the example from Barglow, Vaughn, and Molitor (1987), chi-square distribution ($df = 2$) showing the cutoff for rejecting the null hypothesis at the .05 level.

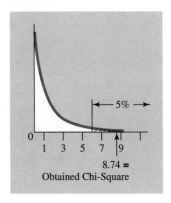

8.74 =
Obtained Chi-Square

Assumptions for Chi-Square Tests

One of the great advantages of a chi-square test over most other inferential statistical procedures is that it has minimal assumptions. For example, you do not need to have a normal distribution of anything. (Thus chi-square tests are examples of what are sometimes called "nonparametric" or "distribution-free" tests. Other tests of this kind are discussed in Chapter 15.)

There is, however, one key assumption: Each observed case must be independent of all the others. That is, chi-square (in its ordinary applications) requires that selecting any one particular subject cannot in any way make it more likely that some other particular subject will be selected. Certainly, if the same subject appeared in two cells, that would violate the assumption. Thus the chi-square test you have learned in this chapter would not apply (at least not in a direct way) in a situation in which each subject was tested twice, as in a repeated-measures design (for example, a study in which 20 people were tested to see if the distribution of their preferred brand of breakfast cereal changed from before to after a recent nutritional campaign).

Effect Size and Power for Chi-Square Tests for Independence

Estimated Effect Size for 2 × 2 Contingency Tables: The Phi Coefficient

In chi-square tests of independence, it is possible to convert the chi-square statistic into a number that describes the degree of association. In the case of a 2 × 2 contingency table, the measure of association is called the **phi coefficient.** It is the square root of chi-square divided by the number of cases in the entire sample. In terms of a formula,

$$\phi = \sqrt{\frac{\chi^2}{N}}, \qquad\qquad (14\text{-}4)$$

phi coefficient

where ϕ (Greek letter "phi") is the phi coefficient, χ^2 is the chi-square computed for a 2 × 2 contingency table, and N is the number of cases in the entire sample observed in the study.

The phi coefficient has a minimum of 0 and a maximum of 1 and is interpreted like a correlation coefficient. In fact, if you were to take the two variables in a 2 × 2 contingency table and arbitrarily make one of the values of each equal to 1 and the other equal to 2 (or any other two numbers), you could then compute a correlation coefficient between the two variables and the result would be exactly the same as the phi coefficient. (Note, however, that the correlation can come out positive or negative, depending on which column gets the 1s and which the 2s. A phi coefficient, by contrast, is always positive. This is because it is the positive square root of dividing chi-square, which is always positive, by the number of subjects, which is also always positive.)

Cohen's (1988) conventions for the phi coefficient are that .10 is a small effect size, .30 is a medium effect size, and .50 is a large effect size. (These are exactly the same conventions as for a correlation coefficient.)

For example, in the Russell (1991) study of whether or not pride was considered an emotion, the 2 × 2 test for independence gave a chi-square of 2.27 with a sample size of 117. Applying the formula for the phi coefficient,

$$\phi = \sqrt{\frac{\chi^2}{N}} = \sqrt{\frac{2.27}{117}} = \sqrt{.0194} = .14$$

This is equivalent to a correlation of .14 between saying pride is an emotion or not and definition of pride given. This is not a large effect size, and having this clear indicator of effect size supports Russell's contention that whether or not people consider pride an emotion is not much affected by the definition they are using. (We will return yet again to this example shortly when we look directly at the issue of power.)

Estimated Effect Size for Contingency Tables Larger Than 2 × 2: Cramer's Phi

Cramer's phi statistic can be thought of as an extension of the ordinary phi coefficient so that it can be applied to contingency tables that are larger than 2 × 2. (Cramer's phi is also known as Cramer's V and is sometimes written ϕ_C or V_C.) It is computed identically to the phi coefficient, except that instead of dividing by N, you divide by N times the degrees of freedom of the smaller dimension. Here it is stated as a formula:

$$\text{Cramer's } \phi = \sqrt{\frac{\chi^2}{(N)(df_S)}} \tag{14-5}$$

where df_S is the degrees of freedom for the smaller dimension of the contingency table, the dimension with the lesser degrees of freedom.

In the transportation preference example, the chi-square statistic was 16.07, the total number of subjects was 200, and the degrees of freedom for the smaller dimension (the rows) was 1. Thus Cramer's phi is the square root of what you obtain when you divide 16.07 by 200 times 1, which comes out to .28. In terms of the formula,

$$\text{Cramer's } \phi = \sqrt{\frac{\chi^2}{(N)(df_S)}} = \sqrt{\frac{16.07}{(200)(1)}} = \sqrt{\frac{16.07}{200}} = \sqrt{.08} = .28$$

In the Barglow et al. (1987) study, the chi-square statistic was 8.74, the total number of infants was 110, and the degrees of freedom for the smaller dimension (again the rows) was 1. Thus to compute Cramer's phi, you first divide 8.74 by 110 (the number of subjects times 1) and then take the square root of this number. This yields .28. In terms of the formula,

$$\text{Cramer's } \phi = \sqrt{\frac{\chi^2}{(N)(df_S)}} = \sqrt{\frac{8.74}{(110)(1)}} = \sqrt{\frac{8.74}{110}} = \sqrt{.08} = .28$$

In both of these cases, because the degrees of freedom for the smaller dimension was 1, Cramer's phi gives the same result as when using the ordinary phi coefficient. But in cases where the degrees of freedom for the smaller dimension is greater than 1, Cramer's phi gives a different and more appropriate result.

The relation of Cramer's phi to power depends on the size of the smaller dimension of the table (df_S). Table 14-11 shows Cohen's (1988) effect size conventions for Cramer's phi for tables in which the smallest dimension is 2, 3, and 4. Note that when the smallest dimension is 2, and thus degrees of freedom is 1, the effect sizes given in the table for this situation are the same as for the ordinary phi coefficient.

TABLE 14-11
Cohen's Conventions for Cramer's Phi

Smallest Dimension of Contingency Table	Effect Size		
	Small	Medium	Large
2 ($df_s = 1$)	.10	.30	.50
3 ($df_s = 2$)	.07	.21	.35
4 ($df_s = 3$)	.06	.17	.29

Power

The power of a study testing hypotheses using nominal variables is determined by the same two main factors that determine power in any study: effect size and sample size. The larger the effect size and the larger the sample size, the greater the power.

Table 14-12 shows the approximate power at the .05 significance level for small, medium, and large effect sizes and *total* sample sizes of 25, 50, 100, and 200. Values are given for tables with 1, 2, 3, and 4 degrees of freedom.[3]

For example, the power of a planned 2×4 study (thus $df = 3$) of 50 subjects with an expected medium effect size (Cramer's $\phi = .30$), to be carried

[3]More detailed tables are provided in Cohen (1988, pp. 228–248). Cohen's tables are based on an effect size called w, which is equivalent to phi but not to Cramer's phi. He provides a helpful conversion table of Cramer's phi to w on page 222.

TABLE 14-12
Approximate Power for the Chi-Square Test of Independence for Testing Hypotheses at the .05 Significance Level

Total df	Total N	Effect Size		
		Small ($\phi = .10$)	Medium ($\phi = .30$)	Large ($\phi = .50$)
1	25	.08	.32	.70
	50	.11	.56	.94
	100	.17	.85	*
	200	.29	.99	*
2	25	.07	.25	.60
	50	.09	.46	.90
	100	.13	.77	*
	200	.23	.97	*
3	25	.07	.21	.54
	50	.08	.40	.86
	100	.12	.71	.99
	200	.19	.96	*
4	25	.06	.19	.50
	50	.08	.36	.82
	100	.11	.66	.99
	200	.17	.94	*

*Nearly 1.

TABLE 14-13
**Approximate Total Number of Subjects Needed to Achieve 80% Power
for the Chi-Square Test of Independence for Testing Hypotheses
at the .05 Significance Level**

Total *df*	Effect Size		
	Small *($\phi = .10$)*	*Medium* *($\phi = .30$)*	*Large* *($\phi = .50$)*
1	785	87	26
2	964	107	39
3	1,090	121	44
4	1,194	133	48

out using the .05 level, would be .40. This means that if the research hypothesis is in fact true, and there is a true medium effect size, there is about a 40% chance that the study will come out significant.

Also consider the implications for interpreting a completed study. In the Russell 2×2 study, if there is a true small effect size in the population, then with about 100 subjects, the power to find significance at the .05 level is only .17. Thus one cannot rule out from these results that such a small effect might exist. However, the power table shows that were there a large effect size in the population, there is almost no chance that it would have failed to show up in this study.

Planning Sample Size

Table 14-13 gives the approximate total number of subjects needed to achieve 80% power for small, medium, and large effect sizes at the .05 significance level for chi-square tests of independence of 2, 3, 4, and 5 degrees of freedom.[4] For example, if you are planning a study involving a 3×3 (*df* = 4) contingency table and you expect a large effect size and will use the .05 significance level, you would only need 48 subjects (about 5 or 6 per cell).

Controversies and Limitations

In 1949, Lewis and Burke published a landmark paper on the misuse of chi-square. They listed nine common errors that had appeared in published papers, giving many examples of each. With one exception, their work has held up very well through the years. The errors are still being made, and they are still seen as errors.

The one exception to this critical picture is the error that Lewis and Burke considered the most common weakness in the use of chi-square: expected frequencies that are too low. Now it seems that low expected numbers in cells may not be much of a problem after all. Lewis and Burke, as did most statistics textbook authors of their time, held that every cell of a contingency table (and every category of a goodness of fit test) should have a reasonable-sized expected frequency. Lewis and Burke recommended a minimum of 10, with 5 as the very bottom limit. Others recommended figures ranging from 1 to 20. Even Sir Ronald Fisher (1938) got into the act, recom-

[4]More detailed tables are provided in Cohen (1988, pp. 253–267).

mending 10 as his minimum. Still others recommended that the minimum should be some proportion of the total or that it depended on whether the expected frequencies were equal or not. (Incidentally, notice that what was being debated are minimum *expected* frequencies, not observed frequencies.)

Since 1949, when Lewis and Burke published their article, there has been some systematic research on just what the effects of low expected frequencies are. (These studies use Monte Carlo methods—see Box 10-1.) And what is the conclusion? As in most areas, the matter is still not completely settled. However, a major review of the research on the topic (Delucchi, 1983) draws two main conclusions:

1. "As a general rule, the chi-square statistic may be properly used in cases where the expected values are much lower than previously considered permissible" (p. 168). Even expected frequencies as low as 1 per cell may be acceptable in terms of Type I error, provided that there are a reasonable number of subjects. The most important principle seems to be that there should be at least five times as many subjects as there are cells. For example, a low expected frequency would be acceptable in a 2×2 contingency table if there were at least 20 subjects.[5]

2. However, Delucchi cites one researcher as concluding that even though using chi-square with small expected frequencies may be acceptable (in the sense of not giving too many Type I errors in the long run), it may still not be a wise approach. This is because the chance of obtaining a significant result, even if your research hypothesis is true, may be quite slim (power is very low). So you run the risk of Type II errors instead.

Chi-Square Tests as Reported in Research Articles

The reporting of chi-square tests almost always includes the information that you would need to repeat the calculation. In the case of a goodness of fit test, the number of cases in each category, the expected frequencies, and some description of the basis for determining the expected frequencies will usually be described. If the expected frequencies are not described, ordinarily it is assumed that what is expected is an equal distribution across categories. In the case of a contingency table (by far the most common use of chi-square in psychology research), the contingency table itself will usually be given. Ordinarily, it will show only observed frequencies, but it may also show their percentages.

The actual chi-square test result is sometimes given with the table of observed frequencies, sometimes in the text (and occasionally in both places). Ordinarily, it is reported in a way that indicates the degrees of freedom, number of subjects, computed chi-square, and significance level. For example, for the check on whether there was initially equal preferences for

[5]If, in a table larger than 2×2, a category or cell has an extremely small expected frequency (or even a moderately small expected frequency if the number of subjects is also small), one solution is to combine related categories to increase the expected frequency and reduce the total number of cells. But this is a solution of last resort if you are making the adjustment based on the results of the experiment, since you are then capitalizing on knowing the outcome. The best solution is to add more subjects to the study. If this is not feasible, an alternative procedure, called "Fisher's exact test," is sometimes possible. It is described in some intermediate statistics texts.

the three fictional candidates in the Stasser et al. (1989) study described earlier in the chapter, the result of the chi-square test was as follows:

> The relative frequencies of prediscussion preferences, presented in Table 1 [a version of the same data as in the first column of our Table 14-1], suggest that we were not entirely successful in constructing equally attractive candidates. Although Candidates A and C were chosen about equally often . . . before group discussion, B was noticeably less popular. For these prediscussion preferences, the hypothesis of equal popularity can be confidently rejected, $\chi^2(2, N = 531) = 28.35, p < .001$. (p. 71)

As another example, Pugh and Boer (1991) administered a questionnaire version of the WAIS-R Information Subtest (the WAIS-R is one of the most widely used adult intelligence tests) to 200 Canadian students. The concern was that some of the items in the test, which was constructed in the United States, are based on information that U.S. citizens are more likely to know. For example, one item asks for the name of two recent U.S. presidents, and another asks about the U.S. Civil War.

Since the WAIS-R is such a widely used test, data are available—called standardized norms (see Chapter 7)—that represent reasonably well what the expected percentage of correct answers should be on each item for people in the United States. Pugh and Boer simply compared the numbers correct in their Canadian sample with the numbers that would have been expected in the United States. For example, 73% of U.S. adults typically give correct answers to the Civil War question. If the Canadians were no different, of the 200 tested, 146 should get the item correct; in fact, only 85 did. (The Canadians did as well or better on the items that were not culturally biased toward the United States.)

Pugh and Boer present the numbers in a table. In the text, they discuss the five key items as follows: "Chi-square analyses showed these items to be significantly more difficult when [probabilities of getting the item correct for the Canadians tested] . . . were compared with the standardization norm group ($p < .001$)" (p. 152).

Regarding the chi-square test for independence, an example of results reported in a table would be the one we produced directly from the Results section of Russell's (1991) study of whether or not people consider pride an emotion (see Figure 14-4). As an example of a verbal description of a chi-square test for independence in the text of an article, Barglow and colleagues (1987) reported their result on infants of working and nonworking mothers as follows: "Analysis of these data showed that the distribution of attachment classifications [the secure and insecure categories] were significantly different for the two groups, $\chi^2(2) = 8.74, p < .02$" (p. 949). Their paper also gave the contingency table and discussed the percentages of cases in each cell.

Summary

Chi-square tests are used for hypothesis tests involving nominal variables (variables whose levels are categories).

The chi-square statistic measures the amount of discrepancy between expected and observed frequencies of cases over several levels or categories. It is computed by making a table and finding for each category or cell the difference between observed frequency and expected frequency, squaring this difference (to eliminate positive and negative signs), and dividing by the expected frequency (to help make the squared differences more proportionate to the number of cases involved). The results are then added over all the categories or cells. The distribution of the chi-square statistic is known, and standard tables are available indicating the significance-level cutoffs for various degrees of freedom (based on the number of categories or cells that are free to vary).

The chi-square test for goodness of fit is used to test hypotheses about whether a distribution of frequencies over two or more levels or categories of one nominal variable matches an expected distribution. (These expected frequencies are based, for example, on theory or on a distribution in another study or circumstance). Hence in this test, the expected frequencies are given in advance. The degrees of freedom are the number of categories minus 1.

The chi-square test of independence is used to test hypotheses about the relationship between two nominal variables—whether the distribution of cases over the categories or levels of one variable has the same proportional pattern within each of the categories of the other variable. The data are set up in a contingency table, in which the two variables are crossed and the number of cases that fall into each combination are entered into each of the resulting cells. The frequency expected for a given cell if the two variables are independent is the percentage of all the scores in that cell's row times the total number of cases in that cell's column. The degrees of freedom for the test of independence are the number of columns minus 1 times the number of rows minus 1.

Chi-square tests make no assumptions about normal distributions of their variables, but they do require that the category or cell that a case falls in be independent of every other case.

The estimated effect size for a chi-square test of independence (that is, the degree of association) for a 2×2 contingency table is the phi (ϕ) coefficient, and for larger tables, Cramer's phi. Phi is the square root of the result of dividing the computed chi-square by the number of cases. Cramer's phi is the square root of the result of dividing the computed chi-square by the product of the number of cases times the degrees of freedom in the smaller dimension of the contingency table. These coefficients range from 0 to 1 and can be interpreted in approximately the same way as a correlation coefficient. A phi of .10 is considered a small effect, .30 a medium effect, and .50 a large effect.

The minimum acceptable frequency for a category or cell has been a subject of controversy. Currently, the best advice is that even very small expected frequencies do not seriously increase the chance of a Type I error provided that there are at least five times as many subjects as categories (or cells). However, low expected frequencies seriously reduce power and should be avoided if possible.

Chi-square tests reported in research articles often include all information about the numbers in each category or cell as well as the computed chi-square and its significance.

Key Terms

categorical variable
chi-square distribution
chi-square statistic
chi-square table
chi-square test for goodness of fit

chi-square test for independence
contingency table
Cramer's phi statistic
expected frequency
independence

marginal frequencies
nominal variable
observed frequency
phi coefficient

Practice Problems

These problems involve computation (with the assistance of a calculator). Most real-life statistics problems are done on a computer. But even if you have a computer, do these by hand to ingrain the method in your mind.

For practice in using a computer to solve statistical problems, refer to the computer section of each chapter of the study guide that accompanies this text.

All data are fictional (unless an actual citation is given).

Answers to Set I are given at the back of the book.

SET I

1. Compute a chi-square test of goodness of fit for each of the following (use the .05 level for each):

(a)

Category	Expected	Observed
A	20%	19
B	20%	11
C	40%	10
D	10%	5
E	10%	5
		50

(b)

Category	Expected	Observed
I	30%	100
II	50%	100
III	20%	100
		300

(c)

Category	Number in the Past	Observed
1	100	38
2	300	124
3	50	22
4	50	16
		200

(d)

Category	Observed[a]
Arts	37
Sciences	21
Humanities	32

[a]Expected is the same number in each category.

2. A director of a small psychotherapy clinic is trying to plan hiring of temporary staff to assist with intake and is wondering if there is any difference in the use of the clinic at different seasons of the year. Last year there were 28 new clients in the winter, 33 in the spring, 16 in the summer, and 51 in the fall. On the basis of last year's data, should the director conclude that season makes a difference? (Use the .05 level.) Explain your answer to a person who has never taken a course in statistics.

3. Compute a chi-square test for independence for each of the following contingency tables (use the .01 level, and compute phi or Cramer's phi for each):

(a)

10	16
16	10

(b)

100	106
106	100

(c)

100	160
160	100

(d)

10	16	10
16	10	10

(e)

10	16	16
16	10	16

(f)

10	16	10
16	10	16

4. An educational researcher is interested in whether students who use a typewriter or a word processor (or neither) when writing in their private room tend to use a pen or a pencil when they are taking notes in class. The researcher surveys 200 students and obtains the results shown in the accompanying table. Is there a significant relationship between these two variables? (Use the .05 level, and compute Cramer's phi.) Explain your answer to a person who has never taken a course in statistics.

		Device Used in Their Room		
		Typewriter	Word processor	Neither
Implement Used for Notes	Pen	42	62	26
	Pencil	18	38	14

5. A political analyst is interested in whether the community a person lives in is related to that person's opinion on an upcoming water conservation ballot initiative. The analyst surveys 90 people by phone and obtains the results shown here. Is opinion related to community at the .05 level? Also compute Cramer's phi. Explain your answer to a person who has never taken a course in statistics.

	Community A	Community B	Community C
For	12	6	3
Against	18	3	15
No opinion	12	9	12

6. Blass (1991), as part of a discussion of studies of obedience to authority, considered a possible cross-cultural difference. In obedience-to-authority studies, individuals are led to believe that they will be giving a series of increasingly strong and painful electric shocks to another subject. In one version of these studies, the subject meets the person who will receive the shocks and then goes into the next room where the subject can hear what the subject believes is the person screaming and complaining. The issue in these studies (which have raised considerable ethical debate) is how many subjects under these conditions will obey the experimenter and continue to give the shocks.

In his article, Blass compares the results of the original version of these studies conducted by Milgram (1974) in the United States to some Australian studies done shortly thereafter:

> In Australia, Kilham and Mann (1974) found a significantly lower rate of obedience (28% [14 of 50]) than Milgram (1974) did in a comparable voice-feedback condition (Experiment 2; 62.5% [25 of 40]) with his American subjects, $\chi^2(1, N = 90) = 10.77$, $p < .01$. (p. 407)

A footnote at this point in Blass's article says, "Chi-square was computed by me."

Explain this result to a person who has never had a course in statistics.

SET II

1. Compute a chi-square test of goodness of fit for each of the following (use the .01 level for each):

(a)	Category	Expected	Observed
	1	2%	5
	2	14%	15
	3	34%	90
	4	34%	120
	5	14%	50
	6	2%	20

(b)	Category	Proportion Expected	Observed
	A	1/3	10
	B	1/6	10
	C	1/2	10

2. Compute a chi-square test of goodness of fit for each of the following, using the .05 level for each. In each case, the expected distribution is equal frequencies in each category.

(a) 5 10 5   (b) 10 15 10   (c) 10 20 10   (d) 5 15 5

3. A U.S. researcher wants to be sure that the sample in her study is not unrepresentative of the distribution of ethnic groups in her community. Her sample includes 300 whites, 80 African-Americans, 100 Latinos, 40 Asians, and 80 others. In her community, according to census records, there are 48% whites, 12% African-Americans, 18% Latinos, 9% Asians, and 13% others. Is her sample unrepresentative of the population? (Use the .05 level.) Explain your answer to a person who has never taken a course in statistics.

4. Compute a chi-square test for independence for each of the following contingency tables (use the .05 level, and also compute phi or Cramer's phi for each):

(a)
8	8
8	16

(b)
8	8
8	32

(c)
8	8
8	48

(d)
8	8	8
8	8	8
8	8	16

(e)
8	8	8
8	8	8
8	8	32

(f)
8	8	8
8	8	8
8	8	48

5. The following chart shows the results of a survey of a sample of people attending a ballet, distributed according to the type of seat they purchased and how regularly they attend. Is there a significant relation? (Use the .05 level, and compute Cramer's phi.) Explain your answer to someone who has never had a course in statistics.

		Attendance	
		Regular	*Occasional*
Seating Category	*Orchestra*	20	80
	Dress circle	20	20
	Balcony	40	80

6. As part of a study about attitudes of heterosexuals toward homosexuality, Whitley (1990) asked 366 heterosexual students on an anonymous questionnaire whether or not they knew anyone who was a homosexual. Whitley reports, "Female (61.9%) and male (59.5%) respondents were equally likely to report knowing a gay person, $\chi^2(1, N = 366) < 1$." Whitley, continues, "However, among the respondents knowing a gay person, women were more likely to report knowing a lesbian (63.4%) than men were to report knowing a gay man (14.4%), $\chi^2(1, N = 223) = 12.602, p < .001$" (p. 374).

Compute the phi coefficient for the second result, and explain the finding and your computation to a person who has never had a course in statistics.

15

Strategies When Population Distributions Are Not Normal
Data Transformations, Rank-Order Tests, and Computer-Intensive Methods

THIS chapter examines the various strategies employed when analyzing the results of a study in which the variables are numerical, not nominal, as in Chapter 14, but the assumption of a normal population distribution is clearly violated—an assumption that underlies most ordinary hypothesis-testing procedures, such as the t test and the analysis of variance. First we briefly review the role of assumptions in the standard hypothesis-testing procedures. Then we examine three approaches that can be applied when the assumptions have not been met: data transformations, rank-order tests, and computer-intensive methods.

Assumptions in the Standard Hypothesis-Testing Procedures

As we saw in Chapters 9 through 13, you have to make certain assumptions to carry out a t test or an analysis of variance. In these hypothesis-testing procedures, we treat the data in our experiment as if they came from some larger, though unknown, population or populations. One assumption we make is that the population or populations involved have a normal (bell-shaped) distribution. (If the populations are not normal, the appropriate comparison distribution is not necessarily a precise t or F distribution, on which the corresponding tables of significance cutoffs are based.) The other main assumption we make is that the populations from which the different experimental groups come have equal variances. (This assumption permits us to pool variances in the *t* test for independent means and to determine a within-group variance estimate in the analysis of variance that averages the variance estimates from the different groups.)[1]

When Assumptions Are Violated

As we noted in previous chapters, the *t* test and the analysis of variance are thought to be generally robust to violations of assumptions. That is, according to Monte Carlo studies (see Box 10-1), in most cases that have been tried in which the population distributions are known not to be normal, they still give acceptably accurate results. (But review our discussion in Chapter 5 about whether populations are more than rarely normal or follow any other consistent patterns.) In any case, the general view among psychology researchers is that only when the data suggest that the assumptions are violated to an extreme extent or in certain combinations do the standard procedures give unacceptable results.

In previous chapters, we considered what happens when the assumption of equal population variances is violated and mentioned ways to deal with the situation (for example, using separate variance estimates in the *t* test and using reduced degrees of freedom in both the *t* test and the analysis of variance). In this chapter, we focus primarily on what happens when there is an extreme violation of the normality assumption. However, some of the procedures we examine are also applicable when the equal-variance assumption is not met.

When the normal curve assumption is strongly violated, the ordinary *t* test or analysis of variance yields an incorrect result. Usually that incorrect result is to make a Type I error more likely—though the table says .05, the real probability of getting these data if the null hypothesis were true might actually be much higher, sometimes as much as .15 or higher. But using the standard procedure when the assumptions have not been met can also make Type II errors more likely. In other words, failure to meet the normal curve assumption can lead to the worst of both worlds—the procedures can turn out too reckless when you want them to be cautious or too stingy when you want them to be generous. In many cases, this is just not predictable.

Recognizing Violations of the Normality Assumption

It is important to keep in mind that assumptions are about populations and not about samples. It is quite possible for a sample not to be normally distributed even though it comes from a population that is normal. Figure 15-1 shows histograms for several random samples, each of which is drawn from a normal population. (Notice that the smaller the sample, the harder it is to

---

[1]These two assumptions—and the various solutions we will discuss for dealing with the situation in which they are not met—also apply when we test hypotheses about correlations and regression coefficients (as introduced briefly in the second appendix to Chapter 3). In the case of regression, we assume that in the population, at each level of the predictor variable, the dependent variable is normal and also that the variance of the dependent variable is the same at each level of the predictor variable. In correlation, the requirement is even stricter, requiring each variable and the combinations of variables to be normally distributed. Sophisticated methods for identifying whether these assumptions may have been violated are presented in more advanced texts. But we can at least assume that the assumptions have *not* been met if the sample data suggest that in the population the overall distribution is not normal for the dependent variable (in regression) or for both (in correlation).

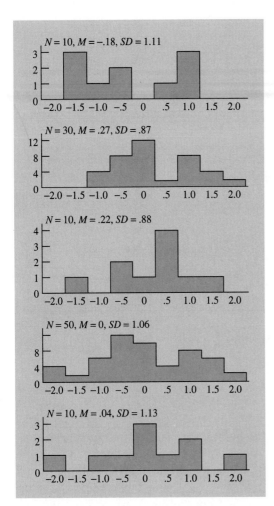

FIGURE 15-1
Histograms for several random samples, each drawn from a normal population with $\mu = 0$ and $\sigma = 1$.

see that it came from a normal population.) Of course, it is quite possible for nonnormal populations to produce any of these samples as well.

Unfortunately, all we have available when conducting a study is the distribution of the sample. Consequently, the usual practice is to look at the histogram for the sample, and unless it is drastically divergent from normal, we assume that the population it came from is normal. When it comes to normality, most researchers consider a distribution innocent until proven guilty.

One common situation in which we are led to doubt the normal distribution assumption is when there is a ceiling or floor effect. As we discussed in Chapter 1, this situation arises when there is some upper or lower limit on the measuring instrument that keeps the underlying variable from being distributed across its full range of values.

Another common situation that raises doubts about normality is when the sample has outliers (discussed in Chapter 2)—extreme cases at one or both ends of the sample distribution. Figure 15-2 shows some examples of distributions with outliers. Outliers are technically a special case of skewness (or if at both ends of the distribution, of kurtosis), but they are sufficiently important in their own right to bear special attention. (However, if you notice an outlier in a sample, first check to be sure it is not due to an error in recording or entering the data into the computer.)

FIGURE 15-2
Distributions with outliers at one or both ends.

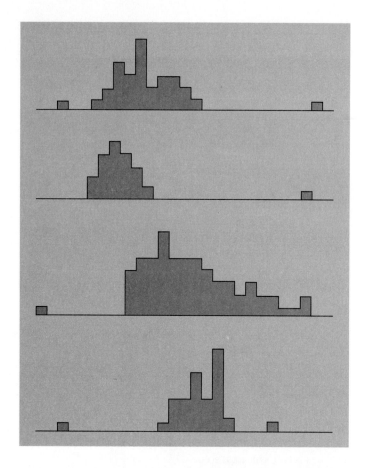

Outliers are a big problem in the statistical methods we ordinarily use because these methods rely, ultimately, on squared deviations from the mean. An outlier, because it is so far from the mean, has a disproportionately large influence when its deviation is squared. The result is that a single outlier, if it is extreme enough, can cause a statistical test to give a significant result even when all the other scores suggest that in fact there is no difference. Conversely, an outlier, if it is opposite to the predicted direction, can undermine what would otherwise turn out to be a significant difference.

Data Transformations

A widely used procedure when the sample data do not appear to come from a normal population is to change the data! Not by fudging—although at first it may sound that way, until we explain. The researcher simply takes each score in the original distribution and applies some mathematical procedure to it, such as taking the square root. The goal is to make a nonnormal distribution closer to normal. (Sometimes this can also make the variances of two or more groups more similar as well—though it can also have the effect of making them more different.) This is called a **data transformation.** Once you have made a data transformation, if the other assumptions are met, you can then proceed to apply the usual *t* test or analysis of variance, and you will get accurate results.

data transformation

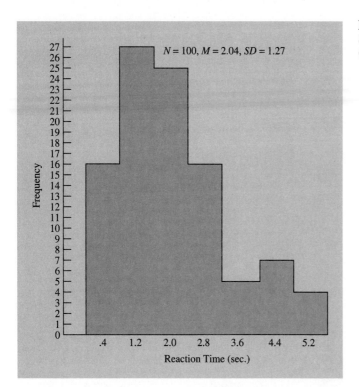

FIGURE 15-3
Skewed distribution of reaction times (fictional data).

$N = 100$, $M = 2.04$, $SD = 1.27$

Data transformation has an advantage over other procedures of coping with nonnormal populations that you will learn about in that it permits the use of familiar and sophisticated hypothesis-testing procedures.

Consider an example. Measures of reaction time are usually highly skewed to the right—there are many short (quick) responses and a few, but sometimes quite extreme, long (slow) ones. It is hard to imagine that the reaction times shown in Figure 15-3 come from a normally distributed population. The population of reaction time scores itself is probably skewed.

However, consider what happens if you take the square root of each reaction time. Most reaction times are affected only a little—a reaction time of 1 s stays 1 s; a reaction time of 1.5 s reduces to 1.22. But very long reaction times, the ones that create the long tail to the right, are substantially reduced—for example, a reaction time of 9 s is reduced to 3, and a reaction time of 16 s (the person was really distracted and forgot about the task) reduces to 4 s. Figure 15-4 shows the result of taking the square root of each score in the skewed distribution shown in Figure 15-3. As you can see, this distribution, of scores subjected to **square-root transformation,** seems **square-root transformation** much more likely to have come from a population with a normal distribution (of transformed scores).

Legitimacy of Data Transformation

Do you feel that this is somehow cheating? It would be if it were done to only some scores or done in any other way to make the result more favorable to the researcher's predictions. However, in actual research practice, the first step after the data are collected and recorded is to check that they meet assumptions and then to carry out transformations if they don't; com-

FIGURE 15-4
Data from Figure 15-3 after square-root transformation.

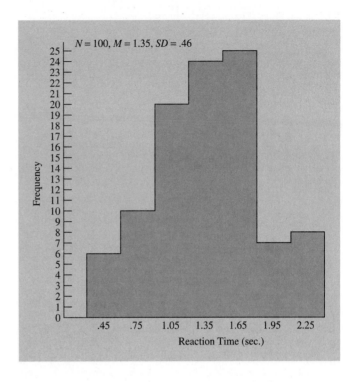

parisons among groups and significance tests are carried out only after this has been done. Also, of course, any transformation of scores on a variable is applied to scores on that variable for all subjects, not just those in a particular experimental condition or group. And most important, no matter what transformation procedure we use, the *order* of the scores always stays the same—a raw score that is the second highest in a group of scores will still be second highest in the group of transformed scores.

Still, the procedure may seem somehow to distort reality to fit the statistics. In some cases, this is a legitimate concern. If you are looking at the difference in income between two groups, you are probably interested not in how much the two groups differ in the square root of their income but in how much the actual dollar earnings differ.

By contrast, precise scores on a self-esteem questionnaire do not have any direct meaning. Higher scores mean greater self-esteem; lower scores, less self-esteem. But each unit of increase on the test is not necessarily related to an equal amount of increase in an individual's self-esteem. It is just as likely that the square root of each unit's increase is directly related to the person's self-esteem. The example we used earlier of reaction time, measured in seconds, would seem to have a direct meaning. But even in this case, the underlying variable, efficiency of processing of the nervous system, may be a complex operation that follows some unknown mathematical rule (though we would still expect that shorter times go with more efficient processing and longer times with less efficient processing).

So in cases in which the underlying "yardstick" of the variable is not known, there is no reason to think that the transformed version is any less accurate a reflection of the reality than the original version. And the transformed version may meet the normality assumption.

Kinds of Data Transformations

There are several types of data transformations. We have already illustrated a square-root transformation: Instead of using each score, you use the square root of each score. We gave an example in Figures 15-3 and 15-4. The general effect is shown in Figure 15-5a. As you can see, a distribution skewed to the right becomes less skewed to the right after square-root transformation. To put it numerically, moderate numbers become only slightly lower and high numbers become much lower; as a result, the right-hand side is pulled in toward the middle.

Probably the most common transformation is the **log transformation.** A log transformation has the same general effect as a square-root transformation: It makes a distribution skewed to the right less skewed to the right. But the log transformation is more severe—it can pull into normal shape an even more extremely right-skewed distribution. This is illustrated in Figure 15-5b.

log transformation

As you may recall from high school trigonometry, a logarithm is the exponent to which you raise some base number (such as 10) to obtain the original number. For example, with base 10, the log of 100 is 2—to get the number 100, you take 10 to the second power (you square it). So if a score was 100 and the base was 10, its score would become a 2. The log for 1,000 would be 3; 10 to the third power (cubed) is 1,000. A score of 1,000 would become 3. The log for 10 is 1 (any number to the first power is itself), and the log for 1 is 0 (any number to the power 0 is 1). A score of 10 becomes 1, and a score of 1 becomes 0. In-between numbers have logs with fractions. The log for 50 is 1.70, for 60 is 1.78, for 8 is .90, and for 328 is 2.52. A range of 1 to 1,000 has contracted to a range of 0 to 3, with much greater effect on larger numbers.

It is not necessary to calculate logs—tables of them are easy to find, and log computations are available on many calculators. The main point to remember is that a log transformation does just what a square-root transformation does, only more so. You would use it when your data are so skewed

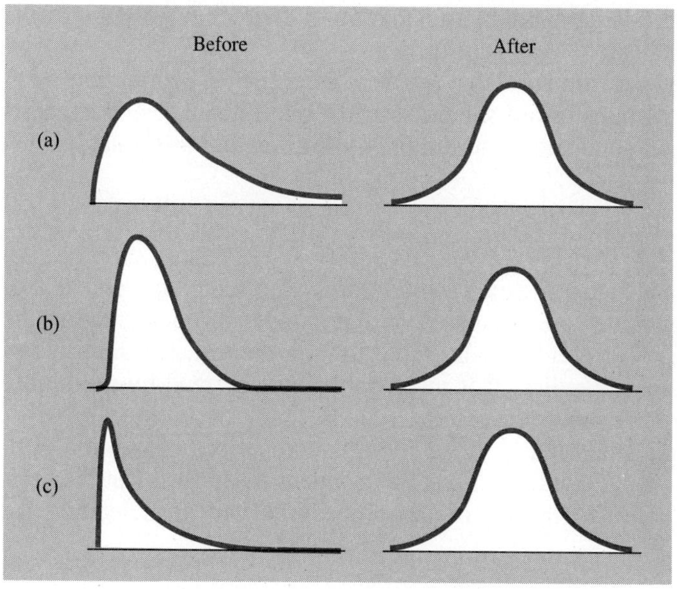

FIGURE 15-5
Distributions to which transformations are appropriately applied: (a) moderately skewed to the right—apply square-root transformation; (b) strongly skewed to the right—apply log transformation; (c) extremely skewed to the right—apply inverse transformation.

to the right that a square-root transformation still does not make the distribution approximate normal.

Another common transformation is an **inverse transformation.** In this case, you take the inverse of each number—that is, you make it the denominator of a fraction in which 1 is the numerator. The inverse of 10 is 1/10; the inverse of 5 is 1/5; the inverse of 1,000 is 1/1,000. (The inverse of 1/10 is 10 and of 1/5 is 5.) The important point is that an inverse transformation also does the same thing as the square-root and the log transformation but has an effect even more extreme than the log transformation, for use on data that are even more skewed. This is illustrated in Figure 15-5c.

Other transformations are also available. For one thing, all of the transformations we have considered so far operate to correct a distribution that is skewed to the right. When a distribution is skewed to the left, you can instead use the square of the numbers or the "antilog." Sometimes researchers "reflect" the variables (reverse all the scores, making highs lows and lows highs by subtracting each score from the same high score), then apply a square-root, log, or inverse transformation. Other transformations deal with problems of kurtosis and of "lumpy" distributions. But in this chapter, for purposes of introducing the key ideas, we will restrict ourselves to the most common types of transformations and focus on problems associated with right-skewed distributions. But remember that the transformation procedures that psychologists use have one feature in common: They keep the order of the scores in a distribution the same. If Subject B's raw score is between Subject A's and Subject C's, after the transformation it will still be between A's and C's.

Steps of Data Transformations

Data transformations can be summarized in the following steps:
1. Examine the sample data to estimate the kind and degree of nonnormal shape of the population distribution. (If there are two or more groups, examine the distribution within each group. Also, when sample sizes are large enough, a histogram or frequency polygon of the sample data can be very helpful.)
2. Apply the transformation that seems to offer the best correction.
3. Examine the transformed sample distribution; if it still clearly suggests a nonnormal population distribution, try a different transformation.

An Example of Data Transformation

Consider a fictional study in which four children who score high on a test of being "highly sensitive" are compared on the number of books read in the preceding year to four children who score low on the test. On the basis of theory, the researcher predicts that more books will be read by the highly sensitives. Table 15-1 shows the results.

Ordinarily in a study like this, involving a comparison of two independent groups, we would conduct a *t* test for independent means. But the *t* test for independent means, like all of the procedures you have learned for

inverse transformation

TABLE 15-1
Results of a Study Comparing Highly Sensitive and Not Highly Sensitive Children on the Number of Books Read in the Past Year (Fictional Data)

	Highly Sensitive	
	No	*Yes*
	0	17
	3	36
	10	45
	22	75
Σ:	35	173
$M =$	8.75	43.25
$S^2 =$	95.58	584.00

hypothesis testing (except chi-square), requires that the parent populations of scores for each group be normally distributed. We also noted that the t test, particularly in a case like this involving equal sample sizes, is fairly robust to violations of this assumption. But this case is quite extreme. In both groups, the distribution of the sample is clearly skewed to the right— the scores tend to bunch up at the left, leaving a long tail to the right. It thus seems likely that the population of scores of number of books read (for both sensitives and nonsensitives) is also skewed to the right. In fact, this seems reasonable, considering that a child cannot read less than zero books, but once a child starts reading, it is not hard to read a lot of books in a year. (Also note that the estimated population variances based on the two samples are dramatically different, 95.58 versus 584, a condition that also precludes conducting an ordinary t test for independent means. But in this case, as often happens, we will see that when we transform scores to make them more nearly normally distributed, we will also solve the problem of different variances.)

It would seem inappropriate to compute an ordinary t test with these data. But the clear and consistent skew in the same direction in both groups suggests that a transformation might solve the problem. In fact, the logic of what number of books read means also suggests that a transformation might be called for. If number of books read is meant as a measure of interest in things literary, the difference between 0 and 1 book is a much greater difference than the difference between 20 and 21 books.

Let's follow the steps listed earlier:

1. Examine the sample data to estimate the kind and degree of nonnormal shape of the population distribution. The sample data suggest population distributions that are skewed to the right to a reasonable degree.

2. Apply the transformation that seems to offer the best correction. We will start with the least severe of those we have considered, the square-root transformation. This means taking the square root of each score, as shown in Table 15-2.

3. Examine the transformed sample distribution; if it still clearly suggests a nonnormal population distribution, try a different transformation. Inspection of the transformed sample scores indicates that for each group, the four cases are no longer arranged so that three are at one end and a fourth far off at 22 or 75. Instead, they are brought together much more, nearer the center, and are less dense at the two extremes in a fairly symmetrical fashion. No further transformation seems necessary.

TABLE 15-2
Square-Root Transformation of the Data in Table 15-1

	Highly Sensitive		
	No		Yes
X	$\sqrt{X}$	X	$\sqrt{X}$
0	0.00	17	4.12
3	1.73	36	6.00
10	3.16	45	6.71
22	4.69	75	8.66

TABLE 15-3
Computations for a *t* Test for Independent Means Using Square-Root-Transformed Data for the Study of Books Read by Highly Sensitive Versus Not Highly Sensitive Children (Fictional Data)

t needed for .05 significance level, $df = (4-1) + (4-1) = 6$, one tailed = 1.943.

Highly Sensitive

	No	*Yes*
	0.00	4.12
	1.73	6.00
	3.16	6.71
	4.69	8.66
Σ:	9.58	25.49
$M =$	9.58/4 = 2.40	25.49/4 = 6.37
$S^2 =$	12.03/3 = 4.01	10.56/3 = 3.52

$$S_P^2 = 3.77$$

$S_M^2 =$	3.77/4 = .94	3.77/4 = .94

$S_{DIF}^2 = .94 + .94 = 1.88$
$S_{DIF} = \sqrt{1.88} = 1.37$
$t = (6.37 - 2.40)/1.37 = 2.90$

Conclusion: Reject the null hypothesis.

Having made what seems to be an appropriate transformation of the data so that the assumption of normal population distributions appears to be reasonably met, we can now proceed with our *t* test. The calculations are shown in Table 15-3. As can be seen from the table, the difference is clearly significant.[2]

Another Example of Data Transformation

Consider another example, this time involving a correlation. A study is conducted on the association between score on an algebra test and grade in school. Four individuals are tested. The scatter diagram is shown in Figure 15-6, and the data and computation of the correlation coefficient are shown in Table 15-4.

As can be seen from the table, there is some degree of correlation, but as is apparent from both the scatter diagram and the raw data, the person with the algebra test score of 95 is clearly an outlier on that variable. Or to put it the other way, the algebra test scores are skewed to the right, bunching up near the lower limit of the test scores with a long tail reaching to the score of 95 on the far right. The grade-level data look reasonably evenly distributed, with scores bunching near the middle (the 6 and 7) and then spreading out evenly a little more on either side (the 4 and 9). Thus there is no reason to suspect a nonnormal distribution for that variable.

What to do about the clearly nonnormal algebra test distribution? First, does it even matter? The correlation coefficient makes no assumptions—it is

[2]Incidentally, had we conducted the analysis using the original untransformed scores, $t = (43.25 - 8.75)/13.04 = 2.65$, a slightly lower but still significant level. Of course, it would not have been correct to carry out such an analysis, and had it yielded a different result, the result based on the transformed data would be the correct one to use.

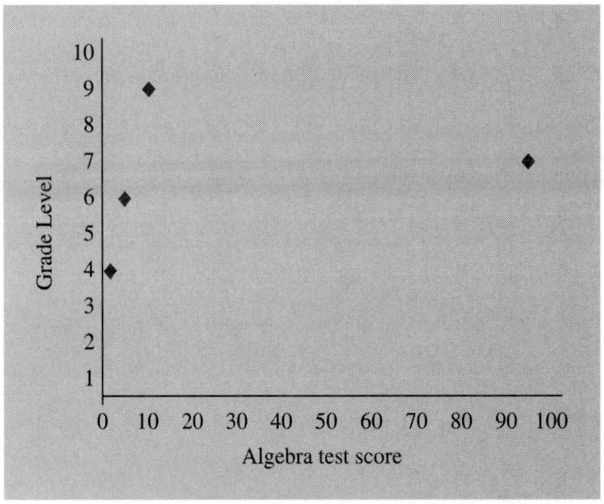

FIGURE 15-6
Scatter diagram for a study of grade level and algebra test scores (fictional data).

simply a description of the degree of linear correlation between two variables. However, if the variables are not normally distributed, there are two problems: (a) The correlation will probably be lowered because a skewed distribution tends to create a curvilinear relationship that the linear approach cannot take into account, and (b) calculating the *significance* of a correlation coefficient does require assumptions, and these are usually not met unless the populations of both variables are normally distributed.[3]

So what is the solution? First, in a case like this where there is a single clear outlier, we would probably check for errors in scoring or try to learn whether the particular subject was in some way atypical of the population being studied (such as someone who was in an accelerated math program or whose parent was a famous mathematician). But assuming that nothing is known or can be learned, another solution is to transform the test score data so that they are no longer skewed. This also seems reasonable in this case, as there is no special value in knowing the raw number of items correct on the test. So let us go through the steps of data transformation for this example.

1. Examine the sample data to estimate the kind and degree of nonnormal shape of the population distribution. The distribution of algebra test scores is highly skewed to the right.

[3]See footnote 1.

TABLE 15-4
Data and Computation for a Study Correlating Grade Level and Algebra Test Scores (Fictional Data)

	Test Score		Grade Level		Cross-Product
	Raw	Z_X	*Raw*	Z_Y	$Z_X Z_Y$
	1	− .68	4	−1.47	1.00
	4	− .60	6	− .29	.17
	10	− .45	9	1.47	− .66
	95	1.73	7	.29	.50
Σ:	110		26		1.01
$M =$	27.5		6.5		$r =$ .25
$SD =$	39.1		1.7		

FIGURE 15-7
Scatter diagram for the study of grade level and algebra test scores shown in Figure 15-6 after a log transformation of the algebra scores (fictional data).

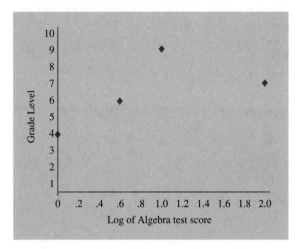

2. Apply the transformation that seems to offer the best correction. We could first try a square-root transformation. This would change the test scores from 1, 4, 10, and 95 to 1, 2, 3.2, and 9.7.

3. Examine the transformed sample distribution; if it still clearly suggests a nonnormal population distribution, try a different transformation. The square-root transformation is still quite skewed to the right. A more extreme transformation is called for. So we would next try a log transformation. Using a calculator (with a key for log to the base 10), we computed the logs of 1, 4, 10, and 95 to be 0, .6, 1, and 1.98. This distribution is only slightly skewed to the right and seems to be a likely candidate to have been sampled from a population (of log-transformed scores) in which most of the scores bunch in the middle and there are fewer but equal numbers at the two extremes.

Having found an appropriate transformation, we can now try our correlation again. The scatter diagram is shown in Figure 15-7 and the computations in Table 15-5. As you can see from the computations, the correlation computed with the transformed scores come out to .65. The correlation using the untransformed scores, as shown in Table 15-4, comes out to only .25.

Table 15-5 also shows the computation of the significance of the correlation coefficient, using the procedure for computing t described in the second appendix to Chapter 3. Even with a correlation as high as .65, with only four subjects there is insufficient power to reject the null hypothesis. (With a correlation, the null hypothesis is that the correlation in the population is 0.) Nevertheless, at least it was correct to compute this t test, in the sense that we had met the assumption of normal distributions. (Had we incorrectly computed t for the correlation of .25 from the untransformed scores, t would have come out to only .37, versus the 1.21 found with the transformed scores.)

Rank-Order Methods

Another way of coping with nonnormal distributions is to transform the scores to ranks. If you have a sample with scores 4, 8, 12, and 64 (a rather surprising sample from a normal population), you could convert the scores to 1, 2, 3, and 4—the 1 referring to the lowest number in the group, the 2 to the second lowest, and so forth. (The only complication is when you have

TABLE 15-5
Data and Computation for a Study Correlating Grade Level and Log-Transformed Algebra Test Scores (Fictional Data)

	Test Score		Grade Level		Cross-Product
	Raw	Z_X	Raw	Z_Y	$Z_X Z_Y$
	0.00	−1.25	4	−1.47	1.84
	.60	− .42	6	− .29	.12
	1.00	.14	9	1.47	.21
	1.98	1.50	7	.29	.44
Σ:	3.58		26		2.61
M =	.90		6.5		r = .65
SD =	.72		1.7		

Significance test:

t needed (.05 level, $df = 2$, one-tailed) = 2.920

$t = (r\sqrt{N-2})/\sqrt{1-r^2} = (.65)(1.41)/\sqrt{1-.65^2} = .92/.76 = 1.21$

Conclusion: Do not reject the null hypothesis that $r = 0$.

two or more scores that are the same. The standard solution in this case is to give them each the average rank. For example, the scores 12, 81, 81, 107, and 154 would be ranked 1, 2.5, 2.5, 4, and 5, respectively.)

Converting the scores to ranks is a kind of data transformation. But unlike the ones we have considered so far, a rank-order transformation is not used to produce a normal distribution. It does, however, produce a particular distribution—one that is rectangular (except for ties), with equal numbers of cases (one) at each value. Ranks have the effect of spreading the scores out evenly.

There are several special hypothesis-testing procedures that make use of rank-ordered data. These are called **rank-order tests.** They also have two other common names. Because data from a population with any shaped distribution can be transformed into ranks, these tests are sometimes called **distribution-free tests.** And because the distribution of rank-order data is known exactly rather than estimated, rank-order tests do not require estimating any parameters (population values). (For example, there is no need to estimate a population variance because you can determine exactly what it will be if you know that ranks are involved.) Hence hypothesis-testing procedures based on ranks are also called **nonparametric tests.** The ordinary hypothesis-testing procedures you have learned (t test and analysis of variance) are examples of **parametric tests.** Chi-square, like the rank-order tests, is considered a nonparametric test, but it is distribution-free only in the sense that no assumptions are made about the shape of the population distributions. However, the terms *distribution-free* and *nonparametric* are typically used interchangeably; the subtleties of differences between them are a matter of ongoing debate among statisticians.

rank-order tests

distribution-free tests

nonparametric tests

parametric tests

Overview of Rank-Order Tests

Table 15-6 shows the rank-order test corresponding to each of the parametric hypothesis-testing procedures you have learned. Where more than one possible test is listed, the procedures are approximately equivalent.

TABLE 15-6
Major Rank-Order Tests Corresponding to Major Parametric Tests

Parametric Test	Corresponding Rank-Order Test
t test for dependent means	Wilcoxin signed-rank test
t test for independent means	Wilcoxin rank-sum test or Mann-Whitney *U* test
Analysis of variance	Kruskal-Wallis *H* test
t test for correlation	Spearman rho or Kendall's tau

Next we will describe how such tests are done in a general way, including an example. However, we do not actually provide all the needed information for you to carry them out in practice. We introduce you to these techniques because you will see them used in articles you read and because their logic is the foundation of an alternative procedure that we do teach you to use. This alternative procedure accomplishes approximately the same thing as these rank-order tests and is more closely based on procedures with which you are already familiar.

Basic Logic of Rank-Order Tests

The idea of rank-order tests can be illustrated by considering a study involving an experimental group and a control group. (This is the kind of situation for which, if all assumptions were met, most researchers would use a *t* test for independent means.) If you wanted to apply a rank-order test, you would first transform all the data into ranks, ranking all the scores from lowest to highest, regardless of whether a score was in the experimental or the control group. If the two groups were randomly drawn from a single population (the null hypothesis of no difference), there should be about equal amounts of high ranks and low ranks in each group. In fact, because the distribution of ranks can be worked out exactly, it is fairly straightforward for statisticians to compute the exact probability of getting any particular distribution of ranks divided into two groups if in fact the two groups were randomly drawn.

So the basic logic is one of determining the total of the ranks in the group with the lower scores, then comparing this to a cutoff figure of the maximum total of ranks that represents the point at which a total that high would occur more than 5% of the time. The particular cutoff depends on how many subjects are in each group and is an exact number, not an estimate based on any assumptions about population shapes or anything else. If the total of the ranks in a group predicted to have lower scores is below the cutoff, the null hypothesis that the subjects are randomly divided between the two groups is rejected.

Example of a Rank-Order Test

Table 15-7 shows a computation of the Wilcoxin rank-sum test for the kind of situation we have just described, using the same data as for our first data transformation example (the fictional study of number of books read by

TABLE 15-7
Computations for a Wilcoxin Rank-Sum Test for the Study of Books Read by Highly Sensitive Versus Not Highly Sensitive Children (Fictional Data)

Cutoff for significance: Maximum sum of ranks in the not highly sensitive group for significance at the .05 level, one-tailed (from a standard table) = 11.

Highly Sensitive

No			Yes	
X	Rank		X	Rank
0	1		17	4
3	2		36	6
10	3		45	7
22	5		75	8
Σ:	11			

Comparison to cutoff: Sum of ranks of group predicted to have lower scores, 11, equals but does not exceed cutoff for significance.

Conclusion: Reject the null hypothesis.

highly sensitive versus not highly sensitive children). The logic is a little different, so be patient until we explain it.

Notice that the significance cutoff was first established, as would be the case in any hypothesis-testing procedure. (This cutoff is based on a table of exact cutoffs for rank totals for different combinations of sample sizes for the two groups. This table is not included in this book but is available in most intermediate statistics texts.)

The next steps were to rank the scores from lowest to highest, then to determine the sum of ranks in the group hypothesized to have the smaller sum, and then to compare it to the cutoff. Nothing at all has to be done to the group with the higher rank, other than use its numbers when doing the ranking. (The procedure and cutoff could just as well have been done using the group hypothesized to have the larger sum of ranks because for any given number of cases overall in both groups, the sum of ranks is fixed. But it is traditional to use the smaller sum.)

In the example, the rank total for the lower group did not exceed the cutoff, so the null hypothesis was rejected. (Although we used the Wilcoxin rank-sum test in the example in the table, we could have used the Mann-Whitney U test instead—it gives an exactly mathematically equivalent final result and is based on the same logic. It differs only in the computational details.)

The Null Hypothesis in a Rank-Order Test

The null hypothesis in the case of a rank-order test is not quite the same as in an ordinary parametric test. A parametric test compares the means of the two groups; its null hypothesis is that the two populations have the same mean. The equivalent to the mean in a rank-order test is the middle rank, which is the median of the nonranked scores. (For example, if five non-ranked scores were 11, 12, 14, 19, and 20, their corresponding ranks are 1, 2, 3, 4, and 5. The middle rank is 3, which corresponds to the median of the nonranked scores, which is the score of 14.) Thus a rank-order test compares the medians of the two groups; its null hypothesis is that the two populations have the same median.[4]

Normal Curve Approximations in Rank-Order Tests

Tables like those described for the maximum sum of ranks for rejecting the null hypothesis become quite cumbersome if moderate to large sample sizes with unequal groups have to be included. And the problem becomes truly unmanageable with more complicated designs. So several approximations have been developed that use the rank sums in a formula to produce a Z score. If the Z score is in the upper 5% (2.5% for a two-tailed test) of the normal curve, the result is considered significant. Often when rank-order tests are reported in research articles, this Z score will be given.

Using Parametric Tests with Rank-Transformed Data

Having introduced the logic of the rank-order tests and given an example of how one is carried out, we now turn to a somewhat different approach that accomplishes about the same thing using procedures with which you are more familiar. This time we will provide sufficient information for you to compute the tests on your own.

Two statisticians (Conover & Iman, 1981) have shown that instead of using the special computational procedures involved in the rank-order tests, you can obtain approximately the same results if you simply transform the data into ranks and then apply all the usual arithmetic for calculating an ordinary parametric statistic, such as a t test.

The result of using a parametric test with data transformed into ranks will not be quite as accurate as either the ordinary parametric test or the rank-order test. It won't be as accurate as the ordinary parametric test because the assumption of normal distributions is clearly violated—the distribution is in fact rectangular when ranks are involved. And it will not be as accurate as the rank-order test because the parametric test uses the t or F distribution instead of the special tables that rank-order tests use, which are based on exact probabilities of getting certain divisions of ranks. However, the approximation seems to be quite close.[5]

---

[4]Technically, the null hypothesis in a rank-order test has to be that the original population distributions for the nonranked scores in the different groups are the same in all ways, because any difference in shapes or medians will affect the ranks. (For example, if two samples represent populations with the same median, when using these tests you might still reject the null hypothesis because, for example, one population is highly skewed to the right and one is highly skewed to the left.) So if you want to be sure that your hypothesis test is really a test of the difference between population medians—which is what one usually wants to know in a nonparametric test—you have to be able to assume that the two populations do not differ in any other way. In sum, it is technically true that rank-order tests are distribution-free, in the sense that no particular assumptions need be made about the nature of the populations. But when you are using such a test to determine whether there is a difference between the *medians* of the two populations, you must assume that whatever the shapes of the two distributions, both have the same shape.

[5]A researcher who is particularly concerned about accuracy could calculate t or F using the rank-transformed scores and then convert the result to the rank-order statistic result (using one of the conversion formulas given by Conover & Iman) and look up that number in the appropriate rank-order test's table.

TABLE 15-8
Computations for a t test for Independent Means Using Ranks Instead of Raw Scores for the Study of Books Read by Highly Sensitive Versus Not Highly Sensitive Children (Fictional Data)

t needed for .05 significance level, $df = (4 - 1) + (4 - 1) = 6$, one-tailed $= -1.943$

	Highly Sensitive	
	_No_	_Yes_
	1	4
	2	6
	3	7
	5	8
Σ	11	25
$M =$	$11/4 = 2.75$	$25/4 = 6.25$
$S^2 =$	$8.75/3 = 2.92$	$8.75/3 = 2.92$

$$S_P^2 = 2.92$$

$S_M^2 =$	$2.92/4 = .73$	$2.92/4 = .73$

$S_{DIF}^2 = .73 + .73 = 1.46$
$S_{DIF} = \sqrt{1.46} = 1.21$
$t = (2.75 - 6.25)/1.21 = -2.89$

Conclusion: Reject the null hypothesis.

An Example of Conducting an Ordinary Parametric Test After a Rank-Order Transformation

Table 15-8 shows the computations of an ordinary t test for independent means for the fictional sensitive children data, using each subject's rank instead of actual number of books read. Again we get a significant result.

Levels of Measurement

Most of the time, measurement in psychology is what is called **equal-interval measurement.** This means that the difference between a score of 8 and 9 means about the same underlying amount of difference on the variable being measured as the difference between 15 and 16.

For example, a ruler as a measure of length uses equal-interval measurement. The difference between 8 and 9 inches is the same as the difference between 15 and 16 inches. But consider another example, the number of items correct on a skills test as a measure of skill. Suppose that there are 15 easy items on the test and all the others are very hard. In that case, a difference between 8 and 9 means much less than the difference between 15 and 16. The intervals are not equal. This is a common situation in psychological measurement.

One example of measurement that is not equal interval is **rank-order measurement.** For example, class standing is sometimes used as a measure of academic achievement. However, the person who is first in the class may have done only very slightly better than the person who is second, whereas the person who is second might have done considerably better than the person who was third. Knowing that one person has a higher rank than the other does tell us who has the better performance, but the exact degree by which the performance is better is not clear from the rank. Another name for rank-order measurement is **ordinal measurement.**

equal-interval measurement

rank-order measurement

ordinal measurement

(You may recall that in Chapter 14, on chi-square tests, we considered the nominal level of measurement—measurement by categories. Nominal measurement provides even less information than rank-order measurement.)

Levels of Measurement and Rank-Order Tests

One advantage of rank-order tests is that they are very appropriate for situations in which the variable being studied is measured with a rank-order measure. Such situations do arise occasionally.

More common is the situation in which the measure appears to be equal-interval but is actually questionable. The exam in which there were 15 easy items and several very difficult ones is an example. But in many situations in psychology, we do not really know that the intervals are equal. How do we know, for example, that a scale marked "1 = Disagree, 2 = Mildly disagree, 3 = Mildly agree, and 4 = Agree" is really equal-interval? But even in these cases, it is clear that the results are meaningful as rank-order information—certainly, 2 shows more agreement than 1, 3 more than 2, and 4 more than 3.

Hence some psychologists argue that in most cases, we should not assume that we have equal-interval measurement and should convert our data to ranks and use a rank-order significance test. Other researchers argue that even with true rank-order measurement, parametric statistical tests have been found to do a reasonably accurate job and that changing all the data to ranks can lose valuable information. The issue remains unresolved.

Computer-Intensive Methods

randomization tests

In recent years, thanks to the availability of computers, a whole new set of hypothesis-testing methods have become practicable. The main techniques are called **randomization tests,** "bootstrap tests," and the "jackknife." Although these methods differ in important details, their logic is sufficiently similar that we can illustrate the basic idea by focusing on one of them, randomization tests.

The Basic Randomization Test

Suppose that you have two groups of scores, one for an experimental group and one for a control group. If these scores were all mixed up, what is the chance that you could, by chance, get a division in which they would differ as much as is found in the actual division? A randomization test actually sets up rapidly, by computer, every single possible allocation of the scores into two groups of these sizes. Then it determines how many of these possible organizations have a difference as extreme as the actually observed differences between your two groups. If fewer than 5% of the possible organizations yield differences this extreme, your result is significant—the null hypothesis that the two groups could have been this different by a chance division is rejected. (This logic is like that used for working out the probabilities for rank-order tests, but in this case, scores are not first converted to ranks.)

Example of a Randomization Test

Table 15-9 shows a worked-out example of what a computer would actually do for a randomization test for the same two-group fictional study we have been using involving number of books read.

The steps for conducting a randomization test involving a difference between the means of two groups are shown next. (Remember, in the real world, computers would do all of this—we lead you through it here and in the practice problems so that you can readily grasp results using this procedure when you see them on a printout or in a journal article. This may become a very common approach in the future as psychology researchers adjust to all that high-speed computers make possible.)

1. Determine the difference between the means of the actual two groups. In the example, the mean difference was 34.5.

2. Determine how many possible divisions of groups there are and how high the actual mean difference would have to be to be in the top 5% (or 1%). There are rules for determining how many possible combinations you would need. These rules are described in some intermediate statistics textbooks, under the topic of permutations and combinations. But since you would never in an actual research study carry out a randomization test by hand, we will leave these rules for you to learn in future courses. (In the practice problems for this chapter, you will carry out some randomization tests with small numbers of cases to help engrain the principle in your mind. In those examples, we will tell you how many combinations are involved.)

In the present situation of eight subjects in two groups of four, there are 70 possible combinations. Out of 70 differences, the top 5% are the top 3.5 cases. Our mean difference will have to be among the top three in order to reject the null hypothesis (unless there is a tie for third place). (If we wanted to use a two-tailed test, we would use the top and bottom 2.5% of the 70 combinations—that is, the single top and bottom cases by themselves.)

3. Lay out the scores in every possible division into two groups (of the sizes of the original groupings). Again, there are systematic procedures for coming up with all the combinations, but this is something the computer would do for you in an actual research situation. In any case, we have shown the 70 combinations in Table 15-9.

4. Compute the difference between groups for each division. For example, in the second division shown in the example, the means are 7.5 for the low group and 44.5 for the high group, making a difference between the means of 37. We have shown the difference between means under each of the 35 combinations.

5. Order the differences from lowest (most negative) to highest. In the example, there are 70 differences, ranging from a difference of −37, where the not highly sensitives have a higher number of books read, to +37, where the highly sensitives have a higher number of books read.

6. Compare the cutoff to where your actual difference falls in the ordered listing to determine whether to reject the null hypothesis. In the example, the actual difference of +34.5 is third from the top, putting it within the required top three. The null hypothesis can be rejected.

TABLE 15-9
Randomization Test Computations for the Study Comparing Highly Sensitive and Not Highly Sensitive Children on the Number of Books Read in the Past Year (Fictional Data)

Actual Results:

Highly Sensitive

	No	*Yes*
	0	17
	3	36
	10	45
	22	75
Σ	35	173
$M =$	8.75	43.25

Actual difference $= M_{Yes} - M_{No} = 34.5$
Needed to reject the null hypothesis: This mean difference must be in top 5% of mean differences. With 70 mean differences, it must be among the three highest differences.

All Possible Divisions (70) of the Eight Scores into Two Groups of Four Each:

Actual

	No	*Yes*		*No*	*Yes*		*No*	*Yes*		*No*	*Yes*		*No*	*Yes*		*No*	*Yes*		*No*	*Yes*
	0	17		0	22		0	22		0	22		0	22		0	10		0	10
	3	36		3	36		3	17		3	17		3	17		3	36		3	17
	10	45		10	45		10	45		10	36		10	36		22	45		22	45
	22	75		17	75		36	75		45	75		75	45		17	75		36	75
$M_{Yes} - M_{No}$	34.5			37			27.5			23			8			31			21.5	

	No	*Yes*		*No*	*Yes*		*No*	*Yes*		*No*	*Yes*		*No*	*Yes*		*No*	*Yes*		*No*	*Yes*
	0	10		0	10		0	10		0	22		0	10		0	10		0	10
	3	17		3	17		3	22		3	45		3	22		3	22		3	22
	22	36		22	36		17	45		17	36		17	36		36	17		36	17
	45	75		75	45		36	75		10	75		75	45		45	75		75	45
$M_{Yes} - M_{No}$	17			2			24			37			4.5			10			−5	

	No	*Yes*		*No*	*Yes*		*No*	*Yes*		*No*	*Yes*		*No*	*Yes*		*No*	*Yes*		*No*	*Yes*
	0	10		0	3		0	3		0	3		0	3		0	3		0	3
	3	22		10	36		10	17		10	17		10	17		10	22		10	22
	45	17		22	45		22	45		22	36		22	36		17	45		17	36
	75	36		17	75		36	75		45	75		75	45		36	75		45	75
$M_{Yes} - M_{No}$	−9.5			27.5			18			13.5			−1.5			20.5			16	

	No	*Yes*		*No*	*Yes*		*No*	*Yes*		*No*	*Yes*		*No*	*Yes*		*No*	*Yes*		*No*	*Yes*
	0	3		0	3		0	3		0	3		0	3		0	3		0	3
	10	22		10	22		10	22		10	22		22	10		22	10		22	10
	17	36		36	17		36	17		45	17		17	45		17	36		17	36
	75	45		45	75		75	45		75	36		36	75		45	75		75	45
$M_{Yes} - M_{No}$	1			6.5			−8.5			−13			14.5			10			−5	

	No	*Yes*		*No*	*Yes*		*No*	*Yes*		*No*	*Yes*		*No*	*Yes*		*No*	*Yes*		*No*	*Yes*
	0	3		0	3		0	3		0	3		0	3		0	3		0	3
	22	10		22	10		22	10		17	10		17	10		17	10		36	10
	17	36		17	36		45	17		36	22		36	22		45	22		45	22
	45	75		75	45		75	36		45	75		75	45		75	36		75	17
$M_{Yes} - M_{No}$	10			−5			−19			3			−12			−16.5			−26	

No	Yes	No	Yes	No	Yes	No	Yes	No	Yes	No	Yes	No	Yes
17	0	22	0	22	0	22	0	22	0	10	0	10	0
3	3	36	3	17	3	17	3	17	3	36	3	17	3
10	10	45	10	45	10	36	10	36	10	45	22	45	22
22	22	75	17	75	36	75	45	45	75	75	17	75	36

$M_{Yes} - M_{No}$: −34.5 −37 −27.5 −23 −8 −31 −21.5

No	Yes	No	Yes	No	Yes	No	Yes	No	Yes	No	Yes	No	Yes
10	0	10	0	10	0	22	0	10	0	10	0	10	0
17	3	17	3	22	3	45	3	22	3	22	3	22	3
36	22	36	22	45	17	36	17	36	17	17	36	17	36
75	45	45	75	75	36	75	10	45	75	75	45	45	75

$M_{Yes} - M_{No}$: −17 −2 −24 −37 −4.5 −10 5

No	Yes	No	Yes	No	Yes	No	Yes	No	Yes	No	Yes	No	Yes
10	0	3	0	3	0	3	0	3	0	3	0	3	0
22	3	36	10	17	10	17	10	17	10	22	10	22	10
17	45	45	22	45	22	36	22	36	22	45	17	36	17
36	75	75	17	75	36	75	45	45	75	75	36	75	45

$M_{Yes} - M_{No}$: 9.5 −27.5 −18 −13.5 1.5 −20.5 −16

No	Yes	No	Yes	No	Yes	No	Yes	No	Yes	No	Yes	No	Yes
3	0	3	0	3	0	3	0	3	0	3	0	3	0
22	10	22	10	22	10	22	10	10	22	10	22	10	22
36	17	17	36	17	36	17	45	45	17	36	17	36	17
45	75	75	45	45	75	36	75	75	36	75	45	45	75

$M_{Yes} - M_{No}$: −1 −6.5 8.5 13 −14.5 −10 5

No	Yes	No	Yes	No	Yes	No	Yes	No	Yes	No	Yes	No	Yes
3	0	3	0	3	0	3	0	3	0	3	0	3	0
10	22	10	22	10	22	10	17	10	17	10	17	10	36
36	17	36	17	17	45	22	36	22	36	22	45	22	45
75	45	45	75	36	75	75	45	45	75	36	75	17	75

$M_{Yes} - M_{No}$: −10 5 19 −3 12 16.5 26

Seventy Differences Ordered from Lowest (Most Negative) to Highest:

−37, −37, −34.5, −32, −27.5, −27.5, −26, −21.5, −24, −23, −20.5, −16, −16.5, −17, −18, −19, −14.5, −13.5, −13, −12, −10, −10, −10, −9.5, −8.5, −8, −6.5, −5, −5, −5, −4.5, −1.5, −3, −2, −1, 1, 1.5, 2, 3, 4.5, 5, 5, 5, 6.5, 8, 8.5, 9.5, 10, 10, 10, 12, 13, 13.5, 14.5, 16, 16.5, 17, 18, 19, 20.5, 21.5, 23, 24, 26, 27.5, 27.5, 31, [34.5,] 37, 37

Conclusion: Actual mean difference is among the three highest. Reject the null hypothesis.

Another Example of a Randomization Test

Let's look again at the fictional correlation study of algebra test scores and grade level. One way of doing a randomization test for a correlation involves computing a correlation between every possible pairing of the scores for the two variables (but never pairing two scores of the same variable). In the case of four subjects, there are 24 possible pairings of this kind. So for a correlation to be significant at the 5% level, the correlation of the actual pairing of scores in the real sample has to be the highest of the 24 possible correlations. Table 15-10 shows the computations for the randomization test. As you can see, the correlation was not significant using this procedure. (This is the same outcome we obtained with these data using the log transformation earlier in the chapter.)

TABLE 15-10
Randomization Test Computation for the Study Correlating Grade Level and Algebra Test Scores (Fictional Data)

Needed to reject the null hypothesis: The actual correlation must be the highest of the 24 possible correlations to reject null hypothesis at the 5% level, one-tailed.

Correlations of All Possible Pairings of Algebra Test Scores (ATS) with Grade Level (GL)

Actual

ATS	GL		ATS	GL		ATS	GL		ATS	GL		ATS	GL
1	4		1	6		1	9		1	7		1	9
4	6		4	9		4	7		4	4		4	6
10	9		10	7		10	4		10	6		10	7
95	7		95	4		95	6		95	9		95	4
$r = .25$			$r = -.79$			$r = -.24$			$r = .79$			$r = -.82$	

ATS	GL		ATS	GL		ATS	GL		ATS	GL		ATS	GL
1	7		1	9		1	7		1	4		1	4
4	6		4	4		4	6		4	7		4	9
10	9		10	6		10	4		10	6		10	7
95	4		95	7		95	9		95	9		95	6
$r = -.76$			$r = .12$			$r = .75$			$r = .82$			$r = .52$	

ATS	GL		ATS	GL		ATS	GL		ATS	GL		ATS	GL
1	7		1	4		1	4		1	6		1	6
4	4		4	9		4	7		4	4		4	4
10	9		10	6		10	9		10	9		10	7
95	6		95	7		95	6		95	7		95	9
$r = -.11$			$r = .18$			$r = -.08$			$r = .22$			$r = .82$	

ATS	GL		ATS	GL		ATS	GL		ATS	GL		ATS	GL
1	6		1	6		1	9		1	9		1	7
4	9		4	7		4	4		4	7		4	9
10	4		10	4		10	7		10	6		10	6
95	7		95	9		95	6		95	4		95	4
$r = .11$			$r = .76$			$r = .18$			$r = -.84$			$r = .82$	

ATS	GL		ATS	GL		ATS	GL		ATS	GL
1	4		1	6		1	9		1	7
4	6		4	9		4	7		4	9
10	7		10	4		10	6		10	4
95	9		95	7		95	4		95	6
$r = .84$			$r = .11$			$r = -.84$			$r = -.22$	

Correlations from Lowest to Highest:

−.84, −.84, −.82, −.79, −.76, −.24, −.22, −.18, −.11, −.08, .11, .11, .12, .18, .22, .25, .52, .75, .76, .79, .82, .82, .82, .84

Conclusion: Do not reject the null hypothesis.

The Approximate Randomization Test

We have illustrated the randomization test using very small samples. Even so, there were quite a few possible organizations of the data in each case. With larger (and more realistic) sample sizes, the number of different organizations quickly becomes unmanageable, even for most computers. For example, a comparison between two groups of seven subjects has 3,432 possible divisions; a comparison of 10 subjects per group has 184,756. With 20 per group, there are 155,120,000! In practice, even most computers cannot handle true randomization tests with the size of samples usually used in psychology research.

To deal with this problem, statisticians have developed what are called **approximate randomization tests.** The principle is that the computer randomly selects a large number of possible rearrangements of the sample—perhaps 100 or even 1,000. These are considered representative of what you would find if you were actually to use every possible division. (This is similar to a Monte Carlo study, which we described in Box 10-1. And how does something as orderly as a computer come up with so many random numbers? See Box 15-1.)

approximate randomization tests

The other methods we mentioned at the outset—the bootstrap and the jackknife—also work in this kind of way: The computer generates a large number of random selections, and the actual result is compared to the theoretically possible ones the computer has sampled. The only differences among the procedures are in the kinds of combinations that are selected randomly; these are technical issues beyond the scope of an introductory book.

Comparison of Methods

We have considered three methods of conducting hypothesis tests when samples appear to come from nonnormal populations: data transformation, rank-order tests, and computer-intensive methods such as the randomization test. How does a researcher decide which to use?

General Advantages and Disadvantages of the Data Transformation Approach

Data transformations have the advantage of permitting the use of familiar parametric techniques on the transformed data. But transformations cannot always be applied (that is, there may not be any reasonable transformation that makes the data normal in all groups). Also, transformations may distort the scores in ways that lose the original meaning.

General Advantages and Disadvantages of Rank-Order Tests

Rank-order methods can always be applied. And they are especially appropriate when the original data are ranks or are not clearly equal-interval (which may be true of psychological measures more often than we like to think). Further, the logic of rank-order methods is simple and direct, requir-

BOX 15-1

Where Do Random Numbers Come From?

To be random, numbers must be selected with equal odds, so that the odds of each one's appearance are totally independent of the odds of the one before and after it. One of the many important uses of random numbers is in computer-intensive statistical methods, as discussed in this chapter. They are also essential to Monte Carlo studies (see Box 10-1), which are used to test the effect of violating normality and other assumptions of parametric statistical tests—one way for psychologists to know whether they need to use the methods described in this chapter. But random numbers in themselves are an interesting topic.

The first random number table was created in 1927. Before that, mechanical methods such as shuffling devices were used. Remember William S. ("Student") Gosset (Box 9-1)? To obtain his random numbers, he shuffled and drew from a deck of 3,000 cards. Then in 1927, Karl Pearson encouraged L. H. C. Tippett to publish a table. Tippett found drawing numbered cards from a bag "unsatisfactory," so he selected digits from the 1925 census report. Later, in 1938, R. A. Fisher and Frank Yates published a list based on logarithms. And at about the same time, a number of methods of checking for randomness were also introduced.

Later more sophisticated physical solutions became common. Flashing a beam of light at irregular intervals onto a sectioned rotating disk was one. Another used the radiation of radioactive substances. It recorded the number of particles detected during a certain time span; if the number was odd, it set a counter to 1, and if even, to 0, and then generated lists of numbers from groupings of these binary digits. A third system employed an electronic valve that made noise that could be amplified; the fluctuating output values were random.

All of these physical methods were a nuisance: They required storing the numbers if they were to be reproduced or reused, and all this apparatus was hard to maintain. So computers are now often used, to create "pseudorandom numbers," using some special equation, such as squaring large numbers and taking a central group of the resulting digits. But these numbers are in some subtle sense not random but predictable because of the very fact that there was an intention in the equation's design—to create randomness (quite a paradox). There is also the problem of whether equations will "degenerate" and begin to repeat sequences. Finally, no matter how the list is generated, there is controversy about the consequences of repeated use of the same table.

The whole topic of how difficult it is to create something free of order or intelligence seems to say something. What that is, we will leave for you to decide.

---

ing no elaborate construction of hypothetical distributions or estimated parameters. However, rank-order methods are not as familiar to readers of research, and for many complex situations, such methods have not even been developed. Finally, rank-order methods, like data transformation methods, distort the original data, losing information—for example, in the same sample, a difference between 6.1 and 6.2 could be one rank, but the difference between 3.4 and 5.8 might also be one rank.[6]

[6]Another traditional advantage of rank-order tests has been their ease of computation. Except for the labor of converting the data to ranks, the actual computation for most of these procedures is very simple compared to that of parametric tests. However, today, with computers, it is as easy to calculate either kind of procedure—and on some standard statistical computer packages, there is actually less trouble involved in computing the parametric test. Also, sometimes the appropriate rank-order test may not be available.

General Advantages and Disadvantages of Computer-Intensive Methods

Computer-intensive methods, such as approximate randomization tests, do not require either of the two main assumptions of parametric tests. Further, like rank-order tests, they have a direct logic of their own that is very appealing in its bypassing of the whole process of constructing estimated population distributions, distributions of means, and so forth. They are also extremely flexible, being applicable to virtually any situation imaginable in which hypothesis testing could be applied. Thus they can often be applied when no existing test—parametric or otherwise—exists.

The main disadvantage of the computer-intensive methods is that they are quite new, so the details and relative advantages of various approaches have not been well worked out. Further, because they are new, in most cases the standard computer statistical packages do not include procedures for conducting them. They are only beginning to be seen in published articles, but their use is likely to increase rapidly.

Relative Risk of Type I and Type II Errors

How accurate are the various methods in terms of the 5% level really meaning that there is a 5% chance of incorrectly rejecting the null hypothesis? And how do the different methods affect power?

When the assumptions for parametric tests are met, the parametric tests are as good as or better than any of the alternatives, in terms of protection against both Type I and Type II errors. This is as would be expected; these are the conditions for which the parametric tests were designed.

However, when the assumptions for a parametric test are not met, the relative advantages of the three possible alternative procedures we have considered are not at all clear. In fact, the relative merits of the various procedures are topics of current and very lively controversy, with many articles appearing in statistics-oriented journals every year for more than a decade.

The reason for the controversy is that which procedure works best depends on the kinds of distributions involved. A distribution that is not normal can be nonnormal in many ways (see Chapter 5). And it turns out that the effects of the different methods on Type I and Type II errors vary according to the kind of distribution involved. In fact, even for a particular kind of distribution, one technique might be better when there are equal numbers in the groups and another when there are unequal numbers, or one method might be better with a large sample size and another with a small sample size. And when comparing groups, the distributions of the groups may involve different kinds of nonnormal distributions.

So even though many studies have been done comparing the various methods (see Box 10-1 on Monte Carlo studies), we still know very little about the relative effectiveness of these methods in most situations. Worse, in many situations, a researcher may have some idea that a sample does not come from a normal population but not much of an idea of the particular kind of nonnormal population it does come from. So even the studies that have been done comparing the various procedures using particular nonnormal population shapes may not be of much use when facing an actual set of data.

It is possible that some day enough research on enough different situations will be done that patterns will emerge that will permit some good practical guidelines. At the moment, in our opinion, researchers must rely on other criteria (such as those presented in this chapter) to select from among the various alternatives when assumptions have not been met. However, from the point of view of reading research (a topic we turn to next), what you need is to be able to understand the logic of the particular procedure the researcher has chosen. Deciding whether it was chosen correctly will usually be beyond your ken at this point, so you can relax about it until later courses and greater advances in the field.

Controversies

Everything we have covered in this chapter is controversial. Especially controversial are the appropriateness of data transformations, the risks of using parametric procedures when the population distributions are unknown, the extent to which it is appropriate to treat typical measures in psychology as yielding equal-interval measurement, and the advantages and disadvantages of computer-intensive methods.

Procedures Used When Populations Appear Nonnormal as Described in Research Articles

The use of the procedures we have described in this chapter seem to wax and wane in popularity in different areas of psychology. In some fields, during certain years, you may see many studies using data transformations and never see a rank-order test. In other areas, during certain years, you may see just the reverse. And the application of computer-intensive methods in psychology is such a new development that you are likely to encounter them in only a few of the most recent studies you read—often in circumstances where there is no obvious alternative procedure.

Data transformations are usually mentioned in the Results section, just prior to the description of the analysis using the data that were transformed. For example, Dixon, Heppner, and Anderson (1991) conducted a study in which they were looking at the relation of problem-solving skills to thoughts about suicide. Nearly 1,300 students completed measures of these and related variables, and a multiple regression analysis was planned. However, prior to describing the statistical analysis, Dixon and colleagues noted,

> As scores on the SSI [Scale for Suicide Ideation] range from 0 to 38, the mean of 1.5 suggests that the majority of students appraised themselves as very low

suicide ideators. . . . Because of the statistical difficulties inherent in the positive skewness of the suicide scores, a square root transformation . . . was conducted to help normalize the SSI scores. (p. 53)

A study by Manning, Hall, and Gold (1990) on the effects of sugar on memory in older people provides an example of rank-order tests reported in a research article. In this case, just prior to presenting the results, the authors wrote a short paragraph headed "Statistical Analysis":

Reliabilities of the tests, relationships between increases in glucose levels and performance, and relationships across neuropsychological tests were assessed using Spearman rank-order correlations. Comparisons of performance on treatment and control days used Wilcoxin rank comparisons of two samples . . . (two-tailed). (p. 308)

The specific tests were not mentioned again in their Results section. Nevertheless, when reporting significant differences, the Z score was given (as opposed to a t or an F score, which would ordinarily be expected in such comparisons), reminding the reader that a normal curve approximation for a rank-order test is being used: "Performance on the Logical Memory Test at both recalls and Long-Term Word Memory on the SRT [Selective Reminding Test] was significantly enhanced after glucose ingestion ($z = 2.98$, $p < .005$; $z = 2.81$, $p < .005$; $z = 1.99$, $p < .05$, respectively)" (p. 308).

Finally, a study by Caspi and Herbener (1990) provides an example of a computer-intensive method reported in a research article. As part of this study, the researchers examined the long-term stability of personality for 252 subjects who were first tested in 1970 and then again in 1981. At each testing, the subjects completed a "Q sort" personality test. This is a special kind of testing procedure in which the subject is given a certain number of cards, each with a personality trait on it. The subject then places these cards in piles, rating them from *not at all descriptive* to *highly descriptive*. What is unique about the method, however, is that the subject must place the cards in piles of particular sizes, sizes that correspond to a normal curve, with more cases in the middle and fewer at each extreme.

To study stability, Caspi and Herbener had to correlate the Q sorts from the two periods. However, these authors noted that correlations between Q sorts ("Q correlations"), as they were being used in their study, have some unusual statistical properties. The authors explained,

We carried out what essentially amounts to a randomization test. Specifically, each subject's 1970 Q-sort profile was correlated with the Q-sort profiles of all same-sex subjects in 1981. . . . For each sex . . . we generated 100 random samples for comparison with the actual personality stability Q correlations. . . . For the . . . women, the 100 trials yielded no values that exceeded the sample mean [of correlations of each subject's 1970 and 1981 profiles] (.49). (p. 253)

(Similar results were found for men.)

Summary

The *t* test, the analysis of variance, and the significance tests for the correlation coefficient and regression analysis all assume that populations are normally distributed. Although these parametric statistical tests seem to be robust over many types of moderate violations of the normal curve assumption, they can permit too many Type I errors or have relatively low power when the population is severely nonnormal. Unfortunately, it is difficult to assess from the sample whether a population is normal. However, outliers are clearly a problem, as is extreme skewness or kurtosis.

One approach when the populations appear to be nonnormal is to transform the scores mathematically, such as taking the square root, log, or inverse of each score so that the distribution of the transformed scores appears to represent a normally distributed population; the ordinary hypothesis-testing procedures can then be applied.

Another approach is to rank all of the subjects on the basis of their scores on a variable. Special rank-order statistical tests (sometimes called nonparametric or distribution-free tests) use simple principles of probability to determine the chance of the ranks being unevenly distributed across experimental groups. However, in many cases, using the rank-transformed data in an ordinary parametric test produces an acceptable approximation.

An example of a computer-intensive method is a randomization test, which considers every possible rearrangement of the scores obtained in a study to determine the probability that the obtained arrangement (in terms, for example, of the difference in means between groups) arose by chance. However, because even with computers randomization tests are currently impracticable for reasonable sample sizes, other computer-intensive methods are used, in which, for example, 1,000 of the possible arrangements are randomly selected and the distribution of their mean differences compared to that obtained in the actual sample.

As for the comparative advantages of all these methods, data transformations permit the use of familiar parametric techniques but cannot always be applied and may distort the meaning of the data. Rank-order methods can be applied to any data set, are especially appropriate with rank or similar data, and have a straightforward conceptual foundation. But because rank-order techniques are not widely familiar, they have not been developed for many complex data analysis situations. And as with other data transformations, information may be lost or meaning distorted. Computer-intensive methods are widely applicable—sometimes to situations for which no other method exists—and have an appealing direct logic. But they are unfamiliar to researchers; being new, their possible limitations are not well worked out; and they can be difficult to set up as they are not provided on standard computer programs. Under conditions in which the population is assumed to be nonnormal, there is little consensus about how the various techniques compare in terms the relative risks of Type I and Type II errors.

In research articles, data transformations are usually described and justified at the beginning of the Results sections, and rank-order methods are described much like any other kind of hypothesis test. Computer-intensive methods, being less familiar, are typically described in more than the usual detail.

Key Terms

approximate randomization tests
data transformation
distribution-free tests
equal-interval measurement
inverse transformation

log transformation
nonparametric tests
ordinal measurement
parametric tests
randomization tests

rank-order measurement
rank-order tests
square-root transformation

Practice Problems

These problems involve computation (with the assistance of a calculator). Most real-life statistics problems are done on a computer. But even if you have a computer, do these by hand to ingrain the method in your mind.

For practice in using a computer to solve statistical problems, refer to the computer section of each chapter of the study guide that accompanies this text.

All data are fictional (unless an actual citation is given).

Answers to Set I are given at the back of the book.

SET I

1. For the distribution of 30 scores given here, (a) make a histogram (based on grouped frequencies) of the scores as they are, (b) carry out a square-root transformation and make a histogram (of grouped frequencies) of the transformed scores, and (c) convert the original scores to ranks and make a histogram (grouped) of the ranks.

9, 28, 4, 16, 0, 7, 25, 1, 4, 10, 4, 2, 1, 9, 16, 11, 12, 1, 18, 2, 5, 10, 3, 17, 6, 4, 2, 23, 21, 20

2. Which of the following sample distributions suggest that the population distribution is probably not normal?

(a) 41, 52, 74, 107, 617
(b) 221, 228, 241, 503, 511, 521
(c) .2, .3, .5, .6, .7, .9, .11
(d) –6, –5, –3, 10
(e) 11, 20, 32, 41, 49, 62

3. A researcher compares the typical family size in 10 cultures, 5 from Language Group A and 5 from Language Group B. The figures for the Group A cultures are 1.2, 2.5, 4.3, 3.8, and 7.2. The figures for the Group B cultures are 2.1, 9.2, 5.7, 6.7, and 4.8. Based on these 10 cultures, does typical family size differ in cultures with different language groups? Use the .05 level, and conduct a square-root transformation (to keep things simple, round off the transformed scores to one decimal place). Explain what you have done and why to someone who is familiar with the t test but not with data transformation.

4. A researcher randomly assigns subjects to watch one of three kinds of films: one that tends to make people sad, one that tends to make people exuberant, and one that tends to make people angry. They are then asked to rate a series of photos of individuals of the opposite gender on their attractiveness. The ratings for the sad-film group were 201, 523, and 614; the ratings for the angry-film group were 136, 340, and 301; and the ratings for the exuberant-film group were 838, 911, and 1,007. First make a rank transform of the data, and then conduct a one-way analysis of variance. Explain what you have done and why to a person who understands the analysis of variance but not rank transformations or nonparametric tests.

5. A study compares performance on a novel task for people who carry out the task either alone or in the presence of a friend (using random assignment to conditions). The scores for the subjects in the alone condition are 9, 5, and 4; the scores of the subjects in the friend condition are 3, 1, and 0. Conduct a randomization test comparing these two groups (use $p < .05$, one-tailed, predicting higher scores for alone). Explain what you did to a person who has never had a course in statistics.

With three subjects in each group, there are 20 different ways of forming two groupings of the six scores:

9 3	9 4	9 4	9 4	9 5	9 5	9 5	9 5	9 5	9 5
5 1	5 1	5 3	5 3	4 1	4 3	4 3	3 4	3 4	1 4
4 0	3 0	1 0	0 1	3 0	1 0	0 1	1 0	0 1	0 3

3 9	4 9	4 9	4 9	5 9	5 9	5 9	5 9	5 9	5 9
1 5	1 5	3 5	3 5	1 4	3 4	3 4	4 3	4 3	4 1
0 4	0 3	0 1	1 0	0 3	0 1	1 0	0 1	1 0	3 0

6. Kivlighan and Angelone (1991) conducted a study of the relation of clients' introversion to the intentions used by novice counselors (intentions were "set limits," "get information," "support," etc.). These authors begin their Results section as follows: "The 19 intentions used by the novice counselors were not normally distributed; accordingly, we used arc sine transformations. . . . We based all subsequent analyses on the transformed scores of these 19 intentions" (p. 27). (An arc sine transformation is a particular mathematical rule designed to adjust a nonnormal distribution.) Explain what is being described here (and why it is being done) to a person who understands ordinary parametric statistics but has never heard of data transformations.

SET II

1. For the distribution of 20 scores given here, (a) make a histogram (based on grouped frequencies) of the scores as they are, (b) carry out a log transformation and make a histogram (of grouped frequencies) of the transformed scores, and (c) transform the original scores to ranks and make a histogram (grouped) of the ranks.
2, 207, 894, 107, 11, 79, 112, 938, 791, 3, 13, 89, 1,004, 92, 1,016, 107, 87, 91, 870, 921

2. Which of the following sample distributions suggest that the population distribution is probably not normal?

(a) 281, 283, 287, 289, 291, 300, 302

(b) 1, 4, 6, 6, 7, 7, 9, 13

(c) 7, 104, 104, 104, 1,245, 1,247, 1,248, 1,251

(d) 68, 74, 76, 1,938

(e) 407.2, 407.5, 407.6, 407.9

3. A study of six unemployed electrical workers correlates number of weeks unemployed with marital satisfaction. The data are shown in the table. Make a square-root transformation of the weeks-unemployed data; make scatter diagrams and compute correlations for both the untransformed and the transformed data.

Weeks Unemployed	Marital Satisfaction
2	8
1	9
9	6
16	3
25	5
4	7

4. A researcher set up an experiment organized around a major televised address by the U.S. president. After the address, three subjects were randomly assigned to listen to the commentaries immediately following, provided by the television network's political commentators. The other three were assigned to spend the same time with the television off, reflecting quietly about the speech. Subjects in both groups then completed a questionnaire that assessed how much of the content of the speech they remembered accurately. The group that heard the commentators had scores of 4, 0, and 1. The group that reflected quietly had scores of 9, 3, and 8. Conduct a randomization test on these data (use the 5% significance level, one-tailed, predicting higher scores for the reflected-alone group). Compare your result to using an ordinary t test for independent means, and explain what you have done and your results to someone who is familiar with the t test but not with randomization tests.

The 20 different ways of forming two groupings of these six scores are as follows:

4 9	4 1	4 1	4 1	4 0	4 0	4 0	4 0	4 0	4 0
0 3	0 3	0 9	0 9	1 3	1 9	1 9	9 1	9 1	3 1
1 8	9 8	3 8	8 3	9 8	3 8	8 3	3 8	8 3	8 9

9 4	1 4	1 4	1 4	0 4	0 4	0 4	0 4	0 4	0 4
3 0	3 0	9 0	9 0	3 1	9 1	9 1	1 9	1 9	1 3
8 1	8 9	8 3	3 8	8 9	8 3	3 8	8 3	3 8	9 8

5. A study compared first- and second-year college students on number of close friends. It was predicted that second-year students would have more close friends. The five first-year students tested reported 2, 0, 2, 1, and 1. The five second-year students tested reported 3, 4, 1, 2, and 6. Conduct an approximate randomization test on these data, as follows: (a) Compute the mean difference between the two actual groups. (b) Write the number of close friends for each subject on an index card. (c) Shuffle the 10 cards, and lay them out face up in two groups of five. Find the mean of the first five and compute the difference from the mean of the second five, and write it down. (d) Reshuffle and repeat this process a total of 40 times. (e) Determine how many of the 40 random shuffles had mean differences as high as the actual sample.

6. June, Curry, and Gear (1990) surveyed black students at a midwestern university about problems in their use of college services. Surveys were conducted of about

250 students each time, at the end of the spring quarter in 1976, 1978, 1980, 1982, and 1987. The researchers ranked the nine main problem areas for each of the years. One of their analyses then proceeded as follows: "A major question of interest was whether the ranking of most serious problems and use of services varied by years. Thus, a Kruskal-Wallis one-way analysis of variance (ANOVA) was performed on the rankings but was not significant . . ." (p. 180). Explain why the researchers used the Kruskal-Wallis test instead of an ordinary analysis of variance and what conclusions can be drawn from this result.

16 Integrating What You Have Learned
The General Linear Model

THIS chapter is intended to integrate and deepen your knowledge about the major statistical techniques you have learned—analysis of variance, *t* test, correlation, and regression. Equally important, it provides a thorough review of those techniques.

The Relationships Among Major Statistical Methods

More than 90% of the studies in the 1988 issues of the major social psychology journals employed *t* tests, analysis of variance, correlation, or multiple regression (Reis & Stiller, 1992). And by now you have probably noticed the many similarities among these four and the other statistical techniques that you have learned in this book as well. In fact, the techniques are more closely related than you might have realized: Many of them are simply mathematically equivalent variations of each other, and most of them can be derived from the same general formula. This is because there is a central logic that serves as the basis for all these methods—a general formula that the mathematical statisticians call the **general linear model.**   **general linear model** (This has no special relation to the structural model approach to the analysis of variance.)

So let's focus on the Big Four, which are all special cases of the general linear model and therefore systematically related. And perhaps in the process, many of your half-sensed intuitions about what you've learned will emerge into the light.

To put it all very briefly (and then proceed in depth), the most general technique is multiple regression/correlation (Chapter 4), of which bivariate

FIGURE 16-1
The relationships among the four major statistical techniques.

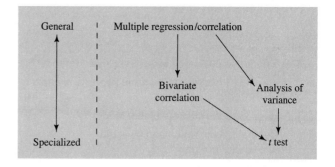

correlation (Chapter 3) is a special case. At the same time, the analysis of variance (Chapters 11–13) can also be shown to be a special case of multiple regression/correlation. Finally, the *t* test (Chapters 9 and 10) can be derived directly from either bivariate correlation or the analysis of variance. We have tried to show all of these relationships in Figure 16-1.

When we say that one procedure is a special case of another, we mean that it can be derived from the formula for the other. Thus when using the more specialized procedures, you obtain the same result as if you had used the more general procedure. Indeed, if you were working with a computer program, the program for the more general procedure could be used just as well.

Or to put it in more concrete terms, if you were going to a desert island to do psychology research and could take only one computer program with you to do statistical tests, you would want to choose one that does multiple regression/correlation. With that one program you could accomplish all of what is done by more specialized programs for bivariate correlation, *t* tests, and analyses of variance.[1]

We explore these links in this chapter. First we briefly review the idea of multiple regression/correlation as introduced in Chapter 4, and in this context we consider a formal statement of the general linear model. Then we examine each of the links in turn: multiple regression/correlation with bivariate correlation, analysis of variance with the *t* test, bivariate correlation with the *t* test, and multiple regression/correlation with the analysis of variance.

Review of the Principles of Multiple Regression and Correlation

Recall from Chapter 4 that the basic principle of bivariate prediction (also called bivariate regression) is that you formulate a systematic rule for predicting a person's score on a particular dependent variable by considering that person's score on a predictor (or independent) variable. For example, we predicted new managers' stress levels from knowing how many people the new managers would be supervising. Multiple regression is the situation in which you make your predictions on the basis of two or more predictor variables—for example, predicting new managers' stress level using the number to be supervised plus the noise level and number of decisions to be made per month.

---

[1]Technically, it is also possible to derive certain cases of the chi-square tests from the general linear model, as well as some of the rank-order procedures we considered in Chapter 15. However, in this chapter we focus primarily on the four most widely used statistical procedures.

Prediction rules can be in either a *Z*-score form or a raw-score form. Here we focus on the raw-score form because that form makes it easier to see the relation to the general linear model. A multiple regression prediction rule with three predictor variables, when working with raw scores, goes like this: The score you predict for a person on the dependent variable is the sum of some particular number (the regression constant, called *a*), plus a raw score regression coefficient (b_1) times the person's score on the first predictor variable (X_1), plus a second raw score regression coefficient (b_2) times the person's score on the second predictor variable (X_2), plus a third raw score regression coefficient (b_3) times the person's score on the third predictor variable (X_3).

Here it is stated as a formula:

$$\hat{Y} = a + (b_1)(X_1) + (b_2)(X_2) + (b_3)(X_3), \qquad (16\text{-}1)$$

where $\hat{Y}$ is the person's predicted score on the dependent variable.

For example, in the managers' stress example from Chapter 4, we suggested that a possible raw score prediction rule in the situation with three predictor variables might be this:

$$\text{Predicted Stress} = -4.70 + (.56)(\text{number supervised})$$
$$+ (.06)(\text{noise in decibels})$$
$$+ (.86)(\text{number of deadlines per month})$$

So if a prospective manager were to supervise only four people in a 50-db work area with only one deadline per month, the predicted stress would be computed this way:

$$\text{Predicted stress} = -4.70 + (.56)(4) + (.06)(50) + (.86)(1)$$
$$= -4.70 + 2.24 + 3 + .86 = 1.40$$

The manager would be predicted to have a very low level of stress (1.40).

It is also possible to describe the overall degree of association between the dependent variable and the combination of the predictor variables. This is called a multiple correlation coefficient and is symbolized by *R*. *R* must be at least as large as the smallest bivariate correlation of any of the predictor variables with the dependent variable and can be no larger than the sum of those bivariate correlations (and never larger than 1). R^2 is the proportionate reduction in squared error gained by using the multiple regression prediction rule compared to simply predicting the dependent variable from its mean.

Finally, a multiple correlation (and the associated proportionate reduction in error) can be tested for significance using a procedure in which the null hypothesis is that in the population the multiple correlation is 0.

In this chapter, we will refer to the whole procedure of multiple regression and multiple correlation together as "multiple regression/correlation." This is a widely used convention and simplifies exposition.

Introduction to the General Linear Model

One way of expressing the general linear model is as a mathematical relation between a dependent variable and one or more predictor variables. The principle is that any person's score on a particular dependent variable (such as level of stress) can be conceived of as the sum of several influences:

1. Some fixed influence that will be the same for all individuals—such as the nature of the testing procedure or impacts of human biology and society
2. Influences of other variables we have measured on which people have different scores—such as number of people supervised, noise level, and number of decisions per month
3. Other influences not measured—this is what makes error

Influence 1 corresponds to the a in a raw score multiple regression prediction rule. Influence 2 corresponds to all of the b and X pairs—$(b_1)(X_1)$, $(b_2)(X_2)$, etc.—in a multiple regression equation. Influence 3 is what accounts for the errors in prediction. (If there were a 1.0 multiple correlation, there would be no Influence 3.) Thus the general linear model can be stated in symbols as

$$Y = a + (b_1)(X_1) + (b_2)(X_2) + (b_3)(X_3) + \ldots + e, \qquad (16\text{-}2)$$

where Y is a person's actual score on some dependent variable; a is the fixed influence that applies to all individuals (Influence 1); b_1 is the degree of influence of the first predictor variable (Influence 2)—it is the raw score regression coefficient, which you then multiply by the person's raw score on the first predictor variable, X_1; b_2, b_3, and so forth represent the influences of predictor variables 2, 3, and so forth; and e is the error, the sum of all other influences on the person's score on Y (Influence 3)—that is, e is what is left over after everything else has been taken into account in making the prediction.

Notice that this formula is virtually identical to that for multiple regression, with two exceptions. First, instead of having the predicted Y value ($\hat{Y}$) on the left, you have the actual value of Y. Second, because the formula refers to the actual value of Y and because a and b values ordinarily don't predict perfectly, an error term (e) is added to account for the discrepancy.

Thus the general linear model is a statement of the influences that make up an individual's score on a particular variable. It is called a *linear model* because if you graphed the relationship between the dependent and predictor variables, the relationship would be constant in the sense of not being curvilinear—the rate-of-exchange influence (the regression coefficient) of each predictor variable always stays the same. In mathematical terms, the equation is said to be linear because there are no squared (or higher power) terms in it.[2]

least-squares model

You may also have heard that various statistical procedures use a **least-squares model.** This means that the a and b values of the general linear model (or of a multiple regression prediction rule) for a particular dependent variable are determined in such a way as to create the smallest amount of squared error—an idea that we have focused on extensively.

[2]There are clever ways of sneaking squared and higher power terms into linear model procedures. For example, you could create a new, transformed variable in which each score was squared. This transformed variable can then be entered into a linear model equation as an ordinary variable, so that no squared term actually appears in the equation. It turns out that this little trick can be extraordinarily valuable. For example, textbooks on multiple regression (e.g., Cohen & Cohen, 1983; Darlington, 1990) show how you can use this kind of procedure to handle curvilinear relationships with statistical methods designed for linear relationships.

The General Linear Model and Multiple Regression/Correlation

The link between the general linear model and multiple regression is clearly very intimate—they are virtually the same. Traditionally, they have not been equated because the general linear model is ordinarily understood to be behind other techniques, such as bivariate correlation and the analysis of variance, in addition to multiple regression/correlation. However, in recent years, psychologists have been made very aware (e.g., Cohen & Cohen, 1983) that these other techniques can be derived from multiple regression/correlation as well as from the general linear model.

Bivariate Regression and Correlation as Special Cases of Multiple Regression/Correlation

Bivariate regression, prediction from one predictor variable to one dependent variable, is a special case of multiple regression, which is prediction from any number of predictor variables to one dependent variable. Similarly, bivariate correlation, the association between one predictor variable and one dependent variable, is a special case of multiple correlation, the association of any number of predictor variables with one dependent variable.

The t Test as a Special Case of the Analysis of Variance

The relationship of the general linear model to correlation and regression is reasonably straightforward. But the relationship of the general linear model (or of correlation and regression) to the t test and the analysis of variance is considerably less straightforward. However, before turning to that relationship, let us first examine the link between the t test and the analysis of variance.

Both the t test and the analysis of variance are procedures for testing the difference among means of groups. The t test is used when there are only two groups.[3] The analysis of variance is usually used only when there are more than two groups. However, there is no reason that the analysis of variance cannot be used with just two groups. And when there are only two groups, the t test and the analysis of variance lead to identical conclusions. Of course, the strict identity of t and F applies only in this two-group case. When there are more than two groups, you cannot compute an ordinary t test. This is why we say that the t test is a *special case* of the analysis of variance—it is mathematically identical to the analysis of variance in the particular case where there are only two groups. (We consider an example shortly.)

[3]We focus on the t test for independent means (and also the analysis of variance for between-subject designs). The discussion of the equivalence of the dependent-means t test and the corresponding repeated-measures analysis of variance procedures (not covered in this book) leads to the same kind of conclusions: They are each part of the general linear model—both are special cases of multiple regression, with the t test for dependent means being a special case of the repeated-measures analysis of variance.

Intuitive Understanding of the Relationship of the Two Procedures

One way to get a sense of the link of the two procedures is through the analogy of signal-to-noise ratio that we introduced in explaining the analysis of variance in Chapter 11. The idea is that the analysis of variance F ratio is a measure of the extent to which the signal (analogous to the difference between group means) exceeds the noise (analogous to the variation within each of the groups). The same idea applies to a t test, which is also really about the extent to which the signal (the difference between the two group means) exceeds the noise (the standard deviation of the distribution of differences between means, which is also based on the variation within the groups).

Parallels in the Basic Logic of the Two Procedures

The analysis of variance is based on computing an F ratio (which is then compared to a cutoff from a table based on an F distribution). The F ratio is the population variance estimate based on the variation between the means of the two or more groups divided by the population variance estimate based on the variation within each of these groups. That is, the F ratio is a fraction in which the numerator is based on the differences among the groups, comparing their means, and the denominator is based on the variation within each of the groups.

The t test is based on computing a t score (which is then compared to a preset cutoff from a table based on a t distribution). The t score is the difference between the means of the two groups divided by the standard deviation of the distribution of differences between means. This latter is computed using the pooled variance estimate, which is based on averaging the variance within each of the two groups. That is, the t score is a fraction in which the numerator is the difference between the groups, comparing their means, and the denominator is based on the variation within each of the groups.

In other words, as shown in Table 16-1, an F ratio and a t score are both fractions with a numerator term based on the differences between the group means and a denominator term based on the variances within the groups.

Mathematical Relationship of the Two Procedures

The formula for a t score can be shown to be exactly the square root of the formula for the F ratio in the case where there are only two groups. Most students will not be interested in the precise derivation, but one implication is that for any two particular samples, if you calculate a t score, it will come out as exactly the square root of what you would get if you calculated an F ratio for those two groups. For example, if you computed a t of 3 and then you computed F for the same data, it would come out to 9. And the cutoff figures that are shown in a t table are exactly the square roots of the figures in the column of an F table that you use when doing an analysis of variance for two groups (that is, the part of the F table in which the numerator's degrees of freedom is 1).

A brief discussion of one aspect of the mathematical equivalence may help you see how two such seemingly different sets of calculations are actually the same underneath. One apparent difference between the two proce-

TABLE 16-1
Some Links Between the *t* Test for Independent Means
and the Analysis of Variance

t Test	Analysis of Variance
Numerator of *t* is the difference between the means of the two groups.	Numerator of *F* is partly based on variation between the means of the two or more groups.
Denominator of *t* is partly based on pooling the population variance estimates computed from each group.	Denominator of *F* is computed by pooling the population variance estimates computed from each group.
Denominator of *t* involves dividing by total number of subjects.	Numerator of *F* involves multiplying by total number of subjects. (Multiplying a numerator by a number has the same effect as dividing the denominator by that number.)
When using two groups, $t = \sqrt{F}$	When using two groups, $F = t^2$
$df = (N_1 - 1) + (N_2 - 1)$	$df_W = (n_1 - 1) + (n_2 - 1) + \ldots + (n_{Last} - 1)$

dures is how they are affected by sample size. In the analysis of variance, the sample size is part of the numerator—the numerator of the *F* ratio (following the method of Chapter 11) is the population variance estimate using the difference among the means multiplied by the number of subjects in each group: $S_B^2 = (S_M^2)(n)$. And in the *t* test, the sample size is part of the denominator—the denominator of the *t* test uses the pooled population variance estimate divided by the number of subjects in each group: ($S_{DIF} = \sqrt{S_{DIF}^2}$; $S_{DIF}^2 = S_{M1}^2 + S_{M2}^2$; $S_{M1}^2 = S_P^2/N_1$; $S_{M2}^2 = S_P^2/N_2$). This apparent contradiction is resolved, however, because multiplying the numerator of a fraction by a number has exactly the same effect as dividing the denominator by that number. (For example, take the fraction 3/8. Multiplying the numerator by 2 gives 6/8, or 3/4; dividing the denominator of 3/8 by 2 also gives 3/4.)[4]

Computed Example Showing the Identity of the Two Procedures

To help make the equivalence more vivid, Table 16-2 shows the *t* and *F* computations for one of the *t* test examples from Chapter 10, the fictional experiment testing the effectiveness of a new job skills training program. Notice the following: (a) The pooled population variance estimate in the *t* test (S_P^2) is the same as the within-group variance estimate for the analysis of variance (S_W^2) both computed as part of the denominator. (b) The degrees of freedom for the *t* distribution ($df = 12$) is exactly the same as the denominator degrees of freedom for the *F* distribution ($df_W = 12$). (c) The cutoff *t* for rejecting the null hypothesis (2.179) is the square root of the cutoff *F* for rejecting the null hypothesis ($\sqrt{4.75} = 2.179$). (d) The computed *t* statistic for these data (2.73) is the square root of the computed *F* ($\sqrt{7.55} = 2.75$, the slight difference being due to rounding error). And (e) the conclusion is the same.

---

[4]Other apparent differences (such as the seeming difference that the *F*-ratio numerator is based on a variance estimate and the *t*-score numerator is a simple difference between means) have similar underlying unities. But we will not pursue those here.

TABLE 16-2

t Test and Analysis of Variance Computations for an Experiment Examining the Effectiveness of a New Job Skills Program for People Who Have Previously Not Been Able to Hold Jobs (Fictional Data)

	Experimental Group (Special Program)				Control Group (Standard Program)		
	X_1	$X_1 - M_1$	$(X_1 - M_1)^2$		X_2	$X_2 - M_2$	$(X_2 - M_2)^2$
	6	0	0		6	3	9
	4	−2	4		1	−2	4
	9	3	9		5	2	4
	7	1	1		3	0	0
	7	1	1		1	−2	4
	3	−3	9		1	−2	4
	6	0	0		4	1	1
Σ	42	0	24		21	0	26

$M_1 = 6$ $S_1^2 = 24/6 = 4$
$N_1 = 7$ $df_1 = N_1 - 1 = 6$

$M_2 = 3$ $S_2^2 = 26/6 = 4.33$
$N_2 = 7$ $df_2 = N_2 - 1 = 6$

t test Computations	ANOVA Computations

Numerator

Mean difference = 6.00 − 3.00 = 3.00

$df_B = N_G - 1 = 2 - 1 = 1$

$GM = (6 + 3)/2 = 9/2 = 4.5$

$\Sigma(M - GM)^2 = (6 - 4.5)^2 + (3 - 4.5)^2$
$= 1.5^2 + -1.5^2$
$= 2.25 + 2.25 = 4.5$

$S_B^2 \text{ or } MS_B = \left(\dfrac{\Sigma(M - GM^2)}{df_B}\right)(n) = \left(\dfrac{4.5}{1}\right)(7) = 31.5$

Denominator

$S_P^2 = \left(\dfrac{df_1}{df_T}\right)(S_1^2) + \left(\dfrac{df_2}{df_T}\right)(S_2^2) = \left(\dfrac{6}{12}\right)(4) + \left(\dfrac{6}{12}\right)(4.33)$

$\quad = (.5)(4) + (.5)(4.33) = 2.00 + 2.17 = 4.17$

$S_{DIF}^2 = S_{M1}^2 + S_{M2}^2 = (S_P^2/N_1) + (S_P^2/N_2)$
$\quad = (4.17/7) + (4.17/7)$
$\quad = .60 + .60 = 1.20$

$S_{DIF} = \sqrt{S_{DIF}^2} = \sqrt{1.20} = 1.10$

$S_W^2 \text{ or } MS_W = \dfrac{S_1^2 + S_2^2 + \ldots + S_{Last}^2}{N_G} = \dfrac{4 + 4.33}{2}$

$\quad = \dfrac{8.33}{2} = 4.17$

Degrees of Freedom

$df_T = df_1 + df_2 = 6 + 6 = 12$

$df_W = df_1 + df_2 \ldots df_{Last} = 6 + 6 = 12$

Cutoff

Needed t with $df = 12$ at 5% level, two-tailed = ±2.179

Needed F with $df = 1, 12$ at 5% level = 4.75

Score on Comparison Distribution

$t = (M_1 - M_2)/S_{DIF} = (6.00 - 3.00)/1.10 = 3.00/1.10 = 2.73$

$F = S_B^2/S_W^2 \text{ or } MS_B/MS_W = 31.5/4.17 = 7.55$

Conclusions

Reject the null hypothesis; the research hypothesis is supported.

Reject the null hypothesis; the research hypothesis is supported.

The *t* Test as a Special Case of the Significance Test for the Correlation Coefficient

The relationship of the correlation coefficient to the *t* test is far from obvious. Even psychology researchers have only recently become aware of the link. The correlation coefficient is about the degree of association between two variables; the *t* test is about the significance of the difference between two population means. What is the possible connection?

One connection is that both use the *t* distribution to determine significance. In Chapter 3, we had not yet considered the logic of hypothesis testing, so we could discuss the significance of a correlation coefficient only in very general terms. With what you now understand, the procedure can be explained more precisely. The procedure follows the standard five steps of hypothesis testing. Its particular features are (a) the null hypothesis is that the population has a correlation of 0, (b) the comparison distribution is a *t* distrib-

---

BOX 16-1

The Golden Age of Statistics: Four Guys Around London

In the last chapter of his little book *The Statistical Pioneers*, James Tankard (1984) discusses the interesting fact that the four most common statistical techniques were created by four Englishmen born within 68 years of each other, three of whom worked in the vicinity of London (and the fourth, Gosset, stuck at his brewery in Dublin, nevertheless visited London to study and kept in good touch with all that was happening in that city). What were the reasons?

First, Tankard feels that their closeness and communication were important for creating the "critical mass" of minds sometimes associated with a golden age of discovery or creativity. Second, as is often the case with important discoveries, each man faced difficult practical problems or "anomalies" that pushed him to the solution he arrived at. (None simply set out to invent a statistical method in itself). Galton (Box 3-1) was interested in the characteristics of parents and children, Pearson (Box 14-1) in measuring the fit between a set of observations and a theoretical curve. Gosset (Box 9-1) had his problem of small samples caused by the economics of the brewery industry. And Fisher (Box 11-1) was studying the effects of manure on potatoes. (Age was not a factor, Tankard notes. The age when these four made their major contributions ranged from 31 to 66.)

Tankard also discusses three important social factors specific to this "golden age of statistics." First, there was the role of biometrics, which was attempting to test the theory of evolution mathematically. Biometrics had its influence through Galton's reading of Darwin and his subsequent influence on Pearson. Second, this period saw the beginning of mass hiring by industry and agriculture of university graduates with "high-powered" mathematical training. Third, since the time of Newton, Cambridge University had been a particular, centralized source for England of brilliant mathematicians. They could spread out through British industry and still, through their common alma mater, remain in contact with students and each other and conversant with the most recent breakthroughs.

Finally, about the entire history of this field, but its golden age in particular, Tankard has some warm, almost poetic words:

Indeed, it is difficult to see how statistics can be labeled as dull or inanimate. After peering beneath the surface of this practical and powerful discipline, we can see that it has succeeded more than once in eliciting strong passions and lively debate among people. And statistics being a product of the human mind, it will doubtless continue to do so. (p. 141)

---

ution with degrees of freedom equal to the number of subjects minus 2, and (c) the score on the comparison distribution is a t score calculated from the correlation coefficient using the formula $t = r\sqrt{N - 2}/\sqrt{1 - r^2}$. (For more details, including an example and considerations of issues of effect size and power, see the second appendix to Chapter 3.) Note that the key to the entire process is converting the correlation coefficient to a t score.

However, knowing about this procedure does not give much insight into *why* the correlation coefficient can be turned into a t score for purposes of hypothesis testing or what the connection is between this t based on the correlation coefficient and the t test as applied to testing the difference between means of two groups. It is to this issue that we now turn.

Group Differences as Associations Among Variables

The correlation coefficient can be seen as being about the association between a predictor or independent variable and a dependent variable. Testing the significance of a correlation coefficient asks whether we can reject the null hypothesis that in the population there is no association between the two variables (that in the population, $r = 0$).

The t test for independent means examines the difference between two population means, based on the data from means of two samples. The samples are measured on a dependent variable. What makes the two groups different is the independent or predictor variable—for example, whether subjects get the new job skills program or get the ordinary job skills program. The null hypothesis being tested is that the group the subject is in (the predictor variable) has no effect on the dependent variable. The t test is testing whether or not in the population at large there is any association between the predictor and the dependent variable. You might want to read this paragraph again.

In other words, a significant correlation coefficient tells you that the predictor and dependent variables are related, and a significant t test for independent means tells you that the predictor and dependent variables are related. If the experimental design permits a causal interpretation (as when individuals are randomly assigned to levels of the predictor variable—rarely the case when using correlation but often the case when using the t test for independent means), then a significant correlation coefficient is a basis for concluding that the predictor variable affects the dependent variable, and a significant t test for independent means is a basis for saying that the predictor variable affects the dependent variable.

Numerical, Multivalued Predictor Variables Versus Those That Represent Two Categories

"But wait!" you may say. "The predictor variable in a correlation coefficient is a numerical variable, such as number of people supervised or high school GPA, whereas the predictor variable in a t test for independent means is a variable with exactly two values, the two categories, such as experimental group versus control group."

Yes, you are quite correct. This is precisely the difference between the situations in which we ordinarily use a correlation coefficient and those in which we ordinarily use a t test for independent means.

Usually, for both the correlation coefficient and the t test for independent means, the dependent variable can take a range of numerical values. However, when it comes to the predictor variable, there is a difference. For the correlation coefficient, the predictor variable, like the dependent variable, is typically a numerical variable—for example, a correlation between number supervised and stress level is between two numerical variables. But in a t test for independent means, the predictor variable has exactly two values, and these are not numbers at all. That is, the predictor variable in a t test is a dichotomous, nominal variable with only two discrete categories—for example, being in the experimental group or the control group.

Bridging the Gap Between Numerical and Two-Category Nominal Variables

How can this gap be bridged? Suppose that we arbitrarily gave two numbers to the two-category nominal variable—for example, call the experimental group 1 and the control group 2. (Using any other two numbers will, in the end, yield exactly the same result when everything is converted to Z scores to compute the correlation coefficient. Which two numbers you use—specifically, which category gets the higher number—determines the plus or minus sign of the final result, nothing more.)

Once you have converted in this way the two-category nominal predictor (independent) variable of a t test for independent means to a numerical variable (with, admittedly, only two values), you can then proceed to calculate the correlation coefficient and, eventually, determine its significance.

Example of the Computational Equivalence of the t Test and the Correlation Coefficient Significance Test

Table 16-3 shows the computations for the same t-test example we used earlier when looking at the equivalence of the t test and the analysis of variance (except, to make the table less busy, we have left out the computations of the standard deviation of each variable that is used to compute the Z scores). Notice that in this setup, each individual has two scores—(a) a 1 or a 2, depending on whether the person is in the experimental group (the group given the new job skills program) or the control group (the group given the standard job skills program), and (b) a score on the dependent variable, which is the employer's job performance rating a month later. The resulting correlation is $-.62$. Using the formula for converting a correlation to a t score yields a t of -2.72, which is, within rounding error (and ignoring the sign, which is arbitrary in this case), what we had calculated earlier (2.73) using the ordinary t-test procedures (see Table 10-3 or 16-2). The degrees of freedom and thus the needed t for significance and conclusion are also the same as when we calculated the t test for independent means with these data.

As illustrated in this example, the significance test of the correlation coefficient gives the same result as the ordinary t test. We say that the t test is a special case of the correlation coefficient, however, because the t test is only a particular instance of the correlation coefficient—the situation in which the predictor variable has only two values.

TABLE 16-3
Computation of the Correlation Coefficient and a Hypothesis Test of the Correlation Coefficient Using the Data From Table 10-3 and Converting the Predictor (Independent) Variable Into a Numerical Variable Having Values of 1 (for the Experimental Group) or 2 (for the Control Group)

Predictor Variable (Experimental Versus Control)		Dependent Variable (Employer's Rating)		Cross-Product
Raw	Z_X	Raw	Z_Y	$Z_X Z_Y$
1	−1	6	.62	− .62
1	−1	4	− .21	.21
1	−1	9	1.87	−1.87
1	−1	7	1.04	−1.04
1	−1	7	1.04	−1.04
1	−1	3	− .62	.62
1	−1	6	.62	− .62
2	1	6	.62	.62
2	1	1	−1.45	−1.45
2	1	5	.21	.21
2	1	3	− .62	− .62
2	1	1	−1.45	−1.45
2	1	1	−1.45	−1.45
2	1	4	− .21	− .21
Σ 21	0	63	0	−8.71
$M = 1.5$	0	4.5	0	$r = − .62$
($SD = .5$)		($SD = 2.41$)		

$df = N − 2 = 14 − 2 = 12$.

t needed with $df = 12$ at 5% level, two-tailed $= \pm 2.179$.

$t = r\sqrt{N − 2}/\sqrt{1 − r^2} = −.62\sqrt{14 − 2}/\sqrt{1 − (−.62)^2} = −.62\sqrt{12}/\sqrt{1 − .38} = −.62(3.46)/\sqrt{.62} = −2.15/.79 = −2.72$

Conclusion: Reject the null hypothesis; the research hypothesis is supported.

Graphic Interpretation of the Relationship of the *t* Test to the Correlation Coefficient

You can gain considerable additional insight into the relationship between *t* and *r* by looking at the situation graphically. It is possible to graph the data for a *t* test for independent means using a scatter diagram, just as you would for a correlation coefficient with only two values of the predictor variable. In fact, the graphs of the same data are the same. Let's look at one. Figure 16-2 shows the scatter diagram and the regression line for the data for the job skills training study. As you can see from the figure, because the predictor (independent) variable has only two values, on the scatter diagram the dots all line up above these two points. Note that the regression line passes through the middle of each set of dots. In fact, if you were to calculate it, when making a scatter diagram of the results of a *t* test, it always turns out that the regression line falls exactly at the mean of each set of dots (that is, at the mean of each group). This is because for any single set of scores, the best single-number predictor (in the sense of producing the least squared error) is always the mean.

Now consider a few possible patterns on such a scatter diagram. Figure 16-3a shows a situation in which the two means are nearly the same. In this case, the slope of the regression line is about 0; the correlation is low and not significant. In fact, for the data in the example, the correlation is .10, which

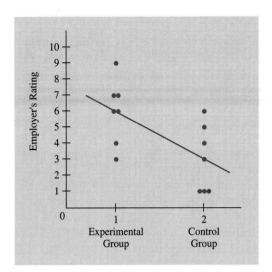

FIGURE 16-3
Three possible scatter diagrams of data analyzed with a *t* test for independent means, in which the means for the two groups are (a) nearly the same, (b) different but the data are widely spread (largely pooled variance, or large standard deviation of the distribution of differences between sample means), and (c) very different, with data not widely spread.

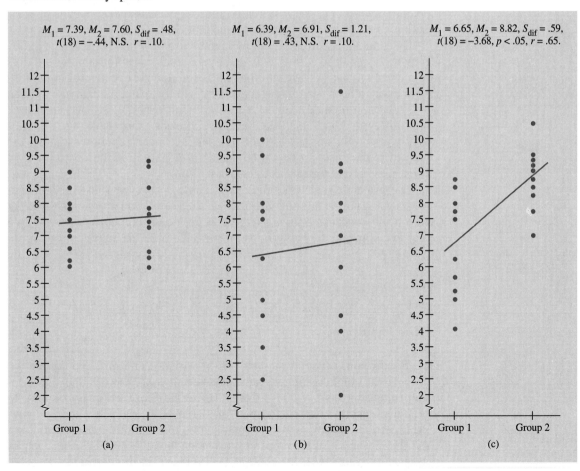

489

with 20 subjects, using the formula for the t test for the correlation coefficient, gives a t of .43: $t = r\sqrt{N-2}/\sqrt{1-r^2} = .1\sqrt{20-2}/\sqrt{1-.1^2} = .43$. Likewise, thinking in terms of a t test for independent means, because there is little difference between the means of the two groups, the t test will not be significant. The data in this example have a mean difference of $7.39 - 7.60 = .21$, which, with a standard deviation of the distribution of differences between means of .48, leads to a t of $-.44$: $t = (M_1 - M_2)/S_{DIF} = (7.39 - 7.60)/.48 = -.44$—the same result, within rounding error (and ignoring sign), that we obtain using the correlation approach.

Figure 16-3b shows the situation in which the means of the two groups are somewhat different but the dots in each group are even more widely spread out. In this case, the regression line again makes a very poor predictor, so that once again the correlation coefficient, though not 0, would nevertheless be quite low and not significant. In fact, for the data in the example, $r = .10$, which is not statistically significant. In the t test for independent means for these same data, the effect of the spread of the dots is to make a larger estimated population variance for each group. This results in a large pooled variance estimate and thus a large standard deviation of the distribution of differences between means. Because in a t test you divide the mean difference by the standard deviation of the distribution of differences between means, the larger this standard deviation, the smaller the t score. The data in the example have a mean difference of .52 and a standard deviation of the distribution of differences between means of 1.21, making a t of .43, which is clearly not significant.

By contrast, Figure 16-3c shows a situation in which there is a large difference between the means with relatively small variation among the dots around each mean. As a result, the regression line is very helpful in predicting, making a high correlation coefficient. (In the example data, $r = .65$ and $t = 3.63$, as computed from r to test its significance.) Similarly, the large mean difference and small variance within each group make for a large t when computed using a t test for independent means. In this example, the mean difference is -2.17 and the standard deviation of the distribution of differences between means is .59, so t is -3.68.

The principle that these figures illustrate is that the t test for independent means and the significance test for the correlation coefficient give the same results because both are largest when the difference between the two means is large and the variation among the scores in each group is small.

The Analysis of Variance as a Special Case of the Significance Test of the Multiple Correlation Coefficient

The relationship between the analysis of variance and multiple correlation parallels the relationship we have just considered between the t test for independent means and the ordinary (bivariate) correlation coefficient. In both relationships, one of the pair of statistics is ostensibly about differences between means and the other about associations among variables. And the resolution of this apparent discrepancy is the same. The analysis of variance examines whether there is a difference on the dependent variable between means of groups representing different levels of a predictor (or independent) variable. The correlation approach sees this as a relationship between the dependent variable and these different levels of the predictor variable. For example, in the Hazan and Shaver (1987) study that examined attachment style and jealousy, discussed in Chapter 11, the researchers found that the analysis of variance showed a significant difference among the three attachment styles (the independent or predictor variable) on jealousy (the dependent variable). A correlational approach, by contrast, would describe this result as a significant association between the attachment style variable and the jealousy variable.

Analysis of Variance for Two Groups as a Special Case of the Significance of a Bivariate Correlation

The link between the analysis of variance and correlation is easiest to see if you interpret the correlation coefficient as the square root of the proportionate reduction in error with raw scores (see Chapter 4) and interpret the analysis of variance using the structural model approach (Chapter 12). The top of Table 16-4 shows the correlation data for the job skills training experiment example. However, this time we show the raw score predicted scores and the errors and squared errors. We also show the computations for the proportionate reduction in error. The bottom of Table 16-4 shows the analysis of variance computations, using the structural model approach, for the same data.

There are several clear links. First, the sum of squared error computed in the correlation when using the bivariate prediction rule ($SS_E = 50$) is the same as the within-group sum of squared deviations (SS_W) for the analysis of variance. Why are they the same? The correlation analysis is computing error as the difference from the predicted value, which is the mean of each group. That is, in the correlation analysis, the sum of squared error turns out to be the result of squaring and summing the difference of each score from its group's mean (which is the predicted score for each case in its group). The analysis of variance is computing the sum of squared error within groups as precisely the same thing—the sum of the squared deviations of each score from its group's mean.

Second, the sum of squared error in the correlation analysis when using the overall mean of the dependent variable to predict ($SS_T = 81.34$) is the same, within rounding error, as SS_T in the analysis of variance. They are the same because the correlation analysis is computing this error as the squared deviation of each score from the overall mean of all the dependent variable scores and the analysis of variance is computing the sum of squared deviations of each score from the grand mean, which is the overall mean of all the dependent variable scores.

Third, the reduction in squared error—the sum of squared error using the mean to predict (81.34) minus the sum of squared error using the bivariate prediction rule (50)—comes out to 31.34. This is the same, within rounding error, as the sum of squared error between groups (SS_B, which equals 31.5) in the analysis of variance. The reduction in error in the correlational analysis amounts to what the prediction rule adds over knowing just the mean. In this case, the prediction rule predicts the mean of each group,

TABLE 16-4
Computation of the Proportionate Reduction in Error With Raw Scores and Analysis of Variance, Structural Model Approach, Using the Data From Table 10-3

PROPORTIONATE REDUCTION IN ERROR

Predictor Variable (Experimental Versus Control)	Dependent Variable (Employer's Rating)			
Raw	Score	Predicted	Difference	Squared Difference
1	6	6	0	0
1	4	6	−2	4
1	9	6	3	9
1	7	6	1	1
1	7	6	1	1
1	3	6	−3	9
1	6	6	0	0
2	6	3	3	9
2	1	3	−2	4
2	5	3	2	4
2	3	3	0	0
2	1	3	−2	4
2	1	3	−2	4
2	4	3	1	1

$$\Sigma = SS_E = 50$$

Sum of squared error using the overall mean as a prediction rule (computation not shown): $SS_T = 81.34$

$$\text{Proportionate reduction in squared error} = \frac{SS_T - SS_E}{SS_T} = \frac{81.34 - 50}{81.34} = \frac{31.34}{81.34} = .39$$

$r^2 = .39; \ r = \sqrt{r^2} = \sqrt{.39} = \pm.62.$

ONE-WAY ANALYSIS OF VARIANCE STRUCTURAL MODEL CALCULATION

$GM = 4.5$

	Experimental Group (Special Program)							Control Group (Standard Program)						
X_1	$X - GM$		$X - M$		$M - GM$		X	$X - GM$		$X - M$		$M - GM$		
	Dev	Dev²	Dev	Dev²	Dev	Dev²		Dev	Dev²	Dev	Dev²	Dev	Dev²
6	1.5	2.25	0	0	1.5	2.25	6	1.5	2.25	3	9	−1.5	2.25
4	− .5	.25	−2	4	1.5	2.25	1	−3.5	12.25	−2	4	−1.5	2.25
9	4.5	20.25	3	9	1.5	2.25	5	.5	.25	2	4	−1.5	2.25
7	2.5	6.25	1	1	1.5	2.25	3	−1.5	2.25	0	0	−1.5	2.25
7	2.5	6.25	1	1	1.5	2.25	1	−3.5	12.25	−2	4	−1.5	2.25
3	−1.5	2.25	−3	9	1.5	2.25	1	−3.5	12.25	−2	4	−1.5	2.25
6	1.5	2.25	0	0	1.5	2.25	4	− .5	.25	1	1	−1.5	2.25
Σ:		39.75		24		15.75			41.75		26		15.75

Note: Dev = Deviation; Dev² = Squared deviation

Sums of squared deviations:
$\Sigma(X - GM)^2$ or $SS_T = 39.75 + 41.75 = 81.5$
$\Sigma(X - M)^2$ or $SS_W = 24 + 26 = 50$
$\Sigma(M - GM)^2$ or $SS_B = 15.75 + 15.75 = 31.5$
Check ($SS_T = SS_W + SS_B$): $81.5 = 50 + 31.5$

TABLE 16-4 (cont.)

Degrees of freedom:
$df_T = N - 1 = 14 - 1 = 13$
$df_W = df_1 + df_2 + \ldots + df_{Last} = 6 + 6 = 12$
$df_B = N_G - 1 = 2 - 1 = 1$
Check ($df_T = df_W + df_B$): $13 = 12 + 1$

Population variance estimates:
S_T^2 or $MS_T = SS_T/df_T = 81.5/13 = 6.27$
S_W^2 or $MS_W = SS_W/df_W = 50/12 = 4.17$
S_B^2 or $MS_B = SS_B/df_B = 31.5/1 = 31.5$
F ratio: $F = S_B^2/S_W^2$ or $MS_B/MS_W = 31.5/4.17 = 7.55$
$R^2 = SS_B/SS_T = 31.5/81.5 = .39$

so the reduction in squared error for each score is the squared difference between the mean of that score's group and the overall mean. SS_B in the analysis of variance is calculated by adding up, for each subject, the squared differences between the subject's group's mean and the grand mean.

Finally, the proportionate reduction in error (r^2, also called the proportion of variance accounted for) in the correlation analysis comes out exactly the same as the proportion of variance accounted for (R^2), one of the measures of effect size we considered in the analysis of variance (both are .39). Both tell us the proportion of the total variation in the dependent variable that is accounted for by its association with the independent variable. That these numbers should come out the same should be no surprise by now; we have already seen that the terms that make up both the numerator and the denominator are the same for the formulas for both r^2 and R^2.

Thus the links between correlation and the analysis of variance are quite deep. In fact, some researchers compute the significance of a correlation coefficient by plugging the various sums of squared error figures it produces into an analysis of variance table and computing F. The result is identical to any other way of computing the significance of the correlation coefficient—if you compute the t for the correlation it comes out to the square root of the F you would get using this procedure.

Analysis of Variance for More Than Two Groups as a Special Case of Multiple Correlation

Recall the tactic we used when considering the t test for independent means a special case of testing the significance of the correlation coefficient. In that discussion, we were able to compute a correlation coefficient for the t-test data by converting the two categories of the nominal predictor variable into any arbitrary two different numbers (in the example, we used 1 for the experimental group and 2 for the control group). The problem is more difficult when the predictor variable involves more than two categories, as is the case in an analysis of variance for more than two groups.

We could get away with assigning any two arbitrary numbers in the two-category situation because particular numbers do not matter. They must merely be different. The conversion to Z scores that is done when r is computed takes care of the degree of difference between the two numbers. But when there are three or more groups, assigning them any three or more numbers will not work. Whatever three numbers we pick imply some particular relation among the groups, and not all relations will be the same.

For example, in Chapter 11 we examined the case in which a researcher compared subjects' ratings of a defendant's degree of guilt under conditions in which the subjects believed the defendant had either a criminal record or a clean record or in which nothing was said about the defendant's record. Suppose that we arbitrarily assigned a 1 to the first group, a 2 to the second, and a 3 to the third. This would imply that we consider these three levels to be equally spaced values on a numerical variable that represents something about knowledge about the criminal record; converting these 1, 2, and 3 values to Z scores would not help, as they would still be evenly spread and in this order. In this case, it might make some sense to think of the three groups as ordered from criminal record to clean record, with no information in between (although the fictional results we considered in Chapter 11 suggest that the effects might be quite different from that order). But even then it would not be clear that they are evenly spaced on this dimension.

In other examples, it makes no sense at all even to order the groups, let alone to decide how they should be spaced. For example, in a study comparing attitudes of four different European nationalities, nationality is the predictor variable. But these four nationalities are not convertible in any meaningful way to four values of a single numerical variable.

There is, however, a clever solution to this problem. Instead of trying to make a nominal variable with more than two categories into a single numerical variable, you can make it into several numerical variables with two levels each.

Here is how this is done: Suppose that the predictor variable comprises four categories—for example, four European nationalities, French, Spanish, Italian, and German. One predictor variable can be whether or not the subject is French—1 if French, 0 if not. A second predictor variable is whether or not the subject is Spanish, 1 or 0. A third predictor variable is whether or not the subject is Italian, 1 or 0. We could also have a fourth variable, about whether or not the subject is German, but it turns out that if the subject has 0s on the first three variables, the subject must be German by elimination (because there are only the four possibilities). In general, to identify all the levels of a nominal variable requires one variable fewer than the nominal variable has.

Using this procedure, any subject's nationality is described by the score on three numerical variables, each having the possibilities of 1 or 0. For example, a subject who was French would have a 1 for French and 0s for Spanish and Italian. A subject who was Spanish would have a 1 for Spanish but 0s for French and Italian. An Italian subject would have 0s for French and Spanish. A German subject would have 0s on all three variables. (Incidentally, any two numbers can be used for each two-valued nominal variable; we just used 1 and 0 for convenience.) Table 16-5 shows how this coding works out for 10 fictional subjects.

nominal coding

This entire procedure is called **nominal coding.** (Our converting the scores in the t-test example to 1s and 2s to compute a correlation coefficient was also an example of nominal coding—for a two-category nominal variable.) The result is that the predictor variable, instead of being a nominal variable with four categories, is now three numerical variables but with only two values each—what we needed to avoid a false ranking of the four.

TABLE 16-5
Example of Nominal Coding for Ten Subjects' Nationality in a Fictional Study of Subjects of Four European Nationalities

Subject	Nationality	Variable 1 French or Not	Variable 2 Spanish or Not	Variable 3 Italian or Not
1	Spanish	0	1	0
2	Italian	0	0	1
3	German	0	0	0
4	Italian	0	0	1
5	French	1	0	0
6	French	1	0	0
7	German	0	0	0
8	Italian	0	0	1
9	French	1	0	0
10	Spanish	0	1	0

Table 16-6 shows another example of nominal coding, this time applied to the subjects in the criminal record example. The result is that the predictor variable, instead of being a nominal variable with three categories, is now two numerical variables (with only two values each, 0 or 1). More generally, any nominal independent variable in an analysis of variance can be coded into a set of two-value numerical variables. The set will consist of exactly one less such variable than there are levels in the nominal variable. (This comes out, not coincidentally, the same as the number of degrees of freedom for the between-subject variance estimate.)

This ability to code a nominal independent variable in an analysis of variance into a set of two-value numerical variables is an important transition because it permits us to conduct a multiple correlation analysis. We can now compute the multiple correlation of these two numerical predictor vari-

TABLE 16-6
Example of Nominal Coding for Fifteen Subjects' Experimental Condition in the Criminal Record Example (Fictional Data)

	Predictor or Independent Variable		Dependent Variable
Subject	Experimental Condition	Variable 1: Criminal Record or Not	Variable 2: Clean Record or Not	Subject's Rating of Defendant's Guilt
1	Criminal record	1	0	10
2	Criminal record	1	0	7
3	Criminal record	1	0	5
4	Criminal record	1	0	10
5	Criminal record	1	0	8
6	Clean record	0	1	5
7	Clean record	0	1	1
8	Clean record	0	1	3
9	Clean record	0	1	7
10	Clean record	0	1	4
11	No information	0	0	4
12	No information	0	0	6
13	No information	0	0	9
14	No information	0	0	3
15	No information	0	0	3

ables taken together with the dependent variable, rating of guilt. The eventual result (in terms of significance level) will be identical to having done the analysis of variance.

The nominal coding procedure we have sketched here—converting a nominal predictor variable in an analysis of variance into several two-level numerical variables in a multiple correlation—is extremely flexible and can be extended to the most complex factorial designs. It is not important that you be able to do nominal coding, as in most cases a computer does it for you. But we did want you to see the principle so that you could understand how it is possible to convert an analysis of variance problem into a multiple regression problem. (If you are interested in nominal coding, it is described in very readable detail in Cohen & Cohen, 1983, chap. 5.)

Choice of Statistical Tests

Considering that the four major statistical procedures we have discussed can be considered special cases of multiple regression/correlation, the question may arise as to why we don't learn just one technique—multiple regression/correlation—and do everything using it. We could. And if we did so, we would produce entirely correct results in each case. Indeed, as we noted at the outset, if you were to learn only one procedure for analyzing statistical data by computer, you should learn multiple regression/correlation.

So why, then, should anyone use, say, a t test instead of an analysis of variance? The reason is simply that it is a procedure that is widely understood. Most researchers today expect to see a t test when two groups are compared. It is traditional. (However, the situation is changing very rapidly as researchers become more statistically sophisticated.) It seems strange, and somehow grandiose, to see an analysis of variance when a t test would do—though in fact the sense of grandiosity is simply a holdover from the days when computations were done by hand and an analysis of variance was harder to do than a t test.

Similarly, in the two-group situation, to use a correlation coefficient (and its associated significance test) instead of an ordinary t test would confuse people who were not very statistically sophisticated (such as yourself before reading this chapter). And analyzing an experiment with several groups using multiple regression/correlation instead of analysis of variance would confuse those same unsophisticated readers.

Part of the confusion in these cases rests on an issue that we discussed in Chapter 3 but bears repeating here. Many people mix up the distinction between an experimental and a correlational *research design* with the distinction between statistical methods. A true experimental research design is one in which individuals are randomly assigned to different levels of the predictor variable (such as an experimental versus a control condition), making it easier to say that different levels of the predictor variables *caused* any differences that occur in the dependent variable. In a correlational research design, the predictor and dependent variables are both measured as they exist (as in a survey of the relationship between time spent together and marital satisfaction), making a clear case for any *association* they have but not for one *causing* the other. A third variable might well have caused both.

BOX 16-2

Two Women Make a Point About Gender and Statistics

One of the most useful advanced statistics books written so far is *Using Multivariate Statistics* by Barbara Tabachnick and Linda Fidell (1989), two experimental psychologists at California State University at Northridge. These two met at a faculty luncheon soon after Tabachnick was hired. Fidell recalls that she had just finished a course on French and one on matrix algebra, for the pleasure of learning them ("I was very serious at the time") and was wondering what to tackle next when Tabachnick suggested that Fidell join her in taking a belly dancing course. Fidell thought, "Something frivolous for a change." Little did she know.

Thus their collaboration began. After the lessons, they had long discussions about statistics. In particular, the two found that they shared a fascination—and consternation—with the latest statistics made possible through all the new statistical packages for computers. The problem was making sense of the results.

Fidell described it this way: "I had this enormous data set to analyze, and out came lots of pretty numbers in nice neat little columns, but I was not sure what all of it meant, or even whether my data had violated any critical assumptions. I knew there were some, but I didn't know anything about them. That was in 1975. I had been trained at the University of Michigan; I knew statistics up through the analysis of variance. But none of us were taught the multivariate analysis of variance at that time. Then along came these statistical packages to do it. But how to comprehend them?" (You will be introduced to the multivariate analysis of variance in Chapter 17.)

Both Fidell and Tabachnick had gone out and learned on their own, taking the necessary courses, reading, asking others who knew the programs better, trying out what would happen if they did this with the data, what would happen if they did that. Now the two women asked each other, why must this be so hard? And were others reinventing this same wheel at the very same time? They decided to put their wheel into a book.

"And so began fifteen years of conflict-free collaboration," reports Fidell. (That is something to compare to the feuds recounted in other boxes in this book.) The authors had no trouble finding a publisher, and the book, now in its second edition, has sold "nicely." (This despite the fact that their preferred titles—*Fatima and Scherazzad's Multivariate Statistics Book: A Thousand and One Variables; The Fuzzy Pink Statistics Book; Weight Loss Through Multivariate Statistics*—were overruled by the publisher. However, if you look closely at the first edition's cover, you will see a belly dancer buried in the design.)

Fidell emphasizes that both she and Tabachnick consider themselves data analysts and teachers, not statistics developers or theorists—they have not invented methods but have merely popularized them by making them more accessible. But they can name dozens of women who have risen to the fore as theoretical statisticians. In Fidell's opinion, statistics is a field in which women seem particularly to excel and feel comfortable. In teaching new students, the math-shy ones in particular, she finds that once she can "get them to relax," they often find that they thoroughly enjoy statistics. She tells them, "I intend to win you over. And if you will give me half a chance, I will do it."

She has also observed that it is geometry that often causes female students to decide that math is not for them. There is some evidence that spatial abilities may be more difficult for some women, and if this is a difference in any way governed by hormones interacting with brain functioning, it is probably increased at the time of puberty, the age when girls take geometry—or so Fidell speculates.

Whatever the reason, statistics is a branch of mathematics that, according to Fidell, women often come to find "perfectly logical, perfectly reasonable—and then, with time, something they can truly enjoy."

Reference: Personal interview with Linda Fidell.

Usually, true experimental research designs involve assignment to two or a few levels of the predictor variable. Such experiments have been traditionally analyzed using a *t* test or an analysis of variance. Indeed, until recently, many experimental psychologists were not even taught multiple regression/correlation as part of their graduate training. They were *experimentalists* and were not to stoop to correlations.

Correlational research designs are usually used when experiments are not possible. They often measure people on two or more numerical variables, without being able to assign them to experience one of these variables fully (for example, age and divorce or income and education). Because bivariate or multiple regression/correlation is the appropriate method of analysis, sociologists, economists, and other social scientists who must rely entirely on such research designs are often not taught *t* tests and analyses of variance as part of their training.

Clearly, experimental designs are advantageous. Both correlational designs and correlational statistics, by association, are considered less impressive—the two are simply confused. However, there is no reason why a true experiment could not randomly assign people to several numerically different levels of a numerical predictor variable. (We used an example of this in Chapter 3, where people were assigned to different numbers of exposures to a word.) Such a true experiment is appropriately analyzed only with a correlation coefficient (and its associated significance test). If you were to try to reduce these levels of exposure down to two groups—for example, those with high versus low numbers of exposures to words—this would lose information and be a much poorer statistical approach (among other things, you would have less power).

Similarly, there are studies that use correlational research designs but in which one of the variables has only two levels—for example, gender. Or you might conduct a study with a category-type variable with more than two levels, such as nationality. In such cases, you could certainly analyze results using a *t* test or an analysis of variance, but this would not change the fact that the studies used correlational research designs in which cause and effect are hard to sort out.

Again, when researchers select one statistical method over another, the decision may have more to do with tradition, what "looks good," or even confusion rather than with any mathematical or logical difference among procedures.

There is a big advantage in using correlation (or multiple regression/correlation if needed) over the *t* test or an analysis of variance: The correlational approach gives you direct information on the degree of relationship between the predictor variable(s) and the dependent variable as well as permitting a significance test. The *t* test and the analysis of variance give only statistical significance. (Although you can compute an effect size for either of these, with a correlation coefficient or a multiple correlation coefficient, you automatically have an indication of the effect size.)

Another advantage of the correlation (and multiple regression/correlation) approach is that it automatically handles situations of unequal numbers of subjects in the groups being compared. With a *t* test or a one-way analysis of variance, you must use more complicated procedures when the numbers of subjects in each group are unequal. But at least in these cases, the *t* test and one-way analysis of variance provide accurate results. When conducting a two-way or higher analysis of variance, if there are unequal numbers in the cells, the standard procedures for the analysis of variance actually fail in the sense that applying them gives distorted results. In most cases, the best solution is to recast the problem as a multiple regression/correlation problem.[5]

Assumptions and the General Linear Model

Another way in which the various techniques based on the general linear model are similar is that the hypothesis-testing procedures all share the same assumptions. With the t test and the analysis of variance, the assumptions are that the population variances for the groups are equal and that the populations represented by the groups are normally distributed. In the case of significance tests for correlation and multiple regression/correlation, the assumptions are basically the same but are a bit more complicated to express.

The assumption of equal population variances in the t test and the analysis of variance equates in correlation (and multiple correlation) to equal variances in the part of the population associated with each level of the predictor variable. If you think in terms of a scatter diagram, the variance of the line at points above a particular score on the independent variable should be the same as the variance of the line of points above any other particular score on the independent variables. (This is called "homoscedasticity.")

The assumption of normal population distributions becomes a requirement that each variable be normally distributed and that their joint distribution also be normally distributed (called "bivariate normal").

It also turns out that except when the number of subjects is very small or when assumptions are drastically violated, all of the general linear model techniques give quite accurate results over a wide variety of situations. Indeed, they are the workhorses of psychology research.

Controversies and Limitations

The general linear model itself is not very controversial; it is simply a mathematical statement of a relationship among variables. In fact, its role as the foundation of the major statistical techniques has not even been widely realized among practicing researchers.

However, the least-squares method within the general linear model is a little more controversial. One alternative idea is that we should minimize absolute error instead of squared error. (One advantage of this approach is that instead of using as our most common measure of variation the square root of the average of the squared deviations, we would just use the average of the absolute values of the deviations, thus giving much less distorting influence to outliers.)

The main criticisms associated with the general linear model, however, are the ones having to do with hypothesis testing. These criticisms are the ones we have been discussing all along, including robustness to violation of assumptions and emphasis on effect size or significance testing.

[5]Some computer programs do this automatically when told to do a factorial analysis of variance where the numbers of cases in the cells are not all the same. However, some programs must be specially told to do this, or they will compute using the ordinary analysis of variance formulas and give a misleading result.

There is another area of criticism that is appropriate to mention here, however. It has to do with the role of statistics in science generally, but in practice it is most often raised in the context of the major general-linear-model-based procedures. This is the issue of causality. We have already addressed this issue at one level in Chapter 3 and again in this chapter, where we considered the problem of inferring a direction of causality from a study that does not use random assignment to groups. But there is a deeper level to the issue still: What does causality mean?

Baumrind (1983) has outlined two main understandings of causality that are used in science. One understanding, which she calls the "regularity" theory of causality, has its roots in philosophers like David Hume and John Stuart Mill (as well as early scientists, including Galileo). This view holds that we recognize X as a cause of Y if (a) X and Y are regularly associated, (b) X precedes Y, and (c) there are no other causes that precede X that might cause both X and Y. In psychology, we address the (a) part by finding a significant correlation between X and Y. We address the (b) part, if possible, by our knowledge of the situation (in a correlation of whether or not one was the firstborn in one's family with anxiety later in life, we can rule out the possibility that anxiety later in life caused the person to be firstborn) or designing it into an experiment (by manipulating X prior to measuring Y). The (c) part has to do with the issue of a correlation between X and Y being due to some third variable causing both. Ideally, we address this by random assignment to groups. But if that is not possible, various statistical methods of equating groups on proposed third factors are used as a makeshift strategy (we explore some of these in Chapter 17).

The fact is that as psychologists, we are only sometimes in a position to conduct the kind of rigorous experimental research that provides a strong basis for drawing conclusions about cause and effect. Much of the criticism and controversy involving research of practical importance, where it is usually least easy to apply rigorous methods, often hinges on such issues. For example, if marriage correlates with happiness, does marriage make people happier, or do happy people get and stay married?

There is another view of causality, a still more stringent view that sees the regularity theory conditions as a prerequisite to calling something a cause, but these conditions are not sufficient alone. This other view, which Baumrind calls the "generative" theory of causality, has its roots in Aristotle, Thomas Aquinas, and Immanuel Kant. The focus of this view is on the dynamics of just how X affects Y—the intrinsic process in which one is connected to the other. This is the way most nonscientists (and non-philosophers) understand causality. The very idea of causality may have its roots as a metaphor of experiences such as willing my arm to move (Event X) and it moves (Event Y). Scientists also take this view of causality very much to heart, even if it offers much more difficult challenges. It is addressed primarily by theory and by careful analysis of mediating processes. But even those who emphasize this view would recognize that demonstrating a reliable connection between X and Y (by finding statistical significance, for example) plays an important role at least in identifying linkages that require scrutiny for determining the real causal connection.

Finally, there are also those who hold—with some good arguments—that demonstrating causality should not be a goal of scientific psychology at all. But we have already had enough controversy for one chapter.

Summary

The general linear model equates the value of a variable for any individual case with the sum of a constant, plus the partial, weighted influence of each of several other variables, plus error. The correlation coefficient and multiple correlation/regression (and associated significance tests), the t test, and the analysis of variance are all special cases of the general linear model.

Multiple regression/correlation is almost identical to the general linear model, and bivariate correlation and regression are the special cases of multiple regression/correlation in which there is only one predictor variable.

The t test for independent means can be mathematically derived from the analysis of variance and can be thought of as a special case of the analysis of variance in which there are only two groups. The computed t score for the same data is the square root of the F ratio. There are many similarities in how the two procedures are computed: The numerators of both t and F are built on the differences between group means; the denominators of both are built on the variance within the groups; the denominator of t involves dividing by the number of subjects, and the numerator of F involves multiplying by the number of subjects; and the t degrees of freedom are the same as the F denominator degrees of freedom.

The t test for independent means can also be considered a special case of the significance test for the correlation coefficient. A correlation measures the degree of association of a predictor or independent variable with a dependent variable. In the same way, by showing a difference between group means, the t test identifies an association of the variable on which the groups are divided, the independent or predictor variable, with the dependent variable. If you assign a score of 1 to each subject in one of the two groups and a 2 to each subject in the other group (or any two different numbers) and then compute a correlation of these scores with the dependent variable, the significance of that correlation will be the same as the t test would produce. Drawing a scatter diagram of these data would make a column of scores for each group, with the regression line passing through the means of each group. The more the means are different, the greater the proportionate reduction in error over using the grand mean and the greater the t score based on a comparison of the two groups' means.

The analysis of variance and correlation/regression also have many similarities. SS_T in regression and in the analysis of variance are both about the deviations of each score from the mean of all the dependent-variable scores. Since the group means in an analysis of variance are the predicted score for each case in regression, SS_E and SS_W are the same. The reduction in squared error ($SS_T - SS_E$) in regression is the same as the sum of squared deviations of scores' group means from the grand mean (SS_B) in the analysis of variance. Finally, regression's proportionate reduction in error (r^2) is the same as the proportion of variance accounted for (R^2), an indicator of effect size in the analysis of variance.

Any analysis of variance can be set up as a multiple regression by making the categories that represent the different groups into one or more dichotomous numerical variables. Strictly speaking, the analysis of variance is a special case of multiple regression in which the predictor variables are set up in this way.

All of these methods share the same assumptions that population distributions are normal and have constant variance over levels of the predictor variable.

Although the *t* test, analysis of variance, and correlation can all be done as multiple regression/correlation, conventional practice (and sometimes confusion) leads to these conceptually identical procedures being used in different research contexts, as if they were actually different.

About causality, the regularity view identifies *X* as a cause of *Y* if *X* and *Y* are associated, *X* precedes *Y*, and no other third factors precede *X* that could cause them both. The generative view argues that in addition there must be a clear understanding of the mechanism by which *X* affects *Y*. Statistical procedures can demonstrate an association between *X* and *Y* and can sometimes give evidence against particular proposed third variables being the cause of *X* and *Y*. All further evidence for *X* causing *Y* depends on knowledge of the situation, experimental design, and theoretical analysis.

Key Terms

general linear model

least-squares model

nominal coding

Practice Problems

These problems involve computation (with the assistance of a calculator). Most real-life statistics problems are done on a computer. But even if you have a computer, do these by hand to ingrain the method in your mind.

For practice in using a computer to solve statistical problems, refer to the computer section of each chapter of the study guide that accompanies this text.

All data are fictional (unless an actual citation is given).

Answers to Set I are given at the back of the book.

SET I

1. Look up the *t* cutoff at the .05 level (two-tailed) for 5, 10, 15, and 20 degrees of freedom, square each of them, and compare the result to the cutoffs for *F* distributions with 1 degree of freedom in the numerator and 5, 10, 15, and 20 degrees of freedom as the denominators.

2. Presented here are three data sets. For the first two data sets, in addition to the means and estimated population variances, we have shown the *t* test information. You should compute the third. Also, in each case, compute a one-way analysis of variance. Note the similarities of (a) *t* *df* to *F* denominator *df*, (b) *t* cutoff to square root of *F* cutoff, (c) S_P^2 to S_W^2, and (d) the *t* score to the square root of the *F* ratio. *t* and *F* are at the .05 level; *t* tests are two-tailed.

	Experimental Group			Control Group			t test			
	N	*M*	*S²*	*N*	*M*	*S²*	*df*	*t* needed	S_P^2	*t*
(i)	30	12.0	2.4	30	11.1	2.8	58	2.004	2.6	2.16
(ii)	36	100	40	36	104	48	70	1.995	44	2.56
(iii)	16	73	8	16	75	6				

3. Group A consists of 10 people whose scores have a mean of 170 and yield a population variance estimate of 48. Group B also consists of 10 people: *M* = 150, *S²* = 32. Conduct a *t* test for independent means (two-tailed) and an analysis of variance, computing the two on two halves of the same page, with parallel computations next to each other. Use the .05 level.

4. For the data given, compute an analysis of variance; then compute a regression analysis, including making a scatter diagram (and drawing in the regression line), finding the correlation coefficient (between the group that subjects are in and their score), determining the proportionate reduction in error using the long method of computing predicted scores, and finding the average squared error using them; finally, make a chart showing the parallels in the results.

Group A	Group B
13	11
16	7
19	9
18	
19	

5. For the data given, compute a t test for independent means (using the .05 level, one-tailed), the correlation coefficient (between the group that subjects are in and their score), and the t for significance of the correlation coefficient (using the formula $t = r\sqrt{N-2}/\sqrt{1-r^2}$).

Group A	Group B
.7	.6
.9	.4
.8	.2

6. Explain the major links between multiple regression and the analysis of variance.

SET II

1. Look up the F cutoff at the .01 level for distributions with 1 degree of freedom in the numerator and 10, 20, 30, and 60 degrees of freedom in the denominator. Take the square root of each, and compare it to the cutoff for the t distribution at the .01 level (two-tailed) using 10, 20, 30, and 60 degrees of freedom.

2. Presented here are three data sets, all from Practice Problem 2, Set II, in Chapter 10. If you never computed the t tests for these, do so now, this time using the .01 level, two-tailed. Then, in each case, also compute a one-way analysis of variance (also .01 level). Note the similarities of (a) t df to F denominator df, (b) t cutoff to square root of F cutoff, (c) S_P^2 to MS_W, and (d) the t score to the square root of the F ratio.

	Experimental Group			Control Group		
	N	M	S^2	N	M	S^2
(i)	10	604	60	10	607	50
(ii)	40	604	60	40	607	50
(iii)	10	604	20	10	607	16

3. For the following data set, conduct a t test for independent means (two-tailed) and an analysis of variance, computing the two on two halves of the same page, with parallel computations next to each other. Use the .01 level.

Group A	Group B
0	4
1	5
0	6
	5

4. For the data in Problem 3, compute a regression analysis, including making a scatter diagram, computing the correlation coefficient (between the group that subjects are in and their score), determining the proportionate reduction in error using the long method of computing predicted scores, and finding the average squared error using them; then compute the significance of the correlation (using the formula $t = r\sqrt{N-2}/\sqrt{1-r^2}$ and then squaring t). Finally, make a chart showing the parallels in the results.

5. For the data given, compute (a) a t test for independent means (.05 level, two-tailed); (b) the correlation coefficient (between the group that subjects are in and their score) and the t for significance of the correlation coefficient; (c) an analysis of variance (.05 level); and (d) a chi-square and phi coefficient (for the chi-square, create a 2×2 contingency table in which one dimension is group and the other dimension is subject score 0 or 1, on the dependent measure). Make a table of similarities in computations and results.

Group A	Group B
0	0
0	0
0	0
0	0
0	0
0	0
0	1
0	1
0	1
0	1
0	1
0	1
1	1
1	1
1	1
1	1

6. Explain nominal coding.

17 Making Sense of Advanced Statistical Procedures in Research Articles

M OST research you will read as a psychology student was done employing one or more of the procedures you have learned in this book. But sometimes you will see procedures that you will not learn to do yourself until you take more advanced courses in statistics. Fortunately, these more advanced procedures are often straightforward extensions of what you have learned—not straightforward enough that you will understand all their subtleties or limitations, but straightforward enough that you will be able to make sense of the general idea of what's being done to the data in the study you are reading.

We can divide these advanced statistical techniques, and statistical techniques in general, into those that focus on associations among variables and those that focus on differences among groups (although, as you learned in Chapter 16, this is a bit of an artificial distinction). The procedures we cover first focus on associations among variables and are all basically extensions and elaborations—in some cases, highly sophisticated ones—of what you learned in Chapters 3 and 4 on correlation and regression: After a brief review of the basics of multiple regression as a foundation, we introduce hierarchical and stepwise multiple regression, partial correlation, reliability, factor analysis, and causal modeling. We then turn to techniques that focus on differences between groups, all of which are basically extensions or elaborations of what you learned in Chapters 11–13 on the analysis of variance. These procedures include the analysis of covariance, multivariate analysis of variance, and multivariate analysis of covariance. The remainder of the chapter discusses the controversy over whether statistics ought to be controversial and considers what to do when you read a research article that uses a statistical technique you have never heard of.

Multiple Regression/Correlation and Some of Its Extensions

In 1988, one article in five in the *Journal of Personality and Social Psychology* used some form of multiple regression or multiple correlation (Reis & Stiller, 1992). The proportion is probably higher still in developmental, clinical, and various applied areas of psychology. We will briefly review the fundamentals of multiple regression and correlation from Chapters 4 and 16. Then we will proceed to consider two of its direct extensions—hierarchical and stepwise regression.

Brief Review of Multiple Correlation and Regression

As noted in Chapters 4 and 16, multiple correlation is about the association of one dependent variable with the combination of two or more predictor variables. In a fictional example we used in those chapters, there was a multiple correlation (R) of .96 between amount of stress that managers experienced and the combination of the number of employees they supervise, the amount of noise in the workplace, and the number of decisions they must make each month.

Also, as we have noted, multiple regression is about predicting a dependent variable on the basis of two or more predictor variables. (Regression, recall, is just the prediction aspect of correlation.) A multiple regression prediction rule includes a set of regression coefficients, one to be multiplied by each predictor variable. The sum of these multiplications is the predicted value on the dependent variable. When working with Z scores, the regression coefficients are standardized regression coefficients, called beta weights (β). For example, with three independent variables, the form of the prediction rule is as follows:

$$\hat{Z}_Y = (\beta_1)(Z_{X1}) + (\beta_2)(Z_{X2}) + (\beta_3)(Z_{X3}) \tag{17-1}$$

In the managers' stress example, the Z-score multiple regression prediction rule was as follows:

$$\hat{Z}_{\text{Stress}} = (.51)(Z_{\text{Employees}}) + (.11)(Z_{\text{Noise}}) + (.33)(Z_{\text{Decisions}}) \tag{17-2}$$

When working with raw scores, the raw score regression coefficient (b) is multiplied by the raw score of each predictor variable, and a particular number (the raw score regression constant, a, is also added in). Here is the standard form of the formula:

$$\hat{Y} = a + (b_1)(X_1) + (b_2)(X_2) + (b_3)(X_3) \tag{17-3}$$

In the managers' stress example, the raw-score multiple-regression prediction rule was as follows:

$$\hat{Y} = -4.70 + (.56)(X_1) + (.06)(X_2) + (.86)(X_3) \tag{17-4}$$

Hypothesis Testing and Significance in Multiple Regression/Correlation

In multiple correlation and regression, researchers can test hypotheses (that is, determine the statistical significance) of both the overall multiple correlation coefficient, R, as well as for each beta (or b) individually. In most cases, however, if the overall R is not significant, the individual betas will not be tested. Yet it is quite possible for the overall R to be significant but for some of the individual betas not to be significant—for example, the overall significant correlation might be due to the strong influence of only one predictor variable, with the others having a negligible contribution.

Hierarchical Multiple Regression

Sometimes researchers are interested in looking at the influence of several predictor variables in a sequential fashion. That is, they want to know what the correlation will be of the first predictor variable with the dependent variable, and then how much is added to the overall multiple correlation by including a second predictor variable, and then perhaps how much more is added by including a third predictor variable, and so on. This is known as **hierarchical multiple regression.**

hierarchical multiple regression

For example, Barocas and his colleagues (1991) conducted a study involving 159 four-year-old children and their mothers to investigate various possible predictors of a child's IQ. Three main categories of predictors were measured: (a) the "contextual risk," the extent to which the family situations put the child at risk for problems, such as poverty, many children in the family, or mental illness of the mother; (b) "maternal teaching style" (MTS), the way the mother instructed the child to carry out a standard task as observed in the researcher's laboratory (variables included mother's positive, negative, or flattened emotional tone; how involved she was with her child; and how much thinking she demanded of the child, called "mental operational demand," or MOD); and (c) the child's ability to direct attention and willfully control his or her own actions as measured by two laboratory tasks ("Luria errors" and "delayed-match-to-sample task"). A hierarchical regression analysis was carried out to see whether each set of predictors, when added to the preceding, yielded any significant additional proportionate reduction in squared error (or increase in "variance explained," which is another term for the same thing). The researchers described their results as follows:

> Table [17-1] shows the hierarchical multiple-regression analysis in which maternal- and family-risk factors are entered in the prediction equation first, followed by the maternal teaching measures and by the child's laboratory-attention measures. . . . When maternal teaching is added, a significant increase of 9% in variance explained is achieved; when the attention measures are entered, an additional significant increase of 7% is obtained. Taken together, these measures of maternal and family risk, MTS, . . . and the child's attention and self-regulation as assessed in the DMS and Luria situations account for more than half the variance in IQ. (p. 483)

Hierarchical multiple regression has become widely used only recently in psychology, and no standard way of describing it or setting up a table has yet emerged. Often descriptions do not give the amount of increased variance or the increment from one R^2 to the next R^2 which includes the additional variable or variables. However, if this is not given, you can determine it by simple subtraction. Also, the significance figures given at each step are sometimes for the entire set of predictor variables (which is not nearly as useful) and sometimes for the extent to which adding the additional variable or variables enhances the predictability (which is what you usually want). So *caveat lector*—read the fine print of the tables or the text.

TABLE 17-1

Summary of Hierarchical Multiple Regression Analysis With Verbal IQ as Criterion

Predictor Variables	R^2	R^2 Change	F (Change)
Step 1			
Contextual risk	.376	.376	94.43*
Step 2			
MTS positive			
MTS negative			
MTS flattened			
MTS involved			
MTS low MOD			
MTS medium MOD	.468	.092	4.35*
Step 3			
Luria errors			
DMS group	.538	.071	11.38*

Note. MTS = maternal teaching style. MOD = mental operational demand. DMS = delayed-match-to-sample task. IQ = intelligence quotient.

From Barocas, R., Seifer, R., Sameroff, A. J., Andrews, T. A., Croft, R. T., & Ostrow, E. (1991), tab. 2. Social and interpersonal determinants of developmental risk. *Developmental Psychology*, *27*, 479–488. Copyright, 1991, by the American Psychological Association. Reprinted by permission of the author.

Stepwise Multiple Regression

stepwise multiple regression

Often, especially in an exploratory study, a researcher may have measured many potential predictor variables and wants to pick out which ones make a useful contribution to the overall prediction. In **stepwise multiple regression,** a computer program goes through a systematic procedure in which it first determines which variable has the highest bivariate correlation with the dependent variable. If this correlation is not significant, no further analysis is done, since even the best predictor is not of any use. But if this correlation is significant, the computer tries each of the other variables in combination with this one to see which combination produces the highest multiple R. It then checks this to see whether this combination is a significant improvement over the best single variable alone. If it is not, the process stops. If it is a significant improvement, the next step is to take these two variables in combination with each of the other remaining predictors, one at a time, to find the best combination of three—which is then tested to see if it is a significant improvement over the two-predictor situation. The process continues until either all the predictor variables are included or adding any of the remaining ones fails to produce a significant improvement. Because this procedure, diagrammed in Table 17-2, proceeds one step at a time, it is called "stepwise."[1]

Here is an example. Mooney, Sherman, and Lo Presto (1991) examined predictors of adjustment to college (the dependent variable) among 82 women in their fourth week of their first semester at college, all of whom were living away from home. The predictor variables were distance from

[1]Technically, what we have described is a "forward stepwise regression." Some researchers prefer to start with the whole set of all the predictor variables and see how much predictability is lost when the least useful predictor is eliminated. If not much is lost, the next least useful is eliminated, and so forth. This process continues until they get a small set of variables in which eliminating the least useful predictor significantly reduces the strength of the prediction. This alternative procedure is called "backward stepwise regression." In most cases, forward and backward stepwise regression give about the same results. Which is used is a matter of the researcher's preference.

TABLE 17-2
The Process of a Stepwise Multiple Regression

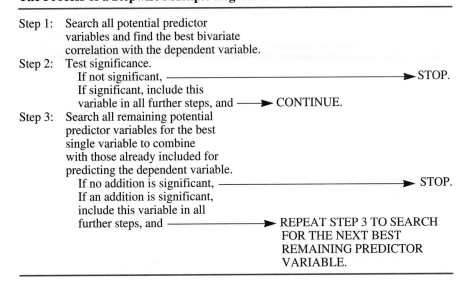

Step 1: Search all potential predictor variables and find the best bivariate correlation with the dependent variable.

Step 2: Test significance.
  If not significant, ─────────────────────────► STOP.
  If significant, include this variable in all further steps, and ──► CONTINUE.

Step 3: Search all remaining potential predictor variables for the best single variable to combine with those already included for predicting the dependent variable.
  If no addition is significant, ─────────────────► STOP.
  If an addition is significant, include this variable in all further steps, and ───────────► REPEAT STEP 3 TO SEARCH FOR THE NEXT BEST REMAINING PREDICTOR VARIABLE.

home (in miles), perceived distance from home (a scale from *just right* to *too far*), a self-esteem scale, and an "academic locus of control" scale that measures the extent to which persons feel in control over their success at school. One question these researchers posed was whether all of these variables made unique contributions to predicting college adjustment, and if not all of them, which ones? The authors describe the procedure they used as follows:

> For this analysis, a stepwise procedure was employed, with forward entry of predictor variables continuing until significant relationships with remaining partialed variables were exhausted. Three predictors were retained: academic locus of control, perceived distance from home, and self-esteem. . . . With these variables in the equation, 59% of the variance in the dependent variable was accounted for ($R = .77$, $R^2 = .59$ . . .). The standardized beta coefficients [of the regression equation including these three predictor variables] indicated that academic locus of control was weighted the most, followed by self-esteem and perceived distance. . . . (p. 447)

The message of this analysis is that of the four potential predictors, using the best three provided a proportionate reduction in error that was not improved by including the fourth as well. Thus actual distance from home was excluded from the final regression equation as unnecessary.

One caution in interpreting results of stepwise regression. The prediction formula that results is the optimal small set of variables for predicting the dependent variable *as determined from the sample studied*. It often happens that when the same variables are studied with a new sample of subjects, a somewhat different combination of variables turns out to be optimal.

Relationship of Hierarchical and Stepwise Regression

Hierarchical and stepwise regression are similar in that in both cases you are adding one variable at a time and checking whether the addition makes a significant improvement in the prediction. The difference between the two procedures is that in hierarchical regression, the order in which the predictor variables are added is determined by some theory or plan, decided in advance by the experimenter on the basis of knowledge of the field. In stepwise regression, there is no initial plan. The computer simply selects the best variables to add until adding more makes no additional contribution.

Thus hierarchical regression is used in research that is based on theory or some substantial previous knowledge. Stepwise regression is useful in exploratory research where we don't know what to expect or in applied research where we are looking for the best prediction formula without caring about its theoretical meaning.

Partial Correlation

partial correlation

Partial correlation is another technique that is widely used in areas such as personality and applied fields, in which researchers are often in the position of trying to sort out the relation among variables and experiments are not possible. Partial correlation is the degree of association between two variables, over and above the influence of one or more other variables. Suppose that a researcher wants to know how much a person's marital satisfaction is associated with how long the person has been married, over and above any influence from the fact that people who have been married longer tend to have more children. Simply computing the correlation between marital satisfaction and length of marriage would be misleading. The researcher wants to know the relation between satisfaction and length that would occur if everyone had the same number of children. Or to put it another way, the researcher wants somehow to subtract the information provided by number of children from the information provided by marital satisfaction. Partial correlation accomplishes this.

holding constant
partialing out
controlling for

partial correlation coefficient

In this case, the researcher would compute a partial correlation between marital satisfaction and length of marriage, **holding constant,** or **partialing out**, or **controlling for** number of children. (All of these terms mean the same thing and are used interchangeably.) The actual measure of partial correlation is the **partial correlation coefficient,** which has values from −1 to +1 and is interpreted like an ordinary bivariate correlation except for remembering that some third variable is being controlled for. The significance of a partial r can also be determined and is commonly reported in research articles in which partial correlation is used.

Here is another way of thinking of partial correlations. In the example, the researcher could compute a correlation between satisfaction and length of marriage using only the subjects who had no children, then compute the correlation for only those with one child, and so on. Each of these correlations would not be affected by number of children, since in each case the number of children of the subjects used in computing that particular correlation would be the same. Then the researcher could average these various correlations (taking into account that some were based on more subjects than others), and the result would be the partial correlation.

In fact, computing the partial correlation is fairly simple and does not require figuring all these individual correlations and averaging them. But the result of the process amounts to doing this.[2]

Partial correlation is often used to help sort out alternative explanations in a correlational study. For example, if it were found that marital satisfaction and marriage length were negatively correlated, the researcher might want to use this result as support for a theory that the effect of time is to make people less satisfied because they take their partners for granted. But the researcher would also be aware that an alternative explanation is that when people are married longer, they are likely to have more children, and having children might reduce marital satisfaction. If the negative correlation between satisfaction and length is found, even after controlling for number of children, this alternate explanation about children is made unlikely.

A study by Baer (1991) provides a specific example of research that used partial correlations to sort out the relationships among variables. Baer was interested in whether verbal creativity (storytelling, poetry, etc.) is a single, general trait or a set of individual abilities of which you can have some but not others. In the past, researchers had found that creativity tests tend to correlate to a moderate degree with each other, and this was taken as evidence for the general, single trait idea. Baer, however, reasoned that the correlations among these measures may be due to various third factors, such as IQ, that may make people do better on any kind of test. In one of his studies, Baer administered to 50 eighth-grade students a number of creativity tests along with IQ and scholastic achievement tests. When the correlations were computed among the creativity tests, low to moderate correlations were found among the verbal creativity measures, as had been found in previous research. But then the correlations were recomputed, partialing out scores on verbal IQ, reading achievement, math IQ, math achievement, and gender (that is, all of these variables were partialed out at once). The partial correlations were in most cases clearly lower. For example, the correlation between creativity in the story task and creativity in the poetry task dropped from a direct bivariate correlation of .23 to a partial correlation of −.01; the correlation between creativity on poetry and creativity on a word problem task dropped from .31 (which was significant) to .19 (which was not significant).

Reliability Coefficients

As we noted briefly in Chapter 3 and describe in more detail in Appendix A, measures in psychology are rarely perfectly accurate (in the sense of stable or consistent). The degree of accuracy is called **reliability.** Roughly

reliability

[2]Partial correlation is closely related to multiple regression. For example, a regression coefficient tells you the extent to which the particular variable predicts the dependent variable at any given level of all the other variables in the equation. (In fact, the formal full name for a regression coefficient is a "partial regression coefficient.") Also, in hierarchical multiple regression, the contribution of adding a variable to all those already in the equation is, in effect, telling what that variable adds over and above all the others. (The formal name for what a variable adds in hierarchical multiple regression is the "semipartial correlation.") For purposes of gaining a general understanding of a research article, a partial correlation, a regression coefficient, and the amount added by a variable in hierarchical regression are all telling you something similar: the relationship of two variables over and above one or more other variables.

speaking, reliability is the extent to which you would obtain the same result if you were to administer the same measure again to the same person under the same circumstances. Computing the reliability of a measurement is central to almost all areas of psychological research, and you will often see reliability statistics in articles.

One index of a measure's reliability is obtained by administering the measure to a group of people twice. The correlation between the two testings is called **test-retest reliability.** However, a study of test-retest reliability is often impracticable or inappropriate, especially if having taken the test once would influence the second taking (as in an intelligence test, for example).

test-retest reliability

For many measures, such as most questionnaires, you can also obtain an index of reliability by correlating the responses of half the items (such as all the even-numbered items) to the other half (all the odd-numbered items). If the person is answering consistently, this should be a high correlation. This is called **split-half reliability.**[3]

split-half reliability

A problem with the split-half method is which way to split the halves. Odd item–even item makes sense in most cases, but by chance it could give too low or too high a correlation. A more general solution is to divide the test up into halves in all possible ways and compute the correlation using each division. The average of these correlations is called **Cronbach's alpha,** which is the most widely used measure of reliability. (This method can also be thought of as describing how much each item is correlated with each other item—the overall consistency of the test, the extent to which high responses go with highs and lows with lows over all the test items.)

Cronbach's alpha(α)

You may also see references to **Kuder-Richardson-20** or **KR-20.** This is a special formula that is used when all the test items are dichotomous (such as yes-no or true-false). The result with KR-20 is the same as with Cronbach's alpha.

Kuder-Richardson-20 (KR-20)

In general, in psychology, a test should have a reliability of at least .7, and preferably closer to .9, to be considered useful.

One context in which reliabilities are nearly always discussed is when a research article is mainly about the development of a new measure. For example, Berscheid, Snyder, and Omoto (1989) developed a questionnaire to assess interpersonal closeness. They asked students to answer their questionnaires with regard to the person with whom they have the "closest, deepest, most involved and most intimate relationship" (p. 793). (Some indicated family members, others close friends, others romantic partners.) The researchers reported on the reliability of their "strength" subscale (34 questions about the extent to which this close other influenced the student): "We found high internal-consistency reliability for this measure across all relationship types ($\alpha = .90$), as well as within the three main relationship types" (p. 795). The Greek letter "alpha" (α) refers to Cronbach's alpha (not to be confused with alpha as the probability of a Type I error in hypothesis testing). They tested a subgroup of 75 of their subjects a second time, 3 to 5 weeks later, and reported that "the correlation between . . . scores at Time 1 and Time 2 [for the entire questionnaire] was $r(75) = .82$,

[3]Because a correlation measuring split-half reliability is based on a smaller number of total items than one measuring test-retest reliability, it produces a somewhat smaller correlation. Thus when a split-half method is used, the researchers usually make a mathematical adjustment, using what is known as the Spearman-Brown formula, to make it comparable to what would be expected if twice the number of items were used. This kind of adjustment is also made in determining Cronbach's alpha and KR-20, described in the next paragraph.

p < .001" (p. 797). They also reported the "test-retest coefficient" for specific subscales, which for strength was ".81 (*p* < .001)" (p. 797).

Reliabilities are also discussed, though usually only briefly, with regard to measures being used in a study (as opposed to a study about the development of a new measure). For example, Hart (1991) conducted a study comparing obsessive-compulsive personality traits in 50 obese weight-loss patients versus 50 normal-weight control subjects. In the Methods section, in the context of justifying the choice of the measure he used for obsessive-compulsive personality, Hart cites studies showing that "measures of internal reliability are reported to be adequate . . . and a 2-week test-retest reliability of .92 has been reported" (p. 359). Furthermore, right at the beginning of his Results section, before proceeding to describe the comparison of obese with normals, Hart is first careful to describe the degree of reliability of the measure as found in the subjects he studied: "Cronbach's alpha . . . was .922, which indicates a very high degree of internal consistency" (p. 359). (However, there was not a significant difference on this test between the two groups. Hart did find a significant difference between the two groups on a different test—one that also had high reliability in his sample, α = .924—which measures obsessive-compulsiveness specifically with regard to eating behavior.)

Evaluating the reliability of a measure used in a study is quite important. As we noted in Chapter 3, low levels of reliability not only undermine the usefulness of the measure but also tend to lower the correlation of that test score with any other variables. (In the context of hypothesis testing, low reliability lowers power and effect size.) We also noted a possible solution: If you know the reliability of two measures and their correlation with each other, it is possible to estimate what the correlation between these two variables would be if they were both measured by perfectly reliable measures. This is called a *correction for attenuation* and has the result of increasing the correlation.

By the way, correction for attenuation is usually not practical in multiple or partial correlation, and the effect of unreliable measures in these cases is often unpredictable—that is, when the variable being partialed out is unreliable, the effect on the partial correlation of the other two variables can be either an increase or a decrease. Hence psychologists conducting complex studies especially try to avoid using measures with low reliability.

Factor Analysis

In the study we mentioned earlier of statistical procedures used in the 1988 issues of the *Journal of Personality and Social Psychology*, the procedure we will consider in this section, **factor analysis,** was found to have been used in about one article in six (Reis & Stiller, 1992). (Be sure you don't confuse factor analysis with the factorial analysis of variance.)

Factor analysis is used when a researcher has measured people on a large number of variables. Factor analysis tells the researcher which variables tend to clump together—which ones tend to be correlated with each other and not with other variables. Each such clump (group of variables) is called a **factor.** The relative connection of each of the original variables to a factor is called that variable's **factor loading** on that factor. (Variables have

factor analysis

factor
factor loading

TABLE 17-3
Factor Analysis of All Love Scales Combined

Individual Measures	Factor Structure and Loadings				
	1	*2*	*3*	*4*	*5*
Attachment Styles					
Avoidant	—	—	—	−.81	—
Anxious-Ambivalent	—	—	.80	—	—
Secure	—	—	—	.83	—
Love Attitudes Scale					
Eros	.76	—	—	—	—
Ludus	—	−.65	—	—	—
Storge	—	—	—	—	.80
Pragma	—	−.39	—	—	.73
Mania	.39	—	.68	—	—
Agape	.54	—	—	—	—
Triangular Theory of Love Scale					
Intimacy	.72	.44	—	—	—
Passion	.85	—	—	—	—
Commitment	.82	—	—	—	—
Passionate Love Scale					
Passionate Love	.80	—	—	—	—
Relationship Rating Form					
Viability	.51	.67	—	—	—
Intimacy	.58	.52	—	—	—
Passion	.82	—	—	—	—
Care	.72	.43	—	—	—
Satisfaction	.78	.38	—	—	—
Conflict	—	−.70	—	—	—
% variance	32	14	8	8	7

Note. Only factor loadings of .35 or larger are shown. $N = 391$.

From Hendrick, C., & Hendrick, S. S. (1989), tab. 4. Research on love: Does it measure up? *Journal of Personality and Social Psychology*, *56*, 784–794. Copyright, 1989, by the American Psychological Association. Reprinted by permission of the author.

loadings on each factor but usually will have high loadings on only one.) Factor loadings can be thought of as the correlation of the variable with the factor, and like correlations, they range from −1, a perfect negative association with the factor, through 0, no relation to the factor, to +1, a perfect positive correlation with the factor. Normally, a variable is considered to contribute meaningfully to a factor only if it has a loading of at least about .3 (or below −.3). This is an arbitrary cutoff based on the idea that since a factor loading is a correlation of the variable with the factor, squaring a correlation of less than about .3 gives a proportionate reduction in error of less than 10%. Some researchers use .35, .40, or even higher levels as the cutoff.

Which variables end up in which factor is determined by the mathematics of the procedure (although the researcher can use a variety of methods of factor analysis and has some leeway as to how many factors to include in the final solution, all of which may yield slightly different results). But the name given to a factor is an entirely arbitrary decision of the researcher and in many cases may imply a closer match to the researcher's theory than follows from the actual set of variables contained in each factor.

Consider an example of factor analysis. Hendrick and Hendrick (1989) administered five measures of love (which, because several measures had subscales, actually amounted to 19 different scales) to 391 undergraduates and then conducted a factor analysis of their scores to "determine commonalities among the scales" (p. 791). Table 17-3 presents the results of this analysis. The names of the love scales are self-explanatory, except for the Love Attitudes Scale's six styles of love: "Eros (passionate, romantic love), Ludus (game-playing love), Storge (friendship-based love), Pragma (practical love), Mania (possessive, dependent love), and Agape (altruistic love)" (p. 785).

In this particular table, factor loadings below .35 are omitted (a short line appears instead) in order to make the structure of the factors clear. Factor analysis tables are not always so easy to read, although some researchers make the table easier to read by reordering the variables so that all of those that load on the same factor appear next to each other.

Also, the last line of this table tells you the percentage of variance that the factor as a whole accounts for (that is, what the R^2 would be of this factor with all the variables). Notice that the five factors, even taken together, do not account for all the variance in the set of 19 variables. But then, accounting for a total of 69% (32% + 14% + 8% + 8% + 7%) of the variance in 19 variables with only five factors is an impressive simplification of the situation, which is the goal of factor analysis.

Hendrick and Hendrick interpret each of the factors in some detail. For example, with regard to the first factor:

> The first factor that emerged included the love styles of Eros, Mania, and Agape; Sternberg's Intimacy, Passion, and Commitment; the Passionate Love Scale; and Davis's Viability, Intimacy, Passion, Care, and Satisfaction. The highest loadings on the factor were those of Commitment and the three measures of Passion, although the other variables also had substantial loadings. Passionate love was certainly a major component of the factor, but intimacy, commitment, satisfaction, and aspects of caring love also appeared to be important. (p. 791)

After describing each factor in this way, they concluded:

> In summary, the various love scales primarily tap passionate love (Factor 1); however, two types of bipolar closeness-distance dimensions (Factors 2 and 4) are also important, as well as ambivalence-mania (Factor 3) and practicality-friendship (Factor 5). (p. 791)

Causal Modeling

Causal modeling techniques are used in only a small percentage of psychology studies (about 4%, according to Reis & Stiller, 1992). However, their use appears to be growing rapidly. We first introduce the older method of path analysis, then proceed to the newer and more powerful development of latent variable models.

Path Analysis

Path analysis is another technique in which a researcher has measured people on several variables. But the goal in path analysis is to analyze the causal structure, the pathways by which the variables influence each other. The procedure involves first making a diagram with arrows connecting the

path analysis

path coefficients

exogenous variable

endogenous variable

variables. Then the researcher calculates **path coefficients** that indicate the extent to which the variable at the start of an arrow is associated with the variable at the end of the arrow, after controlling for all other variables that have arrows to the variable at the end of the arrow. (A path coefficient is the same as a beta in multiple regression, with the variable at the start of the arrow as a predictor variable, the variable at the end of the arrow the dependent variable, and all other variables with arrows to the variable at the end of the arrow as other predictor variables in the regression equation.)

Variables in path analysis are divided into two major categories. A variable that is at the start of a causal chain, having no arrows to it within the path diagram, is called an **exogenous variable** (*exogenous* means "outside"). It is assumed that other variables, not included in the diagram, determine its level. That is, it is not part of the system of variables in the diagram but rather causes those variables from outside. A variable that has arrows to it, within the diagram, is called an **endogenous variable** (*endogenous* means "inside"). However, an endogenous variable is also usually influenced, to some extent, by variables other than those in the diagram. Thus a path diagram may explicitly emphasize that there are other unknown variables influencing an endogenous variable by putting an arrow to it with a blank stem or with the letter *E* (for error).

Bierman and Smoot (1991) interviewed parents of 75 grade school boys about parental discipline practices, parental hostility, marital satisfaction, and the boys' "home conduct problems." The researchers also administered questionnaires to the boys' teachers about "school conduct problems" and collected ratings from schoolmates of how much they liked these boys as a measure of "peer social performance." The purpose of the study was to examine a theoretical model that predicted a specific pattern of relationship among the variables measured. Bierman and Smoot's path diagram is reproduced in Figure 17-1. (This is somewhat complicated in that for variables collected separately from mother and father, which are the four exogenous variables on the left and home conduct problems, there are separate figures

FIGURE 17-1
A path analysis. [Figure 1 from Bierman, K. L., and Smoot, D. L. (1991). Linking family characteristics with poor peer relations: The mediating role of conduct problems. *Journal of Abnormal Child Psychology, 19,* 341–356. Copyright, 1991, by Plenum Publishing Corporation. Reprinted by permission.]

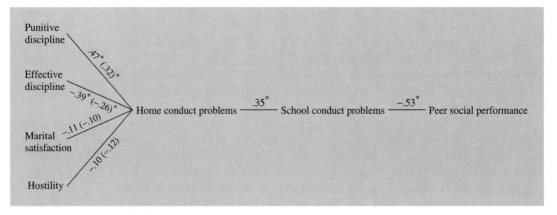

for mothers and fathers, the fathers' path coefficient being in parentheses. But the overall model is considerably simpler than most path models.)

Although for some reason Bierman and Smoot do not actually put in the arrowheads (usually they do appear), it is clear that the causality is intended to go from left to right. In interpreting this path diagram, be sure to notice that some of the signs of the paths are negative. For example, the path from home conduct problems to school conduct problems has a positive path coefficient, meaning the more of one, the more of the other. But the coefficient for the final path, from school conduct problems to peer social performance, is negative, indicating that the more school conduct problems, the less the peer social performance.

Since the major arrows in the path diagram representing their model had significant coefficients in the predicted directions, Bierman and Smoot consider the results to be encouraging support for their conceptualization.

Latent Variable Models

Latent variable modeling is also known as **structural equation modeling.** Often it is referred to as **LISREL,** after the name of a specific computer program that can be used to calculate an analysis of this kind. Basically, latent variable modeling is just a special extension of path analysis. It also involves a path diagram with arrows between variables and path coefficients for each arrow. However, the new method has several important advantages that have attracted psychology researchers. In particular, the computer calculates an overall measure of how good the model fits the data and, in addition, a kind of significance test.

latent variable modeling
structural equation modeling
LISREL

The measure of overall fit (there are several, including the Bentler-Bonnett Normed Fit Index), indicates how well the particular path diagram fits the data. If there is a good fit, the measure of fit is usually above .9 (the maximum is 1).

Further, as we noted, one can compute a kind of significance test. We say a "kind of significance test" because the null hypothesis in this case is that the model fits—meaning that a significant result is saying that the model does *not* fit. In other words, a researcher trying to demonstrate a theory hopes for a nonsignificant result in this significance test!

A second major advantage of the latent variable modeling approach over ordinary path analysis is that it analyzes the links among what are called, not surprisingly, **latent variables.** A latent variable is an artificial construction representing the true value of what the researcher is interested in, as opposed to the fallible **manifest variables,** which are the particular measures used to assess the latent variable. For example, a latent variable might be socioeconomic status, and the manifest variables to measure it might be reported level of income, years of education, prestige of occupation, and home square footage. No one of these manifest variables by itself is a very good measure of socioeconomic status, though some are better indicators than others. What is needed is a weighted average that also takes into account that as a whole, the set of indicators is not perfect. In latent variable modeling, the mathematics is set up so that a latent variable is a combination of the manifest variables that measure it, which are combined in such a way as to use only what they have in common with each other.

latent variables

manifest variables

FIGURE 17-2
A latent variable modeling path diagram.

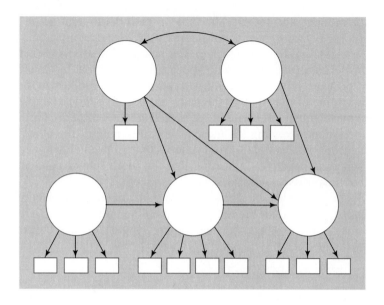

The idea is that what they have in common is the true score on the thing they are all getting at parts of.[4]

In a latent variable modeling path diagram, the manifest variables are usually shown in squares and the latent variables in circles, as illustrated in the example in Figure 17-2. Notice in the figure that the arrows from the latent variables (the ones in circles) go to the manifest variables (the ones in boxes). The idea is that the latent variable is the underlying cause of the manifest variables, the latter being the best we can do to measure the former. Also notice that all of the other arrows are between latent variables. In most cases, a latent variable causal model is structured in this way. As a result, the analysis is sometimes conceptualized as having two parts: (a) the relation of the manifest to the latent variables, called the **measurement model,** and (b) the relationships among the latent variables, called the **causal model.** Often the measurement model part is described only in the text of an article, and the authors present a diagram that shows only the causal model.

Consider an example studying a similar topic to the one we considered in the path analysis example. In this research, Capaldi and Patterson (1991) studied 169 boys in fourth grade and then the same boys again in sixth grade. A large number of measures were used, permitting there to be several manifest variables for each of their hypothesized latent variables. For example, the latent variable Maternal Antisocial Behavior was indicated by four manifest variables relating to the mother: Arrests and license suspensions (factor loading = .40), drug use (.59), score on a personality test measuring deviancy (.34), and age at first birth (–.44). Capaldi and Patterson present only the causal model in their diagram (Figure 17-3). Notice that at the bottom of the diagram, the authors present statistics showing that the model could *not* be significantly rejected—"$\chi^2(61, N = 169) = 76.13, p = .09$"—

measurement model
causal model

[4]A latent variable is the same as a factor in factor analysis. Thus one application of latent variable modeling is to test a particular, predicted pattern of factor analysis—that is, that particular variables will fall into particular factors. This is done by considering the variables to be manifest variables and the predicted factors to be latent variables. If the result of the analysis is a good fit (and the significance test comes out appropriately), it supports the predicted factor structure. This whole procedure is called "confirmatory factor analysis."

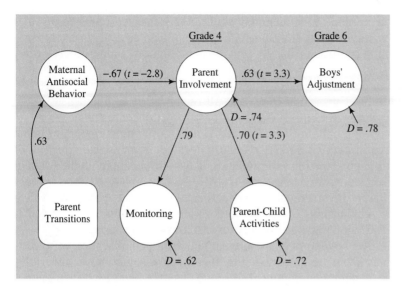

FIGURE 17-3
Mediated model. ($\chi^2(61, N = 169) = 76.13$, $p = .09$. Bentler-Bonett normed fit index = .84; Bentler-Bonett nonnormed fit index = .95; comparative fit index = .96.) [Example of causal modeling from Capaldi, D. M., & Patterson, G. R. (1991). Relation of parental transitions to boys' adjustment problems: I. A linear hypothesis. II. Mothers at risk for transitions and unskilled parenting. *Developmental Psychology, 27,* 489–504. Copyright, 1991, by the American Psychological Association. Reprinted by permission of the author.]

and that the various fit indexes were all fairly high. (*D*, not usually included in such diagrams, represents, roughly speaking, the variation not accounted for by the variable with the arrow leading to it.)

Some Limitations of Causal Modeling

It is important to realize how little magic there is behind these wonderful methods—they still rely entirely on a researcher's deep thinking. Even when all the predicted paths in a path analysis diagram are significant and even when in a latent variable model there is an overall good fit and the significance test comes out appropriately, it is quite possible that other patterns of causality could work equally well or better. Alternatives could have arrows that go in the opposite direction or make different connections, or the pattern could include additional variables not in the original diagram. If these possible alternative arrangements are not sought, they will not be found. The computer does not try alternatives for the researcher.

For example, in the Bierman and Smoot path analysis (see Figure 17-1), an alternative theory might be that school conduct problems cause home conduct problems or that parental hostility directly causes poor peer relations. Similarly, in the Capaldi and Patterson study (see Figure 17-3), it could well be that instead of Maternal Antisocial Behavior having a causal, negative effect on Parent Involvement, maybe Parent Involvement has a causal, negative effect on Maternal Social Behavior. And maybe the most important variable, perhaps class size or father's presence in the home, was never considered.

A path diagram is a statement of a theory, and if the outcome of the analysis is positive, that provides some support for the theory. But it does not provide any evidence against competing theories (other patterns of causality might be as good as or better than those tested). To do that, you would have to construct a path diagram for a competing theory and show that some of its paths are not significant or that it has an overall worse fit to the data than your theory. (This is sometimes done.) Since an infinite number of other possible path diagrams could be constructed (considering that alternatives may involve additional variables), a path analysis or latent variable modeling analysis can never provide unambiguous support for a particular theory; it is always possible that there is some untested alternative that is as good or better.

In addition, causal modeling, and all of the other techniques we have considered so far, which rely basically on correlations, are subject to all of the cautions we emphasized in Chapters 3 and 4. The most important is the one we have just considered: Association does not demonstrate direction of causality (though sometimes the situation does—for example, in the Capaldi and Patterson study, we can assume that Boy's Adjustment at Grade 6 could not cause Parent Involvement 2 years earlier). Further, these techniques take only linear relationships directly into account. And results are distorted if there is a restriction in range (usually toward lower associations).

So don't be bowled over by the mathematical sophistication of a technique such as latent variable modeling. It is useful—sometimes wonderfully useful—but if random assignment to groups has not been used, you cannot make an unambiguous determination of causality. And if the underlying relationships are curvilinear or if other limitations apply, such as restriction in range, the more sophisticated procedures are generally more likely to give distorted results than simple bivariate correlations.

Analysis of Covariance (ANCOVA)

So far in this chapter, we have been exploring statistical procedures that emphasize associations among variables and are basically sophisticated extensions of correlation and regression. Next we turn to procedures that focus on differences between group means, procedures that are basically extensions of the analysis of variance.

**analysis of covariance
ANCOVA**

One of the most widely used of these extensions is called the **analysis of covariance,** or **ANCOVA** for short. In this procedure an ordinary analysis of variance is carried out, but only after first adjusting the variables to eliminate the effect of some unwanted additional variable. So the analysis of covariance does for the analysis of variance what partial correlation does for ordinary correlation. The variable controlled for or partialed out is called

covariate

the **covariate.** The rest of the results are interpreted like any other analysis of variance.

For example, in another part of the article by Capaldi and Patterson (1991) on boys' adjustment in grades 4 and 6, these researchers compared the adjustment of boys who had experienced different levels of parental transitions since birth. (The different levels of parental transition were no transition, loss of father, new stepfather, and two or more new stepfathers.) The authors report, "An ANOVA showed that there were significant differences among the transition groups, $F(3, 170) = 7.53, p < .001$." (The pattern of means for the four levels was in the predicted direction of the more parental transitions, the poorer the adjustment of the boy.) But the authors were aware that the boys' families in the four transition levels were of different socioeconomic status (SES) and had different income levels. Could these differences, and not the differences in transition level, be the underlying cause of the difference in adjustment?

Next, we tested the hypothesis that the differences among transition groups were primarily a function of the differences in SES and income. To test this assumption, an ANOVA was run with SES and per capita income as covariates. The difference among the transition groups remained significant, $F(5, 167) = 4.0, p < .01$. (pp. 492–493)

(The pattern of means was also the same in this analysis as in the original.) Although they did not use the term, an ANOVA with covariates is an analysis of covariance.

The analysis of covariance is generally used in one of two cases: (a) in the analysis of a true experiment involving random assignment in which there is some nuisance variable, such as age of subject, that is adding noise to the interpretation, or (b) where it was not possible to construct a true experiment, in which case an analysis of covariance is used to control for variables on which the groups being compared may differ. Our example was of the second kind, in that the boys were not randomly assigned to their transition-level group.

The analysis of covariance, particularly when of the second kind, only gives accurate results when the correlation between the covariates and the dependent variable is the same in all the cells. Thus in our example, an assumption of the analysis of covariance (in addition to all the usual assumptions of an analysis of variance) is that the correlation of family SES and income with boys' adjustment is the same in the populations at all four transition levels. (*Note:* The requirement is not that the means of these variables be the same at all four levels—they clearly are not—but that the *correlations* of the dependent variable with the covariates stay fairly constant.)

Multivariate Analysis of Variance (MANOVA) and Multivariate Analysis of Covariance (MANCOVA)

In all of the analyses we have considered so far in this chapter (and in this book), there is only one dependent variable. There may be two or even many independent variables, as in the factorial analysis of variance or multiple regression. But in all cases, there has been only one dependent variable. **Multivariate statistical techniques** are procedures involving more than one dependent variable. There are actually several such procedures, including procedures that extend multiple correlation to include more than one dependent variable (this is called "canonical correlation"). But the most widely used of these is the multivariate versions of the analysis of variance and the analysis of covariance, which we consider here.

multivariate statistical techniques

The **multivariate analysis of variance** (**MANOVA** for short) is simply an analysis of variance in which there is more than one dependent variable. Normally these would be two or more different measures of approximately the same thing, such as three different tests of anxiety or two different measures of visual acuity. The overall results of the analysis, however, are interpreted basically the same as an ordinary analysis of variance. If it is a 3×2 MANOVA with four dependent variables, you would examine the significance of each of the two main effects and the interaction, each being considered in relation to its effect on the combination of all the dependent variables.

multivariate analysis of variance (MANOVA)

The only complication is that any significant effects might be due to the impact of the independent variables on only some of the dependent variables. Thus after finding an overall significant effect in a multivariate analysis of variance, researchers will often follow this up with a series of ordinary analyses of variance, each using only one of the dependent variables (and hence sometimes described as "univariate" analyses). (Also, additional technical terminology may be used, such as reference to "Wilks' lambda" or special multivariate multiple comparison procedures. For the most part, however, you can ignore these and still understand the gist of the results.)

Consider an example. Lynn and his colleagues (1991) conducted a 2 × 2 factorial design study of hypnosis in which the independent variables were context (whether the hypnotist did or did not create a strong rapport with the subject—an experimentally manipulated variable) and hypnotizability (high versus low—a personality trait variable). After the hypnotic session, subjects completed a questionnaire (the "AIM") about their relationship with the hypnotist that included three scales: hypnotist power, emotional bond, and fear of negative appraisal.

Lynn and co-workers describe the analysis for the AIM scales (as joint dependent variables) as follows:

> A 2 (context) × 2 (hypnotizability) MANOVA performed on the three scales of the AIM revealed a significant multivariate effect for hypnotizability, $F(3, 39) = 4.08$, $p = .01$. For this factor, significant univariate effects were obtained for the measures of hypnotist power, $F(1, 41) = 4.49$, $p < .05$ (M high hypnotizable $= 29.54$, $SD = 7.82$ vs. M low hypnotizable $= 24.29$, $SD = 7.82$), and emotional bond with the hypnotist, $F(1, 41) = 8.35$, $p < .01$ (M high hypnotizable $= 32.46$, $SD = 9.29$ vs. M low hypnotizable $= 24.76$, $SD = 9.33$). Neither the multivariate Context effect nor the multivariate Context × Hypnotizability interaction achieved significance. (p. 741)

(This analysis, incidently, was a secondary aspect of the study, which was mainly about hypnotic performance. In that analysis, which was not a MANOVA, their predicted effect was found: The highly hypnotizable subjects were about equally responsive to hypnosis regardless of the degree of rapport with the hypnotist, but low-hypnotizable subjects were much more responsive to hypnosis when there was a strong sense of rapport.)

multivariate analysis of covariance (MANCOVA)

An analysis of covariance in which there is more than one dependent variable is called a **multivariate analysis of covariance** (**MANCOVA** for short). The difference between it and an ordinary analysis of covariance is precisely parallel to the difference between a MANOVA and an ordinary analysis of variance.

Overview of Statistical Techniques Considered

Table 17-4 shows in a systematic way the various techniques we have considered in this chapter, along with the other parametric procedures covered throughout the book. Just to prove to yourself how much you've learned, you might cover the right-hand column and play "Name That Statistic."

Controversy: Should Statistics Be Controversial?

Most statistics books, this one included, teach you statistical methods in a fairly cut-and-dried way, almost as if imparting absolute truth. But we have also tried as we went along to mess up this tidy picture with our discussions

TABLE 17-4
Major Statistical Techniques

Association or Difference	Number of Independent Variables	Number of Dependent Variables	Any Variables Controlled?	Name of Technique
Association	1	1	No	Bivariate correlation/regression
Association	Any number	1	No	Multiple regression (including hierarchical and stepwise regression)
Association	1	1	Yes	Partial correlation
Association	Many, not differentiated		No	Reliability coefficients Factor analysis
Association	Many, with specified causal patterns			Path analysis Latent variable modeling
Difference	1	1	No	One-way analysis of variance; *t* test
Difference	Any number	1	No	Analysis of variance
Difference	Any number	1	Yes	Analysis of covariance
Difference	Any number	Any number	No	Multivariate analysis of variance
Difference	Any number	Any number	Yes	Multivariate analysis of covariance

of controversies. Usually, this is thought to be confusing to students. (Although when you learned other fields of psychology, your understanding was built, we hope, from the presentation of controversy—this person's research demonstrated one thing, but this other person did a study showing a flaw, but that one's student showed that this was an exception, and so forth.) So now, here in this last section on controversy, we are going to try to mess things up even more.

In Box 17-1, we describe the historical development of today's statistics out of a hybrid of two views, known as the Fisher and the Neyman-Pearson approaches. This wedding was supposed to end the feud as to which was the better method, but in fact, although most psychologists are content with this hybrid, others, such as Gigerenzer and his associates (Gigerenzer & Murray, 1987; Gigerenzer et al., 1989; Sedlmeier & Gigerenzer, 1989), are not at all content. Neither are Jacob Cohen (1990) and Robert Rosenthal (e.g., Rosnow & Rosenthal, 1989b), two psychologists who have become very well known for their contributions to statistical techniques and whose work on topics such as power, effect size, the null hypothesis, meta-analysis, and other topics we have mentioned throughout the book.

Gigerenzer and Murray (1987) argue that the viewpoints of Fisher and of Pearson and Neyman—which to these early statisticians themselves were always fundamentally contradictory—have been misunderstood and misused as a result of being blended. The marriage was entirely of convenience, with little thought of the long-term effect. Gigerenzer and Murray regard the hybrid as the result of so many of the first statistics textbooks having been written under the influence of the dogmatic and persuasive Sir Ronald Fisher (recall Box 11-1). But then after World War II, the Pearson-Neyman view became known and had to be integrated without admitting that the original texts could have been wrong. (The desire was to present psychology as a science having as its basis a unified, mechanical, flawless method of decision making.)

The result of all of this, Gigerenzer and Murray claim, is a neglect of controversy and of alternative approaches, and statistics textbooks "filled with conceptual confusion, ambiguity, and errors" (p. 23). Further, these two argue that these dominant statistical methods, which were originally only tools, are now shaping the way psychologists view human cognition and perception itself (recall Boxes 12-1 and 13-1).

BOX 17-1

The Forced Marriage of Fisher and Neyman-Pearson

Let's take one final look at the history of the development of statistical methods in psychology, adding some tidbits of interest. We told you in Box 11-1 that Sir Ronald Fisher more or less invented the experimental method as it is now employed; that it arose from his work in agriculture (mostly on soil fertility, the weight of pigs, and the effect of manure on potato fields); that he was a pretty difficult man to get along with; and that Fisher and another great British statistician, Karl Pearson, were particular enemies.

Well, Pearson had a son, Egon, who worked at his father's Galton Laboratory at University College, London. In 1925, the young Egon formed a lasting friendship with Jerzy Neyman, a youthful lecturer at the University of Warsaw who had just arrived at the Galton Laboratory. In the next years, the two worked very closely.

In 1933, Karl Pearson retired. Ironically, Fisher was given Pearson's old position as head of the department of eugenics, originally founded by Galton. And because of the feud between Fisher and the senior Pearson, a new department of statistics was created to smooth the retiring bird's feathers, to be headed by Pearson's son, Egon.

As hard as Pearson and his friend Neyman claim to have tried to avoid the continuation of the old feud between Sir Ronald and the senior Pearson, it was soon as bitter as ever. Pearson and Neyman actually were in many ways far more supportive of Fisher's ideas than of Karl Pearson's, but their extensions and elaborations of Fisher's approaches, intended to be friendly, infuriated the cranky Sir Ronald. (See, you don't want to change your major to history after all—keeping these names straight is at least as hard as learning statistics was!)

What was at issue? To simplify a very complicated set of ideas, Fisher had rejected what is called Bayesian theory, a whole approach to statistics we touched on in Chapter 5, holding the position that scientific research is conducted in order to adjust preexisting beliefs in the light of new evidence as it is collected. In disagreeing, Fisher held that inductive inference is carried out mainly by objectively disproving the null hypothesis, not by testing prior probabilities arrived at subjectively. Fisher was very dogmatic about his ideas, referring to his approach as "absolutely rigorous" and "perfectly rigorous." He called it the only case of "unequivocal inference." And he had a great mind. And he wrote a huge amount.

The greatest problem lies with Fisher's original emphasis, although now distorted into an overemphasis, on the null hypothesis, alpha, and $p < .05$ as a rigid cutoff point and sole determinant of the worth of a piece of research.

Gigerenzer and Murray quote Paul Meehl as saying,

> I suggest to you that Sir Ronald has befuddled us, mesmerized us, and led us down the primrose path. I believe that the almost universal reliance on merely refuting the null hypothesis . . . [is] one of the worst things that ever happened in the history of psychology. (p. 27)

Jacob Cohen, however, is not so sure of the primroses. Of Fisher's agronomy background and studies of manure application he says rather emphatically, "But we [in psychology] do not deal in manure, at least not knowingly. . . . Things are not quite so clearly decision-oriented in the development of scientific theories" (p. 1307).

As a last word, we must say that the majority of psychologists and statisticians are fairly comfortable with the methods to be found in today's

---

He became very influential throughout the world.

Pearson and Neyman also rejected Bayesian theory, but they proposed the method of testing two opposing hypotheses rather than just the null hypothesis. And as a result of this innovation, there would be two types of errors. Type I errors would be when the null hypothesis is rejected even though it is true (and they called its probability alpha, or the level of significance—does all this sound familiar?). Type II errors would be when the research hypothesis is rejected even though it is true (and the probability of that error was beta—again familiar). Which type of error you preferred to minimize depended on the impact of each on your purposes, as Neyman and Pearson were frequently thinking in terms of applied research. Fisher never talked about any hypothesis but the null and therefore never considered Type II errors.

Now you can see what happened: Statistics today is a hybrid of Fisher's ideas, with Pearson and Neyman's added when they could no longer be ignored. The concept of testing the null hypothesis comes from Fisher, the somewhat less influential concepts of Type II error, beta, power, and effect size from his younger enemies.

It was a wedding none of them would have probably approved of, for both camps eventually came to see their approaches as fundamentally in opposition. Fisher compared Neyman and Pearson to the stereotype of the Soviets of his day in their determination to reduce science to technology "in the comprehensive organized effort of a five-year plan for the nation" and remarked sarcastically after Neyman gave a talk before the Royal Statistical Society in London that Neyman should have chosen a topic "on which he could speak with authority." Neyman, for his part, stated that Fisher's methods of testing were in a "mathematically specifiable sense worse than useless." Ah, how rational.

As we have noted throughout these boxes, statistics is, for better and for worse, a product of human intellect and human passions operating together (ideally, for the sake of science, though the latter perhaps to a lesser extent). The results have not always been perfect, but they can be far more interesting than they might seem on the surface.

Reference: Quotations from Gigerenzer and Murray (1987), p. 17.

textbooks, be they mechanical or not. Whether this majority ought to be so complacent, time and careful thinking will tell. But no one is going to figure it out for us. We will all have to do it together. Therefore, we truly hope that once you master the methods in this book, you will have the confidence to look further and not be continuing to apply what is here in a mindless, rote way 20 years from now. If you are a psychologist who either reads research or does it, then whatever else your interests, you must also be a good citizen within the larger discipline and keep up at least a little with developments in methods of data analysis, accepting and even demanding change when it is warranted. After all, if our tools become out of date, what hope is there for our findings?

How to Read Results Involving Unfamiliar Statistical Techniques

Between what you have learned in the first 16 chapters and the brief introduction to advanced techniques covered in this chapter, you should be well prepared to read and understand, at least in a general way, the results of the vast majority of research articles you will encounter as a psychology student. However, you will still periodically come up against new techniques (and sometimes unfamiliar names for old techniques). This happens even to well-seasoned researchers. The field of statistics is simply too large and diverse and growing too fast for anyone to know every possible obscure procedure. So what do you do when you run into something you have never heard of before?

First, don't panic. In most cases, you can figure out the basic idea. Almost always a p level will be given, and it should be clear just what pattern of results is being considered significant or not. In addition, there will usually be some indication of the size of the effect—of the degree of association or the size of the difference. If it is a measure of association, it is probably stronger as the result gets closer to 1 and weaker as the result gets closer to 0. The main thing is not to expect to understand every word in a case like this but to be sure that you grasp as much as you can about the meaning of the result.

Consider an example. Biernat and Wortman (1991) conducted a study of the home lives of women professionals. Near the beginning of their Results section, the researchers mention that in some of their analyses, they will be comparing women academics to businesswomen, and therefore they checked whether the variables to be compared seemed to meet the assumption of equal population variances. Regarding one problematic variable they comment, "Variability in education was higher for businesswomen ($SD = 1.26$) than for academic women ($SD = 0.12$), Cochran's $C(2, 136) = .99$, $p < .0001$" (p. 848). You have probably never heard of Cochran's C, but from the context you can see that it is a significance test comparing the variability of two groups. And while you probably cannot figure out what the numbers in parentheses after the C mean exactly or what the .99 refers to at all, you *can* make sense of the "$p < .0001$." Clearly this tells you that the difference in variabilities of the two groups is significant and that the null hypothesis that they are equal can be handily rejected. Indeed, you could even go further and look directly at the two standard deviations, which give a quite clear idea of how very different they are.

If you really cannot figure out anything about a statistical technique in a research article, you can always try to look up the procedure in a statistics book. Intermediate and advanced statistics textbooks are sometimes a good bet, but you may find these rather hard going, especially if you stray beyond those aimed at psychologists. So eventually, if this happens too often, you also might want to take more statistics courses. Usually the next would be an intermediate statistics course focused on the analysis of variance and perhaps some of the details of multiple regression and correlation. Courses beyond that are generally at the graduate level, although they may accept undergraduates who have a strong interest. These include a very thorough course on analysis of variance methods, called "experimental design," as well as courses on multiple regression/correlation and multivariate statistical techniques and advanced courses on various specialized techniques such as factor analysis or latent variable modeling. In fact, some people find statistics so fascinating that they choose to make a career of it. You might very well be one.

In short, new statistical methods are being invented constantly; we all encounter unfamiliar numbers and symbols in the journals we read. But we puzzle them out, and so will you. We say that with confidence because you have arrived, safe and knowledgeable, at the back pages of this book. You have mastered a thorough introduction to a complex topic. And that should give you complete confidence that with a little time and attention you can understand anything further in statistics. Congratulations on your accomplishment.

Summary

In hierarchical multiple regression, predictor variables are included in the prediction rule in a planned sequential fashion, permitting the researcher to determine the relative contribution of each successive variable over and above those already included. Stepwise multiple regression is an exploratory procedure in which potential predictor variables are searched in order to find the best predictor, then the remaining variables are searched for the predictor which in combination with the first produces the best prediction. This process continues until adding the best remaining variable does not provide a significant improvement.

Partial correlation describes the degree of correlation between two variables while holding one or more other variables constant.

Reliability coefficients measure the extent to which scores on a test are internally consistent (usually with Cronbach's alpha) or consistent over time (test-retest reliability).

Factor analysis identifies groupings of variables that correlate maximally with each other and minimally with other variables.

Causal analysis examines whether the correlations among a set of variables is consistent with a systematic, hypothesized pattern of causal relationships among them. Path analysis describes these relationships with arrows pointing from cause to effect, each with a path coefficient indicating the influence of the hypothesized causal variable on the hypothesized effect variable. Path coefficients are standardized regression coefficients from a multiple regression prediction rule in which the variable at the end of the arrow is the dependent variable and the variable at the start of the arrow is the predictor, along with all other variables leading to that dependent variable.

Latent variable modeling is a sophisticated version of path analysis that includes paths involving latent, unmeasured theoretical variables (each of which consists of the common elements of several measured variables). It also permits a kind of significance test and provides measures of the overall fit of the data to the hypothesized causal pattern.

The analysis of covariance is an analysis of variance that controls for one or more variables. The multivariate analysis of variance is an analysis of variance with more than one dependent variable; the multivariate analysis of covariance is an analysis of covariance with more than one dependent variable.

Key Terms

analysis of covariance (ANCOVA)
causal model
controlling for
covariate
Cronbach's alpha (α)
endogenous variable
exogenous variable
factor
factor analysis
factor loading
hierarchical multiple regression
holding constant

Kuder-Richardson-20 (KR-20)
latent variable
latent variable modeling
LISREL
manifest variable
measurement model
multivariate analysis of covariance (MANCOVA)
multivariate analysis of variance (MANOVA)
multivariate statistical techniques
partial correlation

partial correlation coefficient
partialing out
path analysis
path coefficient
reliability
split-half reliability
stepwise multiple regression
structural equation modeling
test-retest reliability

Practice Problems

For Problems 1 through 5 in each set, you are expected only to explain the general meaning of the results at the level at which the various methods were described in the chapter. You are not, of course, expected to describe the logic of the statistical procedures covered here in the way that you have been doing in previous chapters.

Answers to Set I are given at the back of the book.

SET I

1. Meier (1991) studied the relationship of various stress and related measures to number of physical symptoms (stomachaches, sleeplessness, headaches, etc.) during the past 2 weeks. Gender and social desirability (SD—the tendency to give the responses on a test that make you look good) were also measured so that these could be controlled when analyzing the relationship of stress measures to symptoms. Meier explains one analysis as follows:

A hierarchical regression analysis was calculated with gender, social desirability, and the [other] measures as independent variables. Gender . . . alone accounted for 15% of the symptoms variance. Next SD was entered, but failed to contribute further to explained variance. The MBA [Meir Burnout Assessment] was entered, accounting for only 2% additional variance. However, when the MBI [Maslach Burnout Inventory] was entered, it contributed 10% more of the symptom variance. State anxiety was entered next and accounted for 3% additional variance, bringing the [R^2 to .30]. The final variable, depression, did not add to the proportion of variance explained. (p. 94)

Explain this result to a person who is familiar in a general way with ordinary multiple regression but has never heard of hierarchical multiple regression.

2. Snyder et al. (1991) developed a Hope Scale (sample item, "Even when others get discouraged, I know I can find a way to solve the problem," p. 585). The scale was administered to eight different samples of about 250

TABLE 17-5
Rotated Factor Pattern on the 15 Marker Scales

Marker Scale	Factor 1	Factor 2
Like vs. dislike	.99	.06
Pleasant vs. unpleasant	.99	.07
Good vs. bad[a]	−.98	−.06
Open-minded vs. closed-minded	.96	.00
Friendly vs. unfriendly	.96	.07
Warm vs. cold[a]	−.96	.08
Important vs. unimportant[a]	−.96	−.17
Interesting vs. boring	.90	.33
Social good vs. bad	.90	.38
Intellectual good vs. bad	.78	.31
Dominant vs. submissive	−.09	.97
Impulsive vs. inhibited	−.06	.92
Extraverted vs. introverted	.29	.92
Independent vs. dependent[a]	−.12	−.86
Active vs. passive	.41	.88

[a]These scales were reversed in the presentation format to subjects.

Note. From Anderson, C. A. & Sedikides, C. (1991), tab. 2. Thinking about people: Contributions of a typological alternative to associationistic and dimensional models of person perception. *Journal of Personality and Social Psychology, 60,* 203–217. Copyright, 1991, by the American Psychological Association. Reprinted by permission of the author.

each. In the Results section, the researchers explain that "Cronbach's alphas ranged from .74 to .84" (p. 572), the "range" referring to results obtained from the eight different samples. They also explain, later in the same section, "The test-retest correlations were .85, $p < .001$, over a 3-week interval" (p. 572). Explain what this all means to a person who understands correlation but has never heard of reliability or the statistics associated with it.

3. In a study by Anderson and Sedikides (1991), 108 different kinds of individuals were rated on 15 personality scales (which the researchers called "marker scales" for reasons not important to this problem). They then conducted a factor analysis of these 15 marker scales. Their table of results is reproduced in Table 17-5. In the text of their article, they identified Factor 1 as being about "general evaluation" and Factor 2 as being about "dynamism." Explain these results to a person who is familiar with correlation but knows nothing about factor analysis.

4. Bandura and Jourden (1991) conducted a study of the relationship of self-efficacy (belief that one can be effective) and other variables to actual performance in a laboratory simulation of a business organization. The subjects were all graduate students in a business school. Figure 17-4, which is reproduced from the Results section of their article, shows a path diagram for the major variables they studied. Note that subjects were tested three times in succession, and the left half of the diagram represents the situation prior to the second testing, the middle "Performance" refers to the performance on the second testing, and the far-right "Performance" to their performance on the third testing. Explain the general principles

of interpreting a path diagram (including the limitations), using this diagram as an example, to a person who understands multiple regression in a general way but knows nothing about path diagrams. (You may ignore the figures in parentheses, which are ordinary bivariate correlations.)

5. Pryor, Reeder, and McManus (1991) conducted a 2×2 factorial design study in which one independent variable was whether subjects (undergraduates) scored high or low on a test of attitudes toward homosexuals taken prior to the experiment and the other independent variable was whether the subject saw an AIDS education film or a control film (on robotics). After seeing the film, subjects completed a questionnaire about attitudes toward interacting with an AIDS-infected co-worker under three different scenarios (bookstore, dormitory desk, sandwich shop).

> These attitude ratings were analyzed in a 2×2 multivariate analysis of variance. . . . The principal hypothesis of this study was that the persuasive message in the AIDS education film would be differentially effective for people who differed in their attitudes toward homosexuality. This hypothesis was supported by a Film Type × Homosexuality Attitude multivariate interaction, $F(3, 143) = 3.59, p < .02$. The three univariate interactions related to this multivariate interaction were also statistically significant ($ps < .05$). Multivariate and univariate main effects were also detected for film type and homosexuality attitude; however, these effects seem best understood within the context of the interaction between these variables. (p. 135)

The means for the bookstore scenario for subjects watching the control film were 14.35 for control film pro-homosexual subjects and 13.21 for the antihomosexual

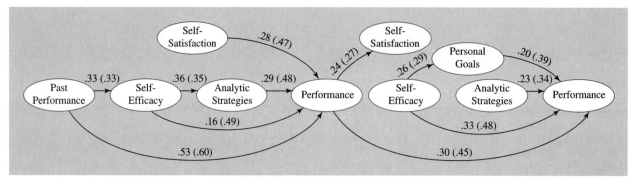

FIGURE 17-4
Path analysis of causal structures in the second and third phase of the experiment. (The initial numbers in the paths of influence are the significant standardized path coefficients, *p*s < .05; the numbers in parentheses are the first-order correlations. The network of relations on the left half of the figure are for the second phase, and those on the right are those for the third phase.) [Figure 3 from Bandura, A., & Jourden, F. J. (1991). Self-regulatory mechanisms governing the impact of social comparison on complex decision making. *Journal of Personality and Social Psychology, 60,* 941–951. Copyright, 1991, by the American Psychological Association. Reprinted by permission of the author.]

subjects; the corresponding means for those watching the AIDS film were 17.59 and 13.49, respectively. The figures for the other two scenarios were similar.

Explain these results to someone who is familiar with ordinary factorial analysis of variance but not with MANOVA.

6. For each of the following fictional studies, what would be the most appropriate statistical technique?

(a) A study in which the researcher has a complex theory of the pattern of cause and effect among several variables

(b) A study of the degree of association among two variables

(c) A study to determine whether a measure is internally consistent and consistent over time in giving the same result

(d) A 3 × 2 factorial design with three dependent measures

(e) A study in which seven variables have been measured that are thought to predict a particular dependent variable, and the researcher wants to determine which variables contribute significantly to the prediction (but has no theory about which ones might be the most likely)

(f) A study in which a researcher measures 16 variables in a large number of subjects and wants to explore whether there is any simpler, underlying structure among them

(g) A study in which an experimental group and a control group are being compared on a single dependent variable

(h) A study comparing five groups of individuals on a single dependent variable

(i) A study in which the researcher is studying the effect of several predictor variables on a single dependent variable, has a specific theory about their relative importance, and wants to check whether each successive additional predictor adds anything to what the preceding variables predict

SET II

1. Zuckerman, Miyake, and Hodgins (1991) collected ratings of the attractiveness of 100 female and 100 male students who appeared on videotape reading a prepared text. Some of the ratings were of physical attractiveness that were made with no sound—"pure physical attractiveness" ratings. Other ratings were of physical attractiveness, but the raters were also able to hear the person's voice— "mixed physical attractiveness" ratings. And some ratings were of the how attractive the person *sounded*, based only on hearing the person's voice (with no picture)—"pure vocal attractiveness." Referring to Table 17-6, which is part of a table in their Results section, describe what Zuckerman and colleagues found to a person who is familiar in a general way with ordinary multiple regression but has never heard of hierarchical regression. (Studies 1 and 2 are different only in what the person being taped was reading. Your answer can focus just on the Study 1 results.)

2. Rusbult et al. (1991) conducted several studies of the way in which people in close relationships deal with a partner doing something destructive to the relationship. At the start of the Results section for their first two studies in this article, under a section headed "Reliability of Measures," they explain that they calculated "reliability coefficients" for their major measures and that "these analyses revealed sizable alphas for the measures of destructive reactions (. . . .91 for Study 1 and .86 for Study 2) and constructive reactions (. . . .61 and .67)." Explain these results to someone who is familiar with correlation but has never heard of reliability or the statistics associated with it.

3. In a study by Naglieri and Das (1988) in which individuals carried out nine different cognitive tasks, a table (Table 17-7) reports the results of a factor analysis on

TABLE 17-6
Hierarchical Regressions of Mixed Attractiveness Ratings Onto Pure Attractiveness Ratings

Predictor Variable	Study 1			Study 2		
	R^2	Partial R[a]	F[b]	R^2	Partial R[a]	F[b]
Mixed vocal attractiveness						
Sex	.00	−.01	0.02	.03	−.16	5.22*
Pure vocal attractiveness	.60	.78	300.41**	.45	.66	153.10**
Pure physical attractiveness	.64	.30	19.45**	.50	.30	19.76**

[a]Partial correlations between predictor and dependent variable.
[b]F test of the increment in variance accounted for. The dfs vary from (1, 198) to (1, 196) depending on the number of variables in the equation.
*$p < .05$. **$p < .001$.
Note. From Zuckerman, M., Miyake, K., & Hodgins, H. S. (1991), tab. 4. Cross-channel effects of vocal and physical attractiveness and their implications for interpersonal perception. *Journal of Personality and Social Psychology, 60*, 545–554. Copyright, 1991, by the American Psychological Association. Reprinted by permission of the author.

scores on these tasks. Explain these results to a person who is familiar with correlation but knows nothing about factor analysis.

4. Carlin and Saniga (1990) compared a group of special education children (mentally retarded or emotionally disturbed) to a group of regular education students in terms of their teacher's and their own ratings of voice problems. The mean ratings for the special education students were 53.8 for self-ratings and 53.2 for teachers' ratings; for regular education students, the corresponding ratings were 53.2 and 56.8 (high scores mean *fewer* voice problems). The researchers reported:

A two-way analysis of covariance with . . . age as the covariate yielded an F of 4.17 (*df*: 1, 129, $p < 0.04$) for the main effect of placement [special versus regular education]. . . . The main effect of the teachers' versus the children's ratings was nonsignificant ($F_{1,130} = 0.37$). . . .

The interaction of placement and rater was significant at the .001 level ($F_{1,130} = 11.19$). (pp. 301–302)

Explain these results to someone who understands the analysis of variance and correlation but not the analysis of covariance.

5. Yukl and Falbe (1991) collected ratings from workers in several companies about the ways in which their managers exert power. Four main measures were used. The two measures of personal power (expertise, persuasiveness, etc.) focused on power "downward" over subordinates and power over people at the same level. Two other measures were of "position power" (formal status, ability to give rewards and punishments, etc.)—again, the two measures being downward and toward those at the same level. In one of their analyses, the researchers compared middle managers with supervisors (lower-level managers) on these four measures of power:

TABLE 17-7
Varimax Factor Loadings of Tasks

Task	Factor		
	I	*II*	*III*
Tokens	−16	42*	20
Figure recognition	−14	40*	13
Matrices	−14	51*	15
Hand movements	− 8	15	44*
Successive ordering	−28	18	44*
Word recall	− 3	11	43*
Matching numbers	51*	−18	−19
Visual search	54*	−11	− 4
Trails	53*	−21	−12

Note. N = 430. Decimal points are omitted. Loadings > .30 are noted [with asterisks]. Factor I is defined by the three marker tests of planning, Factor II by the three marker tests of simultaneous coding, and Factor III by the three marker tests of successive coding.

From Kirby, J. R., and Das, J. P. (1990), tab. 1. A cognitive approach to intelligence: Attention, coding, and planning. *Canadian Psychology, 31*, 320–333. Copyright, 1990, by the Canadian Psychological Association. Reprinted by permission.

The MANOVA . . . on the four composite measures of position and personal power indicated significant power differences between middle managers and supervisors, $F(4, 181) = 2.8$, $p < .05$. Univariate F tests showed that the differences occurred only for the scales measuring position power, $F(1, 184) = 8.0$. . . . Middle managers had more downward position power ($M = 3.7$) than did supervisors ($M = 3.4$). (p. 420)

Explain this result to someone who understands the ordinary analysis of variance but knows nothing about MANOVA.

6. At the library, find an article in a recent issue of a psychology journal that uses one of the statistical procedures described in this chapter. Write a brief summary of what the study found, referring specifically to the statistics.

A

Overview of the Logic and Language of Psychology Research

STATISTICAL methods are tools used in the research process. You will find the statistical procedures in this book easier to understand if you appreciate the larger context in which they are embedded. This appendix provides an overview of the central logic and language of the research process in psychology.

In most cases, the purpose of a research study in psychology is to evaluate the validity of a theory or the effectiveness of a practical application.[1] There are many approaches that a researcher can employ. The strongest research procedures lead to unambiguous conclusions that pertain to a wide variety of other situations and people. Weak research designs, even if their results are consistent with the researcher's predictions, leave open many alternative interpretations as to why those results were obtained or apply only to a narrow group of people or situations.

However, sometimes circumstances limit the sort of research procedure that is possible, yet the research may still seem worth pursuing, even if in a less than rigorous way. In fact, especially in the case of applied research, much of the most important work has been done by psychologists using (of necessity) less than perfect methods, but in very creative ways.

Nevertheless, most psychologists think about the logic of research in terms of a kind of ideal approach, and a real-life study is evaluated in terms of the various ways in which it approximates or fails to approximate this ideal. In this appendix, we first discuss this ideal, the "true experiment," including

---

[1]Research is sometimes conducted for other purposes, such as to explore relationships among various measures, to determine the incidence of some characteristic in the population, or to develop a measure or technique for use in other research. However, the basic logic of the usual kind of research (the focus of this appendix) serves as the underpinning of psychologists' approach to almost all systematic research.

the key terminology associated with it, and then turn to a discussion of four key areas in which studies approximate or fail to approximate it: equivalence of subjects across experimental groups, equivalence of circumstances across experimental groups, generalizability, and adequacy of measurement.

The Traditionally Ideal Research Approach

The True Experiment

true experiment

The research procedure that usually leads to the least ambiguity is the **true experiment.** It is the prototype against which all other methods are compared. Beginning with the hypothesis "Changing the level of X causes a change in the score on Y," the true experiment systematically varies the level of X, keeping everything else the same, and looks at the effect on Y. For example, suppose that a researcher is interested in whether having flashing lights in a room affects people's scores on a math test. X is whether or not there are flashing lights in the room, and Y is score on the math test. In a true experiment, one group of students might be tested in a room with the flashing lights, and another, an initially identical group of students, would be tested under conditions that are completely identical, except there are no flashing lights in the room. Thus the only difference between the two groups is the level of X, the presence or absence of flashing lights in the room. If the students in the room with flashing lights have lower scores on the math test (Y), it must be due to the lighting. (If they have higher scores, that would also be due to the flashing light.)

Basic Terminology of the Experiment

experimental group
control group

subjects
independent variable

experimental manipulation
manipulating the independent variable
dependent variable
population

sample

Much of the terminology of research comes from this approach. A group in which the level of X is changed is usually called the **experimental group.** The comparison group in which X is kept the same is called the **control group.** The individuals studied (the participants in the research) are called **subjects.** The variable that is systematically changed (X—for example, whether the lights flash or not) is called the **independent variable.** The procedure of systematically changing the independent variable is sometimes called an **experimental manipulation** or **manipulating the independent variable.** The variable that is supposed to change as a result of the study (Y, if X causes Y—for example, score on the math test) is called the **dependent variable.** Subjects are taken from the **population**—the group containing all the people on earth belonging to the type being studied. The particular subjects selected to be studied from that population are called the **sample.**

To apply this terminology to another very basic example, imagine that a researcher has two identical cans of a soft drink. The hypothesis is that heating a can of soft drink will make it explode. That is, among soft drink cans, increasing the heat will cause an explosion. The researcher might then put a match under one can (the experimental can) and not put a match under the other (the control can). If the experimental can explodes and the control can does not, the hypothesis is confirmed. Each can is a subject, heating or not is the independent variable, whether or not a can explodes is the dependent variable, and these two cans are samples, respectively, of the populations of all soft drink cans that are and are not heated (see Figure A-1).

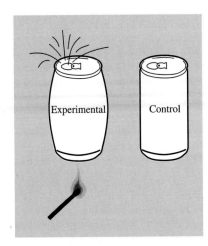

FIGURE A-1
An ideal experiment: One of two identical soft drink cans is heated, and the researcher observes to see if it will explode while the other does not explode.

Four Characteristics of the Ideal Research Design

There are four key characteristics of an ideal research design:

1. The subjects in the experimental and control groups are identical.
2. The experimental and control groups are exposed to identical situations (*except* for the manipulation of the independent variable).
3. The sample studied perfectly represents the intended population.
4. The measurement of the dependent variable is completely accurate and appropriate for what it is supposed to be measuring.

The rest of this appendix examines the various ways that real-life research tries to approximate each of these ideal conditions.

Equivalence of Subjects in Experimental and Control Groups

Ordinarily, the primary consideration in evaluating whether a study's results lead to unambiguous conclusions is the equivalence of subjects in the experimental and control groups. For example, suppose that the math ability of the members of the group in the room with the flashing lights was initially different from those in the room without the flashing lights. Whatever difference in math scores was found between the two groups at the end of the study could be due to either the manipulation of the independent variable—having the flashing lights or not—*or* to their initial differences in ability. The result of the experiment would be ambiguous. To avoid such ambiguous results, researchers aim for strict equivalence of the experimental and control groups. Five main strategies are employed: random assignment to groups, matched-group designs, repeated-measures designs, correlational research designs, and single-subject research.

Random Assignment to Groups

The research procedure that produces the closest real-life approximation to two identical groups is called **random assignment to groups.** For example, if 100 people were available to be in the experiment, each person could be

random assignment to groups

put in either the experimental group or the control group by flipping a coin. Although the two groups of 50 created in this way are not identical, there will at least be no *systematic* difference between them.

It is important to emphasize that "random" means using a strictly random procedure, not just haphazardly picking people to go into the two groups. Any haphazard procedure is likely to produce unintended systematic differences. For example, had the researcher chosen one group from students attending a morning class and the others from students attending an evening class, the two groups might differ because the kinds of people taking classes at these different times of day might differ. Or if one group consists of volunteers to undergo a self-esteem enhancement program and the control group is simply whoever is willing to take a job satisfaction test, the kinds of people in the experimental and control groups might be quite different.

Because random assignment rules out initial systematic differences between groups, any actual difference that exists will be due to random processes. And true random processes follow the laws of probability. Hence if differences are revealed in the dependent variable after the experiment, they can be due either to the manipulation of the independent variable or to random processes. The hypothesis-testing procedures that are covered starting in Chapter 6 of this book are used to check the probability of whether the difference found in a study could have been due to these random procedures. If the statistical analysis indicates that this is unlikely, the only reasonable remaining explanation is that the independent variable caused the difference. This is the basic logic behind the analysis of results of experiments and explains why random assignment and statistical methods are so important in psychology research.

Matched-Group Designs

Sometimes random assignment to groups is not practical. For example, ethics would require that all students in a school district who need a certain reading program be given it; some cannot be randomly chosen to miss out. How can the program be shown to be the cause of improvements in the students? One widely used alternative research approach is the **matched-group research design.** For example, a researcher might compare an experimental group of students who have been selected for the program in one school district to a control group of subjects in another district also needing such a program but not having it available. Every member of this control group could be matched to a member of the experimental group in terms of age, social class, sex, reading problem, and so forth.

Matched-group designs are much better than having no control group at all. And if both groups are tested before and after, the matched-group design can lead to relatively unambiguous results. This case, which is called a **matched-group pretest-posttest design,** is an example of a **quasi-experimental design.** A quasi-experimental design is any approach that is reasonably close to a true experiment but does not use random assignment.

However, no matter how well matched two groups are, and even when before-and-after testing is used, a researcher can never know for certain that there is no systematic initial difference between the groups. Indeed, in most cases, if you have not used random assignment, you know that there *is* a

matched-group research design

matched-group pretest-posttest design
quasi-experimental design

systematic initial difference—whatever it was that put people into one group or the other. (In the reading program example, the systematic difference might be that one group of students lives in a school district not progressive enough or well enough funded to offer the reading program.)

Repeated-Measures Designs

Another research approach is to create two identical groups by testing the same people twice. This is called a **repeated-measures research design** (also called a **within-subject research design**). The students in our example could be tested before and after the reading program.

The simplest repeated-measures design is a **single-group pretest-posttest design** in which, as the name implies, a single group of individuals is tested twice, once before and once after some experimental treatment. This kind of research design, however, is very weak in the sense that if a change is found, there are many possible alternative explanations for it. Merely being tested the first time can change a subject, so that when tested again, the person is not identical but different—different due to the initial testing, not to the experimental treatment. And time itself produces change. For example, if a researcher tested the same group of people before and after the reading program, without any other control group, it would be impossible to know if any change was due to the reading program or to whatever else happened to the subjects during that time period. Or there could be preexisting trends for improvement, or the change could be due to general maturation and experience, or to people starting at a very low point that would naturally improve without the treatment, and so forth.

Because it is such a weak research design, the single-group pretest-posttest design is considered a **preexperimental design.** Research of this kind is often extremely important as a first stage in exploring a research area, but any conclusions from a study of this type are tentative and should be followed up by a stronger research design (such as a quasi-experimental or true experimental design).

In a laboratory setting, however, repeated-measures designs are often used in a way that makes them a true experiment. Suppose that a researcher is interested in the effect of lighting on performance at a complicated task. The researcher might test people's performance under bright lights (the experimental condition) and then test their performance again under ordinary lighting (the control condition). A problem with this approach, however, is that the subjects could be more familiar with the test the second time, creating a *practice effect* or *carry-over effect*, or they could be tired out by the time they get to the second task, creating a *fatigue effect*. To deal with problems of this kind, researchers use a procedure called **counterbalancing,** in which half the subjects are tested first in one condition and the other half first in the other condition. In this way, any practice, carry-over, fatigue, or similar effects are balanced out over the two conditions. If counterbalancing is employed so that the condition a subject experiences first is determined by random assignment, the study becomes a true experiment. Indeed, repeated-measures designs with counterbalancing and random assignment are among the most powerful research methods psychologists use because they make groups so very equivalent.

repeated-measures research design
within-subject research design
single-group pretest-posttest design

preexperimental design

counterbalancing

Correlational Research Designs

correlational research design

A **correlational research design** examines the degree of association between two variables as they exist in a group of people, without any attempt at experimental manipulation. Thus a correlational approach to studying self-esteem and job satisfaction would simply be to survey a group of middle managers as to their self-esteem and their job satisfaction. Then the researcher would see whether those scoring high on self-esteem tended also to score high on job satisfaction. (The actual degree to which there is an association between the two scores is computed using a statistical technique called a "correlation coefficient," described in Chapter 3.)

The correlational approach is often the best that can be done under the circumstances and is widely used. But it is a fairly weak research design in that its results are open to many alternative explanations besides "X caused Y." For example, suppose that self-esteem and job satisfaction are found to be associated in a correlational study. This could be due to high self-esteem causing high job satisfaction. But it could also be that high job satisfaction causes high self-esteem. The association between self-esteem and job satisfaction could even be due to other differences among the managers, such as age—perhaps being older causes middle managers to have both high self-esteem and high job satisfaction, and self-esteem itself causes nothing. (The various possible causal interpretations of the results of a correlational study are discussed in some detail in Chapter 3.) Thus one advantage of a true experiment (when it is feasible) over a correlational study is that the true experiment manipulates the independent variable and then sees the effect on the dependent variable, making causal conclusions unambiguous.

Researchers are well aware of the limits of correlational designs, and when possible, they attempt to rule out some alternative explanations, mainly by using sophisticated statistical procedures such as partial correlation (summarized in Chapter 17). But the correlational approach never produces results as unambiguous as a true experiment or, in most cases, even as clear-cut as a quasi-experiment. However, in a very large number of situations, it is the strongest research approach that is practical—for example, one cannot randomly assign people to marry certain other types of people. And even when experiments are possible, they may be very costly to conduct, so that researchers are not willing or able to test an untried idea experimentally. In these cases, correlational studies often provide a valuable first step in opening up a new area of research.

Single-Subject Research

single-subject research

Finally, some research studies involve an intense examination of a single group, organization, or individual, using the "case study" or "participant observation" approach. Such **single-subject research** is not considered experimental or even correlational. However, in clinical psychology and in some other social science fields, such as sociology and anthropology (and the sociological and anthropological approaches to organizational behavior, education, criminology, communication, and so forth), this kind of research is considered valuable because it gives a rich understanding of all the complexities of what is being studied rather than forcing attention onto a few variables that may or may not be the most critical. And in all areas of psychology, as well as the other social sciences, single-subject research is considered valuable as a precursor to other, more rigorous research approaches. (These topics are also discussed in Chapter 2.)

Single-subject research is also employed in a highly systematic way by researchers in the behaviorist tradition developed by B. F. Skinner. A single subject—whether an animal, like a rat or a pigeon, or a client in a behavior therapy program—is studied over time, with the researcher systematically manipulating the conditions that affect the subject and observing the changes that result. Statistics are not usually employed to analyze the results of such studies; the pattern of results should be sufficiently clear to make statistics unnecessary.

Summary of Research Designs

Table A-1 summarizes the various research designs we have considered, noting their advantages and disadvantages as compared to the ideal of identical experimental and control groups.

TABLE A-1
Major Research Designs and Their Advantages and Disadvantages

Design	Advantages	Disadvantages
True experiment (random assignment to conditions)	Ensures no systematic difference between conditions.	Can be impractical or unethical to implement.
Matched-group (without random assignment)	Controls for obvious differences between conditions; may be most practical with intact groups.	Groups may differ systematically on variables on which they were not matched.
Matched-group pretest-posttest	Controls fairly strongly for initial differences among subjects; is often practical where random assignment is not.	Systematic differences between groups may influence impact; pretest measuring procedure can confound results.
Repeated-measures true experiment (random assignment)	Ensures no systematic difference; minimizes random differences by making subjects their own controls.	Practice or carry-over effects; procedure may be difficult to implement.
Single-group pretest-posttest	Provides some control; is often the only practical approach.	Impossible to know if change would have occurred without the experimental treatment.
Correlational	Is relatively easy to implement with intact groups.	Difficult to determine causality.
Single-subject	Permits deep understanding of processes.	Difficult to generalize results.

Equivalence of Circumstances for Experimental and Control Groups

The ideal study involves not only identical groups but also their being tested under identical circumstances.

In practice, it is very difficult to test different groups under identical circumstances with the sole difference being the manipulation of the independent variable. In a physics laboratory such equivalence may be possible, but when conducting research with human beings, circumstances are never equivalent. One strategy designed to maximize equivalence is to use an isolated location, such as a cubicle in a psychology building or a seminar room in which group interaction in an organization is studied. This minimizes external influences and interruptions that might make one session of the experiment different from another. A related approach is to standardize the situation as much as possible. For example, the instructions to subjects may be tape-recorded.

There are, however, two special problems that plague much social science research—particularly applied research—with regard to equivalence of circumstances: experimenter effects and placebo or Hawthorne effects.

Experimenter Effects

experimenter effects
experimenter bias

Experimenter effects, including **experimenter bias,** are the unintended influences of the researcher on the study. For example, in a study of the effects of psychotherapy, suppose that the researcher is a therapist evaluating the mental health of the subjects. In this case, it is quite possible that the therapist's desire to see the experiment work creates a predisposition to see subjects in the experimental group as having improved more. Even if an independent observer rates the two groups but knows who is in which group, a desire for the experiment to come out a particular way may unintentionally influence the observer's evaluations.

blind conditions of testing

The preferred solution to this problem is called **blind conditions of testing.** This means that the experimenter, at the time of interacting with the subject, is not aware of whether the subject is in the experimental or control group.

Placebo and Hawthorne Effects

placebo effects
Hawthorne effects

Placebo effects involve the influence of a subject's expectation or motivation to do well. **Hawthorne effects** involve the influence of the attention the subject receives and of the subject's reaction to being a participant. For example, if one wing of a factory is trained in a new program and one wing is not, there are several differences between the groups. One is that one wing uses the new way of operating resulting from the program and the other wing does not—this is the manipulation of the independent variable. But another difference is that one wing has been led to expect benefits and the other wing has not (creating a placebo effect). Yet another is that one wing has received special attention and the other wing has not (creating a Hawthorne effect—the term comes from a 1927 study done at the Hawthorne Works plant of the Western Electric Company in Cicero,

Illinois). These additional differences between groups greatly confuse the interpretation of the effect of the manipulation of the independent variable.

The best solution to these undesired differences in circumstances is to conduct a study in which both groups receive some treatment that they believe should be helpful but only one actually receives a treatment consisting of more than mere attention and raised expectations. For example, in medical research, both groups would receive pills that look and taste identical, but one group's pills contain the active ingredient and the other group's do not. No one in the experiment knows who is receiving the real drug. A drug that looks and tastes like the real thing but is actually inactive is called a *placebo* (Latin for "I shall please").

However, in psychology, it is often impossible or unethical to set up a control group condition wherein a person receives a treatment that is believed to be effective but in fact is not. Where it is feasible to use a true placebo control group and the people working with the subjects are unaware of who is in which group, this is called a **double-blind procedure.**

double-blind procedure

Placebo and Hawthorne effects are the most common problems in drawing unambiguous conclusions from results of applied research in areas such as clinical, educational, and organizational psychology.

Representativeness of the Sample

The third requirement for an ideal study is that the sample of subjects studied accurately represent the population to which the study is supposed to apply. This representativeness is called **generalizability** or **external validity.** (**Internal validity** refers to the issues of equivalence of the experimental and control groups and equivalence of circumstances.)

generalizability
external validity
internal validity

Much psychology research is conducted with college students, and it is assumed that what is discovered about them applies to the larger population of people in general. In a study of the effect of a flashing light on performance, for example, the general pattern of results with college students probably applies to most other human beings. However, in many other types of research, the nature of the subjects is very important. For example, college students would probably not be suitable subjects for studies of attitudes toward children—their experience does not commonly include parenthood. One cannot study reading skills in suburban schools and generalize to all students in all schools or study job satisfaction in the computer industry and generalize to all industries.

Another problem involves how a study's subjects are recruited. For example, in a mail survey of knowledge about an issue, some individuals will return the questionnaire and some will not, and presumably there are systematic differences between those who do and do not—it is likely that those who do may know more about the issue being studied. Using only the questionnaires that are returned, the researcher may conclude that people are more knowledgeable about an issue than if the researcher had been able to study the entire population. Similarly, people who volunteer to participate in an experiment may differ from those who do not. For example, volunteers may have personalities that are more responsive to the needs of others.

Random sampling is considered the optimal method for ensuring that a sample is representative of its population. Random sampling means that researchers begin with a list of everyone in the population about which they want to generalize their results, such as a list of all psychotherapists in the nation, then uses a random procedure (such as a random number table) to select a sample from this population. This produces what is called a **probability sample** because every member of the population being studied has an equal probability of being included in the study's sample.

Do not confuse random sampling with random assignment to groups, which we discussed earlier. Both procedures use true random procedures, but random sampling refers to a method of obtaining a sample; random assignment to groups refers to the procedure of deciding which members of the sample will be in the experimental group and which in the control group.

Measurement

The fourth condition we noted for an ideal study is that the measures should be accurate and appropriate.

There are three main kinds of measures used in psychology research: **self-report measures** such as questionnaires or interviews; **observational or behavioral measures** such as rating scales of children's play behavior, number of customers who go through a turnstile, number of milliseconds to respond in a reaction time experiment, or number of times a rat presses a bar; and **physiological measures,** such as hormone levels or heart rate. All three kinds of measure are evaluated primarily in terms of their reliability and validity.

Reliability

The **reliability** of a measure is its accuracy or consistency. That is, when you apply the same measure to the same thing, under identical circumstances, how similar are the results? In psychology, the results are not necessarily similar at all—for example, questionnaires given to the same people on different days often yield different results. Sometimes questions are ambiguous, so that a person may respond in one way at one time and in another way at another time. Or people may simply mark some or all of their answers in the wrong place on one or more occasions. And self-report measures are not the only ones that can be unreliable. Observational measures may be unreliable because observers may disagree. Physiological measures are often highly erratic from moment to moment.

There are three types of measures for reliability: (a) **test-retest reliability,** in which the same group is tested twice; (b) **internal consistency,** in which, for example, scores on half the questions are compared to scores on the other (Cronbach's alpha, the most common approach to internal consistency, is described briefly in Chapter 17); and (c) **interjudge reliability,** used for observational measures, which is the degree of agreement between observers. These kinds of reliability are summarized in Table A-2.

In each of these three cases, reliability is usually reported as a statistic, called a "reliability coefficient."

TABLE A-2
Types of Reliability

Test-retest reliability	Correlation of tests administered to the same people on different occasions
Internal consistency	Correlation among the items
Interjudge reliability	Correlation among different raters' scores when rating the same group of people or objects

Validity

The **validity** of a measure refers to whether the measure actually measures what it claims to measure. (The word is also applied to entire studies, when it refers to the appropriateness of the conclusions that can be drawn from the results.)

A measure that is not reliable cannot be valid. An unreliable measure does not measure anything. But even if a measure is reliable (accurate and repeatable), it is not necessarily valid for measuring what it is meant to measure. For example, consider a marital satisfaction questionnaire that asks, "How likely are you to stay with your spouse over the next several years?" The questionnaire may turn out to be highly reliable (for example, people may answer all the questions on it quite consistently). But instead of measuring marital satisfaction, it might really be measuring commitment to the marriage. Yet respondents might be committed not because they are satisfied but because they have no alternative to married life or because they feel they are very unattractive and could only do worse if they left their partner.

Another reason that a test may not be valid, even if it is reliable, is that it is actually measuring a tendency for the respondents to try to make a good impression or to say yes or some other **response bias** rather than the intended variable. (One way to address this problem is to include a "social desirability scale," sometimes also called a "lie scale." When a subject's score on such a scale is high, the researcher may simply throw out that subject's test. Alternatively, scores on a social desirability scale may be used in a statistical procedure—such as partial correlation of an analysis of covariance, both briefly described in Chapter 17—to adjust the person's score on the regular part of the measure.)

Validity of a measure is more difficult to assess than reliability. There are several methods used. **Content validity** results when the content of the measure appears to get at all the different aspects of the things being measured. Usually this is determined by the judgment of the researcher or other experts.

There are also more systematic means of evaluating the validity of a measure. Determining **criterion-related validity** involves conducting a special study in which the researcher compares scores on the measure in question to some other probable indicator of the same variable. For example, a researcher might test the validity of a measure of mental health by comparing scores of people in a mental hospital to people from the general population. One type of criterion-related validity is a measure's **predictive validity**—for example, whether scores on a job skills test taken when applying for a job predict effective performance on the job. Predictive validity is used especially where a measure is designed for predictive pur-

validity

response bias

content validity

criterion-related validity

predictive validity

TABLE A-3
Types of Validity of a Measure

Content validity	The content of the test appears to experts to encompass the full range of what the test claims to measure.
Criterion-related validity	Scores on the test correlate with some other indicator of what the test is supposed to measure.
Predictive validity	The test score predicts scores on another variable that ought to be predicted by the test, given what it is claimed to measure; a type of criterion-related validity.
Concurrent validity	The test score correlates with another variable measured at the same time that is already known to be related to what the test is claimed to measure; a type of criterion-related validity.

concurrent validity

poses, such as job or educational placement. Another type of criterion-related validity is **concurrent validity.** This refers to the procedure of comparing scores on one measure to those on another that directly measures the same thing—for example, a new, short intelligence test being compared with an existing, longer intelligence test.

These ways of assessing validity are summarized in Table A-3.

You may also see the term *construct validity*, which is used in a variety of ways and often ambiguously. Even the textbooks on psychological measurement disagree about it. Sometimes it includes criterion-related validity and sometimes even content validity. Often it is used to refer to the measure's being used in a study in which there was a predicted result borne out by the study. Because the measure used was successful in producing the predicted result, it shows that the idea (or "construct") behind that measure has proved itself under the theory.

Key Terms

behavioral measures
blind conditions of testing
concurrent validity
content validity
control group
correlational research design
counterbalancing
criterion-related validity
dependent variable
double-blind procedure
experimental group
experimental manipulation
experimenter bias
experimenter effects
external validity
generalizability

Hawthorne effects
independent variable
inter-item consistency
interjudge reliability
internal validity
manipulating the independent variable
matched-group pretest-posttest design
matched-group research design
observational measures
physiological measures
placebo effects
population
predictive validity
preexperimental design

probability sample
quasi-experimental design
random assignment to groups
random sampling
reliability
repeated-measures research design
response bias
sample
self-report measures
single-group pretest-posttest design
single-subject research
subjects
test-retest reliability
true experiment
validity
within-subject research design

B

Tables

TABLE B-1
Normal Curve Areas:
Percentage of the Normal Curve Between the Mean and the Z Scores Shown

Z	% Mean to Z	Z	% Mean to Z	Z	% Mean to Z
.00	.00	.24	9.48	.47	18.08
.01	.40	.25	9.87	.48	18.44
.02	.80	.26	10.26	.49	18.79
.03	1.20	.27	10.64	.50	19.15
.04	1.60	.28	11.03	.51	19.50
.05	1.99	.29	11.41	.52	19.85
.06	2.39	.30	11.79	.53	20.19
.07	2.79	.31	12.17	.54	20.54
.08	3.19	.32	12.55	.55	20.88
.09	3.59	.59	22.24	.56	21.23
.10	3.98	.33	12.93	.57	21.57
.11	4.38	.34	13.31	.58	21.90
.12	4.78	.35	13.68	.59	22.24
.13	5.17	.36	14.06	.60	22.57
.14	5.57	.37	14.43	.61	22.91
.15	5.96	.38	14.80	.62	23.24
.16	6.36	.39	15.17	.63	23.57
.17	6.75	.40	15.54	.64	23.89
.18	7.14	.41	15.91	.65	24.22
.19	7.53	.42	16.28	.66	24.54
.20	7.93	.43	16.64	.67	24.86
.21	8.32	.44	17.00	.68	25.17
.22	8.71	.45	17.36	.69	25.49
.23	9.10	.46	17.72	.70	25.80

TABLE B-1 (cont.)

Z	% Mean to Z	Z	% Mean to Z	Z	% Mean to Z
.71	26.11	1.28	39.97	1.85	46.78
.72	26.42	1.29	40.15	1.86	46.86
.73	26.73	1.30	40.32	1.87	46.93
.74	27.04	1.31	40.49	1.88	46.99
.75	27.34	1.32	40.66	1.89	47.06
.76	27.64	1.33	40.82	1.90	47.13
.77	27.94	1.34	40.99	1.91	47.19
.78	28.23	1.35	41.15	1.92	47.26
.79	28.52	1.36	41.31	1.93	47.32
.80	28.81	1.37	41.47	1.94	47.38
.81	29.10	1.38	41.62	1.95	47.44
.82	29.39	1.39	41.77	1.96	47.50
.83	29.67	1.40	41.92	1.97	47.56
.84	29.95	1.41	42.07	1.98	47.61
.85	30.23	1.42	42.22	1.99	47.67
.86	30.51	1.43	42.36	2.00	47.72
.87	30.78	1.44	42.51	2.01	47.78
.88	31.06	1.45	42.65	2.02	47.83
.89	31.33	1.46	42.79	2.03	47.88
.90	31.59	1.47	42.92	2.04	47.93
.91	31.86	1.48	43.06	2.05	47.98
.92	32.12	1.49	43.19	2.06	48.03
.93	32.38	1.50	43.32	2.07	48.08
.94	32.64	1.51	43.45	2.08	48.12
.95	32.89	1.52	43.57	2.09	48.17
.96	33.15	1.53	43.70	2.10	48.21
.97	33.40	1.54	43.82	2.11	48.26
.98	33.65	1.55	43.94	2.12	48.30
.99	33.89	1.56	44.06	2.13	48.34
1.00	34.13	1.57	44.18	2.14	48.38
1.01	34.38	1.58	44.29	2.15	48.42
1.02	34.61	1.59	44.41	2.16	48.46
1.03	34.85	1.60	44.52	2.17	48.50
1.04	35.08	1.61	44.63	2.18	48.54
1.05	35.31	1.62	44.74	2.19	48.57
1.06	35.54	1.63	44.84	2.20	48.61
1.07	35.77	1.64	44.95	2.21	48.64
1.08	35.99	1.65	45.05	2.22	48.68
1.09	36.21	1.66	45.15	2.23	48.71
1.10	36.43	1.67	45.25	2.24	48.75
1.11	36.65	1.68	45.35	2.25	48.78
1.12	36.86	1.69	45.45	2.26	48.81
1.13	37.08	1.70	45.54	2.27	48.84
1.14	37.29	1.71	45.64	2.28	48.87
1.15	37.49	1.72	45.73	2.29	48.90
1.16	37.70	1.73	45.82	2.30	48.93
1.17	37.90	1.74	45.91	2.31	48.96
1.18	38.10	1.75	45.99	2.32	48.98
1.19	38.30	1.76	46.08	2.33	49.01
1.20	38.49	1.77	46.16	2.34	49.04
1.21	38.69	1.78	46.25	2.35	49.06
1.22	38.88	1.79	46.33	2.36	49.09
1.23	39.07	1.80	46.41	2.37	49.11
1.24	39.25	1.81	46.49	2.38	49.13
1.25	39.44	1.82	46.56	2.39	49.16
1.26	39.62	1.83	46.64	2.40	49.18
1.27	39.80	1.84	46.71	2.41	49.20

TABLE B-1 (cont.)

Z	% Mean to Z	Z	% Mean to Z	Z	% Mean to Z
2.42	49.22	2.63	49.57	2.84	49.77
2.43	49.25	2.64	49.59	2.85	49.78
2.44	49.27	2.65	49.60	2.86	49.79
2.45	49.29	2.66	49.61	2.87	49.79
2.46	49.31	2.67	49.62	2.88	49.80
2.47	49.32	2.68	49.63	2.89	49.81
2.48	49.34	2.69	49.64	2.90	49.81
2.49	49.36	2.70	49.65	2.91	49.82
2.50	49.38	2.71	49.66	2.92	49.82
2.51	49.40	2.72	49.67	2.93	49.83
2.52	49.41	2.73	49.68	2.94	49.84
2.53	49.43	2.74	49.69	2.95	49.84
2.54	49.45	2.75	49.70	2.96	49.85
2.55	49.46	2.76	49.71	2.97	49.85
2.56	49.48	2.77	49.72	2.98	49.86
2.57	49.49	2.78	49.73	2.99	49.86
2.58	49.51	2.79	49.74	3.00	49.87
2.59	49.52	2.80	49.74	3.50	49.98
2.60	49.53	2.81	49.75	4.00	50.00
2.61	49.55	2.82	49.76	4.50	50.00
2.62	49.56	2.83	49.77		

TABLE B-2
Cutoff Scores for the *t* Distribution

	One-Tailed Tests			Two-Tailed Tests		
df	*.10*	*.05*	*.01*	*.10*	*.05*	*.01*
1	3.078	6.314	31.821	6.314	12.706	63.657
2	1.886	2.920	6.965	2.920	4.303	9.925
3	1.638	2.353	4.541	2.353	3.182	5.841
4	1.533	2.132	3.747	2.132	2.776	4.604
5	1.476	2.015	3.365	2.015	2.571	4.032
6	1.440	1.943	3.143	1.943	2.447	3.708
7	1.415	1.895	2.998	1.895	2.365	3.500
8	1.397	1.860	2.897	1.860	2.306	3.356
9	1.383	1.833	2.822	1.833	2.262	3.250
10	1.372	1.813	2.764	1.813	2.228	3.170
11	1.364	1.796	2.718	1.796	2.201	3.106
12	1.356	1.783	2.681	1.783	2.179	3.055
13	1.350	1.771	2.651	1.771	2.161	3.013
14	1.345	1.762	2.625	1.762	2.145	2.977
15	1.341	1.753	2.603	1.753	2.132	2.947
16	1.337	1.746	2.584	1.746	2.120	2.921
17	1.334	1.740	2.567	1.740	2.110	2.898
18	1.331	1.734	2.553	1.734	2.101	2.879
19	1.328	1.729	2.540	1.729	2.093	2.861
20	1.326	1.725	2.528	1.725	2.086	2.846
21	1.323	1.721	2.518	1.721	2.080	2.832
22	1.321	1.717	2.509	1.717	2.074	2.819
23	1.320	1.714	2.500	1.714	2.069	2.808
24	1.318	1.711	2.492	1.711	2.064	2.797
25	1.317	1.708	2.485	1.708	2.060	2.788
26	1.315	1.706	2.479	1.706	2.056	2.779
27	1.314	1.704	2.473	1.704	2.052	2.771
28	1.313	1.701	2.467	1.701	2.049	2.764
29	1.312	1.699	2.462	1.699	2.045	2.757
30	1.311	1.698	2.458	1.698	2.043	2.750
35	1.306	1.690	2.438	1.690	2.030	2.724
40	1.303	1.684	2.424	1.684	2.021	2.705
45	1.301	1.680	2.412	1.680	2.014	2.690
50	1.299	1.676	2.404	1.676	2.009	2.678
55	1.297	1.673	2.396	1.673	2.004	2.668
60	1.296	1.671	2.390	1.671	2.001	2.661
65	1.295	1.669	2.385	1.669	1.997	2.654
70	1.294	1.667	2.381	1.667	1.995	2.648
75	1.293	1.666	2.377	1.666	1.992	2.643
80	1.292	1.664	2.374	1.664	1.990	2.639
85	1.292	1.663	2.371	1.663	1.989	2.635
90	1.291	1.662	2.369	1.662	1.987	2.632
95	1.291	1.661	2.366	1.661	1.986	2.629
100	1.290	1.660	2.364	1.660	1.984	2.626
∞	1.282	1.645	2.327	1.645	1.960	2.576

TABLE B-3
Cutoff Scores for the *F* Distribution

Denominator df	Significance Level	Numerator Degrees of Freedom					
		1	2	3	4	5	6
1	.01	4,052	5,000	5,404	5,625	5,764	5,859
	.05	162	200	216	225	230	234
	.10	39.9	49.5	53.6	55.8	57.2	58.2
2	.01	98.50	99.00	99.17	99.25	99.30	99.33
	.05	18.51	19.00	19.17	19.25	19.30	19.33
	.10	8.53	9.00	9.16	9.24	9.29	9.33
3	.01	34.12	30.82	29.46	28.71	28.24	27.91
	.05	10.13	9.55	9.28	9.12	9.01	8.94
	.10	5.54	5.46	5.39	5.34	5.31	5.28
4	.01	21.20	18.00	16.70	15.98	15.52	15.21
	.05	7.71	6.95	6.59	6.39	6.26	6.16
	.10	4.55	4.33	4.19	4.11	4.05	4.01
5	.01	16.26	13.27	12.06	11.39	10.97	10.67
	.05	6.61	5.79	5.41	5.19	5.05	4.95
	.10	4.06	3.78	3.62	3.52	3.45	3.41
6	.01	13.75	10.93	9.78	9.15	8.75	8.47
	.05	5.99	5.14	4.76	4.53	4.39	4.28
	.10	3.78	3.46	3.29	3.18	3.11	3.06
7	.01	12.25	9.55	8.45	7.85	7.46	7.19
	.05	5.59	4.74	4.35	4.12	3.97	3.87
	.10	3.59	3.26	3.08	2.96	2.88	2.83
8	.01	11.26	8.65	7.59	7.01	6.63	6.37
	.05	5.32	4.46	4.07	3.84	3.69	3.58
	.10	3.46	3.11	2.92	2.81	2.73	2.67
9	.01	10.56	8.02	6.99	6.42	6.06	5.80
	.05	5.12	4.26	3.86	3.63	3.48	3.37
	.10	3.36	3.01	2.81	2.69	2.61	2.55
10	.01	10.05	7.56	6.55	6.00	5.64	5.39
	.05	4.97	4.10	3.71	3.48	3.33	3.22
	.10	3.29	2.93	2.73	2.61	2.52	2.46
11	.01	9.65	7.21	6.22	5.67	5.32	5.07
	.05	4.85	3.98	3.59	3.36	3.20	3.10
	.10	3.23	2.86	2.66	2.54	2.45	2.39
12	.01	9.33	6.93	5.95	5.41	5.07	4.82
	.05	4.75	3.89	3.49	3.26	3.11	3.00
	.10	3.18	2.81	2.61	2.48	2.40	2.33
13	.01	9.07	6.70	5.74	5.21	4.86	4.62
	.05	4.67	3.81	3.41	3.18	3.03	2.92
	.10	3.14	2.76	2.56	2.43	2.35	2.28
14	.01	8.86	6.52	5.56	5.04	4.70	4.46
	.05	4.60	3.74	3.34	3.11	2.96	2.85
	.10	3.10	2.73	2.52	2.40	2.31	2.24

TABLE B-3 (cont.)

Denominator df	Significance Level	Numerator Degrees of Freedom					
		1	*2*	*3*	*4*	*5*	*6*
15	.01	8.68	6.36	5.42	4.89	4.56	4.32
	.05	4.54	3.68	3.29	3.06	2.90	2.79
	.10	3.07	2.70	2.49	2.36	2.27	2.21
16	.01	8.53	6.23	5.29	4.77	4.44	4.20
	.05	4.49	3.63	3.24	3.01	2.85	2.74
	.10	3.05	2.67	2.46	2.33	2.24	2.18
17	.01	8.40	6.11	5.19	4.67	4.34	4.10
	.05	4.45	3.59	3.20	2.97	2.81	2.70
	.10	3.03	2.65	2.44	2.31	2.22	2.15
18	.01	8.29	6.01	5.09	4.58	4.25	4.02
	.05	4.41	3.56	3.16	2.93	2.77	2.66
	.10	3.01	2.62	2.42	2.29	2.20	2.13
19	.01	8.19	5.93	5.01	4.50	4.17	3.94
	.05	4.38	3.52	3.13	2.90	2.74	2.63
	.10	2.99	2.61	2.40	2.27	2.18	2.11
20	.01	8.10	5.85	4.94	4.43	4.10	3.87
	.05	4.35	3.49	3.10	2.87	2.71	2.60
	.10	2.98	2.59	2.38	2.25	2.16	2.09
21	.01	8.02	5.78	4.88	4.37	4.04	3.81
	.05	4.33	3.47	3.07	2.84	2.69	2.57
	.10	2.96	2.58	2.37	2.23	2.14	2.08
22	.01	7.95	5.72	4.82	4.31	3.99	3.76
	.05	4.30	3.44	3.05	2.82	2.66	2.55
	.10	2.95	2.56	2.35	2.22	2.13	2.06
23	.01	7.88	5.66	4.77	4.26	3.94	3.71
	.05	4.28	3.42	3.03	2.80	2.64	2.53
	.10	2.94	2.55	2.34	2.21	2.12	2.05
24	.01	7.82	5.61	4.72	4.22	3.90	3.67
	.05	4.26	3.40	3.01	2.78	2.62	2.51
	.10	2.93	2.54	2.33	2.20	2.10	2.04
25	.01	7.77	5.57	4.68	4.18	3.86	3.63
	.05	4.24	3.39	2.99	2.76	2.60	2.49
	.10	2.92	2.53	2.32	2.19	2.09	2.03
26	.01	7.72	5.53	4.64	4.14	3.82	3.59
	.05	4.23	3.37	2.98	2.74	2.59	2.48
	.10	2.91	2.52	2.31	2.18	2.08	2.01
27	.01	7.68	5.49	4.60	4.11	3.79	3.56
	.05	4.21	3.36	2.96	2.73	2.57	2.46
	.10	2.90	2.51	2.30	2.17	2.07	2.01
28	.01	7.64	5.45	4.57	4.08	3.75	3.53
	.05	4.20	3.34	2.95	2.72	2.56	2.45
	.10	2.89	2.50	2.29	2.16	2.07	2.00

TABLE B-3 (cont.)

Denom- inator df	Signi- ficance Level	Numerator Degrees of Freedom					
		1	2	3	4	5	6
29	.01	7.60	5.42	4.54	4.05	3.73	3.50
	.05	4.18	3.33	2.94	2.70	2.55	2.43
	.10	2.89	2.50	2.28	2.15	2.06	1.99
30	.01	7.56	5.39	4.51	4.02	3.70	3.47
	.05	4.17	3.32	2.92	2.69	2.53	2.42
	.10	2.88	2.49	2.28	2.14	2.05	1.98
35	.01	7.42	5.27	4.40	3.91	3.59	3.37
	.05	4.12	3.27	2.88	2.64	2.49	2.37
	.10	2.86	2.46	2.25	2.11	2.02	1.95
40	.01	7.32	5.18	4.31	3.83	3.51	3.29
	.05	4.09	3.23	2.84	2.61	2.45	2.34
	.10	2.84	2.44	2.23	2.09	2.00	1.93
45	.01	7.23	5.11	4.25	3.77	3.46	3.23
	.05	4.06	3.21	2.81	2.58	2.42	2.31
	.10	2.82	2.43	2.21	2.08	1.98	1.91
50	.01	7.17	5.06	4.20	3.72	3.41	3.19
	.05	4.04	3.18	2.79	2.56	2.40	2.29
	.10	2.81	2.41	2.20	2.06	1.97	1.90
55	.01	7.12	5.01	4.16	3.68	3.37	3.15
	.05	4.02	3.17	2.77	2.54	2.38	2.27
	.10	2.80	2.40	2.19	2.05	1.96	1.89
60	.01	7.08	4.98	4.13	3.65	3.34	3.12
	.05	4.00	3.15	2.76	2.53	2.37	2.26
	.10	2.79	2.39	2.18	2.04	1.95	1.88
65	.01	7.04	4.95	4.10	3.62	3.31	3.09
	.05	3.99	3.14	2.75	2.51	2.36	2.24
	.10	2.79	2.39	2.17	2.03	1.94	1.87
70	.01	7.01	4.92	4.08	3.60	3.29	3.07
	.05	3.98	3.13	2.74	2.50	2.35	2.23
	.10	2.78	2.38	2.16	2.03	1.93	1.86
75	.01	6.99	4.90	4.06	3.58	3.27	3.05
	.05	3.97	3.12	2.73	2.49	2.34	2.22
	.10	2.77	2.38	2.16	2.02	1.93	1.86
80	.01	6.96	4.88	4.04	3.56	3.26	3.04
	.05	3.96	3.11	2.72	2.49	2.33	2.22
	.10	2.77	2.37	2.15	2.02	1.92	1.85
85	.01	6.94	4.86	4.02	3.55	3.24	3.02
	.05	3.95	3.10	2.71	2.48	2.32	2.21
	.10	2.77	2.37	2.15	2.01	1.92	1.85
90	.01	6.93	4.85	4.01	3.54	3.23	3.01
	.05	3.95	3.10	2.71	2.47	2.32	2.20
	.10	2.76	2.36	2.15	2.01	1.91	1.84

TABLE B-3 (cont.)

Denom-inator df	Significance Level	Numerator Degrees of Freedom					
		1	*2*	*3*	*4*	*5*	*6*
95	.01	6.91	4.84	4.00	3.52	3.22	3.00
	.05	3.94	3.09	2.70	2.47	2.31	2.20
	.10	2.76	2.36	2.14	2.01	1.91	1.84
100	.01	6.90	4.82	3.98	3.51	3.21	2.99
	.05	3.94	3.09	2.70	2.46	2.31	2.19
	.10	2.76	2.36	2.14	2.00	1.91	1.83
∞	.01	6.64	4.61	3.78	3.32	3.02	2.80
	.05	3.84	3.00	2.61	2.37	2.22	2.10
	.10	2.71	2.30	2.08	1.95	1.85	1.78

TABLE B-4
Cutoff Scores for the Chi-Square Distribution

df	Significance Level		
	.10	*.05*	*.01*
1	2.706	3.841	6.635
2	4.605	5.992	9.211
3	6.252	7.815	11.345
4	7.780	9.488	13.277
5	9.237	11.071	15.087
6	10.645	12.592	16.812
7	12.017	14.067	18.475
8	13.362	15.507	20.090
9	14.684	16.919	21.666
10	15.987	18.307	23.209

TABLE B-5
Index to Power Tables and Tables Giving Number of Subjects Needed for 80% Power

Hypothesis-Testing Procedure	Chapter	Power Table	Number of Subjects Table
Correlation coefficient (*r*)	3	100	100
t test for dependent means	9	272	273
t test for independent means	10	301	302
One-way analysis of variance	11	331	332
Two-way analysis of variance	13	401	402
Chi-square test of independence	14	437	438

Answers
Set I Practice Problems

Chapter 1

1. (a) Frequency table.

Score	Frequency	Score	Frequency
96	1	72	0
95	0	71	1
94	0	70	1
93	0	69	1
92	1	68	2
91	1	67	1
90·	0	66	0
89	0	65	0
88	0	64	2
87	1	63	0
86	0	62	0
85	1	61	0
84	0	60	0
83	2	59	1
82	0	58	0
81	1	57	0
80	1	56	0
79	0	55	0
78	0	54	0
77	0	53	0
76	2	52	0
75	2	51	0
74	1	50	1
73	1		

(b) Grouped frequency table (one possibility).

Interval	Frequency
95–99	1
90–94	2
85–89	2
80–84	4
75–79	4
70–74	4
65–69	4
60–64	2
55–59	1
50–54	1

(c) Histogram (based on table in b).

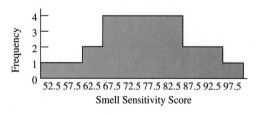

(d) General shape of the distribution: Unimodal, approximately symmetrical (slightly negatively skewed).

2. (a) Grouped frequency table (one possibility).

Interval	Frequency
80–89	10
70–79	0
60–69	5
50–59	0
40–49	5
30–39	7
20–29	7

(b) Histogram (based on table in a).

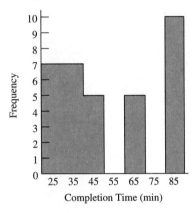

3. (a) Frequency table.

Number of Hours	Frequency	Number of Hours	Frequency
18	1	8	5
17	0	7	11
16	0	6	4
15	1	5	2
14	0	4	3
13	2	3	4
12	1	2	2
11	3	1	1
10	5	0	1
9	4		

(b) Grouped frequency table (one possibility).

Interval	Frequency
18–20	1
15–17	1
12–14	3
9–11	12
6–8	20
3–5	9
0–2	4

(c) Frequency polygon (based on table in b).

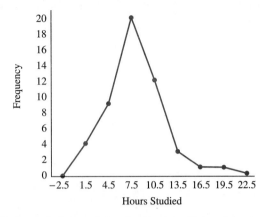

(d) General shape of the distribution: Unimodal, skewed to the right (positively skewed).

4. (a) Bimodal; **(b)** approximately normal (or unimodal or symmetrical); **(c)** multimodal.

5.

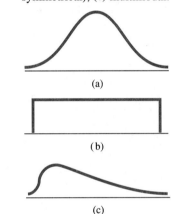

6. (a) A distribution is the way a group of numbers are spread out over the different possible values they can have. One way to describe such a distribution is with a graph. If you make a histogram (a bar graph with one unit of height for each time a particular value occurs and the possible values from low to high in even increments across the bottom), a symmetrical distribution has a symmetrical shape, meaning that the right and left halves are mirror images. Loosely speaking, this means that there are about as many high numbers as there are low numbers, and the way the number of instances at each value decreases as you move from a middle value to the highest value is the same as the way the number of instances at each value decreases as you move from a middle value to the lowest value.

A distribution is unimodal if the histogram graph has one high point. This means that there is a single particular level that has more cases than any other single level. (This level is called the "mode," and being "unimodal" means having only one mode.)

(b) A negatively skewed unimodal distribution is not symmetrical, and its tail—the long, low side—extends to the left (where the negative numbers go on a graph).

Chapter 2

1. Set A. **(a)** $M = 261/9 = 29$.
   (b) Median = 28.
   (c) $SS = (32 - 29)^2 + (28 - 29)^2 + (24 - 29)^2$
   $+ (28 - 29)^2 + (28 - 29)^2 + (31 - 29)^2$
   $+ (35 - 29)^2 + (29 - 29)^2 + (26 - 29)^2$
   $= 3^2 + (-1)^2 + (-5)^2 + (-1)^2 + (-1)^2$
   $+ 2^2 + 6^2 + 0^2 + (-3)^2$
   $= 9 + 1 + 25 + 1 + 1 + 4 + 36 + 0 + 9 = 86$.
   (d) $SD^2 = SS/N = 86/9 = 9.56$.
   (e) $SD = \sqrt{9.56} = 3.09$.
   Set B. **(a)** $M = 4$; **(b)** Median = 4; **(c)** $SS = 26$;
   (d) $SD^2 = 3.25$; **(e)** $SD = 1.80$.

2. The average temperature, in the sense of adding up the 10 readings and dividing by 10, was –7 ˚C. However, if you were to line the temperatures up from lowest to highest, the middle two numbers, determining what is called the median temperature, would both be –5 ˚C. Another way of figuring the typical temperature would be to take the specific temperature that came up most often—which in this case was –1 and –5, both of which came up twice. But this is not very useful information in this case.

As for the variation, you can figure by how much each temperature diverges from the average: Square each of these "deviation scores" (multiply each deviation score times itself to get rid of the minus and plus signs), and take the average of these squared deviation scores. For example, the first temperature's deviation is 2 (–5 minus –7), which multiplied times itself is 4. Squaring each deviation and adding up all the results gives 468. Dividing this by 10 gives an average squared deviation of 46.8. This is called the variance (an index of how spread out a group of numbers is) and is an important part of many statistical calculations. Unfortunately, however, it does not give a very direct sense of how much numbers vary. But if you take the square root of the variance—in this case the square root of 46.8 is 6.84—this gives what is called the standard deviation, a number that very nearly indicates the average amount by which each temperature varies from the average temperature.

3. This result has two parts. First, the "mean" refers to the ordinary arithmetic average—add the numbers and divide by the number of numbers. In this case, the average number of dreams reported over the 2 weeks was 6.84. Second, the "$SD = 3.18$" says that the standard deviation—which, roughly speaking, is the average amount that the numbers of dreams are spread out from their average—is 3.18. This is quite a lot of spread. To be more precise, the standard deviation is computed by taking each person's number of dreams and subtracting 6.84 from it and squaring this difference; the standard deviation is the square root of the average of these squared differences.

4. **(a)** $Z = (X - M)/SD = (91 - 79)/12 = 12/12 = 1.00$.
   (b) $Z = (X - M)/SD = (68 - 79)/12 = -11/12 = -0.92$.
   (c) $Z = (X - M)/SD = (103 - 79)/12 = 24/12 = 2.00$.

5. **(a)** If IQ = 107, $Z = (X - M)/SD = (107 - 100)/16$
   $= 7/16 = .44$.
   $X = (Z)(SD) + M = (.44)(41) + 231 = 18.04 + 231 = 249$.
   (The final answer is rounded off to a whole number because the actual score on the test is the number of items correct, which cannot be a fraction.)
   (b) $Z = -1.06$; $X = 188$.
   (c) $Z = 0$; $X = 231$.

6. Wife: $Z = (X - M)/SD = (63 - 60)/6 = 3/6 = .5$.
   Husband: $Z = (X - M)/SD = (59 - 55)/4 = 4/4 = 1$.

The husband has a higher Z score, so he has adjusted better in relation to other divorced men than the wife has adjusted in relation to other divorced women.

Explanation to person who has never had a course in statistics: For wives, a score of 63 is 3 points better than the average of 60 for divorced women in general (the "mean" in the problem is a statistical term for the ordinary average—the sum of the numbers divided by the number of numbers). But there is, of course, some variation in scores among divorced women. The approximate average amount that women's scores differ from the average is 6 points—this is the SD referred to in the problem. (Actually, SD, which stands for *standard deviation*, is only approximately the average amount that scores differ from the average—to be precise, it is the square root of the average of the square of the difference of each score from the mean.)

Thus the wife differs only half as much as women in general. This gives her what is called a Z score of +.5, which gives her location on a scale that compares her score to that of divorced women in general. Using the same logic to examine the husband's divorce adjustment compared to other divorced men, he is as much above the average as the average amount that men differ from the average; that is, he has a Z score of +1. Therefore, the conclusion is that although both have adjusted better than the average for their gender, the husband has adjusted better in relation to other divorced men than the wife has adjusted in relation to other divorced women.

Chapter 3

1. (a)

(b) Positive linear correlation—as therapist empathy increases, patient satisfaction also increases.

(c)

	Therapist Empathy		Patient Satisfaction		$Z_X Z_Y$
	Raw	Z_X	*Raw*	Z_Y	
1	70	.36	4	.63	.23
2	94	1.45	5	1.26	1.83
3	36	−1.17	2	− .63	.74
4	48	− .63	1	−1.26	.80
					$\Sigma = 3.60$

$$r = 3.60/4 = .90.$$

(d) The first step in a correlation problem is to make a graph, assigning one variable to each axis, then putting a dot where each score falls on that graph. This is called a scatter diagram, and it provides a visual impression of the degree of relationship between the two variables. In this case, high scores seem to go with high, and low with low, making this what is called a positive linear correlation. (The basic idea of correlation is the extent to which high scores go with high scores and low scores go with low scores.) Also, because the dots fall roughly near a straight line, this is an example of a linear correlation.

The next step in the process is to convert all scores to Z scores. This makes it easier to compute the extent to which highs go with highs and lows with lows. Z scores make this easier because they are the best indicator of the extent to which a score is low or high relative to the other scores in its distribution.

The correlation coefficient is a numerical indicator of the degree of association. It is computed by multiplying the two Z scores for each subject times each other, totaling up these products, and then averaging this total over the number of subjects. This will be a high number if highs go with highs and lows with lows, since with Z scores, highs are always positive (and the higher they are, the more positive), and positive times positive is positive. Also, lows with Z scores are always negative (and the lower the score, the more negative the Z score), and negatives times negatives become positives too.

Statisticians can prove that by following this procedure, the highest number you can get, if the scores for the two variables are perfectly correlated, is +1. If there were no linear relationship between the variables, the result of this procedure would be 0 (that would happen if highs were sometimes multiplied with highs and sometimes with lows, and lows sometimes with highs and sometimes with lows, giving a mixture of positive and negative numbers that would cancel out).

In the present case, the total of the products of the Z scores was 3.6, which when divided by the number of subjects is .9. This is called a *Pearson correlation coefficient* (*r*) of .9 and indicates a strong, positive linear correlation between satisfaction and empathy.

(e) Three logical possibilities for direction of causality: (i) If a therapist has more empathy, this causes the patient to feel more satisfied (empathy → satisfaction); (ii) if a patient feels more satisfied, this may cause the therapist to feel more empathic toward the patient (satisfaction → empathy); or (iii) some third factor, such as a good match of the patient's problem with the therapist's ability, may cause clients to be more satisfied and therapists to be more empathic (third factor → satisfaction and empathy).

2. (a)

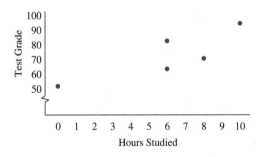

(b) A positive linear correlation—as hours studied goes up, so do test grades.

(c)

Hours Studied		Test Grade		$Z_X Z_Y$
Raw	Z_X	*Raw*	Z_Y	
0	−1.79	52	−1.41	2.52
10	1.19	95	1.48	1.76
6	0.00	83	0.67	0.00
8	0.60	71	−0.13	−0.08
6	0.00	64	−0.60	0.00
$M = 6$; $SD = 3.35$		$M = 73$; $SD = 14.90$		$\Sigma = 4.20$

$$r = 4.20/5 = .84.$$

(d) See answer to Problem 1d for an example of how to write an essay of this kind.

(e) Three logically possible directions of causality: (i) Studying more hours causes improved test grades (hours → grades); (ii) getting a better test grade causes more hours studied (grade → hours; note that although this is theoretically possible, it is not possible in reality to have a future event, the score on the test, cause a previous event, hours studied); or (iii) a third factor, such as interest in the subject matter, could be causing the student to study more and also to do better on the test (interest → grades and hours).

3. (a)

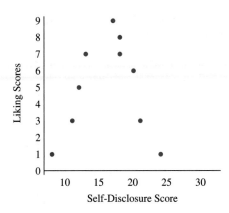

(b) Curvilinear correlation (inverted U shape), so that as self-disclosure increases, liking increases—up to a point. But then as self-disclosure increases further, liking decreases.

(c)

Partner's Self-Disclosure		Liking for Partner		$Z_X Z_Y$
Score	Z Score	Score	Z Score	
18	.37	8	1.10	.407
17	.17	9	1.47	.245
20	.80	6	.37	.296
8	−1.72	1	−1.47	2.528
13	− .67	7	.74	− .496
24	1.63	1	−1.47	−2.396
11	−1.09	3	− .74	.807
12	− .88	5	0.00	0.000
18	.38	7	.74	.281
21	1.00	3	− .74	− .740
				Σ = .932

$r = .932/10 = .09.$

4. This table shows the degree of association among several tests—that is, the extent to which scoring high or low on one test is associated with scoring similarly high or low on the other test. The actual numbers are called *correlation coefficients*. A correlation coefficient of 1 means that the scores on the two tests are perfectly linked—knowing a person's score on one test would be all you would need to know to figure out that person's score on the other. (Such perfect associations are almost never found in real life.) A correlation coefficient of 0 means that there is no association at all between the two tests—a person's score on one test is completely unrelated to his or her score on the other. Finally, a correlation coefficient of −1 means that there is a perfect inverse association—scoring high on the one test is perfectly associated with scoring low on the other, and vice versa. Most correlations fall between 0 and +1 or 0 and −1.

(See the answer to Problem 1d for how you would describe how the correlation coefficient is actually computed.)

Also notice that some of the correlations in the table are marked with asterisks. These asterisks indicate that these correlations are "statistically significant." This means that if in the world at large there was really no association, the chance of getting a correlation this large in this study would be quite slim. It is a kind of statistical reassurance that the association is probably not due to chance factors such as the people that happened to be included in this study.

In this particular set of correlations, we see that behavioral and emotional jealousy and behavioral and cognitive jealousy are significantly and moderately associated, but emotional and cognitive jealousy are not much related. The relation of these three aspects of jealousy to the other measures is also of interest: Emotional and behavioral jealousy, but not cognitive jealousy, are slightly associated with the happiness measure (MUNSH); and all three aspects of jealousy are moderately negatively associated with loving and liking and somewhat more strongly positively associated with White's jealousy scale (the WRJS). Finally, looking at the associations of the other measures among themselves, the happiness scale is associated to any reasonable degree only with liking; the love scale is associated only with the liking scale; and White's jealousy scale is associated negatively with liking.

These associations, particularly the ones marked with asterisks, should be interpreted as representing real degrees of association among the various tests. But the specific direction of cause and effect in these associations cannot be determined from the pattern of associations. For example, the correlation between feeling jealous and jealous behavior could be due to feelings causing the behavior, the behavior creating the feelings, or some third factor, such as not liking the other, causing both.

5. (a) Both measures may have low reliability, thus reducing (attenuating) the possible correlation between them.

(b) Among millionaires, there may not be a very great range of comfort of living situation (they probably all have quite comfortable living situations), so the correlation with any variable (including happiness) is limited.

6. Set A

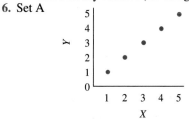

	X		Y		Cross-Product of Z Scores
Raw	Z	Raw	Z	
1	−1.41	1	−1.41	2.0
2	− .71	2	− .71	.5
3	0.00	3	0.00	0.0
4	.71	4	.71	.5
5	1.41	5	1.41	2.0
M = 3; SD = 1.41				5.0
				$r = 5.0/5 = 1.00.$

Set B

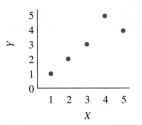

	X		Y	Cross-Product of Z Scores
Raw	Z	Raw	Z	
1	−1.41	1	−1.41	2.0
2	−.71	2	−.71	.5
3	0.00	3	0.00	0.0
4	.71	5	1.41	1.0
5	1.41	4	.71	1.0
				4.5
				$r = 4.5/5 = .90$.

7. Set A

Take Drug		Get Cold		Cross-Product of Z Scores
Raw	Z	Raw	Z	
0	−1	1	1	−1
0	−1	1	1	−1
0	−1	1	1	−1
0	−1	1	1	−1
1	1	0	−1	−1
1	1	0	−1	−1
1	1	0	−1	−1
1	1	0	−1	−1
				−8
				$r = -8/8 = -1.00$.

Set B

Take Drug		Get Cold		Cross-Product of Z Scores
Raw	Z	Raw	Z	
0	−1	1	1	−1
0	−1	1	1	−1
0	−1	1	1	−1
0	−1	0	−1	1
1	1	1	1	1
1	1	0	−1	−1
1	1	0	−1	−1
1	1	0	−1	−1
				−4
				$r = -4/8 = -.50$.

Chapter 4

1. (a) Predictor variable = score on test of knowledge of physiology. Dependent variable = number of injuries over subsequent year. Beta = .4 (the correlation coefficient).
   (b) $(\hat{Z})_{\text{Injuries}} = (.4)(Z_{\text{Score}})$.
   (c) $(.4)(-2) = -.8$; $(.4)(-1) = -.4$; $(.4)(0) = 0$; $(.4)(1) = .4$; $(.4)(2) = .8$.
2. (a) $b = (\beta)(SD_Y/SD_X) = (.4)(2/2) = .4$; $a = M_Y - (b)(M_X) = 10 - (.4)(10) = 10 - 4 = 6$; $\hat{Y} = 6 + (.4)(X)$.
   (b) $\hat{Y} = 16 + (.4)(X)$.
   (c) $\hat{Y} = 2 + (.4)(X)$.
   (d) $\hat{Y} = 8 + (.2)(X)$.
   (e) $\hat{Y} = 2 + (.8)(X)$.
   (f) $\hat{Y} = 14 + (-.4)(X)$.
   (g) $\hat{Y} = 2 + (.8)(X)$.

3.

Midterm	Prediction Model	Predicted Final
30	40 + (.5)(30)	55
40	40 + (.5)(40)	60
50	40 + (.5)(50)	65
60	40 + (.5)(60)	70
70	40 + (.5)(70)	75
80	40 + (.5)(80)	80
90	40 + (.5)(90)	85
100	40 + (.5)(100)	90

4. (a) $b = (\beta)(SD_Y/SD_X) = (.9)(1.58/22.14) = .064$; $a = M_Y - (b)(M_X) = 3 - (.064)(62) = -.97$; Predicted satisfaction $= -.97 + (.064)$ (empathy).

(b)

Pair Number	Therapist Empathy	Patient Satisfaction	
		Actual	*Predicted*
1	70	4	3.51
2	94	5	5.05
3	36	2	1.33
4	48	1	2.10

(c)

Error	Error²
.49	.24
− .05	.00
.67	.45
−1.10	1.21

(d)

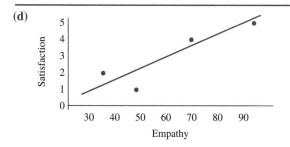

(e) Proportionate reduction in error $= (SS_T - SS_E)/SS_T = (10 - 1.9)/10 = .81$.

(f) $\sqrt{.81} = .9$; $r = .9$.

(g) It can be proven mathematically that the most accurate approach for predicting a person's Z score on one variable (call it Y) based on that person's Z score on another variable (call it X) is to multiply the Z score on X by the correlation coefficient. This procedure can be simplified into a single formula (not requiring conversions to and from Z scores) in which the raw score on Y can be predicted directly from the raw score on X. In this particular case, the single formula comes out so that to predict a patient's raw score on satisfaction, you begin with a score of −.97 and then add the result of multiplying .064 times the therapist's empathy score.

To evaluate the accuracy of this formula, I first determined what I would have predicted using this formula for each patient in the four pairs that I used to find the initial correlation coefficient. For example, using this formula for the first pair, taking −.97 and then adding the result of multiplying .064 times the therapist's empathy (.064 × 70 = 4.48) gives 3.51. For each such prediction, I can compute the error I would make using this model by subtracting the predicted score from the actual score—for example, for the first pair, 4 minus 3.51 gives an error of .49. Because the errors would all cancel each other out when adding them up (because some are negative and some positive), I square the errors. To illustrate this graphically, I drew a line (called a regression line) showing the predictions using this formula on the scatter diagram for these data—as you can see, the dots representing the actual scores fall pretty close to the regression line; the distance of each dot from the line is the error.

I then compare the error I would make using the prediction formula to the error I would make predicting without it (predicting without it means predicting just from the mean of the patient satisfaction scores). The statistic that is actually used is called the proportionate reduction in error. It is the reduction in squared error from using the formula (the total squared error predicting from the mean, which was computed for me to be 10, minus the sum of squared error using the formula, which I calculated as 1.9), divided by the total squared error when using the mean to predict. This comes out to .81—meaning that I have reduced my squared error by 81% over just using the mean to predict. Since proportionate reduction in error is mathematically equivalent to the correlation coefficient squared, I checked my result by taking the square root of the proportionate reduction in error. The square root of .81 is .9, which is exactly the correlation coefficient.

5. (a) $b = (\beta)(SD_Y/SD_X) = (.84)(14.9/3.35) = 3.74$; $a = M_Y - (b)(M_X) = 73 - (3.74)(6) = 50.56$. Predicted test grade $= 50.56 + (3.74)$ (hours studied).

(b)

Hours Studied (X)	Test Grade (Y)	
	Actual	*Predicted*
0	52	50.56
10	95	87.96
6	83	73.00
8	71	80.48
6	64	73.00

(c)

Error	Error²
1.44	2.07
7.04	49.56
10.00	100.00
−9.48	89.87
−9.00	81.00

(d)

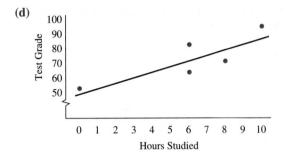

(e) Proportionate reduction in error $= (SS_T - SS_E)/SS_T$
$= (1{,}110 - 322.5)/1{,}110 = .71$.

(f) $\sqrt{.71} = .84$; $r = .84$.

(g) Similar to answer to Problem 4g.

6. This study used a statistical procedure called multiple regression. This procedure determines a formula for predicting a person's score on a dependent variable (in this case, the manager's effectiveness) from his or her scores on a set of predictor variables (in this case, the three types of influence strategies). The formula is of the form that you multiply the person's score on each of the predictor variables by some particular number, called a regression coefficient, and then add up the products. The procedure produces the most accurate prediction rule of this kind.

In this case, the prediction rule for the Z score for manager's effectiveness is $-.66$ times the Z score for "hard," plus .14 times the Z score for "soft," plus .09 times the Z score for "rational." (These are the numbers in the table under each predictor variable in the row for manager effectiveness.)

These regression coefficients suggest that manager effectiveness is most strongly related in a negative direction to using "hard" influence strategies (that is, the more hard influence strategies, the less effective the manager) and that use of soft and rational influence strategies have a positive but slight relation to effectiveness. It is important to note, however, that the regression coefficients for each of these types of strategies reflect what the scores on each strategy contribute to the prediction, over and above what the others contribute. Thus if we were to consider ordinary correlations between each of the predictor variables with the dependent variable, their relative importance could be quite different. (Those correlations, however, were not provided.)

Another important piece of information in this table is the "Adjusted R²." (Which is approximately the same as what is usually just called "R²"—and I will describe it here as if it were an ordinary R², as per the instructions for the problem.) This number tells the proportion of squared error in making predictions that is reduced by using this best prediction rule over just using the mean manager's effectiveness to predict each score. This is a standard way of describing how good this best possible prediction rule is. In this case, the proportionate reduction in error is 23%.

Finally, it turns out that the square root of the proportionate reduction in error is always the same as the correlation coefficient. Since there is more than one predictor, we call this a "multiple correlation coefficient." It comes out to .48.

7.

	Subordinate's Scores		
Subordinate	*Hard*	*Soft*	*Rational*
A	−1	−1	−1
B	0	0	0
C	1	1	1
D	1	0	0
E	0	1	0
F	0	0	1
G	3	1	1
H	1	3	1
I	3	1	3

Prediction Rule

(−.66H)	+	*(.14S)*	+	*(.09R)*
.66		− .14		− .09
0.00		0.00		0.00
− .66		.14		.09
− .66		0.00		0.00
0.00		.14		0.00
0.00		0.00		.09
−1.98		.14		.09
− .66		.42		.09
−1.98		.14		.27

Predicted Manager Effectiveness

.43
0.00
− .43
− .66
.14
.09
−1.79 −1.75
− .15
−1.57

Chapter 5

1. (a) 50%, **(b)** 16%, **(c)** 98%, **(d)** 84%, **(e)** 50%, **(f)** 84%, **(g)** 2%, **(h)** 16%; **(i)** 50, **(j)** 45, **(k)** 40, **(l)** 35, **(m)** 30.

Note: It will be much easier to answer problems like this if you draw a picture of a normal curve and mark it as shown here and on the next page.

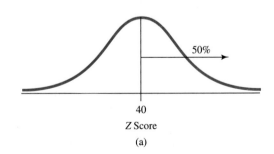

40

Z Score

(a)

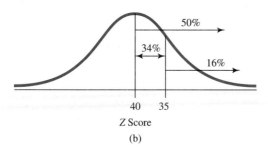

(b)

2. (a) From the normal curve table in Appendix B, 43% (.43) have Z scores between the mean and 1.5, and by definition 50% have Z scores below the mean, so the total percentage below 1.5 is 50% + 43% = 93%.

(b) 43% have Z scores between 1.5 and the mean, and since there are 50% total above the mean, 50% – 43% = 7% remain above 1.5 (or you could take the 93% from 2a and figure that only 7% remain out of the total of 100%).

(c) 43% of cases fall between the mean and 1.5, and since the normal curve is symmetrical, 43% are between the mean and –1.5; since 50% are below the mean, that leaves 7% below 1.5.

(d) 93%, (e) 2%, (f) 98%, (g) 33%, (h) 4%, (i) 5%. (Again, all of these problems are easier to answer if you make a picture of a normal curve and mark in the areas.)

3. (a) Top 10% means 90% are below; of those, 50% are below the mean, so that the top 10% is the point where 40% of cases are between it and the mean. Looking up 40.0 in the normal curve table (the closest actual value is 39.97), you find that this is equivalent to a Z score of +1.28.

(b) 2.33.

4. Needed Z = 1.64 corresponds to raw score of 50 + (10)(1.64) = 66.4.

Explanation: Many things in nature occur in numbers that approximately follow a particular pattern shown here, called a normal curve, in which most of the cases occur near the middle and fewer but equal numbers at each extreme. Because it is mathematically defined, the precise proportion of cases that fall at any particular section of it can be calculated, and these have been listed in special tables.

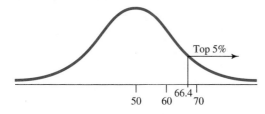

The normal curve tables are based on what are called Z scores. Z scores are in turn based on the *mean* and the *standard deviation*. The mean is the ordinary average—the sum of the numbers divided by the number of numbers. The standard deviation is a measure of how spread out a group of numbers are. Roughly speaking, it indicates the average amount that scores differ from the aver-

age. (To be exact, it is the square root of the average of the squared amounts by which each score differs from the average.) The Z score is the number of standard deviations a score is from the mean. The normal curve table tells the percentage of cases in the normal curve that fall between the mean and any particular Z score.

Since the coordination test scores are known to follow a normal curve, you can look up in the table the Z score that corresponds to the point on the normal curve at which 45% of the cases fall between it and the mean (since the normal curve is completely symmetrical, 50% of the cases fall above the mean, leaving 5% above 45%). This turns out to be a Z score of 1.64 (actually there is not an exact point on the table for 45%, so I could have used either 1.64 or 1.65).

With a standard deviation of 10, a Z score of 1.64 is 16.4 points above the mean. Adding that to the mean of 50 makes the score needed to be in the top 5% turn out to be 66.4.

5. (a) 10/50: p = 10/50 = .2; (b) .4; (c) (10 + 20)/50 = .6; (d) .6; (e) 1.

6. A *sample* is a group of people studied that represent the entire group to which the results are intended to apply, called the *population*. (In this case, the population is all U.S. high school students.) A sample is studied because it would be impracticable or impossible to test the entire population.

One way of ensuring that the sample is not systematically unrepresentative is to select the sample randomly. This does not mean haphazardly. For example, just taking the students that are easily available to test would be haphazard sampling. But this would not be a good method because whatever factors made them easily available— such as living in a nearby town—might make them unrepresentative of the population as a whole. An example of a truly random method would be to acquire a list of all the high school students in the nation, number each student, and then use a table of random numbers to pick as many as are to be surveyed.

Chapter 6

1. (a) A research hypothesis is a statement of the predicted relationship among populations (for example, that they will have different means).

(b) The null hypothesis is a statement of a relation between populations that is opposite to what is predicted in the research hypothesis (for example, that the two populations of interest do not have different means).

(c) Hypothesis testing is the logical and statistical procedure for examining the likelihood of obtaining a particular set of data if the null hypothesis is true.

(d) The comparison distribution is the distribution that represents the situation if the null hypothesis is true.

(e) The ".05 significance level" refers to the situation in hypothesis testing in which we decide to reject the null hypothesis because the probability of getting our particular data if the null hypothesis were true is less than 5%.

(f) A one-tailed test refers to using the hypothesis-testing procedure when the research hypothesis specifies a particular direction of difference (for example, that one population's mean will be higher than the other's).

2. (i) (a) Population 1: Canadian children of librarians; Population 2: All Canadian children.

(b) Research hypothesis: Population 1 children have generally better reading abilities than Population 2 children.

(c) Null hypothesis: Population 1's reading abilities are not better than Population 2's.

(d) One-tailed, because the question is whether they "do better," so only one direction of difference is of interest.

(ii) (a) Population 1: People who live in a particular city; Population 2: All people who live in the region.

(b) Research hypothesis: Populations 1 and 2 have different incomes.

(c) Null hypothesis: Populations 1 and 2 have the same income.

(d) Two-tailed, because the question is whether the income of the people in the city is "different" from the other, so a difference in either direction would be of interest.

(iii) (a) Population 1: People who have experienced an earthquake; Population 2: People in general.

(b) Research hypothesis: Populations 1 and 2 have different levels of self-confidence.

(c) Null hypothesis: Populations 1 and 2 have the same level of self-confidence.

(d) Two-tailed, because they might have either more or less.

3.

Study	Cutoff	Score on Comparison Distribution	Decision
A	+1.64	2.0	Reject null hypothesis
B	±1.96	2.0	Reject null hypothesis
C	+2.33	2.0	Inconclusive
D	±2.57	2.0	Inconclusive
E	+1.64	1.0	Inconclusive
F	±2.57	4.0	Reject null hypothesis
G	±2.57	3.0	Reject null hypothesis
H	±2.57	2.0	Inconclusive
I	−1.64	−2.0	Reject null hypothesis

4. Reject the null hypothesis: Not having a sense of smell makes for fewer correct identifications.

In brief, you solve this problem by considering the likelihood of the scenario in which being without a sense of smell makes no difference. If the sense of smell made no difference, the probability of the student studied getting any particular number correct is simply the probability of students in general getting any particular number correct. And since we know the distribution of the number correct that students get in general, that probability can be deter-

mined. It turns out that it would be fairly unlikely to get only 5 correct—so the researcher concludes that not having the sense of smell does make a difference.

To go into the details a bit, the key issue is determining these probabilities. We are told that the number correct for the students in general are "normally distributed." This tells us that the probabilities of getting any particular number correct follow a specific mathematical pattern, the normal curve, sometimes called "bell-shaped," in which most of the cases fall in the middle and progressively fewer occur as the numbers get higher or lower. There are tables showing exactly what proportion of cases fall between the middle and any particular point on the normal curve. These tables use "Z scores," transformed versions of the original scores reflecting the number of standard deviations above the mean. The mean is the ordinary average (the sum of the numbers divided by the number of numbers). The standard deviation can be thought of as the average amount by which scores differ from the mean. (Strictly speaking, it is the square root of the average of the squares of each score's difference from the mean.)

When evaluating the outcome of an experiment, many researchers use a convention of deciding that if a result could have occurred by chance less than 5% of the time under a particular scenario, that scenario will be considered unlikely. The normal curve tables show that the top 5% of the normal curve begins with a Z score of 1.64. Since the normal curve is completely symmetrical, the bottom 5% includes all Z scores below −1.64. Thus the researcher, even before doing the experiment, would probably set the following rule: The scenario in which being without the sense of smell makes no difference will be rejected as unlikely if the number correct, converted to a Z score using the mean and standard deviation for students in general, is less than −1.64.

The actual number correct for the student who could not use the sense of smell was 5. The normal curve for the students in general we are told had a mean of 14 and a standard deviation of 4. Getting 5 correct is 9 below the mean of 14; in terms of standard deviation units of 4 each, it is 9/4 below the mean, for a Z score of −2.25.

Since −2.25 is lower than −1.64, the researcher concludes that the scenario in which being without smell has no effect is unlikely. This is illustrated as follows:

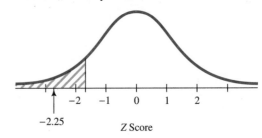

5. The cutoff (.01 level, one-tailed) = −2.326; the Z score on the comparison distribution for the patient studied is +1.2; the experiment is inconclusive.

The explanation is similar to that in Problem 4 except that it may be shorter since the result is opposite to the hypothesis and also you don't need to explain *M*, *SD*, and *Z*.

6. The two means and the "$p < .005$" are crucial. The two means tell us that subjects high on ego development also had higher empathy than those low on ego development. The "$p < .005$" tells us that this difference is statistically significant at the .005 level. This means that if ego development made no difference, the chances of getting two groups of girls who were this different would be less than .005 (less than $\frac{1}{2}$%). Hence we reject that possibility as unlikely and conclude that the level of ego development did make a difference.

Chapter 7

1. The standard deviation of the distribution of means is smaller than the standard deviation of the distribution of the population of individual cases because there is less variation among means of samples of more than one case than there are among individual cases. There is less variation because the likelihood of two extreme scores in the same direction randomly ending up in the same sample is less than the probability of each of those extreme scores being chosen individually.

2. (a) $\sigma_M^2 = \sigma^2/N = 100/2 = 50$; $\sigma_M = \sqrt{50} = 7.07$; (b) 5.77; (c) 5; (d) 4.47; (e) 3.16; (f) 2.24; (g) 1.

3. Since the distribution of the population of individual cases is normal, so will be the distribution of means. Thus, based on the normal curve table, a Z score of at least 1.64 is needed to be in the top 5%. For sample (a): $\sigma_M = \sqrt{36/10} = 1.90$. Z (on the distribution of means) $= (M - \mu)/\sigma_M = (44 - 40)/1.90 = 4/1.90 = 2.11$. Since 2.11 is more extreme than 1.64, this sample is less likely than 5%. The distributions are shown in the graph. Final answer for (b) is more likely than 5%, for (c), less likely, and for (d), more likely than 5%.

4. This is a standard hypothesis-testing problem, except that you cannot compare the reaction time result for the group of women directly to the distribution of reaction times for individual women who don't take the special program. This is because the distribution of women who don't take the special program is a distribution of individual cases, and we have an average of a group of women.

The probability of a group of scores having an extreme mean is considerably less than any one case having an extreme score just by chance. (This is because when taking scores at random, when you take several scores, any extreme scores are likely to be balanced out by less extreme or oppositely extreme scores). Thus the appropriate distribution to compare the mean of the group of 25 scores is a distribution of what would happen if you were to take many random sets of 25 scores and find the mean of each. Such a distribution of many means of samples has the same mean as the original distribution of individual scores (since there is no reason for it to be otherwise), but it is a narrower curve, since the chances of extremes are less. In fact, it is known mathematically that its variance will be exactly the variance of the original distribution of individual cases divided by the number of scores in each sample. This makes a distribution of means with a mean of 1.8 and a standard deviation of .1 ($\sqrt{.5^2/25}$). This will be a normal distribution because a distribution of many means from a normally distributed population is also normal.

The cutoff for significance, using the .01 level and a one-tailed test (the prediction was for a decrease in reaction time), is –2.33. The mean of the group of women tested, 1.5, is 3 standard deviations below the mean of the distribution of means, making it more extreme than the cutoff. Thus we can reject the null hypothesis and conclude that the data support the hypothesis that the program decreases reaction time in women of this age group.

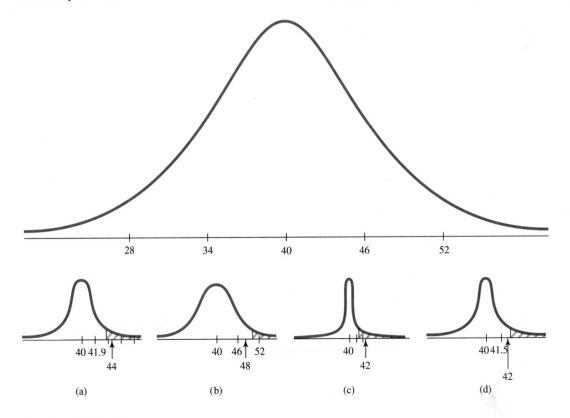

40 41.9	40 46 52
44	48
(a)	(b)

40	40 41.5
42	42
(c)	(d)

5. The distribution of means will be normally distributed with a mean of 5.5 and a standard deviation of .2 ($\sqrt{.8^2/16}$). Using a one-tailed test at the .05 level, the needed cutoff is 1.64. The obtained sample's mean rating of 5.9 is 2 standard deviations above the mean on this distribution: $(5.9 - 5.5)/.2$. Thus the null hypothesis is rejected.

The description to a person who has never had a course in statistics would follow the description in the answer to Problem 4 in Set I Chapter 6 plus the additional material in the answer to Problem 4 in Set I in this chapter.

6.

Conclusion from Hypothesis Testing	Real Status of the Research Hypothesis
	True
(a) Reject null	Decide that more recess improves behavior—correct decision; in fact, it does.
Inconclusive	Decide that the relation of recess to behavior is unknown—poor decision; in fact, more recess improves behavior.
(b) Reject null	Decide that the colorblind distinguish better—correct decision; in fact, they do.
Inconclusive	Decide that whether the colorblind distinguish better is unknown—poor decision; in fact, they do.
(c) Reject null	Decide that former therapy clients are more tolerant—correct decision; they are.
Inconclusive	Decide that whether or not they are more tolerant is unknown—poor decision; they are.
	False
(a) Reject null	Decide that more recess improves behavior—wrong decision; in fact, it does not.
Inconclusive	Decide that the relation of recess to behavior is unknown—good decision; in fact, they are unrelated.
(b) Reject null	Decide that the colorblind distinguish better—wrong decision; in fact, they do not.
Inconclusive	Decide that whether the color blind distinguish better is unknown—good decision; in fact, they do not.
(c) Reject null	Decide that former therapy clients are more tolerant—wrong decision; they are not.
Inconclusive	Decide that whether or not they are more tolerant is unknown—good decision; they aren't.

Chapter 8

1. Alpha is the probability of falsely rejecting the null hypothesis. Beta is the probability of failing to reject the null hypothesis when in fact the null hypothesis is false.

2.

	Z Needed for Significance	σ_M	Score for Significance
(a)	1.64	.4	90.66
(b)	1.64	.4	90.66
(c)	1.64	.2	90.33
(d)	1.64	1.0	91.64
(e)	2.33	.4	90.93
(f)	1.96	.4	90.78

	Z for Significance on the Predicted Population	Beta	Power	Effect Size
(a)	$(90.66 - 91)/.4 = -.85$	.20	.80	1/4
(b)	$(90.66 - 92)/.4 = -3.35$	<.01	>.99	1/2
(c)	$(90.33 - 91)/.2 = -3.35$	<.01	>.99	1/2
(d)	$(91.64 - 91)/1 = .64$	.74	.26	1/4
(e)	$(90.93 - 91)/.4 = -.18$	.43	.57	1/4
(f)	$(90.78 - 91)/.4 = -.55$	.29	.71	1/4

Drawing of overlapping distributions for version (a) appears at the top of page 565.

3. Z needed for significance = 1.64, $\sigma_M = 2$ ($\sqrt{144/36}$), raw score needed for significance = 53.28 (50 + [1.64][2]), corresponding Z score on predicted distribution = $-.86$ ([53.28 – 55]/2), beta = .19, power = .81 (1 – .19).

Explanation: Power is the chance of rejecting the null hypothesis if the research hypothesis is true. To compute power, the first step is to determine the characteristics of the comparison distribution. In this experiment, it will be a distribution of means (of samples of 36 artists each) that is normally distributed (since the population is) with a mean of 50 and a standard deviation of 2 (calculations as shown). To reject the null hypothesis, the sample mean's Z score must be higher than 1.64 (this is a one-tailed test at the .05 level), corresponding to a raw score sample mean of 53.28.

Now come the power computations. The researcher hypothesizes that the mean of the population of artists is 55 (and implicitly that this population is also normal with the same σ of 12). The distribution of means from this population would be normal with mean = 55 and $\sigma_M = 2$. We already determined that any mean above 53.28 will be significant in terms of the comparison distribution. But a score of 53.28 has a Z score of only $-.86$ on the distribution based on the researcher's hypothesis. Using the normal curve table, 81% of the curve is above this point. Assuming that the researcher's predictions are correct, there is an 81% chance that a sample of 36 artists will produce a result high enough to reject the null hypothesis. That is, power is 81%.

The two distributions of means involved and the areas of significance and power are shown at the bottom of page 565.

4. (a) Not affected (that is what the significance level tests).
(b) Probably of small importance (due to small effect size).

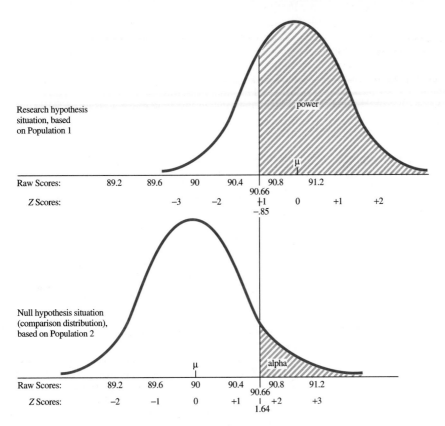

Research hypothesis
situation, based
on Population 1

power

μ

Raw Scores: 89.2   89.6   90   90.4   90.8   91.2

90.66

Z Scores: −3   −2   +1   0   +1   +2

−.85

Null hypothesis situation
(comparison distribution),
based on Population 2

μ

alpha

Raw Scores: 89.2   89.6   90   90.4   90.8   91.2

90.66

Z Scores: −2   −1   0   +1   +2   +3

1.64

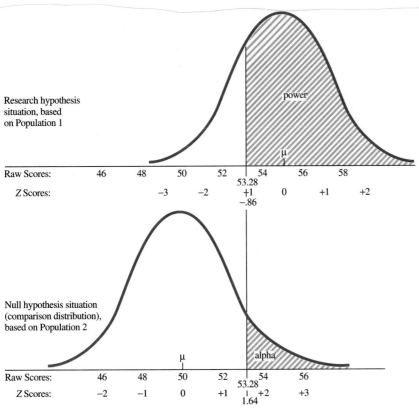

Research hypothesis
situation, based
on Population 1

power

μ

Raw Scores: 46   48   50   52   54   56   58

53.28

Z Scores: −3   −2   +1   0   +1   +2

−.86

Null hypothesis situation
(comparison distribution),
based on Population 2

μ

alpha

Raw Scores: 46   48   50   52   54   56

53.28

Z Scores: −2   −1   0   +1   +2   +3

1.64

5. (a) Increases power; (b) decreases power; (c) increases power; (d) decreases power; (e) decreases power.

6. (a) When planning an experiment, to permit changes of various kinds (or even abandon the project) if power is too low. (Or possibly make the study less costly, for example, by reducing number of subjects, if power is higher than reasonably needed.)

   (b) After a study is done that had nonsignificant results, to evaluate whether the failure of the study should be attributed to the null hypothesis's being false (in the high-power situation) or to inadequate power so that it is still reasonable to think that future research might have a chance of being significant. (Also, in the case of a significant result with a large sample, if power is very high, this suggests that a low effect size is possible, indicating that although the result is significant, it may not be very important.)

Chapter 9

1. (a) t needed ($df = 63, p < .05$, one-tailed) $= -1.671$.
   $S_M = \sqrt{S^2/N} = \sqrt{9/64} = \sqrt{.141} = .38$.
   $t = (M - \mu)/S_M = (11 - 12.40)/.38 = -1.40/.38 = -3.68$; reject null hypothesis.

   (b) t needed $= 2.690$; $S_M = 2.55$; $t = 1.32$; do not reject null hypothesis.

   (c) t needed $= 2.364$; $S_M = .13$; $t = 3.15$; reject null hypothesis.

2. t needed ($df = 9, p < .05$, one-tailed): -1.833.
   $S^2 = \Sigma(X - M)^2/(N - 1) = SS/df = 124/(10 - 1) = 13.78$.
   $M = \Sigma X/N = 280/10 = 28$.
   $S_M = \sqrt{S^2/N} = \sqrt{13.78/10} = 1.17$.
   $\mu = 30$.
   $t = (M - \mu)/S_M = (28 - 30)/1.17 = -1.71$; do not reject null hypothesis.

   Explanation is the same as that for Problem 4 in this chapter, except that here instead of difference scores, actual scores are used, and the expected population mean is the 30 min ($\frac{1}{2}$ h) that the sheriff had promised when a candidate.

3. (a) t needed ($df = 19, p < .05$, one-tailed) $= 1.729$.
   $S_M = \sqrt{S^2/N} = \sqrt{8.29/20} = \sqrt{.415} = .64$.
   $t = (M - \mu)/S_M = (1.7 - 0)/.64 = 2.66$; reject null hypothesis.
   $d = M/S = 1.7/\sqrt{8.29} = .59$.

   (b) t needed $= \pm 1.980$; $S_M = \sqrt{414.53/164} = 1.59$; $t = (2.3 - 0)/1.59 = 1.45$; do not reject null hypothesis; $d = .11$.

   (c) t needed $= -2.624$; $S_M = .52$; $t = -4.23$; reject null hypothesis; $d = -1.1$.

4. t needed ($df = 3, p < .01$, one-tailed) $= 4.541$.
   Difference scores $= 7, 6, -1, 8$; $M = 20/4 = 5$; $S^2 = 50/3 = 16.67$; $S_M = \sqrt{S^2/N} = \sqrt{16.67/4} = \sqrt{4.17} = 2.04$; $t = (5 - 0)/2.04 = 2.45$; do not reject null hypothesis.

   Explanation: The first thing I did was to simplify things by converting the numbers to "difference scores"—preprogram litter minus postprogram litter for each city. Then I found the mean difference score, which was a decrease of 5.

   The next step was to see whether this result represents some real difference due to being in this program. The

alternative is the possibility that this much change could have occurred in four randomly selected cities. That is, we imagine that the average change for cities in general that implement this program is actually 0, and maybe this study just happened to pick four cities that would have decreased this much anyway.

I then determined just how much a group of four cites would have to change before I could conclude that they have changed too much to chalk it up to chance. This required figuring out the characteristics of this hypothetical population of cities in which on the average there is no change. Its mean would be 0 change (by definition). Since I don't know the variance in this hypothetical distribution of cities that don't change, I estimated it from the information in the sample of cities. If the sample was just a chance draw from the hypothetical population, its variance should be representative of the hypothetical population. But because a sample of four is less likely to have quite as high a proportion of extreme cases as the hypothetical infinite population it was drawn from, I had to modify the variance formula to take this into account: Instead of dividing the sum of the squared deviations by the number of cases, I divided it instead by the "degrees of freedom," which is the number of cases minus 1—in this case, 3. As shown in the calculations, this gave an estimated population variance (S^2) of 16.67.

Since I was interested not in individual cities but in a group of four, what I really needed to know was the characteristics of a distribution of all possible means of samples of four drawn from this hypothetical population of individual city change scores. Such a distribution of means will have the same mean (since there is no reason to expect the means of such groups of four drawn randomly to be systematically higher or lower than 0) but will have a smaller variance (because the average of a group of four is less likely to be extreme than any individual case). Fortunately, it is known (and can be proved mathematically) that in such cases, the variance of the distribution of means is the variance of the distribution of individual cases divided by the number in each sample—in this case, 16.67 divided by 4, which comes out to 4.17. The standard deviation of this distribution is thus the square root of 4.17, or 2.04.

It also turns out that if we can assume that the hypothetical population of individual cities' change scores is normally distributed (and we have no reason to think otherwise), the distribution of means of samples from that distribution can be thought of as having a precise known shape, called a t distribution (which has slightly higher tails than a normal curve). Looking in a table for a t distribution for the situation in which there are 3 degrees of freedom used to estimate the population variance, the table shows that there is a less than 1% chance of getting a score that is 4.541 standard deviations from the mean of this distribution.

The mean change score for the present sample of four cities was 5, which would be 2.45 (5/2.04) standard deviations above the mean of 0 change on this distribution of means of change scores. Since this is not as extreme as 4.541, there is more than a 1% chance that these results could have come from a hypothetical distribution with no change—so the researcher would not rule out that possibility, and the experiment would be said to be inconclusive.

The various distributions are illustrated.

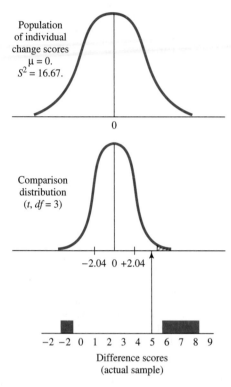

Population of individual change scores $\mu = 0$. $S^2 = 16.67$.

Comparison distribution (t, $df = 3$)

−2.04 0 +2.04

−2 −2 0 1 2 3 4 5 6 7 8 9

Difference scores (actual sample)

5. From Table 9-9: (a) .22; (b) .71; (c) .86; (d) .77; (e) .99.
6. The mean is the ordinary average (the sum of the numbers divided by the number of numbers). The first part of this result thus says that the average scores under bright light were slightly higher than under dim light. But the important part is the last part. By saying that the "difference was not significant," the researcher is telling us that this small degree of difference could easily have been found among the 20 particular individuals tested, even if people in general do not differ between brightly and dimly lit conditions.

The last part—"$t(19) = 1.62$"—refers to the details of how it was determined that the difference was "not significant." The underlying logic depends on first imagining a hypothetical distribution of differences between bright and dim lighting in which the average difference is 0. It will also have a specific amount of variation, which the researcher must estimate on the basis of the variation in the 20 people's differences obtained in the experiment. The formula for estimating this variation requires taking each person's difference minus the mean of all the differences. These "deviation scores" are then each squared and all added up. Dividing this sum by the number of cases (20 in this study) gives the "variance." However, to estimate the variance of the larger hypothetical group of scores, some adjustment must be made: The sum of squared deviations is divided not by the number of cases, but by the number of cases minus 1 (19 in this study).

What is actually needed, however, is to imagine a hypothetical distribution of *averages* of groups of 20 people's differences—the 20 differences for each average coming from our first hypothetical distribution mentioned earlier of individuals' differences in a world in which the overall average difference is 0. This new hypothetical distribution of averages of 20 differences will also have an average of 0, but its variance will be much smaller (because such a distribution of averages will be less likely to have extreme cases). Its variance, in fact, comes out to be the variance of the first hypothetical distribution's variance divided by the number in each group (in this case, 20).

This distribution of averages of groups of 20 difference scores will also have a known shape, called a "t distribution." (Actually, it need not have such a shape, but since the researcher used t in the description, the researcher must have assumed that the appropriate conditions apply.) There are different t distributions according to the number that was used to make the division to estimate the variance of the hypothetical distribution of individual differences—which in our case was 19. (This is where the 19 comes from in the parentheses.)

Finally, it turns out that you can look up in a table how high an average of 20 difference scores would have to be to fall in the highest 5% of such a t distribution. This figure comes out to 1.729 standard deviations (a standard deviation is the square root of the variance, a standard measure of variation) from the average of this distribution of averages. In this particular study, however, the researcher has told us that the number of standard deviations that the average of the actual 20 difference scores would fall above the mean on this hypothetical distribution was only 1.62 (this is the t score). Since this number is not in the top 5% (the part that starts at 1.729), the researcher cannot feel comfortable in ruling out the possibility that this group of 20 could have come from this hypothetical distribution in which the average difference is in fact 0.

It is a conventional rule in psychology that a result is considered "significant" only if its chances of arising from a situation in which there is really no difference are less than 5%.
7. Anxiety: $S_M = \sqrt{S^2/N} = \sqrt{(1.85)^2/100} = \sqrt{.034} = .185$; $t = 1.50/.185 = 8.11$.
Depression: $S_M = \sqrt{(4.23)^2/100} = .423$; $t = 3.08/.423 = 7.28$.
Introversion: $S_M = .222$; $t = .23/.222 = 1.04$.
Neuroticism: $S_M = .421$; $t = .89/.421 = 2.11$.
Explanation of the t test is basically the same as for Problem 6.

Chapter 10

1. Use a t test for dependent means when each subject is tested under two conditions (such as before and after some treatment) and a t test for independent means when each subject is tested under different conditions, so that there is only one score per subject.

2. (a) t needed ($df = 58$, $p < .05$, two-tailed) $= \pm 2.004$; S_p^2 (for equal N) $= (S_1^2 + S_2^2)/2 = (2.4 + 2.8)/2 = 2.6$; $S_{M1}^2 = S_p^2/N_1 = 2.6/30 = .087$; $S_{M2}^2 = .087$; $S_{DIF}^2 = S_{M1}^2 + S_{M2}^2 = .174$; $S_{DIF} = \sqrt{S_{DIF}^2} = \sqrt{.174} = .417$; $t = (M_1 - M_2)/S_{DIF} = (12 - 11.1)/.417 = .9/.417 = 2.16$. Conclusion: Reject the null hypothesis. The difference is significant. Effect size: $d = (M_1 - M_2)/S_p = (12 - 11.1)/\sqrt{2.6} = .9/1.6 = .56$ (approximately medium effect size). Power (from table) $= .47$.

(b) t needed ($df = 58$, $p < .05$, two-tailed) $= \pm 2.004$; S_p^2 (for unequal N) $= [df_1/(df_1 + df_2)](S_1^2) + [df_2/(df_1 + df_2)](S_2^2) = (19/58)(2.4) + (39/58)(2.8) = (.328)(2.4) + (.672)(2.8) = .787 + 1.882 = 2.7$; $S_{M1}^2 = S_p^2/N_1 = 2.7/20 = .135$; $S_{M2}^2 = 2.7/40 = .068$; $S_{DIF}^2 = S_{M1}^2 + S_{M2}^2 = .203$; $S_{DIF} = \sqrt{S_{DIF}^2} = \sqrt{.203} = .451$; $t = (M_1 - M_2)/S_{DIF} = (12 - 11.1)/.451 = .9/.451 = 2.00$. Conclusion: Do not reject the null hypothesis. Difference is not significant. Effect size: $d = .9/\sqrt{2.7} = .55$ (approximately medium effect size). Power: $N' = [(2)(20)(40)]/(20 + 40) = 26.7$; power (from table) is between $.33$ and $.47$.

(c) t needed ($df = 58$, $p < .05$, two-tailed) $= \pm 2.004$; $S_p^2 = (2.2 + 3.0)/2 = 2.6$; $S_{M1}^2 = .087$; $S_{M2}^2 = .087$; $S_{DIF} = .417$; $t = 2.16$. Conclusion: Reject the null hypothesis. The difference is significant. Effect size: $d = .9/\sqrt{2.6} = .56$ (approximately medium effect size). Power $= .47$.

3. t needed with $df = 80$ for a two-tailed test at the .01 level $= \pm 2.639$. TV group: $N = 61$; $M = 24$; $S^2 = 4$. Radio group: $N = 21$; $M = 26$; $S^2 = 6$. $S_p^2 = (60/80)(4) + (20/80)(6) = 3.0 + 1.5 = 4.5$; $S_{M1}^2 = 4.5/61 = .074$; $S_{M2}^2 = 4.5/21 = .214$; $S_{DIF}^2 = .074 + .214 = .288$; $S_{DIF} = .54$; $t = (24 - 26)/.54 = -2/.54 = -3.70$. Reject the null hypothesis; conclude that the theory is supported by the experiment.

Explanation: The mean is the arithmetic average (the sum of the numbers divided by the number of numbers)—in this case, the radio group had a higher average on the test than the TV group. S^2 refers to the estimate of the variance of scores in the general population based on the variance of scores in the group of people studied (called the sample). The variance is a measure of the amount of variation in a group of scores. When estimating the population variance from the variance of the sample, each score's difference from the mean is squared and the sum of these squared differences is divided by the degrees of freedom—the number of subjects in the sample minus 1. (The degrees of freedom represents the amount of unique information available in the sample to use in estimating the population. Using the sample's variance, which is the sum of squared differences divided by the number of cases, would give too small an estimate of the population variance.) In this case, I have two estimates, one from each sample.

Now that I have considered the results given in the problem, let us turn to the issue of how to draw conclusions. The way I frame the question is to ask what is the probability of getting this much difference in knowledge scores between the two groups even if radio versus television made no difference. That is, if the TV and radio groups actually represented two larger populations that were not different, how likely is it that I could have drawn a sample from each population that is this different from the other?

To answer this required figuring out what such nondifferent populations would look like. The estimates of the population variance that I made apply here. In fact, even if the two groups represented different populations, only the means would be different—the variance is assumed to be the same. Hence these are two estimates of the same population variance, and I can average both estimates to get a better estimate still. In averaging, however, I want to give more weight to the estimate based on larger degrees of freedom. So I compute a weighted average, multiplying each estimate by its proportion of the total degrees of freedom and adding up the results. This pooled estimate of the population variance (S_p^2) comes out to 4.5. At this point I had estimated the variance of the populations of individuals' knowledge scores.

Now, because I was interested not in individual scores but in the difference between the mean of a group of 61 and the mean of another group of 21, I needed to figure out what would be the characteristics of a distribution of all possible differences between means of groups of 61 and 21 that are randomly drawn from the two identical populations whose variance I just estimated. This required two steps.

First I needed to figure out the characteristics of an intermediate distribution for each sample—the distribution of means of all possible samples of that size drawn from its population. For the TV group, this would be a distribution of means of samples of 61 each. Such a distribution will have a variance smaller than the variance of the population of individual cases from which the samples were drawn because any one mean is less likely to be extreme than any single score (because the mean of several scores is likely to include some scores that balance out or reduce the effect of any extremes). In fact, it can be shown mathematically that the variance of a distribution of means of all possible samples will be exactly the variance of the parent population of individual cases divided by the number of cases in each sample. For the TV group, this distribution would be 4.5 divided by 61, or .074. The corresponding figure for the radio group is .214.

The second step refers directly to the distribution of differences between means. It is like a distribution that would arise if you took a mean from the distribution of means of all possible samples from the TV group and took one from the comparable distribution for the radio group and computed their difference. After doing this many times, the distribution of the differences so obtained would create a new distribution, of differences between means. Because we are assuming (if radio versus TV made no difference) that the two original populations have the same means, the two distributions of many means of samples should have the same mean. And on the average, the difference between a sample drawn from the TV group and a sample drawn from the radio group should come out to 0 (since sometimes one will be bigger and sometimes the other, but in the long run these random fluctuations should balance out). The variance of this distribution of differences between means will be affected by the variation in both distributions of means—in fact, it will be simply the sum of the two. Thus its variance will be .074 plus .214 or .288. Actually, the variation in such distributions is most often described in terms of what is called the standard deviation (the square root of the variance), which in this case is the square root of .288, or .54.

It also turns out that such distributions of differences between means have a precise known shape, so it is possible to look up in a table the probability of being a certain distance from its mean. The distance is measured in standard deviations. In this case, the table shows that for my distribution (with my total of 80 degrees of freedom), there is less than a 1% chance of getting a score (a difference between means) that is 2.639 or more standard deviations from the mean in either direction. (I took into account both directions because I was studying whether there was a difference in either direction between the TV and radio groups. The "1% level" refers to the conventional point at which psychologists, who are very concerned about the risk of concluding in error that an experiment has made a difference, decide that something is too unlikely to have happened by chance.) I have illustrated these various distributions (see below).

The difference between my particular two means was –2 (24 – 26). This would be 3.70 (2/.54) standard deviations below the mean in the distribution of all possible differences between means of groups of this size. Since this is more extreme than –2.639, I could reject as too unlikely the possibility that I could get a difference this large by taking any two groups of subjects at random

regardless of whether they had been getting their news through TV or radio. Thus the researcher can take the results of this study as support for his or her prediction.

4. t needed ($df = 9$, two-tailed, $p < .05$) = ±2.262. Normals: $M = 36/6 = 6$; $S^2 = 28/5 = 5.6$; Own-name: $M = 48/5 = 9.6$; $S^2 = 77.2/4 = 19.3$; $S_P^2 = (5/9)(5.6) + (4/9)(19.3) = 3.11 + 8.58 = 11.69$; $S_{M1}^2 = 11.69/6 = 1.95$; $S_{M2}^2 = 11.69/5 = 2.34$; $S_{DIF}^2 = 1.95 + 2.34 = 4.29$; $S_{DIF} = 2.07$; $t = (6 – 9.6)/2.07 = -3.6/2.07 = -1.73$.

Do not reject the null hypothesis; the experiment is inconclusive as to whether including the child's name makes a difference. *Note:* This problem actually has a flaw in that it seems to fail to meet the assumption of equal population variances. However, since the result was not significant even using the ordinary procedure, we can assume that it would not be significant using a modified procedure.

Explanation: See the answer to Problem 3.

5. Your answer should explain the following but should be written to explain all the terms and concepts (as in the answer to Problem 3, for example).

This study shows that using a conventional .05 significance level, infants of teenage mothers showed significantly more persistence but were significantly less happy. The results on competence were inconclusive. Since effect size was not reported, the importance of the two significant results is not clear. On the one hand, both

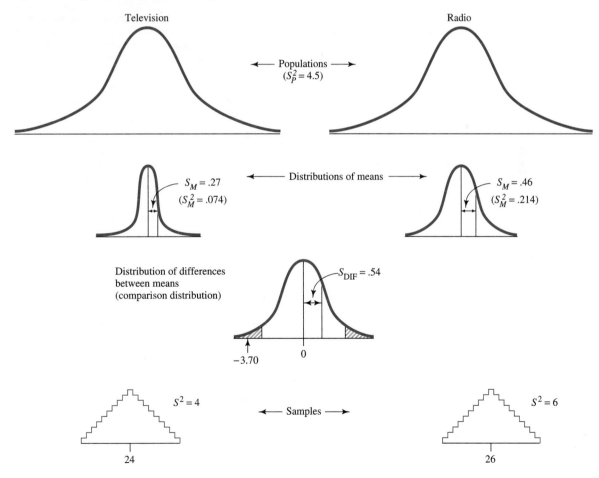

results are more than just barely significant, and 63 is not an extremely large number of subjects. Thus effect size may be high. On the other hand, 63 is a large enough number of subjects, so combined with the clear failure to find significance, it seems that competence may differ only very little, if at all, between these two groups of infants. (Actually, effect size could be calculated, with some ingenuity, from the information available—the t scores, the means, and the number of subjects; what you would need to do is figure out S_p.)

6. Effect size = $(M_1 - M_2)/S_p$.
   2. (a) $.9/\sqrt{2.6} = .9/1.61 = .56$; (b) $.9/\sqrt{2.7} = .9/1.64 = .55$; (c) .56.
   3. $-2/\sqrt{4.5} = -2/2.12 = -.94$.
   4. $-3.6/\sqrt{11.69} = -3.6/3.42 = -1.05$.

Chapter 11

1. (a) F needed ($df = 2, 27; p < .05$) = 3.36; $S_B^2 = (SS/df)(n)$ = $\{[(7.4 - 7)^2 + (6.8 - 7)^2 + (6.8 - 7)^2]/(3 - 1)\}(10) = (.24/2)(10) = 1.2$; $S_W^2 = (.82 + .90 + .80)/3 = .84$; $F = 1.2/.84 = 1.43$; do not reject the null hypothesis, groups are not significantly different at the .05 level. Effect size: $f = \sqrt{1.43}/\sqrt{10} = 1.20/3.16 = .40$ (large effect size). Power = .45.
   (b) F needed ($df = 3, 96; p < .05$) = 2.70 (actually using $df = 3, 95$); $S_B^2 = (164.67)(25) = 4,116.75$; $S_W^2 = (24^2 + 28^2 + 31^2 + 25^2)/4 = 736.5$; $F = 4,116.75/736.5 = 5.59$; reject the null hypothesis; groups are significantly different at the .05 level. Effect size: $f = \sqrt{5.59}/\sqrt{25} = .47$ (large effect size). Power between .85 and .96.
   (c) F needed ($df = 4, 120; p < .05$) = 2.46 (actually using $df = 4, 100$); $S_B^2 = (123.5)(25) = 3,087.5$; $S_W^2 = (24^2 + 18^2 + 31^2 + 25^2 + 27^2)/5 = 735$; $F = 3,087.5/735 = 4.20$; reject null hypothesis; groups are significantly different at the .05 level. Effect size: $f = \sqrt{4.20}/\sqrt{25} = .41$ (large effect size). Power between .90 and .98.

2. (a) F needed ($df = 2, 9; p < .01$) = 8.02;
   Group 1: $M = 8, S^2 = .67$; Group 2: $M = 6, S^2 = .67$;
   Group 3: $M = 4, S^2 = .67$.
   $S_B^2 = (4)(4) = 16$; $S_W^2 = .67$; $F = 16/.67 = 23.88$; reject the null hypothesis; groups are significantly different at the .01 level.
   (b) F needed ($df = 2, 9; p < .01$) = 8.02;
   Group 1: $M = 8, S^2 = 21.33$; Group 2: $M = 6, S^2 = 21.33$; Group 3: $M = 4, S^2 = 21.33$.
   $S_B^2 = (4)(4) = 16$; $S_W^2 = 21.33$; $F = 16/21.33 = .75$; do not reject the null hypothesis; groups are not significantly different at the .01 level.

3. F needed ($df = 2, 9; p < .05$) = 4.26;
   Affective: $M = 6, S^2 = .67$; Cognitive: $M = 10, S^2 = 3.33$; Drug: $M = 10, S^2 = 2.67$.
   $S_B^2 = (5.33)(4) = 21.32$; $S_W^2 = 2.22$; $F = 21.32/2.22 = 9.60$; reject the null hypothesis; there is a significant difference.
   Explanation: The null hypothesis is that the three groups represent populations of length-of-stay scores with equal means (and, as with a t test, we must be able to

assume that they have equal variances). If this null hypothesis is true, then you can estimate the variance of these equal populations in two ways:
(1) You can estimate from the variation within each of the three groups and then average them (just as you would do in a t test for independent means, except now three are being averaged instead of just two). In this case, the three variance estimates were .67, 3.33, and 2.67, which gave a pooled estimate of 2.22—called S_W^2.
(2) Because the means of the three groups are drawn from populations with identical means (assuming that the null hypothesis is true), the actual variation of these means is a basis for estimating the variance of a distribution of all possible means of samples taken from populations of individual cases like any of our populations. In this study, the three means of 6, 10, and 10 yield an estimated variance of 5.33 for this distribution of means. But since this is an estimate of a distribution of means, it must be multiplied by the size of the samples to get an estimate of the parent population of individual cases (this is just the reverse of the dividing you do when going from a population of individual cases to a distribution of means). Thus the estimate based on the variation of the means of groups is 5.33 times 4, or 21.32.
   If the null hypothesis is true, the two estimates should be about the same because they are estimates of essentially the same populations. But if the null hypothesis is false and the three populations these groups represent have different means, the estimate based on the variation among the group means will be bigger than the one based on the variation within the groups. The ratio of the estimate based on the variation among the means to the estimate based on the variation within the groups is called an F ratio. If the null hypothesis is true, this ratio will be about 1; if false, bigger than 1. In this example, our F ratio is 21.32 to 2.22: 21.32/2.22 = 9.60.
   Statisticians have constructed tables of what happens when you compute F ratios based on the situation in which you randomly take a group of four cases from each of three identical populations. This is the situation in which our null hypothesis is true. Looking at these tables, it turns out that there is less than a 5% chance of getting an F ratio larger than 4.26. Since our actual F ratio is bigger than this, the null hypothesis is rejected.

4. F needed ($df = 2, 147; p < .01$) = 4.82 (actually using $df = 2, 100$); $S_B^2 = (.09)(50) = 4.5$; $S_W^2 = (5.2 + 5.8 + 4.8)/3 = 5.27$; $F = 4.5/5.27 = .85$; do not reject the null hypothesis; groups are not significantly different at the .01 level.
   Explanation: See the answer to Problem 3; also use material in the answers to the t test problems in Chapter 10.

5. This result supports the hypothesis that inmates in the three types of prisons have different degrees of need for mental health care. The effect size is .38. (A full explanation would include the material in the answer to Problem 3 plus material in the answers to the t test problems in Chapter 10.)

6. Power = .45; 21 per group (63 total) needed for 80% power.

Chapter 12

1. $df_T = N - 1 = 12 - 1 = 11$.
$df_W = df_1 + df_2 + \cdots + df_{Last} = (4 - 1) + (4 - 1) + (4 - 1)$
$= 3 + 3 + 3 = 9$.
$df_B = N_G - 1 = 3 - 1 = 2$.
F needed for $df = 2, 9$ at the .01 level = 8.02.

Group 1

X	$X - GM$		$X - M$		$M - GM$	
	Dev	Dev²	Dev	Dev²	Dev	Dev²
8	2	4	0	0	2	4
8	2	4	0	0	2	4
7	1	1	−1	1	2	4
9	3	9	1	1	2	4
Σ 32		18		2		16

$M = 32/4 = 8$.

Group 2

X	$X - GM$		$X - M$		$M - GM$	
	Dev	Dev²	Dev	Dev²	Dev	Dev²
6	0	0	0	0	0	0
6	0	0	0	0	0	0
5	−1	1	−1	1	0	0
7	1	1	1	1	0	0
Σ 24		2		2		0

$M = 24/4 = 6$.

Group 3

X	$X - GM$		$X - M$		$M - GM$	
	Dev	Dev²	Dev	Dev²	Dev	Dev²
4	−2	4	0	0	−2	4
4	−2	4	0	0	−2	4
3	−3	9	−1	1	−2	4
5	−1	1	1	1	−2	4
Σ 16		18		2		16

$M = 16/4 = 4$.

$GM = (32 + 24 + 16)/12 = 72/12 = 6$.

$SS_T = 18 + 2 + 18 = 38$.
$SS_W = 2 + 2 + 2 = 6$.
$SS_B = 16 + 0 + 16 = 32$.

Analysis of variance table:

Source	SS	df	MS	F
Between	32	2	16	23.88
Within	6	9	.67	
Total	38	11		

Conclusion: Reject the null hypothesis.

All df as in Chapter 11; MS_B, MS_W, and $F = S_B^2$, S_W^2, and F of Chapter 11.

2. F needed ($df = 3, 5$; $p < .01$) = 12.06.

Source	SS	df	MS	F
Between	298.89	3	99.63	41.51
Within	12	5	2.4	

Conclusion: Reject the null hypothesis.

3. (i) (a) $M_1 = 4$; $M_2 = 1$; $M_3 = 2$.
(b) F needed ($df = 2, 6$; $p < .05$) = 5.14. (*Note: GM =* 2.33.)

Source	SS	df	MS	F
Between	14	2	7	7.00
Within	6	6	1	

Conclusion: Reject the null hypothesis.

(c) $R^2 = 14/20 = .70$.
(ii) (a) $M_1 = 4$; $M_2 = 1$; $M_3 = 2$.
(b) F needed ($df = 2, 6$; $p < .05$) = 5.14.
(*Note: GM =* 1.89.)

Source	SS	df	MS	F
Between	12.89	2	6.45	4.85
Within	8.00	6	1.33	

Conclusion: Do not reject the null hypothesis.

(c) $R^2 = 12.89/20.89 = .62$.
4. F needed ($df = 2, 9$; $p < .05$) = 4.26.

Source	SS	df	MS	F
Between	84	2	42	9.95
Within	38	9	4.22	

Conclusion: Reject the null hypothesis. There is a significant difference in self-esteem among teacher types.

Explanation: The overall logic is to examine whether the variation in self-esteem among the three samples could have occurred more than 5% of the time if in fact the three samples had been drawn at random from three populations of teachers with the same mean self-esteem level. Specifically, the procedure is to consider that if they were just randomly drawn samples, the variation in self-esteem level for each group of teachers would be a reasonable basis for estimating the population's variation, as would the variation of the means of the groups (since any variation among these means can only be due to variation in scores within the three populations). If both estimates are the same, their ratio should be 1:1, or 1. But if the groups are really from populations with different means, the estimate of the variation from the means of the groups should be larger than that based on the variation within each group of teachers, so the ratio (if the between-group variation is put on top) would be more than 1.

Because the number of cases in each group is unequal, it is not simple to pool the information from the three samples (or even to determine precisely the variation among the three groups) because the information provided by the groups is of different weights. However, there is a procedure to simplify this process. It makes use of the principle that for each score, its deviation from the overall mean of all cases is equal to its deviation from the mean of its own group plus the deviation of the mean of its group from the overall mean. It also turns out (and can be proved mathematically) that if you square each of these different deviations, the sum of all the squared deviations from the grand mean is equal to the sum of the squared deviations of each score from its mean plus the sum of the squared deviation of each score's group's mean from the grand mean. The latter two sums of squares, when divided by the degrees of freedom involved in each computation, yield the two estimates of the population variance.

In the present case, the sum of the squared deviations of each score's group's mean from the overall mean (of 6) was 84. Since only three group's means are involved, the degrees of freedom are 2, and the population variance estimate is 84/2, or 42. Similarly, the sum of each score's squared deviation from its group's mean was 38. The total degrees of freedom (each group's number of scores minus 1 for all groups) was 9, making the population variance estimate using the within-group variations 4.22 (38/9).

The overall ratio of estimated population variance based on the variation among the groups to the estimated population variance based on the variation within the groups is 9.95 (42/4.22). This is called the F ratio.

It turns out that the distribution of all possible F ratios is known—though it differs with the degrees of freedom on which the between- and within-group variance estimates are based. In this case, looking up the point at which an F would occur 5% of the time or less is 4.26 on a distribution of F ratios based on 2 and 9 degrees of freedom. Since 9.95 is a considerably larger F ratio than the minimum needed of 4.26, we can conclude that there is a less than 5% chance of getting this much variation among our groups if these self-esteem levels had been actually drawn by chance from three populations of teachers with the same mean.

5. F needed ($df = 2, 7; p < .05) = 4.74$.

Source	SS	df	MS	F
Between	66	2	33	9.62
Within	24	7	3.43	

Conclusion: Reject the null hypothesis.

Explanation: See the answer to Problem 4 and answers to problems in earlier chapters.

6. This table shows results of overall comparisons among the three different activity groups on enjoyment and the other questions they were asked. For each comparison, the table gives the mean (average) rating for each group for each question. The crucial question of interest to these researchers is whether the differences between any two groups' means on a particular question is greater than would be expected by chance—what is called the "statis-tical significance" of the difference. (Sometimes researchers in a situation like this would examine whether, on each question, the averages of all three groups vary among themselves more than would be expected by chance; the statistical significance of that comparison would be evaluated using what is called an "analysis of variance.")

The note at the bottom of the table is very important. It says, "Means with different subscripts differ significantly at $p < .05$." This indicates that for any one question, if the subscripts (the little letters) by two means are different, then the probability is below .05 (that is, less than 5%) that people in general (of the kind used in this study) doing these two tasks actually would, on the average, rate them the same.

On the enjoyment question, the subscripts are different for all three means (that is, one is an a, one a b, and one a c). This indicates that each mean is significantly different from each other mean—that the Hidden Words activity mean is significantly different from the Copying activity mean, that the Hidden Words activity mean is significantly different from the Lettering mean, and that the Copying activity mean is significantly different from the Lettering mean. Taking into account how high the numbers are in each of the means, this says that we have strong evidence that people in general, on the average, would enjoy the Hidden Words activity more than either of the other two and would enjoy the Lettering activity more than Copying.

On perceived competence, the means for the Hidden Words activity and the Copying activity were both significantly higher than the mean for Lettering, but there was no significant difference between the Hidden Words and the Copying activity.

Chapter 13

1. (a) One possible example: A researcher investigated the difference in heat responsiveness among the different fingers on the two hands. One hundred subjects were asked to respond to very slight changes in heat applied to one of their fingers. The 100 subjects were randomly assigned to one of 10 conditions involving the five fingers and the two hands:

		Finger Used				
		Thumb	*First*	*Second*	*Third*	*Fourth*
Hand Used	Right					
	Left					

(b) One possible example: A researcher studying reading skill compares students receiving two kinds of reading instruction, given in either third or fourth grade, to students who scored either high or low on an intelligence test:

		Instruction Method			
		I		II	
		Third grade	*Fourth grade*	*Third grade*	*Fourth grade*
Intelligence	*High*				
	Low				

2. (i) Main effects for class and age; interaction effect. Income is greater in general for upper-class and for older individuals, but the combination of older and upper class has a higher income than would be expected just from the effects of either variable alone.

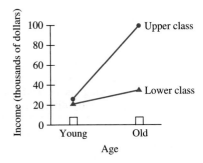

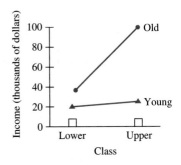

(ii) No main effects; interaction effect. Neither type of college nor type of major, by itself, predicts grades. But there is a clear pattern if one considers the combinations: Grades are highest for community college arts majors and for liberal arts college science majors.

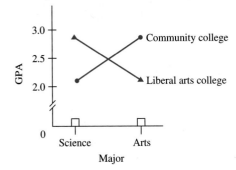

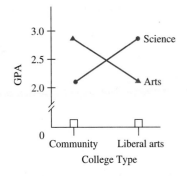

(iii) Both main effects significant; no interaction. Females miss fewer days per month than males; those who exercise miss fewer days per month than controls. Each combination misses the number of days you would expect knowing their level of each independent variable separately.

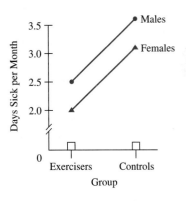

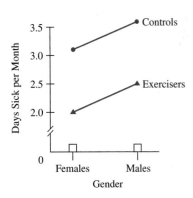

(iv) Main effect for city and price range, plus an interaction. Restaurant quality is different in different cities, with New York highest and Chicago lowest. Restaurant quality is different in different price ranges, with expensive the best and inexpensive the least. The two factors do not simply combine, however: Price makes more difference in New York than in the other cities.

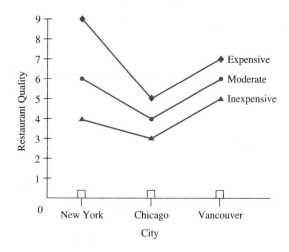

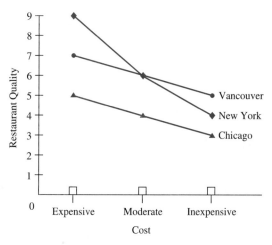

3. The answers are examples only.

Sport

(a)

Condition	Baseball	Football	Basketball	
With motivational program	10	5	6	7
Without motivational program	10	5	6	7
	10	5	6	

(b)

Condition	Baseball	Football	Basketball	
With motivational program	6	6	6	6
Without motivational program	10	10	10	10
	8	8	8	

(c)

Condition	Baseball	Football	Basketball	
With motivational program	6	7	8	7
Without motivational program	8	9	10	9
	7	8	9	

(d)

Condition	Baseball	Football	Basketball	
With motivational program	6	7	8	7
Without motivational program	10	9	8	9
	8	8	8	

(e)

Condition	Baseball	Football	Basketball	
With motivational program	6	7	8	7
Without motivational program	6	8	10	8
	6	7.5	9	

4. (a) Sport effect, .94; condition effect, .97; interaction effect, .94.
(b) Sport, 66; condition, 54; interaction, 66. Thus, at least 66 are needed.

5. F needed for main effect for Diagnosis ($df = 1, 6; p < .05$) = 5.99.
F needed for main effect for Therapy ($df = 2, 6; p < .05$) = 5.14.
F needed for interaction effect ($df = 2, 6; p < .05$) = 5.14.

Therapy A

	X	$(X - GM)^2$	$(X - M)^2$	$(M_C - GM)^2$	$(M_R - GM)^2$	Int^2
I	6	0	4	1	9	0
	2	16	4	1	9	0
M	4	16	8	2	18	0
II	11	25	1	1	9	0
	9	9	1	1	9	0
M	10	34	2	2	18	0

M_C 7

Therapy B

	X	$(X - GM)^2$	$(X - M)^2$	$(M_C - GM)^2$	$(M_R - GM)^2$	Int^2
I	3	9	1	1	9	0
	1	25	1	1	9	0
M	2	34	2	2	18	0
II	7	1	1	1	9	0
	9	9	1	1	9	0
M	8	10	2	2	18	0

M_C 5

Therapy C

	X	$(X-GM)^2$	$(X-M)^2$	$(M_C-GM)^2$	$(M_R-GM)^2$	Int^2	
I	2	16	1	0	9	0	
	4	4	1	0	9	0	
M	3	20	2	0	18	0	3
II	8	4	1	0	9	0	
	10	16	1	0	9	0	
M	9	20	2	0	18	0	9
M_C	6					$GM = 6$	

$SS_T = 16 + 34 + 20 + 34 + 10 + 20 = 134.$
$SS_W = 8 + 2 + 2 + 2 + 2 + 2 = 18.$
$SS_C = 2 + 2 + 0 + 2 + 2 + 0 = 8.$
$SS_R = 18 + 18 + 18 + 18 + 18 + 18 = 108.$
$SS_I = 0 + 0 + 0 + 0 + 0 + 0 = 0.$

Means:

	A	B	C	
I	4	2	3	3
II	10	8	9	9
	7	5	6	

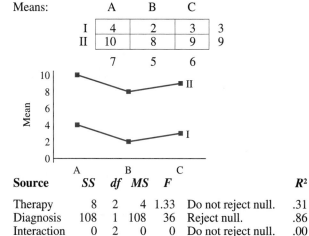

Source	SS	df	MS	F		R^2
Therapy	8	2	4	1.33	Do not reject null.	.31
Diagnosis	108	1	108	36	Reject null.	.86
Interaction	0	2	0	0	Do not reject null.	.00
Within cells	18	6	3			

Description of results in words: These results indicate that there is a significant difference in effectiveness between the two diagnostic categories—therapy is more effective for those with Diagnosis II. However, there was no significant difference among types of therapy, and the types of therapy were not significantly differentially effective for the different diagnostic types. The effect size for the significant effect was extremely large.

6. F needed for main effect for Likability ($df = 1, 8$; $p < .05$) = 5.14.
F needed for main effect for Nervousness ($df = 1, 8$; $p < .05$) = 5.14.
F needed for interaction effect ($df = 1, 8$; $p < .05$) = 5.14.

Likable

	X	$(X-GM)^2$	$(X-M)^2$	$(M_R-GM)^2$	$(M_C-GM)^2$	Int^2
Nervous	7	4	0	0	0	4
	8	9	1	0	0	4
	6	1	1	0	0	4
M	7	14	2	0	0	12
Not Nervous	3	4	0	0	0	4
	3	4	0	0	0	4
	3	4	0	0	0	4
	3	12	0	0	0	12
M_C	5					

Not Likable

	X	$(X-GM)^2$	$(X-M)^2$	$(M_R-GM)^2$	$(M_C-GM)^2$	Int^2	
Nervous	3	4	0	0	0	4	
	4	1	1	0	0	4	
	2	9	1	0	0	4	
M	3	14	2	0	0	12	5
Not Nervous	7	4	0	0	0	4	
	5	0	4	0	0	4	
	9	16	4	0	0	4	
	7	20	8	0	0	12	5
M_C	5					$GM = 5$	

$SS_T = 60.$
$SS_W = 12.$
$SS_C = 0.$
$SS_R = 0.$
$SS_I = 48$

Means:

	Likable	Not Likable	
Nervous	7	3	5
Not Nervous	3	7	5
	5	5	

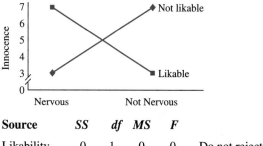

Source	SS	df	MS	F	
Likability	0	1	0	0	Do not reject the null hypothesis.
Nervousness	0	1	0	0	Do not reject the null hypothesis.
Interaction	48	1	48	24	Reject the null hypothesis.
Within cells	12	8	2		

Explanation: These results indicate that there is a significant interaction between nervousness and likability, which in this case means that when the defendant is likable, he is more likely to be rated innocent if he is nervous; but if he is not likable, he is more likely to be rated innocent if he is not nervous. (Perhaps, with a likable person, you can empathize with his nervousness on the stand, and if he were not nervous, you might suspect something funny. With a nonlikable person, nervousness may be a tip-off that he is guilty, but if he is not nervous, it suggests that he has nothing to hide.) There was no overall significant effect for likable or not or for nervous or not—though with the very small sample sizes involved, failures to reject the null hypothesis should not be taken as evidence that such an effect does not exist.

The computation of the significance in this experiment is much like a one-way analysis of variance using the structural model approach. The within-group sum of squares and degrees of freedom are computed in the usual way, considering each of the four cells as its own group. However, in this case, each between-group deviation is divided into parts. One part considers the variation between likability versus not. The deviations for this are computed for each subject by taking the mean for all subjects in that subject's liking versus not-liking condition minus the grand mean. These are then squared and summed to get a sum of squares. The same thing is then done for nervous versus not. The degrees of freedom for each is the number of levels minus one—for example, since there are two levels of likability (likable and not), it has 1 degree of freedom.

This still leaves a part of the between-group effect that considers variations among the means of each of the four subgroups that are not simply the result of summing the effects of likability and nervousness—that is, any variation between likability groups that is different according to which nervousness group they are in. The deviation for this interaction effect is found by taking the deviation of the score from the overall grand mean and then subtracting from this the other three deviations (the score minus its group's mean and those for its likability mean minus the grand mean and for its nervousness mean minus the grand mean). This remainder deviation is then squared and summed to become the interaction sum of squares. Its degrees of freedom are what are left over in the total between-group degrees of freedom. Since there are four subgroups, between-group $df = 3$, and since we have used 1 for likability or not and 1 for nervous or not, that leaves 1 df for the interaction. (All of the computations are shown.)

7. The findings of this study support the hypothesis that female subjects see the person doing the act as more sexist than male subjects do, and this is true regardless of whether the person doing the act is male or female. However, this effect appears to be of relatively small magnitude compared to typical effects in psychology—its "proportion of variance accounted for" is about 3%, while a small effect is considered to be about 1% and a medium effect is about 6%. The findings also support the hypothesis that both male and female subjects who read accounts of people acting in a sexist way toward a female see the act as more sexist if the perpetrator is male. This effect is more substantial, having a proportion of variance accounted for of about 8%. Finally, the finding that there was no significant interaction indicates that the data are inconclusive with regard to the possibility that the difference between male and female subjects in their ratings is greater depending on the sex of the perpetrator of the sexist act. However, although the result is inconclusive, the large number of subjects in this study suggests that if any such interaction effect does exist, it is probably rather small. In fact it can be calculated that if this interaction really exists and is of medium magnitude compared to psychology research generally, there is about a 90% chance it would have shown up unambiguously in this study.

Chapter 14

1. (a) χ^2 needed ($df = 5 - 1 = 4$, 5%) = 9.488.

Category	O	Expected	$O - E$	$(O - E)^2$	$(O - E)^2/E$
A	19	(.2)(50) = 10	9	81	8.10
B	11	(.2)(50) = 10	1	1	.10
C	10	(.4)(50) = 20	−10	100	5.00
D	5	(.1)(50) = 5	0	0	0.00
E	5	(.1)(50) = 5	0	0	0.00
Total	50		50	0	χ^2 = 13.20

Conclusion: Reject the null hypothesis.

(b) χ^2 needed ($df = 3 - 1 = 2$, 5%) = 5.992.

Category	O	Expected	$O - E$	$(O - E)^2$	$(O - E)^2/E$
I	100	(.3)(300) = 90	10	100	1.11
II	100	(.5)(300) = 150	−50	2,500	16.67
III	100	(.2)(300) = 60	40	1,600	26.67
Total	300		300	0	χ^2 = 44.45

Conclusion: Reject the null hypothesis.

(c) χ^2 needed ($df = 4 - 1 = 3$, 5%) = 7.815.

Category	O	Expected	$O - E$	$(O - E)^2$	$(O - E)^2/E$
1	38	(100/500)(200) = 40	−2	4	.10
2	124	(300/500)(200) = 120	4	16	.13
3	22	(50/500)(200) = 20	2	4	.20
4	16	(50/500)(200) = 20	−4	16	.80
Total	200		200	0	χ^2 = 1.23

Conclusion: Do not reject the null hypothesis.

(d) χ^2 needed ($df = 3 - 1 = 2$, 5%) = 5.992.

	O	Expected	$O - E$	$(O - E)^2$	$(O - E)^2/E$
Arts	37	30	7	49	1.63
Sciences	21	30	−9	81	2.70
Humanities	32	30	2	4	.13
Total	90	90	0		χ^2 = 4.46

Conclusion: Do not reject the null hypothesis.

2. χ^2 needed ($df = 4 - 1 = 3$, 5%) = 7.815.

Season	O	Expected	$O - E$	$(O - E)^2$	$(O - E)^2/E$
Winter	28	(1/4)(128) = 32	− 4	16	.50
Spring	33	(1/4)(128) = 32	1	1	.03
Summer	16	(1/4)(128) = 32	−16	256	8.00
Fall	51	(1/4)(128) = 32	19	361	11.28
Total	128		128	0	χ^2 = 19.81

Conclusion: Reject the null hypothesis.

Explanation: If the seasons make no difference, we would expect about 25% of new clients each season (for last year, 25% of the 128 total comes to 32). Are last year's actual numbers in each season so discrepant from these expectations that we should conclude that in general the numbers of new clients are not equally distributed over the seasons?

Chi-square is an index of the degree of difference between observed and expected results. For each category (the four seasons in our case), you compute that discrepancy, square it, and divide by the expected number; then you add up the results. In the winter, 28 less 32 is -4, squared is 16, divided by 32 is 5. Doing the same for the other three seasons and adding up the four gives a total chi-square of 19.81. (Chi-square uses squared discrepancies so that the result is not affected by the directions of the differences. It is divided by the expected number to reduce the impact of the raw number of cases on the result.)

Statisticians have determined mathematically what would happen if you took an infinite number of samples from a population with a fixed proportion of cases in each category and computed chi-square for each such sample. The distribution of such chi-squares depends only on the number of categories free to take on different expected values. (Since the total number expected is the total number of cases, if you know the expected number for any three categories, the number expected for the fourth is easy to determine.) A table of the chi-square distribution when three categories are free to vary shows that there is only a 5% chance of getting a chi-square of 7.815 or greater. Since our chi-square is larger than this, the observed result differs from the expected more than we would reasonably expect by chance—the number of new clients, in the long run, is probably not equal over the four seasons.

3. (a) $df = (N_C - 1)(N_R - 1) = (2 - 1)(2 - 1) = 1$; χ^2 needed $(df = 1, 1\%) = 6.635$.

10 (13)	16 (13)	26 (50%)
16 (13)	10 (13)	26 (50%)
26	26	52

$$\chi^2 = \frac{(10-13)^2}{13} + \frac{(16-13)^2}{13} + \frac{(16-13)^2}{13} + \frac{(10-13)^2}{13}$$
$$= .69 + .69 + .69 + .69 = 2.76.$$

Do not reject the null hypothesis.
$\phi = \sqrt{\chi^2/N} = \sqrt{2.76/52} = \sqrt{.053} = .23.$

(b) $df = (N_C - 1)(N_R - 1) = (2 - 1)(2 - 1) = 1$; χ^2 needed $(df = 1, 1\%) = 6.635$.

100 (103)	106 (103)	206 (50%)
106 (103)	100 (103)	206 (50%)
206	206	412

$$\chi^2 = \frac{(100-103)^2}{103} + \frac{(106-103)^2}{103} + \frac{(106-103)^2}{103} + \frac{(100-103)^2}{103}$$
$$= .09 + .09 + .09 + .09 = .36.$$

Do not reject the null hypothesis.
$\phi = \sqrt{.36/412} = \sqrt{.0009} = .03.$

(c) $df = (N_C - 1)(N_R - 1) = (2 - 1)(2 - 1) = 1$; χ^2 needed $(df = 1, 1\%) = 6.635$.

100 (130)	160 (130)	260 (50%)
160 (130)	100 (130)	260 (50%)
260	260	520

$$\chi^2 = \frac{(100-130)^2}{130} + \frac{(160-130)^2}{130} + \frac{(160-130)^2}{130}$$
$$+ \frac{(100-130)^2}{130}$$
$$= 6.92 + 6.92 + 6.92 + 6.92 = 27.68.$$

Reject the null hypothesis.
$\phi = \sqrt{27.68/520} = \sqrt{.0532} = .23.$

(d) $df = (N_C - 1)(N_R - 1) = (3 - 1)(2 - 1) = 2$; χ^2 needed $(df = 2, 1\%) = 9.211$.

10 (13)	16 (13)	10 (10)	36 50%
16 (13)	10 (13)	10 (10)	36 50%
26	26	20	72

$$\chi^2 = \frac{(10-13)^2}{13} + \frac{(16-13)^2}{13} + \frac{(16-13)^2}{13} + \frac{(10-13)^2}{13}$$
$$+ \frac{(10-10)^2}{10} + \frac{(10-10)^2}{10}$$
$$= .69 + .69 + .69 + .69 + 0 + 0 = 2.76.$$

Do not reject the null hypothesis.
Cramer's $\phi = \sqrt{\chi^2/(N)(df_S)} = \sqrt{2.76/(72)(1)}$
$$= \sqrt{.0383} = .20.$$

(e) $df = (N_C - 1)(N_R - 1) = (3 - 1)(2 - 1) = 2$; χ^2 needed $(df = 2, 1\%) = 9.211$.

10 (13)	16 (13)	16 (16)	42 (50%)
16 (13)	10 (13)	16 (16)	42 (50%)
26	26	32	84

$$\chi^2 = \frac{(10-13)^2}{13} + \frac{(16-13)^2}{13} + \frac{(16-13)^2}{13}$$
$$+ \frac{(10-13)^2}{13} + \frac{(16-16)^2}{16} + \frac{(16-16)^2}{16}$$
$$= .69 + .69 + .69 + .69 + 0 + 0 = 2.76$$

Do not reject the null hypothesis.
Cramer's $\phi = \sqrt{2.76/(84)(1)} = \sqrt{.0329} = .18.$

(f) $df = (N_C - 1)(N_R - 1) = (3 - 1)(2 - 1) = 2$; χ^2 needed $(df = 2, 1\%) = 9.211$

10 (12)	16 (12)	10 (12)	36 46%
16 (14)	10 (14)	16 (14)	42 54%
26	26	26	78

$$\chi^2 = \frac{(10-12)^2}{12} + \frac{(16-12)^2}{12} + \frac{(10-12)^2}{12}$$

$$+ \frac{(16-14)^2}{14} + \frac{(10-14)^2}{14} + \frac{(16-14)^2}{14}$$

$$= .33 + 1.33 + .33 + .29 + 1.14 + .29 = 3.71$$

Do not reject the null hypothesis.

Cramer's $\phi = \sqrt{3.71/(78)(1)} = \sqrt{.0476} = .22$

4. $df = (N_C - 1)(N_R - 1) = (3-1)(2-1) = 2$; χ^2 needed $(df = 2, 5\%) = 5.992$

Device Used
in Their Room

		Word			
		Typewriter	Processor	Neither	
Implement Used for Notes	Pen	42 (39)	62 (65)	26 (26)	130 (65%)
	Pencil	18 (21)	38 (35)	14 (14)	70 (35%)
		60	100	40	200

$$\chi^2 = \frac{(42-39)^2}{39} + \frac{(62-65)^2}{65} + \frac{(26-26)^2}{26} + \frac{(18-21)^2}{21}$$

$$+ \frac{(38-35)^2}{35} + \frac{(14-14)^2}{14}$$

$$= .23 + .14 + 0 + .43 + .26 + 0 = 1.06$$

Do not reject the null hypothesis.

Cramer's $\phi = \sqrt{1.06/(200)(1)} = \sqrt{.0053} = .07$

Explanation: Since 65% of all subjects use pens when taking notes, if pen versus pencil and device used in their room are *not* related, 65% of the people in *each* in-room category should use pens when taking notes. For example, you'd expect 39 of the 60 students who use a typewriter to write with a pen when taking notes. Are the survey results so discrepant from these expectations that we should conclude that the implement that students use to take notes with *is* related to the device that they use to write with in their room?

Chi-square is an index of the degree of difference between observed and expected results. For each combination of the 2 × 3 arrangement, you compute that discrepancy, square it, and divide by the expected number; then you add up the results. In the pen-typewriter combination, 42 minus 39 is 3, squared is 9, divided by 39 is .23. Doing the same for the other five combinations and adding them all up gives 1.06. (Chi-square uses squared discrepancies so that the result is not affected by the directions of the differences. It is divided by the expected number to adjust for the impact of relatively different numbers of cases expected in the combinations.)

Statisticians have determined mathematically what would happen if you took an infinite number of samples from a population with a fixed proportion of cases in each of several groupings and computed chi-square for each

such sample. The distribution of such chi-squares depends only on the number of groupings free to take on different expected values. (For each in-their-room category, if you know the figure for students who take notes with a pen, the figure for those who take notes with a pencil is easily determined. And of the three in-their-room categories for the pen group, if you know two of them, the third is easy to determine because they must add up to the total who use a pen. So only two combinations are "free to vary.")

A table of the chi-square distribution when two groupings are free to vary shows that there is only a 5% chance of getting a chi-square of 5.992 or greater. Since our chi-square is smaller than this, the observed numbers in each category differ from the expected numbers less than they would have to before we would be willing to reject the idea that the implement that people use to take notes is unrelated to the device that they use to write with in their room. The survey is inconclusive.

We can, however, estimate the actual degree of linkage between implement use in class and device use in-their-room. The procedure is called "Cramer's phi," calculated in this case by dividing the computed chi-square by the number of people included in the analysis, then taking the square root of the results—in this case, this comes out to .07. This statistic ranges from 0 (no relationship) to 1 (a perfect relationship; knowing a person's status on one of the dimensions, such as implement use in class, would let you perfectly predict their status on the other dimension, such as what they write with at home). Thus, .07 is a quite low figure. (In fact, Cramer's phi is comparable to what is called a correlation coefficient, and in psychology .07 is very low compared to the correlations found in studies.)

Looking at this another way, we can ask, if there really is a moderate relationship, what is the chance that this whole process would have led to a positive conclusion? Statisticians have provided tables that give this probability. In this case, it turns out that there would be a 97% chance. Thus, given the result of this study, if any relationship exists, it is almost surely fairly small.

5. $df = (N_C - 1)(N_R - 1) = (3-1)(3-1) = 4$; χ^2 needed $(df = 4, 5\%) = 9.488$

	Community			
	A	B	C	Total
For	12 (9.8)	6 (4.2)	3 (7)	21 (23.33%)
Against	18 (16.8)	3 (7.2)	15 (12)	36 (40.00%)
No opinion	12 (15.4)	9 (6.6)	12 (11)	33 (36.67%)
Total	42	18	30	90

$$\chi^2 = \frac{(12-9.8)^2}{9.8} + \frac{(6-4.2)^2}{4.2} + \frac{(3-7)^2}{7} + \frac{(18-16.8)^2}{16.8}$$

$$+ \frac{(3-7.2)^2}{7.2} + \frac{(15-12)^2}{12} + \frac{(12-15.4)^2}{15.4} + \frac{(9-6.6)^2}{6.6}$$

$$+ \frac{(12-11)^2}{11}$$

$$= .49 + .77 + 2.29 + .09 + 2.45 + .75 + .75 + .87 + .09$$
$$= 8.55$$

Do not reject the null hypothesis.

Cramer's $\phi = \sqrt{8.55/(90)(2)} = \sqrt{8.55/180} = \sqrt{.05} = .22$

Power for a small effect = .11; medium = .66; large = .99. (Based on $N = 100$)

Explanation: See the answer to Problem 4.

6. Blass has used the chi-square test of independence to test whether the extent to which subjects obey the command to hurt another person is independent of (unrelated to) the country they are in. The significant chi-square (as indicated by "$p < .01$") means that the chance is less than 1% of getting levels of obedience this different between the two groups if in fact obedience and country were independent. In fact, there is a considerable degree of association, which can be measured statistically using the phi coefficient ($\phi = \sqrt{\chi^2/N} = \sqrt{10.77/90} = \sqrt{.0496} = .35$), which in this case is comparable to a moderate-sized association in comparison to results found in psychology research generally.

The explanation should also explain chi-square more deeply, following the material in the answer to Problem 4.

Chapter 15

1.

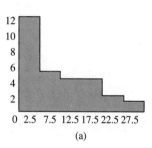

(a)

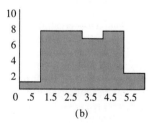

(b)

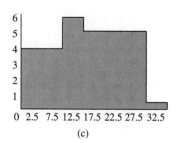

(c)

Untransformed		Square Root		Ranks	
0–4	12	0–.9	1	0–4.9	4
5–9	5	1–1.9	7	5–9.9	4
10–14	4	2–2.9	7	10–14.9	6
15–19	4	3–3.9	6	15–19.9	5
20–24	3	4–4.9	7	20–24.9	5
25–30	2	5–5.9	2	25–29.9	5
				30–34.9	1

Raw	f	Rank	$\sqrt{\ }$	Raw	f	Rank	$\sqrt{\ }$
0/	1	1	0.0	14			
1///	3	3	1.0	15			
2///	3	6	1.4	16//	2	22.5	4.0
3/	1	8	1.7	17/	1	24	4.1
4/////	4	10.5	2.0	18/	1	25	4.2
5/	1	13	2.2	19			
6/	1	14	2.4	20/	1	26	4.5
7/	1	15	2.6	21/	1	27	4.6
8				22			
9//	2	16.5	3.0	23/	1	28	4.8
10//	2	18.5	3.2	24			
11/	1	20	3.3	25/	1	29	5.0
12/	1	21	3.5	26			
13				27			
14				28/	1	30	5.3
15							

2. Probably not normal: (a) skewed right, (b) bimodal, (d) (skewed right)

3. t needed (two-tailed, $p < .05$, $df = 8$) = 2.306

	Square-Root Transformed Scores	
	Group A	*Group B*
	1.1	1.4
	1.6	3.0
	2.1	2.4
	1.9	2.6
	2.7	2.2
$M =$	1.88	2.32
$S^2 =$	.35	.35
$S_p = .35$		
$S_M^2 =$	.07	.07

$S_{DIF}^2 = .07 + .07 = .14$; $S_{DIF} = .37$
$t = (1.88 - 2.32)/.37 = -1.19$
Do not reject the null hypothesis.

Explanation: I could not run a t test on the data as they were because the distributions of the samples were so skewed for both language groups that it seemed likely that the population distribution was also seriously skewed, which violates the assumption for a t test that the underlying population distributions are normal. So I took the square root of each score. This had the virtue of creating a sample distribution that was much closer to normal and therefore probably suggests that the population distribution of square roots of family sizes is nearly normally distributed. I realize that taking the square root of each family size distorts its straightforward meaning. But the impact for the individuals in the family of each additional child is probably not equal. That is, going from no children to 1 child has a huge impact. Going from 1 to 2 has less, and going from 7 to 8 probably makes very much less difference for the family.

In any case, having taken the square root of each score, I then proceeded to conduct an ordinary t test for independent means. The result was inconclusive—the null hypothesis could not be rejected. (And because the sample size was so small, the power was probably also low, making it hard to draw any kind of suggestion from the failure to reject the null hypothesis.)

4.

Score:	201	523	614	136	340	301	838	911	1,007	
Rank:	2	5	6	1	4	3	7	8	9	
M:		$13/3 = 4.33$			$8/3 = 2.67$			$24/3 = 8$		$GM = 5$
S^2:		$8.67/2 = 4.34$	$4.66/2 = 2.33$					$2/2 = 1$		

F needed $(df = 2, 6; p < .05) = 5.14$

$S_B^2 = (SS/df)(n) = \{[(4.33 - 5)^2 + (2.67 - 5)^2$
$\quad + (8 - 5)^2]/(3 - 1)\}(3) = (14.88/2)(3) = 22.32$

$S_W^2 = (4.34 + 2.33 + 1)/3 = 2.56; F = 22.32/2.56 = 8.72$

Conclusion: Reject the null hypothesis.

(*Note:* The structural model approach could have been used instead.)

Explanation: Ordinarily, in this situation of testing the significance of the difference among three means, I would conduct a standard one-way analysis of variance. However, an assumption for the analysis of variance is that the populations corresponding to each group are normally distributed. Based on the sample, the ratings of the sad group looked very skewed to the left, and possibly the ratings of the angry group as well. (Furthermore, there was also quite a discrepancy in the estimate of the population variance between the sad and the exuberant group, which raises a question about another ANOVA assumption, that the population distributions have equal variances.)

To cope with this problem, I changed each of the scores to its rank among all the scores. This had the effect of making the distribution of ratings rectangular (although actually it did not help much within the sad group). In any case, some statisticians recommend that if the assumptions are questionable for an ordinary analysis of variance, one should change the numbers to ranks first and then proceed, and that will give more accurate results. There are actually special procedures that one can use to conduct an analysis of variance by ranks. But the computations are mathematically equivalent to what you do with an analysis of variance. The only difference is that with the rank-order procedure there are special tables that are more accurate in this situation than the F table. However, statisticians suggest that the results using an ordinary F table in this situation are a good approximation. And seeing that our result was clearly more extreme than the cut-off F ratio, we are probably safe to accept this conclusion and reject the null hypothesis.

5. With 20 differences between means, the resultant difference between means has to be the highest to reject the null hypothesis at the .05 level.

The mean differences in the order of the layout in the problem are as follows:

4.67	4	2.67	2	3.33	2	1.33	1.33	.67	−.67
−4.67	−4	−2.67	−2	−3.33	−2	−1.33	−1.33	−.67	.67

The mean differences in order from smallest (most negative) to largest are as follows:

−4.67, −4, −3.33, −2.67, −2, −2, −2, −1.33, −1.33, −.67, −.67, .67, .67, 1.33, 1.33, 2, 2, 2.67, 3.33, 4, 4.67

Conclusion: Reject the null hypothesis.

Explanation: Suppose that being tested alone or with a friend made no difference. In that case, the reason that the scores for the particular people I studied are higher in the alone condition must be the random assignment's having accidentally put more of the people who would have done well anyway into the alone condition. But what is the probability of that? There are only 20 ways in which six people could be put into two groups of three each. These 20 ways were laid out for me in the problem, and I figured out the difference between the average alone score minus the average friend score. Of the 20 possible ways in which the random assignment could work, only one—the one that has the scores of our actual two groups—would have produced this much difference between the two averages. Being the highest one of 20 has only a 5% probability if everything is operating just by chance. That seems too low to consider likely. Thus I concluded that the big difference between the averages of our two groups was not due to chance from the random assignment. Since everything else was the same between groups, the remaining conclusion is that the condition of being alone versus with a friend is what caused the difference.

6. Kivlighan and Angelone wanted to examine the relationships among the variables they are studying, probably including various parametric hypothesis-testing techniques such as the t test or an analysis of variance (or testing the significance of bivariate or multiple correlation or regression results). All of these procedures are based on the assumption that the distributions of the variables in the population follow a normal curve. However, these authors, examining their sample data, concluded that it seemed unlikely that the scores on the intention variables were normally distributed in the population. So they decided to take each score and change it mathematically—this is called a transformation. (Transformations are often done by taking the square root or the log of each score. In this case, the researchers used a different mathematical technique, but the principle is the same. And with any of the transformations, the order of the scores always stays the same.) The particular transformation is selected so as to make the distribution of the sample scores as close to normal as possible (and then, presumably, they will be representing a population of transformed scores that is more normal). Making such a transformation seems particularly appropriate with a new measure in which there is as much reason to think that a transformation of the scores is a representation of the underlying reality as the untransformed scores. Having done the transformation, the transformed scores were presumably then used in the ordinary parametric statistical techniques.

Chapter 16

1.

df:	**5**	**10**	**15**	**20**
t	2.571	2.228	2.132	2.086
t^2	6.61	4.96	4.55	4.35
F	6.61	4.97	4.54	4.35

2. (i) ANOVA:

F needed $(df = 1, 58; p < .05) = 4.02$

$S_B^2 = (SS/df)(n)$
$= \{[(12 - 11.55)^2 + (11.1 - 11.55)^2]/(2 - 1)\}(30)$
$= (.405/1)(30) = 12.15$

$S_W^2 = (2.4 + 2.8)/2 = 2.6;\ F = 12.15/2.6 = 4.67$
Reject the null hypothesis.

Comparison

	df	**Cutoff**	**Within-Group Variance**	**t or F**
t	58	2.004	$S_P^2 = 2.6$	2.16
F	58	4.02 ($\sqrt{\ } = 2.005$)	$S_W^2 = 2.6$	4.67 ($\sqrt{\ } = 2.16$)

(ii) ANOVA:

F needed $(df = 1, 70; p < .05) = 3.98$

$S_B^2 = (SS/df)(n)$
$= \{[(100 - 102)^2 + (104 - 102)^2]/(2 - 1)\}(36)$
$= (8/1)(36) = 288$

$S_W^2 = (40 + 48)/2 = 44;\ F = 288/44 = 6.55$
Reject the null hypothesis.

Comparison:

	df	**Cutoff**	**Within-Group Variance**	**t or F**
t	70	1.995	$S_P^2 = 44$	2.56
F	70	3.98 ($\sqrt{\ } = 1.995$)	$S_W^2 = 44$	6.55 ($\sqrt{\ } = 2.56$)

(iii) t test:

t needed $(df = 30, p < .05,\ \text{two-tailed}) = 2.043$
$S_P^2 = (8 + 6)/2 = 7;\ S_{M1}^2 = 7/16 = .44;\ S_{M2}^2 = 7/16 = .44;$
$S_{DIF}^2 = .44 + .44 = .88;$
$S_{DIF} = .94;\ t = (73 - 75)/.94 = -2.13$
Reject the null hypothesis.

ANOVA:

F needed $(df = 1, 30; p < .05) = 4.17$
$S_B^2 = \{[(73 - 74)^2 + (75 - 74)^2]/(2 - 1)\}(16)$
$= (2/1)(16) = 32$
$S_W^2 = (8 + 6)/2 = 7;\ F = 32/7 = 4.57$
Reject the null hypothesis.

Comparison:

	df	**Cutoff**	**Within-Group Variance**	**t or F**
t	30	2.043	$S_P^2 = 7$	-2.13
F	30	4.17 ($\sqrt{\ } = 2.042$)	$S_W^2 = 7$	4.57 ($\sqrt{\ } = 2.14$)

3. t-Test Computations

Needed t $(df = 18, p < .05,$ two-tailed): 2.101

Mean difference $= 170 - 150$
$= 20$

$df_T = df_1 + df_2 = 9 + 9 = 18$

$S_P^2 = (df_1/df_T)(S_1^2)$
$\quad + (df_2/df_T)(S_2^2)$
$= (.5)(48) + (.5)(32)$
$= 24 + 16 = 40$

$S_{DIF}^2 = S_{M1}^2 + S_{M2}^2$
$= (S_P^2/N_1) + (S_P^2/N_2)$
$= (40/10) + (40/10)$
$= 4 + 4 = 8$

$S_{DIF} = \sqrt{S_{DIF}^2}$
$= \sqrt{8} = 2.83.$
$t = (M_1 - M_2)/S_{DIF}$
$= 20/2.83$
$= 7.07$

Reject the null hypothesis.

ANOVA Computations

Needed F $(df = 1, 18; p < .05)$: 4.41 $\sqrt{\ } = 2.1$)

$GM = (170 + 150)/2 = 320/2$
$= 160$

$\Sigma(M - GM)^2 = (170 - 160)^2$
$\quad + (150 - 160)^2$
$= 10^2 + (-10)^2$
$= 100 + 100$
$= 200$

$S_B^2\ \text{or}\ MS_B = \dfrac{\Sigma(M - GM)^2}{df_B}\ (n)$

$= (200/1)(10)$
$= 2,000$

$df_W = df_1 + df_2 + \cdots + df_{Last}$
$= 9 + 9 = 18$

$S_W^2\ \text{or}\ MS_W = (S_1^2 + S_2^2 + \cdots + S_{Last}^2)/(N_G)$
$= (48 + 32)/2$
$= 40$

$F = S_B^2/S_W^2\ \text{or}\ MS_B/MS_W$
$= 2,000/40$
$= 50\ (\sqrt{\ } = 7.07)$

Reject the null hypothesis.

4. $GM = (85 + 27)/8 = 14$

Group A

X	$X - GM$		$X - M$		$M - GM$	
	Dev	*Dev²*	*Dev*	*Dev²*	*Dev*	*Dev²*
13	−1	1	−4	16	3	9
16	2	4	−1	1	3	9
19	5	25	2	4	3	9
18	4	16	1	1	3	9
19	5	25	2	4	3	9
Σ 85		71		26		45
$M =$ 17						

Group B

X_2	$X - GM$		$X - M$		$M - GM$	
	Dev	*Dev²*	*Dev*	*Dev²*	*Dev*	*Dev²*
11	−3	9	2	4	−5	25
7	−7	49	−2	4	−5	25
9	−5	25	0	0	−5	25
Σ 27		83		8		75
$M =$ 9						

Note: Dev = Deviation; Dev² = Squared deviation

$\Sigma(X - GM)^2$ or $SS_T = 71 + 83 = 154$
$\Sigma(X - M)^2$ or $SS_W = 26 + 8 = 34$
$\Sigma(M - GM)^2$ or $SS_B = 45 + 75 = 120$
Check $(SS_T = SS_W + SS_B)$: $154 = 34 + 120$

Degrees of freedom:
$df_T = N - 1 = 8 - 1 = 7$
$df_W = df_1 + df_2 + \ldots + df_{Last} = 4 + 2 = 6$
$df_B = N_G - 1 = 2 - 1 = 1$
Check $(df_T = df_W + df_B)$: $7 = 6 + 1$

Population variance estimates:
S_W^2 or $MS_W = SS_W/df_W = 34/6 = 5.67$
S_B^2 or $MS_B = SS_B/df_B = 120/1 = 120$

F ratio: $F = S_B^2/S_W^2$ or $MS_B/MS_W = 120/5.67 = 21.16$

Proportion of variance accounted for: $R^2 = SS_B/SS_T = 120/154 = .78$

Correlation (Group A = 1, Group B = 0):

Group (X)		Score (Y)					
X		Y					
Raw	Z	Raw	Z	$Z_X Z_Y$	$\hat{Y}$	Error	Error²
1	.77	13	−.22	−.17	17	−4	16
1	.77	16	.46	.35	17	−1	1
1	.77	19	1.14	.88	17	2	4
1	.77	18	.92	.71	17	1	1
1	.77	19	1.14	.88	17	2	4
0	−1.29	11	−.68	.88	9	2	4
0	−1.29	7	−1.60	2.06	9	−2	4
0	−1.29	9	−1.14	1.47	9	0	0
Σ: 5		112		7.06			34
$M = .625$		14			$r = .88$	$r^2 = .77$	
$SS = 1.874$		154					
$SD = .484$		4.387					

Proportionate reduction in error $= r^2 =$ reduction in error/total error $= (SS_T - SS_E)/SS_T = (154 - 34)/154 = 120/154 = .78$

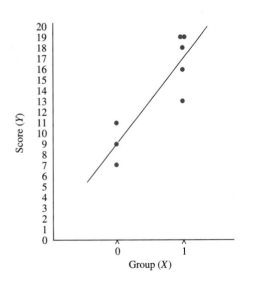

Parallels:

r	F
Mean of Y = 14	Grand mean = 14
$SS_T = 154$	$SS_T = 154$
Predicted Y for Group A = 17	Mean of Group A = 17
Predicted Y for Group B = 9	Mean of Group B = 9
$SS_E = 34$	$SS_W = 34$
Reduction in error = 120	$SS_B = 120$
$r^2 = .77$	$R^2 = .78$

5. t-test:
t needed $(df = 4, p < .05,$ one-tailed$) = 2.132$
Group A: $M = .8$, $S^2 = .01$; Group B: $M = .4$, $S^2 = .04$
$S_P^2 = (.01 + .04)/2 = .025$; $S_{MA}^2 = .025/3 = .0083$; $S_{MB}^2 = .0083$;
$S_{DIF}^2 = .0083 + .0083 = .017$; $S_{DIF} = .13$; $t = (.8 - .4)/.13 = 3.08$
Reject the null hypothesis.

Correlation (Group A = 1, Group B = 0):

	Group (X)		Score (Y)		
	Raw	Z_X	Raw	Z_Y	$Z_X Z_Y$
	1	1	.7	.42	.42
	1	1	.9	1.26	1.26
	1	1	.8	.84	.84
	0	−1	.6	0.00	0.00
	0	−1	.4	− .84	.84
	0	−1	.2	−1.68	1.68
Σ	3		3.6		5.04
	$M = .5$		.6		$r = .84$
	$SD = .5$		.238		

$t = r\sqrt{N - 2}/\sqrt{1 - r^2} = .84\sqrt{6 - 2}/\sqrt{1 - .84^2} = .84\sqrt{4}/\sqrt{1 - .71}$
$= (.84)(2)/\sqrt{.29} = 1.68/.54 = 3.11$

6. You can think of the analysis of variance as examining the relationship between the independent variable (the variable on which the groups differ, such as the "experimental condition") and a dependent variable. In this sense, it is doing the same thing as regression and correlation, which also examine the relationship between a dependent variable and an independent variable. In fact, if you were to take a two-group analysis of variance and code the people in one of the groups as 1s and those in the other group as 2s (any two numbers would do, these are just examples) and you compute the correlation between this group membership number and the dependent variable, the significance of that correlation will be the same as the significance of the analysis of variance.

Looking at the computations' connections, the first is that in both regression and the analysis of variance, you compute the total squared deviations from the overall mean. In both regression and the analysis of variance, this is called the sum of squares total. Another, deeper link arises because the best predictor for members of a group is the mean of that group. Thus the regression equation predicts the mean for the members of each group. The result is that the errors of predictions are deviations of the scores from the mean. If you square these and add them up, they are called the sum of squared errors in regression and the "sum of squares within" in an analysis of variance. In regression, as a preliminary to computing the proportionate reduction in error, you compute the reduction in error ($SS_T - SS_E$). This represents what the regression approach has saved. It turns out to be the same as the "sum of squares between" in an analysis of variance. This is because when there are only two group means involved, regression is able to improve on prediction only to the extent that the means of the two groups are different. Finally, because SS_T is the same in both cases and reduction in error = SS_B, it follows that r^2 will equal R^2.

There is one complication, however, in this link of regression and the analysis of variance. Regression, even multiple regression, uses only ordinary numerical variables. When there are only two groups, coding them with two numbers creates a numeric variable that works fine. But when there are three or more groups, the nominal variable on which these groups differ cannot be used directly in regression analysis. The solution is to create more than one of these two-valued numerical variables to account for this nominal predictor variable. Then a multiple correlation carried out using these specially coded variables gives the same result (in terms of statistical significance) as an analysis of variance.

Chapter 17

1. A hierarchical multiple regression is a variation of ordinary multiple regression in which each predictor variable is added to the equation, one at a time (or sometimes a set of variables is added as a group), and the *additional* contribution of that variable (in addition to the variable added in the previous step) is computed. The order in which the predictor variables are entered is determined by the researcher in advance. In this case, the dependent variable was symptoms. The first predictor variable considered was gender, which, Meier reports, accounted for 15% of the variance. This means that using gender to predict number of symptoms reduced the squared error (compared to predicting just from the mean of number of symptoms) by 15% (that is, r^2 would be .15). This is an ordinary bivariate prediction situation. The next predictor variable added was social desirability. The researcher reports that it did not add anything—thus the overall proportion of error reduced would still be 15%. The next variable added was score on the Meir Burnout Assessment measure, which improved the prediction slightly, reducing the squared error by another 2% (that is, with these three measures as predictor variables, R^2 is up to 17%). The addition of the Maslach test was a big contribution, however, reducing squared error by an additional 10% (raising the overall R^2 to 27%). Adding the anxiety measure reduced squared error by another 3%, and adding depression made no further reduction, so that with all variables considered, the total squared error reduced was 30%.

2. Snyder et al. are describing results that bear on the degree of reliability of their new measure. Reliability is the extent to which the test measures something consis-

tently—the extent to which, if the test were taken again by the same person under identical circumstances, it would give the same result. One way of assessing reliability is by looking at how one half of the test correlates with the other half of the test, the idea being that the same person is taking two tests (the two halves of the test) at the same time under the same circumstances. Cronbach's alpha tells the overall average of correlations between every possible way of splitting the test in half and then adjusts this to take into account the fact that with only half as many items, the correlations are a bit lower than if the full test were correlated with another full test like itself. A Cronbach's alpha of .74 to .84 is considered a moderate degree of reliability.

Another way of assessing reliability is actually to give the test twice to the same people and compute the correlation of scores from the two testings. This is what Snyder et al. describe as "test-retest reliability." Their result of .85 over a 3-week period between the two testings is also acceptably high. Taking both Cronbach's alpha and test-retest reliability together, it is reasonable to conclude that this test has a moderate to high level of reliability.

3. A factor analysis helps a researcher who has collected data on a large number of variables to uncover the underlying pattern (if any exists) among them—to find which variables group together in the sense of correlating with each other but not with variables not in the grouping. In this case, the researchers had ratings of 108 people on 15 variables. The factor analysis results suggest that the best underlying pattern has two groupings (called "factors"). The table shows the correlations of each individual variable with the grouping (called "loadings"). When Anderson and Sedikides made up the table, they listed the variables in order so that those with high loadings on the first factor come first and those with high loadings on the second factor are printed at the bottom, after the break. The authors also suggested in their article general descriptive terms for each factor. They described the first factor as "general evaluation," presumably because the 10 variables with high loadings on it (such as "Like vs. dislike" and "Pleasant vs. unpleasant"), taken as a group, seem to relate to an overall positive or negative judgment of the person. They described the second factor as "dynamism," presumably because the five variables with high loadings on it (such as "Active vs. passive" and "Impulsive vs. unpleasant"), taken as a group, seem to relate to an overall sense of active, energetic characteristics.

4. Path analysis is a technique in which the researcher specifies a pattern of causal relationships among variables, diagrammed with arrows connecting each cause to its effects. The statistical aspect of path analysis involves computing a "path coefficient" for each arrow, which tells the degree to which changes on the variable of the tail of the arrow are associated with changes in the variable at the head of the arrow (under conditions in which all other causes for that effect variable are held constant). That is, the path coefficient is a standardized regression coefficient (a "beta") for the causal variable in an equation in which the effect variable is the dependent variable and all of the causal variables are predictor variables.

The figure is an example of a path diagram, and the

numbers shown along the arrows are the path coefficients (ignore the numbers in parentheses). For example, the arrow from Self-Satisfaction (at the top left, which is for the second phase of the study) to Performance (in the middle, which is performance in the second phase) tells you that the researchers hypothesized that in the second phase of the study, Self-Satisfaction would have a causal effect on Performance. The .28 means that after controlling for the other three variables also hypothesized to have a direct causal effect on Performance (Analytic Strategies, Self-Efficacy, and Past Performance), an increase of 1 standard deviation on Self-Satisfaction predicts an increase of .28 of a standard deviation on Performance.

5. The "2 × 2 multivariate analysis of variance" described in this article is the same thing as an ordinary 2 × 2 analysis of variance, except that in a multivariate analysis, several dependent variables are included at the same time. Thus the "multivariate interaction" refers to an interaction effect of the two independent variables (Film Type and Homosexuality Attitudes) on the combination of the three dependent variables (which were attitudes about interacting with an AIDS-infected worker in three different situations). The researchers also reported that the interaction was found when doing ordinary ("univariate") 2 × 2 analyses of variance, one for each of the dependent variables. Using the bookstore scenario as an example, the pattern of means in this case was that subjects watching the AIDS film who had initially prohomosexual attitudes were much more positive about interacting with an AIDS-infected person than any of the other three groups. Put another way, the film did not seem to have any effect on subjects with initially antihomosexual attitudes, and those with initially prohomosexual attitudes who saw the control film were not much more positive about interacting with an AIDS-infected person than those with initially antihomosexual attitudes.

6. (a) Causal modeling (path analysis or latent variable modeling)
   (b) Bivariate correlation and regression
   (c) Reliability statistics, such as Cronbach's alpha and test-retest reliability
   (d) A 3 × 2 multivariate analysis of variance, probably followed up by univariate 3 × 2 analyses of variance and possibly also by multivariate and/or univariate multiple comparisons among specific pairs or groups of means
   (e) Stepwise regression
   (f) Factor analysis
   (g) A t test for independent means
   (h) A one-way analysis of variance, possibly followed up by multiple comparisons among specific pairs or groups of means
   (i) Hierarchical multiple regression

Glossary

Numbers in parentheses refer to chapters in which the term is introduced or substantially discussed.

Alpha (α) The probability of a Type I error; same as *significance level.* (8)

Analysis of covariance (ANCOVA) An analysis of variance that is conducted after first adjusting the variables to control for the effect of one or more unwanted additional variables. (17)

Analysis of variance (ANOVA) A hypothesis-testing procedure for studies involving two or more groups. (11)

Analysis of variance table A chart showing the major elements in computing an analysis of variance using the structural-model approach. (12, 13)

Approximate randomization test An alternative to a randomization test used when a sample is too large for a randomization test that looks at every possible reorganization of a sample's data; the computer-intensive approximate randomization method generates a large number, such as 1,000, of the possible reorganizations of the data. (15)

Assumption A condition, such as a population's having a normal distribution, required for carrying out a particular hypothesis-testing procedure; a part of the mathematical foundation for the accuracy of the tables used in determining cutoff values. (9)

Beta (β) Standardized regression coefficient (4); also probability of a Type II error in hypothesis testing. (8)

Between-group degrees of freedom (df_B) Same as *numerator degrees of freedom.* (11)

Between-group population variance estimate (S_B^2, MS_B) In an analysis of variance, the estimate of the variance of the population distribution of individual cases based on the variation among the means of the groups studied; same as *mean squares between.* (11)

Between-group sum of squares (SS_B) Same as *sum of squared deviations between groups.* (12)

Biased estimate An estimate of a population parameter that is likely systematically to overestimate or underestimate the true population value; SD^2 would be a biased estimate of the population variance (it would systematically underestimate it). (9)

Bimodal distribution A frequency distribution with two approximately equal frequencies, each clearly larger than any of the others. (1)

Binomial effect-size display A table showing the relation between two variables in which each variable is divided in half at the median and the percentage of cases in each of the four combinations (high scores on one variable with highs on the other, highs with lows, lows with highs, and lows with lows) are shown. (3)

Bivariate prediction The prediction of scores on one variable based on scores of one other variable. (4)

Bivariate regression Same as *bivariate prediction.* (4)

Bonferroni procedure A multiple-comparison procedure in which the total alpha percentage is divided among the set of comparisons so that each is tested at a more stringent significance level. (12)

Categorical variable Same as *nominal variable.* (14)

Causal analysis A procedure, such as path analysis or latent variable modeling, that analyzes correlations among a group of variables in terms of a predicted pattern of causal relations among them. (17)

Causal model In latent variable modeling, the set of causal paths among latent variables. (17)

Ceiling effect The situation in which many scores pile up at the high end because it is not possible to have a higher score. (1)

Cell In a factorial design, a particular combination of levels of the independent variables; also, in chi-square, the particular combination of categories for two variables in a contingency table. (13, 14)

Cell mean The mean of a particular combination of levels of the independent variables in a factorial design. (13)

Central tendency The typical or most representative value of a group of scores. (2)

Chi-square statistic (χ^2) A statistic that reflects the overall lack of fit between the expected and observed frequencies; the sum, over all the categories or cells, of the squared difference between observed and expected frequencies divided by the expected frequency. (14)

Chi-square table A table providing cutoff scores on the chi-square distribution for various degrees of freedom and significance levels. (14)

Chi-square test for goodness of fit A hypothesis-testing procedure that examines how well an observed frequency distribution of a categorical variable fits some expected pattern of frequencies. (14)

Chi-square test for independence A hypothesis-testing procedure that examines whether the distribution of frequencies over the categories of one categorical variable are unrelated to the distribution of frequencies over the categories of another categorical variable. (14)

Collapsing over factors A procedure in a factorial analysis of variance in which one of the dimensions (independent variables) is ignored, reducing the overall analysis to one less dimension, but with the same total number of subjects. (13)

Column mean The mean score for all the subjects at a particular level of the independent variable whose levels correspond to columns in the diagrammed layout of a factorial design. (13)

Comparison distribution The distribution representing the situation if the null hypothesis is true; the distribution to which a sample statistic is compared. (6)

Computational formula An equation mathematically equivalent to the definitional formula that is easier to use for hand computation but does not directly display the meaning of the procedure it symbolizes. (2)

Computer-intensive methods Statistical methods, including hypothesis-testing procedures, involving large numbers of repeated computations that have become practical only recently due to the availability of computers. (15)

Contingency table A two-dimensional chart showing frequencies in each combination of categories of two categorical variables. (14)

Controlling for In multiple regression, partial correlation, or analysis of covariance, removing the influence of a variable from the association among the other variables; same as *partialing out* and *holding constant*. (17)

Conventional levels of significance ($p < .05, p < .01$) The levels of significance widely used in psychology. (6)

Correction for attenuation A statistical procedure that computes the correlation between two variables that would be expected if both variables were measured with perfect reliability. (3)

Correlation coefficient (r) The average of the cross-products of Z scores of two variables; a measure of the degree of linear correlation ranging from –1 (a perfect negative linear correlation) through 0 (no correlation) to +1 (a perfect positive correlation); the square root of the proportionate reduction in error. (3, 4)

Correlation matrix A common way of reporting the correlations among several variables in research articles; a table in which the variables are named on the top and along the side and the correlations among them are all shown (only half of the resulting square, above or below the diagonal, is usually filled in, the other half being redundant). (3)

Covariate A variable controlled for in an analysis of covariance. (17)

Cramer's phi A measure of association between two categorical variables; an effect-size measure for a chi-square test of independence with a contingency table that is larger than 2×2; also known as *Cramer's V* and sometimes written as φ_c or V_c. (14)

Cronbach's alpha A widely used index of a measure's reliability that is equivalent to the average of the split-half correlations from all possible splits into halves of the items on the test. (17)

Crossed variables In a factorial design, the situation in which each level of one independent variable is measured at each level of the other independent variable. (13)

Curvilinear correlation A relation between two variables that shows up on a scatter diagram as dots following a systematic pattern that is not a straight line; any association between two variables other than a linear correlation. (3)

Cutoff sample score The point on the comparison distribution at which, if reached or exceeded by the sample score, the null hypothesis will be rejected. (6)

Data transformation The application of one of several mathematical procedures (such as taking the square root) to each score in a sample, usually carried out in order to make the sample distribution closer to normal. (15)

Definitional formula The equation directly displaying the meaning of the procedure it symbolizes. (2)

Degree of correlation The extent to which there is a clear pattern of some particular relationship (usually linear) between the distributions of the two variables. (3)

Degrees of freedom (df) The number of scores free to vary when estimating a population parameter; it is usually part of an equation for making that estimate—for example, in the formula for estimating the population variance from a single sample, the degrees of freedom is the number of scores minus 1. (9)

Denominator degrees of freedom (df_w) The degrees of freedom used in the within-group variance estimate in an analysis of variance, the denominator of the F ratio; the number of scores free to vary (number of scores in each group minus 1, summed over all the groups) in computing the within-group variance estimate; within-group degrees of freedom. (11)

Dependent variable (usually Y**)** A variable that is considered to be an effect; also used in regression for any variable that is predicted about. (3, 4)

Descriptive statistics Procedures for summarizing a set of scores or otherwise making them more comprehensible. (1)

Deviation score A score minus the mean of all scores. (2)

Difference score The difference between a subject's score on one testing and the same subject's score on another testing; often an after score minus a before score; also called a *change score.* (9)

Dimension In a factorial design, one of the independent variables crossed with another independent variable. (13)

Directional hypothesis A research hypothesis predicting a particular direction of difference between populations (for example, one population having a higher mean than the other). (6)

Distribution-free test A hypothesis-testing procedure making no assumptions about the shape of the underlying populations; approximately the same as a nonparametric test. (15)

Distribution of differences between means The distribution of all possible differences between means of two samples such that for each pair of means, one is from one population and the other is from a second population; the comparison distribution in a t test for independent means. (10)

Distribution of means A distribution of all the possible means of samples of a given size from a particular population (also called a sampling distribution of the mean); the comparison distribution when testing hypotheses involving a sample of more than one case. (7)

Effect size The separation (lack of overlap) between or among populations due to the independent variable; it increases with greater differences between or among means and decreases with smaller standard deviations in any of the populations but is not affected by sample size. (8)

Effect-size conventions Conventions about what to consider a small, medium, and large effect size, based on what is typical in psychology research; often known as *Cohen's conventions.* (8)

Effect size for studies involving one or two means (d**)** Number of population standard deviations by which the population means differ. (8–10)

Effect size in the analysis of variance (f**)** The standard deviation of the means of the groups divided by the standard deviation of the individual cases. (11)

Endogenous variable A variable in a path analysis (including latent variable models) that has arrows leading to it. (17)

Equal-interval measurement Measurement in which the difference between any two scores represents an equal amount of difference in the underlying thing being measured. (15)

Error In prediction, the actual score minus the predicted score. (4)

Exogenous variable A variable in a path analysis (including latent variable models) that is at the start of a causal chain, having no arrows leading to it within the path diagram. (17)

Expected frequency In a chi-square test, the number of cases in a category or cell expected if the null hypothesis were true. (14)

Factor In a factor analysis, a subset of variables all correlating with each other but not with variables not in the subset. (17)

Factor analysis An exploratory statistical procedure, applied in situations where many variables are measured, that identifies groupings of variables correlating maximally with each other and minimally with other variables. (17)

Factorial analysis of variance In a factorial design, an analysis of variance for the differences among the means in each dimension and for the interaction of the variables in different dimensions. (13)

Factorial design A way of organizing a study in which the influence of two or more variables is studied at once by constructing groupings that include every combination of the levels of the variables. (13)

Factor loading In a factor analysis, the correlation of a variable with a factor. (17)

F distribution A mathematically defined curve describing the comparison distribution used in an analysis of variance; the distribution of F ratios when the null hypothesis is true. (11)

Floor effect The situation in which many scores pile up at the low end because it is not possible to have any lower score. (1)

F ratio In the analysis of variance, the ratio of the between-group population variance estimate to the within-group population variance estimate; a score on the comparison distribution (an F distribution) in an analysis of variance. (11)

Frequency distribution The pattern of frequencies over the various values; what a frequency table, histogram, or frequency polygon describes. (1)

Frequency polygon A line graph of a distribution in which the values (or intervals of values, as in a grouped frequency table) are plotted along the horizontal axis and the height of each point corresponds to the frequency of that value (or interval); the lines begin and end at the horizontal axis, and the graph resembles a mountainous skyline. (1)

Frequency table A listing of the number of subjects receiving each of the possible values that the scores on the variable being measured can take. (1)

F table A table providing cutoff scores on the F distribution for various degrees of freedom and significance levels. (11)

General linear model A general formula that is the basis of most of the statistical methods covered in this text; the formula describes a score as the sum of a constant, the weighted influence of several variables, and error; the formula is similar to a multiple regression equation except that error is included and the sum of the influences is the actual score, not the predicted score, on the dependent variable. (16)

Grouped frequency table A frequency table in which the number of subjects is indicated for each interval of values. (1)

Haphazard selection A procedure of selecting a sample of individuals to study by taking whoever is available or happens to be first on a list; should not be confused with true random selection. (5)

Harmonic mean (N'**)** A special average that is influenced more by smaller scores; the harmonic mean of the sample sizes in a t test for independent means in which the sample sizes are different is used as the equivalent of each group's sample size when computing power. (10)

Hierarchical multiple regression An approach to multiple regression in which predictor variables are added to the prediction rule, one or a few at a time, in a planned sequential fashion, permitting the researcher to determine the relative contribution of each successive variable over and above those already included. (17)

Histogram A barlike graph of a distribution in which the values (or intervals of values, as in a grouped frequency table) are plotted along the horizontal axis and the height of each bar corresponds to the frequency of that value (or interval); the bars are placed next to each other without spaces, giving the appearance of a city skyline. (1)

Holding constant In multiple regression, partial correlation, or analysis of covariance, removing the influence of a variable from the association among the other variables; same as *partialing out* and *controlling for*. (17)

Hypothesis testing A systematic procedure for determining whether results of an experiment (which studies a sample) provide support for a particular theory or practical innovation (which is thought to be applicable to a population). (6)

Independence The situation of no systematic relationship between two variables; a term usually used in the context of chi-square. (14)

Independent variable (usually *X*) A variable that is considered to be a cause; also, in regression, sometimes any predictor variable, whether or not it is regarded as a cause. (3, 4)

Inferential statistics Procedures for drawing conclusions based on the scores collected in a research study but going beyond them. (1)

Interaction effect Situation in the factorial analysis of variance in which the combination of variables has a special effect that could not be predicted from knowledge of the effects of the two variables individually. (13)

Interval In a grouped frequency table, each of a specified-sized grouping of values for which frequencies are reported (for example, if the interval size was 10, one of the intervals might be from 10.00 to 19.99). (1)

Interval size In a grouped frequency table, the difference between the start of one interval and the start of the next. (1)

Inverse transformation A data transformation in which the researcher uses the inverse (1 divided by the number) of each score. (15)

Kuder-Richardson-20 (KR-20) A special formula that is used to compute an index of a measure's reliability when all the test items are dichotomous (such as yes-no or true-false); the result with the KR-20 is the same as with Cronbach's alpha. (17)

Kurtosis The extent to which a frequency distribution deviates from a normal curve, being either too peaked and pinched together or too flat and spread out. (1)

Latent variable In latent variable modeling, an unmeasured theoretical variable assumed to be the underlying cause of several measured variables included in the overall analysis. (17)

Latent variable modeling A sophisticated version of path analysis that includes paths involving latent, unmeasured, theo-

retical variables and that also permits a kind of significance test and provides measures of the overall fit of the data to the hypothesized causal pattern; also called *structured equation modeling* and *LISREL*. (17)

Least-squares analysis of variance The recommended approach to the factorial analysis of variance when the subjects in the cells are not all equal in number. (13)

Least-squares model The usual method of determining the optimal values of regression coefficients; these optimal values are those that produce the least squared error between predicted and actual values. (16)

Level of significance (α) The probability of obtaining statistical significance if the null hypothesis is actually true; the probability of a Type I error. (6–8)

Levels of independent variables or factors The divisions of a dimension or a variable in the factorial analysis of variance. (13)

Levels of measurement Types of underlying numerical information provided by a measure, such as equal-interval, rank-order, and nominal (categorical). (15)

Linear contrast A planned comparison that resembles a correlation in which, for each subject, one variable is the predicted influence of the group the subject is in and the other variable is the score on what is being measured. (12)

Linear correlation A relation between two variables that shows up on a scatter diagram as dots following a straight line; a correlation of r unequal to 0. (3)

LISREL A computer program for latent variable modeling; sometimes used as a generic name for the procedure itself. (17)

Log transformation A data transformation in which the researcher uses the log of each score. (15)

Long-run relative-frequency interpretation of probability Understanding probability as the proportion of a particular outcome that would be obtained if the experiment were repeated many times. (5)

Main effect The difference between groups on one dimension of a factorial design; the result for a variable, averaging across the other variable or variables (sometimes used only for significant differences). (13)

Manifest variable In latent variable modeling, an ordinary, measured variable—in contrast to a latent variable. (17)

Marginal frequency In chi-square, the frequency (number of cases) in a row or column of a contingency table. (14)

Marginal mean In a factorial design, the mean score for all the subjects at a particular level of one of the independent variables; often shortened to *marginal*. (13)

Mean (M, μ) The arithmetic average of a group of scores; the sum of the scores divided by the number of scores. (2)

Mean of a distribution of means (μ_M) The mean of the population of individual cases from which the samples are taken. (7)

Mean squares between (MS_B) Same as *between-group population variance estimate* (S_B^2). (11)

Mean squares within (MS_W) Same as *within-group population variance estimate* (S_W^2). (11)

Measurement model In latent variable modeling, the set of causal paths between latent and manifest variables. (17)

Median The middle score of a sequence of all the scores in a distribution arranged from highest to lowest. (2)

Meta-analysis A statistical method for combining the results of independent studies, usually focusing on effect sizes. (8)

Midpoint In a histogram or frequency polygon based on a grouped frequency table, the middle of an interval; the point halfway between the start of the interval and the start of the next interval. (1)

Minimum meaningful difference The smallest amount by which two populations might differ without jeopardizing the effect's theoretical interest or practical usefulness. (8)

Mode The value with the greatest frequency in a distribution. (2)

Multicollinearity The situation in multiple regression in which the predictor variables are correlated with each other. (4)

Multimodal distribution A frequency distribution with two or more approximately equal frequencies, each clearly larger than any of the others; a bimodal distribution is a special case. (1)

Multiple comparisons Procedures for examining the differences among particular means in the context of an overall analysis of variance. (12)

Multiple correlation coefficient (R) A measure of the overall association between a dependent variable and the combination of two or more predictor variables; the positive square root of the proportionate reduction in error (R^2) obtained in a multiple regression analysis. (4)

Multiple regression The prediction of scores on one variable (the dependent variable) based on scores of two or more other variables (predictor or independent variables). (4)

Multivariate analysis of covariance (MANCOVA) An analysis of covariance in which there is more than one dependent variable. (17)

Multivariate analysis of variance (MANOVA) An analysis of variance in which there is more than one dependent variable. (17)

Multivariate statistical technique A statistical procedure involving more than one dependent variable. (17)

Negative linear correlation A relation between two variables in which high scores on one go with low scores on the other, mediums with mediums, and lows with highs; on a scatter diagram, the dots roughly follow a straight line sloping down and to the right; a correlation of r less than 0. (3)

No correlation No systematic relation between two variables. (3)

Nominal coding Converting a nominal (categorical) predictor variable in an analysis of variance into several two-level numerical variables that can be used in a multiple regression analysis. (16)

Nominal variable A variable with values that are categories, with no numerical relation (that is, they are names rather than numbers); same as *categorical variable*. (14)

Nondirectional hypothesis A research hypothesis that does not predict a particular direction of difference between populations. (6)

Nonparametric test A hypothesis-testing procedure making no assumptions about population parameters; approximately the same as a distribution-free test. (15)

Normal curve A specific, mathematically defined, bell-shaped frequency distribution that is symmetrical and unimodal; distributions observed in psychology research commonly approximate it. (1, 5)

Normal curve table A table showing percentages of cases in a normally distributed distribution that fall between the mean and various numbers of standard deviations above the mean (Z scores). (5)

Normal distribution A frequency distribution following a normal curve. (5)

Norms Known population parameters on standardized tests (such as personality or aptitude tests) that serve as standards of comparison for any individual who takes the test. (7)

Null hypothesis A statement about a relation between populations that represents the crucial opposite of the research hypothesis; a statement that in the population there is no difference (or a difference opposite to that predicted) between populations; a contrived statement set up to examine whether it can be rejected as part of the hypothesis-testing process. (6)

Numerator degrees of freedom (df_B) The degrees of freedom used in the between-group variance estimate in an analysis of variance, the numerator of the F ratio; the number of scores free to vary (number of means minus 1) in computing the between-group variance estimate; between-group degrees of freedom. (11)

Observed frequency In a chi-square test, the number of cases in a category or cell actually obtained in the study. (14)

One-tailed test The hypothesis-testing procedure for a directional hypothesis; the situation in which the region of the comparison distribution in which the null hypothesis would be rejected is all on one side of the distribution. (6)

One-way analysis of variance An analysis of variance in which there is only one independent variable. (11, 12)

Open-ended interval In a grouped frequency table, a highest (or lowest) interval that includes all values above (or below) a particular value. (1)

Ordinal measurement Same as *rank-order measurement*. (15)

Outcome The result of an experiment (or virtually any event, such as a coin coming up heads or it raining tomorrow). (5)

Outlier A score with an extreme (very high or very low) value in relation to the rest of the scores in the distribution. (2)

Parametric test An ordinary hypothesis-testing procedure, such as a t test or an analysis of variance, that makes assumptions about the shape and other parameters of the populations. (15)

Partial correlation The procedure of determining a partial correlation coefficient. (17)

Partial correlation coefficient The correlation between two variables, over and above the influence of one or more other variables. (17)

Partialing out In multiple regression, partial correlation, or analysis of covariance, removing the influence of a variable from the association among the other variables; same as *holding constant* and *controlling for*. (17)

Path analysis A method of analyzing the correlations among a group of variables in terms of a predicted pattern of causal relations that diagrams the causal links as arrows and computes an index of the degree of relation associated with each arrow in the context of the entire predicted pattern. (17)

Path coefficient The degree of relation associated with an arrow in a path analysis (including latent variable models); same as a standardized regression coefficient from a multiple regression prediction rule in which the variable at the end of the arrow is the dependent variable and the variable at the start of the arrow is the predictor, along with all the other variables that have arrows leading to that dependent variable. (17)

Perfect correlation A relation between two variables that shows up on a scatter diagram as the dots exactly following a straight line; a correlation of $r = 1$ or -1; a situation in which each subject's Z score on one variable is exactly the same as that subject's Z score on the other variable. (3)

Phi coefficient (φ) A measure of association between two dichotomous categorical variables; an effect-size measure for a chi-square test of independence with a 2×2 contingency table. (14)

Planned comparisons Multiple comparisons in which the particular means to be compared were designated in advance; same as *planned contrasts*. (12)

Planned contrasts Same as *planned comparisons*. (12)

Pooled estimate of the population variance (S_p^2) A weighted average of the estimates of the population variance from two samples, each estimate weighted by the proportion of its degrees of freedom divided by the total degrees of freedom for both estimates; one of the figures computed as part of a t test for independent means. (10)

Population The entire group of subjects to which a researcher intends the results of a study to apply; the larger group to which inferences are made on the basis of the particular set of subjects studied. (5)

Population mean (μ) The mean of the population (usually not known). (5)

Population parameter A descriptive statistic for a population, such as the mean or the standard deviation (usually not known, though sometimes estimated); population parameters are usually symbolized by Greek letters. (5)

Population standard deviation (σ) The standard deviation of the population (usually not known). (5)

Population variance (σ^2) The variance of the population (usually not known). (5)

Positive linear correlation A relation between two variables in which high scores on one go with high scores on the other, mediums with mediums, and lows with lows; on a scatter diagram, the dots roughly follow a straight line sloping up and to the right; a correlation of r greater than 0. (3)

Post hoc comparisons Multiple comparisons among particular means that were not designated in advance but are being conducted as part of an exploratory analysis after the study has been completed. (12)

Power Same as *statistical power*. (8)

Power table Table for a hypothesis-testing procedure showing the statistical power of a study for various effect sizes and significance levels. (8)

Prediction model A formula for making predictions; for example, a bivariate prediction model is a formula for predicting a person's score on a dependent variable based on the person's score on an independent variable. (4)

Predictor variable (usually X) A variable that is used as a basis for estimating scores of individuals on another variable. (3, 4)

Probability (p) The expected relative frequency of a particular outcome. (5)

Proportionate reduction in error (r^2, R^2) The measure of association between variables that is used when comparing associations obtained in different studies or with different variables; the correlation coefficient squared; the reduction in squared error, using a bivariate or multiple regression prediction rule, over the squared error using the mean to predict, expressed as a proportion of the squared error when using the mean to predict. (3, 4, 12, 13, 16, 17)

Proportion of variance accounted for (r^2, R^2) An indicator of effect size in an analysis of variance; same as *proportionate reduction in error* in multiple regression. (4, 12, 13, 16)

Randomization test A hypothesis-testing procedure (usually computer-intensive) that operates by considering every possible reorganization of the data in the sample to determine if the organization of the actual sample data was unlikely to occur by chance. (15)

Random selection A method for selecting a sample of individuals to study that uses truly random procedures (usually meaning that each individual in the population has an equal chance of being selected); one method is for the researcher to obtain a complete list of all the members of the population and select a set to study using a table of random numbers; should not be confused with haphazard selection. (5)

Rank-order measurement Measurement in which higher values represent more of the underlying thing being measured, but the difference between any two scores does not represent an equal amount of difference in the underlying thing being measured; same as *ordinal measurement*. (15)

Rank-order test A hypothesis-testing procedure that makes use of rank-ordered data. (15)

Raw score An ordinary measurement (or any other number in a distribution before it has been made into a Z score or otherwise transformed). (2)

Raw score prediction formula A prediction rule using raw scores. (4)

Raw score regression coefficient (b) The regression coefficient in a bivariate or multiple prediction model using raw scores. (4)

Rectangular distribution A frequency distribution in which all values have approximately the same frequency. (1)

Regression coefficient The number multiplied by a person's score on the independent variable as part of a formula (prediction rule) for predicting scores on the dependent variable. (4)

Regression constant (a) In a bivariate or multiple prediction model using raw scores, a particular fixed number added into the prediction. (4)

Regression line A line on a graph representing the predicted value of the dependent variable for each value of the independent variable. (4)

Reliability The degree of consistency of a measure; the extent to which, if the same measure were given again to the same person under the same circumstances, the same result would be obtained. (3, 17)

Repeated-measures analysis of variance An analysis of variance in which all the levels of the independent variable or variables are measured for the same subjects. (13)

Repeated-measures design A research strategy in which each subject is tested more than once; same as *within-subject design*. (9)

Research hypothesis A statement about the predicted relation between populations. (6)

Restriction in range The situation in which a correlation is computed when only a limited range of the possible values on one of the variables are included in the group studied. (3)

Robustness The extent to which a particular hypothesis-testing procedure is reasonably accurate even when its assumptions are violated. (9)

Row mean In a factorial design, the mean score for all the subjects at a particular level of the independent variable whose levels correspond to the rows in the diagrammed layout. (13)

Sample The scores of the particular set of subjects studied that are intended to represent the scores in some larger population. (5)

Sample statistic A descriptive statistic, such as the mean or the standard deviation, computed from the data about a particular sample of scores; sample statistics are usually symbolized by ordinary (as opposed to Greek) letters. (5)

Scatter diagram A graphic display of the relationship pattern between two variables; the values of the predictor or independent variable are scaled along the vertical axis, the values of the dependent variable are scaled along the horizontal axis, and each score is represented as a dot in this two-dimensional space. (3)

Score A particular subject's value on a variable. (1)

Shape of a distribution of means The characteristics of a distribution of means such as modality, skewness, and kurtosis; in general, a distribution of means will tend to be unimodal and symmetrical and is often normal. (7)

Skewness The extent to which the preponderance of cases in a frequency distribution fall to one side of the middle. (1)

Slope The steepness of the angle of a line on a two-variable graph, such as the regression line in a graph of the relation of a dependent and independent variable; it is the number of units the line goes up for every unit it goes across (in raw score regression, slope = b). (4)

Split-half reliability One index of a measure's reliability, based on a correlation of the scores from items representing the two halves of the test. (17)

Squared deviation score The square of the difference between a score and the mean. (2)

Square-root transformation A data transformation in which the researcher uses the square root of each score. (15)

Standard deviation (SD, S, σ) The square root of the average of the squared deviations from the mean; the most common descriptive statistic for variation; approximately (but not exactly) the average amount by which scores in a distribution vary from the mean. (2)

Standard deviation of a distribution of means (σ_M, S_M) The square root of the variance of the distribution of means. (7)

Standardized regression coefficient (beta, β) The regression coefficient in a bivariate or multiple prediction model using Z scores; also called *beta weight*. (4)

Standard score A Z score in a distribution that follows a normal curve; sometimes refers to any Z score. (2)

Statistical power The probability that the study will yield a significant result if the research hypothesis is true. (8)

Statistical significance The extent to which the results of a study would be unlikely if in fact there were no association or difference in the populations the measured scores represent; an outcome of hypothesis testing in which the null hypothesis is rejected. (3, 6)

Stepwise multiple regression An exploratory procedure in which all the potential predictor variables that have been measured are tried in order to find the variable that produces the best prediction, then each of the remaining variables is tried to find the variable that in combination with the first produces the best prediction; this process continues until adding the best remaining variable does not provide a significant improvement. (17)

Structural equation modeling Same as *latent variable modeling*. (17)

Structural model A way of understanding the analysis of variance as a division of the deviation of each score from the overall mean into parts corresponding to the variation within groups (its deviation from its group's mean) and between groups (its group's mean's deviation from the overall mean); an alternative (but mathematically equivalent way) of understanding the analysis of variance. (12, 13)

Subjective interpretation of probability Understanding probability as the degree of certainty that a particular outcome will occur. (5)

Sum of squared deviations (SS) The total over all the scores of each score's squared difference from the mean. (2)

Sum of squared deviations between groups (SS_B) The sum of squared deviations of each score's group's mean from the grand mean; same as *between-group sum of squares*. (12)

Sum of squared deviations within groups (SS_W) The sum of squared deviations of each score from its group's mean; same as *within-groups sum of squares*. (12)

Sum of squared deviations total (SS_T) In an analysis of variance, the sum of squared deviations of each score from the overall mean of all scores, completely ignoring the group a score is in; in regression, the sum of squared differences of each score from the predicted score when predicting from the mean. (4, 12)

Sum of squared errors (SS_E) The sum of the squared differences between each score and its predicted score. (4)

Symmetrical distribution A distribution in which the pattern of frequencies on the left side and right side are mirror images. (1)

***t* distribution** A mathematically defined curve describing the comparison distribution used in a *t* test. (9)

Test-retest reliability One index of a measure's reliability, obtained by administering the measure to a group of people twice; the correlation between scores obtained on the two testings. (17)

Total sum of squares (SS_T) The sum of the squared differences between each score and the overall mean of all scores; same as *sum of squared deviations from the mean* (SS). (4, 12, 13)

***t* score** On a *t* distribution, the number of standard deviations from the mean (hence, it is like a *Z* score). (9)

***t* table** A table providing cutoff scores on the *t* distribution for various degrees of freedom, significance levels, and one- and two-tailed tests. (9)

***t* test** A hypothesis-testing procedure in which the population variance is unknown; it compares *t* scores from a sample to a comparison distribution called a *t* distribution. (9, 10)

***t* test for dependent means** A hypothesis-testing procedure in which there are two scores for each subject (or the subjects are in matched pairs) and the population variance is not known; it determines the significance of a hypothesis that is being tested using difference scores from a single group of subjects. (9)

***t* test for independent means** A hypothesis-testing procedure in which there are two separate groups of subjects whose scores are independent (that is, not paired across groups in any systematic way) and in which the population variance is not known; it determines the significance of a hypothesis tested from a study involving two groups of subjects. (10)

Two-tailed test The hypothesis-testing procedure for a nondirectional hypothesis; the situation in which the region of the comparison distribution in which the null hypothesis would be rejected is divided between the two sides of the distribution. (6)

Two-way analysis of variance An analysis of variance for a two-way factorial design. (13)

Two-way factorial design A factorial design with two independent variables. (13)

Type I error Rejecting the null hypothesis when in fact it is true; obtaining a statistically significant result when in fact the research hypothesis is not true. (7, 8)

Type II error Failing to reject the null hypothesis when in fact it is false; failing to get a statistically significant result when in fact the research hypothesis is true. (7, 8)

Unbiased estimate of the population variance (S^2) An estimate of the population variance, based on sample scores, that has been corrected (by dividing the sum of squared deviations by the sample size minus 1 instead of the usual procedure of dividing by the sample size directly) so that it is equally likely to overestimate or underestimate the true population variance. (9)

Unimodal distribution A frequency distribution with one value clearly having a larger frequency than any other. (1)

Value A possible number or category that a score can have. (1)

Variable A characteristic that can take on different values. (1)

Variance (SD^2, S^2, σ^2, *MS*) The average of the squared deviations from the mean; a common measure of variation in a group of scores. (2, 5, 9, 11)

Variance of a distribution of differences between means (S^2_{DIF}) One of the figures computed as part of a *t* test for independent means; it equals the sum of the variances of the distributions of means corresponding to each of two samples. (10)

Variance of a distribution of means (σ^2_M) The variance of the population divided by the number of cases in each sample. (7)

Weighted average An average in which the scores being averaged do not have equal influence on the total. (10)

Within-group degrees of freedom (df_W) Same as *denominator degrees of freedom*. (11)

Within-group population variance estimate (S^2_W, MS_W) In an analysis of variance, the estimate of the variance of the distribution of the population of individual cases based on the variation among the scores within each of the groups studied; also called *mean squares within;* same as *error variance* (S^2_E) and *mean squares error* (MS_E). (11)

Within-group sum of squares (SS_W) Same as *sum of squared deviations within groups.* (12)

Within-subject design Same as *repeated-measures design.* (9)

Z score The number of standard deviations a score is above (or below, if negative) the mean in its distribution; an ordinary score transformed so that it better describes that score's location in a distribution. (2)

Z test A hypothesis-testing procedure in which there is a single sample and the population variance is known. (7)

Glossary of Symbols

α Significance level; probability of a Type I error. (8)

β Standardized regression coefficient (4); also probability of a Type II error in hypothesis testing. (8)

μ Population mean. (5)

μ_M Mean of a distribution of means. (7)

σ Population standard deviation. (5)

σ_M Standard deviation of a distribution of means. (7)

σ^2 Population variance. (5)

σ_M^2 Variance of a distribution of means. (7)

Σ Sum of; add up all the scores following. (2)

φ Phi coefficient; effect size in chi-square analysis of a 2×2 contingency table. (14)

χ^2 Chi-square statistic. (14)

a Regression constant. (4)

b Raw score regression coefficient. (4)

d Effect size for studies involving one or two means. (8–10)

df Degrees of freedom. (9–14)

df_1, df_2, etc. Degrees of freedom for the first group, second group, etc. (10–13)

df_B Numerator degrees of freedom in the analysis of variance. (11)

df_C, df_R, df_I Degrees of freedom for columns, rows, and interactions (in the factorial analysis of variance). (13)

df_T Total degrees of freedom over all groups. (10–13)

df_W Denominator degrees of freedom in the analysis of variance. (11)

f Measure of effect size in the analysis of variance. (11)

F ratio In the analysis of variance, ratio of between-group population variance estimate to within-group population variance estimate. (11)

GM In the analysis of variance, mean of all scores. (11–13)

M Mean. (2)

M_1, M_2, etc. Mean of the first group, second group, etc. (10–13)

M_C, M_R Mean of the scores in a particular column or a particular row (in the factorial analysis of variance). (13)

MS_B Mean squares between. (11)

MS_C, MS_R, MS_I Mean squares between for columns, rows, interaction. (13)

MS_E Mean squares error. (11)

MS_W Mean squares within. (11)

n In the analysis of variance, number of cases in each group. (11)

N Number of cases overall. (2)

N_1, N_2, etc. Number of cases in the first group, second group, etc. (10–13)

N' Harmonic mean of two unequal sample sizes. (10)

N_C, N_R Number of columns, number of rows (in factorial analysis of variance). (13)

N_{Cells} Number of cells in a factorial design. (13)

N_G In the analysis of variance, number of groups.

p Probability. (5)

r Correlation coefficient. (3)

r^2 Proportionate reduction in error (proportion of variance accounted for) in bivariate regression. (3)

R Multiple correlation coefficient. (4, 12)

R^2 Proportionate reduction in error (proportion of variance accounted for) in multiple regression and analysis of variance. (4, 12, 13)

R_C^2, R_R^2, R_I^2 Proportion of variance accounted for (a measure of effect size in the factorial analysis of variance) for columns, rows, interaction. (13)

S Unbiased estimate of the population standard deviation. (9)

S^2 Unbiased estimate of the population variance. (9)

S_1^2, S_2^2, etc. Unbiased estimate of the population variance based on scores in the first sample, second sample, etc. (10–13)

S_B^2 Between-group population variance estimate. (11)

S_C^2, S_R^2, S_I^2 Estimated population variance between groups for columns, rows, interaction (in the factorial analysis of variance). (13)

S_{DIF} Standard deviation of the distribution of differences between means. (10)

S_{DIF}^2 Variance of the distribution of differences between means. (10)

S_E^2 Error variance. (11)

S_M Standard deviation of the distribution of means based on an estimated population variance. (9)

S_M^2 Variance of a distribution of means based on an estimated population variance in a t test or as estimated from the variation among means of groups in the analysis of variance. (9, 11)

S_{M1}^2, S_{M2}^2, etc. Variance of the distribution of means based on a pooled population variance estimate, corresponding to the first sample, second sample, etc. (10, 11)

S_P Pooled estimate of the population standard deviation. (10)

S_P^2 Pooled estimate of the population variance. (10)

S_W^2 Within-group population variance estimate. (11)

SD Standard deviation. (2)

SD^2 Variance. (2)

SS Sum of squared deviations. (2)

SS_B Sum of squared deviations between groups. (12)

SS_C, SS_R, SS_I Sum of squared deviations between columns or rows or due to interaction (in the factorial analysis of variance). (13)

SS_T Total sum of squared deviations from the mean (or from the grand mean, in the analysis of variance). (4, 12, 13)

SS_W Sum of squared deviations within groups (or within cells). (12, 13)

t score Number of standard deviations from the mean on a t distribution. (9)

X Score on a particular variable; in regression, X is the usual designation for the independent or predictor variable. (1–4)

X_1, X_2, etc. First predictor or independent variable, second predictor or independent variable, etc. (4)

$\overline{X}$ Mean of variable designated X. (2)

Y Usually, the dependent variable in regression. (3, 4)

$\hat{Y}$ Predicted value of the variable designated Y. (4)

Z Number of standard deviations from the mean. (2)

Z_X Z score for the variable designated X. (3, 4)

Z_{X1}, Z_{X2}, etc. See score for the first predictor or independent variable, see score for the second predictor or independent variable, etc. (4)

Z_Y Z score for variable designated Y. (3, 4)

$\hat{Z}_Y$ Predicted value of the Z score for the variable designated Y. (4)

Other Symbols

$\wedge$ Predicted value of the variable. (4)

$^{—}$ Mean of the variable. (2)

References

ABRAMS, R. A., & BALOTA, D. A. (1991). Mental chronometry: Beyond reaction time. *Psychological Science, 2,* 153–157.

ALEXANDER, C. N., LANGER, E. J., NEWMAN R. I., CHANDLER, H. M., & DAVIES, J. L. (1989). Transcendental Meditation, mindfulness, and longevity: An experimental study with the elderly. *Journal of Personality and Social Psychology, 57,* 950–964.

ANDERSON, C. A., & FORD, C. M. (1986). Affect of the game player: Short-term effects of highly and mildly aggressive video games. *Personality and Social Psychology Bulletin, 12,* 390–402.

ANDERSON, C. A., & SEDIKIDES, C. (1991). Thinking about people: Contributions of a typological alternative to associationistic and dimensional models of person perception. *Journal of Personality and Social Psychology, 60,* 203–217.

ARON, A., & ARON, E. N. (1989). *The heart of social psychology.* Lexington, MA: Heath.

ARON, A., ARON, E. N., & SMOLLAN, D. (1992). Inclusion of Other in the Self Scale and the structure of interpersonal closeness. *Journal of Personality and Social Psychology, 63,* 596–612.

ARON, A., ARON, E. N., TUDOR, M., & NELSON, G. (1991). Close relationships as including other in the self. *Journal of Personality and Social Psychology, 60,* 241–253.

ARON, A., & GILMORE, J. (1992). *The one-and-one-quarter-tailed test.* Unpublished essay.

ARON, A., PARIS, M., & ARON, E. N. (1993). *Falling in love and other earth-shaking experiences: A prospective study of self-concept change.* Manuscript under review.

BAER, J. (1991). Generality of creativity across performance domains. *Creativity Research Journal, 4,* 23–39.

BANDURA, A., & JOURDEN, F. J. (1991). Self-regulatory mechanisms governing the impact of social comparison on complex decision making. *Journal of Personality and Social Psychology, 60,* 941–951.

BANKSTON, W., THOMPSON, C., JENKINS, Q., & FORSYTH, C. (1990). The influence of fear of crime, gender, and southern culture on carrying firearms for protection. *Sociological Quarterly, 31,* 287–305.

BARGLOW, P., VAUGHN, B. E., & MOLITOR, N. (1987). Effects of maternal absence due to employment on the quality of infant-mother attachment in a low-risk sample. *Child Development, 58,* 945–954.

BAROCAS, R., SEIFER, R., SAMEROFF, A. J., ANDREWS, T. A., CROFT, R. T., & OSTROW, E. (1991). Social and interpersonal determinants of developmental risk. *Developmental Psychology, 27,* 479–488.

BARON, R. S., BURGESS, M. L., & KAO, C. F. (1991). Detecting and labeling prejudice: Do female perpetrators go undetected? *Personality and Social Psychology Bulletin, 17,* 115–123.

BAUMRIND, D. (1983). Specious causal attributions in the social sciences: The reformulated stepping-stone theory of heroin use as exemplar. *Journal of Personality and Social Psychology, 45,* 1289–1298.

BEAMAN, A. L. (1991). An empirical comparison of meta-analytic and traditional reviews. *Personality and Social Psychology Bulletin, 17,* 252–257.

BECKINGHAM, A. C., & LUBIN, B. (1991). Reliability and validity of the trait form of Set 2 of the Depression Adjective Check Lists with Canadian elderly. *Journal of Clinical Psychology, 47,* 407–414.

BERSCHEID, E., SNYDER, M., & OMOTO, A. M. (1989). The Relationship Closeness Inventory: Assessing the closeness of interpersonal relationships. *Journal of Personality and Social Psychology, 57,* 792–807.

BIERMAN, K. L., & SMOOT, D. L. (1991). Linking family characteristics with poor peer relations: The mediating role of conduct problems. *Journal of Abnormal Child Psychology, 19,* 341–356.

BIERNAT, M., & WORTMAN, C. B. (1991). Sharing of home responsibilities between professionally employed women and their husbands. *Journal of Personality and Social Psychology, 60,* 844–860.

BINER, P. M. (1991). Effects of lighting-induced arousal on the magnitude of goal valence. *Personality and Social Psychology Bulletin, 17,* 219–226.

BLANCHARD, F. A., LILLY, T., & VAUGHN, L. A. (1991). Reducing the expression of racial prejudice. *Psychological Science, 2,* 101–105.

BLASS, T. (1991). Understanding behavior in the Milgram obedience experiment: The role of personality, situations, and their interactions. *Journal of Personality and Social Psychology, 60,* 398–413.

BREWER, J. K. (1972). On the power of statistical tests in the *American Education Research Journal. American Educational Research Journal, 9,* 391–401.

BRICKMAN, P., COATES, D., & JANOFF-BULMAN, R. (1978). Lottery winners and accident victims: Is happiness relative? *Journal of Personality and Social Psychology, 36,* 917–927.

BROWN, J. D., & SILBERSCHATZ, G. (1989). Dependency, self-criticism, and depressive attributional style. *Journal of Abnormal Psychology, 98,* 187–188.

BUCK, J. L. (1985). A failure to find gender differences in statistics achievement. *Teaching of Psychology, 12,* 100.

CAPALDI, D. M., & PATTERSON, G. R. (1991). Relation of parental transitions to boys' adjustment problems: 1. A linear hypothesis 2. Mothers at risk for transitions and unskilled parenting. *Developmental Psychology, 27,* 489–504.

CARLIN, M. F., & SANIGA, R. D. (1990). Relationship between academic placement and perception of abuse of the voice. *Perception and Motor Skills, 71,* 299–304.

CASPI, A., & HERBENER, E. S. (1990). Continuity and change: Assortative marriage and the consistency of personality in adulthood. *Journal of Personality and Social Psychology, 58,* 250–258.

CHASE, L. J., & CHASE, R. B. (1976). A statistical power analysis of applied psychological research. *Journal of Applied Psychology, 61,* 234–237.

CHOW, S. L. (1988). Significance test or effect size. *Psychological Bulletin, 103,* 105–110.

CHRISTENSEN, L., & BURROWS, R. (1991). Criterion validity of the Christensen Dietary Distress Inventory. *Canadian Journal of Behavioural Science, 23,* 245–247.

CLIFF, N. (1983). Some cautions concerning the application of causal modeling methods. *Multivariate Behavioral Research, 18,* 115–126.

COHEN, J. (1962). The statistical power of abnormal-social psychological research: A review. *Journal of Abnormal and Social Psychology, 65,* 145–153.

COHEN, J. (1988). *Statistical power analysis for the behavioral sciences.* Hillsdale, NJ: Erlbaum.

COHEN, J. (1990). Things I have learned (so far). *American Psychologist, 45,* 1304–1312.

COHEN, J., & COHEN, P. (1983). *Applied multiple regression/correlation analysis for the behavioral sciences.* Hillsdale, NJ: Erlbaum.

Commission payments to travel agents. (1978, August 8). *New York Times,* p. D-1.

CONOVER, W., & IMAN, R. L. (1981). Rank transformations as a bridge between parametric and nonparametric statistics. *American Statistician, 35,* 124–129.

COOK, T. D., & CAMPBELL, D. T. (1979). *Quasi-experimentation: Design and analysis issues for field settings.* Skokie, IL: Rand McNally.

COOPER, H. M., & LEMKE, K. M. (1991). On the role of meta-analysis in personality and social psychology. *Personality and Social Psychology Bulletin, 17,* 245–251.

COOPER, S. E., & ROBINSON, D. A. G. (1989). The influence of gender and anxiety on mathematics performance. *Journal of College Student Development, 30,* 459–461.

DAHLSTROM, W. G., LARBAR, D., & DAHLSTROM, L. E. (1986). *MMPI patterns of American minorities.* Minneapolis: University of Minnesota Press.

DANE, F. C., & WRIGHTSMAN, L. S. (1982). Effects of defendants' and victims' characteristics on jurors' verdicts. In N. L. Kerr & R. M. Bray (Eds.), *The psychology of the courtroom.* Orlando, FL: Academic Press.

DARLINGTON, R. B. (1990). *Regression and linear models.* New York: McGraw-Hill.

DELUCCHI, K. L. (1983). The use and misuse of chi-square: Lewis and Burke revisited. *Psychological Bulletin, 94,* 166–176.

DELUGA, R. J. (1991). The relationship of subordinate upward-influencing behavior, health care manager interpersonal stress, and performance. *Journal of Applied Social Psychology, 21,* 78–88.

DIXON, W. A., HEPPNER, P., & ANDERSON, W. P. (1991). Problem-solving appraisal, stress, hopelessness, and suicide ideation in a college population. *Journal of Counseling Psychology, 38,* 51–56.

DWINELL, P. E., & HIGBEE, J. L. (1991). Affective variables related to mathematics achievement among high-risk college freshmen. *Psychological Reports, 69,* 399–403.

DYKMAN, B. M., HOROWITZ, L. M., ABRAMSON, L. Y., & USHER, M. (1991). Schematic and situational determinants of depressed and nondepressed students' interpretation of feedback. *Journal of Abnormal Psychology, 100,* 45–55.

ENDLER, N. S., & MAGNUSSON, D. (1976). Toward an interactional psychology of personality. *Psychological Bulletin, 83,* 956–974.

EPPLEY, K. R., ABRAMS, A. I., & SHEAR, J. (1989). Differential effects of relaxation techniques on trait anxiety: A meta-analysis. *Journal of Clinical Psychology, 45,* 957–974.

EVANS, R. (1976). *The making of psychology.* New York: Knopf.

EYSENCK, H. J. (1981). *A model for personality.* Berlin: Springer-Verlag.

FEHR, B. (1988). Prototype analysis of the concepts of love and commitment. *Journal of Personality and Social Psychology, 55,* 557–579.

FISHER, B. (1978). *Fisher Divorce Adjustment Scale.* Boulder, CO: Family Relations Learning Center.

FISHER, R. A. (1938). *Statistical methods for research workers* (7th ed.). London: Oliver & Boyd.

FOA, E. B., FESKE, U., MURDOCK, T. B., KOZAK, M., & MCCARTHY, P. R. (1991). Processing of threat-related information in rape victims. *Journal of Abnormal Psychology, 100,* 156–162.

FRANZ, M. L. VON. (1979). *The problem of puer aeternus.* New York: Springer-Verlag.

FREUND, R. D., RUSSELL, T. T., & SCHWEITZER, S. (1991). Influence of length of delay between intake session and initial counseling session on client perceptions of counselors and counseling outcomes. *Journal of Counseling Psychology, 38,* 3–8.

FRODI, A., GROLNICK, W., BRIDGES, L., & BERKO, J. (1990). Infants of adolescents and adult mothers: Two indices of socioemotional development. *Adolescence, 25,* 363–374.

GALLUP, D. G. H. (1972). *The Gallup poll: Public opinion, 1935–1971.* New York: Random House.

GALTON, F. (1889). *Natural inheritance.* London: Macmillan.

GAMES, P. A. (1988). Theory-free statistics and theory-based statistics: Their appropriate roles in the reporting of scientific results. *Journal of Experimental Education, 57,* 47–58.

GARIEPY, J., HOOD, K. E., & CAIRNS, R. B. (1988). A developmental-genetic analysis of aggressive behavior in mice (*Mus musculus*): III. Behavioral mediation by heightened reactivity or immobility? *Journal of Comparative Psychology, 102,* 392–399.

GEISSER, S., & GREENHOUSE, S. (1958). An extension of Box's results on the use of the *F* distribution in multivariate analysis. *Annals of Mathematical Statistics, 29,* 885–891.

GIGERENZER, G., & MURRAY, D. J. (1987). *Cognition as intuitive statistics.* Hillsdale, NJ: Erlbaum.

GIGERENZER, G., SWIJTINK, Z., PORTER, Y., DASTON, L., BEATTY, J., & KRUGER, L. (1989). *The empire of chance.* Cambridge: Cambridge University Press.

GLADUE, B. A., & DELANEY, H. J. (1990). Gender differences in perception of attractiveness of men and women in bars. *Personality and Social Psychology Bulletin, 16,* 378–39.

GOSSET, W. S. (1947). *"Student's" collected papers.* London: University College.

GOUGH, H., & HEILBRUN, A. (1983). *The Adjective Check List manual.* Palo Alto, CA: Consulting Psychologist Press.

GREENWALD, A. G. (1975). Consequences of prejudice against the null hypothesis. *Psychological Bulletin, 82,* 1–19.

HAMILTON, D. (1981). *Cognitive processes in stereotyping and intergroup behavior.* Hillsdale, NJ: Erlbaum.

HAMILTON, D., & GIFFORD, R. (1976). Illusory correlation in interpersonal perception: A cognitive basis of stereotypic judgments. *Journal of Experimental Social Psychology, 12,* 392–407.

HARRIS, G., THOMAS, A., & BOOTH, D. A. (1990). Development of salt taste in infancy. *Developmental Psychology, 26,* 534–538.

HART, K. E. (1991). Obsessive-compulsiveness in obese weight-loss patients and normal-weight adults. *Journal of Clinical Psychology, 47,* 358–360.

HAZAN, C., & SHAVER, P. (1987). Romantic love conceptualized as an attachment process. *Journal of Personality and Social Psychology, 52,* 511–524.

HEATHERTON, T. F., POLIVY, J., & HERMAN, C. P. (1991). Restraint, weight loss, and variability of body weight. *Journal of Abnormal Psychology, 100,* 78–83.

HENDRICK, C., & HENDRICK, S. S. (1989). Research on love: Does it measure up? *Journal of Personality and Social Psychology, 56,* 784–794.

HILGARD, E. R. (1987). *Psychology in America: A historical perspective.* Orlando, FL: Harcourt Brace Jovanovich.

HINDLEY, C., FILLIOZAT, A., KLACKENBERG, G., NICOLET-MEISTER, D., & SAND, E. (1966). Differences in age of walking in five European longitudinal samples. *Human Biology, 38,* 364–379.

HOBFOLL, S. E., & LEIBERMAN, J. R. (1987). Personality and social resources in immediate and continued stress resistance among women. *Journal of Personality and Social Psychology, 52,* 18–26.

HOPKINS, K. D., & GLASS, G. V. (1978). *Basic statistics for the behavioral sciences.* Englewood Cliffs, NJ: Prentice Hall.

HUBER, V. L. (1991). Comparison of supervisor-incumbent and female-male multidimensional job evaluation ratings. *Journal of Applied Psychology, 76,* 115–121.

HUNSLEY, J., & LEFEBVRE, M. (1990). A survey of the practices and activities of Canadian clinical psychologists. *Canadian Psychology, 31,* 350–358.

HUSSERL, E. (1970). *The crisis of European sciences and transcendental phenomenology: An introduction to phenomenological philosophy* (D. C. Carr, Trans.). Evanston, IL: Northwestern University Press.

INHOFF, A., LIMA, S., & CARROLL, P. (1984). Contextural effects on metaphor comprehension in reading. *Memory and Cognition, 12*, 558–567.

INTROINI-COLLISON, I. B., & MCGAUGH, J. L. (1986). Epinephrine modulates long-term retention of an aversively motivated discrimination. *Behavioral and Neural Biology, 45*, 358–365.

JOHNSON-LAIRD, P., & OATLEY, K. (1986). The meaning of emotions: A cognitive theory and a semantic analysis. Unpublished essay, Cambridge University.

JUNE, L. N., CURRY, B. P., & GEAR, C. L. (1990). An 11-year analysis of black students' experience of problems and use of services: Implications for counseling professionals. *Journal of Counseling Psychology, 37*, 178–184.

KAISER, H. (1960). Directional statistical decisions. *Psychological Review, 67*, 160–167.

KELLEY, H. H. (1971). Attribution in social interaction. Morristown, NJ: General Learning Press.

KEPPEL, G. (1982). *Design and analysis: A researcher's handbook*. Engelwood Cliffs, NJ: Prentice Hall.

KERLINGER, F. N. (1973). *Foundations of behavioral research*. New York: Holt, Rinehart and Winston.

KILHAM, W., & MANN, L. (1974). Level of destructive obedience as a function of transmitter and executant roles in the Milgram obedience paradigm. *Journal of Personality and Social Psychology, 29*, 696–702.

KIRBY, J. R., & DAS, J. P. (1990). A cognitive approach to intelligence: Attention, coding and planning. *Canadian Psychology, 31*, 320–333.

KIRK, R. E. (1982). *Experimental design*. Pacific Grove, CA: Brooks/Cole.

KIVLIGHAN, D. M., & ANGELONE, E. O. (1991). Helpee introversion, novice counselor intention use, and helpee-rated session impact. *Journal of Counseling Psychology, 38*, 25–29.

KLEINMUNTZ, B. (1990). Why we still use our heads instead of formulas: Toward an integrative approach. *Psychological Bulletin, 107*, 296–310.

KRAEMER, H. C., & THIEMANN, S. (1987). *How many subjects? Statistical power analysis in research*. Newbury Park, CA: Sage.

KUPFERSMID, J., & FIALA, M. (1991). Comparison of EPPP scores among graduates of varying psychology programs. *American Psychologist, 46*, 534–535.

LANGLOIS, J. H., & ROGGMAN, L. A. (1990). Attractive faces are only average. *Psychological Science, 1*, 115–121.

LEVENSON, M. R. (1990). Risk taking and personality. *Journal of Personality and Social Psychology, 58*, 1073–1080.

LEWIS, D., & BURKE, C. J. (1949). The use and misuse of the chi-square test. *Psychological Bulletin, 46*, 433–489.

LYNN, S. J., WEEKES, J. R., NEUFELD, V., ZIVNEY, O., BRENTAR, J., & WEISS, F. (1991). Interpersonal climate and hypnotizability level: Effects on hypnotic performance, rapport, and archaic involvement. *Journal of Personality and Social Psychology, 60*, 739–743.

MALIPHANT, R., HUME, F., & FURNHAM, A. (1990). Autonomic nervous system (ANS) activity, personality characteristics, and disruptive behavior in girls. *Journal of Child Psychology Psychiatry, 31*, 619–628.

MANNING, C., HALL, J., & GOLD, P. (1990). Glucose effects on memory and other neuropsychological tests in elderly humans. *Psychological Science, 1*, 307–311.

MAXWELL, S. E., & DELANEY, H. D. (1990). *Designing experiments and analyzing data*. Belmont, CA: Wadsworth.

MCCRACKEN, G. (1988). *The long interview*. London: Sage.

MEEHL, P. E. (1954). *Clinical versus statistical prediction: A theoretical analysis and a review of the evidence*. Minneapolis: University of Minnesota Press.

MEIER, S. T. (1991). Tests of the construct validity of occupational stress measures with college students: Failure to support discriminant validity. *Journal of Counseling Psychology, 38*, 91–97.

MICCERI, T. (1989). The unicorn, the normal curve, and other improbable creatures. *Psychological Bulletin, 105*, 156–166.

MILGRAM, S. (1974). *Obedience to authority: An experimental view*. New York: Harper Collins.

MILLIGAN, G. W., WONG, D. S., & THOMPSON, P. A. (1987). Robustness properties of nonorthogonal analysis of variance. *Psychological Bulletin, 101*, 464–470.

MIRVIS, P., & LAWLER, E. (1977). Measuring the financial impact of employee attitudes. *Journal of Applied Psychology, 62*, 1–8.

MISCHEL, W. (1968). *Personality and assessment*. New York: Wiley.

MOONEY, S. P., SHERMAN, M. F., & LO PRESTO, C. T. (1991). Academic locus of control, self-esteem, and perceived distance from home as predictors of college adjustment. *Journal of Counseling and Development, 69*, 445–448.

MOOREHOUSE, M. J., & SANDERS, P. E. (1992). Children's feelings of school competence and perceptions of parents' work in four sociocultural contexts. *Social Development, 1*, 185–200.

MOSES, R. P., KAMII, M., SWAP, S. M., & HOWARD, J. (1989). The Algebra Project: Organizing in the spirit of Ella. *Harvard Educational Review, 59*, 423–442.

MYERS, D. G. (1991). Union is strength: A consumer's view of meta-analysis. *Personality and Social Psychology Bulletin, 17*, 265–266.

NAGLIERI, J. A., & DAS, J. P. (1988). Planning-Arousal-Simultaneous-Successive: A model for assessment. *Journal of School Psychology, 26*, 35–48.

NOLEN-HOEKSEMA, S. (1987). Sex differences in unipolar depression: Evidence and theory. *Psychological Bulletin, 101*, 259–282.

OAKES, M. (1982). Intuiting strength of association from a correlation coefficient. *British Journal of Psychology, 73*, 51–56.

OLTHOFF, R., & ARON, A. (1993). *Premarital communication-skills training on marital satisfaction*. Unpublished manuscript.

PEARSON, K. (1978). *The history of statistics in the 17th and 18th centuries*. London: Griffin.

PECUKONIS, E. V. (1990). A cognitive/affective empathy training program as a function of ego development in aggressive adolescent females. *Adolescence*, *25*, 59–76.

PETERS, W. S. (1987). *Counting for something: Statistical principles and personalities*. New York: Springer-Verlag.

PFEIFFER, S. M., & WONG, P. T. (1989). Multidimensional jealousy. *Journal of Social and Personal Relationships*, *6*, 181–196.

PHILLIPS, L. D. (1973). *Bayesian statistics for social scientists*. London: Nelson.

POLLARD, C. A., POLLARD, H. J., & CORN, K. J. (1989). Panic onset and major events in the lives of agoraphobics: A test of contiguity. *Journal of Abnormal Psychology*, *98*, 318–321.

PRYOR, J. B., REEDER, G. D., & MCMANUS, J. A. (1991). Fear and loathing in the workplace: Reactions to AIDS-infected co-workers. *Personality and Social Psychology Bulletin*, *17*, 133–139.

PUGH, G. M., & BOER, D. P. (1991). Normative data on the validity of Canadian substitute items for the WAIS-R information subtest. *Canadian Journal of Behavioural Science*, *23*, 149–158.

REGIER, D., MYERS, J., KRAMER, M., ROBINS, L., BLAZER, D., HOUGH, R., EATON, W., & LOCKE, B. (1984). The NIMH Epidemiologic Catchment Area Program. *Archives of General Psychiatry*, *41*, 934–941.

REIS, H. T., & STILLER, J. (1992). Publication trends in *JPSP*: A three-decade review. *Personality and Social Psychology Bulletin*, *18*, 465–472.

RIESSMAN, C. (1991). *Shared activities and marital satisfaction: Self-expansion vs. boredom*. Unpublished doctoral dissertation, California Graduate School of Family Psychology, San Francisco.

REISSMAN, C., ARON, A., & BERGEN, M. R. (1993). Shared activities and marital satisfaction: Causal direction and self-expansion versus boredom. *Journal of Social and Personal Relationships*, *10*, 253–254.

ROSNOW, R. L., & ROSENTHAL, R. (1989a). Definition and interpretation of interaction effects. *Psychological Bulletin*, *105*, 143–146.

ROSNOW, R. L., & ROSENTHAL, R. (1989b) Statistical procedures and the justification of knowledge in psychological science. *American Psychologist*, *44*, 1276–1284.

ROSS, D. C., & KLEIN, D. F. (1988). Group matching: Is this a research technique to be avoided? *Educational and Psychological Measurement*, *48*, 281–295.

RUSBULT, C. E., VERETTE, J., WHITNEY, G. A., SLOVIK, L. F., & LIPKUS, I. (1991). Accommodation processes in close relationships: Theory and preliminary empirical evidence. *Journal of Personality and Social Psychology*, *60*, 53–78.

RUSSELL, J. A. (1991). In defense of a prototype approach to emotion concepts. *Journal of Personality and Social Psychology*, *60*, 37–47.

SANSONE, C., WEIR, C., HARPSTER, L., & MORGAN, C. (1992). Once a boring task, always a boring task? Interest as a self-regulatory mechanism. *Journal of Personality and Social Psychology*, *63*, 379–390.

SAWILOWSKY, S. S., & BLAIR, R. C. (1992). A more realistic look at the robustness and Type II error properties of the *t* test to departures from population normality. *Psychological Bulletin*, *111*, 352–360.

SCHACHTER, S., CHRISTENFELD, N., RAVINA, B., & BILOUS, F. (1991). Speech disfluency and the structure of knowledge. *Journal of Personality and Social Psychology*, *60*, 362–367.

SEDLMEIER, P., & GIGERENZER, G. (1989). Do studies of statistical power have an effect on the power of studies? *Psychological Bulletin*, *105*, 309–316.

SELIGMAN, M. E., NOLEN-HOEKSEMA, S., THORTON, N., & THORTON, K. M. (1990). Explanatory style as a mechanism of disappointing athletic performance. *Psychological Science*, *1*, 143–146.

SHAPIRO, D. A., & SHAPIRO, D. (1983). Comparative therapy outcome research: Methodological implications of meta-analysis. *Journal of Consulting and Clinial Psychology*, *51*, 42–53.

SHREIDER, YU. A. (1966). Preface to the English edition. In N. P. Bushlenko, D. I. Golenko, Yu. A. Shreider, L. M. Sobol', & V. G. Sragovich (Yu. A. Shreider, Ed.), *The Monte Carlo method: The method of statistical trials* (G. J. Tee, Trans.), (p. vii). Elmsford, NY: Pergamon Press.

SINGER, J. A. (1990). Affective responses to autobiographical memories and their relationship to long-term goals. *Journal of Personality*, *58*, 535–549.

SKINNER, B. F. (1956). A case history in scientific method. *American Psychologist*, *11*, 221–233.

SNYDER, C. R., HARRIS, C., ANDERSON, J. R., HOLLERAN, S. A., IRVING, L. M., SIGMON, S. T., YOSHINOBU, L., GIBB, J., LANGELLE, J., LANGELLE, C., & HARNEY, P. (1991). The will and the ways: Development and validation of an individual-differences measure of hope. *Journal of Personality and Social Psychology*, *60*, 570–585.

SOLANO, C. H., & KOESTER, N. H. (1989). Loneliness and communication problems: Subjective anxiety or objective skills? *Personality and Social Psychology Bulletin*, *15*, 126–133.

STASSER, G., TAYLOR, L. A., & HANNA, C. (1989). Information sampling in structured and unstructured discussions of three- and six-person groups. *Journal of Personality and Social Psychology*, *57*, 67–78.

STEEN, L. A. (1987). Forward. In S. Tobias, *Succeed with math: Every student's guide to conquering math anxiety* (pp. xvii–xviii). New York: College Entrance Examination Board.

STEERING COMMITTEE OF THE PHYSICIANS HEALTH STUDY RESEARCH GROUP. (1988). Preliminary report: Findings from the Aspirin component of the ongoing Physicians Health Study. *New England Journal of Medicine, 318,* 262–264.

STIGLER, S. M. (1986). *The history of statistics.* Cambridge, MA: Belknap Press.

TABACHNICK, B. G., & FIDELL, L. S. (1989). *Using multivariate statistics* (2nd ed.). New York: Harper Collins.

TABACHNICK, B. G., KEITH-SPIEGEL, P., & POPE, K. S. (1991). Ethics of teaching: Beliefs and behaviors of psychologists as educators. *American Psychologists, 46,* 506–515.

TAGESON, C. W. (1982). *A humanistic approach.* Homewood, IL: Dorsey Press.

TANKARD, J., JR. (1984). *The statistical pioneers.* Cambridge, MA: Schenkman.

THOMAS, A., & CHESS, S. (1977). *Temperament and development.* New York: Bruner/Mazel.

TOBIAS, S. (1982, January). Sexist equations. *Psychology Today,* pp. 14–17.

TOBIAS, S. (1987). *Succeed with math: Every student's guide to conquering math anxiety.* New York: College Entrance Examination Board.

TUFTE, E. R. (1983). *The visual display of quantitative information.* Cheshire, CT: Graphic Press.

U.S. BUREAU OF THE CENSUS. (1990). *Statistical abstracts of the United States.* Washington, DC: U.S. Government Printing Office.

U.S. DEPARTMENT OF EDUCATION. (1990). *The condition of education.* Washington, DC: U.S. Government Printing Office.

WALBERG, H. J., STRYKOWSKI, B. F., ROVAI, E., & HUNG, S. S. (1984). Exceptional performance. *Review of Educational Research, 54,* 87–112.

WARD, S. E., LEVENTHAL, H., & LOVE, R. (1988). Repression revisited: Tactics used in coping with a severe health threat. *Personality and Social Psychology Bulletin, 14,* 735–746.

WATTS, W., & WRIGHT, L. (1990). The relationship of alcohol, tobacco, marijuana, and other illegal drug use to delinquency among Mexican-American, black, and white adolescent males. *Adolescence, 25,* 171–181.

WHITLEY, B. E. (1990). The relationship of heterosexuals' attributions for the causes of homosexuality to attitudes toward lesbians and gay men. *Personality and Social Psychology Bulletin, 16,* 369–377.

WINER, B. (1971). *Statistical principles in experimental design.* New York: McGraw-Hill.

WONG, M. M., & CSIKSZENTMIHALYI, M. (1991). Affiliation motivation and daily experience: Some issues on gender differences. *Journal of Personality and Social Psychology, 60,* 154–164.

YUKL, G., & FALBE, C. M. (1991). Importance of different power sources in downward and lateral relations. *Journal of Applied Psychology, 76,* 416–423.

ZEIDNER, M. (1991). Statistics and mathematics anxiety in social science students: Some interesting parallels. *British Journal of Education, 61,* 319–329.

ZUCKERMAN, M. (1979). *Sensation seeking: Beyond the optimal level of arousal.* Hillsdale, NJ: Erlbaum.

ZUCKERMAN, M., & LUBIN, B. (1965). *Manual for the Multiple Affect Adjective Checklist.* San Diego, CA: Educational and Industrial Testing Service.

ZUCKERMAN, M., MIYAKE, K., & HODGINS, H. S. (1991). Cross-channel effects of vocal and physical attractiveness and their implications for interpersonal perception. *Journal of Personality and Social Psychology, 60,* 545–554.

Index

D

Data transformation, 448–56, 467, 470–72
  inverse transformation, 452, 472
  legitimacy of, 449–50
  log transformation, 451–52, 472
  rank-order methods, 456–62, 472
  reflecting variables, 452
  in research articles, 470–72
  square-root transformation, 448–51, 472
Dahlstrom, L. E., 172
Dahlstrom, W. G., 172
Dane, F. C., n326
Darlington, R. B., n480
Das, J. P., 530–31
Daston, L., 523
Davies, J. L., 359–60
Decision aids, 123
Definitional formula, 47
Degree of correlation, 74–78, 93–94. *See also* Correlation
  coefficient
Degrees of freedom, 253, 261, 276
  in analysis of variance table, 346–47
  and chi-square distribution, 419
  in computing Cramer's phi, 436, 441
  in computing weighted average, 284–85, 361
  in contingency table, 428–29, 441
  denominator, 324–25, 329, 335, 344–46, 353
  in factorial analysis of variance, 386–88, 397
  and F distribution, 324–25, 329, 335
  numerator, 324–25, 329, 335, 344–46, 353
  in research articles, 274–76, 303–5, 439–40
  and t distribution, 255, 287, 305
  in t table, 256
Delaney, H. D., 402, 404
Delaney, H. J., 411
Delucchi, K. L., 439
Deluga, R. J., 129–30
De Moivre, A., 134–35
Dependent means, 262. *See also* t test for dependent means
Dependent variable, 66–67, 103–4
Descriptive statistics, 2, 31
Deviation score, 38
Difference score, 262
Dimension, 369
  in contingency table, 426
  in factorial design, 311–12, 369
Directional hypothesis, 169, 176
Distribution-free test, 457, 472
Distribution of differences between means, 281–83, 286–88, 305
  mean of, 283, 305
  shape of, 287, 305
  standard deviation of, 287, 305
  in t test for independent means, 281–305
  variance of, 286–87, 305
Distribution of means, 181–90, 202–3
  and comparison distribution, 191, n255
  in hypothesis testing, 191–92, 202–3
  mean of, 184, 187, 202
  shape of, 186–87, 202
  standard deviation of, 186–87, 202

variance of, 185–87, 202
Dixon, W. A., 470–71
Double-blind procedure, 541
Dwinell, P. E., 14
Dykman, B. M., 179

E

Eaton, W., 421–22
Effect size, 215–24, 231, 245
  for analysis of variance, 328–30, 335, 356–58, 362
  for chi-square test for independence, 435–38, 441
  comparison to statistical significance, 236–40, 245
  conventions, 222–24, 245
  for correlation coefficient, 100–101
  for factorial analysis of variance, 398–402, 408
  and meta-analysis, 241–45
  in research articles, 244
  for t test for dependent means, 270–73, 276
  for t test for independent means, 299–302, 305
Effect size for analysis of variance (f), 328–30, 335, 356, 399
Endler, N. S., 383
Endogenous variable, 516
Eppley, K. R., 242
Equal interval measurement, 461–62, 470
Equal interval size, failure to use, 21–22, 28
Error. *See also* Proportion of variance accounted for; Standard
  deviation of a distribution of means; Sum of squared errors;
  Type I error; Type II error
  in analysis of variance table, 346
  deviation scores, n39
  in general linear model, 480
  graphic interpretation of, 111–12
  in least-squares model, 480, 499
  in path diagram, 516
  in prediction model, 110–15
Error variance. *See* Within-group variance estimate
Ethnicity, and math performance, 22–23
Eugenics, 75, 319, 417
Evans, R., 54
Exogenous variable, 516
Expected frequency, in chi-square tests, 416–18, 427–28, 438–41
Experimental group, 534–41
Experimenter bias, 540
Experimenter effects, 540
External validity, 541–42
Eysenk, H. J., 15

F

Factor, 513–15, n518
Factor analysis, 513–15, 527
  comparison to other statistical techniques, 523
  in latent variable modeling, n518
  table of results, 514–15
Factorial analysis of variance, 367, 396–408. *See also* Interaction effect
  assumptions of, 396
  computational formula, 411–12
  effect size, 398–402, 408

least-squares analysis of variance, 403
and power, 398, 400–402, 408
repeated-measures analysis of variance, 403–4, 408
in research articles, 406–7
structural model approach in, 344, 385–97
three-way and higher analysis of variance, 402, 408
two-way analysis of variance, 382–97, 407, 411–12
Factorial design, 357–72, 407–8. *See also* Factorial analysis of variance
Factor loading, 513–15
Falbe, C. M., 531–32
Fatigue effect, 537
F distribution, 323–24, 329, 335, 353
Fehr, B., 25, 27
Fermat, P., 141
Feske, U., 57
Fiala, M., 361
Fidell, L. S., 497
File drawer problem, 243
Filliozat, A., 158
Fisher, B., 200
Fisher, R. A., 316, 318–19, 417, 438–39, n439, 468, 524–25
Fisher approach, 523–25
Fisher's exact test, n439
Floor effect, 20, 447
Foa, E. B., 57
Ford, C. M., 364
Formula, computational and definitional, 47
Forsyth, C., 126
Franz, M. L. von, 56–57
F ratio, 315–16, 329, 334. *See also* Analysis of variance
Frequency distribution, 18. *See also* Normal curve; Skew
shape of, 18–20
Frequency polygon, 12–17, 28
exaggeration of proportions, 23–25, 28
in media, 21, 23–25, 28
and mode, 36
in research articles, 25, 28
Frequency table, 2–9, 28
and frequency polygon, 12–17
grouped, 6–9, 28
and histogram, 11
in media, 21–22, 28
and mode, 36
in research articles, 25, 28
use of equal interval sizes, 21–22, 28
Freund, R. D., 243
Frodi, A., 306–7
F table, 316–17, 324–25, 549–52
F test. *See* Analysis of variance
Furnham, A., 130–31

G

Galileo, 500
Gallup, D. G. H., 146
Galton, F., 75, 77, 150–51, 319, 417, 485
Games, P. A., 151
Gariepy, J., 201–2
Gauss, K. F., 134

Gaussian distribution. *See* Normal curve
Gear, C. L., 474–75
Geisser, S., 404
Gender
and math performance, 22–23
and statistics performance, 22, 497
Generalizability, 541–42
General linear model, 477–81, 499–501
assumptions of, 499, 501
least-squares model, 480, 499
Generative theory of causality, 500, 502
Gibb, J., 528–29
Gifford, R., 87
Gigerenzer, G., 151, 233, 383, 523–25
Gilmore, J., 174
Gladue, B. A., 411
Glass, G. V., 149
Gold, P., 471
Gosset, W. S., 75, 233, 250–51, 273–74, 318, 417, 468
Grand mean, 320–21, 329, 340–42, 353, 361
Graziano, B., 49
Greenhouse, S., 404
Greenwald, A. G., 165
Grolnick, W., 306–7
Grouped frequency table, 6–9, 28. *See also* Frequency table
Group matching
comparison to random assignment, 332–35
matched-group designs, 536–37, 539

H

Hall, J., 471
Hamilton, D., 87
Hanna, C., 415–21, 439–40
Haphazard selection, 146–47
Harmonic mean, 301–2
Harney, P., 528–29
Harpster, L., 363
Harris, C., 528–29
Harris, G., 275
Hart, K. E., 513
Hawthorne effect, 540–41
Hazan, C., 311–13, 316–17, 360–61, 491
Heatherton, T. F., 304
Hendrick, C., 514–15
Hendrick, S. S., 514–15
Heppner, P., 470–71
Herbener, E. S., 471
Herman, C. P., 304
Hierarchical regression, 507–10, 527
comparison to other statistical techniques, 523
and partial correlation, n511
and stepwise regression, 509–10
Higbee, J. L., 14
Hilgard, E. R., 55
Hindley, C., 158
Histogram, 10–12
exaggeration of proportions, 23–25, 28
in media, 21, 23–25, 28
and mode, 36